E762. R6 1964

AN
AMERICAN
FAMILY

Also by Ishbel Ross

*A*N
*A*MERICAN *F*AMILY

THE TAFTS ⌐ 1678 to 1964

Ishbel Ross

THE WORLD PUBLISHING COMPANY

CLEVELAND AND NEW YORK

Published by the World Publishing Company
2231 West 110th Street, Cleveland 2, Ohio

Published simultaneously in Canada by
Nelson, Foster & Scott Ltd.

Library of Congress Catalog Number: 64–23540

SECOND EDITION

ACKNOWLEDGMENTS

THIS HISTORY of the Taft family is based largely on the vast William Howard Taft collection of papers in the Library of Congress. I have drawn from Mr. Taft's presidential papers, general correspondence, letter books and, in particular, from the assembled family papers. The greatest riches for my purpose lay in the letters and diaries under the last classification and, above all, in Mr. Taft's letters to his wife, which run from the 1880's to his death in 1930. I found his letters to his daughter, Mrs. Frederick J. Manning, especially enlightening on his days as chief justice. The correspondence of his mother, Mrs. Alphonso Taft, and her sister, Miss Delia Torrey, with William Howard Taft gives a spirited view of the social and political panorama of the late nineteenth and early twentieth centuries.

I am indebted to Mrs. Manning, Charles Phelps Taft, II, and Congressman Robert Taft, Jr. for their generous cooperation in my use of the papers in the general William Howard Taft collection. Charles Taft was also good enough to guide me to papers of his own in the William Howard Taft Memorial Association in Cincinnati. Mrs. Hulbert Taft very kindly shared with me some reminiscences of her husband and gave me an inside view of Indian Hill, where Senator Robert A. Taft and Hulbert

Taft resided outside Cincinnati. Charles Taft, Congressman Taft and William Howard Taft, III, were most helpful to me in interviews; and Mrs. Donald R. Morris, Seth Chase Taft and Peter Rawson Taft were generous in their cooperation. I am also indebted to Richard H. Lovelace, of the Taft Alumni Association.

Mrs. Willa Beall, executive director of the William Howard Taft Memorial Association in Cincinnati, has been tireless in supplying me with family material, genealogical details, and up-to-date information on the various branches of the young Tafts—an ever-spreading clan. I am much indebted to Mrs. Beall for all her aid. As collector and custodian of memorabilia designed for the restoration of the Mount Auburn house where William Howard Taft was born, she has had access to family sources hitherto untapped.

Mrs. Darrah Dunham Wunder, of Cincinnati, has been kind and helpful at all stages of my work on this book, and I should like to express my appreciation of all the authoritative information she was able to give me on the lives of the Tafts in Cincinnati, Washington, and at Murray Bay. As an old family friend of the Robert A. Tafts and the Charles Phelps Tafts, Mrs. Wunder has been enlightening on many points.

In the Manuscript Division of the Library of Congress I had the utmost cooperation from its chief, David C. Mearns, and I am grateful to him and to many members of his staff for their unfailing courtesy during the months I spent there doing research for this book. Special credit is due Miss Kate M. Stewart, a specialist on the Taft papers, for her good offices, deep background knowledge, and general helpfulness. Among others to whom I am indebted are: Fred Shelley, in charge of presidential papers, Edwin A. Thompson, Russell M. Smith, Dr. C. P. Powell, Joseph Meredith, Joseph Sullivan, Roger Preston, and John McDonough. In arranging for illustrations Miss Virginia Daiker and Carl E. Stange, of the Prints and Photographs Division, were as helpful to me as always, and I should also like to thank Legare Obear for special courtesies. Among the fellow researchers to whom I am especially indebted are: Mrs. Ona Griffin Jeffries, Mrs. Bliss Treat, Dr. David Danelski, and Harold Hollingsworth.

At the National Archives I was aided by Mrs. Julia Bland Carroll, Miss Jane Smith, Richard S. Maxwell, and E. O. Parker, and I wish to give special thanks to H. B. Fant, who is with the National Historical Publications Commission, for countless good offices in the course of my research.

I am indebted to more persons in Cincinnati than I could name for help of one kind or another, but I should like to express my gratitude in particular to Dr. Louis L. Tucker, director of the Historical and Philosophical Society of Ohio, and his assistants, Mrs. Alice Hook and Miss Ruth Brill; and to Ernest I. Miller, Mrs. Jacob M. Plaut, Mrs. Elizabeth Cameron, Miss Karline Brown, Mrs. Mabel Schell, and Miss Jean Hamer, of the Cincinnati Public Library. Among many others to whom I am indebted in Cincinnati are: Mrs. Russell Wilson, Dr. Francis J. Moore, Dr. Paul Herget, Miss Ethel L. Hutchins, Mrs. Allen Brown, Mrs. Eleanor Adams, Miss Betty L. Zimmerman, Miss M. E. McCormick, Mr. and Mrs. George Rosenthal, E. R. Bellinger, and Leonard Sive.

At Uxbridge and Mendon, where the Taft family had their beginnings in this country, I was shown the early landmarks by Mr. and Mrs. Jefferson O. Rawson. Mrs. Rawson is one of the numerous Tafts who live in this part of Massachusetts. At the American Antiquarian Society in Worcester I had the friendly cooperation of Dr. Clifford K. Shipton, its director, and Miss Mary Brown, Miss Avis G. Clarke, and Mrs. Laura Paletta. I am also indebted to James de T. Abajian, of the California Historical Society, and to Robert W. Hill, the ever-helpful Chief of Manuscripts in the New York Public Library

I.R.

CONTENTS

AN
AMERICAN
FAMILY

CHAPTER 1

FROM VERMONT
TO CINCINNATI

ALPHONSO TAFT arrived in Cincinnati from Vermont in 1838 with a box of law books, a degree from Yale, and a strong strain of ambition. He was six feet tall, rugged in bearing, with deep-set hazel eyes and a cautious way of talking. Through him the family tree took root in Ohio, its branches spreading in all directions until scholars, lawyers, business-men, journalists, a senator, a chief justice and President, made the Taft name familiar to the country at large. Through two gifted wives of New England ancestry Alphonso had one daughter and five sons who lived to grow up. Although his own beginnings were in New England his career developed in Ohio and eventually on the national scene. His sons and grandchildren carried the family tradition full sweep into public affairs until in the course of a century the Tafts were deeply entrenched in national history.

Alphonso's ancestry went back to the days of the Massachusetts Bay Colony through both parents. The first Taft to settle in America was of yeoman descent and bore the name Robert. He came from England to Weymouth in the late 1670's—a "plain, unlettered man" and a carpenter by trade. At first he settled in Braintree, Massachusetts, where he had pasture and orchard land, salt marshes, pigs, oxen, and cows. By 1679 he had moved to nearby Mendon, a settlement in the Blackstone River valley, and was serving as a town selectman. The house he built was close to Lake Nimpuc, which came to be known as Taft's Pond. The land was potentially fertile and he farmed and acquired substantial tracts of property. There was more need for farmers than for joiners and his interest turned naturally to agriculture, although he put up some houses and with the help of his sons built two bridges across the Blackstone River. Robert and his wife Sarah had twelve children in all, founding a strong line that scattered throughout New England. For the most part their offspring married young and had large families—in one instance thirty children.

A tradition of public service was discernible in the Tafts from the beginning. At first they shared in the hardships of other pioneers—coping with Indians, clearing land, and carving out small farmlands in the wilderness. As they prospered they took part in town government and public affairs. Although the farming tradition was paramount in these early days, later generations bred ministers and schoolmasters, physicians, lawyers, bankers, and merchants—"men who knew how to get rich and men who dared to be poor," said Alphonso of his ancestors. In course of time they held judicial office on the local level and promoted education. Their wives for the most part were women of education, sometimes of piety, and usually of strong opinion.

Little was heard of them in the late seventeenth or early eighteenth century, but George Washington made a brief stop in 1789 at Samuel Taft's farm and tavern on the old turnpike road running from Boston to Hartford. He was charmed by Polly and Patty Taft, the two daughters of the house who waited on him, and later wrote to their father commenting on their "modest and innocent looks." At the same time the first President sent the girls five guineas and pieces of chintz for gowns.

The nationally known Tafts of today are descended from Joseph, the fourth son of Robert, the first arrival in this country. Joseph married Elizabeth Emerson in 1708, so that Ralph Waldo Emerson was distantly related to the Tafts. Joseph's grandson, Aaron Taft, a Princeton man, was town clerk of Uxbridge in 1799 when he joined a migration of farmers who had decided to test the good land in the new state of Vermont. He bought a hundred acres at West Townshend in Windham County for $567 and journeyed to his new home in the depths of winter, with five ox-teams drawing sleds piled with family belongings. Aaron's fourteen-year-old boy Peter walked most of the eighty miles through snow, driving the family cow. They settled on a rising that came to be known as Taft's Hill. When spring came and the landscape flowered Mrs. Aaron Taft gazed with satisfaction on the magnificent view from their plain house on the hill. Born Rhoda Rawson, she had brought another strong pioneer strain into the Taft family. She was descended from Edward Rawson, of English ancestry, who had settled in Newburyport in 1637, become a large property owner, and served as town clerk there for twelve years.

Peter Rawson Taft, the son of Aaron and Rhoda, taught, did surveying, and at an early age filled town and county offices. It was he who initiated the judicial history of the Tafts. He was an active figure in the Vermont legislature, a judge in the probate and county courts, and a justice of the peace. At the age of twenty-five Peter married Sylvia Howard, daughter of Henry Howard, whose farm lay close to Taft's Hill. His father-in-law had fought in the War of the Revolution and Sylvia was descended from Samuel Hayward, who settled in Braintree in 1642, and from Deacon Josiah Chapin, of Mendon. She was of Scotch and Irish stock and had grown up in the first frame house built at Townshend. Solemn-faced Sylvia was a devout Baptist, a temperance advocate, and a woman of spirit, although narrow-minded toward other faiths. She and Peter were undemonstrative but deeply devoted in their family life. Unlike the other more prolific Tafts they had only one child, Alphonso, who was born on November 5, 1810. With him the family history shifted to Cincinnati and eventually flowered in the national spotlight. In time Alphonso became the first Taft of national reputation.

From childhood he was lectured on the evils of drink, the importance of politics, the inviolability of family life. While Sylvia stressed the word of God for her growing son, his father, cautious in all his convictions, reminded him when he left home to reserve judgment and to stay clear of the currents of passion and prejudice. In his future development Alphonso showed the combined qualities of the Tafts, the Haywards, the Chapins, and the Rawsons—a blend of independence, enterprise, and stability. He had a powerful physique and energy that sometimes drove him to extraordinary effort. His boyhood followed the Spartan New England tradition. Money was tight. The teachers at the local academy his father helped to found boarded with the Tafts and it was an accepted fact that he would go to college. After getting all he could from the local school he attended Amherst in 1827 and 1828, making the trip from Brattleboro to North Hadley by boat, then walking the remaining miles to the small college town. He tutored and taught in the village high school until he entered Yale in 1829 at the age of nineteen.

Arriving in a black broadcloth coat, with a massive black bow tie, Alphonso looked huge and somber among the assembled students. His dark hair was brushed in heavy strands over his temples, giving him a clerical air. His thin mouth seemed grim in moments of thought and his brilliant dark eyes burned with zeal. Occasionally he walked from West Townshend to New Haven and once he went to New York by sloop, then sailed up the Hudson and tramped over the mountains to his home. At an early age Alphonso decided that he had no wish to be a farmer. The young men of Vermont and Massachusetts were moving west and were working their way to success in the growing towns of Ohio. As he labored in the orchard and tended the stock on his trips home he thought constantly of a more expansive life, an ambition sympathetically viewed by his father, who was often away from home attending to legislative matters in Montpelier. His mother, too, was well aware that nothing could stop the drive of the young people who were moving away from their parents' farms. The hills, dark forests, and rocky streams of Vermont had great charm for Alphonso, but he was a practical youth and he saw no future for himself in these surroundings. "I should like right well to live in Vermont, but I can't, at any rate for the present," he wrote to his parents on November 8, 1835. When finally he moved away, he wrote that Vermont "was a noble state to emigrate from."

His days at college were crowded with work and interest as he formed the first link in the long Taft family connection with Yale. Jeremiah Day was president while Alphonso was there and the Calvinist influence was so strong that religious observances were embedded in the life of the college. Students joined the Congregational Church in droves during a religious revival, but in spite of his devout mother Alphonso was cold to evangelicism. However, he wrote reassuringly to his parents that he did not spend his days in frivolity and social exchanges. He was one of the organizers of the honor society Skull and Bones, a tradition highly valued in his family, and he belonged to the group known as Brothers in Unity. Alphonso was class orator and spoke on "Political Integrity" when he was graduated in 1833, a Phi Beta Kappa and third in a class of ninety-three.

For a time he considered going south to teach. Letters from Amherst classmates who had scattered to various parts of the country piqued his interest. In the end he raised funds by teaching at Ellington Academy in a village close to Hartford, Connecticut, and in 1837 he was able to return to Yale, where he studied law after a term of tutoring in philosophy. Sylvia, pleased that he had chosen so sound a profession, wrote that she hoped he would never deviate from the "pathway of rectitude," but would show that a man could live and die with an untarnished character in the practice of law. He, in turn, assured her that he viewed his profession as an avenue for service to his country and his fellow citizens. The preparation was interminable, however, and from time to time his parents sent him money to help him complete his education. It was not always easy for them, but they never weakened in helping Alphonso to realize his ambitions.

The tall young man from Vermont had lofty dreams as he walked under the elms of New Haven, or shared in the lusty debates at his boarding house, where Whigs and adherents of Andrew Jackson battled things out. During this period he developed great reverence for Daniel Webster and his interest was engaged in the growing antislavery sentiment throughout New England. It had become strong in Vermont, as in Massachusetts, and his parents were involved in the society formed in their region to push this cause. As he read his mother's letters telling him of these developments he reflected on the incompatibility of this fever with the cool climate of Vermont.

When the time came to break away, Alphonso, like other young men of his generation heading west, sought a wife from his own surroundings. The daughters of Charles Phelps seemed to be the most likely prospects. Phelps was a man of property in West Townshend, a judge much respected in local affairs, a scholar, and a member of a noted New England family. He had six children and his oldest daughter, Elisa, seemed the most suitable choice. While Alphonso was at Yale she was attending Miss Emma Willard's school in Troy, and was already deep in Virgil's *Bucolics* and the second book of Euclid, but in the end his interest shifted to Fanny, her frail and pretty sister who had seemed immature to Alphonso when he wrote to his father:

> As to Fanny she is so young, & her character so little formed, I don't think it worth while to take any trouble about her. If I should make no bargain until she becomes of proper age, then it will be in season to think of her. . . . If Elisa won't do I had better cast an eye around for another, by and by I suppose. I would rather some one would do it for me. I have enough else to do. Besides, my opportunities are not good.

This curious system of mating was not uncommon at the time and Sylvia kept a weather eye on the two Phelps girls for Alphonso. When he took the first major step in his career and left Vermont in September, 1838, he had no idea where he would settle. First he went to New York, which then had a population of 300,000. He quickly decided that "intellectual superiority" was disregarded in its grimy operations. "I dislike the character of the New York Bar exceedingly," he wrote to Fanny. "The notorious selfishness, or dishonesty of the great mass of the men you find in New York is in my mind a serious objection to settling there." Philadelphia, on the other hand, struck him as being a noble and moral city. However, he deduced that it would take years to make headway at the bar in this well-ordered community, for the competition would be formidable. Next he struck out for the West and by October was on his way to Ohio, traveling by canal boat, stage, and railroad. The journey took him three weeks and all of it was a revelation to Alphonso as he studied the landscape, the surge of a pioneer population, the growing towns.

He found Pittsburgh prosperous and substantial, with much bustle and a ceaseless scramble for riches, but the legal outlook there seemed discouraging and the dirt dismayed him. The city was veiled in darkness from the use of bituminous coal. He was warmly received in Columbus with its tight little population of 8,000 and Alphonso would have settled there had he not been persuaded that Cincinnati, five times as large, would be a livelier center for legal work. He was struck at once by the natural beauty of its surrounding hills, the majesty of the winding river, the intense activity on the waterfront. "I do not look upon Cincinnati as a paradise," he wrote to Fanny immediately after his arrival. But he predicted that it would grow to be a mighty place, with its canals, its macadamized roads, its railroads.

He went to work in the office of Nathaniel Wright, a Vermonter who had been practicing law in Cincinnati for a score of years. His home consisted of two rooms in the market section, close to the wharf, and his first year's work, while he read for his Ohio bar examinations, was exacting and tedious. But he never tired of his exhilarating walks in the hills, or the excitement at the public landing where steamers came and went, whistles blew at all hours, gamblers and roustabouts sang chanteys on the riverboats, and assorted merchandise lay on the wharf waiting to be shipped. The broad landing sloped down to the river, and drays and carts rattled over its shining limestone surface at a sharp tilt. The fashionable and the dowdy, the frontiersman and the city dude, all traversed it with a list. Sometimes the water rose so high that the steamboats actually moved in the street, sixty feet above the normal water level.

Alphonso listened attentively to the blended accents of the crowds at the wharf. Immigrants poured in during his early days in Cincinnati— Germans, Irish, Poles, English, and Dutch. Coffeehouses and taverns abounded and hard drinking led to disorder along the waterfront. The echoes of frontier life had not yet died out. But Cincinnati had sixty lawyers and thirty-five physicians when Alphonso settled there. It had twelve pork packers, eight brewers, nine dry-goods dealers, sixteen booksellers, and nine printers and publishers. Salmon Portland Chase, Ohio's famous lawyer and politician, swung along the street with godlike majesty of bearing. Nicholas Longworth, whose devotion to law was exceeded only by his passion for horticulture, decked the hillsides with his grapevines. John Shillito was building up a reputation as a merchant prince. William Procter and James Gamble, two Britons who had started separate candle factories and married sisters, had amalgamated their operations in 1837, the start of a great soap fortune. Young Rudolph Wurlitzer had arrived from Vienna with a violin under his arm and was soon supplying the market with organs and other musical instruments. David Sinton, of Irish birth, was laying the foundation of an iron fortune.

Menageries and carnivals were popular and shutters were put up on circus day. Dorfeuille's Western Museum was a chamber of horrors and the Apollonian Gardens drew crowds on summer evenings to listen to a German band. The public took phrenology as seriously as politics, and revivals were in the air. The Millerites were stirring up frenzy as they sang hymns and prayed on the hills while waiting in spotless robes for the end of the world. The Germans had brought with them their deep love of music, and choral and instrumental societies were fostering good music in the community. There were thirty-eight Protestant and two Catholic churches. Dr. Lyman Beecher, the controversial head of Lane Seminary, was pounding away for temperance and was fighting licenses for the coffeehouses. Alphonso studied him with great interest on his first visit to Walnut Hills, and he quickly decided that Catharine Beecher was a knowing old maid.

In the spring of 1839 he returned briefly to West Townshend. Again he helped his parents on the farm and this time he courted Fanny seriously, for she was now seventeen and seemed more attractive than Elisa. He had passed his bar examinations in Ohio and so he felt free to give her an engagement ring before starting west again. On his return he corresponded with her as if she were his own Galatea, advising her on her reading, her use of words, her spelling and punctuation. Alphonso laced his letters with homilies and advice and urged her to exchange her geometry problems with him. He reminded her to get out in the fresh air and take exercise, assuring her that tight lacing was more destructive to the body than intemperance. But his mother told Fanny that the Gospel was the study that really mattered.

Fanny accepted all this with a docile spirit, but she was not lacking in cultivation or common sense. She had quiet wit, an interest of her own in public affairs, and considerable family tradition. As time went on her letters became quite spirited and his more sentimental. He had urged her father to send Fanny to the Misses Edwards' School in Troy, where she had a stiff drilling in Latin, Greek, algebra, geometry, and history, as well as the customary feminine whirl in French, sewing, music, and deportment. Her father went out to Ohio to see how Alphonso was doing before committing his delicate daughter to the Vermonter's care. He was pleased with what he saw and decided to move to Cincinnati himself. Alphonso had made $200 in his first seven months of practice and $600 by the end of the year; he had bought a hundred dollars' worth of books but had not spent a farthing on worldly amusement, he assured his parents. Nor had he touched liquor except for one glass of wine at the home of Nathaniel Wright, who was a strong temperance man. When another hundred dollars reached him from his parents he wrote: "You have undertaken to make a man of me. God only knows with what success. It would have cost but little to bring me up a ninny. . . ."

Alphonso was offered a law partnership with the Wright firm, where he had served his apprenticeship in a minor capacity, and by 1840 he was also getting involved in politics. Every evening the Whigs and the Locofocos had big gatherings as the "Tippecanoe and Tyler Too" campaign was lustily waged in Ohio. Martin van Buren was viewed as the mouthpiece of Wall Street, but echoes of the rowdiest campaign within memory died down quickly with the sudden death of President Harrison. Alphonso, strong, buoyant, with life ahead of him, wrote to Fanny of the fierce political currents in Ohio. He noted that the people of the West seemed less refined than the Yankees.

By the summer of 1841 the Phelps family were ready to accept Alphonso Taft as a son-in-law. Fanny was nineteen and he was thirty when they were married at the bride's home on August 29, 1841. They went to Niagara Falls on their wedding trip and then to Cleveland, before settling down in a house at the corner of Fourth and Vine streets that Alphonso had bought for $3,000. His parents had decided to move west with him and they helped him to pay for the house. He had said good-bye to his bachelor life, to boardinghouse meals, to long evenings passed reading to his blind friend, Ethan Stone, with whom he had boarded.

Regardless of the way in which his romance had begun it was now a true love match and he wrote that the pleasure of living at home with a wife surpassed his most sanguine expectations. He enjoyed the solid comfort of Fanny's housekeeping and the tranquillity of her sweet nature. For the time being he was content to attend the Baptist Church with the Phelps family. When he traveled, Fanny followed him with adoring letters. She read deeply, took piano lessons, and sang. In her diary she noted when Washington Irving left for Spain to serve as ambassador, when Henry Clay resigned his seat in the Senate, when the great temperance celebration of 1842 took Cincinnati by storm. She visited Longworth's gardens and on summer mornings got up at five o'clock to go to market, where she could buy a quart of strawberries for seven cents, beef for eight cents a pound, flour for three dollars a barrel, and butter for ten cents a pound.

The Tafts had a chance to observe Mr. and Mrs. Charles Dickens at the Broadway Hotel, to hear him lecture, and later to read his comments on their city:

Cincinnati is a beautiful city, cheerful, thriving, animated, I have not often seen a place that commends itself so favorably and pleasantly to a stranger at the first glance as this does, with its clean houses of red and white, its well-paved roads and footways of bright tile. . . . I was quite charmed with the appearance of the town and its neighboring suburb of Mount Auburn. . . .

Fanny was popular in her new surroundings. She engaged in church and charitable work and she was ambitious for Alphonso, urging him to strike for high attainment. Like her father, she was broad-minded politically and took an eager interest in her husband's affairs when they first flowed into national currents in 1847. He had finally established contact with Daniel Webster when he won his fight in court over Edward McMicken's bequest to the city of property valued at $500,000. The wealthy trader wished this sum to be used for educational purposes but his heirs tried to break the will. Taft fought them and won the case. This decision paved the way for the University of Cincinnati, which was founded later on the McMicken land. Webster, who had waged a similar fight for Girard College in Philadelphia, followed the McMicken case with interest and congratulated Taft on his victory. Soon the two men were corresponding about the common schools and other public issues. Alphonso was already deep in municipal politics, serving as a member of the city council and at the same time keeping a weather eye on state and national politics. On the local front he steered clear of party labels although he inclined toward the Whigs.

In June, 1848, he visited Washington and called on the eleventh President—James Knox Polk. He was received in the "elegant elyptical saloon" and observed the Chief Executive with close attention. He had a talk with John C. Calhoun, whose views on slavery and other questions offended him. He met Daniel Webster face to face for the first time and found him depressed over the presidential election. They dined together and Alphonso reported to Fanny that he was a noble-looking man, humble in his feelings, his appearance, and his words. He could find no trace of the arrogance that some observed in Webster.

Fanny followed Alphonso to Washington later that summer on her way to Vermont. She climbed steps in the Capitol to view the city and attended a levee at the White House but was disappointed that Mrs. Polk had not seen fit to open the East Room. Fanny made diary notes on the Polks and on Dolley Madison:

Mrs. Polk is a good looking woman. She is not the plain, unassuming person that I had always supposed. She was dressed at the top of the fashion & like a girl of 18—James is quite gray—he combs his hair straight over his head, and lets it hang loose, for the reason that he hasn't enough to braid. On the whole he is not so bad a looking man

as he might be. Lady Madison was present. She received more attention than any other person in the room—even the generals had to stand
to one side for Mrs. Madison—she was dressed very richly & very becomingly—she always wears the Turkish turban. She is a noble specimen of American woman.

Mr. and Mrs. Alphonso Taft now had two growing sons—Charles
Phelps, born in 1843, and Peter Rawson (Rossy) in 1845. Of their five
children these were the only two who survived, and both were frail until
they grew into their teens. Charles was five when he accompanied his
mother East on this occasion and had his first glimpse of Washington
and of New York—a city of church spires, low rooftops, and green
stretches. The boy gazed with wonder at Castle Garden and asked his
mother innumerable questions as they moved around the city. They
drove up Broadway to Union Square, passing drays, carts, and carriages.
Fanny admired the shops and took her small son to Thompson's confectionery for ice cream, strawberries, and oysters. The year was 1848 and
she was already going into decline. Rossy, who had stayed at home with
his father, was ailing, too. At first the family doctor thought that he had
consumption but in the end he diagnosed his illness as stomach trouble.
Fanny's descendants would always be less sturdy than those of Alphonso's second wife. Rossy was not boisterous in his play, like Charles, for he
was much too feeble to exert himself. Fanny missed Alphonso when they
were separated and wrote that she found it "dull music to live alone."
She described their marriage as an "unbroken sea of happiness, without
suspicion or jealousy" and added:

> I am fully inclined to the belief that I am the happiest wife in this
> broad land. I know I have a husband that cannot be equaled, and if he
> is as happy in my love as I am in his, I think he is a totally happy man.
> You are just the man for me, and I would not have a trait in your char-
> acter changed. . . . There is one thing I cannot divide with anybody,
> and that is your love. I must have your whole heart. I can have no part-
> nership there.

Alphonso's law business was flourishing and he went often to Columbus for the trial of cases. He was an impressive figure in the courtroom,
earnest and quiet in argument, slightly brooding in manner, gentle and
forceful at the same time. In his city council work he was constantly on
the lookout for civic improvement and he did not hesitate to break away
from party lines when he felt he was in the right. He spoke at street corn-
ers, defending unpopular issues, and he was unwavering and stubborn
in his convictions. Together he and Fanny worked for the establishment of the House of Refuge, which he opened officially in October,

1850. He was an early advocate of the theory that the children were unfortunate rather than criminal and that all too often their delinquency was due to parental neglect.

That same year he spoke to the Young Men's Mercantile Library Association on "The Railroads of Cincinnati." Fanny corrected his proofs and this speech was considered a significant one in its era. Railroads became a major interest in the Taft family from the time Alphonso first saw the importance of rail communication to the development of Ohio. He advocated subsidizing the existing lines and establishing new ones to link the city with other states. Time and again he predicted that with an adequate railroad system Cincinnati would be enthroned as "Queen of the Mighty West." This prophecy was fulfilled in his lifetime, as a thick network of lines brought life and business to the city when the river traffic dwindled after the opening of the Erie Canal. Alphonso was an incorporator of the Ohio and Missouri Railroad and of the Marietta and Cincinnati Railroad. For many years he was a director of the Little Miami Railroad.

One of his most decisive moves affecting the railroads was a judicial decision in which he affirmed the constitutionality of the laws permitting Cincinnati to build the Southern Railway, an opinion later sustained by the superior court. After the Civil War this railway became of the utmost importance to the development of Cincinnati and of the South. Towns sprang up along the line and the village of Chattanooga grew to the proportions of a city.

Alphonso was just beginning to function effectively in railway matters in 1851 when he moved his family into the square, substantial home on Mount Auburn that later became famous as the birthplace of a President. He bought it for $10,000 and later enlarged it. At the moment he felt that they would all be healthier on the heights, away from the miasmic valley, but the move to higher land was too late to save Fanny. She had been ailing since the birth and death of her last child and she now became desperately ill with "congestion of the lungs and of the brain."

Charles Phelps, her somber and adoring father, was a witness to her lingering death. She was twenty-nine and had been delicate all her life. As she lay in a half-comatose condition she was asked—after the fashion of her era—if she "felt as if she were dying."

"I don't know," said Fanny calmly. "Do you think I am?"

Alphonso told her that she was.

She spoke of the children and hoped that they would remember her. She said she would place her trust in the Saviour and that she was not anxious about living. Then Fanny kissed each member of the family and quietly died. The date was June 2, 1852. Afterwards Alphonso wrote and distributed among his friends a memoir extolling her virtues and graces, which were many. Some of Fanny's gentle qualities were to show up in her son Charles, who later became an important figure in Cincinnati life. Her own letters and diary, impeccably written, suggest a high degree of literacy, independence, deep interest in Alphonso's work, and a passionate love for him.

In the year of Fanny's death he wrote another memoir that was widely quoted across the country. This time the subject was Daniel Webster, who had become his idol. His lecture "Daniel Webster, Statesman and Lawyer" was delivered scores of times by Alphonso. As the Whig party broke up in 1852 Taft became irrevocably dedicated to the embryo Republican party—a tradition that would run through his family for the next hundred years.

The repeal of the Missouri Compromise and the passage of the Kansas-Nebraska Act had intensified the work of the antislavery men. The Compromise doomed the Whig party, which had flourished ever since Henry Clay assembled the anti-Jackson men into a new party in 1832. Webster visited Taft in Cincinnati in 1852 to discuss party matters before the convention at Philadelphia in which he went down to defeat. Both Taft and his alternate, Thomas Spooner, a Cincinnati merchant and clerk of the court, were in the Ohio delegation on this occasion. William H. Seward, of New York State, led the fight against Webster. Winfield Scott was nominated and Alphonso supported the ticket, but without enthusiasm. Webster was unable to make this compromise with his conscience. It made no difference in the long run since Franklin Pierce defeated Scott. And by the end of 1852 Clay, Calhoun, and Webster, three Titans of the slavery struggle with diverse views, were all dead. This meant the close of an era in national politics, but men like Chase, Taft, and others across the country were already deeply committed to pushing the antislavery cause.

With the disintegration of the Whig party groups of men were gathering in various parts of the country in 1854 to form a new political party. Two years later the Republican party took shape when Lewis Clephane of Washington rounded up a number of sympathizers to meet informally in Pittsburgh and issue a call for a national convention. Nearly a score of well-known Cincinnatians crowded into Taft's back office to lay preliminary plans. Alphonso was chosen to represent Hamilton County at the first Republican convention, which was held that year in Philadelphia. He backed Justice John McLean of the Supreme Court but when John C. Frémont was the party choice he supported him loyally. In the end the Republicans went down to defeat and James Buchanan moved into the White House. The political conflict grew harsher as the nation moved irrevocably toward war. Many of the Whigs had joined the Democratic party and the lines were clearly drawn as the Southern Democrats pledged themselves to the protection of slavery. Meanwhile Alphonso Taft was one of those who helped to lay the foundations of the party to which his descendants would be dedicated.

CHAPTER 2

THE TORREY SISTERS

Eighteen months after the death of Fanny, Alphonso Taft married for the second time. Both wives were unusual women—intellectual in their interests, attractive, devoted, and firm in their views. Fanny was delicate and idealistic; her successor was practical and worldly. Both were New Englanders, selected for their suitability as Taft wives. They were chosen with forethought, yet Alphonso married them without knowing them well, except by correspondence. Having made his choice, he gave them single-minded devotion and they, in turn, worshiped him. The warmth, stability, and loyalty of family feeling that pervaded Alphonso's home became a pattern for ensuing generations.

His second wife, Louisa Maria Torrey, always known as Louise, was the daughter of Samuel Davenport Torrey and Susan Holman Waters Torrey, of Millbury, Massachusetts. Her family line reached back to William Torrey, who came from Combe St. Nicholas in Somersetshire, England, in 1640 and settled in Weymouth. Louise's father was a Boston merchant who dealt with the West Indian trade until he developed heart trouble and retired to Millbury. His first wife, Delia Chapin, died in 1821. Three years later he married Susan Waters, a clever and independent girl who followed Dr. William Ellery Channing into the Unitarian fold and shared in the intellectual movements of the day in Boston. Susan was descended from Colonel Jonathan Holman and Colonel Asa Waters, two well-known New Englanders of the Revolutionary era.

Louise was born in Boston on September 11, 1827, and was only four when her family moved to the small New England town in the Blackstone valley and occupied a handsome pillared house across the street from the Waters mansion. Her mother had made an impetuous choice in marrying Samuel Torrey, who seemed to his small grandchildren to be as tall and straight as his own grandfather clock. He was awe-inspiring to the young, who did not always understand his wry wit, but he was a courteous man, strong in family pride, exacting in his standards. In some respects his views were narrow and he clamped down from time to time on his wife's free-wheeling instincts. Since Samuel would not let Susan spread her wings, she felt unbearably cramped at times, and had even been known to batter down a door with an ax in defiance of her husband's wishes.

Mrs. Torrey studied the political scene with passion and was a gifted but dissatisfied housekeeper who could never become reconciled to living away from Boston. In moments of revolt she worked furiously at her easel, doing landscape paintings. Although her eyes failed her in her later years, for most of her lifetime she was the best read and most vital member of the family, and she kept her children politically alert. Her daughters—Delia Chapin, Louisa Maria, Anna Davenport, and Susan H. Torrey, known as Susie—were spirited girls and she gave them an uncommon degree of freedom and education. She had attended Amherst Academy during 1822 and 1823, studying astronomy, logic, and the catch-all course, philosophy. Although Samuel read the newspapers faithfully he had none of his wife's devotion to books. He was powerful, healthy, and lived to be eighty-nine, but Susan, always delicate and often overwrought, died in her early sixties.

Like the Tafts, the Torreys scattered through New England, various branches settling in Connecticut, Vermont, and Maine, but most of them remaining in Massachusetts. The Torrey and Waters families of Millbury were well known in the Boston area as people of culture and substance. The lyceum circuit was in full play, with a constant parade of lecturers, and Susan saw to it that none of them missed the Torrey home. Louise and Delia enjoyed all the celebrities from Oliver Wendell Holmes and Horace Greeley to Lucy Stone. Their mother studied them attentively and sharpened her own wits on their talents. Greeley and she exchanged notes on spiritualism and Lucy Stone surprised them all with her feminine bearing and gentle manner. No one enjoyed these exchanges more than Delia, who usually contributed sprightly conversation and unorthodox views. She knew how much the company of brilliant and original visitors meant to her mother and in a moment of insight she wrote to Louise in the 1850's: "Mother, you know, is very ambitious and ambition in a woman is synonymous with unhappiness. She has great mental and physical activity, and there is not a man or woman in town with whom she can have any satisfactory intellectual conversation."

Mrs. Torrey was determined that her daughters should not suffer from a limited view of life. When they were still quite young she let them move freely between Millbury, Worcester, and Boston. They visited Washington and New York and stayed at the fashionable spas. They were familiar with the theater, with Boston's most advanced lecturers, with skating parties and dances. They watched a balloon ascension in Boston on Independence Day, 1843. But, above all, their mother was determined that they should attend college, a rising interest in the feminine spectrum. They arrived at South Hadley on an October day in 1843 to find that academic study and domestic training were impartially imposed on her students by Miss Mary Lyon, founder of Mount Holyoke College. Both sisters felt unbearably confined, since they were used to great freedom of movement and speech. "Oh, I shall be so glad to get home where I can speak above a whisper and not have to move by a line and plummet," Louise wrote to her mother in April, 1844. But Mrs. Torrey sternly reminded them that they must "imbibe the true spirit of self-culture."

In retrospect Delia came to admire Miss Lyon, and years later she primed William Howard Taft with reminiscences for a commencement address at Mount Holyoke. But for the time being life seemed desolate and the prospect of becoming teachers remote. Louise cherished the fancy that she might be a writer. Her mother, a purist, never failed to point out the inelegancies in the compositions of her girls. The letters and diaries left by the sisters suggest considerable literary sophistication; in fact, all the Torreys were as keen in their literary interests as they were demanding in their social standards.

Louise stayed at Mount Holyoke for a year, but Delia left at the end of six months, ill with bilious colic. From the rigors of this experience they switched to the free air of New Haven, where the Torreys had many friends. Here they studied with Miss Mary Dutton and attended lectures by Professor Denison Olmsted, the scientist who introduced laboratory work at Yale. Through him they acquired a smattering of meteorology, physiology, geology, and philosophy. Meanwhile, they lived at the home of their Aunt Harriet, who was married to the Reverend Samuel Dutton, a Yale friend of Alphonso Taft's. Louise attended dances given by Governor Roger Sherman Baldwin of Connecticut and she was a close friend of his daughter, Lizzie. She received more attention in New Haven than Delia, a distinction that Aunt Harriet ascribed to her fine figure, her manners, musical gifts, and confidence in herself. She went to soirees of all kinds and, like other young girls of her day, attended a Bible class and a sewing society known as the Beehive. Louise's thoughts, however, were already attuned to the larger world.

In 1847 the two sisters taught at Monson Academy in Maine, where they had horses to ride and meager salaries of $2.25 a week, which gave them a feeling of emancipation, however, and enabled them to take the fashionable grand tour of the period. They visited Niagara, Quebec, Saratoga, and Burlington, winding up in New York, where they stayed at the Astor House and swung recklessly from sermons by noted preachers to Palmo's Opera House. This was a period when they could attend anything from Shakespearean readings by Fanny Kemble to dabblings in animal magnetism, as popular a fad as hypnotism.

Both girls had beaux but they were hard to please. Now and again they had qualms about how much they cost their father. "How you could husband your property if you could only husband your daughters!" Louise wrote to him in January, 1853. By this time she was studying music and was giving music lessons in Boston. Her marriage hopes were dwindling, and she wrote to Delia: "Tell everybody that I have come to the same conclusion as yourself—viz.—not to marry."

However, before the end of that year Louise had been caught up in a somewhat impersonal courtship with Alphonso Taft, who had come East to select a second New England wife. He met Louise through the Duttons and was struck by her grace and intelligence. On his return to Cincinnati he wrote to Mrs. Dutton asking if she were "extravagant, undomestic, wilful, or had been badly crossed in love." Aunt Harriet, amused and somewhat dismayed by this calculating form of courtship, let Louise know that she was being appraised. But the Duttons were so reassuring that Alphonso quickly wrote to Samuel: "I need not be told that Louise is a splendid woman, one of whom a man might be proud. I sincerely believe that it will turn out that she is just the companion I want and I hope I would be a fair match. Whether she may think so is more doubtful."

Louise liked Alphonso from her first glimpse of him and his inquiries only amused her. He returned to Millbury in November and urged her to marry him at once, since he had to get back to his legal work in Cincinnati. Their romance had developed so rapidly that Louise bargained for a quiet wedding and they were married in the Torrey home in Millbury on December 26, 1853. Louise was twenty-six; Alphonso was forty-three. A great snowstorm raged as they journeyed to Albany and on to New York, where they stayed at the St. Nicholas Hotel. They went to a Jullien concert, visited the Crystal Palace, and bought books for Charles and Rossy. On the last lap of their wedding journey they stopped in Columbus and visited Aaron and Elizabeth Perry, who had been close friends of Fanny's. Perry, like Taft, was a Vermonter who went west fresh from law school, settled in Columbus, and became a successful lawyer and legislator.

The elder Tafts welcomed Louise warmly to Mount Auburn. She found Peter Rawson Taft—by this time contentedly transplanted from Vermont—a jovial old gentleman, amazingly well informed and eager to preserve peace on all sides. Sylvia, still a fine-looking woman with a lean face and keen dark eyes, struck her as being a "truly good, honest, warm-hearted woman." She knew she was stepping into a difficult situation but she felt at once that her mother-in-law would not be jealous of her rights. However, small flurries developed, involving authority, until Peter smoothed the troubled waters and mollified Sylvia. Louise had little trouble with the children. She found Charles, aged ten, and Rossy, seven, bright boys who seemed chiefly to need a mother's training in grooming and manners. "They are easily influenced and are ambitious to please me," she wrote home. "It seems very strange to be called 'Mother' but they take to it so naturally that I am getting used to it." Mr. and Mrs. Phelps accepted her without a visible chill, although Charles Phelps was a man of deep reserve, uncompromising in spirit. Rossy was too young to remember much about his own mother and within six months Alphonso was praising Louise for the "great care and attention she had given his boys," drilling them in manners, stirring them up on their schoolwork.

Again Alphonso had made a good choice in a wife. He confided at once to Delia that he was exceedingly happy with her sister. "No man was ever more fortunate than I have been in forming this connection," he wrote a week after their marriage. Alphonso and Delia became good friends at sight and they soon started a lifelong correspondence that would throw much light on Taft history. From the beginning Louise was as certain as Alphonso of the wisdom of their marriage. "I want to confide to you that I have the best husband in the United States and strange enough he seems to have a similar opinion about his wife," she wrote to Delia, who missed her clever sister and wrote: "Oh, Louise, Louise, how can I live the rest of my life without you? I am but half a pair of scissors."

The newly married Mrs. Alphonso Taft found the Mount Auburn house spacious and comfortable, but she missed the silver, fine china, and period furniture of the Torrey home. Characteristically, she made the best of things and set forth with Alphonso to spend three hundred dollars of wedding-gift money on a sixty-five-dollar parlor table with a marble top, a Gothic chair upholstered with figured plush, and a twenty-five-dollar whatnot. Her piano, shipped from the East, helped to furnish the parlor. Her clothes, hastily rounded up in Boston or sewn at home, were a success, for Louise wore her garments with a flourish. The Tafts had thirty callers on New Year's Eve and she moved majestically among them, wearing a black and green silk gown. "I felt no embarrassment in receiving them and Mr. Taft seemed pleased and proud of me," she wrote to Delia with satisfaction. He was always to be "Mr. Taft" to Louise and her family.

Alphonso, who had set up a new law partnership known as Taft, Key & Dixon, was busy with railroad matters and he and his bride had long, contented evenings at home, while she read and he worked over his papers. He encouraged her to keep posted on political events and he often quoted from congressional speeches as he studied them. Louise was dubious of her skill in the kitchen when her mother-in-law watched her with a penetrating eye, and sometimes she wished that she had paid more attention to this side of her education. Her mother was so thoroughly gifted as a housekeeper that she had rarely been called on to help at home. Delia was the domestic jewel among the daughters, as skilled in the household arts as she was knowing in her critical opinions.

But aside from minor domestic worries Louise flourished in her new surroundings. She had not envisioned the bold contours and fluctuating colors of the hills of Cincinnati, or the silver sweep of the winding river. The roads twisting up around the hills were rough but a young Irishman drove her carriage. About fifty families lived on Mount Auburn and many were from New England. Nearly all called on her and she was surprised to find that a number of the women had their hair professionally dressed, and that some took maids to parties to help them in and out of their cumbersome wraps. She had not counted on the dirt of Cincinnati and a month after her arrival she wrote to Delia:

> The soft coal spreads such a dust that everything is black with it. It is worse in the city than on the hill. When there I hardly dare make a call or enter a store without satisfying myself that I have not a large beauty spot on my nose or other part of my face—a small blemish of that sort is not worth noticing for everybody you meet has a similar ornament. It is a serious extravagance to wear light kids and I hardly think I can keep tidy in white underclothes.

The surrounding hills were being settled at this time and new fortunes were in the making. Some of the older houses had spacious grounds, conservatories, and rooms paneled with tapestry; there were a few pure Georgian types with interiors to match. Rock gardens bloomed with azaleas and rhododendrons. Roses blazed on the terraced levels. Great oak and chestnut trees threw shade on farms and country estates. In spring, masses of pink and white blossoms flowered from the apple, peach, and plum trees. Vines flourished on the terrace stretches, with the Longworth family cultivating the native Catawba grape.

The city was already famous for its hospitality to strangers. The banquets, the crystal and silver, the wine and food, were commented on by

travelers, one of whom exclaimed: "Talk of the backwoods—these people live in the style of princes." But the Tafts saw little of this during
their early years on Mount Auburn. Their lives were frugal and austere.
Louise soon picked up the traditions of the region, however, and
watched developments as the early settlers moved to other parts of the
city, and new ones came in. The first sale of land on Mount Auburn
dated back to 1792 and in 1819, when James Key built a splendid house
on the brow of the hill, the surrounding area took its name from his
home. But in 1837 it was renamed Mount Auburn when an Englishwoman named Mrs. Sumner put up a painted signboard at the foot of the
hill with the inscription: "Mt. Auburn, 1 mile." The name took hold
and the legend spread that this visitor had named it after Mount Auburn
Cemetery in Cambridge.

The Tafts lived at 2038 Auburn Avenue in a house still standing in
1964. By 1870 both sides of the street were substantially built up but
when the Tafts settled there, it was open farming country. Rabbits,
squirrels, and possum darted about on their property. Fifty different
kinds of birds wheeled over the woods and originally a vineyard ran along
the slope below the house. When Louise looked from her back windows
she could see woods, fields, and country lanes, with pastoral glimpses
of cows grazing.

Early in 1852 the Perrys moved to Cincinnati and settled close to the
Tafts on Mount Auburn. Alphonso and Aaron formed a law partnership, and celebrated the occasion with oysters and champagne. "Had
we been told at New Haven, what has since happened to us, I doubt if
either of us would not have considered the predictions somewhat
highly colored," Perry remarked. Louise and Elizabeth Perry found
that they had much in common; both were widely read and discriminating in their tastes.

Alphonso had often attended the Second Presbyterian Church to hear
Dr. Lyman Beecher preach, but in the late 1840's he moved to the Unitarian Church, where he soon became a trustee and a guiding force. His
wife, liberal in her religious as in her political beliefs, first attended the
Baptist Church with the elder Tafts but in time she followed Alphonso
into the denomination that her mother approved. His Unitarianism
created problems for Alphonso, since it was the least popular of all de-
nominations in Ohio, and the choice of a church was an important matter in a community where the freshly minted fortunes of the pioneers
were being turned to account in substantial homes, in trips to Europe
and to the fashionable spas.

One of the most notable of the settlers, whose descendants would be
closely linked with the Tafts, was Thomas J. Emery, an Englishman
whose trimly curtained shop with bright yellow shutters had borne for

years the sign: "Emigrant Office. Houses, Stores, and Lots for Sale." He
had landed in Cincinnati in 1832 and at first had manufactured lard oil
and candles, but as time went on he made a specialty of selling "country
seats." After one bankruptcy he prospered again. Two years before Louise moved west he fell through a hatchway at his plant and was killed,
but his sons, Thomas J. Emery and John J. Emery, continued in the
family tradition, building up a real estate empire. Eventually the Emery
name would be identified with the city's greatest philanthropies and
Robert A. Taft would supervise their estate.

Visitors to Mount Auburn invariably showed interest in the gabled
house identified with William Holmes McGuffey, author of *McGuffey's
Readers*, and his brother, Alexander Hamilton McGuffey. It was remembered that Fanny F. Crosby, the blind poet who wrote "Safe in the Arms
of Jesus," had sometimes stayed at the home of William Howard Doane,
author of "Tell me the Old, Old Story" and other hymns. Bars of music
were carved on the walls of Doane's Mount Auburn home. Up on Walnut Hills the Beecher family clustered around Lane Seminary and
stirred up constant agitation with new educational theory, antislavery agitation, and temperance crusading. Down by the river the dancing,
drinking, and fiddling places abounded. The city had growing pains of
every kind, with a mixed population that ranged from the most conservative traditions to wild experimentation. Scholars, writers, travelers
of all kinds, were aware of the surging vitality of Cincinnati, of its debating and literary clubs and its cultural gropings, from the time that Mrs.
Frances Trollope hurled her verbal brickbats at the young city. Cholera
had decimated its population in 1830 and again in 1849. But it wore the
air of a prosperous and beautiful city when Louise and Alphonso
founded their family on the hill. "Mount Auburn is in its glory now—the
country could not look more beautiful than it does," Louise wrote
home early in June, 1854. Flower beds ran beside their front walk and
honeysuckle tangled with the rose bushes. Blossoms foamed from the
fruit trees like pink mist against the blue sky. Sylvia nurtured their
garden, rounding up roots and seeds from neighbors, and in time they
planted silver maples, mountain ash, and horse-chestnut trees.

Alphonso took his wife to the national antislavery convention held in
Cincinnati in 1854 and she listened attentively to Lucy Stone and Frederick Douglass, the Negro lecturer and writer. All antislavery developments were carefully weighed in the Taft home as the drive to free
the slaves grew strong in Ohio, with its big New England population.
Chase had become one of the most discussed men in the country since
his defense of John Van Zandt, the farmer who helped nine Negro fugi-
tives to escape in his produce wagon. Even though he lost the case he had
focused national attention on the issue and was much in the public eye.

In 1855 he presided at the opening of Zion College, nucleus of the Hebrew Union College, which was the first Jewish theological seminary in the country. Reformed Judaism soon spread out from this focus. Cincinnati already had more than six thousand Jews in its population, with many filling important positions in the life of the city. They had their synagogues, a hospital, club, schools, and literary societies, and were already contributing largely to the cultural life of Cincinnati.

In 1857 the opening of the State House in Columbus was another event of special interest to Alphonso Taft. This public building would become a familiar background for successive generations of Tafts as their political history took root in the capital of Ohio. Alphonso soon became a frequent visitor as his career brought him close to the focus of state government. That same year Delia surprised her family by becoming engaged to a man named Moody. She had no sooner taken this step and confessed to a "little fountain of joy" in her heart than she began to doubt the wisdom of her choice. Her young man came from Lowell, where he had furniture shops and property estimated at $20,000. Since he belonged to the school committee, the lyceum, and other public enterprises, he met the Torrey requirements of public service. But Delia decided that although he had some appreciation of poetry and art, and could play chess well, he was not an "accomplished gentleman—not a person of boots, gloves and whiskers." Her father thought that Moody was neither "bold enough nor swaggering enough" for his exacting daughter and her mother considered him "deaconish and puritanic." Delia liked her beaux to have wit and more than a little learning.

The entire family conferred over this romance. Samuel Torrey was not particularly anxious to have his invaluable daughter leave home. Delia's friends in general decided that Moody was no match for her. "An arbitrary unreasonable man has no title to your heart or hand," Alphonso assured her. "I by no means think single blessedness the worst fate of a lady. Old unmarried ladies have a full share of respect and, I trust, of happiness." But Delia grieved that her romance should be over almost before it had begun. "I'm all broken to pieces," she wrote to Louise, a month after her engagement was announced. She met her young man once more in Boston, played for time, gave further thought to the matter, then finally returned his letters. When he wrote reproachfully to her about her strong-mindedness Delia had her final say in the matter:

> You paid me quite a compliment though perhaps unintentional when you intimate that my strength of mind will be an obstacle to my pleasing gentlemen. . . . If "ladies of strong minds seldom marry" I suppose the reverse proves true and ladies with weak minds usually do. I prefer to belong to the first class even though it precluded me from marrying.

But Delia soon forgot all about Mr. Moody and went on to other romances. They followed much the same pattern until Louise, happily married herself, lost all patience with her shilly-shallying. "We very naturally think everybody ought to do just as we did—get married as soon as they can possibly get ready—having never seen any reason to regret our course," she wrote to self-willed Delia, who was firmly entrenched in the Victorian tradition of setting her duty to her parents above all else.

CHAPTER 3

BIRTH OF A PRESIDENT

Aﬀﬀﬀer the birth of their first son, Samuel Davenport Torrey, who lived only fourteen months and died of whooping cough in 1856, Mr. and Mrs. Alphonso Taft welcomed the stout and lusty child born to them on September 15, 1857. When he was six days old his father wrote to Increase N. Tarbox, a relative by marriage, that Louise was getting along astonishingly well, and the baby was fat and healthy. He thanked providence for this wise ordering of events "so highly important to us." This child's birth was important not only to his parents but to the nation at large, since he would serve as President of the United States from 1909 to 1913 and as Chief Justice of the Supreme Court from 1921 to 1930.

There was rejoicing in Millbury and Susan Torrey wrote to her daughter Louise: "Kiss the dear baby for me. It will be a long time before he will be aware of my existence, but I already take a lively interest in his." Delia suggested that he be named Andrew but she approved the name William Howard Taft given him by his parents. The "Howard" was in honor of his grandmother, Sylvia Howard, whose husband, Peter Rawson Taft, made a casual note of the baby's birth in his diary: "Sept. Tuesday 15. Fair and pleasant. Population of Iowa 509,414. Went over the Seminary with Dr. (E.A.) Crawley. William born."

Louise watched her second son apprehensively, remembering how Samuel had slipped away from them so soon after his birth. But by the time Willie was six weeks old she was writing to her sister Susie that she took great comfort in his perfect health. He was an aggressive baby who insisted on being held whenever he was awake. She could not leave him to go to the city. His father thought him peevish but Louise was convinced that he cried just enough to be healthy. She described his eyes as being "deeply, darkly, beautifully blue" but they would become much lighter as time went on and thousands of Americans would take note of William Howard Taft's clear blue eyes. When he was only seven weeks old Louise was dismayed to find that he had outgrown the slips her mother had made for him. "He has such a large waist that he cannot wear any of the dresses that are made with belts," she wrote to Delia, and went on to describe him in detail:

> Our little Willie is well and hearty and a most charming baby as you would wish to see. He is a great contrast to Sammie who though good and quiet was never very playful. Willie laughs and plays constantly. . . . He has a round and not very large head—a broad, rather than high, forehead. His eyes, though blue have, I still insist, the expression of his father's. His nose is like Rossy's. He has the short upper lip making the triangular fish-shaped mouth common to the babies of our family, but his chin is peculiar and just like his father's and grandfather's.

To Alphonso his new son was a "noble, healthy, fast-growing boy," built more like Rossy than like slim, boyish-looking Charles. But Charles was growing up fast and at Christmas that year he wore his first frock coat. Anna Torrey, Louise's young sister who helped her with the children, stayed with them for the winter and attended the Mount Auburn Young Ladies Institute that had just opened on the hill. She excelled in Latin and French and was the best music student in the school. Anna, like all the Torreys, was deeply interested in history and the political picture, and they all took note of the fact that this was the year of the Dred Scott decision, of the Indian Mutiny, and of the laying of the Atlantic cable.

At home times were hard, for there had been a business collapse and most of the banks had suspended specie payments. Shillito's stayed open but other dry-goods stores in Ohio closed in the autumn of 1857. With the coming of spring and a rush of blossoms all around them, Louise planned improvements for the house—plastering, painting, new carpets. She took Willie with her when she drove to the city to shop. His face lighted up with smiles at the slightest provocation and he spread out his chubby fists to anyone who would look in his direction. His mother took time off now and again from attending him to read *The Virginians* or some other book of the hour. Louise felt that she was becoming too deeply immersed in domestic affairs and she was doubly sure of this when Alphonso wrote to her with an unaccustomed note of reproach after she had taken Willie back to Millbury in the summer of 1858. Her husband had stayed in Cincinnati to attend to his legal affairs, and his mother, who had seemed so amiable to Louise, had been stirring up discontent behind her back. The tenor of Alphonso's complaint was that she was too deeply absorbed in clothes, dressmaking, and sewing, and was neglecting her reading and her interest in public affairs. Actually, she was a woman of exceptional intellect but Willie was absorbing all her time and attention at this point. She was deeply hurt and wrote to Alphonso on August 22, 1858:

> I received in all humility what you say of my need of application to some course of reading and the danger of letting the mind run to waste for want of systematic culture. . . . I have been dismayed and discouraged to find that my mind was so occupied with household matters—the care of the family—of the house but chiefly, the complicated machinery of the kitchen, that even when you found time to read to me I found it difficult to listen with undivided attention. . . .

At this point Louise spoke up briskly in her own defense, reminding Alphonso that in his reading he had been concentrating on ancient history, so as to bring his father within the range of his literary sympathies. Personally she inclined more "to the blooming flowers and fresh foliage in preference to the dyed and preserved specimens—to the living, breathing representatives of animated nature rather than to their fossil remains." But a truce was declared when Louise returned from Millbury in the fall. On her way home she visited Niagara and from there wrote to Delia that "it will be something to tell Willie years hence that he crossed the Niagara River in a little row-boat within reach of the spray from the Fall—before he was a year old."

Willie had become somewhat wild during his summer in the East. His grandfather Torrey had spoiled him and had made a practice of carrying him out to the fields in his nightgown before the family were up in the morning. He could now say Papa and Mamma and had a way of scurrying off with a merry laugh when he was up to mischief. He burned himself several times through his passion for meddling with the stove or picking up lumps of coal. But his mother found him excellent company as he reeled around in a plaid-trimmed dress that bulged around his middle. His father thought him a "delightful little fellow who seemed willing to make the best of the ills of this life."

Alphonso appreciated his family more than ever after their summer separation and the chill that had developed between them. He was careful not to reproach Louise again and she, in turn, tried to accustom herself to his rapidly changing interests and to make some contribution to his studies. Alphonso demanded considerable response from his wives on public affairs. He was a zealot for any cause he took up, and he kept turning constantly to fresh interests. For a period he delved into Egyptian history. Then he studied the life and works of Cicero. He helped Professor O. M. Mitchel start the Cincinnati Observatory and he had a passion for astronomy. His telescope was always focused on the stars and he kept up with the latest in scientific discovery, from the Darwin theory to a new comet. Alphonso took up shorthand enthusiastically when Benn Pitman, brother of Isaac Pitman, came to the United States to promote the science of phonography that they had perfected. The public was skeptical of this elliptical method but Taft was one of Benn's first pupils when he gave demonstrations in Cincinnati. Such was his concentration in a succession of interests that Louise felt that she could count on him for anything but social events. "We might almost as well ask a train of cars to go out of its course to carry a passenger as to expect Mr. Taft to turn aside from his business for the pursuit of pleasure," she commented.

But he took his wife and her sister Anna to observe Donati's comet through the telescope in October, 1858. Charles was deep in Greek and Latin by this time and Rossy had come up with another round of "perfect lessons" at the public school they attended. Both boys played whist and chess when they had free time. They were heroes to Willie as he grew older and he followed them around slavishly, chuckling with delight when they played marbles or frolicked with him.

By Christmas, 1858, Louise reported regretfully to Delia that Willie was "fast growing out of the charming age of babyhood" but the crib would not be empty for long, since she was expecting another child. She felt strong and well and believed it better to have her children in close succession. "I delight in large families and if my health is spared to me I intend to make it the business of my life for a few years," she wrote. The tradition of large families continued with future generations of Tafts. But Willie gave them all a scare early in 1859 by becoming seriously ill, and his parents feared for a time that they would lose him. He was desperately weakened by dysentery, the plague that took the lives of many children of that era.

As he recovered another son was born to the Tafts on May 27, 1859. He weighed nine pounds and was fat, like Willie. His parents named him Henry Waters Taft. Willie, who had long flaxen curls by this time and whose eyes had lightened to a cerulean blue, showed jealousy of the new baby. But his mother was firm with him and he soon learned that he could no longer be rocked to sleep. Even when he was unruly his mother could detect something "arch and interesting" in little Willie's reactions. He now resorted to playing with a dog, to shoveling ground with Rossy's spade, to watching pigeons flutter around the house. He was much too boisterous for his grandmother Torrey, when she visited Cincinnati in the summer of 1859.

The fastidious Susan enjoyed her first glimpse of the western city. She observed that horse railroads were being laid, that Cincinnatians seemed to be heading in droves for Europe, and that large weddings with hundreds of guests, band music, and bridesmaids in white silk with veils were the prevailing fashion among the well-to-do. She was amused to find that Peter and Sylvia Taft were critical of the younger Tafts for having removed themselves from what Susan considered "regular Baptist fogeyism." This enabled Susan to slip into the Unitarian fold without comment.

Alphonso went East late in 1859 to enter Charles at Andover. His parents hoped that this would ensure their eldest son getting into Yale. On his way from Boston to Andover Cincinnati's future millionaire and benefactor spent six cents for coffee, nine cents for peaches, three cents for a cake, sixty-five cents for his fare, thirty cents for a hack, and three cents for a Boston newspaper. There were sixty youths in Charles's class, some green, others smart, but all were bent on getting into Yale. He played chess and cricket, split wood, and used dumbbells for exercise. Charles wrote home that the chapel pews were so high that only his head and neck were visible and the seats were six inches wide. He added a postscript to his first letter home that would become a familiar Taft refrain from school and college: $8.03 in the Treasury and lowering."

His grandmother Torrey, who now saw something of Charles during vacations, considered him a youth of fine manners and obvious promise. His father urged him to correspond with him in phonography—a poser for Charles, who knew nothing of this magic art. But by this time Louise had relaxed sufficiently on her domestic duties to give Alphonso more of the intellectual companionship that he expected of her. She devoted less of her time to sewing and tried to stay awake while he read theology, philosophy, and metaphysics to her at the end of the day. "I have settled it with my conscience that sewing is not my mission or even my duty," she wrote to her mother. "Willie's serious illness was a good lesson to me. It prepared me to feel that while he was spared to us no small trials should make me unhappy." She added that life had never looked so pleasant to her as during the last year, even though it had brought her increasing cares and duties.

By 1860 the Tafts were spreading out in many ways and were entering more into the social life of the city. Alphonso was becoming an important figure in the community and Louise was getting recognition as a New Englander of background and sophistication. They were invited to some of the more elaborate parties of the era and Mrs. Jacob Burnet and Mrs. William S. Groesbeck had at last decided to call on Mrs. Taft. The Perrys had taken a larger house and moved away. With money of her own Mrs. Perry was stocking up on choice pieces for her home in the spring of 1859. Louise observed these developments with interest and took note of her friend's costly new silver tea service. Her own husband had built a stone wall around their house that spring, but she regarded it with mixed feelings, thinking that she could have used the $300 put into it for new carpeting and curtains. It seemed to Louise that an iron fence would have made more show, but the stone wall became a distinctive feature of the Taft house on Mount Auburn and the growing boys liked to sit on it and swing their legs.

Alphonso was a charter member of the Literary Club and among his fellow members were Rutherford B. Hayes, John Williamson Herron, a jurist and father of the future Mrs. William Howard Taft, and Ainsworth R. Spofford, who later headed the Library of Congress. When the new Opera House opened in 1859 Louise attended, draped in an Indian shawl. She and Alphonso invariably created interest when they entered a public place. Both were uncommonly tall, bore themselves well, and had strongly modeled features. They soon became familiar figures at the Opera House with which the Taft name would always be associated. At this time they heard Maria Piccolomini in *Don Giovanni* and attended performances in which Theresa Parodi was the star. In February, 1860, they met Ralph Waldo Emerson at the home of fellow Unitarians. He had lectured at their church and Louise discussed Worcester and Concord affairs with him. "He is social and genial and talks well but he has not repose of manner but is nervous and fidgety," she reported to Delia, while Alphonso added that Emerson was a rare character, an original genius. He approved of his ideas on beauty and its effect on the human race.

With these developments even the preoccupied Mr. Taft conceded that they were getting to be a "party-going family." In one week they attended four soirees, a play, and a lecture on the war in Italy by Henry J. Raymond, of the *New York Times*. Alphonso believed in widening the social spectrum and including all manner of people in their circle. His friend Perry was concerned because he felt that his children were associating almost entirely with the boys and girls of wealthy families, which was not in the Vermont tradition. Louise wrote home that she was not disposed to hold herself aloof but was as "democratic as could be desired."

The social scramble intensified when the Prince of Wales, traveling as

Baron Renfrew, stopped at the Queen City on his American tour of 1860. The Tafts were not invited to the ball given in his honor, since they had "no young ladies to dance with the Prince." But their neighbor, Miss Helen McGregor, was one of his favorite dancing partners, and Rebecca Groesbeck, in white tulle puffed at the waist, was the belle of the evening.

Across the country there was an air of unrest and tension that Louise felt to the full when she went to New England with her small boys in the summer of 1860. The slavery question and the threat of war were discussed in every home. Samuel Torrey could think of little else as he watched small Harry, a strong and forceful child, pushing a chair around with violent movements. Through observing her sons Louise was developing positive theories on the training of the young that she put into effect as she brought up her family. There was nothing haphazard about the Taft training, and it became traditional. She believed that parents could not love their children too much, nor could they afford to forget the profound influence of their own behavior. "It is what we *are*, not what we do in reference to them, which will make its impress on their lives," she wrote to her mother. "They will be sure to find out our weak points whatever professions we make."

Rossy by this time was an inveterate hunter and was always out bagging rabbits, rats, or birds. Charles, about to enter Yale, took Willie to his first circus. His small brother watched with interest while he bought a stove for ten dollars and an overcoat for sixteen to keep him warm in college. Charles was well aware that his father had turned down a place on the superior court bench because he wished to maintain his law practice until he and Rossy were qualified to step into the firm. Later Alphonso changed his mind and became a judge, but in the meantime he continued his fight for civic improvement. He was beset by problems involving the street railroad going up Mount Auburn. The older women opposed it, feeling that it would disturb the tranquillity of the region, but Alphonso expected support from the young, since it would bring them more beaux from other parts of the city.

By December the Tafts were in Washington, where there was no mistaking the war clouds that hung over the country. On their way there they paid close attention to the scene at Harpers Ferry, where the echoes of John Brown still were strong. They saw the engine house where he had entrenched himself, and the hole in the wall made by the cannon ball that hit the mayor. The raid was fresh in the public mind, one of the irritants that led to the ultimate explosion. They were conscious at once of the suppressed excitement in the capital. The Southerners gathered in small groups and all the usual social exchanges were ignored as grave-faced men and women seemed to be waiting breathlessly for the storm to break. Alphonso had cases before the Supreme Court but his major interest lay in observing the drama in the capital. Both he and Louise met Abraham Lincoln at the New Willard, a tall, awkward figure who was still an unknown quantity to the country at large. He looked at them with mournful eyes and had little to say.

Alphonso sought out the Southern leaders, many of whom he knew, and had long talks with them. The depth of purpose that underlay their smooth words was quite apparent to him, and he and Louise were spellbound as they declared themselves in the Senate. The fiery performance staged by Senator Robert Toombs of Georgia, and Judah P. Benjamin's impassioned plea to crowded galleries, made a deep impression on the Tafts. The steps and aisles were jammed with grave-faced spectators as the specter of war assumed reality. Alphonso thought that Stephen A. Douglas's speech was one of the worst he had ever heard anywhere. He wrote about it to his friend Perry:

> Its characteristics were the boldest falsehood, and a total absence of patriotism. It is not compromise but decision and prompt action that is wanted. Everybody is perfectly conscious of that though many have axes which they think will be best ground by compromise.

In spite of the imminence of war as one Southern state after another broke away, Louise found gravity but no alarm among Washingtonians. The Committee of Thirty-three was working for peace, and Thomas Corwin, who had been governor of Ohio and was well known to Taft, reported regularly to him on their progress. But Alphonso was sure that the hour had struck and that peace was out of the question. He and Louise attended President Buchanan's reception on New Year's Day and "saw the old traitor himself, and also Miss Lane." The White House seemed less imposing to Louise than she had expected but the conversation around her was so absorbing that she had only a fleeting impression of the furnishings. Driving through the streets as rain fell, she decided that the general effect of the city was one of mud and disorder. The Capitol dominated the scene; the avenues were wide but the houses were so scattered and so varied in design that Washington as a whole had a "straggling, untidy air." The Tafts were shepherded about by two Cincinnati friends—Larz Anderson and Mrs. John McLean, wife of Justice McLean.

Alphonso Taft was widely recognized in Washington. Many of the politicians both of the North and the South knew him. He had attended the Republican convention of 1860 as an alternate delegate and had watched the political shift from William H. Seward to Lincoln. Ohio was behind Salmon Portland Chase but when Vermont made the first break from Seward to Lincoln, Taft was credited with using influence to this end. He never made this claim himself and he was not a Lincoln man in the beginning, but he strongly urged Chase to become secretary of the treasury at a moment when the brooding Ohio senator, who had longed for the greater prize, was inclined to sulk and hesitate.

CHAPTER 4

THE CIVIL WAR

THE SHOT AT FORT SUMTER in April, 1861, echoed as sharply in Cincinnati as anywhere in the Union. The city, ranged on its encircling hills, was strategically open to attack should Kentucky secede. It was feared that the Confederates might plant batteries on their side of the river, and one alarm followed another in the early days of the Civil War. Cincinnati's population exceeded 160,000 and many of its citizens had Southern sympathies. It lay in the heart of a rich agricultural region, with railroads threading their way northward. Cannon rumbled through the streets and troops left for Washington. Wagons went from house to house collecting comforts for the soldiers.

The Mount Auburn men organized a Home Guard and drilled every night. Eventually twenty-six boys from the local high school formed a junior division for the same purpose. Small boys ran around tugging at army caps and playing at war. "I see little boys not larger than Willie in paper uniforms, trailing round to the music of a drum," Louise wrote to her mother in the early days of the war. "The Stars and Stripes float from almost every house in the city, and disloyalty to the Union is no more tolerated than Unionism was in South Carolina."

Louise reported that the newspapers were Alphonso's "meat, drink and lodging." He stayed downtown until ten o'clock at night to catch the late dispatches. The excitement was intense. His own sympathies had always been strongly antislavery, and from the start he was opposed to any compromise. He ordered ammunition, spy glasses, and books on military strategy. As a leading citizen he was in demand to back patriotic causes and war benevolences. He helped to sell Government bonds, and he made speeches urging emancipation. When recruiting lagged Taft went into action with his own brand of simple, earnest oratory.

Delia stayed with her sister that summer to look after the small children, for Louise was expecting another baby. On December 28, 1861, the future head of the Taft School was born on Mount Auburn. Horace Dutton Taft had a large, muscular frame at birth and Louise thought that he looked like his father. She advocated the name Horace since Alphonso was reading Roman history as the Civil War was fought, and she felt it was less pretentious than some that he proposed. "Robert I like very well, but the inevitable nickname Bob Taft discouraged me," she wrote. Horace proved to be the quietest of all her babies; in fact, sometimes she thought him too good to live, while Willie and Harry had enough "human nature in them to seem to belong to this world."

During the war years the three youngest Taft boys—Willie, Harry, and Horace—grew strong and sturdy, in spite of childish fevers and minor illnesses. Each one early in life showed the characteristics that were to become pronounced in his later years. Willie was tractable and learned with ease. He attended Sunday School at the Western Unitarian Conference Church and behaved well. Harry was so eager to follow him there that his mother had to chase him over a fence and bring him back. He was the Taft son who could not be tamed into any sort of application, but he was ambitious to imitate Willie and to know as much as his older brother. It was also Harry's fate to wear the hand-me-down pants in the family. Horace, clumsy and splay-footed in his first attempts to walk, was an amiable child from the start. Before he was three his father predicted that he would be a giant. He was three feet two inches at twenty-five months of age.

Alphonso took a farm half an hour's ride from Mount Auburn, and Charles and Rossy, when on holiday, benefited by the good air away from Cincinnati's perpetual veil of smoke. Each had a double-barreled gun and their father used a rifle to bring down quail, pigeon, and woodpeckers. Charles's health was frail at the end of his first year at Yale and he needed all the fresh air he could get. He was developing a taste for music at this time and went with his mother to hear Louis Moreau Gottschalk, the popular pianist and composer from New Orleans. In spite of the war Louise noted that music-loving Cincinnatians turned out in opera cloaks and hats. Things did not stand still because of the distant battlefields and she tried to furbish the house on Mount Auburn with new trees and shrubs for the yard. Indoors, vines and ivy hung from baskets in the library window, Dodge patent grates were installed, and the Tafts enjoyed the fresh magic of gaslight. They had turned one room into a library equipped with cherrywood bookcases.

"There is a spirit of improvement going through the hill, to correspond with the sidewalks and fences," Louise wrote to Delia even as the city shuddered with the impact of war and the river trade turned from commerce to wartime traffic. Mrs. Perry had a baby girl in 1862 but Louise saw less of her after they moved away. Her close friend now was Mrs. Harry Smith and they were together at the Opera House early in 1862 when Wendell Phillips, antislavery protagonist, was mobbed. Eggs rained down on them and the scene aroused Louise's desire to defend free speech. She blamed the mayor, whose secessionist sympathies were well known, for refusing to give protection to speakers.

During the war years Louise coped with constant shifts in help, with wayward girls and uproar in the kitchen, with petty pilfering and various domestic annoyances. She had three maids whose pay she cut from $1.75 to $1.50 a week as the war raged on. The outdoor man was dropped for economy and she learned to manage the kitchen range herself, buckling down to making bread that her father-in-law assured her was better than that of their German baker. She found some relief when the daughter of a Lutheran minister joined their household, to look after the children and teach them German. Louise, too, studied the language, for Alphonso was away so much of the time that she felt isolated on Mount Auburn. His rents lagged and his law business had slowed down through war's exigencies but his patriotic duties kept him busy day and night. Louise refrained from buying new clothes since she had enough to do to keep her growing boys fed and clothed under wartime conditions. On his fourth birthday Willie's fair curls were cut and his big blue eyes had a better view of the world.

They were all apprehensive when the rumor spread that Major General Edmund Kirby Smith, with 15,000 soldiers, was heading through Kentucky toward the city. Martial law was imposed on Cincinnati, and on Newport and Covington, Kentucky. A civilian corps of older men was mustered and detachments were posted in the hills. But this scare subsided when it developed that the Confederate general was only staging a demonstration. Taft was highly critical of the conduct of the war. By the summer of 1862 he was convinced that General George B. McClellan would be relieved for incompetency. He had lost all patience with the slow-moving Union leader and considered him a "poor patriot," doing the Confederacy more service than the picturesque Beauregard. Both McClellan and Major General Henry W. Halleck seemed to Alphonso to be "brutally pro-slavery and lacking in republican sentiment." After expecting much from Major General John Pope, he watched the collapse of his vainglorious gestures and deplored his treatment of John Charles Frémont.

Taft kept up a steady barrage of letters to congressmen, judges, friends, and, in particular, to Delia, for whom he reserved his most personal and critical views. At one point he was ready "to pitch Lincoln and his Cabinet into the Potomac, and cudgel his Generals as cowards and traitors." He could see nothing but cold conservatism in their failure to come to grips with the slavery issue. He and Louise, old friends of Frémont, had become his ardent backers during the war years. They were still slow to acknowledge the growing power of Abraham Lincoln and Alphonso wrote with candor to Delia near the close of 1862:

> You see I am not satisfied yet with Lincoln's performance. He must come up to the work and do his duty before this great war rendered threefold greater by his "vacillations and inefficiency" can be brought to a successful conclusion. . . . Nothing can be clearer than that there has been no consistent plan made, or adhered to, in this war. . . . As to politics, you know my sentiments so well that it is unnecessary for me to write. You know I am radical, and find a good deal of fault with the administration, but am hopeful nevertheless.

But Taft's mood changed swiftly when President Lincoln issued the Emancipation Proclamation after Antietam. He was in Washington when this step was taken and he studied the capital in its hectic wartime mood. On his return home he took to the hustings with redoubled enthusiasm and spoke for emancipation at patriotic rallies. The slavery issue was for Taft the inner core of the war. By July he and his fellow townsmen were again stirred up when John Hunt Morgan circled the city with his marauding cavalry, foraged in Clifton and Glendale, and stole horses. They cut the railroad line, shot at a train, and marched the passengers to Morgan's headquarters for parole. They were headed off by Major General Ambrose E. Burnside's cavalry. Gunboats guarded the river lest they recross and eventually they were captured. But Gettysburg and the fall of Vicksburg that month brought hope to the Union forces. The nation's credit was good, Alphonso assured Delia. He had faith in Ulysses S. Grant and his army. "I believe they are patriotic, if they are yet a little under the hallucinations of slavery," he wrote.

All that summer he was busy countering the Copperhead activities of the anti-war faction, for the Secretary of War had retained him to defend the Government in a series of suits involving this discordant element in the population. The draft riots in New York had caused national consternation, and Alphonso assured his father that the time was coming when the Copperheads would call on the rocks and the mountains to fall on them and hide them from the scorn of mankind. Cincinnati was a Copperhead center, with bombs, arms, and other munitions being made there and distributed farther west. Against this was the strong role the city played in outfitting regiments and recruiting men from southern Ohio, Indiana, and Kentucky.

But casualties mounted steadily in 1863 and the city reflected the darkness of death. The wounded came home in droves. The sorrows induced by war affected nearly every household. Dr. Lyman Beecher no longer pushed his abolitionist work on Walnut Hills for he died that year, but Levi Coffin had headquarters in the suburbs for the underground railway. With the Byronic flair of his earlier years subdued to a more somber note, induced by grief and experience, Salmon Portland Chase had now become a respected national figure as he financed the war with masterly effect. Echoes of his interference with Union generals kept reaching his native state, and his daughter, the beautiful Kate, visited Cincinnati with trunkloads of fashionable clothes on her wedding trip in 1863. She had married Governor William Sprague of Rhode Island, and Abraham Lincoln had walked quietly along the street all by himself to attend her wedding, at a moment when her father was making life bitter for him.

Late in 1863 Louise worked for the great Sanitary Fair held in Cincinnati to raise money for war relief. A temporary building was put up in the square between Main and Walnut streets, leaving scarcely enough room for carriages to pass on either side. Refreshment booths stood in the Palace Garden grounds on Vine Street and the horticultural exhibits were in the Mechanics Institute. Pictures and statuary were displayed in Mozart Hall and war trophies were on view. The women worked through their various church groups and Lane Seminary had a table of its own. The Unitarians, an alien group, stood alone in this aggregation of church forces. Louise, busy finishing a Marie Stuart hood for sale, cheerfully commented that "our church invited in all the heathen who didn't belong anywhere." These dissenters clustered under an arch of evergreens surrounding a laden Christmas tree superintended by tall Mrs. Taft. Half the city seemed to have turned out for the fair and crinolines were squashed as women with tilted bonnets and eager eyes moved from booth to booth, buying to help the soldiers. When the smoke cleared away they found they had $230,000 in their coffers.

Toward the end of the war Alphonso dissolved his law partnership with Aaron Perry, who had independent means and who felt he was getting too deaf for court work. The two older Taft boys were heading rapidly toward manhood and would soon be ready to join the family firm. Rossy had distinguished himself at Andover. The great battle was raging around Chattanooga when he entered Yale, with his father's admonition: "There is no place like college to teach the value of each particular moment." Rossy had pleased his father by suddenly displaying a blaze of interest in his studies. Charles was doing well at Yale but Alphonso thought him too worldly in his interests. He was ambitious to get ahead in the business world at a fast pace, convinced that "success could be snatched like a plum from the tree." But his health was so frail in the winter of 1864 that his parents persuaded him to go to Millbury to recuperate. Willie, who had just started going to school on Mount Auburn, begged to be allowed to travel East with his big brother. Louise was criticized for letting her small son set out on this cold and hazardous trip under wartime conditions. But she had perfect faith in Charles's capacity to take care of Willie. "We have concluded that it would be a pretty thorough test of Charley's health," Alphonso wrote to Samuel Torrey on January 10, 1864, as slim, narrow-chested Charles and stout little Willie set forth on their pilgrimage. He had no fears for Willie: "I think you will find Willie a pretty manly little boy. If we had not thought him a good boy, who would not make you much trouble and who would give you a good deal of pleasure, we should not have sent him. It was his own plan. But it struck us favorably under the circumstances. . . . You will find that he means to be a scholar, and studies well. I have never had any little boy show a better spirit in that respect. . . . He has a kind of zeal that is his own."

Willie was soon sledding down the snowy slopes at Millbury and after a mild attack of measles he attended the village school. His father warned him that he need not fight any of the Yankee boys, for Willie was quick with his fists. "They will treat you well, for they will consider you as good a Yankee as the rest of them, and so you are," he wrote to his small son. But he soon learned that Willie was a success all around. He pleased his grandparents and was happy himself. On his return to Cincinnati he went regularly to the district school. He could already read and spell simple words but was behind in arithmetic and writing. Louise decided to coach him. To make all her little boys feel happy she gave Harry a party with ten guests on his fourth birthday, but every festivity, even for children, had its background of shadow. The Battle of the Wilderness raged that May, leaving deep echoes in the nation's homes. "What terrible suspense to those whose friends are in danger," Louise wrote to her sister Anna. "I tremble while I rejoice."

Again the Tafts went East for the summer. Louise visited Saratoga with her sister Anna and they stayed at Congress Hall, drank the waters, and observed the constant dressing up that went on, even in the midst of so much woe and anxiety. Alphonso, who preferred the sea, went to Long Branch for bathing and Rossy joined him there. The boy was worn down from hard study after winning the Woolsey scholarship at Yale, top honor in his class. Louise was concerned, too, to see Charles looking so delicate. "I wish he had better health but we hope to build him up," she wrote to Delia on August 4, 1864. Louise noticed that she could always discuss books, politics, and music with Charles, whom she found energetic, thoughtful, and "caretaking," if not the scholar that Rossy was. At Yellow Springs the two youths met girls from New York boarding schools. In a moment of maternal pride over her grown-up stepsons Louise wrote to her sister in Millbury:

> Our boys can go anywhere and aspire to anybody, without any help from me. If they fulfill their present promise I think no young men will be better worth having. Beaux are so much in demand, they may be in danger of getting an exaggerated idea of their own importance, but their good sense will save them from that.

Charles was deeply interested in the girls he met. Rossy, devoted to outdoor exercise, was less graceful and expert in the ways of society than Charles but he had dignity and quiet humor. His face was thoughtful and expressive and he stood slightly aloof from his fellows. Louise felt that the good conduct of the older boys would set an example for her own sons. "May we never know the sorrow of seeing our sons drunken and worthless," she observed. It had always been the family policy to indulge the boys in reasonable amusements. They installed a billiard table in their home when they saw that Charles was inordinately fond of this diversion. While the little boys were still absorbed in their kites, balls, and tops, their mother helped to start a dancing school on the hill where they would have instruction for their heels as well as their heads, she jested. When a bowling alley was established in the city for family use, the Tafts were among the first to take season tickets and Willie promptly surprised them with good rolls and a ten-strike. She engaged three fiddlers to play at a party she gave for the older boys. With two eligible sons in their home and their own high standing in the community, the Tafts now had the solid social status in Cincinnati that the Torreys had always taken for granted in Massachusetts. But anxious as they were to do everything possible for the advancement of their sons, they were not prepared to compromise on their church affiliations. Many of their friends were moving to the more fashionable Presbyterian churches but Alphonso reported proudly to Mrs. Torrey that her daughter was not one of the herd in this respect.

In spite of the years of wartime suffering there were many brilliant entertainments, but for the most part Mrs. Alphonso Taft entertained her Unitarian friends—the Harrisons and the Goodmans, the Woolsons, Duttons, and the Hoadlys. An occasional *fête champêtre* at Mrs. Harrison's, a party at Mrs. Perry's with a number of generals present, a sprinkling of war heroes at her own board, helped to relieve the strain of existing conditions. She found Major General James A. Garfield a "real wag" who kept the euchre table group roaring with laughter.

Meanwhile in lovely, sequestered Millbury Delia walked from her pillared house along country lanes to attend church meetings, or took shopping trips to Boston and Worcester. Neighbors and relatives came home from the battlefields, wounded, exhausted, with tales of heroism and horror, but not all the young men were on the firing line. Beaux sought Delia out, were weighed by the family circle, and usually were found unfitted for their priceless treasure. They all professed to be anxious to see her married but her father felt that she was needed at home. Her brilliant mother had been failing since she had had a severe bout of influenza in 1862, and Delia had acted as nurse and doctor. "She does not emulate the position of Joan of Arc but rather that of Florence Nightingale," Louise commented. She was the indispensable who tended the sick, ran the house, brought order out of chaos, mollified fractious babies, and argued spiritedly on public issues. She read three newspapers a day and studied the war maps, as well as sharing Alphonso's more serious magazines.

After three years of strenuous work during the war, Delia left for California by way of Panama in 1864. She had no sooner sailed than Susie, the youngest and most frivolous of her sisters, married Samuel Austin Wood, who had traveled East from San Francisco to find a bride in Millbury, his native town. He was an affluent widower, ten years older than Susie, and he owned a boot and shoe business in California. The Torreys were pleased that Susie had made such a good match and they went into action at once preparing for her wedding, but it seemed unthinkable to have an event like this without Delia's guiding hand. More than a hundred guests were invited; a Worcester caterer supplied the wedding feast; and the bride sailed into view looking demure in an elaborate wedding gown trimmed with velvet lace and bugle beading.

But when Susie reached the coast and was installed by Sam Wood at the luxurious Cosmopolitan Hotel her first visitor was Delia, who noticed at once that the bride's hands were "bleached to a shade that displays her diamonds to good advantage." California became more interesting to Delia after the arrival of her young sister. She found much to admire, much to deplore, in her new environment. The misty gray veiling the houses seemed depressing, but the flowers were brilliant, and markets filled with game and vegetables early in February were a novel sight to a New Englander. There were earth tremors from the moment she arrived, a form of excitement that Delia relished, since she thought the amusements and public entertainments dull beside those of Boston. There seemed to be no visiting or partying and she reported sadly that she had not met one unmarried man during her first three months in California other than those she had known before. However, she was entangled in a long-distance romance from the moment she arrived, and was faced with the most important decision of her life.

The brilliant but erratic Samuel Dutton, with whom she had argued and jested for years, poured out his heart to her as soon as she left for the West. He wished to marry her. Delia was appalled since his wife, their Aunt Harriet, had been dead only a few months. The Duttons had been a devoted pair and Harriet was regarded as the ideal minister's wife. They had all visited back and forth and Delia was quite familiar with Samuel's strong and independent views. They had had many discussions on religion, books, and politics, but she had never envisioned him as a suitor. A year earlier she had rejected a young man named Pierce. Like most of Delia's beaux he was a preacher, one of the young men who came to fill the Millbury pulpit for $1,000 a year, usually accompanied by motherless children. These transients were soon aware of Delia's importance in the community, her wit, and her domestic accomplishments.

But with a perfect sense of realism she had never considered herself a good candidate for the parsonage. She had broad views on dogma and she liked to dance and to play cards. Delia even confessed to a vagrant taste for champagne. She believed in woman suffrage and considered herself a worldly woman. But the Reverend Samuel Dutton was a family friend and relative, a clergyman of consequence and some local fame around New Haven. He could not be dismissed too lightly and she was drawn to him as an intellectual peer.

His twenty-page letters were filled with love and persuasion. Delia had never experienced such ardent, if long-range, wooing. While the romantic battle raged she lived in a hotel smothered in roses and taught physiology and calisthenics for sixty dollars a month at the Benicia Seminary, the oldest boarding school in the Bay region. She took trips to Yosemite Valley and saw the Big Trees while she wrote ardent but delaying letters to Samuel Dutton. On her return to Millbury she became more elusive than ever. He had bought a house with a garden for his prospective bride, but she refused to have their engagement announced, although she had declared her love for him in one of her letters. When she insisted that her parents needed her, Louise gave her a severe dressing-down for her vacillation and told her to stop her everlasting dissection of her motives. Delia read her sister's blistering words with some dismay:

Just yield to your first impulse and be happy. . . . You are so bent upon being miserable that anything I can say will be lost upon you. I think it is therefore my duty to warn Mr. D. against marrying such an unreasonable intentional old maid, who has more whims than he has. But he is so infatuated I should inevitably meet the fate of those who try to interfere between man and wife. . . . If I should succeed in alienating him from you, you would go distracted, and reproach me to the end of your days.

When 1865 dawned and the Union forces were closing in for victory, Delia was still playing cat and mouse with Samuel Dutton's affections. She was ever the bellwether of the flock, sharp and observant in her comments, reluctant to give up her freedom, insistent that she could not desert her parents. But the situation solved itself before the minister ever fully understood his fate. Visiting the Torreys in January, 1866, he developed pneumonia and was nursed at the end by Delia.

Feeling apprehensive, Louise wrote to her after his death: "I think and hope for your sake, that no unkindness passed between you in that last visit and I hope he died believing in your affection for him. He had his faults and weaknesses but he was a good and noble man. . . . However it might have terminated, you were seeking his best good, as well as your own."

Delia held her peace and mournfully helped Samuel's sister Mary break up the house that he had bought for her. This was the last of her romances and she laid it away in a package of letters as she continued on her ceaseless round of good deeds for others.

CHAPTER 5

PEACE AT LAST

THE STREETS OF CINCINNATI blazed with lights and fireworks as the war came to an end. The windows of Mount Auburn and the other hillsides sparkled like fireflies. Bands played and flags flew everywhere. All shared in the general belief that the fighting had ended, but the echo of death and suffering muted the rejoicing. Within a few days another crisis had arisen. The victory parade was scarcely over before news of the assassination of Abraham Lincoln reached Cincinnati. Shops closed at once and all business was suspended. Bells tolled and a state of tension prevailed such as the Tafts had never experienced, even in wartime. Years later William Howard Taft recalled his father reading the news to his children in the parlor on Mount Auburn. The symbols of joy turned quickly to mourning. Louise, astute in her appraisal of the political effect of the assassination, wrote to Anna on April 18, 1865:

> The city is draped and craped from one end to the other. . . . All the flags are at half mast and almost every building is festooned with black cambric. . . . Mr. Lincoln could not have died at a happier time for his own fame. Never since his accession has he been so popular with all parties. The success of our armies put everybody in good humor with the Administration and his leniency toward the rebels won the

favor of the Peace men. . . . His views of reconstruction met with great diversity of opinion even among Republicans. There will be many hard questions to settle, and perhaps he was not the man for the coming emergency. Whether Johnson is, remains to be seen. . . .

Alphonso considered President Johnson more likely to hold the Southern leaders responsible for past events than Abraham Lincoln. He had not always approved of the course that the war President had followed, but in the end he had come to honor him without reservation. He believed that the assassination had been planned for an earlier date but, like a torpedo, had gone off at the wrong time. Word of the wounded Seward's fate was awaited as various moves were made in Cincinnati, expressive of the emotions of the people. Junius Brutus Booth, brother of the assassin John Wilkes Booth, had to leave the city secretly because of the violent demonstrations when he was advertised to perform at Pike's Opera House.

At night a band of men made raids and burned secessionist books and papers in the streets. They threatened the homes of prominent secessionists and there was danger of mob rule until the police interfered. But peace finally settled on the city. Freed from a sense of guilt at enjoying themselves while others suffered, people turned to entertaining, to building up their depleted stocks, to looking at the newspapers without mounting apprehension. Even the children seemed relieved and the small Taft boys thrived on Mount Auburn. Willie's appetite for useful knowledge seemed to his father to be healthy and keen and Harry was bright and fond of mischief. Horace, twisting around on a new velocipede, was liked by everyone. Together they created uproar on rainy days and they were all interested in the birth of a baby sister on July 18, 1865. Louise described her to her mother as a doll-like creature with delicate hands and feet, and the "same three-cornered mouth and dimple as Willie." The Tafts had longed for a daughter and "no tongue can tell with what joy she is received. . . . I told Mrs. Perry I should call her Fanny McFlimsey," she added. She soon learned that at about the same time a small nephew had been born in San Francisco. Susie and Sam Wood had named their boy William, and through him the Torrey strain had now been established in California.

By this time Charles was studying law at Columbia University, having been graduated from Yale in 1864. Rossy, or Peter as he was now called, was cramming eight hours a day at Yale, besides his regular studies. He rarely had six hours of sleep a night and his eyes bothered him. He was shocked to find some of his classmates "skinning papers," using elastics, loose coats, and long wristbands for the purpose of cheating. He had seen all of Loomis's Analytics on a roll of paper that could be wound to any portion of the text. His father was astonished to hear this of his honored alma mater.

Alphonso was now a judge of the superior court. Appointed to fill a vacancy, he was elected when the term expired, and he served a third term as the choice of both parties. His judicial spirit thrived on this distinction although it did not fill the family coffers and the Tafts were by no means well-off. The title was no novelty, Louise pointed out, since they were all accustomed to hearing him spoken of as Judge. "As I have no title of my own, being only Mrs. Judge, I shine by a reflected light and shall take on no new airs," she commented.

But to Judge Taft the office was a rare prize. He had thought longingly of the Supreme Court for himself and had written to Salmon P. Chase on December 7, 1864: "To be Chief Justice of the United States is more than to be President, in my estimation. I rejoice beyond what I can express, in the confidence that now the momentous interests of Liberty will be protected in that High Court." He could forgive Lincoln much for having appointed Chase chief justice, added the man whose own son would be the only American to serve both as President and Chief Justice of the United States.

Mrs. Torrey died in 1866 and her importance to the family was summed up in Louise's letter to Delia: "How hard to realize that Mother is not with you to consult and pass judgment upon everything proposed. The loss can never be made up to us." She had been the scholar of the family, stimulating her children with the rich fare of her own intellectual background. Louise urged both Delia and Anna to sustain their mother's interest in public affairs and to read the papers constantly, as their mother had done. The Torrey blood ran strong in the growing generation, as well as the Taft inheritance. After her mother's death Anna wintered again on Mount Auburn, intent on growing a "little citified." She had adopted the fashionable new posture known as the Grecian bend. Although she had developed into an accomplished and attractive girl her health was poor and Alphonso urged the new homeopathic treatment, in which he firmly believed. Social life on the hill was returning to normal and Anna went to the opera with Louise, danced, played croquet at lawn parties, rode, and skated. To celebrate the first Christmas after the war Louise attended a matinee party given by Mrs. Perry. The guests danced in full dress in the afternoon with blinds drawn and candles lit, a fashion popularized in Washington by Harriet Lane. The Longworths, Groesbecks, Andersons, L'Hommedieus, Shillitos, Burnets, and other entrenched Cincinnatians were Mrs. Perry's guests and when it was over Louise wrote revealingly to her family: "I had a sociable time with the ladies & plenty of amusement in watching the butterflies. But the whole affair impressed me with the hopelessness and incongruity of such social aspirations for me, and I came home quite content in my own sphere."

All thought of parties was driven from her mind a few weeks later when Horace and Willie had serious accidents. A new stableman lifted Horace to a horse's back while it was drinking water. The horse reared and kicked and the boy was severely injured in the head. Louise was just coming in the gate when she saw Peter racing for the doctor. She found her son lying in the kitchen, covered with blood and screaming. He had a lump as large as a hen's egg on the left side of his head. A doctor checked the bleeding, cut off Horace's hair around the cut, and drew it together with sticking plaster. He kicked all the time and his mother held him on her lap by main force.

Three weeks later, on a May day in 1866, Willie was in a more serious accident, and at first there seemed to be no hope for his life. The new horse bolted down the hill and the carriage was wrecked. The driver escaped with sundry bruises but Willie was dragged along with the carriage after it overturned, his head banging against the curbstone. His injuries were more severe than Horace's, and his scalp had to be sewn all the way across his head, leaving a scar for life.

Louise was shopping in Shillito's when a friend rushed in to give her the news and drive her home. They went up the hill at a fast pace and passed the wrecked carriage along the way. Willie had been moved to his home from the house on Mulberry Street into which he was carried after the accident. His wound was already dressed when his mother walked in and he looked less battered than Horace had been, but he was much more seriously injured. She nursed him night and day and despaired of his life, but at last she was able to write to Delia: "You must not think of us as depressed and discouraged by our misfortunes. We are happy in the thought that our boys are spared to us, brought as it were from death to life."

Although she never lost her composure Louise was shaken by this experience, and when the boys began to play outdoors again she worried lest they bruise their heads. With deep emotion she wrote to her father: "I had more pride in Willie than in all the rest. He is a very nice boy still and we realize what it would have been to lose him." But illness dogged the Taft family during the spring and summer of 1866. Peter Rawson Taft was close to death and cholera was raging all around them in Cincinnati. Charles and Peter went to Yellow Springs and White Sulphur Springs to escape it. The lives of both youths now broadened out as first one and then the other went abroad to round out his education. Early in 1867 Charles set sail for Europe and by June was deep in Roman law at Heidelberg. That same month Peter was graduated from Yale with a score of 362, the highest on record there. He was valedictorian of his class and his father was elated. Willie was a proud spectator on Presentation Day, but the hours of applause and sunshine for Peter were nearly over. When he joined Charles in Europe he was already worn out. Plagued by headaches and eye trouble he could no longer cope with his studies. Dark days followed as he wandered about, trying first one subject and then another, and always having to put aside his books as headaches oppressed him.

He had hoped to study civil law like Charles, who took his degree at Heidelberg in 1868. Instead he tried to toughen himself with exercise. He walked in the woods and climbed the mountains. The weather was wet and cold and he was acutely conscious of the lack of sunshine, the emptiness of his days after the intensity of his studies at Yale. He caught one cold after another and nothing seemed to help him. Plagued with a sense of guilt where his parents were concerned, he felt that he was failing them. His father's sense of expectation for Peter had been boundless. With Charles things were different. He traveled from country to country, taking in the traditional sights, hearing the finest music, attending the theater, viewing the great art of Europe, and perfecting himself in French and German.

This all took root and affected Charles's taste in the future. He combined what his mother described as a good deal of "pleasuring with a considerable amount of study." He was as lucky at roulette at Wiesbaden as he was with his examinations. His proverbial luck in life was already beginning to show. He wound up in Paris, living with a French family, studying with a professor from one of the *lycées,* and finally taking a degree at the Collège de France. From time to time he entertained visiting Cincinnati girls such as Elizabeth Perry and Mary Shillito. Peter finally joined Charles in Paris and they shared rooms overlooking the garden of the Hôtel de Cluny. The younger Taft felt slightly better in his new environment. Both youths were conscious of the political excitement in Paris as the days of the Commune approached. They watched the Emperor drive along the Champs Élysées and listened to revolutionary talk in the cafes. They visited the Chamber of Deputies and heard Patti sing *Traviata.*

Early in 1869 they were joined by their parents, who had arrived for a brief holiday. Now that Alphonso was assured $5,000 a year as a judge he felt that they could afford this luxury. He was fifty-eight and his dark hair was threaded with gray. Peter acted as their guide and they were scarcely conscious of the restlessness and malaise that beset him. The elder Tafts missed their little boys as they traveled and Alphonso undertook to give them geography lessons through his letters. He had them dipping into encyclopedias and books on natural history to answer his questions. Their mother described for them the glories of Schönbrunn and the Pantheon. Horace had just been entered in the Sixteenth District School that they had all attended and his mother summed up his character with accuracy when she wrote to her father just before sailing for Europe: "We do not call him a handsome or showy boy but somehow he wins his way to all hearts with his well-meaning straightforward simplicity, and he is a favorite with all the neighbors. I am mistaken if he does not prove to have that kind of character of which it is said: 'It will do to tie to.'" His aunt Delia added her own conception of Horace when she wrote after studying one of his photographs: "Horace doesn't handsome up much, but he is a dear boy." She approved his love of history and the way he followed people around the house, describing battles and other historical events. Delia thought Horace was born to be a schoolmaster.

During the long summer days while his parents were abroad Willie worked in the garden and earned eight dollars for his efforts. The grapes were lush that year and apples were ready for eating by July. The catawba vine against the stable had roots which seemed to Willie to grow a yard in a week. Trailing vines and verbena overflowed the large iron vat that Louise had installed in the front yard before going abroad. It delighted both of the Tafts to make improvements in their property. Alphonso had bought another lot close to his house; he had the stable set 150 feet farther back and had a wall built to support the carriage way.

Just before Christmas, 1869, Willie sent Peter a letter that astounded his older brother for its penmanship, maturity, and interest. He had embarked on a correspondence that was to become a lifelong habit. Wherever William Howard Taft was, whatever he was doing, he always took time to communicate entertainingly and at length with his family and friends. Peter, back in Heidelberg after his parents' visit, wrote at once with appreciation to his small brother:

> We expect you younger boys, who have the benefit of our experience in education, to do great things. Never be content until you have done the very best you could have done, for if you always do that you will never be unhappy. I am glad to hear that you boys are doing so well in school. It is a favorable indication as to your future career. You must make Charley and me proud to be able to call you brothers. . . . Work hard, and do your part in building up the reputation of the family.

It was Willie's fate to have precept, example, and encouragement doled out to him by parents and brothers. Charles, who took great interest in the success of his younger brothers, sent Willie his silver watch from Europe when he was first in his class that year, with an average of 95. Horace was second in his, and Harry third, to his dismay, for he was a hard worker and dogged by nature. But his studies came easily to Willie, who was neither a prig nor a bookworm. He played with as much zest as he worked, and he welcomed Charles back to Cincinnati with great joy in the spring of 1870.

The oldest Taft son was now a worldly young man, polished, experienced, ambitious. He went into the practice of law with Edward F. Noyes, who later became governor of Ohio, and threw himself wholeheartedly into local affairs. Cincinnati mothers studied him with interest as a prospective match for their daughters. He was slight in build, keen and quiet in his ways and speech. Charles had absorbed a great deal about the art, music, and politics of Europe during his two years abroad. Every day had been put to good use, for he had drive, well concealed behind a modest and thoughtful manner. His grandfather Phelps, a tenacious and scholarly man, had left Charles and Peter $50,000 each when he died, so that they now had independent means.

While Charles was getting started in Cincinnati, Peter was living through the exciting days of 1870 in Paris. He wrote to his father about the breathless moments when the plebiscite was adopted. Paris was illuminated that May night as he drove around, viewing the public buildings. The Emperor had a big reception, "but forgot to invite me," Peter noted with a flash of humor. Smallpox raged in the city and he was glad to be heading home. "The College education and the European education are no longer projects; they are accomplished facts," he wrote to his father. The months abroad had been as devastating for Peter as they had been stimulating for Charles, who had tried unsuccessfully to help his brother. The Tafts and the Torreys were equally persuaded of the importance of study abroad to round out an American education. Louise and Alphonso were unitedly ambitious for their children and on one occasion his mother stated firmly: "Mediocrity will not do for William."

The Tafts were strong and serene characters themselves, meeting difficulties with spirit and high courage. To some they seemed exacting in the demands they made on their children. Their work was closely surveyed and was analyzed and criticized. They must always excel in their studies or they were asked why they had lagged. This, too, became a family tradition. Louise was the disciplinarian and she could be stern. She did not believe in spoiling her children but she saw to it that their lives were filled with simple and healthy pleasures and that all family observances were kept with warmth and spirit. In this way she created a pattern of family gatherings and family loyalty that flowed down through successive generations. Like his wife, Alphonso expected certain standards of his children and they all felt they had to live up to the wishes of their parents. In later years Horace remembered his father as having a rare combination of strength, gentleness, simplicity, and tolerance. He considered him generous, and completely democratic in spirit.

Their home had the advantages of city and country life. As the children grew up they had all the joys of farm and garden life, of pets and country picnics. The small boys tagged after the big ones and learned to swim and shoot and fish. Horace would swim in the shallow end of the pond while Charles and Peter sought the deep end. They took long country walks and picnicked on sausage and hard-boiled eggs. They ate apples straight from the trees and strawberries from their garden. In their younger years they played marbles and sandlot baseball with the boys from Reading Road and Little Bethlehem and later they went in for football, baseball, and shinny, as well as croquet and billiards. At all ages they skated on the canal and trudged up and down Mount Auburn in storm and sunshine. Actually, the Taft boys devised many of their own amusements. Horace was clumsy at games and failed in many, but he was vigorous in a rough-and-tumble and enjoyed a contest of this kind. His conspicuous height made him shy and awkward, but his homely ways endeared him to his contemporaries as well as to his elders. There was much fighting among the brothers and their mother disliked this intensely. Will was too big and strong to fight with Horace, but Harry and Horace tangled constantly and Will had to act as referee.

After district school they all attended the Woodward High School, named for its notable founder, William Woodward, a formidable schoolmaster whose reputation was nation-wide. It was a grim-looking building, terra-cotta in tone, with an iron fence suggestive of the Bastille. Woodward was vigorous in imposing high standards of education and his school had considerable reputation in its day. He thought nothing of dropping forty percent of the class if they did not meet his stiff standards. It was a free school and the students were expected to work or leave. Five boys in Horace's class went on to Yale and four were Phi Beta Kappa. The school was particularly strong in mathematics. The boys pored over historical books and the young Tafts went in strongly for Scott, Dickens, Thackeray, Cooper, and, in lighter moments, the Oliver Optic books, adventure stories with patriotic undertones. Will spent hours reading *Harper's Weekly* at the home of his friend, Rufus B. Smith.

He had grown to his full height by the time he entered high school and had hardened up physically, although his fellow students chose to call him "Lub" or "Lubber." Willie had become Will to his relatives and Bill to his contemporaries. He was good-natured, with a hearty laugh and a genial spirit that turned to tough determination when he tangled with the gangs that haunted Butchertown, below Mount Auburn. The boys on the hill were fair game for the warriors of the flats and big Bill Taft could stagger them with his strength. He was heavy in build but was light on his feet. He had wrestled for years and could land a smashing blow. When John L. Sullivan visited Cincinnati, Judge Taft invited him to his offices. He felt his biceps and studied him from head to foot. At last he exclaimed: "Well, sir, you are surely a marvelous specimen. But let me tell you, sir, I wanted you up here to decide if you're a better put-up man than my son Will."

Sullivan grinned. "Well?" he asked.

"You'll have to pardon me, sir, but you are not," the Judge replied. "My Will is the better man."

Family pride was strong in Alphonso and Louise. All of the children had profited by their summer visits to Millbury, where Samuel Torrey, with his old-time manners and brisk temper, conveyed a mood of his own. He abhorred idleness and extravagance. It was his custom to do his own marketing and he saw to it that the children sawed wood and earned their keep in practical ways. Samuel was as devout as his wife Susan was free-ranging in her religious views. He took pride in shepherding an assortment of grandchildren down the aisles of the Congregational church in Millbury as the years went on. With his stiff crop of white hair, precise manners, and acid comments, he could wither the boys with his unerring criticism. There was something of her father in Delia; Horace in his maturity considered her an unreconstructed Yankee with a New England conscience.

As the years went on they all liked to jest with Delia about her parsimonious ways but her economies were applied solely to herself. She was always ready to lend money at the prevailing rate of interest to any member of the family who needed it. As the boys and girls were graduated or won special honors Aunt Delia's honorariums arrived without fail. She was a bulwark of strength with her convictions, her solid virtues, her interest in the currents that flowed around her. None could say that her faded romances had left her with the lavender-and-old-lace touch, for she had a wry sense of humor and her bite and wit were proverbial. The people of Millbury took pride in their Miss Torrey. When the Taft boys first visited the little town, the Blackstone River ran clear and beautiful, but as nearby Worcester grew from a village to the proportions of a city it lost its crystal clarity and Delia compared it to a sewer.

Horace thought of his mother, too, as being a Yankee clear through, with exceptional firmness of character and her full share of New England ideals. In bringing up her five sons and one daughter she succeeded in unifying the family heritage of Phelps and Torrey. She treated the boys impartially and was as proud of Fanny Phelps's children as of her own, different though they were. Charles's entertaining tales of his life abroad were of great interest to Louise and she was pleased that he lost no time on his return in getting into action on the political front. He

served a term in the Ohio General Assembly but was defeated when
nominated for Congress by the Republican party. His defeat sat lightly
on him, however, and his father felt that the experience he had had in
public speaking and observing the ways of government would serve him
well in the practice of law.

Alphonso became a headline figure in 1868 through the most publi-
cized decision of his judicial career, and one that was destined to impede
him later on the political front. A petition was laid before the school
board urging the prohibition of religious instruction and Bible reading
in the common schools of Cincinnati, an issue that various groups had
been stirring up for some time. Critics of the petition argued that the
government was responsible for the dissemination of religious and moral
information. Early in 1869 a Protestant organization brought suit to en-
join the school board from abandoning religious instruction. Judge Taft
was one of the three judges who heard the case and he delivered a dissenting opinion on technical grounds. He argued that the school board
had an obligation as well as a right to keep religious partisanship out of
the public schools.

The headlines that accompanied Judge Taft's decision created an impression of godlessness that was most disquieting to the Tafts and the
Torreys and was not a true evaluation of the situation. His decision was
often cited subsequently and he always regarded it as his most important
ruling. He viewed it with pride rather than with regret. The Supreme
Court of Ohio upheld his opinion and reversed the judgment of the
lower court. Actually all of the Tafts were ardent and regular churchgoers but Alphonso's swing from the Baptist to the Unitarian church
had created problems for his family. The breadth and tolerance of
Unitarianism were suspect in the conventional circles to which they belonged. Judge Taft had helped to build up the denomination in Cincinnati, to choose the most likely preachers, and to support them when
they ran into trouble with their independent views.

His stand became public talk when he backed Moncure D. Conway,
the vigorous abolitionist who was editing The Dial in Cincinnati as war
broke out and who moved to London in 1864. Both on dogma and the
slavery question, Conway shared the views of Theodore Parker, the
Massachusetts Unitarian clergyman whose "heresies" rationalizing the
Miracles had stirred up churchmen across the nation. The Tafts considered their fellow Unitarians in Cincinnati people of intellect, who
made no show although many had great wealth. For the most part their
roots were in New England. They dressed plainly and had good books
and fine art in their homes. Louise, on the defensive as Alphonso plunged
deeper into controversy, wrote to her family in Millbury that in the past
her husband had always attended church to please others. Now he was

pleasing himself. And while he was fighting Conway's battle for freedom in the pulpit one legal colleague remarked that when a difficult case involving fundamental principles of law was under consideration, Judge Taft brought up the heavy artillery.

CHAPTER 6

A SINTON MARRIES A TAFT

O N THE AFTERNOON of December 4, 1873, Annie Sinton, dark-eyed, with sparkling Celtic charm, was married to Charles Phelps Taft. This was a significant wedding for Ohio, fusing the Sinton fortune with the Taft ideals and ambition. Their fellow townsmen recognized it as a union of importance. Together the bride and groom would leave an indelible stamp on the artistic and civic life of Cincinnati. The Cincinnati *Enquirer* of December 5 reported that the "fashionable, the wealthy, and the intellectual elements of old Cincinnati" attended the wedding and added: "The widowed father of the bride is perhaps the wealthiest man in the community, and the fair bride is his only surviving child; the groom is a young lawyer, of a family noted for intellectual cultivation."

Annie's white satin bridal gown had a short train, was cut low, and was trimmed with point lace. She wore pearl and diamond jewelry and carried orange blossoms. Charles and she stood under a canopy of evergreens in the fine old mansion on Pike Street where the Sintons lived. A wedding bell of exotics hung over them as Dr. Skinner, of the Second Presbyterian Church, performed the ceremony. Peter Taft was best man and the ushers were Samuel F. Hunt and Charles B. Wilby. Mrs. Elliott Pendleton received with the bride and Currier's band played through the reception that followed. Mrs. Alphonso Taft moved about majestically in black silk with a grenadine overdress and Valenciennes lace. "I never looked so well in my life," she wrote home with satisfaction.

David Sinton approved the marriage of his daughter to young Taft. He was a self-made man who had been brought to the United States from Ireland as an infant and had built up a fortune in iron. He worked first as a boy in a store in a small Ohio town, and then moved to Cincinnati, where he ran a small commission business. At the age of eighteen he tramped to Ironton when he heard of an opening in a blast furnace. He quickly learned all that he could about casting iron and before long leased a furnace of his own. As his business expanded he moved back to Cincinnati in 1849. With the approach of the Civil War he took all his own capital, borrowed as much more as he could, and stocked up on pig iron. In the years that followed he became an immensely wealthy man with a wide range of business interests. He concentrated on real estate, railroads, gas, and civic improvements, and was philanthropic in his own obstinate way. Sinton despised the wasteful, the extravagant, the idlers of the world, and he told William Howard Taft on one occasion that he had thrown all his own energies into making money.

Rugged in demeanor, close-fisted, deeply devoted to his daughter, he was proud of his fortune, yet chary of spending it. His wife died of consumption when Annie was still a baby and he jealously guarded the child's life, ordering her nurse to keep her on a toughening regime of cold baths and light clothing. She was a dark-eyed and vivacious little girl, a romantic adolescent full of Celtic fancies, and a good student at the Mount Auburn Young Ladies Institute, where she was liked for her wit and her generous spirit. Annie was everything that her father was not in the way of warmth and spontaneity. Sinton spoiled her but kept her on a tight rein. Although he was both cautious and autocratic Annie at times could move him in the direction that she wished him to go, or wheedle him into acquiescence.

It was inevitable that she and the Tafts should meet, even though they did not move in the same circles and Mrs. Alphonso Taft knew her only slightly. Charles was an ambitious young lawyer who had just been defeated for Congress. During these early years of practice he was the superior court reporter and he helped to codify the school laws of Ohio. He entertained pretty Miss Sinton with tales of his travels and they often discussed the art and music of Europe. The Sintons lived in the colonial mansion on Pike Street that eventually became the Taft Museum. David Sinton bought it in 1871 and he continued to live in it after his daughter's marriage. It was a house with a history, even before the Tafts made it one of the notable homes of the nation. Martin Baum, a German settler who had bought a tract of land stretching from Pike

Street to the top of Mount Adams, had it built in the early 1820's along
lines suggestive of the White House. When his business failed in 1826
and he had to sell his mills, boatyards, packing plants, and land, his
house, which was then known as Belmont, was deeded to the United
States Bank. It was run as a female seminary until Nicholas Longworth
bought it in 1830 and made it one of the aristocratic homes of Ohio.
The winegrower dwelt in it in patriarchal style, adding to its fame.

For the better part of a century artists, writers, musicians, statesmen,
jurists, and celebrities of all kinds attended functions in this graceful
mansion. From Mrs. Trollope to President Taft the list was long. Harriet
Martineau commented on the "splendid house with garden and con-
servatory" that overlooked the canal. The Tafts delighted in the beauty
and harmonious proportions of the Baum house. Its classical portico
faced west and David Sinton eventually added a wing to the northeast.
Annie's wedding in this setting was the great social event of 1873 in Cincinnati. Louise proceeded at once to introduce her to the Taft friends, for
David Sinton was so tyrannical that she had not shared freely in the social
life of the city. But her gifted mother-in-law took the situation in hand
and watched Annie with approval as she faced the social barrage. Her
earliest impression of the bride was that she was unobtrusive and had
poise.

The quality young Mrs. Taft had in the highest degree was an authentic wit and insouciant spirit that her fellow townsmen would come to
know and appreciate. Charles was a steadying force in the background
and her devotion to him was encompassing from the start. Some found
her imperious as the years went on and her power grew, but she was
generous and thoughtful as long as she lived. Although she deferred to
her father in many respects, Charles led her gradually into asserting
herself in small matters, such as going to Lookout House to listen to a
German band on a Sunday. Annie debated with herself as to whether it
could be wrong to listen to music at any time. "You know I have been
more strictly raised than Charley with regard to Sunday keeping or breaking and what seems all right to him strikes me a little strangely," she confided to Alphonso.

The winter of Charles's wedding was a mild but troubled one. The
country had been shaken by the financial panic of 1873 and there
were breadlines in Cincinnati. River traffic had declined since the war
but the railroads had widened the markets in a steady and dependable
way. The city, with a population that now exceeded 200,000, had been
outstripped by Chicago as a packing center but new industries had
opened up. Four of the surrounding hills had prosperous and well-
cultivated communities. Mount Auburn, the oldest and also the first to
be brought within city limits, had become noted for its gardens. The Taft

home was a sturdy landmark, with its square lines, its observation platform, its narrow porch, its open grounds and stone wall. Clifton, where the Chases had long had their farm, had become the most fashionable of the hilltops. Walnut Hills had many famous families, as well as its echoes of Lane Seminary and the Beecher family. Price Hills had substantial homes, many in rococo style, with iron grills, freestone fronts, and the arabesque architecture characteristic of the growing city. The glimpses of Kentucky and the play of light and color on the winding river were a constant source of delight to the dwellers on the hills. James Parton, visiting Cincinnati in the 1870's, wrote in the *Atlantic Monthly*: "As far as we have seen or read, no inland city in the world surpasses Cincinnati in the beauty of its environs."

Parks and gardens by degrees turned Cincinnati into a show city and its naturally beautiful setting lent itself well to such adornment. The beeches, elms, and sycamores of Mount Adams gave the famous observatory a verdant setting. The Cincinnati Zoological Garden, encompassing a park of forty-five acres of woodland, plateau, and ravine, opened in 1875 with a crowd of 10,000 present. Annie, Louise, and Fanny drove up with a flourish to show their interest and Annie thereafter made it one of her special projects. Downtown, the Tyler Davidson Fountain became a city landmark in 1871. Cincinnatians worked in the valley and lived on the slopes. They still liked to congregate around the public landing where the vivacious flow of river life went on, as paddle-wheel steamers with orchestras and calliopes came to rest at the wharf. Trains and steamboats brought in an endless stream of strangers, and diverse tongues were heard in the city streets.

The last touch of the frontier had passed away, however. Men dressed with more formality, paid Sunday calls, and showed some interest in the arts. Fine equipages drove up and down the hillsides, and dinners and balls of consequence grew in number. But with all this prosperity the crusading touch was strong and a great temperance drive took the city by storm in 1874. The Methodists and Baptists were deeply involved; the Presbyterians were mildly interested; but the Unitarians stood aloof from it all. When women canvassed the hills for temperance pledges Louise kept out of their way. Although approving the basic principle of temperance she considered the movement sectarian. She was equally cold to the women's suffrage convention held at Worcester, a pioneer event attended by Delia. Both sisters were unequivocally committed to the suffrage cause but Louise preferred to have the subject discussed calmly on its merits, instead of being talked of only in women's rights meetings. Neither one approved of Victoria Woodhull, one of the most militant agitators in the field, a beauty who would dare to run for the Presidency. Louise and Mrs. Perry agreed to stand firmly behind the Reverend Dr.

Henry Ward Beecher when Mrs. Woodhull's charges that he had alienated the affections of Theodore Tilton's wife eventually landed him in court. Both women knew the noted preacher well and were incredulous. "The whole pack of his persecutors are so contemptible it is easier to believe that he is innocent than that they can have told the truth," Louise wrote to Delia, but history proved her wrong.

Although the Tafts favored public school education for their boys they decided to send Fanny to a private school run by Miss Edith Nourse. "Is it not best to put Fanny into the fashionable mill and let her take her chances with the rest?" Louise asked Delia, who agreed. Most of the debutantes of the period in Cincinnati were educated and polished by Miss Nourse, a Maine spinster whose school was known as The Nursery. She had 120 students when Fanny came on the scene but some of the fashionable families deserted her when George K. Bartholomew, the compiler of a Latin grammar, opened a school for girls at Fourth and John streets.

With Peter an eligible young bachelor and three other sons heading toward maturity, Louise studied the year's crop of debutantes attentively. Mary Shillito was the girl whose name was linked most often with his. Peter's health had improved and he was now practicing law with Charles. He had moved to the fashionable Second Presbyterian Church and was taking dancing lessons. "Peter lies low as yet," his mother wrote, but she thought that he had never looked so handsome or been so agreeable. Soon she was aware that he had fallen in love with Matilda Hulbert, the daughter of William P. Hulbert, a man of large commercial interests. Like David Sinton, Hulbert was brusque in manner and domineering in spirit—a rugged pioneer. His wife was an invalid and he kept a tight rein on Tillie, who was pretty, intelligent, and popular with the younger set. Her father made her promise to wait until she was nineteen before becoming engaged and Louise, who had disapproved at first because of her youth, capitulated and wrote to Delia that it was pleasant to see young people as happy as Peter and Tillie were.

Harry was showing more talent for music and art than for scholarship at this stage of his life and his parents found him more difficult to satisfy than the other boys. "It may be that he will be the merchant of the family," his father predicted of the son who would become a successful corporation lawyer in New York, with a strong taste for political reform. He seemed to do better after Will left for college, perhaps because his older brother had always overshadowed him. "Willie is foremost, and I am inclined to think he will always be so," Alphonso informed Samuel Torrey.

Will entered Yale in 1874 and landed at once in the first division of a class of 191. He found the chapel seats unduly hard, the sermons dull, and Livy difficult, but he was cheerful over the hazing. His schedule seemed severe to the blond, fine-looking youth from Cincinnati, who described it in detail in a letter to his mother:

> Rise at half past six, generally look over my lesson before breakfast, breakfast, prayers, recitation, grubbing until half past eleven, recitation, dinner, grubbing until 3 o'clock, gymnasium, half an hour study until five, recitation, supper. Here I sometimes go down to the P.O. Then I work till ten, sometimes till eleven. . . . You expect great things of me but you mustn't be disappointed if I don't come up to your expectations.

Young Taft remained deaf to the family injunctions to devote himself entirely to his studies. He was already a friendly and gregarious youth and he informed his mother that if he had to be isolated from his class in order to take a high stand, then he did not pine for the honor. He insisted on some degree of relaxation. Like Peter and his friend, Rufus B. Smith, he was elected to Skull and Bones, but he did not win the Woolsey Prize, as Peter had done, and as his family had expected him to do in his sophomore year. This left no scar and he wrote philosophically to Aunt Delia: "I don't care very much because Father knows I worked hard." His classmates envied him the number of letters he received from home but he cheerfully explained that he had a father who considered letter writing a recreation.

Will visited Millbury that spring and he and Aunt Delia, thoroughly congenial souls, sparred together with merry wit. She teased her big nephew about his girl friends and Will, like his father, upheld his aunt in her spinsterhood. "I wouldn't have you marry for anything because you wouldn't be the same good soul you are now," he wrote to her on April 25, 1875, when it became known that her younger sister Anna had stolen a march on her and become engaged to Professor Edward Orton, a geologist of considerable reputation in Ohio. This match was something of a sensation in the family circle, since quiet Anna had found a prize in the matrimonial sweepstakes. Her fiancé was a widower with four children and she moved with confidence into a happy marriage, becoming a well-known figure in Columbus.

Actively out in the political field for the first time in his life, Judge Alphonso Taft came to the fore in 1875 as a candidate for the governorship of Ohio. New forces were stirring up the Republican party. Discord prevailed and it was felt that a man of Taft's standing and reputation might improve the party prospects. The pre-convention campaign was a violent one, for political alignments had changed since the war and corruption flourished. Bounties, greenback inflation, speculation, and the redistribution of power and wealth had had their effect. George Barns-

dale Cox had come into power in Ohio as a party boss of dubious reputation. He was involved in tax assessment cases, street-paving contracts,
public service franchises, and various court decisions; meanwhile, he
steadily built up a fortune and dominated certain factions in the Republican party.

More than anything else the old issue of the Bible in the public schools
served to defeat Alphonso in his campaign for the governorship. In the
end Rutherford B. Hayes was renominated, although he had said he
would not run if his friend Taft's name were presented. Charles Taft
moved that Hayes be the unanimous choice of the party and Alphonso
gave him full support, making the nominating address and working determinedly for his election. But it was not the governorship that Judge
Taft longed for so much as a place on the Supreme Court. Toward the
end of 1874 he had written frankly to Chief Justice M. R. Waite asking
for consideration if Justice Noah H. Swayne should retire. "But I do not
suppose that anything of that kind is in store for me," he added with
humility. Justice Waite assured him that his sympathies were with him in
his wish but he feared that the President would select someone from the
South. As it happened, Justice Swayne remained on the bench until
1881 and Taft's ambition was never realized, nor did he live to see his
own son become chief justice.

Although defeated on the state level Alphonso became a national
figure in 1876 when President Ulysses S. Grant asked his old friend to become his Secretary of War. He was looking for a man of unblemished
reputation to take the place of William W. Belknap, who was impeached
that year for malfeasance in office. Taft was known far beyond the
boundaries of Ohio for his varied legal experience and his high ideals.
In Washington, he found himself at once in the middle of the roaring
storms of the Grant administration. Although he disliked his role he per-
severed with his official duties and, taking the large view of his situation,
wrote to Samuel Torrey: "One day it is Babcock; another it is Belknap.
But the Government moves on, backed by a mighty people."

After the wild spending and charges of corruption surrounding his
predecessor, Alphonso tried to curb patronage and to cut military expenses. The affairs of the War Department were in great confusion
and he was relieved when President Grant made him Attorney General,
where his talents and judicial experience could be used to better advantage. He always considered this period the peak of his career and he
looked back with satisfaction on his role in the Hayes-Tilden election
dispute of 1876. Both Rutherford B. Hayes, the Republican candidate
for the Presidency, and Samuel J. Tilden, his Democratic opponent,
claimed victory when the count was in. Taft, as Attorney General, was
called on to help frame a bill for the creation of an electoral commission

that would have power to settle questions arising from a disputed vote for the Presidency. In this instance the commission found in favor of Hayes and he was elected, although the murmurs of dissent continued. Taft was called to the White House by President Grant and stood by while Hayes was privately sworn into office in the Red Room two days before the official ceremony in the Capitol.

During this period the Tafts lived at the Ebbitt House and the Washington papers took note of the striking pair who spread dignity and confidence as they moved about in a somewhat checkered society. Taft was described as a "splendid specimen of American manhood, one of the ripest scholars, ablest jurists, and wisest men in the United States." The Washington *Chronicle* assayed Mrs. Taft as a "lady of rare perceptive powers, of still rarer common sense—a woman whose mind is above petty rivalries and snobbish affectations." The press agreed that she was handsome, intellectual in her interests, and unpretentious in her manners. Actually, Louise found her new role completely to her liking. From time to time she and Alphonso dined *en famille* with the Grants. Both came to the conclusion that Mrs. Grant was sensible and modest, although Louise thought her impulsive at times and inclined to be governed by prejudice.

"She is simplicity itself—almost *flat* sometimes, with the appearance of a person who has never been criticized or *taken down*," she reported to Delia. Young Frederick D. Grant, the General's oldest son, was away on service. His wife, the exotic-looking Ida Honoré of Chicago, who was Mrs. Potter Palmer's sister, was at the White House, awaiting the birth of her first child. Julia Grant, who later became the Princess Cantacuzene, was born on a June day in 1876 and was baptized in the East Room. Mrs. Taft considered Fred and Ulysses Grant pleasant, unaffected fellows— "like our boys, only I don't believe they are so smart." Altogether she found the Grants an affectionate and happy family, disposed to have a good time and not to worry over the critical things said of them.

Always demanding in her standards, Louise considered many of the women in government circles "platitudinous" but she enjoyed the company of the more gifted men. "Mrs. Blaine is bright and smart—one of our sort of women," she wrote to Delia of the wife of the senator from Maine. She learned to be "wise as a serpent and harmless as a dove" in steering clear of complications in Washington, particularly in the case of Roscoe Conkling, the flamboyant senator from New York. For some time his name had been associated with that of Kate Chase Sprague, the dazzling daughter of the Chief Justice, who had died in 1873. The powerful banking house of Jay Cooke, and the vast cotton interests of Senator Sprague of Rhode Island had crashed in that same year and Kate's fortunes were in eclipse, as waves of scandal gathered around her.

Delia was able to form her own conclusions about Washington when she visited her sister in 1876. She drove to Arlington Heights and the Soldiers Home and decided that the capital streets looked grubby. It gave her great satisfaction to receive with Louise and attend a family dinner at the White House. Delia and Mrs. Grant had much to say to each other but the man who had saved the Union had no small talk. Louise aroused her sisterly pride as she sat at the White House table, wearing a black silk gown with a blue overdress and Spanish lace. Once again her cameos and point lace—the family dress-up symbols—were in full play. "It is a great thing to be in official circles in Washington," Delia reported to their father. "Mr. Taft and Louise bear their high honor with becoming dignity, but their good sense is not impaired, and they do not assume any lofty airs." Before returning to Millbury Delia followed thousands of her fellow countrymen to the Centennial Exposition in Philadelphia.

The Torrey sisters relished life at the seat of government but Louise worried about her small daughter, who had been left at Miss Nourse's school. Fanny sent her mother anguished letters, insisting that she would die if she were not rescued. She raised as much fuss as Nellie Grant did to get away from Miss Porter's at Farmington, or as Jesse Grant did when sent to a succession of boarding schools. Mrs. Perry took her to the Zoological Garden to console her. Annie and her friends rallied around but Fanny wrote frantically to her mother: "I am crying so. O! Mama, please take me to Washington. I am so lonesome. From your darling little girl, Fanny." But, true to the Taft tradition, she wished her father to know that her marks were good.

When fully persuaded that Fanny was making herself really ill, her mother, who could be skeptical of hysterics, brought her to Washington. Horace felt lonely, too, with his parents away from Mount Auburn but he always found a warm welcome on Pike Street. Charles had his feet already well planted on the road to material success. He had plenty of vigor and ambition of his own but the Sinton money and influence were now behind him and he was thinking of giving up law to devote all his time to the family interests. When his father moved to Washington he advertised the law firm of C. P. and P. R. Taft, successors to A. Taft & Sons, but Peter and he were not doing well as partners. Sinton, at the moment, was out of patience with the street railroad companies and some of the city authorities over improvements he planned for Fifth Street. He was prepared to spend from $150,000 to $200,000 on a forum that his enemies said he intended as a monument to himself. The Iron King tartly announced that he did not hanker to squander a fortune glorifying himself. As obstructions developed he refused to wine and dine the officials who might have pushed through his plans. Above all, he believed in independence.

Sinton always kept an interested eye on Will Taft, who was now getting keen enjoyment out of Yale. In his junior year he won a prize in mathematics and one for an essay on "Availability as a Ruling Consideration in the Choice of Presidential Candidates." He could not understand why he slipped from grace in his sophomore year except that he failed to find anything as interesting in "these prosy Greek tragedies as in the sentences of Demosthenes." His college expenses for a year amounted to $400, including the simple furnishings for his room. His years at Yale were smooth and productive. He was popular and his record was good, if not sensational. Many of the friends he made were to figure in his later career. He was handsome, affable, and always willing to do someone a good turn. But he could show flashes of temper, too, and while living in Old South College in his senior year he flung books, pillows, and curses at a couple of invaders who were disturbing the peace and keeping him from his studies.

Will did not smoke or drink, except for an occasional glass of beer. He had to work hard, for he was not brilliant, in the sense that Peter was, and he knew what was expected of him by his parents. He rowed, boxed, wrestled, played football, and worked in the gymnasium, but he preferred not to go in for sports on a competitive basis. Although not an athlete, few could stand up to him in a wrestling match, for he had great strength and physical endurance. Horace recalled that he had a "clear, strong mind" and he resented statements that his brother was fat and lazy in college. On the contrary, he viewed him as working with intense concentration and great ease, even in the midst of noise. Above all, Will was remembered as a moral force at Yale and in many ways he was the most conspicuous man of his year. His senior oration was on "The Professional and Political Prospects of the College Graduate" and he cheerfully prophesied that as students they would all step out into a world lacking in political giants because there were no emergencies to create them. The year was 1878 and William Howard Taft was salutatorian. The valedictory was delivered by Clarence Hill Kelsey, who would be a lifelong friend. Mr. and Mrs. Alphonso Taft were forced to accept the fact that Will was second, not first, in his class, but nevertheless he had made an enviable record for himself and forged a link with Yale that would never be broken.

Will was still in college when he learned that Hayes had been elected President, a matter of great interest to the Tafts as to all Ohioans. When the Alphonso Tafts returned from Washington to Cincinnati in 1877 a fire burned the roof and the second floor of their Mount Auburn house while they were staying a few doors away. Judge Taft's books were damaged by water and much remodeling had to be done before the house was in order again. The ceilings were tinted and frescoed and Peter gave his parents a mantelpiece carved by an artist named Fry that would still be in the house in the 1960's. Louise was called East again that year when her father, Samuel Torrey, died. Delia was now alone in the big house at Millbury.

Judge Taft steered clear of politics after his service in the national government. He was glad to be practicing law again and he had gone into partnership with Major Harmon P. Lloyd when his name came up again for the governorship, but that prospect faded quickly into the mists. The major grief of his life came in the following year when Peter, who had married Tillie in 1876, had a total breakdown and was confined in a sanitarium soon after the birth of his son Hulbert. The Judge wrote to his friends that the doctors thought Peter had studied too hard. But within four months he was at home again in the house on Freeman Street that Hulbert had given to Tillie at the time of her marriage. However, this dark chapter was not ended. Peter's marriage gradually disintegrated until in 1882 Tillie divorced him, with the approval and understanding of the Tafts. Judicial as always, Alphonso wrote that she was young, worthy, and had done as well as she could under the circumstances. All the Tafts were kind and sympathetic to Tillie throughout. Peter maintained that his father-in-law had caused most of the trouble and it was he who had urged the divorce. Annie, always deeply sympathetic to Peter, felt that his health had been impaired by too much study and hard work. She had made up her mind not to put academic pressure on her own children, David and Jane. Will suggested that the distraught Peter attend his graduation from Yale in 1878, believing that it might revive for him the picture of happier days.

Delia sent Will money as a graduation gift and he promptly bought sleeve buttons and a locket. "You may know that I shall always remember the giver," he wrote with the touch of sentiment he always had for this aunt. He was back in Cincinnati and deep in family tradition again just before Christmas, when more than a hundred friends gathered in the parlor of the restored Taft home on Mount Auburn to celebrate the twenty-fifth wedding anniversary of Louise and Alphonso. The dates 1853 and 1878 were woven over the Fry mantelpiece in letters made with evergreens.

Will was now studying at the Cincinnati Law School under the aegis of its famous dean, Rufus King. But he disliked the drudgery of his courses and preferred working for his father's firm of Taft & Lloyd. However, Alphonso was by no means satisfied with Will's performance in his first year. He wrote severely to him on July 2, 1879, when he found that

the genial young lawyer had gone off to the Yale boat race to watch
Harry in action with the crew:

> I do not think that you have accomplished as much this past year as
> you ought with your opportunities. You must not feel that you have
> time enough to while away with every friend who comes. . . . Our
> anxiety for your success is very great and I know that there is but one
> way to attain it, & that is by self-denial and enthusiastic hard work in
> the profession. . . . This gratifying your fondness for society is fruit-
> less. I like to have you enjoy yourself, so far as it can be consistent with
> your success in life. But you will have to be on the alert for business,
> and for influence among men, if you would hope to accomplish success.

In this same letter his father urged him to write for the *Times-Star*,
which had become the family paper. He considered Charles's plunge
into journalism at this time a great enterprise and he felt that the entire
family should contribute to it—"if there is any intellectual activity & culture among us." Charles, in association with Sinton, had bought the
controlling interest in the Cincinnati *Times*, a forty-year-old paper
known originally as *The Spirit of the Times*. They then absorbed the
Evening Star, thereby creating a powerful afternoon paper, the *Times-
Star*, that was to remain in the family until the 1950's. It was strongly Republican and was a political asset as the Taft fortunes expanded. Charles
and his father-in-law were already heavy stockholders in the *Volksblatt*,
Cincinnati's successful German newspaper. Charles occupied the editorial chair at the *Times-Star* and in course of time Annie fell into the habit
of making daily trips to the office to act as unofficial adviser. Their
combined newspaper influence had its effect on the development of Cincinnati and on the extension of its cultural interests.

Will had already had his newspaper initiation, doing court reporting
at six dollars a week for Murat Halstead, editor of the *Commercial Gazette*. In this way he picked up a useful working knowledge of the press,
which he failed to use to good advantage, however, when he became
President. His mother at this time was whipping up interest in the
kindergarten movement and was doing it "*con amore*," she said, because
she did not wish to serve as a mere figurehead. A charity kindergarten
opened in the Spencer House and she persuaded Miss Nourse to start a
small kindergarten that would feed her school. The movement spread all
over the city and money was raised to introduce kindergartens in the
public schools. Louise was the prime mover and she also busied herself
with the Art Association, the Mount Auburn Book Club that she had
founded, and the French Club, where she appeared at a party in the role
of Madame de Maintenon. She was always ready to attend a Kettle Drum
with Alphonso and she had never felt so much at leisure, with her chil-

dren grown-up and a good domestic staff at her beck and call—a laundress, an excellent cook, and two maids to whom she paid $3.50 a week.

All the Tafts who were in Cincinnati gathered at the Grand Hotel in September, 1879, to watch Ulysses Grant's triumphal procession on his return from his two-year trip around the world. Mrs. William T. Sherman stayed with the Tafts and Alphonso and Louise called on the Grants to renew their old friendship. They were much attached to the General and his amiable wife. Alphonso had heard from him while he toured the world, and had sensed at times his longing to be at home instead of in the distant places that his wife Julia favored. The Judge was now backing Grant for a third term. With Louise and Charles he attended the Republican convention in Chicago and saw this prospect fade. He was deeply disappointed although he knew that the General had no heart for another term in the White House.

"Grant is beaten," he wrote to Delia on June 13, 1880. "How it was done will no longer interest you. It was not fairly done but in politics there is no remedy for fraud. . . . Garfield was sprung upon the convention and they took him to get out of a difficulty."

Alphonso trimmed sails at once and decided to uphold his party and support the nominee. Louise, who had attended the sessions night and day, wrote to her sister that they were beaten in good company, but Annie and she were in the mood to become Democrats. "The prospect is that the Tafts are out of politics and it is just as well for them," she wrote to Harry, although this was far from being the case. Alphonso willingly took the stump for Garfield, a fellow Ohioan, and Will had his baptism as a campaigner. He was newly graduated from the Cincinnati Law School when he pitched into action for Garfield. His father coached him in public speaking, and Will wrote drafts of his speeches and rehearsed them, but in the end used them only for reference. He was not a fluent talker but he felt no embarrassment on the platform.

Horace's college life was just getting well under way when Will made his maiden speech, but it was no longer the Yale their father had known. Steam heat now warmed the rooms and the students had adequate bathing facilities. Eleven hours a week were allotted to prescribed studies and four hours to optional work, until the end of the sophomore year. On Sundays the students took long walks with their friends and had time for talk and reading. Looking back at his days in Yale from the accelerated 1940's, Horace decided that there was as much drinking then as later, and plenty of sporadic disorder, but there seemed to have been less criticism and discontent. Times were simpler. No original work was required and the courses in classics and mathematics seemed inferior to those of a later date. He worked hard and was a fair student, although he did not distinguish himself in any way. But Horace enjoyed his years at

Yale in spite of a bad start when he lost his privileges briefly through being conditioned in Greek composition, a disgrace for a Taft son.

Alphonso journeyed East for the Yale commencement of 1881 and he
was joined by Will, Horace, and Harry. He visited Uxbridge and looked
up old family records for the family history he was compiling. Seven years
earlier he had spoken at a great gathering of Tafts held at Uxbridge and
had traced the family history to its beginnings in the United States. The
decision was made on that occasion to put a family marker on the site
where the first Robert Taft's home was supposed to have stood. Family
history was a lifetime hobby with Alphonso Taft, a tenacious quest
closely linked to his pride in each successive generation—an interest
that was not unique at the time, since many other Americans were assem-
bling family history and tracing their descent from the early settlers.

In 1881 the Taft family tree was about to send out fresh shoots, this
time in New York. Harry, freshly graduated from Yale, had fallen in
love with Julia Smith, daughter of the most prominent lawyer in Troy,
New York. She was a striking-looking girl and Harry took her at once to
visit Aunt Delia, since all prospective brides had to pass muster at Millbury. "We are just suited for one another and I don't believe there is
another girl on earth who could manage my restless worrying disposition," he assured his aunt. "Hers is just the opposite, patient, loving and
sweet-tempered."

Harry courted Julia with great earnestness. He was now a handsome,
substantial-looking young man, dark, quiet, and inclined to be morbid.
In college he had gone in strongly for wrestling and rowing but he now
had an atrophied muscle in one knee and was lame at times, using a
cane. It took him years to get a strong foothold in his profession in New
York. When he first tackled this highly competitive legal center he
worked for Chamberlain, Carter & Hornblower at 346 Broadway. Then
he joined forces with Thomas Thacher, but business lagged, since there
was not enough work for two. Harry had taken his law degree at Columbia University and now he was desperately anxious to make enough
money to support Julia, who was the child of wealthy parents. But she
was prepared to wait, and then to live on a modest scale. Meanwhile,
she watched his health and cheered him up when he fell into one of his
depressed moods. While this romance was developing a new name was
appearing with frequency in the family correspondence. Will kept men-
tioning Nellie Herron, daughter of Judge John Williamson Herron, a
law partner of Rutherford Hayes. Howard Hollister, a Yale classmate
and one of Will's closest friends, was interested in Miss Herron, a dainty,
dark-eyed girl, reserved in manner, scholarly in her tastes.

In 1881, with all their children now starting out in life, Alphonso was
drawn into the international field by President Arthur, who appointed

him ambassador to Austria-Hungary in acknowledgement of his long years of political service in Ohio and his work for President Grant. This was one of the diplomatic plums that involved little more than social observances, since the United States was not directly involved in the affairs of Central Europe. Louise had angled boldly for the appointment when she and her husband dined with the President. "It was pleasant to find ourselves very 'near the throne,' " she reported to Delia.

To their surprise they learned on this visit that Will, who had been acting as assistant prosecuting attorney at $1,200 a year since January, 1881, was about to be appointed Collector of Internal Revenue for the First District. Congressman Benjamin Butterworth of Ohio had recommended him as the most popular young man in Hamilton County, showing power and good spirit in helping the Republican party. The President wished to rid himself of a troublesome appointee and Butterworth assured him that Will Taft had no enemies. Alphonso opposed the appointment on the ground that his son was too young, that it would be called favoritism, and in general would not be a sound political appointment.

Louise was against it on less altruistic grounds. She thought that two appointments could not go to one family and, in her own words: "Will is well off and can take care of himself. If he will stand in the way of his father's appointment I never will consent." The member of the family who must have recognition, she firmly stated, was Mr. Taft. In the end both appointments went through. Will became collector of internal revenue, an uncongenial post that he held reluctantly until March, 1883, but never enjoyed, since it gave him a quick indoctrination in the corruption that could cloak federal office-holding.

Louise settled Fanny at Miss Porter's in the winter before they went abroad, but again Fanny was homesick and made a fuss to join her family. Her parents decided to take her with them and leave her in Paris to study French. Will wrote to his sister that he was glad she was going to get her European education at an age when she could not be un-Americanized. "Go in, Fanny, and learn all you can—work will tell," he wrote. Their parents also expected Horace to do the grand tour when he left Yale but they were determined that Will and Harry should stick strictly to business, which meant staying at home and "working with uninterrupted constancy." Alphonso reminded them that their professional standing in law should be their main goal. Before leaving for Vienna he reviewed his own years in Ohio at a dinner given in his honor at the Burnet House:

> The experiences of more than forty years in Cincinnati rise before me and pass in review as I am about to take my leave of Ohio. Though not

a native, Cincinnati is my adopted home and my wife has been thoroughly identified with this city. Here on the banks of the Ohio I hope to end my days and here I shall leave those who inherit my name and my blood among the generous people of the West. . . .

He recalled his own trek west in 1838, traveling a large part of the way by canal. Now he was going abroad on a national mission. The intervening years had tied his family roots firmly to Cincinnati but he had influential friends from coast to coast. Whitelaw Reid, also an Ohioan, gave the Tafts a dinner as they passed through New York and among the guests were such established figures in the national life as John Jay, Edwin L. Godkin, D. O. Mills, William M. Evarts, Edwards Pierrepont, and Charles M. Dickinson. Delia was at the pier to see them sail on the *Alaska* on June 30, 1882. Alphonso was seventy-one and by now his hair was heavily frosted with silver; his furrowed face had a look of experience and a faint suggestion of weariness. Will's parting message to his parents set the tone of the whole experience: "I hope you will make yourselves comfortable and elegant even if it is a little expensive at first. You're off on a lark and we are willing to extend your allowance a little to insure your having a good time."

Alphonso Taft had spent all of his substance educating and bringing up his family. Both he and Louise had worked hard and accomplished much. Now their sons were ready to return some of the benefits that they had received down the years, and both Charles and Will were giving them financial aid. As they left, the elder Tafts learned that Annie had borne a daughter. "To be the founders of a family is a great matter," Alphonso wrote to Charles with satisfaction as he sailed across the Atlantic and into an unfamiliar world.

CHAPTER 7

VIENNA DAYS

The court of the Emperor Franz Josef was at its most brilliant when Mr. and Mrs. Alphonso Taft arrived in Vienna and took up their residence in the United States Legation. They had no preparation for the role they were called on to play, and in spirit they remained staunchly democratic. Alphonso had felt more at home on Commemoration Day at Oxford during a brief stop in England on his way to Austria. He had dined with Robert Browning and Benjamin Jowett, Master of Balliol and famous classicist; then he and Louise had heard Gladstone speak in the House of Commons, and his old abolitionist friend, Moncure Conway, had held a reception for them.

In Vienna the Tafts moved into a world of court ceremonial, knowing little of the language or of the social forms of this milieu. Louise, always poised and self-assured, proceeded with caution but her husband went around absentmindedly, being his natural self. In Cincinnati Will read a letter from his mother with a mixture of amusement and concern:

He believes in the good old Vermont way of doing things "by main strength and awkwardness." Your father borrows no trouble and says

there is no mystery about etiquette, that it is just as it was in Washington. He does not realize the embarrassment of not understanding
the language which makes it impossible to obey signals and save ourselves from blunders.

Alphonso was not abashed and his kindliness and sincerity were recognized by all. He thought the diplomats were like the members of an
agreeable club, with uncommon facilities for knowing what went on in
international circles. He warmed up particularly to the British and German ambassadors. His own presence aroused interest as he stood straight
and observant, without polish or artifice, while uniformed figures ablaze
with decorations whirled around him, bowing, clicking heels, going
through the social gestures of the regime. Alphonso disliked the toadyism and hand-kissing of the court and he quickly decided that a baron in
Austria was the equivalent of a justice of the peace in Vermont.

Alphonso's salary was $17,500 but they found it difficult to make ends
meet with all the entertaining they had to do. The servants were compe-
tent, although given to peculations, and Louise had trouble showing
them how to make such American oddities as corned beef hash or milk
toast for her husband's breakfast. With his usual zest for study Alphonso
took up German and soon was able to read the papers, spelling out the
news with the aid of a dictionary. He went to work enthusiastically on his
new typewriter, a novelty that fitted in with his Pitman shorthand. His
family in Cincinnati now received letters typed in large purple script.

Until they settled in the Legation the Tafts used street cars and entertained at the Imperial Hotel, but they soon had an equipage with liveried men, black horses, and light leather harness heavily studded with
brass nails. They walked often in the Prater and watched the noisy rooks
nesting high in the trees. Deeply conscious of the beauties of the Austrian capital they wandered across the stone bridges and strolled along
the terraced banks of the river. "You could not imagine a more beautiful city than we look out upon in the sunlight—the river—the bridge—
Belvedere in the distance and a beautiful fountain in the Schwarzenberg
Park," Louise wrote to Will soon after their arrival.

Their rooms were gloomy, with brown and crimson paper, dark paneling and high, ornate ceilings, but Louise became adept at hunting up
choice pieces at bargain prices. She soon assembled chandeliers, glass,
china, furniture, and other fittings that the Embassy required. Her red
satin upholstery and various objects of art showed up later in Cincinnati.
By degrees she became used to low-necked gowns and made a handsome
appearance in white satin and crimson velvet when first received by the
Emperor and his consort. Alphonso addressed the Empress in German
but she quickly assured him that she spoke English. He observed that

she was tall and graceful, with a high complexion and dazzling jewels. Her good works and philanthropy made her particularly interesting to the Tafts, who found more hauteur among the nobles than in the rulers themselves. Louise and Alphonso thought it a pity that Annie, who loved ceremonial and the blare of trumpets more than any other member of the family, could not have joined them in Vienna. The various functions seemed to them to be more like spectacles than social affairs.

The court balls, with a succession of rooms filled with women superbly gowned and men in richly decorated uniforms, never ceased to interest Louise. She wrote to Anna of the jewels that flashed under the glittering chandeliers: "I have come to gaze with composure on them and am content with my modest little solitaire." She was dubious of dances that ran over into the Sabbath, a violation of the Puritan tradition. To salve her conscience she gave teas with hymns and Bible reading on Sunday afternoons, and Saturday night suppers for visiting Americans. But she constantly reminded her visitors that she could not arrange invitations for them in the inner circle, since the Viennese court was snobbish to the last degree and inhospitable to outsiders. Although invited to all the official functions because of their official rank, Louise reported indignantly that they were strangers themselves and that they found the servility to rank disgusting, for they gloried in being republicans. "The trouble with us Americans is that we can never get it out of our heads that we are just as good as anybody in the same company," Alphonso wrote to Delia.

Meanwhile, the least happy member of the family was Fanny, whom they had left in Fontainebleau and had then transferred to St. Cloud. She disliked both experiences and conducted a lively correspondence with Horace, commenting wryly on her school life and illustrating her letters with charming sketches of her surroundings. She moped as she walked along winding paths edged with rocks and blackberry bushes in the forest of Fontainebleau. She disliked the walls around the houses in France and deplored the fact that girls could not go anywhere alone. But things improved when her mother settled her in Paris with the French family that had also looked after James G. Blaine's daughter Maggie. Fanny took singing, piano, and French lessons and enjoyed her view of the rooftops.

When she joined her parents in Vienna they found her greatly improved. Although never a beauty, Fanny's figure was exceptionally good and she bore herself with grace. The court circle opened to her at once and with her parents she went to operas and plays, as well as to court balls. They saw Edwin Booth in *King Lear* and heard Pauline Lucca in *Carmen*. They applauded Princess Metternich and Baroness Rothschild in an operetta given at the German Embassy by amateurs.

The Tafts on both sides of the Atlantic kept up a warm interflow of correspondence. Letters were passed around from one member of the family to another. Alphonso avoided discussing international affairs, warning his sons, who were closely allied to the newspaper world, that diplomacy marched with discretion. They heard more about social events and squabbles in Legation affairs than about the Slavic groups in conflict with the German element; the delicate balance of power effected in 1881 by the Dreikaiserbund; the boiling pit of the Balkans, Asia Minor, and Africa. Bismarck, Disraeli, Gladstone, and Boulanger kept their iron grip on the politics of Europe but Alphonso's duties as United States minister did not involve him in any major issues. One matter of business that he settled involved the embargo on American meat threatened by native meat packers who could not compete with low-priced products from the United States. Alphonso soon exposed the trumped-up rumors harmful to American trade and protested so vigorously that the embargo was abandoned. His stand on this issue in Austria had its effect on the meat import trade in surrounding countries.

On a brief trip to Europe with Rufus Smith in the summer of 1883, Will visited his parents in Vienna for three weeks. He took a walking trip in Switzerland and then toured England, Scotland, and Ireland, but he ran out of funds and was almost penniless in London. He had spent $700 in four months and an additional $200 for clothes and gifts. There was little to see in the theater but he heard Gladstone speak in the House of Commons. Will was restless and eager to get home because Nellie Herron was constantly in his thoughts. Back in his law office in Cincinnati in October he wrote to his mother that he "might marry in a jiffy" and that it was about time he and Aunt Delia went into the parlor for some serious conversation. It was a family joke that his maiden aunt must be the first to know of a serious romance.

But Will was not the only Taft footloose in Europe in 1883. Delia went abroad with Horace and Clara Orton, one of Anna's daughters. Horace was so exhausted by his academic efforts that even his favorite aunt could not soothe his restless spirit. To his great disappointment he had just missed capturing the DeForest Prize at Yale but he had won the Townsend Prize—"the only Townsend man in the family," Will noted. The Taft brothers were all on hand to see Horace graduate. Harry came on crutches because his lame knee was worse than usual. Aunt Delia was present to applaud the tall one among her boys. Soon she was touring Europe and finding adventure in every country. She visited Ischia and saw the devastation caused by the earthquake a year earlier. Characteristically she made herself as familiar with London in the course of four weeks as she already was with Boston. She visited the Exposition in Holland and bought clothes in Paris so as to be ready for the gay life in Vienna.

Louise's fashionable friends had given her the addresses of the great couturiers but she did not dare to invade their salons. She chose to buy frugally, except for one velvet gown that "must last as long as I live for a *grand dress*," she wrote to Susie. Two ten-dollar velvet bonnets with ostrich tips standing up straight in front proved to be irresistible. This was not the time to be rash, for she and Susie had been plunging on the market with Alphonso's help and had lost. "We deserve to be punished for dabbling in stocks, having had the experience of everybody else to profit by," she wrote to her fashionable sister in California.

No one enjoyed Vienna more than Delia, who shrewdly appraised the exhilarating scene and made sharp Yankee comments on the frivolity and display. For a court ball in January, 1884, she wore the black velvet, enlivened with red flowers, red plumes in her hair, a diamond pendant, and her solitaire. She may not have glittered like the arch duchesses but her humor sparkled, her conversation was tart, and she was not overawed by the surrounding magnificence. Both she and Louise, who was gowned in cream satin with gold fringe, and plumes in her hair, were amused as they watched Horace's long-legged dash across the ballroom floor in the Viennese waltz. He had firmly made up his mind that he would not bow from the waist.

"Horace was kind enough to be very proud of me," Louise wrote with satisfaction to Will after the tall young scholar had been received by the Austrian rulers. He had scoffed at the ceremonial and had been indifferent about attending but to his surprise Aunt Delia had decided that it was important and they must all do their best for Mr. and Mrs. Taft. As the Empress Elizabeth approached, Horace leaned forward in his natural, unconscious way and forgot to say "Your Majesty" until the audience was almost over. He seemed to his fond mother to appear to good advantage among the more accomplished courtiers. "The Empress is immense," he announced, but he took no part in the frivolity except when his mother entertained. Then he did his best to help her. There were times when she found it tiring to be on the sidelines as a chaperone until five in the morning.

Maria Herron, Nellie's dashing young sister, had been invited to visit the Tafts and Horace rejoiced in the chance to escort her around Vienna, for he was deeply in love with her. In her independent way Maria had traveled to Paris without an escort. Her success with the Austrian officers was sensational and soon she and Fanny were dancing night after night. Horace suffered as he watched the witty and elusive Maria being spun around the ballroom floor by uniformed noblemen. He was beginning to see her as the grown-up Maria, and not just as the schoolgirl he had known for years. Alphonso found Maria somewhat too candid in her comments for the ward of a diplomat. Fanny was more discreet, but

Maria's piquant sallies were a matter of interest to everyone around her. She was slight and graceful, with brilliant dark eyes and a delicately chiseled profile. No one thought her easy to handle, for she could be crisp, witty, diffident, and bold all at the same time. Occasionally she would succumb to self-doubt and would retire into a shell from which no one could rout her. At other times she was effervescent. Her personality was always of great interest to William Howard Taft, although her sister Nellie was the one he loved. But he knew that behind Maria's provocative manner was a dynamic nature and he enjoyed her conversation. All the Herrons were noted for their candor.

As Louise watched Horace she could see that he was far from happy. Although he worked hard over his German, he felt dissatisfied and was haunted by the thought that his classmates were getting started in life while his own activities were aimless. His dyspepsia plagued him; he slept poorly and had headaches. Delia found him difficult and homesick as they toured Europe together. After Maria went home the scene was flat for him and even Fanny found that the rush had tapered off with her departure. Horace passed six weeks in Italy and then three months in Hanover, Paris, and London. Fifty years later he took a nostalgic view of this period as he went on a guided tour through the Palace of the Hapsburgs, paying a few cents to view the residue of the pageantry he had shared with Maria and his parents.

Delia went home in 1884 with memories of the days in Vienna and her sightseeing in Europe that would stay with her for the rest of her life. But her property cares had followed her even to the Viennese capital. Friends were urging her to sell some of her land in Millbury and she was thinking it over. She was anxious to keep up her contributions to foreign missions and "to recognize the duty of sending teachers to the uncivilized." There were all kinds of worlds in the Taft and Torrey spectrum. Louise and Alphonso had drawn much pleasure from a tour they made in 1883 through Italy, Greece, Turkey, Czecho-Slovakia, and Rumania. Their children in America received detailed accounts of their adventures, from their fatigue at Pompeii to their awe at the Acropolis. Louise shopped to her heart's content in Constantinople and Alphonso, who had been studying Cicero for years, drew on his historical background in visiting Italy and Greece.

From his post in Vienna Alphonso followed every move made by his sons, advising them, praising them, keeping the family spirit burning brightly. He urged Charles to throw Cincinnati business in Harry's direction, while he looked out for him in Vienna. "We are bound up in the honor and prosperity of our children," he wrote to Charles, recalling how his own father, Peter Rawson Taft, had burst into tears when he found him in financial difficulties through no fault of his own.

Harry wrote every week to his parents but Will had established himself as the champion family correspondent. In copperplate script he sent his father satisfying accounts of civic and political affairs in Ohio, while he supplied his mother with the social chit-chat of the hour. He assured her that her executive ability was greatly missed in Cincinnati. "When woman's field widens, Mother, you must become President of a Railroad Company," he wrote. "I am sure you would be a success." He described Harry's wedding in such detail that they felt as if they had been there. The ceremony took place at St. John's Church, Troy, on March 28, 1883. Julia's father and stepmother sent out 1,240 invitations. Will was best man and Horace was one of the six ushers. Charles, who admired Harry's grit and persistence with his law business, gave him $500 for a wedding gift and another $200 on behalf of their parents, whose finances he was handling during their absence.

Julia and Harry settled in two rooms on the edge of Gramercy Park, with the elevated trains rumbling past night and day. The young bride set out to show what an able housekeeper she could be on limited means. She initiated treatments for Harry's bad knee. They tried Swedish exercises, electric therapy, massage, and medicine, but he had many ups and downs before the condition improved. Sometimes he worked through a nightmare of pain. As long as he lived he was conscious of this disability, both on the golf course or when he had to walk any distance. For one period his leg was in splints but Julia whiled away the hours reading to him from Irving, Hawthorne, Macaulay, and Taine. He joined the firm of Simpson, Thacher and Barnum, and his business rarely flagged after his marriage to Julia.

Charles and Annie visited them at the end of 1883 and sent enthusiastic reports to Vienna of the bride and groom. On this visit Whitelaw Reid, D. O. Mills, and Eliot F. Shephard all gave dinners in New York for the visitors from Cincinnati. They went to the Metropolitan Opera four times and Annie gloried in the music and the setting. The Grand Opera House in Cincinnati, which had been built largely through their combined efforts, had opened in the fall of 1882 with a minstrel show. It had been remodeled with skill and care. There were twelve proscenium boxes and David Sinton had seen to it that one would be permanently assigned to his family. Will attended the opening and shared in Annie's spontaneous delight over this event. When the May Festival was held in the following spring she filled her box with "agreeable and good-looking people" and Will was again a guest. But he had some reservations about the acoustics of the new Opera House.

Charles was inclined to be critical as he studied the Pike Street household bills at this time. Annie had annoyed her father, too, with a party she had given for 560 guests in honor of Sir John Coleridge, Chief Justice of Queen's Bench. It always gave her pleasure to snare a visiting lion. Her father footed the bills but complained bitterly. Will took another view of this and wrote to his mother: "The house is so well suited to entertaining and he is so rich that it is eminently proper that he should entertain the city's guests." By this time Charles's prosperity had become an accepted fact in the Taft family. His newspaper interests were flourishing and he looked after many of his father-in-law's properties. He had become a man of affairs and was singularly happy in his marriage. Wilful, impulsive, pretty, and full of high spirits, Annie was an affectionate wife, a conscientious mother, and she created an aura of gaiety around her.

Charles played for big stakes and lost when Joseph Pulitzer bought the New York World in 1883. On learning that the paper was on the market he sent a representative to Jay Gould and negotiations for the purchase began. But Pulitzer won this prize and in the years that followed made the most of it. Charles was philosophical, as always. "I am well satisfied with the newspaper business in Cincinnati," he remarked. Some of the rival papers had just introduced space rates, with editorial writers getting seven dollars and reporters five dollars a column. Charles was watching to see how the system worked. He had traveled to Yellowstone over the Northern Pacific Railroad with members of the Western Associated Press. His prestige in newspaper circles was growing, and he was influential in having leased wires introduced for the distribution of news. When the Times-Star building burned in 1883 the loss was covered by insurance and he was able to buy a font of type that had been handed down from the old Chronicle. The paper declared a four per cent dividend that autumn and things were going well.

Jane and David, Charles's children, had begun their school life in a small neighborhood school run by a maiden lady innocent of the progressive ideas that the new kindergartens were fostering. "She is thin, sharp-featured, inartistic, with old-fashioned ideas of enforcing obedience in a most uncompromising manner—in short a relic of the past," Annie wrote to her father-in-law in her easy, slanting script. But she felt that the children learned a great deal from her. They now summered at Kennebunkport, leaving Will to keep David Sinton company on Pike Street. The young lawyer, now in partnership with Major Lloyd, wrote to his father that if any of Mr. Sinton's Presbyterian friends were to stand near the front door on a Sunday afternoon they would hear a sound remarkably like the click of billiard balls.

At the moment Annie's father was engrossed in new ventures. He was trying to devise some way of creating such perfect combustion of gas that it would not blacken the city. In the spring of 1883 he paid $175,000 for a stretch of waterfront property, to be leased to the railroad interests. The object was to use it for a new bridge across the river. He was tearing down one of his buildings on the north side of Fourth Street to put up two modern stores, one for Woodruff, the hatter; the other for Snowden, the carpet man. The Emerys were erecting a building nine stories high on the site of old St. Paul's Church. This pile, with its stone front and iron framework, was destined to be the most conspicuous building in the city for years to come. But Will reported to his father that the town residences in Chicago were much more magnificent than anything in Cincinnati.

Will was now heading into civic battles of his own. One that he fought with all his might was to unhorse Thomas C. Campbell, a lawyer noted for using influence, terrorism, and duress in having his clients freed by the courts. Campbell worked with Cox, the politician who had battered his way to wealth and power until he now controlled the Republican machine in Hamilton County. Public indignation over Campbell's bold piracy and the general corruption in the courts came to a head with riots in 1884, resulting in much loss of life and destruction of property.

Late in March a mob ran loose and burned the courthouse. Campbell's boast that he could obtain favorable verdicts for $5,000 sparked the rioting that continued for days. Will noted in a letter to his father that March 29, 1884, was a sad day in the history of Cincinnati. Louise, reading the papers sent to Vienna by her son, was reminded of Bastille Day. "What a siege of terror you must have had for three days and what a mixture of influences and motives," she wrote. Peter, who lived across from the courthouse, was sitting on his bed when a rifle ball crashed through the front windows and buried itself in the headboard behind him. Most of the court records were saved but 200 old deed books were destroyed, as well as the law library, much mourned by Will. The mob would not let the fire engines get near the burning buildings. Regiments were called in and armed men stood guard for days, with barricades surrounding the jail and courthouse as in the days of the Civil War. Soldiers slept on blankets on the sidewalks.

After the riots the Bar Association sought to have Campbell disbarred. He was the leading criminal lawyer in the city but he had put himself beyond the pale in juggling law, politics, and venality. Young Taft was chosen by the Bar Association as a junior member of the legal staff appointed to prosecute him. He prepared evidence, interviewed witnesses, and did a masterly roundup for the prosecution. As his brother Horace pointed out, it took courage to attack Tom Campbell openly but Will's summation was devastating in its impact and was quoted for years afterwards. However, the case was lost on legal grounds. Only one of the three judges voted for disbarment, which the Tafts all considered an outrageous conclusion to a flagrant case. Will was so disgusted that he felt like abandoning politics altogether but his speech had had its effect and Campbell disappeared from public view.

Taft went about his business, a tall, good-natured young lawyer with an alert eye for the scene around him. It took him some time to feel at home in the legal profession but his father wrote firmly to Charles: "I am glad to learn he (Will) is going to work at law with all his might. That is his destiny and he should be in it." But he had made a poor beginning. He lost his first jury case and also a Supreme Court decision. To his intense chagrin he was beaten in a case he handled for David Sinton. But Alphonso kept assuring him that his arguments were spirited and good, just as he wrote often to Peter with the tenderness he always reserved for this unfortunate son. Peter's work had become aimless and desultory. His father advised him either to take hold of his legal business again or else, if he felt unequal to the strain, to live a retired and quiet life. "You may rely upon one thing, and that is that my heart is always with you," Alphonso wrote to him on June 15, 1883, after the divorce suit had been heard. The case was handled in Major Lloyd's office but all efforts to keep it quiet failed. Peter did not ask for the custody of little Hulbert, but he continued to see his son regularly.

CHAPTER 8

WILL TAFT AND NELLIE HERRON

WHILE WILLIAM HOWARD TAFT was getting his start in law and politics his lifelong romance was developing quietly in the background; but the genial young lawyer, with much to offer, found that Miss Nellie Herron was not easy to captivate. Although her name did not appear in the family letters before 1880, they had known each other for six years and had met first at a coasting party on Mount Auburn when Nellie was eighteen. Charles and Annie, whose house was close to the Herron home on Pike Street, were with them at their first meeting.

The Herrons were firmly entrenched socially and although not particularly well-off they entertained with some distinction in their gray brick house. John Williamson Herron had attended Miami University with Benjamin Harrison and was United States Attorney during his administration. He and Rutherford B. Hayes were law partners for years and the two families were close friends. As a girl of seventeen Nellie had been the guest of the President and Mrs. Hayes at the White House. She had thought then that she would like to be First Lady. Her mother, Harriet Collins, was the daughter of Congressman Eli Collins of Lowville, New York. Harriet moved with her mother to Cincinnati when she was seventeen and lived with her brother, Judge Collins, until she married his law partner, John Herron.

Mrs. Herron was much admired for her striking looks and keen wit. At an early age she had snow-white hair, which contrasted dramatically with her dark eyes and fresh complexion. Will Taft often commented on her beauty and style. He considered her better looking than any of her daughters except Maria, who was the most distinctive of her girls whereas Nellie (or Helen, as she was baptized) was the most reserved. The Herrons were a large family but three of their eleven children died at an early age. Their six girls were Nellie, Maria, Emily, Jane, Eleanor, and Lucy, and their sons were William and John. Lucy was baptized in the White House and was named after the President's wife.

Nellie was twelve when Charles and Annie married and settled in the house along the street from the Herrons. The Larz Anderson family, with ten sons, all older than Nellie, lived across the street in a large red-brick mansion. Jennie eventually married Charles Anderson, one of their sons. All of the Herron girls attended Miss Nourse's School and Nellie was an exceptional student. She was never a beauty; in fact, she was quite outshone by the debutantes of her day in Cincinnati. But she had quiet strength and steadfastness that Will came to know and appreciate. She was slight and active, with a tiny waist, dark hair, and a stubborn mouth and chin. All through her adolescence she was dissatisfied with herself, and her strong ambitions, discontent, and literary tastes show clearly in the diary she kept in these girlhood years. At nineteen she said she felt as if she were fifty. She longed to write a book, to have some occupation, to be independent and prove herself. In general she was happy enough with friends but cold to strangers, and she had persuaded herself that she had no drawing power for men. "I am very exacting, and at the same time unwilling to make the least advance, so what wonder that I am not always satisfied," she wrote on June 19, 1881.

Music and books were her chief diversions and she decided that she would rather have music lessons than the gowns her mother made her buy at Cadwallader's. The debutante's life bored her and she professed to dislike all men under thirty. It was Nellie's fate to have one young man after another snatched from her by more flirtatious friends, while she shrank into herself, shy and silent—"trembling . . . and as stupid as a hitching post" when young men came to call. At last she decided that she must go out more and read less, but she could not overcome her diffidence and nervousness. When she left Miss Nourse's the future First Lady made a sad little note in her diary: "To one who feels as I do that I will probably never marry, this leaving school seems like settling down in life."

Actually, the set in which she moved seemed to be always in pursuit of pleasure. Some of their families had country places on East Walnut Hills, along Madison Road and the Grandin Road. They went to big parties at the Harrisions, the Scarboroughs, and the Keys. They played whist, tennis, poker, picknicked and bowled, and they rarely missed a German at Clifton Hall. They went to the Grand Opera House and to Pike's Opera House where they had the fun of listening to Gilbert and Sullivan's new production *The Pirates of Penzance*. Nellie never missed a musical event and she often helped to get up plays and charades. They went to the baseball grounds to watch athletic events and thought nothing of walking home from Covington after attending the Kentucky races. Nellie had a wide circle of friends but her special confidante was Alice Keys and it was to "Allie" that she wrote when her one-time bobsled partner showed up at Yellow Springs on a July day in 1880:

> Who do you think arrived and stayed until Tuesday but that adorable Will Taft—imagine, just think of it. Unfortunately, I did not recover from my surprise and delight soon enough to make that impression which I would have wished. . . . Oh, it was such a splendid opportunity to make an impression . . . but alas! he strikes me with awe, and I could not make any more out of it.

Will was his most gallant self. He cut up her little sister Eleanor's meat and helped the mothers over brooks. Although "enchanting as ever" he took little notice of Nellie, so that she cried herself to sleep after he left. Her father took her afterwards to Narragansett Pier, where she joined in the usual round of tennis, walks to the beach, bowling, sailing, croquet. The girls were knocked about by the surf. They ate clams at Billington's, or drove through the woods for clambakes. They watched the waves, deep purple as evening fell, rolling in to break up in snowy foam. Nellie sat on the rocks with one of her friends and together they smoked cigarettes. But love was missing, and the fact that she found couples in every rocky recess along the beach added to her melancholy. She made up her mind that she would work to more serious purpose that winter.

When her parents left for California Nellie buckled down to household tasks, reading Carlyle's *Life of Schiller* as she dried the dishes. She was mildly interested in a young man named John Dudley until Howard Hollister came into view and held her interest for a long time. Eventually he became Will Taft's most serious rival. He was much smaller and not as good looking as Will but he was clever, sympathetic, and had a merry wit. Nellie sang duets with him and thought his voice abominable. He was a flirt and whispered the same sweet nonsense to her friends that he did to her. Both joined a walking club and tramped the hills with Annie, Mary Hanna, and other young friends.

But things brightened for Nellie when Will reappeared in February, 1881, and invited her to a German at Annie's. To her surprise he was so aloof at the party that she wondered why he had asked her to go with him. But by 1882 Will was increasingly aware of demure Miss Herron and he frequently went to the Highland House on Tuesdays and Fridays, the fashionable evenings there, in the hope of seeing her. "You may travel to Constantinople or Jerusalem but nowhere I venture to say will you find girls as pretty, as interesting, as stylish, and as fresh as our American girls," he wrote to his father on July 14, 1882. Nellie often went to the Highland House with Howard Hollister and on one June night she sat on a quiet balcony having supper with him and drinking wine—"which was rather fast, I suppose, but there were three," she wrote in her dairy. She fancied herself in love with her escort that night and made an entry: "It is really delightful there sitting on a retired porch, with the lights and crowds of people below, and the gay music, and cool air."

On another occasion she put up her feet on the railing and smoked a cigarette while she viewed the city lights and the river flowing darkly under its two bridges. Lights glowed faintly and an occasional train of cars moved along like a rustling moccasin. They drank beer and ate wienerwurst, which she knew would have horrified some of her friends. Howard and she thought it fun to look down on the pavilion where the dancers whirled around. Although a classicist in music, Nellie was always to like band concerts and beer, tastes that her husband never shared with her. They were apt to joke about this between themselves.

Aware of Howard's interest in Nellie, Will wrote uneasily to his mother about this incipient romance but without revealing his own feelings. He now dwelt on the importance of children to make Christmas count, after spending a merry December 25th at Annie's. But as his interest in Nellie deepened Will did not neglect the other debutantes. In February, 1883, he decided to pay off some of his social debts in a single week while the Opera Festival was under way. It happened that Christine Nilsson, Adelina Patti, and Emma Albani were all singing in Cincinnati that season and he went seven times, costly though it was. His mother in Vienna read the roll call with amusement:

> I took Miss Nellie Herron Monday night, Miss Edith Harrison Tuesday night, Miss Lawton, cousin of Mrs. Austin Goodman, Wednesday afternoon, and Miss Smith's niece Wednesday night. Tomorrow afternoon I take Miss Allie Keys, and tomorrow Miss Agnes Davis. I see Father shake his head when he reads this list and hear him say that a thorough knowledge of the law is not obtained in that way. Well, it is my farewell to the social world.

It was anything but that, since William Howard Taft would become one of the most banqueted men in the history of the United States. Social invitations were irresistible to him, even at this early age, and he promptly reported attending a party given by Mrs. Larz Anderson for Mrs. Frances Hodgson Burnett, the creator of Little Lord Fauntleroy. He was not particularly impressed by this popular author, who seemed to him to be "dressed like a dowdy." From occasions like this he turned with relief to Miss Nellie Herron's Saturday night "Salon" and it was in this atmosphere that their romance flowered. The gatherings were held at Nellie's home and the declared purpose was cultivation rather than recreation, although the discussions veered often from the abstract to the personal level. Will wrote humorously to his mother about the hallowed Saturday nights:

> Tell Maria that I am drinking deep from the fountain of knowledge which her sister has set up in the Salon. The lamps and gas are only lit for the sake of conventionality. The phosphorus that scintillates from the brain of each member is quite sufficient to illuminate two or three rooms as large as Mrs. Herron's parlor.

Will felt that he and the other young men who attended were woefully lacking in literary knowledge as compared with the girls. At first it was humiliating, but by degrees he grew accustomed to being in the learner's seat. He also enjoyed the oysters and strawberries that Miss Herron supplied when the evening's work was ended. They all had heavy reading to do and he usually met Nellie at the Mercantile Library and carried home her books for her. In turn they analyzed the characters of Benjamin Franklin, John Adams, Edmund Burke, Martin Luther, Rousseau, and Voltaire, among others. Nellie was now more at peace with herself and had abandoned her earlier dream of entering a convent. But she had persuaded her parents to let her study chemistry and German at the University of Miami and in spite of their objections she turned to teaching—first at Madame Frédin's, then at a private school on Walnut Hills known as White and Sykes, and finally at Miss Nourse's, her own school. Jennie and David, Annie's children, were attending Madame Frédin's School in 1883 and David was showing a poetical turn of mind, to his mother's delight. The Herrons attended the fashionable Second Presbyterian Church but Nellie drew little comfort from church work—the Salon alone could distract and cheer her.

From books its young members turned to histrionics and Will appeared in a burlesque of *The Sleeping Beauty*. He buffooned his way through *A Scrap of Paper* at Annie's house and not even the presence of a stage manager brought on from New York by Annie saved him from missing his cues and making a "grand botch" of the play. He sent his parents a hilarious account of his malapropisms, pointing out that he would always

feel like a bull in a china shop when he trod the boards, Will regretted
that Fanny and Maria were missing the gayest winter in years. Charles
and Annie had given a magnificent Christmas party, which was followed
by a Salon entertainment devised by Nellie on New Year's Eve to welcome in 1884. Soon afterwards Will, who did not feel well enough off at
this time to propose to any girl, wrote cautiously to his mother:

> I may say that the Richmonds in that field are many and that as yet,
> much as I admire her, I have not felt myself impelled to become one of
> them, nor have I ever had the least reason to think that she would be
> pleased to have me join the number who are struggling for her hand.
> . . . But do not understand me to stop myself from changing my great
> mind on this or any other equally profound subject.

All these personal problems were forgotten briefly in February when
the Ohio River flooded, with the ensuing misery that Cincinnati residents had come to know. The gas works were submerged; the waterworks
closed down and business was at a standstill as the waters rose to a height
of seventy-one feet. Two railroads continued to operate, but the other
companies had their passengers conveyed by canal boats. Will's washer-
woman lived in the submerged area and his laundry floated off. "I am
truly one of the flood sufferers," he wrote cheerfully to his father. "I have
no light to sew with, no water to wash with and no clothes to wear. My
clothes are now going over the falls at Louisville or are being used for
signals of distress in the submerged area—my stock of wearables is getting lower as the river gets higher."

The public responded quickly to calls for help from the homeless and
hungry. Flotsam sailed majestically on the dark waters. Mails were delayed. An occasional electric light sent out a beam in the midst of darkness and desolation. But before the rise of the waters the younger set
were going about their business as usual. Will went to hear Matthew
Arnold lecture and admired his talk on economics. He managed to get
to Nellie's Salon while the river was still sixty-four feet ten inches in the
channel and rising steadily. They all exchanged valentines and Nell gave
Will one of her own composition, chiding him gently for his total im-
mersion in his work:

> Leave your dull cases
> Let them grow dusty
> Turn to the graces!
> Till laughter effaces
> Their pages musty
> Leave your dull cases,
> Let them grow dusty.

Nellie liked to dash off verse, and tucked into her diary of this period are sundry poems, valentines, and cards sent with flowers. Recognition of the Taft-Herron romance was made manifest in this one:

St. Valentine the good!
Now cheer & cheer him still
For giving Will to Nellie
And giving Nellie to Will

To him belongs all praise,
To him your bumpers fill
For giving Will to Nellie
And giving Nellie to Will

And o'er this glass let's pray
While grinding out lore's mill,
He'll give each boy a Nellie
And give each girl a Will

Even as the waters were receding the Opera Festival was held and Will went with Charles, Annie, and Nellie to hear *The Prophet*, but the performance was given under great difficulties because of the gas failure. Few turned out, but Will considered it the most magnificent feast of music he had ever had. Madame Marcella Sembrich, the new soprano, carried off the honors. He compared her with Patti in the precision of her notes but found her voice much richer. He preferred her to Christine Nilsson and he wrote to his father with enthusiasm: "The audience stopped her right in the midst of her singing and yelled. I never have seen an audience in that hall so enthusiastic." Henry Irving and Edwin Booth both played in Cincinnati at this time. There was great diversity in the entertainment available to the townspeople and in addition to grand opera a minstrel festival was given at the Music Hall, with 300 Negroes on the stage.

The young people went with their elders to the major entertainments but provided their own fun, from May parties and dances around the maypole to salon picnics. That summer Nellie visited Eva and Alice Keys at their summer home at Little Boar's Head in New Hampshire. Will, who had now moved strongly into the picture as a suitor, followed her there in August and their romance deepened under the influence of moonlight, picnics, and country rambles. "One by one the roses fall," Will wrote to his mother when Nellie returned and held the first meeting of the Salon. The members were getting married and Will was beginning to view himself as an aging bachelor, although he had always said he would not marry until he was thirty.

Horace, back from Vienna, was lovesick over Maria, who seemed to

Will to be more beautiful than ever since her return from Europe. Both joined the Salon and added interest to the meetings. Will was much impressed with his brother's character and bearing, and wrote to their father that they could all be proud of him, for honesty and gentleness "shone out from Horace." He weighed 202 pounds and Charles looked small and boyish beside his three tall brothers. Horace made every effort to adapt himself to a career in law. He worked in the office of Henry N. Morris and tried to find contentment in his studies. Years later he wrote: "All of us Tafts went into the law as naturally as we went from junior year to senior year in college, yet we have scattered over the face of the country, and our occupations have been extremely varied."

Horace and Will lived together on the west side of Broadway, between Fourth and Fifth streets, and they went to political meetings. The Salon members joined the Blaine campaign of 1884 and watched the procession from Blaine's rooms in the Burnet House when the Republican candidate visited Cincinnati. Charles had a long talk with him and ended up contributing to his campaign, but he could not persuade David Sinton to part with a penny for the senator from Maine. Although Horace voted for Blaine on this occasion he was to become a solid admirer of Cleveland and to vote for him in 1888 and 1892. Will served as chief supervisor of elections to offset the frauds that were all too common in Cincinnati. In the course of his work around polling places he had been known to knock an enemy tackler cold. Many remembered the punishment he gave a man named Lester A. Rose during his law-school days. In a scurrilous paper that he edited, Rose ran a libelous item about Alphonso Taft soon after he was defeated for governor. Will hunted up the slanderer, beat him to a pulp, and ordered him to leave town at once, which he did.

But in general Horace had more genuine zest for the rough and tumble of politics than his brother Will. "My brother did not claim to be a reformer . . . and he often poked fun at me on the subject," Horace noted. None of the Tafts enjoyed supporting the controversial Blaine but while many Republicans veered away from him they voted for Blaine. Horace, however, had developed a passion for political reform and was inclined to dissent from other members of his family. He was not a conformist in any respect and he had become a food faddist, doing gymnastic exercises, eating the health foods that were coming into fashion, and trying in every way to build himself up. Will was skeptical of this, having superb health himself. Both Rufus Smith and Horace, dyspeptic, nervous types, seemed to him to be hipped on the subject. Will could eat like a trencherman and did, without any damage to his health. He had a special passion for fruit, and he ate apples at every opportunity.

Annie was consistently kind to the brothers while their parents were away, and Horace and Will spent so much time at her house that they might as well have lived there. She kept open house for them, served delicious meals, gave them concert tickets as well as beefsteaks, and was the guardian angel of all Charles's brothers. Horace flattered himself that he, in turn, was educating Annie in politics. He enjoyed her wit and originality, and found her flexible in debate. They all kept watch over little Hulbert, who was so delicate that he had to be taken out of school at this time to be built up with cod liver oil and fresh air. He had a goat and a wagon, a dog and some chickens, and he played outdoors much of the time. Horace studied him thoughtfully and wrote to Fanny: "Hulbert is a jewel and will be the brightest one in the family. He is obedient, unselfish, wonderfully intelligent and, what seems to me one of his best traits, doesn't fear Mr. Hulbert a bit or seem to be very much under his influence."

The rich and aging Mr. Hulbert, like David Sinton, was somewhat awesome to the younger generation, but his daughter Tillie was strong enough to hold her own. She busied herself with the Woman's Exchange, a self-supporting charity, and she did not spend her days in idleness. With more enterprise than many of her contemporaries she took French lessons regularly and worked along philanthropic lines. Peter's decline continued and Charles and he had just broken up their law partnership. Charles boxed up his law books and moved to his office at the *Times-Star*. Peter maintained a law office on Third Street but business was slow and he was not in good spirits. Will, feeling gloomy himself, did his best to cheer up Peter and stimulate him to effort. His own affairs came to a head when he finally summoned up courage to propose to Nellie on May 1, 1885, but she kept him in suspense for a month before being definite in her answer. They had been to the Scarborough house and, after driving her back by phaeton to Pike Street, he cornered her in the parlor of her home and, in his own words, "forced a forbidden subject until by an unwilling admission I was able to win the reluctant prize." Neither then nor later did Nellie show the eagerness that consumed young Taft, for Howard Hollister was an alternative always in the background.

It was not Nellie's nature to be demonstrative but she baffled candid Will by insisting that neither of their families be told of the engagement. He went around wearing the tie pin that she had given him for Christmas but he was so miserable and lovesick all through the summer of 1885 that Annie described him as a mountain of misery. At every opportunity he sent flowers and loving messages to Nellie. "For the Woman I Love" he wrote on the card that accompanied his May bouquet. "*Du hast die schönsten Augen*," and "*Ich hab dich geliebst und liebe dich noch*," he was telling her in June. Soon it was "Oh, My Love is Like a Red, Red

Rose." He sat through *Tannhäuser*, conducted by Walter Damrosch, deaf to the music and deeply alive to the gray-eyed sphinx by his side. But total desolation set in when Nellie left for Fenton's in the Adirondacks, a rustic resort some miles from Lowville, where the Collins family had lived for generations. Her father stayed in Cincinnati and every time he met him Will had the guilty feeling that he must know the news they were concealing from him.

Nellie was exhausted and nervous when she left for Fenton's and Will wrote her encouraging letters, trying to still her qualms and lift her depression. Her moods still wavered although she wore a ring that he had given her when she left. He sent her two volumes of the *Geology of the State of New York*, a special interest of hers, accompanied by a lovesick note:

> Oh, Nellie, you must love me. I rely on time to help me. My great good luck must not desert me now. I believe you will be happy with me. The consciousness of having made me a better and a truer man which you can not fail to have when you shall have become my wife will make you happy. . . . Goodbye, my love. God bless you, my own Nellie. Your loving lover, Will.

In his letters Will recalled their moonlight drives along Duck Creek Road, their nightly farewells in the Pike Street doorway, her insistence that she must marry a scientist, her taste for highbrow and sometimes unprocurable books. He pictured little dinners in the future for Skull and Bones men, with a bright fire on the hearth, and evenings alone while she sewed and he worked. Annie laughed at big Will for all this moonshine and advised him never to give up society in favor of the fireside. Nellie answered his letters infrequently and without much warmth, and Will had to keep assuring her that he had not revealed their engagement. But he begged her to let her parents know. "I know I am not good enough for you but that is a criticism which would be made against all the men I know," he wrote.

Nothing he did had any savor for love-sick Will but he passed as much time as he could with David Sinton, who was living in solitary state in the family mansion during the summer of 1885. He had obstinately refused to join Annie at Boar's Head and he was much preoccupied with money matters. He was looking for new investments to make but with $600,000 lying idle in the bank he could not see anything he wanted and so decided that it was "better to eat at the loaf." His most recent interest was a Texas ranch in which he had sunk half a million dollars.

Charles was now spreading out on his own and his father-in-law thought better of his business habits than he did of Will's, although he liked the bulky young lawyer who straddled his chairs and fed him gossip.

During one of their talks he took Will to task for being extravagant. In fact, Sinton considered this a habit in the Taft family, going back to Alphonso, whom he thought might have been a millionaire had he saved his money. "But some men want one thing and some another," he told Will. "I wanted money and I got it. Doubtless your father is satisfied, too." Will assured him that his father was, and that his own extravagance must be due to heredity.

But a thrifty force was about to enter the Taft family in the person of Miss Herron. Her sense of economy was pleasing even to David Sinton. "She is bound to be something more than one of the drones," Horace observed. When Will finally received a letter with some warmth in it he grasped at it like a starving man. "Any act, any expression, any look of yours, Nellie, that show me that you hold me dearer than any other man sets me wild with delight," he wrote. But smooth words did not flow easily from Nellie and she said only what she meant. At last she had decided to tell her mother that she intended to marry him and Will was blissful. He sent her an ecstatic letter and in her reply she enlarged humorously on her own shortcomings as a housewife. She could not make an afghan, a lampshade, or thread a worm on a fishing hook. What sort of wife would she be? Will reminded her that without a wriggle she had hooked one gasping fish weighing 240 pounds.

Late in July young Taft visited the Herrons at Fenton's and the last of his doubts about Nellie's love were dispelled. They went rowing on the lake, picked flowers, and rambled in the woods. She sewed and sketched while he read to her William Dean Howell's *Their Wedding Journey* and George Eliot's *Mill on the Floss*. Will told her that he would "like to shake old Ruskin by the hand" for the delight he had found in reading his works to Nellie on the porch. Maria, handsome and deeply sunburned, sometimes rowed on the lake with Will and Nellie. She talked to them of Vienna, while Will came close to capsizing the boat as he reached for water lilies to give them. One of his most vivid memories of his days of courtship in the Adirondacks was of a picnic in a little clearing in the woods. On his way back from a swim he picked a hatful of raspberries which he offered to Nellie with a flourish. With the potatoes she had fried and sandwiches made with boned chicken it was all as "fine as anything Delmonicos could serve," Will reported to his parents in Vienna.

After that he found it easy to talk to the charming Mrs. Herron of his marriage prospects as he walked in the moonlight with her in Lowville. They had gone there together to see the Collins landmarks and after supper they sat on the verandah of a hotel and talked of days gone by in this picturesque small town. They walked up Collins Street to Clinton Street and "I greeted with respect the ghosts of your grandfather Collins and your grandfather Clinton," Will wrote to Nellie. "Oh, you are blue blood and no mistake."

Mrs. Herron assured him that Nellie and he would be happy because their tastes were much alike. She spoke of her "sweet-tempered and sensitive nature" and said how much she would miss her, since she had often found Nellie the most companionable of her daughters. She had always worried about her future because of her shy nature, whereas she felt that Maria could take care of herself. Greatly reassured by his comforting talk with Mrs. Herron Will returned to Cincinnati and his law office in a cheerful state of mind. But with another shift of mood Nellie turned cold and distant again. Her letters were reserved and she seemed to be uncertain of her own mind. Will wrote that he understood her nature and loved her all the more for it. He assured her that he did not think her cold; in fact, he knew of no tenderer, gentler heart and "when it beats with love for me, Nellie dear, as it must, the sun will shine on no happier man than your loving Will."

As he sat writing to Nellie on August 29, 1885, band music from Mabley's balcony floated through the windows. The esplanade below was crowded with people who had come to hear the concert. He thought there were more plug-uglies and thieves in town than ever before, for John L. Sullivan was there defending the title. Tom Campbell was his attorney and Will reminded Nellie in this connection that she was marrying a man richer in enemies than in worldly goods. Certain Republicans were whetting their knives for him because they blamed him for Charles's persistent newspaper opposition to Campbell.

Will was preparing for the next political convention and was busy with editorial work. He had written a number of articles for the *Times-Star* and the *Volksblatt,* and he was becoming adroit in pre-election battling. Horace thought his brother more of a reformer when in office than when he was a private citizen but Will found the newspapers a good medium to air his views on civic corruption and he was already regarded in Cincinnati as a strong supporter of clean politics. At the moment he was having trouble with Joseph B. Foraker, who was running for the governorship. In a fit of temper Foraker told him over the telephone that he would slap his mouth. He then apologized for his hastiness. Will was not surprised, since he thought that Foraker had an "ungovernable temper and an overbearing disposition." Moreover, he had been a Campbell man and "when a man bears such a brand, I'll none of him," said Will.

His political activities helped to ease his pain over Nellie's variable moods. Will was essentially committed to public affairs and he had listened to political discussion from his earliest years. But everything seemed in order by September and the news of his engagement reached Annie and Horace while they were still at Boar's Head. They went rollicking around outdoors, dancing and demonstrating their joy without reserve. Horace whacked his sister-in-law on the back in his exuberance, and Annie was no less pleased. "We are all as happy as can be over it," she wrote to Will. "It is a thing that I wished for long ago but had little hope of. What a lucky fellow you are, to please yourself and all those who have interest in you."

Horace dashed off a quick note: "In all my acquaintance she is the girl I would have picked for you long ago & ever since and you are the one I would have chosen for her. What a pair you will be!"

Will wrote to Aunt Delia, who was about to leave for California, that Nellie had been slow to accept him, but he hoped he would never give her cause for regret. Moreover, he considered her almost as good a cook as Aunt Delia. Could he say more? "I have a treasure," Will wrote. "You will know her some day, I hope, and will recognize the truth of what I write. She is not a girl of many friends nor one who makes them easily. She is rather reserved in manner, self-contained, independent, and of unusual application."

Will's engagement was a matter of great moment to Aunt Delia, who promptly wrote to Louise in Vienna that Miss Herron was very smart and would certainly make a good wife. "Is she not a lucky girl?" she added, with full appreciation of her favorite nephew's virtues.

Family life was about to begin for Will, but it was nearing a close for Alphonso, who had become desperately ill in the spring of 1885 and was now due to come home. He had been transferred from Vienna to St. Petersburg in the autumn of 1884 but in between he made a quick trip to Britain to do some genealogical research. Although he visited country parishes and examined church registers he was not particularly successful in tracking down Tafts. However, he ran down clues, opened up a large correspondence on the subject, and satisfied himself that Taft had long been an English name. He had often heard that the family name originally was Toft or Taffe or Taafe and probably was of Scotch or Irish origin, but this was one of the obscure points that Alphonso was never able to clear up. He had no trouble tracing the Torreys and found them to have been people of property, a substantial farming group. Although he had no time to look up any descendants during his brief visit to England he visited a 300-year-old stone house in picturesque countryside that was identified as a Torrey dwelling. Alphonso was gratified to find that the Rawson family had considerable luster in England and he had some success with the Haywards, too.

Pleased with these discoveries he hurried back to St. Petersburg to settle in quarters overlooking the Neva. He and Louise were received by the Czar, and Alphonso engaged in his last diplomatic mission for his country. A number of repatriation cases involving Jews who had emigrated to the United States were pending and he went to work on the most flagrant of these and won it. Russia refused to acknowledge the status of Jews who had gone to America, taken out citizenship there, and had then returned to Russia and set up in business. Alphonso was indignant about this, as he was over the fact that Jews in Russia were not permitted to engage in the professions. Many of those who had gone to America and returned were now stranded in a no-man's-land. The Minister planned to take up many of these cases but he had completed only one when he developed typhoid fever, which was complicated later by pneumonia and asthma. The severe winter weather aggravated his condition. Louise sent for Harry and after two months of rest in the mountains Alphonso improved and was able to write to Will, but in a shaky script that was only the shadow of his usual bold handwriting. Will was deeply touched and replied with feeling: "Well, father, you have educated your boys and girl, you have sent them through Yale College and the whole family has been to Europe and you have not been a wealthy man either. Certainly that is something for you to be proud of and for us to be thankful to you for."

In this letter he told his father of his engagement and listed Nellie's virtues—her scholarly interests, her zeal for work, her independence, her three years of teaching, her eagerness for knowledge—all qualities guaranteed to appeal to Alphonso. "I know you will love her when you come to know her and will appreciate as I do her noble character and clear-cut intellect and well-informed mind," Will wrote.

The patriarch responded warmly. He recalled having met Miss Herron at a chemistry class at the university and he was told then that she was an excellent student. Although she had rarely been in the Taft house he had heard enough about her to approve her course in life. Moreover, he knew and admired her parents and hoped that they would be as well pleased with the engagement as he was. He urged Will to make public their plans and added:

> I want to see all our children settled as soon as they can suit themselves
> with partners, and their circumstances render it practicable. My sands
> are so nearly run that I can only hope to live to see them start & make
> some estimate of what is to be the complexion of their future lives. I
> am very happy in your prospects.

But Will made a tactical mistake in showing Nellie a letter his mother sent him about their engagement. It was a worldly letter, and even slightly calculating in tone. Nellie was chilled by its implications. Louise wrote that she would certainly not object to an alliance with the Herron family, since she was not mercenary. Nellie, sensitive and quick to shrink

into herself, promptly concluded that Will had reasoned himself into loving her but that his family did not consider her a good match. He quickly
assured her that she would be welcomed warmly into the Taft family
when his parents returned from Europe. Before the elder Tafts landed,
William Hulbert died and was buried from his home on Freeman Street.
Soon afterwards Tillie, who had a large inheritance from his estate, became engaged to Frank Perin, whom she had known from childhood.
Her father had opposed this match but their friends had expected it.

Alphonso walked feebly ashore from the *Serbia* at the end of August,
1885. He stayed with Harry in New York and when interviewed deplored
the emphasis in Russia on military power rather than on popular education. He had returned without any wish to run for office. At the age of
seventy-five he was now ready to concede that "hereafter the activity of
the Taft family shall be displayed by our children." It was apparent to
all who saw him that he could no longer draw on the strength and energy
that had been phenomenal all his life. When he made his official visit to
Washington to report to the President, Louise went to Millbury for a
family reunion. Susie Wood had come on from California, Anna Orton
from Columbus, and Delia was their hostess. The four sisters were together for the first time in a decade. Their lives had taken widely diver-
gent routes. Louise was now worldly, traveled, and sophisticated. Susie
was well-off, good looking, and happy in her family life. Anna was leading a useful and satisfying life in Columbus. Her husband had just been
appointed state geologist and she was following Louise's example by
engaging in a multiplicity of public duties. "What with art and literature and charity and education to help take care of, she would be a busy
woman without her family cares," her husband commented. Delia studied all three of her sisters with interest. She was the catalyst among
them, unchanging, observant, a true daughter of Massachusetts.

The elder Tafts were back in Cincinnati by the middle of October,
1885, and they had given their personal blessing to Will and Nellie.
Back in occupancy on Mount Auburn, Louise arranged the treasures she
had assembled in London, Vienna, and Constantinople. Will had sent
her money to buy linen for Nellie. The marriage plans were going forward and the young pair hoped to go abroad for their wedding trip but
Will was worried about finances. Her father had given Nellie a lot on
McMillan Street, overlooking the river, and here they proposed to build
a house. But Nellie considered the trip abroad more important than she
did the house and she and Will had some minor disagreements over
money matters in the spring of 1886. He was much hurt by a letter he received from her in March devoid of any expression of affection and he
wrote to her anxiously: "I never felt so hungry for money as I do now but
my little pile seems like the German featherbed used as a covering; when

one's head is protected one's feet are exposed and when one's feet are warm one's head is cold." Nellie had objected to a reduction he proposed in the fund for their travels. But they patched things up and he wrote again, saying he knew she had never regretted his poverty but would meet all exigencies with her customary quiet courage.

Nellie had her wedding gown made in Washington and when she tried it on she decided that she looked a fright in it, or so she wrote to Will, with a footnote that she assumed he would not agree. He replied somewhat prophetically:

> I hope you will think of me tomorrow when you take your Sunday after-noon walk along the beautiful streets of Washington. I wonder, Nellie dear, if you and I will ever be there in any official capacity. Oh yes, I forgot, of course we shall when you become Secretary of the Treasury.

Wedding presents were soon pouring in, but Nellie and Will preferred books to all else. While Nellie was in the capital, Will helped her mother to celebrate her thirty-first wedding anniversay and he decided all over again that she was the most beautiful woman of her age he had ever seen and was "just as charming and good as she was pretty." This occasion led him to hope that he and Nellie would find equal happiness and that their love was not a passing ecstasy that would die out, leaving life tasteless and insipid:

> It will be a growing, widening, developing love that will reveal and has already revealed a depth of feeling I was unconscious of. Oh Nellie dearest, I don't want to put the burden on you but I must. I want you to insist upon my cultivating myself always. You can do it with your sweet quiet persistence and your ambition to know. Ah, my darling, you are a treasure I value more highly every day. I bless the day that opened my eyes to my need for you and the day when you consented to help me on through life. . . .

As June approached Will and Nellie were constantly together. They attended the dog show. They went roller skating and Will sent her a set of dumbbells, for she was suffering from rheumatism that spring and gymnastic exercises were the current cure-all for stiffening of the joints. They went up to Mount Auburn and found Fanny and Horace trying to do what Alphonso had suggested when he went out to California with Louise for his health. The patriarch had commissioned them to get the old family place in order, to cultivate an orchard, to grow sweet corn and flowers. But Will's interest had switched now to plans for his own future home. He and Nellie took morning streetcar rides to survey the McMillan Street property that Mr. Herron had given them. They rode past flowering gardens and the fragrance of May was all around them. One family was breaking up. Another was in the making.

CHAPTER 9

A DAY IN JUNE

W ILLIAM HOWARD TAFT was jovial but nervous on his wedding day, June 19, 1886. The Episcopalian service was conducted in the late afternoon in the Herron house by the Reverend D. N. A. Hoge, of Zanesville, who had married Nellie's parents. The bride looked trim and shy in her gleaming satin gown with embroidered bodice and a veil caught with sprays of white lilac. She held a bouquet of sweet peas and lilies of the valley and seemed tiny beside tall, blue-eyed Will and towering Horace, who was best man. Maria and Fanny, her bridesmaids, were joyous observers in white. A reception was held from five to eight, and Nellie confessed later to having only a blurred recollection of the day's events, because the house was so jammed with guests. But Horace assured Will that things had gone off well—"no complaint, everybody satisfied," he announced in his crisp way.

When young Mrs. Taft walked into the Albemarle Hotel on Madison Avenue on the following day, a new world was opening up for her. She was seeing New York as a young bride and she was on her way to Europe. But as she unpacked she found that she had forgotten her opera glasses, her Satchel Guide to Europe, and the *Vicar of Wakefield*, which she had hoped to read on the steamer. Nellie wrote at once to her mother to send them on, and she also expressed the fear that she and Will were taken for "b. and g." This worried her less than the fact that their bill for one day at the Albemarle was $15.50, including meals. They sailed across the bay to Sandy Hook and took a train to Sea Bright where "for four days our eyes closed in slumber and happiness to the music of the crash and roar of the deep sounding sea," she wrote in her wedding diary. The weather was stormy and waves washed up to the hotel piazza. It rained all the time they were there but they managed a buggy ride to Long Branch, and also to Elberon to see the cottage where President Garfield died. Nellie was seasick crossing the Atlantic on the *City of Chester,* which she described as a slow old tub. The passengers were not the sort who traveled by the White Star and Cunard lines but she soon decided that it was just as well they had chosen the cheapest boat, since most of the time she wore a "fifteen-dollar dress, a six-year-old coat, a tipsy hat minus a hat pin, and a limp veil." The Captain, recovering from a drunken spree in New York, rarely appeared.

They celebrated the Fourth of July on board with songs and recitations and enjoyed the idle, irresponsible days at sea, reading long stanzas from Coleridge and Shelley. At Liverpool they inspected the new tunnel under the Mersey before setting out with two hand valises and a satchel on the traditional tour of England. They visited the cathedrals, the castles, the focal points of interest. Each night they made entries in the joint diary they kept of their wedding trip—a page by Nell, a page by Will, with occasional laughing comments to each other scrawled into the record, such as "Nell loves Will" or "Will loves Nell."

Young Taft viewed England in a different light on his wedding trip. Its spires and towers, its fields and gardens, now had romantic interest with Nellie at his side. They sat in Addison's Walk at Magdalen and listened to the wind rustling through the trees. Sunlight played on the walk and the skies were cloudless for the young pair. But they had their first quarrel on the day they saw the Tower of London. It blew up over a visit to relatives and Nellie sulked as they viewed the crown jewels and the Beefeaters. They stayed at the Royal Hotel Blackfriars since Miss Glossop, who had harbored Will and also his father on other occasions, could not take them in. Will found great delight in strolling through the Inns of the Temple, his only glimpse at this time of "those old nests of the Knights of the law." Later he would be an honored guest in their sacred precincts but in the meantime he was well satisfied with external observation.

When he asked Henry White, the United States Ambassador, for passes to the House of Commons to hear a notable debate, none was available. Instead he received tickets to view the horses and state equipages of Queen Victoria in the Royal Mews, as popular a sight in the 1880's as

the changing of the Guard in the twentieth century. But Nellie was offended and this incident had long-range consequences. Whether by accident or design Henry White was dropped summarily by William Howard
Taft when he became President of the United States. There were other
disillusioning experiences. After a day at Hampton Court and Richmond,
Will decided that he preferred the Ohio River to the Thames. Nellie
roamed happily through Liberty's and lingered with Will at shop windows in the Burlington Arcade. As they moved through the shops they
felt as if they were catching glimpses of Victorian England and the lavish
life of the nobles, but they preferred the republican ideals of their own
land.

Always impassioned theatergoers, the Tafts saw Henry Irving, Ada
Rehan, John Drew, Otis Skinner, and May Irwin from six-shilling seats
at Daly's. The opera season was over, to Nellie's disappointment. They
toured the Lake Country in a ponderous coach and browsed contentedly
over the Wordsworth and Coleridge landmarks. In the old Salon fashion
they recited verse to each other, for Nellie insisted on keeping the literary flame alight. After viewing both York and Lincoln cathedrals in a
single day they felt wearied and confused and were glad to set off for
Scotland. Edinburgh was bedecked for the arrival of Queen Victoria.
They had good seats on a stone block on the sidewalk and saw her clearly
as she drove past in a drizzling rain. The city was brilliantly lit that night,
from Holyrood to the Castle.

Nellie had insisted on a quick trip to Paris. She approached the Pari-
sian dressmakers "with fear and trembling" but came away satisfied with
her three purchases—a reception dress of brown silk, a rose silk dinner
dress, and a green cashmere that Will thought looked particularly well on
his small-waisted bride. He had a strong taste of Nellie's ingrained fru-
gality when she insisted that they use buses for their sightseeing so as to
save cab fare. Will was exhausted but Nellie paraded cheerfully in the
Luxembourg Gardens and shopped in the Bon Marché for gloves and
trifles. They attended services at the Madeleine and were jolted to the
Bastille on top of a bus. Its grim echoes seemed not yet distant. They
enjoyed La Chasse, the horse spectacle at the Hippodrome, and agreed
that the ballet at the Eden Theater was superb. As they left Versailles
they were glad that they had seen the palaces, but Will said he hoped
he would never again have to trail through the labyrinth of salons. In
Holland they picked up some Delft plates that he carried around in straw
until they became a family joke. After being brought safely across the
Atlantic by hand they were smashed to smithereens when sent by express from New York to Cincinnati.

Returning home on the *City of Chicago* they played euchre and
read Sir Walter Scott novels and Holmes's *Autocrat of the Breakfast*

Table. Their steamer collided with a fishing smack in a dense fog off the Newfoundland banks. Will saw the accident through the porthole and pictured a shipwreck. After reassuring Nellie he went up on deck and found the crew launching a small boat for rescue purposes, but the smack was not leaking, nor was their ship damaged.

Nellie brought home a wealth of sentimental reminders of their trip —programs, menus, dried flowers, postcards, souvenirs of all kinds that were to repose eventually in the Library of Congress. Their house was not quite finished on their arrival so they stayed for a month on Mount Auburn, where Nellie for the first time was able to form impressions of the elder Tafts. She saw that as parents they spread serenity and had an "abiding confidence in the future of their children which strongly influenced the latter to justify it." They had created a family atmosphere in which the children absorbed high ideals and strove to meet the family standard of intellectual and moral effort. Nellie decided that both of Will's parents had wide culture and catholic sympathies. At the outset of her own married life she recognized the family pattern that had been set and tried to carry it on with the next generation. She found Louise formal but kind, and she wrote of Alphonso in *Recollections of Full Years:*

> My husband's father was "gentle" beyond anything I ever knew. He was a man of tremendous firmness of purpose and just as set in his views as any one well could be, but he was one of the most lovable men that ever lived because he had a wide tolerance and a strangely "understanding sympathy" for everybody. He had a great many friends and to know him was to know why this was so.

The young Tafts began the year 1887 in their own Victorian home on Walnut Hills. It was far from being an architectural gem, with its redwood-shingled roof, scroll-trimmed porches, and windows with colored glass, but it was roomy and comfortable. A brook twisted like a silver thread down into the valley and their view was magnificent. Not only did they have the vista of the river but their library window opened on the Keys forest, a brilliant sight in autumn. Taft unquestionably was happy in his new surroundings. The romantic mood prevailed as he plunged again into his legal work. Almost at once he was appointed a judge of the Superior Court of Ohio, the post his father had filled twenty years earlier. The salary was $6,000 a year and his work did not take him away from home. Although head of the hostile faction, Governor Foraker had appointed him to fill a temporary vacancy and he was re-elected for a five-year term.

Will, like the elder Tafts, was deeply concerned when Horace suddenly broke away from his law practice late in 1886 and went to Kansas City with the hope of founding a boys' school, his long-cherished ambition. His old friend, Sherman Thacher, was practicing law in Kansas but he was tutoring on the side since he, too, yearned to be a schoolmaster. Horace was heartily sick of law and felt that his practice was "flat on its back" when he left for the West. Reflecting in later years on his abandonment of the profession his father had wished for him, Horace wrote: "I should never have made a good lawyer, but I might have done a good deal better if I had not been so interested in political reform."

Alphonso was baffled by Horace's sudden decision. He wrote to Delia that it was the most trying parting he had ever had with one of his sons. To make matters worse, Horace was heartbroken because Maria had rejected his proposal of marriage. He could not find her to say good-bye on the dismal day on which he left Cincinnati, Down the years Maria would move in and out of his life, as they shared picnics and parties, golfed together at Murray Bay, attended their friends' weddings, exchanged biting views and witty sallies, but their romance died when Horace went west. Soon he was writing home from a tiny room in Kansas City. He had three trunks, a clutter of books, and most uncertain prospects.

Before long he was tutoring George B. Case, later captain of the Yale baseball team and a prominent New York lawyer, but he was full of unrest. Thacher, a man of strong character, high ideals, and sarcastic tongue, had gone to California immediately after his graduation from Yale and had then moved to Kansas. He was still groping for what he wanted. The legal profession was as irksome to him as it was to Horace, and each understood how the other felt, for they had known each other from childhood. Their fathers too, had been close friends at Yale and Thacher had married a cousin of Horace's. After long talks together about their prospects Horace finally decided to return East and tutor in Latin at Yale. Thacher stayed behind but later returned to Yale and eventually founded a boys' school in the Ojai Valley, California. Thus two schoolmasters of consequence were snatched from the courts of law.

From 1887 to 1890 Horace was a familiar figure on the Yale campus but he tutored without inspiration, appraising his own teaching at the time as wooden. He was not a classicist by training and had not consciously chosen this field, but he renewed old friendships in New Haven and made many trips to Millbury to see Aunt Delia. It was a restless, uneasy period for Horace, since he had not yet found his bearings and he could not forget the provocative Maria. He had a deep sense of failure over abandoning his profession in a family that demanded constancy and success. The result was that he slept poorly and worried constantly. By the spring of 1889 he had persuaded himself that even at Yale he was

not regarded as a scholar. But an opportunity came his way in the following year when Mrs. Robert Black, of Pelham Manor, whose brother had
been a classmate of Harry's, decided to open a school in memory of their
father. She offered Horace the post of headmaster and he felt that at
last the way was opening for him to start a boys' school. Harry and Julia
had a cottage in Pelham Manor, so that he knew he would be among
friends. He confided to Nellie that he was glad to be giving up his tutorial
duties although he had been well treated at Yale. Studying one of his
small nephews he wrote:

> Hang it, Nellie, it is these rascally children that make one feel that a
> man who never marries doesn't see one tenth of life. With a lot of
> children around me I think I should be not only happier but a hundred
> per cent better. But mine, if I ever have any, will probably be sickly
> chaps, with weak nervous organizations like their daddy's.

The doors of the red brick house opened in 1890 and it was known as
Mr. Taft's School. At first there were only seventeen boys, representing
all grades. Horace taught everything himself except Greek and modern
languages. To all intents and purposes it was like a tutoring school. His
father recognized the spirit of self-depreciation in Horace and wrote to
Delia that he would be a source of happiness wherever he went to all
except to himself. All of the Tafts rejoiced that at last Horace was
reaching toward his life's ambition and was working with definite purpose. He wrote enthusiastically of his plans to his old confidante Fanny,
who was having troubles of her own. She had decided not to come out, a
course that even independent Maria disapproved. After all the frivolity
of Vienna she had become a rebel and had great contempt for society
as such. She was now more interested in church work than in viewing
the world through what Horace called "society glasses." He considered
hers a good healthy vision and he sympathized when she told him that
she was bored when she stayed with Harry and Julia in New York, and
restless at Narragansett Pier. But between her kindergarten and her
church work she managed to keep busy in Cincinnati, and it amused her
to make five dollars a week singing in the church choir. She saw a good
deal of Mrs. William Howard Taft, who was recognized in the family
by this time as a woman of strength and character.

But in the year that Horace opened his school Fanny surprised her
family by marrying Dr. William Edwards, a surgeon ten years her senior
who had attended her father in California. None but Maria had known
about this romance until the announcement was made. Dr. Edwards
was an experienced and able practitioner and when they visited the
East on their wedding trip he made a good impression on all of Fanny's

relatives. On his return to California he predicted that Will Taft would yet be President, an ambition that had not yet occurred to any member of the family.

Alphonso and Louise, back from California, had settled down to a circumscribed life, to changing family patterns and the development of their young. Alphonso had never fully recovered from his illness in Russia and it was evident to his family that he was failing badly. Louise, the tireless matriarch, busied herself with various causes. The kindergarten movement she had initiated had expanded and she now planned a training class for teachers to be run by Maria Kraus-Boelte, an educator who used Froebel methods. Louise fostered the Art Institute which had evolved from the Women's Art Museum that she and Mrs. Perry had helped to found. The collections in the new Art Institute caught the public interest at once and it was flourishing by 1888. In October of that year Mrs. Alphonso Taft was on the committee that welcomed Mrs. Benjamin Harrison to Cincinnati shortly before she became First Lady.

Meanwhile things had gone so well with Will and Nellie that they felt they could afford to go abroad again that summer. This time they covered more ground and Nellie felt she was having a rare experience when she heard *Parsifal* at Bayreuth and watched Edward Strauss conduct his own orchestra. They toured Germany and proceeded to Venice, where Will read Ruskin to Nellie in St. Mark's Square and also nearly tipped her into a canal as he stepped into their gondola. They stayed at the Villa Trollope in Florence where part of *Romola* was written. In Rome they visited the grave of Keats and hunted in vain for Shelley's. After touring the Italian lakes and Switzerland they made a return trip to London. Both had come down to earth after the romantic aura of their wedding trip, but they were more deeply in love than ever.

Soon after they returned home Peter died of consumption. He had been failing badly and his parents knew that he was dying. His life since leaving Yale had been a sad one and in writing sympathetically to his father Harry recalled the days when Rossy was the "sunniest of us all." Horace wrote with philosophical acceptance: "Nothing is stranger than to see what different records men have made from those they were expected to make when we graduated." Funeral services for Peter were held at Charles's house and Bishop Boyd Vincent, of the diocese of Southern Ohio, conducted the service. He had been chosen because he was an old Yale classmate of Peter's and in his eulogy he recalled his earnestness and simplicity in his college days:

> The self-mastery and self-direction of this man were a constant marvel to us. . . . Steadily, day or night, he held on his way toward his own ideal of excellence. No doubt he thus helped to lay the foundation of

the illness which has now ended his life. But just as surely he did reach his own chosen end at that time of the highest rank in scholarship ever reached at Yale. He had brought lasting honor on himself, his family, his class.

Small Hulbert was at the funeral and heard the eulogy of his father, a memory that he never discussed in his later years. He was already a deeply studious boy although his mother did her best to discourage this tendency in him. Alphonso, with all his memories of their early pride in Rossy, looked a stricken man at the funeral. Will, observing with concern, wrote later to Horace that Peter's tragedy was the great disappointment of his life. "To think of that sweet, kindly, generous, beautiful character who has been such a father to us as never was before or will be again" beaten down by this grief seemed inexpressibly sad to Will. Alphonso was now dropsical and his circulation was failing. He slept propped up on a sofa and had cardiac asthma.

As Alphonso failed, the young Tafts had their first child. Robert A. Taft was born on McMillan Street early on September 8, 1889, with a minimum of fuss or delay. Mrs. Herron had been visiting at the Rutherford Hayes home but she arrived in time for Robert's birth. He weighed eight pounds; his head was large and his mother thought that his hands and feet resembled those of Horace. She cautioned Will not to look conceited on his journey downtown, but he had difficulty restraining himself. "I have been accused of the unjudicial conduct of rushing out into the street after the boy came and yelling 'Hurrah! For a man is born unto me!'" he noted. He wished to name the baby Alphonso but Nellie was adamant about Robert.

Through her excellent management the young Tafts by this time had spent $8,500 on their house and furniture, had freed themselves from debt, and had made two trips to Europe. Her father-in-law described Nellie as an "economical and excellent calculator," and Will freely admitted that all this had been possible only because she was at the helm. His own affairs were expanding. Four months after his son's birth the first suggestion of a place on the Supreme Court reached young Taft and he wrote eagerly to his father that although the chance was only one in a million, even the slightest suggestion of so great a prize was something to dwell on with pleasure. Judge Hiram Peck of Cincinnati had been advocating his appointment but Will felt that his "chances of going to the moon and of donning a silk gown at the hands of President Harrison are about equal." Foraker also claimed to have pushed his cause with the President but Will was skeptical, knowing how cool their relations were.

If he did not make the Supreme Court at this time another opportunity came to him through the good offices of Congressman Ben Butterworth, and he served as solicitor general from 1890 to 1892. Alphonso, who had returned to California in 1889, gloried in this appointment, and urged Will to go ahead and fear not. He thought him young for the honor but he trusted to the "good sense and prudence" of Nellie in the background. She could be sharp with Will but her criticism never riled him. Alphonso remembered his own battles in the same post many years earlier and he reminded Will that the best legal talent in the country would try his mettle.

It pleased the dying warrior that his sons should all be such good friends. The family bond was sustained and potent. Charles was the financier and journalist of the family, Horace the scholar, Harry the lawyer, and Will the judge. Charles had some of his father's tough invincibility in his drive for results and in his family pride. He wrote to Will from the editorial rooms of the *Times-Star* on May 21, 1890, that "we boys are all trying to push along toward success if for no other reason than to convince Father in his ebbing days that he has not spent a life in vain." Charles wrote that he gloried in Harry's nerve, energy, and push. He predicted success for Horace in the academic world and he urged Will to show the Washington chaps how thoroughly he could handle Supreme Court cases.

Will had recently bought thirty additional volumes of the English Chancery Reports to complete the set his father had given him. This supplied him with a better working library in his offices than any lawyer of the Western bar then possessed. Nellie deplored his extravagance in buying so many expensive books but Alphonso felt that Will was proceeding sure-footedly down the judicial road that he had mapped out for him. The Attorney General was ill when he arrived in Washington so that young Taft immediately had experience of considerable range and made the most of it. As Alphonso put it: "He whose plate is always right side up, is sure to catch the porridge." Will sometimes quoted this observation when asked why so many appointments had come his way without any particular effort being put forth by him.

On his first day in office William M. Evarts, the noted senator and lawyer from New York, looked him up and invited him to dinner. He knew and admired Alphonso Taft. The result was that Will, who had been dismayed to find that his legal quarters amounted to a single shabby room three flights up, with no office staff, almost immediately sat between Mrs. Henry Cabot Lodge and Mrs. John Hay at the Evarts dinner table and was warmly welcomed to Washington. Nellie arrived with Robert two weeks later and they settled in a small house on Dupont Circle. Their rent was seventy-five dollars a month and they had two

Welsh maids. Will was urged to drop in any evening at the White House. Washington society in 1890 consisted of the old families of the city, the diplomatic corps, and leading government officials. A dinner party for twelve was considered large and there was little social life around the White House. The Tafts were involved chiefly with the judiciary. Mrs. John Marshall Harlan was kind to Nellie but they went out very little, even when the stimulating Maria was with them.

Alphonso, dying slowly in San Diego, continued to advise, praise, and analyze Will's legal moves. He was critical of his first argument before the Supreme Court, reminding him that he must be duly modest since he was dealing with the "first men of the nation." Up to February, 1891, he had won fifteen and lost two cases. He was soon involved in the Bering Sea dispute, a diplomatic war that had been raging with Great Britain for some time. In this instance the Canadian Government had brought suit against the United States over seal-hunting rights, a moot issue since the acquisition of Alaska from Russia. The case was finally settled by international arbitration. Joseph H. Choate complimented Taft on his brief and his father thought it a good piece of work. It was 300 pages long and represented a staggering amount of research. He next defended the constitutionality of the McKinley tariff law and won his case. He adjudicated important labor cases and eventually won what he considered the most important decision of his term, in the Addyston Pipe & Steel Company case. This was a Government suit to break up a cast iron pipe monopoly and was regarded as a significant anti-trust victory. Taft always felt that the principles laid down in this case set a pattern for much of the work done subsequently to break up monopolies. It was the first time that his own name was drawn into the type of action that would provide high drama for Theodore Roosevelt.

Knowing how strong Nellie was, Alphonso warned his son not to be influenced by his wife's anxiety for him to make great speeches in court. This was not the way to win cases. Louise sent him warnings about the pitfalls of social life in the capital. She preferred the ambience of the Blaine circle to the high-flying social life of the McLeans. Ever watchful for the interests of all her sons she urged Will to invite Harry to Washington, should he be giving a dinner for the judiciary. "Don't be discouraged at the indifference of the old fogies of the Supreme Court," she added. "It is a new experience which you will get used to."

In the summer of 1890 Nellie went with Robert to stay with the Herrons at Magnolia, Massachusetts. She read Dumas, George Sand, Mrs. Humphrey Ward, and mystery stories as she coped with lively Bobby whose disposition, she thought, got worse by the day. He squirmed and yelled when she dressed him but he made good progress in learning to walk. His appetite was huge and she tried to control it by giving him cream and sugar with his first bowl of cereal, milk and sugar with the second, and plain milk with the third.

His father thought him full of charm and wrote humorously to Nellie: "I need not argue with you to establish the fact that our boy is different from other babies in many desirable ways." Nellie, never given to extravagant statement, found him "cute and smart." Soon he was trotting the length of the porch at Magnolia without mishap. At fifteen months he would sit still and look at a picture book but he preferred to dash about and shout. His mother described the effect created by the future senator in a letter to his father: "We are going to have our hands full with him. . . . How I wish you could see him running at full speed from one end of the parlor to the other, or waving his arms and talking at the top of his voice."

Bobby, sometimes also known as Robbie and Bobbie, surprised his mother eventually by turning into a quiet and extremely well-behaved boy, for at this age he was uncommonly rambunctious. He covered himself with boot blacking, roared when he was cutting teeth, and scampered around like an elusive spider. Nellie did not enjoy her summer away from Will. Nothing had any savor for her with her husband in Washington. "You are the dearest, sweetest boy that ever lived," she wrote to him. And again: "Goodnight, my sweet precious darling. I am not a bit happy without you, and it worries me to think of you there without anyone to look after you." She scolded him for spending too much on his laundry and she warned him about the feasting that his position entailed.

Will wrote every day to the absent Nellie, detailing each event of his life and telling her again and again how much he missed her and Bobby. Although deeply involved in large affairs he kept up his interest in the minutiae of family life and Nellie's small anxieties. He had established pleasant relations with the members of the Supreme Court and had occasional glimpses behind the scenes where the drama of government was being enacted. He took firm central control of the business on the docket instead of having it scattered through the department.

Charles, having just sold the *Volksblatt*, visited the capital with Annie in January, 1891, and Nellie gave her first big Washington party in their honor. The Harlans and other Justices attended and she wished that she had some of Mrs. Alphonso Taft's glass and china for the occasion. They all went to the White House reception on New Year's Day. Nellie was beginning to feel at home in Washington, although she still lived on an unpretentious scale. She went regularly to the House and Senate to hear the debates and she had animated exchanges with Will on political issues. Her ambition on his behalf was taking shape.

That same spring another opportunity loomed up for Will. Nine new circuit judges were to be appointed and Judge Peck, Rufus Smith, Howard Hollister, and other Cincinnati friends were urging that young Taft be given the Sixth Circuit. Nellie was against it. She believed that it meant he would be shelved for life. But the prospect appealed strongly to Will. With a point of view that was to be lifelong on this issue he wrote to his father:

> I like judicial life and there is only one higher judicial position in the country than that. . . . Federal judgeships like that don't lie around loose, and if you don't get them when you can you will not get them when you would. It would be in the line of promotion to the Supreme Court, and I am sure would be a fine position to hold. It would keep me poor all my life if I were to get it, but I don't see that people with very modest incomes don't live as happily as those who have fortunes. The salary is $6,000 a year.

Alphonso advised him to accept the offer. He could retire from the bench if better prospects opened up—the governorship of Ohio, for instance. But death hung over the Taft family in the spring of 1891, taking the oldest and one of its youngest members. Little David Taft died of typhoid fever in February, and Charles and Annie were inconsolable. Will and Horace went to Cincinnati for the funeral. They found Charles quiet but unstrung and Annie completely prostrated. She clung to Horace, who wrote to his mother: "Poor Annie! Her sad, sweet face will haunt me for a long time to come. . . . It will be harder for her than for most. The strength of her love for those who are dear to her is extraordinary and David had grown to fill a wonderful place in her life. All of her quaint fun he appreciated and shared. He sympathized with all her tastes and had little touches of the romantic in his character that appealed to her."

David's schoolmates at Woodward High School passed resolutions in his memory. His grandfather Sinton took it stoically. He had intended to buy a ranch of 160,000 acres in Texas for little David, estimating that it would be worth a million dollars by the time he was twenty-one. Louise promptly wrote to Will that she hoped he would use that million —"which might have ruined David"—for a hospital, a college, a charity, some true memorial to their boy. "It seems a ghastly satire on the poverty of riches that all his money could not save the boy," she added. Harry, too, lost a son that year. He was named Walbridge Smith Taft and another son born later would bear the same name.

Alphonso, nearing his own end, dwelt more on the living than the dead. He liked to look at his grandson Robert's picture, which was hung where he could see it from his bed. "He is a noble boy," he wrote to Will.

"There is nothing I think of so much as my children & grandchildren." From their cottage in San Diego he and Louise had a magnificent view of the bay, with the mountains in the background. Watching him sink into the shadows but with his mind still alert, Louise wrote to Will: "What a resource is a cultivated mind! What can people do when old and sick without intellectual resources? I can always entertain him."

In April, 1891, his father sent for Will and when the young judge reached the house on the hill he was shocked to find Alphonso so far gone. Greatly touched, he described their meeting to Nellie. When he gave the dying man some brandy he "looked at me in the sweetest way and said to me, 'Will, I love you beyond expression.'" He spoke of the baby Nellie was expecting at that time and when asked what they should call him if he were a boy he murmured "Call him Robert the Second." He asked Will what he thought of "those old fellows on the Bench in Washington." Actually, none of them was as old as he, but he liked to refer to them in that way, Will noted, and added:

> I am not superstitious as you know, my darling, but I have a kind of presentiment that Father has been a kind of guardian angel to me in that his wishes for my success have been so strong and intense as to bring it and that as his life ebbs away and ends, I shall cease to have the luck which has followed me thus far. . . . In any event, my darling, we can be happy as long as we live, if we only love each other and the children that come to us.

Will assured Nellie that she meant everything to him and that the light went out of his life when she was not with him. He believed firmly that their love gained in strength as time went on. He thought of her as he took long walks in an impressive setting of ocean, headlands, and mountains—all of which he described to her in his letters. At close range he found Dr. Edwards a successful practitioner and skilled surgeon, but inclined to be tactless and hot-tempered. He and Fanny seemed happy together and Will was satisfied to see his sister so well established on the coast.

Alphonso died on May 21, 1891, and he was taken to the house on Mount Auburn for funeral services. He had asked for this, although Leopold Markbreit, president of the *Volksblatt*, was in occupancy. The roots of his life were centered there and his sense of family was deathless. His sons were his pallbearers and he was buried in Spring Grove Cemetery, where Louise in time put up a memorial to the gentle-mannered man who had left so vigorous a family line. She spent that summer with Nellie, who was awaiting the birth of her second child. Maria came often to visit them on the Grandin Road, sometimes in tears, for she was finding her amiable mother difficult at this point. But

Maria was devoted to Bobby and took him buggy riding at every opportunity. She made little horses for him with branches off the trees,
and with a switch for a whip he galloped around contentedly. He had a
small cart and shovel and worked away at the earth. His mother found
him an inquiring and industrious child. Every move he made was reported to his father by Nellie—his cunning ways when he crept into her
bed to waken her in the morning and patted her face, or rolled his
curly head close to hers; how he swallowed a bottle of epipac and hung
a wreath of trumpet flowers on his head; how crazy he was about his engine. She found him excellent company while she read Bret Harte
and Kipling as she sat in a white wrapper under the trees on the hot
summer days.

But Bobby was not so pleased when his little sister was born on August
1, 1891. In fact, he was disturbed. "More baby!" he announced when
brought in to inspect small Helen. For some time after that she was
known as "More Baby" and then as "Helen Blazes" because of her lusty
crying, especially during the night. Bobby cried almost continually, too.
Each child yelled louder than the other and their mother cooked mush in
the chafing dish with one hand while she wrote to Will with the other,
describing her distress. But things soon quietened down and her small
son went back to his concentrated play. He and Helen were always to
be the best of friends. The Longworths, Scarboroughs, and Harrisons all
called to see the new baby and Louise, feeling satisfied that Nellie and
her little daughter could now do without her, left for San Diego with
Delia. The Torrey sisters were now to be together again, as in their girlhood days. They settled in a small house at Fourth and Grape streets
and helped Fanny build and furnish her new bungalow. They joined a
magazine club, made new friends, and had Bill and Fanny in for dinner
on Sundays and holidays, as in the old Mount Auburn days.

The new generation was now on the rise. Louise faded slowly into the
background, although her hold on her children and her pride in them
would never weaken. She was still deferred to in important matters. But
it was only the shadow of her former life as she watched the new
alliances, the growing children, the unquenchable stream of life that
had begun with her and Alphonso.

CHAPTER 10

LE PETIT JUGE

MR. AND MRS. WILLIAM HOWARD TAFT first went to Murray Bay in 1892. They were sailing along the St. Lawrence after a family wedding when they came to the small settlement 114 miles northeast of Quebec and were so charmed by it that they decided to go no farther. From then on it became the summer headquarters of the family, and gatherings that began under rustic conditions continued with each generation for the next seventy years. Old houses were rented and re-modeled and new houses with modern improvements were built. The peninsula in the St. Lawrence eventually became something of a Cincinnati colony. One by one the Taft grandchildren came to know and love the rocky headland overlooking the wide stretch of river. Charles Taft, from his neighboring cottage, told of watching Will pacing solemnly on the moonlit cliffs, trying to soothe a crying baby so that his wife might have peaceful sleep. They all enjoyed the fresh breezes, the rugged landscape, the sunsets, storms, and rains.

Except for the years when he was President, Will rarely failed to summer at Murray Bay, and from the Supreme Court bench, as each term ended, he voiced his longing for the freshness, the freedom, the informality of the resort where, in baggy knickers and bashed hat, he could indulge in his favorite pastime—golf. In time he came to be known affectionately to the French Canadians as *Le Petit Juge*. At first he and Nellie stayed at Chamard's Lorne House that stood where the Manoir Richelieu was later built. Then they rented cottages and kept enlarging and building until they had the space and convenience that they desired. Soon young Robert was imitating his father with tiny golf clubs.

The Tafts had just attended Horace's wedding when they discovered Murray Bay. Horace had surprised them all by getting married on June 29, 1892, to Winifred S. Thompson, a girl from Niagara Falls who taught in New Haven. Fanny had introduced them and she was carefully scrutinized by the family, since Horace was extra dear to them all. Will's first reaction was to write to his wife: "It seems to me she will be getting what was intended for all mankind. But it is rather hard and selfish of us to consign Horace to celibacy."

Everyone remembered Horace's old love for Maria. Winifred was a different type altogether. She was tall and serious and Horace told his brother that she "believed thoroughly with him in the good." He was thirty-one at the time of his marriage and she was a year and a half his senior. She had just been to Europe when she came into the lives of the Tafts and they soon saw that she was independent in all her ways. Her tastes were artistic and bookish and she was obviously a woman of character. Louise and Winifred became fast friends but other members of the family were slow to warm up to Horace's wife. Will, friendly with everyone, thought her sarcastic, and Nellie and she were temperamental opposites. Annie, an absorbed and attentive mother, felt that she failed to show interest in the Pike Street children. Knowing how every member of the family wished to pull Horace to their hearthstones, Winifred did not always fall into the Murray Bay pattern, but persuaded Horace to go to other resorts. She was vigilant of his health and understood his nervous temperament. As time went on she made a separate life for Horace and was the only Taft who did not feel altogether at home in Cincinnati.

To Horace, however, Winifred was a good and loving wife and Louise approved her enthusiasm for his ideals, which were exacting ones. At the time of his marriage he was spreading out in the academic world and the entire family, led by his mother, was backing him. "Horace is so modest he needs somebody to blow his trumpet for him," she wrote to Will. "He says I am a regular drummer and would do well on the road. Aunt Delia says she cannot walk about, but she is willing to have an advertisement on her back, if necessary."

Before the end of his first year at Pelham Horace had decided to seek larger and healthier quarters. Winifred was prepared to live in any remote spot provided they could find a suitable site for the school. They looked at properties in Litchfield and New Milford before finally settling on the Warren House, a run-down old hotel in Watertown, Connecticut. Here the Taft School of today came into being in 1893. Horace leased the property for five years and borrowed $10,000 to make it habitable. Partitions were torn down and the headmaster sat on the platform where the hotel clerk had presided. Water was piped from a spring near the ball field and drinking water came from a well. They lacked city gas and electricity at first and used lamps in the big schoolroom. To add to their early difficulties the gymnasium burned down in the first year.

They began with thirty boarding students and a number of day scholars, with five masters holding classes besides the school head. Parents sometimes worried over Horace's Unitarianism but the boys all attended the Episcopal Church. Both masters and boys shared in the village life and attended town meetings, with their flavor of old New England. Horace gave Sunday suppers in his own apartment for as many boys as he could seat. The old hotel served its purpose for many years and for nearly half a century Horace kept making changes and enlargements to meet his growing needs. Bertram Goodhue was the architect responsible for the buildings designed immediately before the first World War. James Gamble Rogers was called in for further enlargements in 1930 and today there are seven buildings forming a connected unit under one roof. The school has a Horace Dutton Taft Building and a Charles Phelps Taft Hall. Its 3,500 graduates, including fifteen Tafts in the direct family line, have engaged in business, industry, the professions and public service.

The Taft School was part of a general movement in the East to emulate the famous prep schools of Britain and to build up a new academic tradition in the United States. As great fortunes increased, the demands for entrance could scarcely be met by Andover, Exeter, the Hill School, St. Paul's, and St. Mark's, all of which had been in existence since the 1850's. The Episcopal Church influence was strong in the early schools and Groton, founded by the Reverend Endicott Peabody, was already creating its own tradition of service and dedication when Horace Taft opened his school in Pelham Manor. He and Dr. Peabody became lifelong friends.

In the early 1890's a cluster of new prep schools opened in Connecticut—Hotchkiss, Pomfret, and the Choate School, established by Judge William Choate six years after the Taft School came into existence. The Westminister School, established in 1888, was so close to the Taft School that the two kept up constant communication. But the school that interested Horace most of all was the one his friend, Sherman Thacher, had opened in Ojai, California. All of these schools followed the English pattern of the Spartan life, rigid discipline, tough academic standards, and good sportsmanship on the playing fields. In the be-

ginning each school's tradition was built largely around the personality
of its founder—as in the case of Dr. Peabody and Horace Taft. The
schools were still too young to have ivied halls but each set its own stamp
on its graduates and supplied the colleges with a steady stream of youths
bred in the prep-school tradition. Some of the headmasters, like Horace,
placed special emphasis on character and scholarship, and did not always open their doors merely to the sons of the rich. His own brother
Charles had gone to Andover, but the young Tafts of the next three
generations attended the Taft School as a matter of course.

Horace's ideal for his student body was a "small pattern of Will." He
urged his brother to look for likely material for him as he traveled around.
By 1894 he had thirty-nine boarding students and six day boys. He had
refused ten boys because his standards were what his mother thought
to be transcendental. She believed that the ten rejected boys should have
a chance. Horace differed from his family in this as in many other respects, being the only Taft to believe in Grover Cleveland and free
trade. The family accepted these divagations with equanimity, recognizing the philosopher and reformer behind the pedagogue.

Progressive ideas in education had not yet gone beyond kindergarten
level, and Horace followed the established curriculum after a flyer during his early days in new methods of teaching Latin and mathematics.
Athletics flourished at his school and the boys formed their own glee
club and band. Winifred was highly successful in converting their barren
quarters into a homelike setting for the boys and their teachers.

During the early days of Horace's school Will traveled about on the
circuit and Nellie lived with her children at 118 East Third Street in Cincinnati. Their letters flowed back and forth, with Taft returning for occasional weekends. Now and again his mother gave Robbie a paddy-
whacking, as she called it, but she preferred to leave discipline to his
father. On one of his weekends at home when his son was four Judge
Taft marched him upstairs for punishment.

"Papa, are you going to spank me?" he demanded.

"Yes. It's for your own good and will hurt me more than it will you."

"Then," said Bob, "can I kiss you first?"

His father burst out laughing. Nellie, listening downstairs, misunderstood and called up: "Well, if you have to spank Bob, do it, but don't
laugh at him."

That was the last occasion for punishment and Bob soon became a
pupil at the Bartholomew kindergarten. Nellie kept alive the image of
their father for the children, since they rarely saw him. Both children
counted the kisses they sent to their absent father. They studied his pictures and jabbered happily about Papa. Nellie was an indulgent mother
and an observant one. Helen talked earlier and more clearly than Bob

but she was wobbly on her feet and managed to roll downstairs from the bathroom to the library door early in 1893. She had a way of waking up in the middle of the night to sit up in bed and cheerfully rattle off all the words she knew. Soon she and her father would be laughing together. Her grandmother thought that Helen had the "same fish mouth that Robbie has" but that nothing could be more beguiling than the way she sat up and folded her hands before her to have her picture taken.

Young Mrs. Taft, unlike her mother-in-law in the early days of her marriage, did not let herself get swamped in domestic matters. Ambition had not died with the birth of her babies. She attended an art class at the home of Alice Keys and backed a book club. She was interested in a new hospital, the training of nurses, and in kindergarten work, but she declined the presidency of the International Kindergarten Union Branch. Perhaps her chief interest was the establishment of the Cincinnati Symphony Orchestra, which grew out of the Ladies Musical Club, to which she belonged. She was the first president of the symphony association and worked zealously for this cause, which Mrs. Christian R. Holmes and then Annie took over after Mrs. Taft left for the Philippines. After a long and tiring struggle she was responsible for getting Frank Van der Stucken as conductor but Will had to help her in putting through the deal. He encouraged her in all her public interests and urged her to keep up her writing after she delivered a club paper on Robert Schumann. Will always had great respect for his wife's intellect. In February, 1893, he wrote to her from Nashville, where he was holding court:

> My love for you, dear, grows each year and you become more and more indispensable to my life and happiness. This is not the enthusiasm of the wedding journey, but it is the truth deliberately arrived at after full opportunity for me to know. I hate to have the years go on to change the sweetness of our present existence with the children in that most interesting and lovely period of budding intelligence and ourselves sufficiently young to enjoy the things of youth.

There were many pleasant events for Nellie to report on in her letters to Will. She was enraptured when she heard Paderewski play in the Opera House. She found Lillian Russell much less of a beauty than she had expected from the extravagant publicity that surrounded her. They all had a fling in 1893 at the Columbian Exposition in Chicago where Annie squandered money with the joyous abandon that she showed on such occasions. Every night they attended the theater and Nellie enjoyed the neo-classical buildings of the fair, the nonsense of the midway, the wide range of exhibits. They were drawn into Mrs. Potter Palmer's nimbus in the Woman's Building for they already knew her through the Grants. Nellie sometimes found it difficult to catch the spirit of Annie's effervescent wit, but as a traveling companion she kept them all at a sparkling level.

This was the year, too, in which the trial of Lizzie Borden was stirring up arguments across the country. It was followed with close attention in the Taft home on Third Street. Maria read column after column of testimony to Nellie from the New York *Sun*. Will, moving about on his circuit, followed it too and they compared notes. The Judge pointed out that there was no evidence on which to convict Lizzie but, with Nellie, instinct prevailed. She was sure that Lizzie was guilty and she thought that the court should have admitted the prussic acid evidence. "Imagine my going to buy prussic acid to put away furs or to clean them either!" she wrote to Will on June 17, 1893.

Will's own legal experience was broadening greatly at this time. Between 1892 and 1900 he established a national reputation with decisions involving trusts, railroads, and labor unions. As circuit court judge, he was generally recognized among lawyers as contributing in a substantial way to a shifting pattern in legal procedure. He was breaking precedents and taking a firm but unpopular stand on labor questions. There was great unrest among workers; strikes were on the increase. Court dockets were packed with injunction and contempt of court cases. The Pullman strike in Chicago opened the floodgates. The railroad king had not been able to mollify his workers by giving them what he considered idyllic conditions in Pullman Town. They kicked over the traces, went on strike; and violence followed as Eugene V. Debs, in command of the American Railway Union, led the strikers in their efforts to get higher wages.

Frank M. Phelan, a Debs emissary, arrived in Cincinnati to stir up the employees of the Southern Railroad to strike and tie up the road. He instigated violence until he was brought to court before Taft, who heard the case. The courtroom was crowded every day with strikers and their sympathizers. Taft was loudly denounced at meetings held in the evenings. He was greatly troubled over this decision, seeking to be scrupulously fair and to abide by the letter of the law. As usual he confided his doubts to Nellie, who had gone to Murray Bay:

> I am a good deal in doubt as to what I ought to do with him. I do not wish to make a martyr of him nor do I wish to be so easy with him as to encourage him or his fellow conspirators to think that they have nothing to fear from the court. . . . I sleep in the custom house, but strange to say I find it quite noisy and not very cool. It is a bit lonely. . . . I am homesick for you and the children.

In the end Judge Taft found Phelan guilty of contempt of court and sent him to jail for six months. In his decision he defended the right to

strike and took pains to differentiate between a legal strike and an illegal boycott. Experts who observed him over the years all agreed that
Taft stood for strict interpretation of the law. It was his creed that the
law could not err and he never swerved from this conviction. During his
circuit years he handed down other decisions that favored labor as well
as many that riled workers across the country, but he became a natural
target for labor agitators. The Homestead strike in Pittsburgh, the Hay-
market Square bombings in Chicago, and the Pullman strike had un-
leashed violent new forces that could neither be suppressed nor explained
away.

"After us the deluge," Louise wrote to Will as he coped with these
problems. "I do not take these things to heart as I used to, except as
they affect my son."

Will's legal experience broadened greatly as he coped with these developments. In traveling on the circuit he picked up impressions of cities
and public men, and made lifelong friends among members of the legal
profession. He was popular at Bar Association meetings and was recognized as a well-informed and warm-hearted man. His conversation was
anecdotal, allusive, and often witty. Wherever he went he ran into Yale
men. The Southern members of the bar seemed to him to be a particularly genial lot, and Louisville was one of his favorite stops on the circuit.
He considered Toledo a fine-looking city with a good courthouse and
clean air because natural gas was used. He reported more churchgoing
and better use of money in Detroit, Cleveland, and Louisville than in
Cincinnati. "We don't splurge much in Cincinnati," he wrote to Nellie
as he observed the wealth and prosperity of Cleveland, but he thought
that his own city had more cultivation in the arts.

Will dined with Mark Hanna at his "palace on the Lake Shore." It
stood 200 feet from the water, a square, reddish building surrounded by
elm trees. Behind Hanna he visualized the iron and coal interests, the
foundries, forgers, and melters that had made his fortune. Here was the
politician and the big business-man in one, and Judge Taft observed him
with interest. Later he found it hard to understand Hanna's enthusiasm
for William McKinley. "Hanna is a very pleasant man and I like him,"
he wrote to his wife. But at this point he was heartily sick of public dinners and of lavish entertainment.

After his exhausting work on the labor cases of 1894 Taft hurried off
to Murray Bay and was soon doing the nine-hole golf links every
day with Harry and Horace. Charles, who had been desperately ill that
summer, joined them and soon revived in the bracing air. This was the
third time that he had been close to death in recent years and Annie, because of her emotional nature, had not been told how serious his illness

was. He recovered sufficiently at the St. Lawrence resort to run for Congress that autumn as a compromise candidate. He had made up his mind to show his independence of David Sinton, who did not wish Annie to move to Washington. Charles told Will that all through his married life he had arranged his affairs to suit his father-in-law but he did not propose to do so any longer. "The thing is done, the race is begun and Old Man Sinton will have to stomach it," Will wrote to his wife.

When Charles was nominated by acclamation Annie immediately gave a party and served punch "strong enough to curl your hair." The drawing room had been done over and she drew Will's attention to the stunning chandelier from Vienna that his mother had given her. They agreed that it looked well in the Pike Street setting. When Will visited the capital in the spring of 1896 he found Annie in high fettle, enjoying Washington life, but he did not think that she and Charles had made the most of their opportunities. Although potent in action, Charles had a quiet manner and never pushed himself forward on the social front. In the background of Will's visit at this time was the wistful hope of a Supreme Court appointment. He wrote frankly to Nellie of his unslaked longing and the hopelessness of the prospect. Charles and others in Washington seemed to think it a certainty—or so they told him—but Will was convinced that William McKinley would never appoint him.

He swung at once into the familiar groove in the capital. He went to the Ebbitt House to have his hair cut, had oysters at Harvey's, watched a Senate vote, conversed with Mrs. John Hay, and dined with Naval Commander George Dewey, as yet unknown to fame. He sat next to Mrs. Nellie Grant Sartoris, who remembered his father well, then called on Mrs. Ulysses S. Grant who talked to him at length about his parents. She showed him her Oriental treasures and said that the General had destroyed nearly all his papers. In New York Judge Taft dined with Theodore Roosevelt and went to Koster & Beals with Harry. He did not like the smoking, drinking, or the "lubricity of modern days." All his life he scorned the smutty, the suggestive, the scandalous touch. He disliked an off-color story, in or out of the smoking room, and he was critical of earthy realism in a novel.

On his visits to New York Harry and Julia now gave large dinners for him, inviting the leading members of the bar. Harry was not only becoming highly successful in his profession but he was speculating in real estate and making money on it. At the moment he was trying important railroad cases and had won a number in succession. His way of living had become more luxurious after the long, difficult years of trying to make ends meet. He now played golf at the St. Andrews Club in Yonkers and later at Piping Rock. In the summer of 1896 he went to Murray

Bay with a cook, a maid, a man of all work, and a governess, but by this time his wife preferred hotel life to the bare, unpainted cottages of the St. Lawrence resort.

The more her mother-in-law saw of Julia the better she liked her, observing that she handled her children well and was deeply devoted to Harry. They had three altogether, in addition to the boy Walbridge who had died. After him came a second Walbridge Smith Taft, William Howard Taft (known as Howard II), and Louise. Mrs. Alphonso Taft now made a point of visiting the various families and keeping track of the growing children. She had been left less than $5,000 but she still clung to the Vine Street property that Alphonso had willed to her. He had always felt sentimental about it. Since his death she and Delia had become nomads. They wintered in New York or Boston and moved easily from Watertown to Cincinnati to Murray Bay. They whipped off to California to see Fanny from time to time but in the end they always returned thankfully to Millbury. In New York they stayed at a boardinghouse on Murray Hill. It was their custom to look up old friends, join clubs, attend lectures and concerts. They went regularly to the theater and Louise considered it a sacred duty to see the good Shakespearean productions. Delia liked to hear the noted preachers and she held her own at their boardinghouse in a nest of Southerners and Democrats who looked suspiciously at Boston Yankees who were also Unitarians. Lame, but still a sparkling personality, Delia beat them at whist, out-talked them on politics, and made herself useful to the teachers, art students, musicians, and fading gentlemen who gathered at the dining room table. In Boston they lived in a pleasant apartment opposite the public gardens, took a course of lectures with Professor Charles Eliot Norton, and heard Julia Ward Howe speak. An electric railway now passed their gate at Millbury, making Worcester more accessible. Louise traveled in to hear Mrs. Ballington Booth speak on the Salvation Army and Clara Barton make her appeal for the Red Cross mission to Armenia.

Fanny and her husband journeyed East in the summer of 1896. They spent most of their time in New York and were seen at the Horse Show, the opera, and the theater, or they went yachting and coaching. Fanny had taken up bicycling for exercise. Americans now were on wheels from coast to coast and William Howard Taft was considering this new sport as a reducing measure. The summer of 1897 was one of the hottest in Cincinnati's history and he often took streetcar rides at night to cool off. New roads were stringing their way through the hills surrounding the city and Will wrote to Nellie, who was in Murray Bay, of the cars that ran on the Avondale line to Shillito Street and then crossed country to the zoo. Homes and gardens, creeping ever higher on the hillsides, created a dense network of suburban life. The streets meandered to conform to the contour of the hills, making sudden twists through woodland. The population now exceeded 300,000 and all manner of products, from carpet tacks to organs, were being manufactured in Cincinnati.

Judge Taft had undertaken to build up the Cincinnati Law School. With Judson Harmon, Lawrence Maxwell, and other judges, he helped to introduce the Harvard case system and to create a strong law department, of which he was dean. He founded the circuit court library, which soon had 15,000 books. By this time it was widely recognized that Judge Taft was conducting his court work in an economical and effective way. His friends did not call him Will when he mounted the bench, for he functioned with dignity and reserve. It was his custom to work late at night dictating his opinions. He labored over them, writing and rewriting. They were long and often dull, but they covered every point in detail. He became an expert in patent rights, particularly through his work on the Addyston Pipe case.

When holding court in Cincinnati Judge Taft walked to his home and his fellow townsmen became as familiar with his swinging gait as once they had been with Alphonso's. He was particularly friendly with his fellow judges, H. H. Lurton and William R. Day and then, as later, he found great satisfaction in the judicial round. "It is the comfort and dignity and power without worry I like," he said when he had reached the haven of the Supreme Court after his bitter years in the Presidency.

There were times when Nellie accused her husband of spreading too much suavity in his dealings with men. She could bring him down to earth with a few well-chosen words. He valued this critical quality in her and wrote as he was leaving for Murray Bay in 1897:

> I wonder if you miss me as I miss you, darling. You are so much of my life. The thought of you has so much intellectual flavor, and sweet sentiment too. I am so glad that you don't flatter me and sit at my feet with honey. You are my dearest and best critic and are worth so much to me in stirring me up to best endeavor. Goodnight, dearest. Kiss the bairns for me. Tell them to be sure and count the days before my coming and to meet me at the boat.

Helen and Robbie constantly sent little notes to their father and he kept them supplied with puzzles wrapped up in loving messages. "Tell Robbie that I send him as many kisses as there are squares between 3rd and Lawrence and Freeman & Liberty, and as many to Helen as there are squares between Freeman and Liberty and 3rd and Lawrence." He worked out sums for them to do, juggling their ages. Robbie was wrestling with long division and fractions at the Hoffman School by the summer of 1896. He was already showing mathematical skill. Helen observed in later years that he would have been a star on a quiz show for his answers came with lightning speed. Some of his skill at figures was acquired in the firehouse across the street from his home. When he was six he began to calculate how many miles each engine traveled going to and from a fire. After twelve months of this, his friends the firemen put him on a high stool at a desk and let him copy their calls and make out the station reports. He went to the fires whenever possible and it was a source of great grief to him when his family moved away from the block that harbored this fascinating firehouse.

At the age of seven he read a history of the Civil War and wrote his first poem which featured one line that Helen always remembered: "General Pope, who washed his hands with Ivory Soap." When he was eight he moved from checkers to chess, which he taught himself from a book, and he played cribbage at an early age. He joined his father joyfully on the golf links in the summer of 1897 and trotted after the tall figure, bulkily outfitted in a twenty-five-dollar golf suit of Scottish tweed and English grained golf shoes bought at Shillito's. The Judge had decided to abandon the popular knickerbockers; his girth was on the increase, with all the banqueting that his circuit work entailed.

Charles Phelps Taft, their third and last child, was born to the Tafts on September 20, 1897. Louise hoped that he would be named after his father but Charles, who had not repeated the name in full in his own family, was pleased. Charlie proved to be a handsome and gregarious child from the start. He was thriving by the time the family returned to Murray Bay in 1898 and Helen wrote to her father, with her special brand of spelling: "Dear Papa I am having a veary nice time, and I hope you are to, are you. Baby is very well. He steill says papa. I miss you very much. Your little girl, Helen." Bobby wrote at the same time that the boys had been allowed to play golf on the big links and had been around the eighteen holes twice and nine holes once. "I am very sorry that you went home and I am very lonely," he finished. By this time he was reading *St. Nicholas* and his father was sending him the baseball scores.

Helen clung lovingly to her father when he came home for Christmas in 1899, and the baby presented an impish front. The Judge gave Robert a tiny set of golf clubs and Helen a watch to pin on her dress. He danced with Nellie at the holiday parties and reflected on the peace and harmony of his home. On their eleventh wedding anniversary he had sent her a note: "Nellie my darling—never for one moment have I regretted that step I took that day, but each year has only made me happier in the result. Can you say the same, my dear?"

Will, Horace, and Harry Taft all were mentioned for the presidency of Yale at this time. Harry, who had become a partner in the firm of Strong & Cadwalader, thought that Will would be the perfect choice. He pushed hard for his brother's acceptance, but Will was convinced that he had no special qualifications for the position and that his religious views would be against him. In a letter to Harry he set forth his convictions on this issue:

> I am a Unitarian. I believe in God. I do not believe in the divinity of Christ, and there are many other of the postulates of the Orthodox creed to which I can not subscribe. I am not, however, a scoffer at religion but on the contrary I recognize in the fullest manner the elevating influence that it has had and always will have in the history of mankind.

Mrs. Alphonso Taft shared Harry's view that her son Will was amply qualified to fill the role offered him. She went abroad in 1898 and paid a nostalgic visit to Vienna. Henry White gave a dinner for her at the Embassy in Berlin and she was in Amsterdam for the inauguration of Queen Wilhelmina. In London she found John Hay functioning as a "dignified, sensible man." She had hoped that Charles might be appointed to one of the embassies but in spite of her diplomatic connections nothing came of this plan. On her return to America she finally sold the Mount Auburn house in 1899 for $18,000. When the Spanish-American War broke out she was back in Millbury and Will happened to be visiting her, his first return to the family homestead in twenty years. He was greeted like the prodigal son and they all sat on the porch and sang, with Will's booming voice drowning out Aunt Delia's thin treble. But the war news was sobering. Judge Taft felt that President McKinley had taken the wrong course, although later on he conceded that he had no other choice at the time.

Taft was back in Cincinnati two days later and was presiding in court when the news arrived that Admiral William T. Sampson had destroyed the enemy fleet. The sky over Cincinnati was clouded with floating balloons and a celebration was in progress. Taft followed the war news with interest but no enthusiasm. It never occurred to him that his own life would be directly affected by the outcome of this war. Another public figure, whose path would soon cross his, studied the war dispatches with a deep sense of urgency and excitement. Before long Theodore Roosevelt would be writing from Albany to Mrs. Bellamy Storer, Nicholas Longworth's aunt: "Will Taft is a very fine fellow. I wish there was someone like him here in New York, for I am very much alone. I have no real community of principle or feeling with the machine."

A historic friendship was on the horizon.

CHAPTER 11

GOVERNOR OF THE PHILIPPINES

WILLIAM HOWARD TAFT stepped into the international picture when he landed in the Philippine Islands in 1900 as head of a commission charged with establishing a civil government and bringing peace and order to the conquered islands. He no more approved of the acquisition of the Philippines than he had been sympathetic to the clamor for war. The jurist did not consider himself qualified to cope with a colonial administration and when President McKinley appointed him Taft observed: "He might as well have told me that he wanted me to take a flying machine."

Up to this time his relations with President McKinley had been distant and he had not been one of his admirers. The ice was broken first at a friendly meeting in Canton on the night of the Ohio elections of 1899. When the President summoned him to the White House three months later to ask him if he would serve in the Philippines Taft found him uncommonly persuasive, as he urged him to take the post in the interests of public service. Elihu Root, Secretary of War, was present and he told Taft in his crisp way that he thought his help was needed. Taft hesitated and said that he believed a man more sympathetic to the acquisition of the islands should head the proposed commission, to which President McKinley replied: "You don't want them any less than I do, but we have got them and in dealing with them I think I can trust the man who didn't want them better than I can the man who did."

In seeking a man of high integrity, judicial experience, and a sense of the humanities President McKinley had turned to Taft, who was also a fellow Ohioan. His choice had the additional advantage of being a sound political appointment. He promised Taft large powers and wide jurisdiction. Taft asked for a week to think matters over and to discuss it with his family. He knew no more, no less, of the islands than the average well-read man, but he was already widely recognized as an accomplished mediator. However, he had no wish to break up the quiet judicial round into which he had settled so harmoniously.

Mrs. Taft, always keen for change and travel, cast her vote at once in favor of acceptance, and his brothers were in agreement. Horace, characteristically, wrote that he could do more good in the Philippines in one year than on the bench in a dozen and added: "They can't get a better man than you. . . . As for your future it is too bad about that. If you get stuck I can give you a place in the school . . . the chair of Christian manhood."

In the end it became a family pilgrimage. Although warned not to expose her children to the hazards of such a journey, Nellie decided to accompany her husband and to take with them Robert, aged ten, Helen, who was eight, and Charlie, who was only two. They gave up their house in Cincinnati, put their furniture in storage, and persuaded Maria to go with them. The President thought that the commission could complete its work in nine months, if not less. But four years would pass before Taft finished his dramatic job in the Philippines.

They sailed on the army transport *Hancock* on April 17, 1900. There were only forty-five passengers on board the ship and it seemed like a private yacht. The commissioners held business meetings in one of the cabins and Taft walked miles around the deck each day. He missed the newspapers but found the voyage restful. Robert had taught himself chess so well that he usually beat the army officers who engaged him. Helen enjoyed the smooth floating motion as they crossed the Pacific and watched out for the smaller children on board. Maria, like Nellie, had become little Charlie's slave, and his father considered himself the only hope for his son's training. He wrote to the elder Charles: "We call him the 'tornado,' he creates such a sensation when he lands in the midst of the children of the ship. He is very badly in need of discipline, and yet I cannot very well administer it in a crowd."

Charlie had had pneumonia shortly before leaving but his buoyant spirits had revived. When he landed in Honolulu he was taking his first step into a world he would come to know well in the years ahead. Mean-

while, Bob and Helen were quietly taking note of the sweep of Diamond Head, of the waves of perfume rising from the shower trees, of
the chattering people around the dock. Their party went surf-riding at
Waikiki Beach. They attended a poi dinner and were feted continuously
for four days before leaving for Yokohama with leis around their
necks and haunting songs following them to sea. Bubonic plague was
epidemic in Honolulu so that they all came under severe medical scrutiny in Japan. During his week there several bearers were needed to con-
vey Judge Taft's jinrickisha from point to point. By the time he reached
the last hill at Nikko he decided that the whole village was engaged in
the push.

Mr. and Mrs. Taft were received by the Emperor and Empress at the
palace in Tokyo. Nellie had a blurred impression of gold leaf on the
walls and Japanese paintings in muted colors; of the Empress and
her ladies-in-waiting wearing European costume; of the timid looks
and gentle voice of the Empress. Years later she sent Mrs. Taft a Gobelin
tapestry which was hung in the state dining room of the White House.
The Oriental cast of features shown by Columbus and Isabella in this
instance was a phenomenon which bewildered dinner guests during the
Taft administration.

When the commission moved on to Manila Mrs. Taft with Maria and
the children remained for a time in Yokohama in a bungalow on The
Bluff, the foreign residential quarter, which was still buzzing with echoes
of the Boxer Rebellion. Bessie Mullay, Charlie's nurse, who had been
quarantined because of a bad throat, was no sooner released than Robert came down with a mild case of diphtheria and Helen developed ear
trouble. She and Charlie were sent to the Grand Hotel with Bessie
while the others stayed in quarantine with Robert, who studied French
and English history as he convalesced, and took systematic notes from
day to day. They could see the bay from one side of their house and
the snow-tipped cone of Fujiyama from the other. Matsu, the amah,
"toddled after Charlie like a dog and he rules her with a rod of iron,"
Nellie reported to Louise. He was known as Baby San and was the household pet. They all laughed when he rubbed noses with Matsu; obviously
Charlie was fast becoming the family cutup.

Mrs. Taft was a persistent shopper, wherever she happened to be, and
she and Maria hunted up bargains in Yokohama and Kyoto. Will urged
his wife by letter not to stint herself in her buying, since his salary was
now $25,000 a year. This seemed like affluence to the Tafts but it scarcely
covered their expenses when they began to entertain officially. The
earthquakes terrified Helen but Bob made a counting game of them and
wrote to friends in Cincinnati that he had lived through thirteen in one
day. In Kyoto Helen took dancing lessons and when the heat became

intense they went up into the Hakone Mountains to stay in Miyano-shita. On their way there they were caught in a severe storm and their string of jinrickishas lost its bearings. Mrs. Taft and Charlie were cut off from the rest of the party and Bob and Helen were completely lost as the rain came down in torrents and the wind blew wildly. Helen clung to Bob.

"Don't worry, Helen, I'll get you out of this," he assured her, but she was inconsolable.

"It could be worse," he told her. "We might have been prisoners in the Black Hole of Calcutta."

Helen screamed at this outrageous idea but Bob calmed her down with a matter-of-fact account of what the Black Hole would have been like. In the meantime practical Maria, who had insisted on going back for a lantern, cast a beam in the darkness and the entire party was rounded up, with the missing ones appearing like ghosts out of the mist. With one dim lantern to guide them they proceeded to their mountain inn, worn out and hungry. When the sun shone again they were able to enjoy the temples and wayside shrines, the tea houses, the blossoms, and the beauty of their surroundings. Mrs. Taft was cheered when her husband wrote to her from Manila on June 18, in celebration of their fourteenth wedding anniversary:

> On the eve of that day, I wish to record the fact that it was the most fortunate of my life, and that every year only confirms me more strongly in that opinion. Every year I feel more dependent on you; every year I grow more lonely in your absence, and every year my darling, I love you more.

Taft had taken firm hold of his administrative duties after a cool reception from Major General Arthur MacArthur, the military governor of the islands, who resented the invasion of a civilian commission. He had settled in the Arellano house in Malate, a rambling structure in a state of disrepair, needing plumbing, electricity, and fans, which the Judge proceeded to have installed. He wrote to his wife almost daily, detailing each phase of his administrative work. Usually he got up as early as half past five and wrote his letters on the porch as dawn illumined the bay. In the distance he could see Corregidor. Steamers lay offshore and far over at Cavite the white warships of the United States Navy rocked like pale ghosts in the morning light. The mountains across the bay changed from peacock to rose and the water shimmered with rippling streams of gold. Forgetting his political cares for the moment Taft wrote poetically to Nellie of the break of dawn around him. The breeze blew in his face and he felt comfortable in the new pajamas of varying hues that he had picked up in Hong Kong and now wore for many hours of the day. It had not been easy to outfit himself with clothes suitable for the tropics. His bulk did not contain itself well in the customary white linen and duck. Nellie had persuaded him to have all his suits tailored with sack coats. Although made to order his shoes, stockings, underwear, collars, and hats fitted poorly.

The staff he had selected in Hong Kong had turned out well, particularly Ah Sing, the cook, and he soon found that life with so many servants was easier and more luxurious than at home. Despite the fact that ants ran about in armies, cockroaches were rare, and only an occasional lizard showed up at Arellano. When it rained Taft felt as if the "windows of heaven were falling out." The hospitality of the Filipino people was unbounded and he soon wrote to Nellie that the local banquets would be the death of him—a dozen courses, and everything tinctured with garlic.

The commission worked in the Ayuntamiento, General MacArthur's headquarters, where they were squeezed into one small room. Taft made a point of walking home, a health measure he observed wherever he happened to be. He took Spanish lessons since he felt handicapped in not knowing the language. It was clear to him at once that the people were anxious to be free from military control. He was impatient of it himself but he did not think the Filipinos were ready yet for self-government. Before long he became deeply attached to them as a people.

Taft and Root together had worked out the plan for control of the islands. President McKinley had concurred wholeheartedly and when Taft sailed he was already so familiar with the requirements that he moved forward without hesitancy. Later he always gave Root credit for initiating the Philippine policy and for being responsible for its success "from the standpoint of statesmanship and farsightedness." He took pride in this joint document which "offered no promise of independence but secured to the Philippine people all the guaranties of our Bill of Rights except trial by jury and the right to bear arms." The underlying purpose was to give them the maximum degree of influence in their own affairs, to assign them such offices as they were qualified to hold, and ultimately to guide them to a popular Assembly of their own.

Emilio Aguinaldo, who had helped American forces seize the city of Manila during the Spanish-American War and later declared himself president of the Philippine Republic, was at this time a rebel outlaw, stirring up trouble, particularly in Luzon. Taft had to face the fact that although widespread insurrection had been quelled small bands rose up from time to time and spread terror. But within two months the commission had full legislative power and its members tackled problems involving the disposition of public lands, education, health, the postal service, harbor improvements, currency and finance, customs, roads, and railways. Taft assigned tasks to his fellow commissioners and concentrated personally on setting up provincial and municipal government, on the disposition of confiscated lands and on revising the code of laws. He began on the old Roman principle of building roads, believing this to be a civilizing influence. He interviewed scores of the natives and traveled around the islands on observation trips. General MacArthur had 62,000 soldiers stationed throughout the Philippines, which had a total population then of nearly seven million. The Filipinos spoke seven languages and used a variety of dialects. The General was pessimistic about pacification and he was convinced that the chief need was for more troops.

Taft did his best to mollify him but he was indignant when he found that some of the dispatches going to Washington were being censored. General MacArthur continued to deluge Root with letters of complaint. Soon the head commissioner was writing to Washington with equal warmth and finally Taft said they would all resign unless General MacArthur became more cooperative. The President and the Secretary of War stood solidly behind Taft and, bit by bit, MacArthur was stripped of his power. Bewildered and sincerely believing in what he was doing, he fought back, and at times the air was thick with recrimination. But it was largely a battle of letters, for they maintained courteous relations to the end and had respect for each other as men.

Taft reported to Elihu Root that MacArthur was a "courtly, kindly man, lacking in a sense of humor." He informed his half-brother, Charles, that the General was a "good fellow, upright and honest and genial," but timid, narrow, and rigid in his outlook, slow both to comprehend and to act. He felt that MacArthur had little knowledge of men outside of army circles and did not know how to deal with them. This experienced soldier chose to let matters drift, trusting that time would take care of situations that seemed to Taft to need radical handling. The Miliary Governor struck him as being pompous in manner and pretentious and didactic in speech. MacArthur saw military danger where Taft felt that none existed and he fully believed that he should have the power to veto Taft legislation. But Root had given the commission absolute power to control appointments in the Philippines.

One of the first discoveries Taft made was that the army, by drawing the color line, had alienated the more friendly Filipinos in Manila. This was not General MacArthur's policy but it prevailed among the officers' families. When Mrs. Taft arrived with the children on the *Kasuga Maru* later that summer an effort was made immediately to break down this barrier.

Although General MacArthur had made no move to entertain them after their arrival the Tafts gave a dinner for him. Recognizing the importance of some formality Mrs. Taft went to considerable lengths to give atmosphere to her entertainments. Twelve musicians played and the Filipinos were so fond of music that it was always a simple matter to assemble an orchestra for a special occasion. The ground sparkled with colored electric lights strung through the trees, Japanese lanterns swung from the porch, and the newly acquired Oriental pieces were in place. The tile-floored veranda, seventy-five feet long, ran the width of the house and overlooked the bay. The house was so big and barnlike that Mrs. Taft mellowed the bare areas with the natural ferns and orchids brought in from the forest and sold in the streets. Her first Filipino callers sat in embarrassed silence until her husband made them feel at home with his easy laugh and cordiality. He was soon credited with coining the much-used phrase "our little brown brothers," which reflected an affectionate and well-meaning, if somewhat patronizing, attitude.

On New Year's Day, 1901, the Tafts gave a luncheon for fifty guests, both Filipino and American. That same day General MacArthur also held a mixed reception, according to his established custom. Among Judge Taft's favorite Filipinos were Cayetano Arellano, the Chief Justice, Benito Legarda, and Pardo de Tavera, all of whom were on excellent terms with the commissioners and had a poor opinion of the native judiciary. One of Taft's toughest problems, with international aspects, was the disposition of the land formerly held by the friars, a complicated issue involving the Catholic hierarchy that took years to solve. Under Spanish rule four missionary orders, intimately linked with the government in Madrid, had managed Catholic interests in the Philippines. But the friars were more than priests. They had been accused of extorting money from the people, collecting taxes, and functioning as political inquisitors. During the war the Filipinos drove them out, but since they had possession of nearly half a million acres of the best land they planned to return and continue their operations. Taft did not wish them to come back; neither did the people they had oppressed. He proposed that the United States buy title to the disputed lands and restore them to the Filipino farmers.

Mrs. Taft observed that bitter though the friars' controversy was, it had no effect on the Filipino's love for his church. Her husband, with his customary thoroughness, made a study of the Catholic Church under Spanish rule while investigating the friars' title to these vast tracts of land. He was not enthusiastic about the Reverend P. L. Chappelle of New Orleans, chargé d'affaires for the Vatican in the Philippines. Matters similarly were complicated for Taft by Mrs. Bellamy Storer, whose husband was then United States Minister to Spain. As a devout Catholic she was urging the promotion of Archbishop Ireland to ease the situation in the Philippines, and she wished Taft to use his influence with the President to this end, but he resisted her importunity.

The Taft children found their new life in the Philippines exhilarating. They were allowed to drive themselves in a little two-wheeled *quilez* and they had at least one bad spill when they were sideswiped by a passing carriage. They enjoyed their shaggy ponies and Robert and Helen rode every afternoon to the Luneta, a treeless area popular in the early evening, when bands played, carriages congregated, and children shared in games. Charlie's education was of the spontaneous kind. He played with José and Capito, the gardener's sons and learned a language that his father described as "fearfully and wonderfully made of Tagalog, Spanish and English." He communicated with his young friends without any difficulty. Charles enjoyed the monkeys, climbed trees, flew kites, and had so many interests that it was difficult to induce him to come in for meals or a bath. He breakfasted with Miss Bessie, lunched with his family, took his supper in his room, and appeared in his nightgown after play at the Luneta to get chocolate before going off to bed. The children had a soldier guard and Charlie was an object of great interest to the Filipino soldiers.

He soon learned to gallop around the yard on his white pony without being held. In course of time the Taft family acquired five carriages, two smaller vehicles, fourteen ponies, a steam launch, and a large staff of servants. Mrs. Taft had her own victoria driven by matched black ponies and the Governor had a sturdy carriage drawn by two brown horses. The children had a variety of pets—a monkey, a tame young orangutan that Gifford Pinchot had brought them from Borneo, and a pet deer that Fred Grant had sent to Helen. The orangutan had to be shipped off to the Zoo, however, for Mrs. Taft feared that he might attack their irrepressible baby. But Charlie grew quite tall in the Philippines and was no longer pleased to be called Baby. He held the stage at every family gathering and seemed at times to be the most important person present, or so his father jested in letters to Charles: "He is just as notional and just as determined as ever and his mother is just as much a slave to him as she ever was, but she accuses Maria and me of spoiling him whenever we get a chance so that she regards honors as even."

The Tafts were concerned at first about the education of their growing children. Helen attended the Convent of Santa Isabel for a time and picked up some Spanish. Robert was tutored by Mrs. LeRoy, a graduate of the University of Michigan and an excellent teacher who was amazed at his grasp of mathematics. Ultimately they attended a school opened by Frederick W. Atkinson, who was brought to Manila by the Governor to build up the schools and to staff them largely with American teachers. Robert stayed indoors more than the others to read and play chess. When swimming in the Pasig River he was badly stung by a jellyfish and was quite ill afterwards. When the Tafts gave a dinner in Manila for Frederick D. Grant, then serving in northern Luzon as Brigadier General of Volunteers, he invited Robert to his headquarters to appoint him his aide in the name of his grandfather, Alphonso. Robert set off proudly with General Grant's son, accoutered in a small-size khaki suit, the regulation army hat, and cavalry leggings.

Aside from their official entertaining the Taft family life at this time was comparatively simple. They dined early and were usually in bed by nine, although sometimes they sat on the porch after dinner and played cards. The Governor had become fond of mangoes and he had them regularly for breakfast, along with bacon and eggs, toast and coffee. Lunch frequently consisted of crabs, lobsters, or shrimps, beefsteak, cheese and salad, banana fritters, and fruit. The Chinese chef surprised them continually with the variety of his dinner fare. Taft liked his cane-bottomed bed with its thin mat instead of a mattress. In later years he often longed for it as he tossed about on hot summer nights in Washington. A huge bathtub, big enough to hold a dozen Filipino boys, was installed for his use.

In September, just after Nellie and the children arrived, they lived through one of the worst typhoons Manila had had since 1882 but their house stood firm against the wind. The Governor, Nellie, and Maria sat in kimonos in the front room listening to the "awful wind and feeling the house shake every little while." Finally, the head of the house fell asleep in his chair. Roofs were torn off in the city. Trees were uprooted. Thatched houses were flattened. One steamer was carried clear up the beach to the Luneta. But the Tafts soon became used to dramatic effects as they toured the islands in 1901. Mrs. Taft and the children accompanied the commission on a memorable trip through eighteen provinces. A party of sixty sailed on the *Sumner* and Taft was outraged when the trip was characterized at home as a junket. He considered it the hardest work he had ever done in his life. As they visited each area he held meetings wherever halls were available, set up local governments, read and explained the new provincial code, and helped in the selection of local officials. Filipinos were named as governors whenever possible. Taft took soundings on the prevailing situation at each stop, and saw for himself what was needed. He had to deal with hill tribes, with Christians and Mohammedans, with the head-hunting Igorots, with the powerful sultan of Jolo, with the pagan customs of the Moro districts. Contrary to his expectation the Moros of Zamboanga seemed quiet and friendly.

Everywhere they went the Tafts walked under arches of flags, lanterns, and flowers. Palm leaves and bamboo branches decorated the awnings that protected the speakers from the sun. Flags drooped in the sultry air and at banquets the hosts waited on their guests instead of sitting with them. The convention at Dagupan was held in a bamboo theater and was followed by a banquet and a dance, at which Taft enjoyed the rigadoon, an old European dance much like the quadrille. Charlie dashed from one point to another, dazzled by a succession of curious scenes. His father described him as being "intensely full of life, hard in flesh and growing all the time." When his young son raised his voice it sounded like a sea captain's bellow. The children collected shells, coral, and marine oddments as they traveled, and their favorite fiesta took place at Bataan, where the *Insurrectos* were busy. There they were met by a fleet of boats fifty feet long, decked with leaves and flowers, and manned by a score of oarsmen.

But by April Taft was beginning to feel the strain of excessive work and was actually heading into a severe intestinal illness. He had worked unremittingly, without taking the customary siesta needed in a tropical climate. By this time he was tired of driving in flower-decked victorias, of shaking hands, of watching bandsmen in gaudy uniforms whip out "A Hot Time in the Old Town Tonight" and "Won't You Come Home, Bill Bailey?" He wrote to his brother Charles: "Our trip is full of interest, but the ferocious hospitality and enthusiasm with which we are received by the Filipino people and the constant labor, mental and otherwise, which we have to undergo, make the trip a great strain." It had also been a pronounced success from the political point of view.

Taft was at Jolo when word reached him that the insurrection had collapsed and that the rebel Emilio Aguinaldo was a prisoner and had taken the oath of allegiance. He did not consider Aguinaldo formidable, either as a parliamentarian or a speaker, but he conceded his great pertinacity, and believed that he would cause further trouble. He wanted to deport him to Guam, writing to Root that he was a "natural conspirator . . . an intriguer, not of sufficient mental stature to attract the jealousy of able men." Aguinaldo had said he would fight on until independence was achieved but he was downcast over the defeat of William Jennings Bryan in 1900. After taking the oath of allegiance the Filipino warrior turned his attention to economic matters and presented a dignified and law-abiding front to the world until his death in 1964.

After the capture of Aguinaldo Taft felt that it would be possible to round up all the rifles on the islands and to preserve peace. The Taft-Root correspondence of this period contains the seeds of government as these two able men compared notes on the evolution of colonial rule in the Philippines. Taft took the stand from the start that the natives should have self-government in time but were not yet ready for it. He made it amply clear to the Secretary of War that the people were born politicians, "as ambitious as Satan," and jealous of each other's preferment. They liked intrigue but could be educated and trained for self-government. He found them quiet, polite, light-hearted, superstitious, and at times capable of great cruelty.

Shortly after their tour of the Archipelago Mrs. Taft and Maria accompanied General J. Franklin Bell on a trip through the mountains of northern Luzon. This involved riding on horseback for days over dangerous trails where white women had never been seen. They forded rivers, crossed on rafts, rode part of the time in an ambulance, or jolted over deeply rutted roads in army wagons. They sailed in rafts with bamboo awnings and sometimes stuck in the mud. Mrs. Taft kept a diary of this trip, in which she described the magnificent scenery and their encounters with Igorots marching Indian-file on steep rice terraces, carrying baskets of rice on poles. She and Maria rode in slickers through torrents of rain, slept on blankets on the floor, cooked in one tent and ate in another. They were exhausted when they reached the home of Don José Mills, an exile who had established himself at Cervantes. Here they sang operatic arias around the fire, played puss in the corner, flourished harmonicas, and established the Earring Club, their insignia being brass Igorot earrings. Nellie and Maria were always good sports, ready to fall into the party spirit—an old Herron tradition.

They were at Baguio when word reached them that Will had been appointed governor of the Philippines. Nellie hurried home to find that her husband had issued 2,000 invitations to a farewell reception for General MacArthur on July 4, the day of his own installation as governor. MacArthur had taken this turn of events with grace and good spirit. He showed no resentment that he had been displaced, although the situation between the two men had been difficult for a long time. Mrs. Taft's frugal instincts toward such a large guest list had been outraged but overruled and she entered heartily into the plans for the reception. The garden was strung with Japanese lanterns and a refreshment tent was set up on the lawn. The Rizal Orchestra, named after José Rizal, the national hero who was executed in 1896, was summoned to speed General MacArthur on his way, just as it had serenaded her and the children on their arrival.

The installation of William Howard Taft as governor of the Philippines on July 4, 1901, was a landmark in the history of the islands and an event of personal importance to the able judge from Ohio who had come to love the islands and their people. The ceremony was held in a square in the Walled City. Cathedral Plaza—later renamed Plaza McKinley—was filled with thousands of Filipinos in assorted costumes massed around the pavilion where Taft stood, benign and smiling. Nellie thought that he looked even larger than usual in his crisp white linen suit as he towered over Chief Justice Arellano, who administered the oath of office. Trim and poker-straight, General MacArthur presented his successor before he was sworn in.

Signal fires had summoned tribes from distant islands to see their civil governor inaugurated. In a sense it was the birth of a nation. Flags drooped in the still, sunlit air; flowering plants and shrubs spread fragrance. A band coped with "The Star-Spangled Banner" while lines of American soldiers and sailors stood at attention in khaki and duck. The Governor's speech was translated into Spanish as he delivered it. He had just received a message from President McKinley which he included in the text. The Taft children looked on with close attention and never forgot the scene.

Next day they all moved into Malacanan Palace, which General Mac-Arthur had just left. It stood on a peninsula in the bend of the Pasig River and had the barren aspect of a large summer hotel. The public rooms were handsome, with old Spanish portraits and fine porcelains, but the mahogany furniture had been covered with black paint, giving a funereal look to their surroundings. Their living quarters were far from comfortable and they were plagued by mosquitoes. At night they caught cool breezes from the large porch on the second floor. Mrs. Taft was horrified to discover that General MacArthur's electric light bill for his rambling palace had been more than $300 a month. Her husband soon reported to the Secretary of War that they would reduce this expense by shutting it off after they went to bed. Although they were no longer on the seafront their grounds were extensive and palms shaded the house. Governor Taft had a view of the river from his study and Nellie brightened up their own quarters by hanging bolos, hats, spears, and other native adornments on the walls.

An important figure who now appeared on the scene was handsome Major Archibald Butt, who had been a newspaperman and had served in the Quartermaster's Department of the United States Navy. He and Fred W. Carpenter, the Governor's secretary, who lived in the palace, were helpful to Mrs. Taft at her weekly receptions and the balls and dinners she gave that were greatly enjoyed by the Filipinos as well as by the Americans. She had two bands for her concerts and four *señoritas* who played the harp and guitar. Sporadic outbreaks still continued in three or four of the provinces, out of a total of forty-five, but Governor Taft felt that the archipelago was at last at peace.

Louise sent them a large consignment of books for Christmas, knowing their tastes. But they arrived late and Nellie had a hard time making the season seem real in tropical weather. She used red ribbons, cotton wool and glitter dust to embellish the tree. Louise was sorrowing over her sister Anna Orton, who had died in Columbus of a stroke in June, 1900, a year after the death of her husband, Edward Orton. When the family matriarch and Delia revisited Mount Holyoke that autumn they talked of Anna's energy and ambition, her bright mind, her sweetness of character. The two aging sisters surveyed the cluster of buildings, now well endowed, where the old seminary had stood that they once attended. Some of their classmates looked "even older, more venerable and decrepit than ourselves," Louise noted. "Like us perhaps they 'lag superfluous.'" She had just passed her seventy-third birthday and wrote to Will, coping with the problems of colonialism in far-off Manila:

> Old age is still old age. It is the waning, not the crescent moon. But I will not repine. I have had my day. The future looks very much "of a muddle" and I am rather glad I am to have little responsibility about it. You are in the thick of a fight.

All of the Tafts, in Manila as well as in Ohio and Massachusetts, rejoiced when McKinley was re-elected in November. The Governor was particularly concerned over this campaign. He believed that a Bryan victory would be a disaster for the Philippines, since the Great Commoner advocated immediate independence for the Filipinos. Taft's respect and liking for McKinley were sincere by this time. The President had backed him on every point and he and Root had been able to go forward in their plans without any hampering influence from the White House.

In Cincinnati Maria, who had sailed home because Mrs. Herron had had a stroke and needed her, watched the searchlight on top of the *Times-Star* building signaling the Republican victory. Returns were thrown on a canvas stretched across Sixth Street. More than 20,000 persons had gathered in the nearby streets, and pictures and bulletins followed one another in rapid succession. Annie watched it all from a third-story window. Charles had not been able to attend the convention in Philadelphia at which McKinley and Roosevelt were chosen as candidates. He had hoped to go for sentimental reasons since his father had attended the first Republican convention held there in 1856. But David Sinton was dying and Charles dared not leave him or Annie. However, after being in a coma for weeks in mid-summer the patriarch revived and resumed telling stories and reciting poetry. This flicker of life soon failed, however, and he died of uremic poisoning in September, 1900. His entire fortune was left to his daughter and Taft wrote indignantly to Nellie that Charles was not named in the will nor was he co-executor. But the tone of his letter to Charles was bland and respectful. He was well aware that Sinton had profoundly influenced all their lives, and now he wrote with gratitude: "His was a strong and an honest character. I am glad to have known him. He was very kind to me and

I shall always cherish the pleasantest recollection of our relations." Taft considered David Sinton's long life "well lived and well ended."

"What a change at Pike Street! Annie will hardly know what to do with her newfound liberty—or her fifteen millions," his mother wrote to Will. Sinton had held the purse strings so tightly that his daughter had never had the chance to spend money as she wished. Now she embarked with zest on using her money for the public good, as well as in gratifying her own whims. She took Charles's advice in some matters but more often her own will prevailed. Annie had no wish to see her husband in a subservient position because of her money, so she gave him all her father's interest in the *Times-Star*, including the stock, the land, and the building. It seemed to Annie that this was Charles's true field and that he ought to be in full possession of the newspaper interests. Young Hulbert Taft joined the paper at about this time, beginning as a reporter. His uncle Charles told him that he would have to work his way up, and Hulbert showed a willing spirit. Their own son Howard, to whom Annie was most indulgent, had gone back to Horace's school.

Immediately after her father's death Charles and Annie went for a rest to Elberon in New Jersey. From the Holland House in New York they made plans to go abroad. Annie never liked New York. Although she visited it periodically to buy clothes, to attend the opera, to sail for Europe, she was always glad to leave it. New Yorkers struck her as being smug and she disliked crowds, refusing even to attend the Yale celebrations that meant so much to Charles. But she was always a zestful spectator of the Shamrock yacht races at Newport. Annie thought that a man like Sir Thomas Lipton, who would sink half a million dollars in this uncertain venture, was a dead game sport and deserved to win. She never failed to appreciate a good fellow Celt.

Just before the Charles Phelps Tafts sailed for Europe the Grand Opera House in Cincinnati burned down, an event of great significance to them since they were deeply committed to the Cincinnati Orchestra and Annie had taken over Nellie's duties in this field. Van der Stucken had been a success and was so well received in Chicago that Theodore Thomas declared his reading of Wagner and Tchaikovsky to be the best. Now Annie had decided to enlarge her scope and become a patroness of the drama, too. After the fire she and Charles promised that they would rebuild the burned opera house and seek architectual inspiration on their trip abroad. "We shall put up about as fine a theater as we can get, thoroughly modern in all respects," said Charles.

As they made the conventional grand tour in Europe they studied theaters and opera houses, taking notes on their acoustics, their equipment, and their architecture. They had their daughter Louise with them and

Annie threw herself enthusiastically into the delights of sightseeing and shopping. She had decided to pick up treasures for the Pike Street house to give it the period elegance that its own grace and dimensions seemed to suggest. Charles, who had absorbed a good deal about art when he lived in Europe, now rummaged through antiquarian shops looking for treasures. After viewing the collection of Baron Gustave Rothschild at his home he chose a Louis XVI cabinet and shipped it home quietly to surprise Annie.

While in Paris he persuaded her to buy a necklace with a large pearl pendant at Tiffany's. At first she hesitated over its magnificence but it came to be a well-known adornment to the noted visitors at the Pike Street house. Will once suggested teasingly that she hang it from the chandelier. Charles picked up an emerald brooch for her and bought her ruby earrings at Christie's in London that had belonged to the Empress Josephine. Annie played to the hilt the role of the well-off American woman buying Paris gowns, Venetian lace, jewels, and bibelots of every kind. She and Charles traveled to Cairo and as far east as Constantinople on this trip, then wound up in Ireland.

After three months of sightseeing and buying Charles wrote to Will that he had had enough of ruins, monks, and saints. He was anxious to get back to his paper and to supervise the construction of the opera house, which was to be as nearly fireproof as possible, with an enormous amount of iron going into the construction. While in London he had decided that the Cincinnati theater should be better than any he saw in the British capital; he had disliked the poor ventilation and the orchestra seats below street level.

He and Annie sailed home full of plans for the future and at once began enriching the Pike Street house with their treasures. Annie devoted herself to color schemes and the more artistic aspects of the opera house while Charles, in his more practical way, appraised its structural progress. His paper was prospering to the point where he needed larger quarters, so he bought an $18,000 lot adjoining the *Times-Star* from Tom Emery.

All of the Taft brothers were making headway. Harry was ever more deeply involved in New York politics. As an independent Republican and a close friend of Roosevelt's, he was becoming known as an active reformer. But he confided to Will at this time that he had never been able to indulge his own political ambitions because of financial stringency, and he was now so occupied professionally that he could not afford to take office. Comparing his career with his brother's he wrote: "Your career has been such that you have public distinction & could also step into almost any professional position that you might choose." Will responded sympathetically to this, assuring Harry that his career in New York made him feel humble, because it had all been done without the advantageous circumstances that had eased his own path. "I feel the greatest pride in you, old man, and congratulate you from the bottom of my heart," he wrote with the warm family touch that came so easily to William Howard Taft.

CHAPTER 12

TAFT AT THE VATICAN

THE ASSASSINATION of President McKinley in September, 1901, came as a stunning blow to the Governor in Manila. He arrived at Malacanan Palace for luncheon looking white and startled. "The President has been shot," he quietly told Mrs. Taft. His death was keenly felt in the Philippines where the people had regarded him as the sympathetic guardian of their destiny. Now an Olympian moved into office and the Governor in far-off Manila wondered what kind of President Theodore Roosevelt would be. Although they had good relations they did not know each other well. Harry Taft had been closer to him through their political contacts in New York State. Will had some mental reservations about Roosevelt and wrote to Harry on October 21, 1901, that he did not believe the new President "had the capacity for winning people to his support that McKinley had."

For the time being the Governor was heavily engaged with problems of his own. Two weeks after McKinley's death a company of American infantry, stationed on the island of Samar, was surprised at breakfast and fifty men were massacred. It was the biggest loss they had had since being in the Philippines. "It comes like a clap of thunder out of a clear sky, for the reason that everything has been going well in Samar," Taft wrote to Horace. In the days that followed he missed the understanding touch of McKinley as confusing cablegrams came from the White House while Theodore Roosevelt was taking hold. Pistols appeared again in Manila and the situation was tense.

Mrs. Taft decided to go to China at this point to get away from the tropical heat. The Boxer Rebellion was over. The Dowager Empress was still in the West, where she had fled during the siege of Peking. Nellie visited Nagasaki, Peking, Shanghai, Hong Kong, and Canton, buying silks and brocades as she traveled. She had just settled at the Astor House in Shanghai when word reached her that her husband was ill. At first he was thought to have dengue fever. Actually he had a deep-seated abscess that needed immediate surgery. He had been greatly weakened by his last trip through the Archipelago and in October had developed serious symptoms.

"Come, dear, am sick," he cabled to Nellie at the Astor House.

But thinking it over he sent her another cable next day: "Much better, don't shorten trip."

Nellie answered: "What is trouble. Love. Helen H. Taft."

There was no immediate way of getting back to Manila, so Nellie went up the Yangtze River on a houseboat belonging to the wife of the American consul. Lying flat on his back in the First Reserve Hospital her husband wrote to Charles that he preferred to have Nellie finish her trip. "Had matters gone wrong, however, she might have blamed me severely for not telling her the truth," he added. Actually, it was touch and go that he lived.

The children were thoroughly alarmed to see their strong and cheerful father being carried out of the palace on a stretcher. He endured great pain in the days that followed and had to undergo a second operation on Thanksgiving. He read Kipling and weathered his agony with a stoical spirit that Archie Butt, watching him, never forgot. But the situation was so serious that Roosevelt and Root decided he must come home on three months' leave of absence. They needed him for other reasons, too. In January, 1902, a Senate committee was due to begin hearings on the Philippines. Taft knew that many hostile witnesses would be heard and he wished to present the true picture, as he saw it.

On Christmas Eve, 1901, the Taft family left Manila on the *Grant* with both parents prostrated most of the way home. They were all somewhat tired and dispirited as they headed home. Even the children were less joyous than on their way out nineteen months earlier. Mrs. Herron died as they crossed Nebraska on their way home. Nellie was too ill to attend her funeral and her father had just had a stroke, to add to the family woes. She decided to stay in Cincinnati with the children while the Governor went on to Washington. Although due for further surgery he

had to testify first before the Senate committee. This was a severe ordeal for him, ill as he was, but he gave a clear and convincing picture of
the progress being made. His first-hand testimony was presented with
judicial clarity, but he had some uncomfortable hours while being questioned on the adverse aspects of the administration. When asked about
cruel treatment of Filipinos by American soldiers—a subject that had
been thoroughly aired in the newspapers—Taft admitted some isolated
instances. Answering Bryan's charges that American rule in the Philippines was a departure from the principles of the Declaration of Independence, the Governor maintained that American procedure in the Archipelago spread, rather than suppressed, liberty. Taft believed that the
work done in the Philippines was being felt throughout the Orient, particularly in China and India, and that he and his colleagues were pioneers
in spreading Western civilization in the Far East. His views on colonial
administration were considered liberal in terms of the period in which
he functioned, however outdated they might seem half a century later.

On the whole Taft felt more warmth than chill as he moved around
with ease in the capital. He was again deep in the official circle. Roosevelt, Root, and he had long convivial talks. Their sense of intimacy deepened, for they were three men who understood one another. The Secretary of War was Taft's host and he confided to Nellie that Mrs. Root was
a paragon housekeeper, like her own mother. Her scathing comments on
life in Washington amused him. Their daughter Edith struck him as being intellectual and keen. He thought Alice Roosevelt good-looking
and Mrs. Roosevelt quite unchanged in her new role as First Lady.

Nellie was curious to hear more about Mrs. Roosevelt and asked questions: "Is she one of the advanced women? I see she dresses on $300
a year, or did do so. We wonder how she does it." She was greatly chagrined that, through a mishap, Will's dress suit had been left behind
and he showed up at the White House in everyday attire. "Did you just
wear your farmer suit and necktie?" Nellie inquired. The Governor
warned her not to be upset by the onslaughts in the press about his work
in the Philippines. He told her that life had become highly fashionable
and prohibitively expensive in Washington during their absence. The
Roots paid $8,000 a year for their house.

Despite the Governor's official cares and his illness he was drawn into
the social round in Washington. President Roosevelt's first major entertainment was a stag dinner given at the White House for Prince Henry
of Prussia in February, 1902, and Taft reported to Nellie on the dinner
plan. The new state dining room was still incomplete but a horseshoe
table had been set up in the East Room. Hundreds of colored bulbs
formed anchors, stars, and ropes. The patriotic touch was strong as the

vigorous new President walked in to dinner. The famous Monroe glass plateau mirrored primroses and azaleas.

During this period Taft had a chance to observe Roosevelt in the role of President and he soon decided that his impetuosity was likely to get him into trouble. He blurted out information that the Governor felt he should have kept to himself, and in following his usual dynamic course he showed no signs of worry or hard work. "It is very difficult for me to realize that he is the President," he wrote to Nellie. Only a short while earlier Roosevelt had been thinking in terms of Taft as Chief Executive. Now Will confided to his wife that the President was anxious for him to stay in the Philippines and complete his work there. Root had told him that if he returned for two years more nothing would be denied him in the future. Ill, busy, and upset by the hearings, he did not write to Nellie as often as usual and she chided him: "You certainly are not so devoted as you used to be, and no doubt Annie will soon notice the difference."

Back in Cincinnati the Taft children were getting accustomed to their old way of living. They missed the sun and freedom of the tropics but they adapted themselves well to new conditions. Bob skated on Fred Exston's pond. Helen went happily off to school with Cincinnati friends. Nellie soon moved them all to the home of her sister, Mrs. Charles Anderson, on the Grandin Road. She enjoyed herself less at Annie's than the Taft brothers, who were always enthusiastically welcomed there. In any event, the Pike Street house was being restored. Plasterers, paperhangers, carpet dealers, moved in and out as Annie revived some of its early grandeur and style, and displayed the treasures she had bought abroad.

As soon as he could leave Washington Taft joined his family in Cincinnati and prepared to have his third operation in five months. He had debated whether to undergo surgery in New York, Baltimore, or Cincinnati but decided in favor of his native town. He had perfect confidence in Dr. Hiller Rauschoff and Dr. Frederick Forchheimer, the two brilliant medical men, well known to him, who now operated on him successfully in March, 1902.

Already fresh plans were in the making for Governor Taft. President Roosevelt and Elihu Root had decided to send him to Rome to discuss with the Pope the issue of the friars' lands in the Philippines. The entire family prepared to accompany him on the *Trave* in May but Bob developed a mild case of scarlet fever soon after having his tonsils removed. He was confined to the Good Samaritan Hospital in Cincinnati but his mother, anxious and distraught, was still determined to go abroad as soon as Bob recovered. Louise, after a long-distance telephone call,

agreed to step into the breach and go abroad with her son until Nellie
and the children could join him. His health was still in some jeopardy,
and although seventy-four years old his mother was in New York within
twenty-four hours, packed and ready to sail with Will. She had just reproved him by letter for failing to mention his father in the speeches he
had been making. Before a banquet in Cincinnati took place she made
her point emphatically:

> You owe so much to his influence that you might be thought a striking
> exemplification of the influence of heredity, and the environment
> which surrounded you in living in the same atmosphere, and breathing
> the same air—an inspiration to everything that was good. What an ex-
> pansionist he would have been if he could have lived to enjoy your suc-
> cess. Rip Van Winkle says "How soon were we forgotten." It is a com-
> fort that his children will do him honor. An allusion to "my honored
> father" would be a graceful thing in Cincinnati where he is well re-
> membered.

Thus the matriarch spoke, with her never-ending awareness of family
continuity and her deep pride in the Taft inheritance.

Her son went to Baltimore to see Cardinal Gibbons before sailing for
Europe, and Horace wrote that he hoped Will in the course of this mission would not forget his stiff Puritan principles. The Governor had
visited the Taft School and the boys had given him a royal time. Friends
from Watertown poured in to hear him talk on the Philippines. His
visit had heartened Horace the Schoolmaster, and Will had taken note
of the improvements in his flourishing school. The boys' dining room
now had Pompeiian-red walls; the bedrooms were attractively papered;
the library was hung with photographs of authors and heroes. At one
end was the frieze of the Parthenon that his mother had given Horace for
Christmas. Only the Hill School had done better than the Taft School in
the entrance examinations for Yale that year. Horace's good work was beginning to tell, and none rejoiced in this more than his older brother.

Will was soon established in the Grand Hôtel du Quirinal in Rome
and would have enjoyed the life around him but for the stalemate on the
friars question. His mission was delicate and his status unofficial. Root
had clearly defined it as a business negotiation rather than as a diplomatic mission. He found papal politics "serpentine" and Cardinal Ram-
polla, with whom he first dealt, "cold as fate." The Governor's proposal
was simple. He wished to buy the friars' lands for his government on condition that the priests should not return to their parishes. He was determined also to guard against the possibility that they might send
agents who would be as unpopular with the Filipinos as they were themselves.

When finally ushered into the presence of Pope Leo XIII Taft was astonished at his vigor and the resonance of his voice. He was seated under a canopy in a small audience chamber and when the Governor read his declaration, which was immediately translated into French, the Pope bowed and smiled, or waved his hand when he heard something he liked. He talked for ten minutes in reply before breaking off for informal conversation; then he assured the Governor that the questions he brought up would be approached in a broad spirit of conciliation. As the Pope moved down from his dais to chat with members of the commission he "asked for the pleasure of shaking my hand—a privilege which I very graciously accorded him," Will wrote jestingly to Charles. "The old boy is quite bubbling with humor. . . . He was as lively as a cricket."

Taft detected the twinkle in the Pope's eye as he appraised his own Falstaffian proportions, more marked than ever in evening dress. He assured his American guest that he had heard of his illness but did not think his appearance bore it out. At close range his own skin was like parchment and he seemed bowed down by years, but his dark eyes were brilliant and his mind was alert. Taft gave him an eight-volume set of Theodore Roosevelt's writings. Yet he was not sanguine as he left the Vatican, knowing that the agents of the friars were working to defeat his purpose. The influence of the monastic orders in Rome was powerful.

While he waited for the outcome Nellie and the children arrived. Along with his mother they, too, had an audience with the Pope, who gave Bob a special blessing. He called the boy to his side and told him he hoped that he would follow in the footsteps of McKinley and Roosevelt. Then he asked Bob what he intended to be when he grew up. Without a moment's hesitation Bob said that he meant to be chief justice of the United States. He had heard much conversation on the desirability and importance of this office.

Mrs. Taft talked freely to the Pope in French and he spoke of the Roosevelt books and of his own interest in the hunt as a young man. He escorted them to the door and the children went home with a strong impression of the majesty of the Vatican, the Swiss Guard, the paintings, and the pomp. Charles had developed whooping cough on the way over and Helen promptly picked it up. When she first saw her father in Rome she said: "Papa, why is it that we can never go anywhere without catching something?" But the year 1902 seemed to be the Taft year for illnesses. Cholera raged in Manila and the Governor was determined that his family should spend some time in Italy and Switzerland before returning to the East by way of Suez. He thought the children were not old enough to profit by their sightseeing in Rome, but he soon admitted he was mistaken about this. Bob became known as The Guide. He studied books and folders and led the way with an infallible sense of direction, whether they were filing through the Catacombs or visiting the Borghese Gardens. Louise thought him an improving companion, intelligent and precise, but she gave credit to Nellie for including the children in her own explorations, and interesting them in art, architecture, and Roman history.

Before Nellie arrived Mrs. Alphonso Taft presided for a month over a dinner table group that included a colonial governor, a Supreme Court Justice, a Roman Catholic, and an Anglican bishop. She was in her element, for the world seemed to have come back to her again after her quiet years in Millbury and in boardinghouses across the country. Inevitably she ran into old friends who had known Alphonso in his heyday. Although his official business was disturbing to her son he managed to spend some time with his family. Rome had a large American colony and they were as likely to meet a sculptor from New England as a cardinal or marquise. The Governor was in his element speaking to the crimson-cassocked students at the American College.

All the children were taken to see the Coliseum by moonlight, and on Sundays they made trips to Frascati, Albano, and Tivoli. Mr. and Mrs. Taft dined out nearly every night, leaving Louise with the children. Their hotel rooms opened on a balcony and in the daytime they spent happy hours playing in the courtyard garden. Early in July Governor Taft learned that his mission had failed for the time being. Orders reached him from Washington to end negotiations and return to Manila. He felt that this defeat would affect his prestige and possibly that of the United States in the Philippines, but the last word had not been spoken in the matter. Root proposed continuing negotiations by slow stages, without breaking off too abruptly, since they did not wish to shock the Catholics at home or to impair harmony in the Philippines.

In a final audience the Pope lavished gifts on the Tafts and repeated in polished phrases much of what he had said in letters. Although the Governor left Rome with a sense of defeat his aims were finally attained after much complicated negotiation. The Spanish friars did not regain their power. By an agreement reached at the end of 1903, 10,000 out of 400,000 acres were withdrawn from sale and the rest of the land was bought for $7,543,000. In 1912, 50,000 Filipinos were working small farms bought on generous terms from the United States government.

The passage of the Philippine bill in 1903 was some consolation to Governor Taft, for it achieved much that he had desired and recommended. He confessed to Aunt Delia, however, that it had a number of defects which he hoped would be corrected by the next session of Congress. Devoted as he was to Theodore Roosevelt he was annoyed when he heard that the President, speaking at Harvard, had referred to him as a martyr. He wrote about this to Horace:

> I hate to be talked about as a martyr. I have a great opportunity to do good work. It involves no sacrifice. It is full of interest. I appreciate his goodness of heart but I wish he would not think out loud so much. However, he seems to be growing stronger & stronger in the country. I am very glad.

Nevertheless, the impression spread that big Will Taft was going back to the Philippines to die. He sailed from Naples on July 24 after being thrown from a carriage and escaping serious injury because of what he called his heavy "cushioning." Mrs. Taft left Rome reluctantly, having felt while there like an "actor in a medieval pageant whose costume had not been delivered in time for the performance." The ecclesiastical gatherings had been impressive. In Florence Charlie distressed his dignified brother Bob by twirling a paper windwheel in the Duomo. In Venice they swam at the Lido and wandered around St. Mark's, scarred at the moment by the collapse of the campanile. The Palace of the Doges tired Helen—"there was so much of it," she wrote to her father from Salzburg. They moved on to Dresden, Weimar, Nuremberg, Eisenach, Baden Baden, with Helen writing affectionately to her father of each small adventure, from the Iron Virgin charm she got for her chain in Nuremberg to a long walk in the Thuringian Forest. Will wrote to his wife and children with great tenderness after leaving them. He was much concerned over Nellie's poor health and he felt that in his busy life he did not give enough time to her or to the children. In the long hours at sea on his way back to the Philippines he gave much thought to this and wrote to his wife on August 5, 1902:

> I measure every woman I meet with you and they are all found wanting. I chide myself for not having greater patience with the children . . . when they do not show the self-restraint and consideration for you and others that ought only to be expected of older people. I sometimes feel as if I do not deserve such children . . . Who could have a finer boy than Robert? I am proud of him down to the ground. And Helen too. They are both fine children and loving and lovable. As to Charles, he is so attractive even in his naughtiness that he will have to grow into a less attractive age before he can have the necessary discipline. Well, I love them all so dearly and you their mother more than all.

Will assured her that her character, her independence, her straight way of thinking, her quiet planning, loyalty and sympathy when he needed it, her affection, and her love all combined to make him happy. Few

Presidents' wives can have had such constant reminders of their husband's devotion as William Howard Taft lavished on Nellie Herron. Afield or at home, he treated her with uncommon gallantry.

When he reached Malacanan Palace he wrote teasingly to Helen about her spelling, which he had found original—"but I was able to understand what you meant, even if you did not follow Mr. Noah Webster in his dictionary." He reported that her pet deer had been taken to the zoo, that the palace had been painted and decorated in a way that her mother might not like, that the grounds and stables had been improved, that the lanterns were being strung and an orchestra of thirty-five musicians would be on hand for the family's return. José and Capito were eagerly awaiting Charlie's arrival. Dominga was all ready to be his nurse again.

Filipinos had poured down from the hills to welcome the Governor on his return. But he felt lonely in his palace without his family. He longed for Murray Bay as he read of Harry's new house there, of Charles playing golf with Justice Harlan, of the croquet, ping-pong, and tennis tournaments at Pointe au Pic. Bowing to Winifred's wishes Horace was building a house at Wainscott on Long Island. In September he and the other brothers gathered at Millbury for their mother's seventy-fifth birthday. She had returned from Rome full of good tales and now wore an old lady's lace cap with some distinction.

Aunt Delia had made newspaper headlines by chatting with President Roosevelt at the home of Senator Samuel Hoar. The President had expressed a wish to meet her and Delia wrote to Will: "Of course I would not have the President disappointed . . . so you see how your illustrious reputation embraces me." Roosevelt treated her to such extravagant praise of Will at luncheon that for once Miss Torrey was silenced. But she was much amused when one of the participants at the seventy-fifth anniversary of the Millbury Congregational Church remarked: "There's that man Taft. Where would he ever have been if it had not been for a Millbury woman?"

There was no doubt that Mrs. Alphonso Taft was greatly pleased with all the applause that reached her as Governor Taft's mother. She had become what she called a "scissors editor," clipping the papers, but Will did not like to have his mother or his wife worrying over hostile criticism. While Nellie kept his feet on the ground with more deflation than praise, his mother never failed to catch the note of applause. She did not share the family ambition, harbored by all except William Howard Taft himself, that he should aim for the Presidency. Twice President Roosevelt offered him a place on the Supreme Court bench and twice he refused it, arguing that he must finish his work in the Philippines. On his return he had found the people facing cholera, ladrones, locusts, a fall in the value of silver, and possible famine. Revenues were falling off because of a severe drought. The Governor had a relief bill to administer, a new coinage to float, and he was deep in administrative detail at once.

Meanwhile the family had gathered in strength at Harry's place in New York to discuss his future. Should he or should he not accept the opportunity he had always coveted? They had all been thinking along presidential lines since 1901. Harry, working busily in New York, was the chief advocate of this possibility. He had written to Will on June 7, 1901: "I can hardly be reconciled to your being simply Governor of Ohio. . . . As to the Presidency, while I have no doubt that your first impulse would be to say that you would prefer the Supreme Court, at the same time no man can on reflection prefer that to the higher office."

Taft was inclined to laugh at the family proddings where the Presidency was concerned. He wrote to Charles on August 27, 1901, that his labor rulings in themselves would make such a choice ludicrous. Nor did he have the slightest ambition in that direction. Harping on the old refrain he added: "I have but one ambition, and if that cannot be satisfied I am content to return to the practice of the law, with reasonable assurance that if my health holds out I can make a living and make Nellie and the children more comfortable than I could if I went to Washington."

But much had come to pass in the intervening two years and it was January, 1903, when Mr. and Mrs. Charles Phelps Taft and Louise and Delia again conferred with Harry on Will's future. Charles now felt that he could accept the Supreme Court opening and still be available for other public office. Louise and Delia urged him to decline. Nellie, most potent of all, was against it. She made no secret of the fact that the White House was her goal. "Nellie was especially pleased to see that you and Harry and Horace agreed with her that I ought not to go on the bench," Will wrote to his mother. "Still, I venture to differ with you and her."

Governor Taft in Manila had qualms about the President's motives in offering him the spot that he was known to covet. He wondered if he were being kicked upstairs because of the Catholic attacks that had been made on him. But Harry wrote reassuringly that this was not the case. President Roosevelt had dismissed such theories as nonsense. He told Harry that Will's extraordinary talents fitted him to do even better work in public life than on the bench, but he had never stressed this, knowing his strong desire for the Supreme Court.

Actually, Taft found it hard to resist the President's renewed offer and Roosevelt pleaded hard for his acceptance. He told Harry that he had found the right man in Oliver Wendell Holmes and now he wanted Will, who would approach all the industrial questions "without fear of the effect upon himself, of the influence of either the J. P. Morgans or of the labor leaders." But the Filipinos themselves settled the matter. They were determined to keep him. Placards reading "We Want Taft" were hoisted all over Manila. The palace was mobbed by urgent suppliants. Protests poured into Washington and the President surrendered. He cabled to the Governor: "All right, stay where you are. I shall appoint some one else to the Court."

But a few months later he was after Taft again—this time to join the Cabinet. He wanted him to be secretary of war since Elihu Root was pulling out. Taft still stubbornly knew what he wanted most of all but he stalled for time on the Cabinet offer until he heard from his brothers, "on whose judgment, especially concerning my private affairs—I place much dependence," he wrote to the President. Roosevelt summed up his point of view in a letter dated February 14, 1903:

> If only there were three of you. Then I would have one of you on the Supreme Court, as the Ohio member in place of good Day [Justice William R. Day]; one of you in Root's place as Secretary of War, when he goes out; and one of you permanently Governor of the Philippines. No one can quite take your place as Governor, but no one of whom I can now think save only you can at all take Root's place as Secretary.

The only argument that appealed to Governor Taft was the one that as secretary of war he would still have control over Philippine affairs. He wrote to Charles that he would be in the midst of a presidential campaign "which would be most distasteful to me, for I have no love for American politics." Nellie spoke strongly in favor of acceptance. A Cabinet post might take him one step closer to the Presidency; the Supreme Court would not. Actually, Taft was much concerned over the health of his family, should they remain too long in the tropics. Horace wondered if Will himself could stand the pace after what he had been through physically. Louise, down to earth as always, wrote that the Cabinet post would not dazzle her. She would rather see him finish his job in the Philippines, which was peculiarly his own and would go down in history as original. He had founded a civil government under difficult conditions. She had been entertained at the White House in March, 1903, and had not been won by Theodore Roosevelt. "I do not think his personality is agreeable and his manners are explosive and so demonstrative as to seem like affectation," she wrote crisply to Will.

He in turn worried over the expenses he would incur as a Cabinet member in Washington but he accepted the offer on the understanding that Elihu Root would hold the post for another year. Roosevelt brushed aside the financial aspects of the situation, reminding him that when he was Civil Service Commissioner Mrs. Roosevelt had done most of her entertaining at Sunday high tea, since she could not afford champagne for dinners. At Oyster Bay they had two maids and lived like "any family of gentlefolks with small means." He saw no reason why the Tafts could not live as they did when Will was solicitor general. "So, old man, it would really add immensely to my pleasure as an American to have you, who will be the foremost member of my Cabinet in the public eye, live the simplest kind of life."

Taft was not so sure about this. He wrote to his old friend Howard Hollister on September 21, 1903: "You should see Nellie's lip curl at the suggestion of Sunday high teas and dinner parties without champagne." But Charles, always generously alert to his brother's interests, at once offered to make up any deficit in the family expenses. Will could rely on him for $6,000 annually and more if he needed it. This would bring his income in Washington to $14,000 a year. Nellie was satisfied for the time being and commented that his new post was in line with the kind of work she wanted Will to do.

By this time the entire Taft family was united again in the Philippines and in April, 1903, with these matters pending, they went to Baguio in the province of Benguet as a health measure. Will had amebic dysentery and was being dosed with quinine. The region reminded them all of Murray Bay, with its fresh breezes, the barnlike cottage, the pine trees and grass. Will rode twenty-five miles on horseback to reach his destination. When he cabled to Root, who kept close track of his friend's health, that he had stood the ordeal well, the Secretary of War cabled back with the wry touch that both understood:

"How is the horse?"

The Governor planned to make Benguet a summer capital like Simla in India and he conducted business from this mountain retreat. Mrs. Taft had a mountain pony that took her over the hills and kept her in good condition. She was still excessively thin but felt better. The boys' horses looked more like bags of bones than like Bucephalus, their father jested, but they made speed. Charlie's pony was known as "Weary Willie" but there was nothing weary about its rider. The mountain air had done wonders for him. His father wrote to Mr. Herron in June that Charlie reminded him of one of the Mellin's Food children after taking his daily quota. Arrangements were made at this time to send a hundred Filipino boys to American schools and two were entered at the Taft School.

Robert Taft, fourteen years old and self-reliant, traveled home alone from the Philippines in the summer of 1903, bound for his uncle's school in Watertown. His father chose to pay the full tuition fee—"I don't want you to give me ministers' rates," he wrote to Horace. Julia was to outfit him with suitable clothes to make him look "as respectable as a son of mine can look, which I agree is not saying very much." He thought it time for Robert to wear long trousers.

By way of introduction Governor Taft wrote to Horace that he did not think Robert had any bad habits, except that he kept his mouth open and was not too particular about cleaning his nails. He became intensely interested in games and discussions, and could get wrought up to the point of tears if things went against him. He had a decided taste for history and for study of all kinds, a great affinity for mathematics, and considerable skill at card games and chess. His father was not so sure that he would shine at athletics, although he played both tennis and baseball. He had grown fast but was strong. Up to this point Bob had studied elementary algebra, geometry, Spanish, French, and German, and was reading Caesar. Will hoped that Horace would prepare his son for college in three years. Bob would then enter Yale on his seventeenth birthday and would be graduated with the class of 1910 "which I prophesied on the day of his birth." September happened to be the month of birthdays in the Taft family. On September 8, 1903, Robert was fourteen and three days later his grandmother was seventy-six. On September 15 William Howard Taft was forty-six and on September 20 Charlie was six.

Robert was an unobtrusive traveler, playing chess and reading as his ship crossed the Pacific, but already the limelight was playing on him. The San Francisco papers made much of the fact that young Bob Taft was going halfway around the world by himself. He landed on September 18, 1903, just as young Douglas MacArthur was sailing off to Manila to join his father. Their paths would cross significantly in the future. Susie's family, the Woods, gave him a thorough tour of San Francisco before seeing him off to New York on the train. He was two weeks late for the opening of the Taft School and had some catching up to do. Bob was equal to the middle class in algebra, although rusty in the subject. Horace found him slightly behind in Latin and Greek but he went to work to catch up, so that he had 98 in his first examination in Greek.

His uncle studied him carefully and decided that he was a "great boy," taking hold of things firmly and harboring a strong inner drive behind a diffident manner. His marks, relayed regularly to his parents, were impressive from the start. By November Horace conceded that he was the best scholar in his class but Taft wrote urgently to Bob, reminding him that he must show his uncle the stuff he had. "I do not have to tell you how anxious I am for you to study hard and do well in your classes," he added, with more than the usual touch of fatherly concern.

CHAPTER 13

THE WAR OFFICE

B<small>Y THE END</small> of 1903 Governor Taft's work in the Philippines was finished. He would now be Secretary of War. One significant period in his history had come to a close—a period in which he had set up a government, become internationally known, and had unconsciously paved the way for his own ascent to the Presidency. He had laid firm foundations in the Philippines in government, education, public improvements, the judiciary, and transportation. The utmost good will surrounded the Tafts as they left.

They gave one final party—a Venetian fete planned by Mrs. Taft. The guests arrived at the river landing by boat. Canoes, bancas, rafts, barges and launches smothered in flowers, nudged one another as they approached the palace grounds, which were hung with Japanese lanterns and multicolored lights. Mandolins and guitars spread melody through the night. The Filipino women, masked, beautifully gowned, adorned with jewels drawn from old Spanish caskets, were greeted by Governor Taft attired as the Doge. Mrs. Taft was appropriately turned out as his consort. Charlie was a Venetian youth and Helen was dressed in the romantic period mood. Will wrote enthusiastically to his brother Charles about "the moonlight, the beautiful grounds, the great porticoes running over the river, the Chinese lanterns and the brilliant costumes, the constabulary band, and the feeling that an era was ended."

Robert had missed this closing spectacle but he was already entering on a new social phase at his school and in Cincinnati. His father wrote to him of their trip home, of their visit to Japan and the "bigwigs" they had met there, of the reception given him by Elihu Root on his return to Washington. Mrs. Taft had decided to spend the winter in California with the children and the Governor confided to Bob that he did not feel immediately at home, since all his family were missing and the Army was *terra incognita* to him. He found the dining and wining on his arrival overwhelming. Just as Alphonso had guided him through his schooldays so he now counseled his son Robert. With the characteristic Taft instinct for the better things of life he wrote:

> I hope that you find that your roommate and your classmates are pleasant fellows, and that you are making warm friendships with them. You must remember that the friendships you make now and while in college will be the most lasting of your life, and you should select those boys for your friends that are not of a low tone and vulgar because they will not prove to be either the most useful or the best friends that you can make. . . . You will always find that the friends for whom you have respect are the friends worth tying to later on.

The newly appointed Secretary of War wrote plaintively to Nellie about his bachelor state when she upbraided him for writing to her so infrequently. He had taken rooms at the Arlington for $250 a month and he confessed to Nellie that he did not feel he was living at all in her absence, but was just marking time until she arrived. "If there is anything more dreary than hotel life I don't know what it is," wrote the home-loving Secretary of War. "I am longing for you all the time."

Mrs. Taft had settled in Santa Barbara after visiting Fanny. Dr. Edwards had given up his hospital and was in private practice again. Robert's letters both from the Taft School and from Cincinnati, where he had spent his Christmas holidays at the Pike Street house, were reassuring to his mother. He had been entertained by their old friends and had enjoyed it all, from a Yale Glee Club function to coasting on the golf links. His cousin Hulbert had just become engaged to Nellie Leaman, a match that William Howard Taft approved, since he had known and liked her father. Nicholas Longworth had asked Hulbert to be his private secretary in Washington, but Hulbert was devoted to the *Times-Star*. Bob's Aunt Eleanor had just married Dr. Louis Trenchard More, a professor at the University of Cincinnati. All of the Herron sisters were married now, except Maria, who was left alone with her father. Jennie was Mrs. Charles Anderson, Lucy was Mrs. Thomas Laughlin, and Emily had married Gustavus Parsons.

The new *Times-Star* building was finished in 1903 and all the presses were now run by electricity instead of by steam engine. Charles was pushing the gas business in Cincinnati and Annie was reminding him at breakfast every morning that he must run his daily editorial on the smoke nuisance. The sales of the family gas company in Cleveland were fifty per cent more than in his own city and he felt that meters should be installed in homes, so that gas ranges could be introduced as well as light. Mrs. Alphonso Taft thought that Charles did not fight the Cox machine with enough energy and when she visited Cincinnati now she bemoaned the passing of the Titans, and could find no citizens to compare with Alphonso, Rufus King, Aaron Perry, John Herron, William M. Ramsay, Manning F. Force, and other friends of days gone by. But new developments were in sight for her son William and all the Tafts noticed with interest that his name was now appearing in magazines and newspapers as a presidential possibility. Taft was actually embarrassed when the New York *Sun* described a Yale dinner given for him in New York in March, 1904, as a presidential boom for "plain Bill Taft." He warned Nellie at the end of that month "not to be too confident of Teddy's giving me the Chief Justiceship."

In attending this dinner he had stayed with Harry and Julia in New York, as he always did. When a tall youth walked into the room he had difficulty recognizing him at first as his own son Bob, down for his spring vacation. The boy had grown taller and stouter and Julia had outfitted him with suitable clothes. Watching him in the family group that had gathered for the Ohio Society dinner Taft approved his quiet, attentive manner, and after seeing him in his first tuxedo he wrote to Nellie: "Robert is a great joy to me. He looks like the Herrons and while not a beauty, he is a manly-looking boy who attracts people."

It was the first time in two years that Taft had seen his mother and Delia, and he found both greatly saddened by Susie's death, which had occurred early in 1904. She left two sons—William and Samuel Austin Wood, whom Bob had met in California. Horace now weighed 200 pounds and his brother thought that he had gained in health and strength. Will had a long talk with him that night about Bob. Horace, touching on a fundamental in Robert Taft's character, said that he was capable of great concentration and always went to the center of things. His father noticed that his young son had the knack of doing a little here and a little there until he had finished a task—a quality that he wished he shared with Bob. At the moment he was reading up on the Panama Canal to write a composition for the Litchfield County Prize Oration contest, but this did not prevent him from sightseeing in New York. He visited Grant's Tomb, Riverside Drive, and the Cathedral. Downtown he did a thorough tour from the Battery to Trinity Church. He rode over

Brooklyn Bridge and walked back. He then went up in the much discussed Flatiron Building, the skyscraper of the hour, and wound up his day at the theater, seeing *Sweet Kitty Bellairs* with his cousin Howard.

From New York Bob proceeded to Washington and had his first good look at the city where his future lay. Fred Carpenter met him at the station and took him straight to his father at the War Department. The boy whose statue one day would stand under a bell tower close to the Capitol walked four miles that afternoon with his father, who pointed out the different monuments and buildings. He heard his father testify before the Committee on Insular Affairs, his first taste of government inquisition. Next day he went alone to the Senate and walked around Washington, seeing the Smithsonian Institution, the Navy Yard, the Soldiers' Home, and going to the top of the Washington Monument. Herbert Putnam, head of the Library of Congress, took him behind the scenes, a tour that interested Robert greatly. He had lunch and dinner at the White House and met the entire Roosevelt family. The boys were just leaving for Groton when Bob wrote to his mother on April 10, 1904: "Teddy is rather nice, but I think I like Kermit better as he is a good deal quieter. He is just my age, but I am about as big as Teddy."

Robert returned to the Taft School greatly enlightened on governmental matters. He was not selected, however, as one of the ten to speak in the Oratorical Contest, since oratory was still one of his major difficulties. But his averages climbed steadily until they were around 95 in November, 1904. Horace assured his father that Bob did his best in everything and was the brightest boy he had ever had in his school. He used his knowledge of the Philippines to good advantage in a speech on colonization, a subject suggested by his father. Then he engaged in a debate on the tariff, another strong family interest. His classmates called him Aguinaldo when they wished to tease him but Robert or Mr. Taft when they sought help in their problems. When up to mischief they usually tried to rope him in, hoping that in this way they might escape the utmost in punishment, but it did not always work.

Bob was preeminently the scholar, inclined to stay indoors with his books. In the afternoons the boys did track work, threw balls in the gymnasium, or skated. When spring came he played tennis, but as yet he had little taste for social pleasures. Horace tried to interest him in a diversity of things and to stir up his ambition for writing. On Monday nights he had the Glee Club, on Wednesday the Chess Club, on Saturday the Literary Club. He sang at a Kettle Drum in a voice that was singularly unmelodious. Although he was not heavy enough for football he was on the third team and was always ready to take punishment. In spidery handwriting he corresponded zealously, if somewhat prosaically, with his mother about his school activities. He gave her play by play accounts of the football games and relayed the scores of all the big college games. He took dancing and boxing lessons and tried for the school plays. The Taft love of charades helped him on different occasions and he had a small role in a play *The Two Buzzards*. In time he became editor of the *Taft Annual* and took a strong hand in the school magazine, *The Oracle*, and in *Papyrus*, a paper that he helped to start.

Robert was neither a paragon nor the type of student labeled a "greasy grind" by his classmates. Although letter-perfect in class, he never roused animosities among the less successful, either in school or college. Horace observed that he stored facts in his mind as if it were a filing cabinet and he recalled that Bob had memorized the Constitution in his elementary-school days and could come up with the apt point at a moment's notice. Some thought him dull and stodgy, but he could pause to laugh and he reported cheerfully to his mother that "last night six of us had a 'feed' in our room after lights, which was very good while it lasted, but which came to a disastrous end, as we were all caught."

Uncle Horace saw to it that no favors were granted him, and his grand-mother, Mrs. Alphonso Taft, visiting the school, sent reassuring word to his father that he was liked both by the boys and the teachers, and that he seemed to be happy at the Taft School. She noted with pleasure the advances that Horace had made since the day in 1890 when a few boys and a stack of furniture had arrived together at the small Red House in Pelham owned by Mrs. Black. Now an annex had been added to the rambling Warren House, the old hotel that Mr. and Mrs. Horace Taft had converted into a comfortable school. The boys still slid down the banisters of the circular staircase when they could get away with it, and they played tricks with the telephone house-tubes. There were sixty-five resident boys and a large number of day scholars, Mark Hanna's two grandsons among them.

Girls were looming pleasantly on the horizon for Bob by 1905. With exams out of the way he went to the senior dance at St. Margaret's in Waterbury, after the school had won a baseball game and the track meet with Westminister. He wrote to his mother that he had a splendid time although he knew nobody. He managed to dance without mishap "keep-ing my feet to the music but whether I was dancing a waltz or not, I'm not sure." The big gymnasium was so crowded that they could scarcely move. There were many Yale men there, and Bob felt that the Taft boys were shunted off on the girls who were left over, but he managed to enjoy him-self thoroughly. At another dance the full moon dulled the electric deco-rations and Japanese lanterns in the grounds. Many of the girls chose to sit out on the porch and under the trees. "I didn't know anybody, but several I met were very nice," Bob wrote. "On the whole I had a splendid time and felt afterwards that it was also part of my education."

His parents were surprised to learn in the spring that one of the day students had run ahead of Bob, who tried to catch up with his score of 98 but found it hopeless. However, Bob promptly got 99 in a Greek examination and 100 in Greek history. He won second prize and a silver medal for a composition, and "honorable mention" in Latin prose composition. A youth named Arthur Fergusson had outclassed him in this field, but Bob received a ten-dollar prize for having the highest average in the two upper classes. It was nip and tuck all along the line and Bob sometimes felt that his uncle expected too much of him. Marks were a matter of historic concern in the Taft family. Alphonso and Louise had set the pattern and some of their grandchildren suffered for it, although few families can have delivered so consistently and so well. Walbridge, Harry's son, and Howard, the son of Charles and Annie, did not shine in the Taft School but Walbridge did well in college.

While Bob followed a steady and successful course at prep school his father's prestige increased. He worked prodigiously hard on unfamiliar problems in the War Department but he disliked the political aspects of his Cabinet position, which went against his judicial temper. When questions arose involving the Philippines he went into action with knowledge and satisfaction. His correspondence tells little of his War Department work, since President Roosevelt had chosen him as his troubleshooter and moved him about when emergencies arose. The result was that routine army and navy matters were left largely to his chief of staff.

His mother was reproachful because he failed to attend a Sutton and Millbury celebration commemorating General Rufus Putnam. To mollify her he sent a message pointing out that both of his grandfathers and one grandmother and all of his ancestors were citizens of Worcester County. His grandfather, Samuel D. Torrey, and his great-grandfather, Asa Waters, had been residents of the area for half a century. Louise was now collecting family records, perpetuating her husband's interest in Taft history. She had a modest income from the Vine Street property in Cincinnati, which she had finally decided to sell.

The Secretary of War skipped the May Festival in Cincinnati in 1904. There were moments when he and Charles compared notes behind Annie's back over their boredom with some of the lengthier recitals. There was a strong suspicion in the family that William Howard Taft would not have taken his music so seriously had it not been for Annie and Nellie. But he lent himself heartily to backing the elaborate Filipino exhibit at the Louisiana Purchase Exposition that year. Nellie and the children joined him in St. Louis and he decided that her stay in California had done much for her health. On their return to Washington Charlie and Helen were invited constantly to the White House to play and have supper with Archie, Quentin, and Ethel. Taft's stay at Murray Bay that summer was brief but before leaving he had a picturesque birthday celebration when a hundred *habitants* came to the house, waving birchbark torches and singing French-Canadian songs. They serenaded him to one of the large houses at Pointe au Pic, where they danced the Virginia reel, sang, gave presents, and made speeches. "It was a complete surprise to me, which is an indication of how easily fooled I can be, for the whole community seems to have been in on the secret," the Secretary wrote to Howard Hollister. The Tafts now flew an American flag at their house on special occasions.

By this time the presidential campaign was warming up and Roosevelt was anxious to have Taft speak, particularly on the Philippines. But he found him too mild a campaigner, and urged him to attack instead of being on the defensive. One of his letters brought the Secretary to the point of resigning. Taft had no heart for the bellicose touch and he felt he was not by nature a campaigner or spellbinder. He relied on the power of facts to persuade. This was his particular gift. But Nellie and Horace both spoke to him frankly about the length and the dullness of his speeches. At no time in his life did he build up any faith in his own oratory, but in the summer of 1904 he was emerging as a speaker. Always subject to heavy colds he was hoarse so often that he particularly disliked speaking outdoors.

Taft felt rusty on general politics and he had not done much public speaking in twenty-four years. His family suffered with him as he left his addresses until the last minute, and then rushed them out under pressure, a lifelong habit. But he enjoyed campaigning in Vermont and did not fail to make the point that his father's people had come from that state. "The stamp of sincerity and seriousness on the faces of the people is unmistakable," he wrote to Howard Hollister. "It is a wholesome atmosphere one breathes there, and with that kind of people to form the backbone of the country, we may take courage as to the future."

President Roosevelt's acceptance speech seemed to Taft to be the best thing he had done since becoming Chief Executive. He admired his "dignity and force of epigrammatic statement." Working as he now did in close contact with Roosevelt he found him a "sweet-natured man and a very trusting man when he believes in one." He was devoted to his chief and hoped that Nellie would warm up to him when she had had more opportunity for firsthand observation. But Nellie had never been enthusiastic about Theodore Roosevelt and she saw no reason to change her mind. She considered him too ebullient and she doubted his sincerity. However, she could agree with Will when he wrote to her on March 31, 1904: "We never had a President whose family life has been better than Roosevelt's. The people know it. That is why they like him. . . ."

The Tafts dined frequently at the White House during this period. By October, 1904, they were settled in their Washington home at 1603 K Street. Nellie found it difficult to fit her large pieces of furniture into their new quarters. After the barnlike rooms of Malacanan their house seemed of midget proportions. Only their Legardo bed looked right in its new setting, after all the small pieces had been glued together like a Chinese puzzle. The library was dark and gloomy until she applied some homelike touches and filled the cases with her husband's books. Will had great belief in his wife's capacity as a housekeeper and homemaker. Time and again she proved her skill in this respect. Now they called their Washington home the Hotel du Taft and invited Cincinnati friends to use it freely.

Charlie and Helen were escorted to their schools on opening day by their father, who commented that a cyclone had left the house when Charlie settled at a school desk. He went into the third reader but was behind his contemporaries in arithmetic. When he came home for lunch the first day he cried and decided that he would have no more of school, but he quickly became an enthusiastic pupil and the second-best reader in his class. A bicycle ordered by his mother from Wanamaker's for Christmas was of some help, too. Mlle. Jeanne Marret, their French governess, shepherded both children around the capital. Helen, who attended the National Cathedral School, had special gymnastic exercises for curvature of the spine. Her education went on without interruption although she wore a plaster jacket for a time and did special exercises for years.

The Tafts had a War Department carriage, driven by an Irish coachman known as Quade, who had been an artilleryman and always made Theodore Roosevelt feel as if he were on the caisson of a gun wagon going into action. The Secretary had his own horse for riding but would not have it fed at public expense. Arthur Brooks, a major of militia and valued Negro messenger in the War Department, helped Mrs. Taft with her major entertainments. She frankly missed the luxurious simplicity and freedom from household detail that had been her lot in the Philippines. Her cook did not equal Ah Sing, nor did her Negro butler and housemaid take the place of Ah King and Chang, her Chinese boys. Eight bare-footed *muchachos* had polished her hardwood floors to a mirrorlike gloss in Manila. But the Tafts had few quiet evenings at home. They dined out constantly or entertained themselves. Nellie faithfully attended Mrs. Roosevelt's weekly meetings for the Cabinet wives to discuss matters supposed to interest them all. She was caught up in a whirl of calls, a social amenity that she disliked.

Her husband was away so much, on one mission or another, that the cartoonists usually showed him with his hat being lifted off his head by the wind while he hurried along, perspiring and carrying a suitcase. Roosevelt, on the other hand, wore the guise of Mercury in the cartoons, with his heavy eyeglass ribbons streaming backwards. These effects were always a source of great amusement in the Taft household. Father's proportions lent themselves to extravagant caricature. The President remarked that it was a relief to have Will's bulk take the place of his own wide grin and glasses for a change. The Secretary of War had spent $500 on a new wardrobe for himself when he assumed his new post. He kept urging Nellie to equip herself generously and not to stint on clothes for Helen. Her sense of economy sometimes overcame her motherly instincts in this respect.

The children were no sooner settled in school than the election excitement swamped them all as Theodore Roosevelt was returned to office in 1904. Taft was traveling at the time but Charles kept him supplied with bulletins along the way. The reaction in Cincinnati was intense. Annie, as usual, was at the *Times-Star* office to share in it all. Crowds paraded in the streets and the newspaper offices were mobbed. Harry Taft had been offered the Republican nomination for governor of New York State that year and had visited Murray Bay to discuss the matter with Will before turning it down. He now had a large income and was just beginning to reap what he had sown, Will observed. He had managed to save $80,000 but his expenses were high and Julia liked luxurious living. She had persuaded Harry that East Hampton had more diversions than Murray Bay, along with a good deal of its simplicity. But Will that year was happy to be able to rent the Buchanan cottage at Murray Bay for $450.

The golden shower from Pike Street continued when the Tafts settled in Washington. Charles urged his brother to take a good house and not to stint on entertaining. He promised him $10,000 a year and gave him a thousand shares in the Cleveland Gas Company. His own private income at this time was $40,000 a year, aside from Annie's fortune. As usual, the Taft brothers were as ready to help one another in prosperity as they had been in the early days. Charles coveted a diplomatic post, but Roosevelt was not responsive. Fanny wanted some favors, too. She urged a post office appointment for a friend in Coronado, and she asked Will to get her a permit to enter Mexico on hunting expeditions. "Much to your mother's dismay I have made quite a hunter out of Fanny," Dr. Edwards wrote to Will. "She is a very good wing shot, and most excellent at large game with a rifle." They shot on a game preserve of 128,000 acres owned by a Chicago millionaire, but Fanny and Bill had encountered customs complications in crossing the border. Dr. Edwards urged his brother-in-law to join them for a shoot, promising him that it would help to reduce his weight.

Will deplored the idea of killing any living thing and had no taste for hunting, but it interested him that Fanny had become such a good shot. He was concerned at this time about taking off weight. He had gained fifty pounds in the Philippines and was interested in an anti-fat remedy that Julia had used to good effect. Julia was tall and handsome, but she put on weight easily and she and Will kept up a lively interchange on the subject. However, his life was not conducive to austere measures, for the popular Secretary of War was soon being invited to all the liveliest dinner tables, and also some of the dullest, in the capital. "Invitations are as thick as the leaves of Vallombrosa" he wrote as he started on the Washington round that would continue for the rest of his life. The fare at the home of Larz Anderson was particularly epicurean, since he had a French chef. At this time Taft joined the Cosmos Club and the National Geographic Society, to which he was nominated by Alexander Graham Bell. The Tafts and the Bells were all good friends and Gilbert H. Grosvenor, who had married Elsie May Graham Bell, was a relative by marriage.

Late in 1904 President Roosevelt sent his Secretary of War to Panama on the first of many visits he would make as the master overseer and troubleshooter of the great engineering venture there. He supervised the work of the Isthmus Canal Commission, both on the construction of the canal and the exercise of governmental powers, under the treaty made with the new Republic. President Roosevelt had taken possession of the Canal Zone when he recognized the Republic of Panama after it revolted from Colombia in 1903. He had negotiated a treaty giving the United States the right to build the canal. When Colombia rejected the treaty a new government was established and another treaty was signed. This again gave Americans the right to go ahead with construction of the Canal.

Taft was drawn into the situation at a time when there was a legislative lag and Congress made no further provision for the government of the Canal Zone for seven years. The situation was highly confused, with the Secretary of War finding himself immediately involved in problems of labor, politics, engineering, and sanitation. His work in a sense resembled his administrative functions in the Philippines. He held conferences wth officials and private citizens as he investigated the clearance of vessels, postal matters, currency, and judiciary appointments. The Panamanians feared annexation and it was his task to mollify them and still their fears. He gave assurance that there was no intention of establishing a separate colony in the middle of the State of Panama. In the course of his investigations he found monopolies in tobacco, cigars, cigarettes, and opium.

Mrs. Taft went with him on three of his trips, including the first. Her knowledge of Spanish was useful to her husband on this occasion. They crossed the Isthmus by private train and Taft had long talks with Dr.

William Crawford Gorgas, whose work on the mosquito as the bearer of yellow fever was still being ridiculed. This pioneer felt that he was not getting much cooperation in his passion to clean up the swamps and pools where mosquitoes bred. The Secretary of War was open-minded about his work and gave him official support, although he felt in the beginning that Gorgas lacked executive ability. Taft disliked the sort of friction and lack of administrative skill that prevailed in the Panama area. But he was enthusiastic about the role Major George W. Goethals was playing.

The Secretary's trip was considered a success and *vivas* greeted the agreement he reached with the Government of Panama. Harbor boundaries were defined. Public health jurisdiction remained under American control. Years of discord lay ahead, with unscrupulous politicians, contractors, grafters of one kind and another, laying red herrings across the trail, but the Secretary kept an iron grip at the top. This was just the opening wedge, however, and Taft would become all too familiar with locks and climatic difficulties, engineering problems, and conflicting interests.

He was swept into an unfamiliar field again early in 1905 when he served as secretary of state during John Hay's absence. Hay was ill and the President was touring the West. On April 8 Roosevelt wrote to Taft that he was handling everything in the right way. He approved his course during the crisis of that year involving the treaty Britain and France had signed for the partition of Morocco. He was equally satisfied with Taft's handling of the Santo Domingo crisis when President Carlos F. Morales was confronted with revolution over the issue of foreign debts that his countrymen were not prepared to meet. The United States was playing a strong hand at the time in the administration of the island and by the Dominican Treaty of 1907 a continuation of this phase of Dollar Diplomacy was approved.

The relations between Roosevelt and Taft grew increasingly friendly as they worked harmoniously on these issues. Roosevelt had decided to make Taft his attorney general and Taft agreed that the Department of Justice would be much more to his liking than the War Department. In this he repeated the course followed by his father many years earlier. Busy with his antitrust activities President Roosevelt wrote in this connection to Sir George O. Trevelyan, the British historian, that Taft had no more fear in dealing with the interests of great corporate wealth than of the most powerful labor unions. "To strength and courage, clear insight and practical common sense he adds a very noble and disinterested character," Theodore Roosevelt wrote.

With Will established in the Government Mr. and Mrs. Charles Phelps Taft of Cincinnati were considering moving to Washington in the spring of 1905. The smoke in Cincinnati bothered Annie to a marked degree and things did not seem to improve, in spite of all the editorializing they did in their paper. But Charles dreaded the banqueting in Washington and the absence of the work he liked to do in Cincinnati. The situation was somewhat comparable to Mrs. Taft's on her return from the Philippines. One woman approached her at a Washington tea with the exclamation: "Why, out there you were really a Queen, and you come back here and are *just nobody*."

These were the years when Charles and Annie made trips to Europe and bought most of their art collection. They frankly acknowledged that they chose to buy pictures instead of piling up their fortune in bonds and real estate. Annie was eager to use her newly acquired riches in a pleasant and beneficial way. This was a significant decision with far-reaching results for Cincinnati. Moreover, they had considerable pleasure themselves in viewing the pictures and they did some of their most important buying in 1903 and 1904. Charles, who had studied this field years earlier, went back to a close scrutiny of paintings in the galleries and museums, while Annie bought emeralds at Cartier's and gowns at Doucet's. Charles accompanied her to Doucet's one September morning. He watched a dozen models parading by and stayed just long enough to study the fashion procedure. Next day he wrote to Will that a few minutes were enough to give him the idea.

While in Paris in 1903 they started a rare collection of sixteenth-century Limoges enamels, including caskets, plaques, platters, and cruciforms. They added to this group in 1904 and picked up a notable triptych. Charles revisited Heidelberg and found the same family living in the house where he had roomed as a student. After thirty-five years they recognized him at once. In Holland they gave close attention to Dutch art. They were now becoming discriminating critics and Joseph Duveen was advising them on their purchases. In London that summer they bought Constant Troyon's "Vaches à l'Abreuvoir" and Jean François Millet's "La Maternité," which Charles considered one of the most impressive pictures he had ever seen. Both came from private collections and he wrote to Will from Claridge's on July 12, 1903: "As I am on the ground and put up the money, I got the chance." At this time he added a Rousseau, a Sir Joshua Reynolds and Jacob Maris's "Rotterdam" to his collection. A rock crystal piece and a Luca della Robbia were selected by Annie. With a wry touch Charles wrote to his brother in the Philippines about this profitable excursion: "Of course I will not suggest how much these things cost. They are not given away."

Julia and Harry joined the Charles Phelps Tafts in London and they saw the more luxurious side of Victorian England. They had a box for a gala performance at Covent Garden attended by King Edward VII and they sat in the grand tier adjoining the royal box. Charles thought that Joseph H. Choate, the American ambassador, looked profoundly bored in the diplomatic box. Both he and Annie were blinded by the dazzle of diamonds around them. Charles described the scene in a letter to Will:

> Annie's regret was that she did not have some of her jewels. We how-ever saw what others wore. Almost every lady in the boxes in the grand tier had a diamond coronet. Our box was conspicuous by the absence of this ornament. While we all enjoyed the spectacle inside the house, we noted that Covent Garden was the meanest place in London for opera. It took us nearly an hour to find our carriage and get away.

Back in New York Charles and Annie made large art purchases there, too, in 1903. Charles made many trips to the Metropolitan Museum with Joseph Duveen, studying the masters and listening to his advice. He picked up nearly a score of pictures at this time, including a Meissonier, a Gainsborough, a Corot, a Constable, a Troyon, a Diaz de la Peña, and a Vibert. Between their purchases in Europe and New York, Charles and Annie had gone far toward starting the collection with which their names would always be identified. Realizing what their aims were Will wrote to them appreciatively: "I do not know of any direction in which money may be spent to greater advantage than in that way in our country."

The new paintings were taken to Pike Street and were hung by experts. But the Corot gave them trouble. Annie did not wish to diminish the beauty of her music room by having lights dropped from the ceiling. They finally decided to hang it over a mantelpiece, and the Corot and a new Gainsborough made conversation in Cincinnati that winter. So did the paintings of Charles and Annie done by Raimundo de Madrazo, the Spanish artist. Annie traveled far for special fittings for the gown she wore and there was much fussing about the fall of her old Venetian lace ruffles.

But the Taft generosity covered many areas. Annie never tired of her work for the orchestra. She studied the aesthetic effects as well as the musical excellence of Van der Stucken's productions. For a time she considered having a woman in the orchestra to relieve the somber effect of the men grouped in black dress suits, for Annie liked those around her to be good-looking, becomingly attired, and joyous in spirit. She and Charles were concerned to find a big business-building going up on the Anderson lot just south of them when they returned from Europe in 1903. They did not like the idea of a factory until they learned that it was owned by the American Book Company; then they were reconciled and welcomed their new neighbors. Workmen walked all over their place and swung cables across the top of their beautiful house but indoors all was serenity, with the new pictures in place. Anything that fed a cultural interest, anything that beautified Cincinnati, was welcomed by Mr. and Mrs. Charles Phelps Taft.

When Funck-Brentano, the French historian, visited them in 1905 he pronounced "La Maternité" the finest painting by Millet and said it was worth a trip across the ocean to see it. William M. Laffan, art connoisseur and publisher of the New York *Sun*, told Will Taft that Charles's collection was in many respects better than anything of the sort in the United States, and that the pilgrims to view it would increase in number—all of which filled quiet Charles and exuberant Annie with a glow of happiness.

Winifred's mother died in the spring of 1905 at the age of eighty-two and she and Horace decided to spend the summer at their new home in Wainscott instead of going to Murray Bay. All the Tafts were heading in different directions at this time. Again President Roosevelt had called the signals on their destiny. He asked his secretary of war to head a congressional party on a good-will trip to the Philippines and Japan. When Horace read of this in the papers he wrote at once to Will: "I see that you are to have Alice Roosevelt with you. I should think that she would cause more excitement and trouble than half a dozen Filipino tribes. But cheer up, the Summer is short. . . . Bob is not a Demosthenes or Cicero yet, but for a 'fifteen-year-older' he does well."

Mrs. Taft decided to spend the summer in England with her younger children. Bob was to tour Scandinavia with Mr. and Mrs. Charles Phelps Taft and a group of boys; then he would join his mother at the end of his trip. But Bob was tepid in his approach to the British Isles. "Still it will not be bad to have seen England, though it will seem more like education than fun," he wrote to his mother.

Mrs. Taft sailed on the *Zeeland* on July 1, 1905, while her husband left for San Francisco to cross the Pacific. "Recent events make me long to see you out of politics, safely moored on the Supreme Court bench," Mrs. Alphonso Taft wrote to her son as one more leaf was turned in the history of his life. He would soon be in the headlines again, this time with Alice Roosevelt, a girl who had already made a deep impression on the American people.

CHAPTER 14

ALICE ROOSEVELT
AND MR. TAFT

M RS. TAFT settled close to Oxford and Charlie and Helen were
engaged in boating and bicycling as William Howard Taft steamed
across the Pacific on the *Manchuria* in the summer of 1905. There were
fifty-four in the official party, including seven senators and twenty-three
congressmen. Others who joined them along the way brought the final
score to eighty-three. At home the trip was regarded as a congressional
junket. Actually, President Roosevelt had again chosen Taft as his ambassador of peace—this time to conduct some quiet negotiations with the
Japanese before the forthcoming peace conference to be held in the
United States, and also to show the legislators at firsthand what had been
accomplished in the Philippines.

Romance as well as diplomacy flourished as the ship cut through vel-
vety waters, with the moon casting its spell over the decks. Nicholas
Longworth was one of the passengers and although he was wooing
Alice Roosevelt neither one would acknowledge being engaged or even
in love. The worldly young member of Harvard's Porcellian Club, who
played the violin well and sang robustly, was obviously infatuated
with Alice, although she made no secret of the fact that she wished to
marry a man who would be President, or was prominent politically. Miss

Roosevelt did not look forward to the obscurity that she anticipated when her father left the White House. "I don't know whether she thinks Nick will become President or a prominent statesman or not," Will wrote to Nellie. This expedition established her more solidly than ever in the public eye as a personality to be reckoned with, a dynamic girl who cared little for convention. She stole the limelight all along the way and no one minded, least of all William Howard Taft.

Worn out with hard work he found the trip relaxing. He slept deeply at sea and felt rested after months of concentrated effort in an unfamiliar field. Every day he walked four miles around the decks and when he felt in the mood he played poker with the men or danced with the women. Then, and later, there were comments on his light-footed dancing, which became a matter of jest during the presidential campaign. One of the jingles of the day ran:

> That Taft is just a wonder
>> Is a thing which we all know;
> That as Presidential thunder
>> His big boom is like to go.
> But as butterfly, blooms sipping,
>> And as waltzer, simply ripping!
> 'Tis a sight to see Taft tripping
>> On the light fantastic toe.

Mrs. Francis A. Newlands, wife of the senator from Nevada, was the official chaperone for Alice and the other girls, but Taft considered her more attractive than any of her charges. Sitting at his table, in addition to Alice and the Newlands, were Miss Amy McMillan, Miss Mabel Boardman, and Herbert Parsons and his wife, who was a daughter of Henry Clews. They all played bridge, had balls, swimming parties on deck, games and masquerades, a mock trial with Taft presiding, and a pillow fight. They took pictures and tried sleight of hand. Much of the merriment was worked up by Burr McIntosh, a droll character greatly enjoyed by Taft. Martin Egan, the Associated Press correspondent later identified with J. P. Morgan & Company, was in love with Eleanor Franklin, the magazine correspondent whom he married in Yokohama after their romance had developed on the *Manchuria*.

Alice worked off her varied collection of bridesmaids' gowns for the evening parties. In the daytime she lounged about in white linen skirts with blouses and three-quarter length coats, or embroidered linens and muslins. She smoked incessantly from a gold vanity case that she stuffed with cigarettes instead of hairpins. Will reported to his wife that Alice was quite nervous after meals until she had a cigarette alight, and he offered to give up drinking if she would stop smoking. She took great delight in shocking her fellow passengers but got on well with the Secretary of War, whom she genuinely liked. Sometimes he reproved her gently but, in general, he viewed her exhibitionism with good-natured understanding. He wrote to Nellie that she was simple, straightforward, and in some respects younger than her years. She had generous impulses but lacked discipline. He disapproved of her taste for gambling and considered her conversation with Nick too sophisticated at times for her years. Although self-absorbed the Secretary thought Alice completely honest and forthright. He was relieved to find that she made a good impression wherever they went, conducting herself in what Taft considered an attractive and dignified way, except for a few lapses in Japan. In the Philippines his friends Legardo and Tavera were quite bewitched by her.

It took Taft some time to believe that she and Nick were serious in their romance, although he could see that Longworth's knack for saying bright and original things diverted her. At times she became so absorbed in him that she ignored people she was supposed to greet. One day Taft asked her outright if she were engaged to Nick.

"Alice, I think I ought to know," he said.

"More or less, Mr. Secretary, more or less," Alice replied and that was the end of it.

It was not until they reached Nagasaki in August that she finally told him she was engaged but did not expect to be married for a year or more. He still felt skeptical that she would go through with it. They spent five magical days in Honolulu, with songs and leis, flying fish and moonlight to beguile them. Alice learned to dance the hula-hula and a song was written in her honor. They drove to Pali and took a special train to a sugar plantation. When they swam and surf-boated Taft asked the photographers to refrain from taking pictures of Alice in her bathing suit— not that Alice would have minded, since it was quite a creation of mohair with sleeves and a high neck, finished off at the other end with long black stockings. In order to catch the tide the ship sailed off without her, and Alice, Nick, the Newlands, and several others had to pursue the *Manchuria* by motorboat.

As they steamed from Honolulu for Japan Miss Roosevelt made headlines by plunging fully clad into the swimming pool on deck. Her old friend W. Bourke Cochran had joined their party and they were standing together looking at the outdoor pool when Cochran said in his booming voice that it looked so inviting he was tempted to jump in just as he was.

"Come along," Alice challenged him.

She kicked off her shoes and plunged in without a moment's hesitation. Cochran dived after her and the passengers crowded around to watch the President's daughter stroking her way across the pool in a whirl of petticoats. The newspapers lost no time in whipping up this incident on Mr. Taft's Ark in the Pacific.

Both at Yokohama and Tokyo crowds followed the party around and Alice thought that she detected teeth behind the barking roar of "Banzai," but Taft could find no evidence of anti-American feeling. Roosevelt had virtually forced Russia and Japan to agree to the peace conference that was held later that year in New Hampshire and resulted in the Treaty of Portsmouth. Taft was the advance guard on negotiations and the diplomatic reasoning behind his mission was complicated and confidential. Roosevelt wished him to sound out Count Taro Katsura, the Japanese premier, on the destiny of Korea, which Japan meant to absorb now that the war was won. Stories were being circulated in the United States that Japan also had designs on the Philippines. Katsura denied this to the Secretary of War and made it clear that he favored an understanding between the United States, Japan, and Britain to uphold the Open Door principles propounded by John Hay.

The Japanese premier fished blandly for a definite understanding of some sort but Taft told him that the President could not have even the most informal understanding without the approval of the Senate. However, he assured Katsura that Americans were in full accord with the policy of Japan and Great Britain in maintaining peace in the Far East and that he could count on their support.

It was delicate negotiation, since the Secretary could not make promises, but it was the kind at which he excelled. Roosevelt, who believed that the safety of American trade interests depended on a balance of power between Russia and Japan, was pleased with Taft's report. But when the Peace Conference was held in August the Japanese were chagrined that Russia was not required to pay them an indemnity. There were riots in Tokyo in September over this, since the people felt that it denied them total victory. Although they were allowed to dominate Korea there was still a residue of bitter feeling toward the United States.

While in Tokyo Taft was entertained at Shiba Palace, which had been built originally for General Grant's reception on his world tour. The party lunched with the Emperor, who gave Taft a private audience. The Empress showered lacquer and priceless embroideries on Alice. "I did so love my loot," she wrote of the costumes, fans, and souvenirs of all kinds that came her way in Japan. The Cherry Blossom Festival was staged for their benefit and the Government used all its resources to honor Theodore Roosevelt's daughter. Alice finally wearied of the ceremonial and showed a touch of boredom.

Taft sent his wife a detailed account of their reception in the Philippines, knowing how much she cared for the islands. "How I wish you were here for I am very sure that you would enjoy it all," he wrote. A great gathering of Filipinos greeted him and he was entertained by W. Cameron Forbes, a grandson of Ralph Waldo Emerson, who was also a millionaire who wished to serve his country. Surveying the scene with which he was so familiar Taft decided that Forbes had done good work in simplifying governmental methods. At this time the New Englander was a member of the Philippine Commission and would become governor of the islands in 1909.

Once again Taft had an official reception, a parade with floats, cheering crowds of Filipinos. "I love the noble Filipino people," he said in a formal address at Malacanan Palace. "Every face suggests something of crisis or something of interest that filled four years of the life that I spent on these islands." But again he told them that the time had not yet come for independence.

Taft received the gold key of Manila and toured the islands in the old fashion, making speeches, observing, asking questions, listening, urging the people to work hard and to have faith in the justice of the American people. They, in turn, stared with interest at the legislators from Washington and at Alice Roosevelt, who paraded in red linen, swinging a red parasol over a red hat when she and the Secretary of War led a party up the little wharf at Iloilo to be greeted by the Sultan of Sulu. He gave Alice pearls and a saddle, and Taft a Morro cannon. At a military ball the girls danced the rigadoon, wearing the mestizo costume, and Miss Boardman wrote to her mother that "Secty Taft, very light on his feet, danced the rigadoon too."

Before they left they saw native dances, sham battles, bull fights, and fiestas of all kinds. Years later Alice wrote: "The palms and the ocean were like a drop scene, one felt as though a highly colored stage setting had suddenly become real." They were all a little bewitched by the tropical surroundings, the round of parties, the haunting music, but Taft, well used to these conditions, kept them on a steady keel, so that peace and harmony prevailed for the entire period of three months. He sent Mrs. Taft profiles of the personalities on board, with some penetrating character studies, from Cochran's pretentious ways to Alice's latest whim.

The friendships formed on this trip carried over into later years. Taft was always to be fond of Alice, even when she took her father's side with passion after he split with his former favorite. He was also to see much of Miss Boardman after their return home. She was one of three sisters well known in Washington. One was Mrs. Murray Crane, wife of the New England paper manufacturer and a strong figure in the Republican Party. Another was Mrs. Florence Keep. Mabel was engaged in pulling the American Red Cross out of the backwater into which it had sunk. President Roosevelt had appointed her a member of the central committee and she and the Secretary of War had already been in correspondence.

Many years earlier Taft had known her father, William Boardman, in Cleveland. He wrote now to his wife that he was impressed with Miss Boardman's common sense, her good nature, and her wide knowledge of life and affairs. He considered her a steadying influence on their butterfly Alice. She seemed to him to be the strongest character among his fellow diners and Mrs. Newlands the most charming. After another seven weeks he wrote again to his wife about Miss Boardman: "She is a girl of very high character and quite attractive to me and wears better than anyone else on the trip."

While they were in Yokohama Mabel gave him a bronze elephant and he assured her that in moments of self-doubt it would spur him to greater effort. After thirty, few real friendships were made, he wrote, but in her he had found both charm and character and he hoped that they would continue to be friends and that she and his wife would be equally responsive to each other. This was the beginning of a friendship that became more or less historic in Washington and embraced the entire Taft family. William Howard Taft and Mabel Boardman soon embarked on a detailed correspondence that illumined the period, both on the official and social side. On her part it developed into a Sunday night diary of events, recording the week's activites. Since she dined regularly with the diplomats and the leading men and women in government circles, she astutely followed developments during Taft's political rise and at times acted as an unofficial adviser. He wrote to her constantly, too, and sent her copies of his more important official letters, thus creating an informal history of his years in office.

With their mission ended the party split up at Hong Kong. Alice Roosevelt, Nicholas Longworth, Mabel Boardman, Amy McMillan, Bourke Cochran, and the Newlands continued up the coast on a transport. They sailed by way of the Yellow Sea to Tientsin, and then went on to Peking. The Secretary of War at this point sailed for home.

Meanwhile, Mrs. Taft coped with British weather and mishaps of one kind or another in England. There were times when she wished she had chosen to take the Philippine trip with her husband, but she had decided that a quiet life in England would be better for the children than the excitement of a congressional jaunt. They bicycled along country byways and rented a punt, as well as a big family boat. They watched cricket matches and went swimming in a pool. Mrs. Agnes Exston, of Cincinnati, and her children, Frederick and Katharine, shared their house. It rained nearly every day but this did not bother the children. Helen wrote cheerfully to her father: "Frederick and I go out in the canoe together a good deal and when there is any wind we sail with an umbrella. Our one ambition is to turn over and we have come pretty near it once or twice. The river is so narrow that we couldn't drown if we tried."

Robert joined them late in the season after his North Cape trip and he enjoyed the brief period he spent in England. He went canoeing, rowing, bicycling, and played tennis, but, like Helen, he longed for more young companions. Mrs. Taft was determined that they should tour and see the traditional sights, but she found the English snobbish on this un-official visit and came to the conclusion that she would never wish her husband to be an ambassador there. Meanwhile, she followed the reports of the Philippine trip with great interest, and commented from time to time on Alice Roosevelt's actions, as reported in the press. Will's cor-respondence seemed to her to lag and she chided him gently in a letter written on an August day: "I fear the ladies on board have been so fas-cinating as to prevent your writing. I love you very much even if you don't write to me as you used to do." But long before this letter reached him Will had already written: "I try to imagine you in Oxford and on the Thames. Remember, darling, that I might go twice ten thousand miles but I would never find a girl I could love as I do you, darling."

However, what really worried Mrs. Taft, whose ambition never slept, was the fact that Elihu Root had been appointed secretary of state when John Hay died during her husband's absence. She insisted that if he had not gone to the Philippines the post would have been his. Will did not agree with her on this. He was quite without envy of his fellow men and he greatly admired Elihu Root. But he was surprised that Root had accepted the post. Mrs. Root had disliked Washington on their earlier stay, but neither had she found contentment in New York. President Roosevelt had written to Henry Cabot Lodge that he had hesitated be-tween Root and Taft because he liked both men so well that he wished to have their combined services. He had been functioning as his own secre-tary of state with John Hay fading into the shadows. The President had told Root that he was committed to Taft for the Presidency, insofar as his influence might properly go. Taft knew this and he inferred that Root was not thinking in terms of the White House—"though you never can tell," he wrote to Nellie, to whom he always revealed the inner workings of his mind. "If the Chief Justice would retire how simple everything would become," he added, with the old longing coming again to the sur-face.

But the feeling prevailed at home that Taft had lost ground to Root during his absence and that the President was grooming Elihu to be his successor. Actually, it was Taft who had urged the President to keep Root in the Cabinet and there was the utmost good feeling between the two men. He expressed his pleasure at once over the appointment and urged the President to give Root the Panama Canal project to han-dle, but Roosevelt hesitated on this. The State Department was in des-perate need of new life. He had always been devoted to Hay, whose wit and charm had never failed to interest him; but he felt a lack of dynamism in the man who had been so significant a figure on the Washington scene from the days of Lincoln. "I think he was the most delightful man to talk to I ever met," Roosevelt wrote to Lodge on January 28, 1909: "He was at his best at a dinner table or in a drawing room. . . . He had a very ease-loving nature, and a moral timidity which made him shrink from all that was rough in life. . . . But he was not a great Secty of State . . . he was not to be mentioned in the same breath with Root."

Mrs. Roosevelt did not share her husband's enthusiasm for Root. Alice attributed this to the fact that he had once laughed when her athletic father had a severe fall on one of his walking trips. He had made so many of his associates suffer and sweat on these exhausting marathons that Root felt he was getting some of his own medicine. It was a current jest that Root had run out of excuses to avoid these expeditions and that he had killed off his grandmother more than once.

While Taft was heading back from the East and his wife from England, a big family gathering was held at Millbury to celebrate Aunt Delia's eightieth birthday. She and Louise had been following his adventures in the East with intense interest. Will arrived first and waited anxiously for his family to land. There had been a flurry of excitement as they left London. The boys had been assigned to look after the trunks but everything had gone awry when King Edward VII arrived at the station where they were. When Mrs. Taft and Mrs. Exston came on the scene they found that the boys had muffed directions and the trunks were at another station.

Nellie rushed into the stationmaster's office and for once in her life pulled rank. "I am Mrs. William Howard Taft of Washington," she announced. "I must get my trunks on that boat train. They'll be here in a few minutes. Can't you hold it for me? My husband is the Secretary of War of the United States."

The stationmaster looked blank. Then Nellie played her trump card. "He's traveling now with Miss Alice Roosevelt," she told him.

That did it. The train was held; the trunks were handled with expedition; and they caught the ship. This was one of the first stories Taft heard when he welcomed his family in New York. He was chagrined to find that his wife was run-down and frail after her summer abroad. She had not enjoyed the experience, nor was she pleased with the gowns she had picked up in Paris. Above all, she was depressed because Will had missed the political opportunity that might have taken him one step closer to the White House. Annie had returned from Europe with magnificent clothes, new jewels, exciting objects of art. She was now showing keen interest in the family investments but was insouciant when they went wrong. Charles's Packard was a new plaything and she drove around Cincinnati enjoying herself.

Maria was completely charmed by little Charlie on his return from England. She found him "beautiful as an angel in his blue coat and hat and he behaved like one." They had all gone to Cincinnati on their return but were back in Washington for Christmas. As usual, Charles gave his brother a generous sum of money and Will responded: "You brightened a Christmas that has its shadows. I am getting very tired of being abused for mistakes I did not commit. Doubtless I have made enough of my own."

Taft was smarting over the effects of a speech he had made in Akron in October, 1905. It had demoralized the local Republican organization in Cincinnati and was an incident that churned up ill-will in the months that followed. He had gone to Ohio to speak for Myron T. Herrick, who was running for re-election as governor. Herrick had been charged with being subservient to Cox, the party boss. Taft did not believe that he was and said so. He announced that if he were there to vote he would cast his own ballot against the Republican municipal ticket, while supporting his party on the state ticket. In the end the entire list of candidates was elected except Herrick who, however, did not blame Taft for his defeat. Independent Republicans applauded the Secretary of War for his courage in speaking out against the machine. His brother was embarrassed locally but Will wrote to his wife that he would not be classed as a Cox man, even at the expense of "hurting lovable Charles's feelings." Foraker and his friends at once began to beat the drums for reorganization, claiming that he was the legitimate party leader. Taft's son, young Charlie, would pursue the same course for municipal reform, but the Secretary of War had made his last stand as a reform leader in Ohio.

Soon after his return home Taft made a determined effort to lose weight, since he had reached the point where he could scarcely stay awake. Nellie often had to jog him to attention when he dozed off in public. Finally he agreed to observe the dietary rules laid down for him by Dr. N. E. Yorke-Davis, a Harley Street specialist in nutrition. Under his wife's careful management this worked wonders. Taft came closer to his own conception of physical fitness when he reached a low of 255 pounds in the spring of 1906. He had been 314 pounds in the previous December. The experiment cost him $400 for the alteration of his clothes, which he jestingly said was a small price to pay for his improved physical condition.

Mrs. Taft's influence with her husband was a paramount factor early in 1906 in projecting him squarely into the presidential picture. When

Justice Henry B. Brown retired from the Supreme Court Taft again
seemed to be the inevitable candidate. The Tafts were visiting Mr.
and Mrs. John Hays Hammond in Lakewood, New Jersey, when President Roosevelt telephoned Will to ask if he would accept the appointment. Mrs. Taft protested at once. So did Hammond. Each felt that the
presidential nomination could be his in 1908. Had the offer been for the
Chief Justiceship things might have been different. Taft hesitated and
wrote expressing his uncertainty now that the prize was within reach.
Roosevelt called in Mrs. Taft for counsel, knowing how potent her influence was. She had told Will early in March that he would be making the
mistake of his life if he accepted the offer.

Mrs. Taft talked so convincingly to the President that he immediately
wrote to Will saying that after a "half-hour's talk with your dear wife" he
had a different view of matters. He conceded that if he were in the Secretary of War's shoes he would stay with the Department for three more
years, then abide the fall of the dice as to whether he became President,
continued in public office, or went back to the practice of law. But he
urged him not under any circumstances to break loose from Ohio.
Roosevelt told him frankly in this same letter, dated March 15, 1906, that
of all the men who had appeared on the horizon he was the most likely
presidential possibility, and the best man to receive it. Root would be
fully as good a President, he added, but he did not touch the people at as
many points as Taft and he did. The letter continued:

> I think you could do most as President, but you could do very much
> as Chief Justice; and you could do less, but still very much, either as
> Senator or as Associate Justice. Where you can fight best I cannot say,
> for you know what your soul turns to better than I can. . . . But it is
> well to remember that the shadow of the Presidency falls on no man
> twice, save in the most exceptional circumstances. . . . No one can
> with wisdom advise you.

In the social realm Washington was just recovering from the excitement of Alice Roosevelt's wedding.

Her marriage to Nicholas Longworth had taken place in the East
Room on a February morning in front of a window draped in cloth of
gold and roped with smilax and Easter lilies. The Blue Room was solidly
jammed for the reception and the guests talked for days of the brilliant
bride and her Ohio husband; of the necklace of sixty-three matched
pearls given her by the Republic of Cuba; of the dower chest from the
Dowager Empress of China; the antique jewelry from the king of Spain;
the pendant from the emperor of Austria, and the mosaic table from the
king of Italy. Alice was a fabulous bride who needed no bridesmaids to

attend her to the altar. By this time the whole world was aware of her daring and her intelligence.

Once Taft's decision to decline the justiceship was made, the path toward the White House was clearly marked, although he followed it with considerable reluctance of spirit. Some months later, on an October day in 1906, the President again sent for Mrs. Taft at a time when her husband was in the West. Roosevelt's purpose this time was to discuss the fact that Charles Evans Hughes was looming up strongly as a presidential candidate. Elihu Root was present but "as he is perfectly uninterested in me I can never talk to him," she reported later to Will. The conversation at the table was slow and forced, and Nellie had a sense of strain. She had no feminine support since Mrs. Roosevelt and Ethel were out on the river. Finally the President drew her over to a window seat and away from Root for a quiet talk. As usual, his conversation was all about Will, but she quickly saw that he was taking a new line as he emphasized the good campaign that Hughes was making in New York State for the governorship.

Roosevelt made it all too plain to Mrs. Taft that he thought she was consumed with an inordinate ambition to see her husband become President and he wished to warn her that this might never come to pass. He told her that while Will was his own first choice, if he was persona non grata with the party he might feel compelled to support Hughes, should he win in New York.

Mrs. Taft was furious. She reported to her husband that she had to restrain herself from saying: "Support whom you want, for all I care."

Her husband's reaction was to write at once to Roosevelt saying if he, the President, should decide to support Hughes it would be no disappointment to him. Two weeks later Taft told Root that it "would be a great thing for the country to have another term of Roosevelt." Nellie was profoundly irritated by her husband's determination to push the cause of Roosevelt, Hughes, Root, or any but his own. The President promptly assured him that Mrs. Taft had misunderstood what he had said. He had merely wished to get across the idea that he should not be so aloof and indifferent as to dishearten organization supporters.

The Tafts in conclave decided that Roosevelt had been applying a prod—to get Nellie to stir up her husband into taking more interest in the campaign, for the presidential boom for Taft was now in the making. Roosevelt did not propose to run for a third term. However, he held off for a long time from publicly showing his hand about Taft and he told William Allen White that he did not wish to interfere. Speculation was strong all through 1906 and 1907 that he might change his mind and decide to run again, or might be drafted on the spot. When he seemed to lean to Root the political pot bubbled. Then came the swing to Hughes. Neither Roosevelt nor Taft warmed to Hughes although they respected his integrity and ability. It was not until July, 1907, that the public could be sure the President was behind Taft. He considered open advocacy of the Secretary of War's cause to be impolitic.

This was only one of many occasions on which Mrs. Taft swayed her husband's decisions. He had high regard for her knowledge of human nature and was inclined to listen to what she had to say, even if he was not moved when his own convictions conflicted with her point of view. He had a court of four—his wife and three brothers—always in the wings and fully persuaded that Will was destined for the White House. But Taft had the judicial temperament and a will of his own. Roosevelt was never in any doubt about Mrs. Taft's ambition; in fact, she was so intense by nature that she made no secret of her aims. In her autobiography written many years later she disavowed any attempt to pose as a woman endowed with special comprehension of problems that men alone had been trained to handle. "I confess only to a lively interest in my husband's work, which I experienced from the beginning of our association, and which nothing in our long life together, neither monotony nor illness nor misfortune has served to lessen," she wrote.

But Taft was more realistic. He described his wife as the family politician who could meet all issues. Nellie could be sharp with him in giving advice, and even snap at him in public. She had the Herron candor, but functioned with quiet dignity as a Washington hostess. Her burning ambition was never far from the surface. Time and again she urged Will to hold out for the greater prize. But his mother, with her memories of Alphonso and her knowledge of Will's character, alone preferred the Supreme Court for him. Louise thought that Elihu Root should be President and her son chief justice and she did not hesitate to say so, even to the press. "I do not want my son to be president; he is not my candidate," she wrote. "His is a judicial mind, and he loves the law."

But Nellie believed that Will did not fully realize his potentialities. He discussed his political interests with her in detail and she was always an intelligent listener, ready to give him pointed and sharp appraisals of people and events. It was not in her nature to be insincere so she was able to supply the touch of skepticism that Taft lacked. Even when she nagged and criticized him he listened without resentment and gave thought to what she had to say. To observers she sometimes seemed invincible in her determination to see him get on. But in spite of this relentless drive, conscious or unconscious, she was respected and loved by her children and adored by her husband. Her likes and dislikes were well known to her friends. Actually, Mrs. Alphonso Taft had a more tolerant approach than Nellie to the varying temperaments of the women who married into the Taft family. But if some of them did not warm to Nellie they admired the way she ran her home and brought up her children. Although not a demanding mother she achieved results.

In dealing with her sisters-in-law Nellie was more disposed to avoid them than to run into head-on clashes, and the Herron sisters were always close to her. Will was particularly anxious for Nellie and Annie to understand and love each other but they were poles apart in outlook. Annie's munificence and her impetuous ways were foreign to Nellie's frugal, restrained habit of thought. Will, who was on good terms with all members of the family, catered tirelessly to his wife's moods. In return he seemed to find consolation and deep reserves in her. His open and generous nature shows itself clearly in the continuous stream of letters he sent to Nellie over the years.

Louise and Delia passed a lively winter in New York as Will moved closer to the Presidency. "I'm not sure what deviltry they may be up to this winter," he wrote to Charles of their mother and aunt. Actually, they were attending lectures on Browning, seeking out the best Unitarian preachers, playing bridge, and going to the theater. Louise belonged to the League for Political Education and listened quietly to the views of the new generation. There was much she could have told them. "I may be renewing my youth or else getting in my dotage," she wrote to Will on a February day in 1906.

The Tafts had scarcely settled down in Murray Bay that summer before the Secretary had to set off for Cuba. In one of the recurrent Cuban crises, Tomás Palma, first president of this troubled republic, had asked for military aid and President Roosevelt responded. Palma had decided to give up his office and force the United States to assume responsibility for the government. Roosevelt held a conference at Oyster Bay and decided that Taft would be the ideal conciliator. When he arrived on the scene with Robert Bacon, Assistant Secretary of State, he found Palma still in power, but camping outside Havana. There were 20,000 men under arms, ready for trouble. The Secretary of War passed ten of the most miserable days of his life before the insurgents were disarmed and a provisional government was set up without resort to military force. Taft was deeply depressed as he coped with this crisis. He wrote to Nellie that his vitality and optimism were failing him and in a moment of acute depression, quite alien to his cheerful temperament, he added:

> I am in a condition of mind where I can hardly do anything with sequence. I would give a great deal to talk it over with you, my own sweet darling. You could help me so much with your sympathy. . . .
> I am looking out on to Havana Bay and were it not for you and the children and others near and dear I should not regret it if one of the bolts now flashing and resounding struck me. Never in all my life have

I encountered such lack of moral stamina as there is among Cuban
politicians.

A thunderstorm raged as he wrote. In the voluminous correspondence
of a lifetime this was one of the rare occasions on which Taft showed a
flash of despair. It was a letter that also revealed how much he depended
on his wife for comfort and advice. But next day he apologized for the
doleful tone of this letter. He felt that the Cubans were quite unfit to
govern themselves and he wrote that it was harder to find an honest man
in Havana than in Manila. There was strong feeling at this time for annexation by the United States. But order was restored within a month
and the Secretary of War turned over the governorship to Charles E.
Magoon, brought from Panama for the purpose.

With the Palma administration out he asked Nellie to join him in the
historic old palace in Havana. She was mistress of this establishment for
three days, but found it as gloomy as Spring Grove Cemetery. "Had we
come in and at once supported the constituted government, we should
have had a war on our hands," Will wrote to Charles. But the people did
not keep faith in the surrender of their arms. They concealed the good
weapons and gave up the poor ones. American troops were sent to the
island to prevent rioting. A Cuban cabinet was appointed, with American advisers to help them. The local governments were reorganized and
early in 1909 the provisional governor turned over his authority to a duly
elected president, and the Cuban republic entered on the second phase
of its history.

This was one of many difficult missions that Taft undertook. He was
overwhelmed with work as he coped with problems involving the Philippines, the Panama Canal, and Cuba; the San Francisco disaster; and
routine army matters. He had to appear before committees and give testimony on a wide variety of subjects. The constant sniping at the operations in the Canal Zone worried him and he was upset when Poultney
Bigelow, author and journalist, made a savage attack on him. Echoes of
the battle were reflected in the witty, affectionate correspondence that
passed between Root and Taft, two men who understood and valued
each other. Root signed himself Athos and Taft Porthos in their letters.
Porthos was inclined to be diffuse in his; Athos was succinct and slyly
witty. Roosevelt was D'Artagnan. Cartoonists had labeled these three
powerful and congenial men The Three Musketeers and this image became well lodged in the public mind.

Although Taft was always on the brink of a volcano in the War Department these were useful and enjoyable years for him. He and Nellie were
firmly established in the inner circle in Washington and, thanks to
Charles, they were able to serve champagne instead of high tea. "The

truth is . . . that we could not live here at all, we couldn't have come into the Cabinet, if it had not been for you," Will wrote to his brother. But in the spring of 1907, when Cabinet salaries were raised to $12,000 he insisted that Charles reduce his monthy payments. This was a year of financial panic but Taft refused to become excited about the stock market; he thought that the country was becoming more independent of Wall Street influences. In many ways he made it clear that he enjoyed being in the Roosevelt Cabinet and he told his intimates that he felt his own strength lay largely in being the friend of Teddy. Taft brought good cheer to the War Department and tested his own administrative strength. Meanwhile, Nellie enjoyed life in the capital as a Cabinet officer's wife.

Her husband was not so busy that he could not enjoy the lighter moments of his life at home. He was in his office, clearing up business matters before heading west to speak for Roosevelt, when Charlie appeared, looking for a box of elastics to give to his teacher. Quentin Roosevelt had used this beguilement and Charles felt that he must follow suit. He rollicked around on his new roller skates and adapted himself as easily to life in Washington as he had to his rural summer in England, to the Philippines, to Murray Bay, or to Cincinnati. His mother worried when she saw him dashing about with a bottle of cough medicine and a spoon in his pocket, but Charlie always found the original way to cope with things. Like the rest of his family he had become friendly with the Boardmans. The Secretary's prediction that his wife and Miss Boardman would become friends had come to pass and they now saw each other constantly. Charlie stayed overnight at the Boardman house when his parents were away and he liked to practice on the family typewriter. A megaphone he had acquired added to the family noise and gaiety, and on Christmas Eve, 1905, he wrote to his mother: "Please don't get me a kodak, because Miss Boardman gave me one. P.S. Don't make me give it up."

Helen was confirmed early in 1906 and that year she attended her first school dance. She was apt to be shy at social functions, a fact which worried her mother. But her father laughed it off and wrote to Nellie: "You have a nightmare about a lack of the social instinct in your children. Don't worry about Helen. She'll get on because she's got a good head." But Helen grew stronger after entering the Baldwin School in preparation for Bryn Mawr. She played hockey and basketball and took long country walks, sometimes with mud up to her knees. She was delighted with her school but prepared her parents for the worst where marks were concerned. "I love it here but we have to work awfully hard," she wrote to her father on November 18, 1906. "You mustn't be disappointed if my marks seem very low for they have a way here of marking everybody extremely low."

Although she always did well Helen was less zealous about her marks than the other members of the family. She shared her father's sense of fun to a marked degree. Meanwhile Bob plodded along with unvarying success at the Taft School. In the spring of 1906 he led in every class and was perfect in geometry, but debating was a real hurdle for him. He grasped arguments easily but was apt to be tongue-tied, said Horace of the future Mr. Republican. He whose speeches, if not eloquent, would always be arresting, seemed to his uncle to fail in sharp, forceful expression. His voice was harsh in timbre and he was apt to use it too emphatically in debate. But in spite of these flaws Bob was a determined orator. He never missed a chance to get into a debate or a speech contest. And he worked hard to improve his style. He was now almost as tall as his father and was showing great independence in running his affairs. He handled his own funds and paid his own bills, asking fifteen dollars a month for allowance, His handwriting had matured and he was gaining in confidence. Bob had become self-contained. The dinner dances were now of some consequence in his life, in spite of his clumsy footwork. At no time did Robert match his father's grace on the dance floor. By the end of the summer of 1906 he was at peace in the knowledge that he had passed his examinations for Yale. The third generation would now stroll under the elms and add to the academic distinction of the Tafts.

Bob's father became a member of the Yale Corporation that year. He was elected for a second term in 1912 and resigned in 1913. At the moment Taft was proud to see his son step into the familiar quadrangle and in the midst of all the political buffeting in Cuba he took time to give the boy encouragement, writing to him on October 4, 1906:

> I have thought of your beginning college life and wondered whether you had become at all acclimated and accustomed to the atmosphere of old Yale. This last two weeks for me has been so much of a trial, and so full of trouble and excitement, that I have longed for the academic shades of New Haven as a quiet place where I could enjoy a nice rest and take the exercise I need. . . . With the greatest pride in you, my dear boy, and the confidence that you will make the best of your college life. . . .

Taft was equally interested in Helen's start at the Baldwin School. Charles now offered to send him $2,500 a quarter to meet the increased expenses of his children's education since he did not wish Will to have financial worries. But he and Annie declined the invitation sent them by Will and Nellie for the dinner they were giving for President Roosevelt just before Christmas, 1906, The Cincinnati Tafts had engaged F. Hopkinson Smith to lecture at their home on "Plantation Days" and Annie would never abandon an engagement in her native city to go to the capital or anywhere else. Charles had heard Smith speak at the Century Club in New York and decided that he would make good parlor entertainment for their Literary Club. They had just acquired Sir Henry Raeburn's portrait of Edward Satchwell Fraser and Jules Dupré's "Landscape with Cattle."

Charles was trying to get out of the Cleveland Gas Company, which was suffering from competition. He and Annie together had four million dollars invested in it. He was part owner of the Cubs, having bought into the team in 1905. They were National League champions in 1907, 1908, and 1910, and won the World Series in 1907 and 1908. The club had more than paid for itself in the first year. Charles and Annie in a sense were the keystone of the strong arch the Tafts were building across the country. All the members of the family were indebted to this generous pair at one time or another, but in each case it paid off—Horace with his school that prospered; Harry with his practice that grew; Will with his expanding political career.

Harry was making rapid strides ahead and in Will's estimation was "living like a lord." He had a large town house, gave elaborate dinner parties, had a butler, a fine new automobile, and traveled at will. But what seemed important to his brother was his genuine success at the bar. Justice Harlan had spoken of the excellent impression he made in an argument before the Supreme Court in January, 1906. Harry was trying at this time to pull out of the American Tobacco Trust investigation, which he was finding an embarrassment and a burden. He had devoted much of his time to it for two years, at the expense of his law business and his health. Four or five more years of hard work lay ahead if it were to be done thoroughly, and Harry believed in doing things to the limit of his capacity. "I can't do it and be faithful to relations which I formed before I undertook the work," he observed.

With his strong feeling for his profession Harry was perhaps most truly the lawyer of the Taft family, and at the end of 1906 he wrote sympathetically to Will: "In spite of the newspapers' insistence on presidential aspirations and their statements that your Cincinnati and New York brothers are urging you to stay in politics, I for one would be most gratified to see you Chief Justice." But as Will moved steadily into the forefront in 1907 as a presidential candidate he was embarrassed at times by the maneuverings of his zealous brothers. On January 1 he wrote to Charles: "I suppose it is unreasonable but I would be very glad to avoid the slightest appearance of getting into a political contest for I have no spirit for it. I sincerely hope you will keep everything favorable to my candidacy out of the *Times-Star*."

At Easter that year Nellie was storming that Charles should be muzzled for the Foraker row he was stirring up in his paper. It was becoming a national issue as Taft led the presidential race. "You have got yourself in an awful position by allowing him to take his own way," she wrote indignantly to Will. "You simply must make Charlie keep quiet. . . . With dearest love, even if you haven't come up to the scratch as a presidential candidate."

All possible strings were being pulled in Ohio for Taft's election, with Charles fighting like a tiger in a milieu that he understood. Foraker, who had helped to start Taft on the road that he himself now would like to travel, had been urged to support Taft for President if Will in turn would back him for the governorship. But Taft would make no concessions to Foraker, the bitter foe of Roosevelt in Ohio. He denied all patronage links with his native state and insisted that there was not a single appointee in Ohio, except possibly a judicial selection, on which he had advised the President. Foraker shouted defiance and decided to submit the question of the state's choice to direct primary. Charles accepted this with assurance and the Republican State Committee declared itself for Taft, who had told Roosevelt that rather than compromise with Foraker he would give up all hope of the Presidency.

This stirred up a storm on home ground that caused suffering to all the Tafts. Louise, with Alphonso's picture in her trunk wherever she went, wrote sympathetically to her son on a June day that year: "So near the throne you realize that uneasy lies the head that wears a crown. Roosevelt is a good fighter and enjoys it, but the malice of the politicians would make you miserable." Better than most she understood Ohio politics and she predicted that Foraker would now find out he could not rule Ohio. "I have a fancy that if the Taft standard were lifted there 'one blast upon that bugle horn' were worth a thousand men," wrote Louise, with invincible family pride. She knew that her son at heart was not a fighter. He smiled but suffered deeply under antagonism and criticism. Although he had weathered a good deal of both he was essentially a man of courtesy and restraint, floundering helplessly in the midst of political machination. His special skill lay in smoothing out difficulties rather than in doing battle.

As the campaign advanced Harry kept encouraging him, and warning him not to be bitter if defeated. Horace faced a decision also in the summer of 1907. He was offered the post of dean at Yale but decided not to accept it. His school was prospering and he felt he was not particularly suited for the functions of a dean although to Will he seemed the "ablest man in the country." Both brothers were summoned to Millbury in July when their mother's life was threatened by a severe gall bladder attack. Boston specialists were called in and she improved with treatment. Will was shocked by her appearance but she discussed the political situation as vigorously as though she had not been perilously ill. His visit braced up both sisters. He had been turning a deaf ear to their random requests to use his influence in some of their pet causes. He jested with his mother about her drive to have their maid's husband appointed to a marine captaincy. She had even taken up the matter with the Quartermaster when her son was not responsive. Will listened judicially when she and Delia urged him not to yield to the pressure of the engineers on power development for Niagara.

When President Roosevelt made it clear in July that he preferred Taft to Hughes for the nomination he promptly proposed a trip around the world for his candidate. Taft had promised to return to the Philippines for the opening of the first Assembly there and Roosevelt considered this a good opportunity for his favorite to spread his special brand of goodwill in different parts of the world. He was briefed at Oyster Bay, with Root on the scene to make it clear that this was not a diplomatic mission. He was to travel over the Trans-Siberian Railway but was to avoid Paris and London and give no impression anywhere of a royal progress. Nellie at once decided that Charlie and she would go with him.

They had only five weeks at Murray Bay that summer. Bob had finished his freshman year at Yale with a string of "A's." He was rowing, "heeling" for the *News*, and was a shark at his studies, his father told Nellie. They all welcomed Howard, Charles's son, home from a tour of Europe, and at the same time saw Walbridge off to Japan to meet celebrities and enlarge his horizons. Harry and Julia were at their own house at Murray Bay. Winifred and Horace were missing, but all were watching anxiously the prospects of William Howard Taft's try for the Presidency. The main Taft cottage had assumed the air of a campaign headquarters.

Their Canadian friends followed developments with interest. At Murray Bay they had come to know some of the notable public figures of the Dominion. Sir Charles Fitzpatrick, Chief Justice of Canada, and Taft had become good friends. Sir Wilfrid Laurier, the premier, offered him a government ship for a trip to the Gulf of St. Lawrence but he declined it. Justice Harlan, a fellow American, was often one of his associates on the links. Miss Boardman visited Murray Bay for the first time that summer and stayed with the Tafts, after being warned by Will of the austerity she would encounter in their "wooden tent." They all conferred on wedding gifts for Edith Root, Elihu Root's daughter who was marrying Ulysses S. Grant, III, and for Amy McMillan, their traveling companion on the Philippine trip, who was to become the bride of Sir Richard Harrington.

But there were speeches to be prepared before the Secretary of War set off for the Orient, and notably one at Columbus, which he felt would make or mar his chances of election. He had decided to talk on the tariff, the railway rate bill, the trusts, the concentration of wealth. He conceded that it was much too long—15,000 words—to the consternation of Nellie and Charles. "I shall be made fun of because of its length," he wrote to his wife. "But I am made this way and 'I can do no other.' That is the kind of an old slow coach you married. . . . Keep me in your thoughts about this speech. By some mental telepathy you may help me on." Nellie's response to this was consoling. "Never mind if you cannot get off fireworks," she wrote. "It must be known by this time that is not your style. . . . If people don't want you as you are, they can leave you, and we shall both be able to survive it."

In his Columbus speech Taft calmly held his ground in defending the capitalist system. He deplored William Jennings Bryan's wholesale approach to the subject and his desire "to extirpate trusts, root and branch," since his own view was that there were benign trusts and evil ones, and he preferred to judge each case on its own merits. "I believe that such large combinations legitimately conducted greatly add to the prosperity of the country," said Taft. "The captains of legitimate industry . . . are entitled to large reward, and it is impossible to impose a fixed limitation upon the amount which they may accumulate."

Instead of jailing those who had been found guilty of monopolistic practices he argued in favor of curbing their operations by injunction. In defending the Rooseveltian policies Taft said that they were not socialistic; nor was there anything radical or severe in the reforms he proposed. Taft's views, as always, were dictated entirely by his respect for the law, and by his own standards they were liberal, but the Progressives kept up a ceaseless chorus of disapproval.

Taft was received with great enthusiasm in Columbus and things went off better than he had expected. Still, he had doubts about his own prospects and immediately afterwards he wrote to his mother:

> Tell Aunt Delia that she must not get her hopes raised to the point of thinking that she is going to be a guest in the White House. If I am President, she will be a guest, but as that is the one condition upon which she can be a guest, I would tell her not to prepare her dress and wardrobe yet, for there are a great many difficulties in the way, any one of which might easily become insuperable.

As he traveled and made speeches Taft kept up a constant exchange with the President. He soon came to the conclusion that Roosevelt was stronger with the public than he knew, but in his own case he was not lulled to a false sense of security by the cheering crowds around him. Whenever possible he took a strong stand on behalf of the Negroes. He felt that they needed highly educated leaders to plead their cause and on different occasions he expressed indignation over the "blind and unreasonable assaults" on innocent people because of their color. Later, as

President, he tried to find places for them, an old interest of his father's and also of his. "The prejudice against them is so strong that it makes few places available, and yet I must do something for the race, for they are entitled to recognition," he wrote to Mrs. Taft.

On more than one public occasion Taft declared that he had not the slightest race prejudice or feeling, and that recognition of its existence only awakened in his heart deeper sympathy for those who had to suffer from it. He was sensitive on this subject since he had met with considerable criticism over the part he played in a shooting affray in 1906 at an army post in Brownsville, Texas. One man had been killed and two wounded at the post, and a preliminary investigation by army authorities sustained the complaints of the white residents that Negro soldiers were responsible for shooting up the town. All of the soldiers denied knowledge of the crimes but President Roosevelt issued a flat order that the men of the three army units stationed there be discharged.

Since the President was leaving at the time for Panama Taft had to act as disciplinarian. He advised Roosevelt to delay action because of the doubts in the case but the President wished him to go ahead. "I do not think he realizes quite the great feeling that has been aroused on the subject." Taft wrote to his wife on November 21, 1906. But he acknowledged to his brother Charles that although he was not responsible for the Brownsville order and had recommended a rehearing of the testimony, he considered it justified.

During the Senate investigation of this incident Senator Foraker attacked Taft bitterly and although the committee upheld the President's action, the Brownsville incident was later used as a point of attack on Taft, whose attitude to the Negro in general was enlightened and sympathetic. At an early date he was alert to the implications of the Jim Crow laws.

When Mrs. Taft joined him at Yellowstone she learned how strenuous political campaigning could be. They had three days to spend in the park and they drove fifty miles a day. By chance they played cards on a Sunday at Old Faithful Inn, thinking it was Saturday. Fearing repercussions from strict Sabbatarians Taft wrote apologetically to Roosevelt: "The truth is that Mrs. Taft is quite particular about not playing cards on Sunday, inheriting that from her early training, and not deriving it from her marital association." It was an entirely innocent breach of the Commandments and no one seemed to notice, but Taft was sensitive to every passing current. His last word as he sailed was to Horace: " 'Tis all a gamble, and I shall not be disappointed if I come back to find that the whole thing is 'busted.' I have had a run for my money and it has been a novel and not uninteresting experience."

In leaving the War Office he could look back on a considerable record as a conciliator. He had given impetus and order to operations in the Panama Canal. He had done the Philippines additional good from his desk in the War Office and had helped materially in the pacification of Cuba. He was now heading with distaste into a campaign that he knew he would not relish. "Politics makes me sick," he wrote to Nellie on more than one occasion.

Will sent his mother a message on her eightieth birthday and she answered with a faint scrawl at the end of one of Fanny's letters. It was the last word he ever received from her and it ended a long and brilliant correspondence. Knowing that she could not live he proposed giving up his trip to be near at hand. His mother was outraged. "No Taft, to my knowledge, has ever yet neglected a public duty for the sake of gratifying a private desire," she protested. He had promised the Filipinos that he would be present for the opening of their first Assembly and that was enough. Louise had watched his career from its beginning. She had prodded him as zealously as his wife and had done much to establish the family tradition.

CHAPTER 15

AROUND THE WORLD

LATE IN 1907 Mr. and Mrs. Taft, with ten-year-old Charlie, went around the world. They traveled through eight countries and covered 24,000 miles by land and sea. Taft was a worried man when he left, for he knew that his mother was soon to die. He was pessimistic, too, about his political prospects but he relaxed to the familiar hum of a ship headed for distant places. He walked six miles a day around the decks and watched Charlie's diverting games with his playfellows. His small son engaged in pillow fights and showed nimble fist- and foot-work while boxing with boys of his own age.

Their visit to Japan was the reopening of a familiar book. The Secretary's welcome was even warmer than the reception given him when he had arrived with Alice Longworth. Again he stayed at Shiba Palace and this time he had his fourth audience with the Emperor. His diplomacy on this occasion was directed toward Admiral Togo, Prince Oyama, and members of the political hierarchy in Japan. His "peace speech" was delivered at a banquet held at the Imperial Hotel in Tokyo. Contrary to his usual habit of last-minute preparation he had worked on it for weeks and the impact was immediate. It helped to clear the air of discordant currents in the diplomatic approaches following the Portsmouth Treaty.

Tumult broke out under the brilliant canopy of bunting, flowers, and lanterns as Taft bluntly emphasized the absurdity of war between the United States and Japan. He praised the heroism of the Japanese Army, deplored the riots in San Francisco over the so-called "Yellow Peril," and pointed out that the Treaty of Portsmouth had established Japan in the family of great world powers. Nevertheless, the Yellow Peril agitation on the West Coast continued until the time of Woodrow Wilson.

The Empress seemed to Mrs. Taft to be more frail than on her earlier visit and her voice was barely audible. She gave Charlie a small gold cabinet and lavished lacquer treasures on his mother. As a family the Tafts left Japan laden down with gifts, including a silver tea service from the residents of Yokohama. The merchants of Shanghai entertained them royally and Taft made another speech there that reaped a harvest of international attention. Again he promised that the United States would adhere vigorously to the Open Door policy advocated by John Hay. Before leaving the Chinese city he dedicated its Y.M.C.A., fostering an interest that was to become traditional in the Taft family.

For the time being the youngest Taft was a star performer as his family moved from point to point. His picture appeared in the newspapers and Japanese editors took him sightseeing in Tokyo. They gave him masks with which he goggled at the children on the ship. His father, writing to Charles in Cincinnati, pictured his small namesake at the Shiba Palace being waited on by five uniformed lackeys with all the nonchalance of a young prince who had enjoyed this sort of service since babyhood. In Nagasaki Mrs. John J. Pershing took him to see Japanese dances.

In the long run young Charlie was glad to be back in the Philippines, staying at the familiar Malacanan Palace. He and his mother were equally responsive to the blue and gold of Manila Bay, with the tree-filled ravines of Corregidor in the distance. They visited Cameron Forbes at Topside, his country estate 5,000 feet up on the island of Luzon. As he traveled around the islands Taft had a chance to see the results of his road-building policies, particularly where some of the old outposts had been brought into communication with the larger centers. He found conditions better than he had expected and considered Manila well-governed at this time. American businessmen had come round to seeing the value of measures that they had opposed when he was governor.

Familiar faces were all around him at the opening of the Assembly as he defined the terms of the Philippine Act, making it clear that independence was not close at hand but would come when the people as a whole were prepared for self-government. This was chilling to many, but it did not affect the welcome accorded the Tafts. They went through another exhausting round of functions until even Charlie had had enough.

He was soon doing setting-up exercises with the marines on the U.S.S. *Rainbow* as they sailed for Vladivostock in November, 1907, escorted by two naval vessels. Their party included Carpenter, General Clarence R. Edwards, Mr. and Mrs. Martin Egan, and two other correspondents. While in Manila word had reached Taft that his chances for the Presidency had improved. Hughes, his most formidable rival, was definitely out of the running.

A cold north wind blew as they landed in Russia. At Harbin they passed through lines of Chinese soldiers and a guard of Cossacks, mounted on shaggy ponies and carrying lances. Every day the train made several stops and the Tafts stepped out for exercise. Will, with the long fur-lined coat he had bought in Shanghai flapping at his heels, tried to keep up his usual vigorous gait. They came close to a serious accident when another train came at them head-on and stopped only a few feet short of collision. Nellie wakened abruptly when her electric lamp toppled down on her.

From Manchuria they moved into Siberia, and Charles in Cincinnati noted this fact in a letter to Delia: "I see by the papers this morning that Will's train has passed through Harbin on its way through Siberia. I never thought that a Taft would be going through Siberia in winter." Nellie thought that the good grazing land around them resembled the northern states of America, although sparsely populated. When they reached the steppes they passed herds of horses, and sleighs cutting picturesquely through the snowy desolation. While their train moved at a snail's pace Will read and studied reports, or played bridge. Although it was eighteen degrees below zero at Ufa the cars were warm. At the stations the natives crowded around, to sell them aquamarines and amethysts from the Ural Mountains. Questioning eyes stared at them from under hooded lids. Babies and bundles were underfoot wherever they went. A towering cake adorned with flowers and flags, and the date of the *Mayflower* landing mistakenly placed at 1662, was served them for Thanksgiving.

The governor of Moscow arranged that the Kremlin should be opened for them on Sunday. Mrs. Taft and Charlie drove in a droshky to a church service and then joined the rest of their party for a tour of the churches and palaces. The Americans in Moscow gave them a dinner that night at the Metropole Hotel and afterwards they attended a special performance of the ballet, ordered for their benefit by the governor. Since he had a daughter who was Charlie's contemporary, the youngest Taft had a social program of his own in Moscow. Mrs. Taft and Mrs. Egan explored the palace at the Kremlin and the Hall of St. George where the Imperial balls were given; then they visited the three small churches where the Czars were crowned and buried.

In St. Petersburg Taft had an audience with the Czar and again he used the diplomatic approach at which he was so adept. The Russians were resentful at the moment, believing that President Roosevelt and the American press had been partial to Japan at Portsmouth. One aspect of Taft's mission was to mollify the ruffled diplomats in Russia, and in subtle ways he emphasized the President's neutrality. However, the impression prevailed both at home and abroad that Roosevelt and Taft favored Japan. The Czar and Taft discussed the sale of Alaska, a subject on which the jurist was deeply versed since his handling of the Bering Sea dispute. They compared notes on military might, and although the Secretary of War had no predilection for guns and battleships his disciplined mind had absorbed the facts and policies of his department so that he was able to hold his own with the martial-minded Nicholas.

Since the Empress was ill Mrs. Taft was not officially received, but she was entertained by Princess Cantacuzene, the granddaughter of General Grant, who was living near the Russian capital. Heavily wrapped in furs she visited the Winter Palace and the Hermitage, and to see all sides of the picture she prowled in the thieves' market. Mrs. Taft considered the Russian women unfashionable in their attire. After attending a woman's luncheon she wrote in her diary: "My dress, which came from Paris, was quite a success considering that it has never fitted, but was not any better for the price than I could have bought in New York."

At Irkutsk she had an experience that she often described in later years at dinner parties. Roosevelt thought it a droll tale and encouraged her to tell it. In moving into a different train one of the officers meeting the Tafts at this stop whisked her away in a sleigh driven by two Orlovs. He wished to show her the sights. It was a bitterly cold, moonlit night and the pace of his horses alarmed Mrs. Taft, who thought they had bolted. General Edwards tried to follow but soon lost sight of the sleigh. They did a thorough tour and then her host took her to his house to meet his wife. On her return Nellie expected to find Will in a panic over her absence; instead he was peacefully asleep.

Helen and Bob wrote cheerfully to their parents along the way. Bob had made the fraternity he preferred at Yale. Helen was treasurer of the Glee Club at the Baldwin School and assistant business manager of the school annual. At this point her marks were not indicative of the brilliant future in store for her. Helen treated them with mirthful disdain, knowing that her parents expected nothing less than the best. "I send my report in case it may interest you," she wrote. "It doesn't me." Then, with a characteristic touch of the junior Taft brand of fun she added: "Give my respects to the Czar, Kaiser and King and any other big people you may meet."

But on this trip her father kept his meetings with rulers to a minimum.

Root had warned him against official receptions, and after he had fulfilled his delicate mission in Russia and Japan his diplomacy was inci-
dental during the rest of his tour. He was invited to be the guest of the
German emperor, the king of Belgium, and the president of France, but
he hurried through Berlin and on to Hamburg to join his ship, while
Nellie made a fast trip to Paris to buy clothes.

Taft was at sea on the *President Grant* on December 9, 1907, when
word reached him from Harry that his mother was dead. Charles had
sent him a warning cable to the American Embassy in St. Petersburg
four days earlier. Their trip home was shadowed by this news. Will had
impressed on Charles that there must be no formal reception for him
when he landed. Both Roosevelt and Root had emphasized the importance of this before he sailed for Russia. There were times when Will
feared his brother's potency as a newspaper editor and his ardor as a political backer.

After landing he made a quick trip to Cincinnati to lay a wreath on his
mother's grave. She was buried from the Pike Street house with the Reverend George A. Thayer conducting a simple Congregational service.
Verses from Whittier were read. Annie's reception room, looking like an
art gallery, was banked with flowers. Mrs. Perry, Mrs. Smith, Miss
Nourse, and all her old friends attended. The courts of Judges Lurton
and Severance adjourned for the day as lawyers and judges paid their last
respects to Mrs. Alphonso Taft. Annie wrote to Will: "Could one
hope for eighty happier more beautiful years than your mother enjoyed?"

They all remembered how pink-cheeked and vital she had been on her
eightieth birthday and Horace, who had watched her closely as her
time ran out, added his own encompassing view of his mother's life: "I
think the dominant note must be one of thankfulness for a life so exceptionally full of high ideals, practical duty and rich experience." An old
friend, living in Venice, recalled her at Anna's wedding, looking like a
Roman mother, with all the stateliness she had inherited from Samuel
Torrey.

As Louise left the scene, Anna's son, young Samuel T. Orton, whom
she had put through the Taft School, announced his engagement to
Mary P. Follett, a Wellesley graduate. Thus life went on, and no member of the family would deny the profound influence that Mrs. Alphonso
Taft had had on all their lives. Most bereft of all was Delia, forlorn after
a lifetime of close association with her sister. It was to Delia that Will
wrote with deep feeling on the day after Christmas, when he was back at
his desk in the War Department:

Our own sorrow is swallowed up almost in the sympathy with you.
For us, Mother's life of eighty years is a monument of high ideals, of

the pursuit of duty, and usefulness that falls to few people. There was that sturdy element that she got from her Puritan ancestors that was seen in everything she did, everything she said. Her dignity, her interest in her family, her pride in her children, all come back to one with overwhelming force now that she has gone. . . .

Delia was proud as well as poor and Horace proposed that they storm her entrenchments to persuade her to accept the financial plan they had worked out for her benefit. Will, Harry, Horace, and Fanny agreed to divide their mother's estate in five parts, giving Delia the fifth portion of the rent from the Vine Street property. The Herron girls were less well-off when Mrs. Herron's estate was finally appraised. It looked as if Maria would be almost penniless at a time when she was too old to learn to do anything to support herself, but in the end she led a spirited existence and traveled wherever she wished.

On his return from Russia Taft was immediately in the forefront of the presidential race. He began the year 1908 with the knowledge that Roosevelt definitely would not accept the nomination if it were offered to him. Root did not want it. George B. Cortelyou was pulling out. Although no official announcement was made word was subtly conveyed to the correspondents that Taft was the favored contender. On a January night in 1908, when the Tafts and Miss Boardman were dining with the Roosevelts, a significant incident occurred in the White House library. The President sank deep into a chair, threw back his head, closed his eyes and chanted: "I am the seventh son of a seventh daughter. I have clairvoyant powers. I see a man standing before me weighing about 350 pounds. There is something hanging over his head. I cannot make out what it is; it is hanging by a slender thread. At one time it looks like the Presidency—then again it looks like the Chief Justiceship."

"Make it the Presidency!" exclaimed Mrs. Taft.

"Make it the Chief Justiceship!" said William Howard Taft.

His trip had been a success and he had gained in national stature. Horace warned him to limit the length of his report on the Philippines, for Nellie had told him that it was almost as long as the Bible. By February she was deploring his comparison of Roosevelt with Lincoln in one of his speeches. Again her guiding hand was apparent when she wrote to Will:

> I do hope myself that you are not going to make any more speeches on the "Roosevelt policies" as I think they need to be let alone for the present, and you are simply aiding and abetting the President in keeping things stirred up. Let the corporations rest for a while. It is soon enough to talk about it, when something needs to be done.

Charles gave a year of his life to building up his brother's candidacy. He established headquarters in Ohio with A. I. Vorys in charge, and in New York with Charles D. Hilles, who had worked for McKinley in 1900. Gustav J. Karger, Washington correspondent of the *Times-Star*, became Taft's personal press representative. Another zealous aide was his secretary, Carpenter, a graduate of the University of Minnesota and a member of the bar. He had been with Taft in the Philippines and knew every mood and shade of feeling shown by the Governor. An astute observer, who would leave a lively record of his association with the Tafts, was on the scene in the person of Major Butt, Roosevelt's devoted aide whom they had come to know in the Philippines. Later he would apply a vivid touch to the Taft family history in his letters to his mother, Mrs. Joshua W. Butt, and to Mrs. Lewis F. Butt, his sister-in-law.

"He has a wonderfully well trained mind and seems to have none of the trouble of so many people in deciding questions," Archie wrote to his mother as he watched Taft wind up his business in the War Department. It was clear at once that he lacked Roosevelt's relish for publicity. He disliked the constant snapping of cameras and sometimes lost patience with the photographers. As the campaign got under way he was already desperately tired and was observed sound asleep on public platforms, driving in the street, and even when dining out. He would dictate to Carpenter while lying down to snatch some rest before an evening function. In May he caused an uproar by referring in a speech at Grant's Tomb to General Grant's victory over intemperance. Champions of the great General resented this allusion. Taft, like his parents, was devoted to the entire Grant family and he suffered intensely over this incident. It was one of his first ineptitudes as he moved closer to the White House.

That same month he made a return trip to the Canal zone to study the reorganization of the Canal Commission and to smooth out some of the confusion that resulted from jealousy and conflicting interest on financial and civil questions. Characteristically, on his way there he read a history of the Moors in Spain, another of France under Richelieu and Mazarin, and a book on the Congo Free State. Nellie always wished to know what he was reading and how he was observing his diet. But he gave little thought to either as he coped with the problems he found at Panama. By May 20 Horace wrote to him: "I see that you have smoothed things out in Panama after your fashion. Meanwhile everything has gone well in the land of Uncle Sam."

Shortly before his father sailed for Panama Charlie, by this time a regular visitor at the White House, shared in a good dressing-down from the President. Charlie, Quentin, and two other boys had been passing a rainy day indoors, getting more boisterous by the minute. Finally they made spitballs and plastered them on portraits. The President did not discover this until after dinner. He pulled Quentin out of bed and made him go around removing the spitballs. Next morning the other culprits were brought before him and were told that they had acted like boors. It would have been a disgrace to have behaved in this fashion in any gentleman's house, the President said, and it was a double disgrace in the House of the Nation. The punishment decreed was that Quentin would not be allowed any visitors, nor could the others come to the White House until the President felt they had been punished enough. The boys wilted under his glare, but Quentin stuck out his chin and remarked that Charlie was one of them and it would soon be his house anyway.

Charlie was a regular member of Quentin's gang and he participated in more mischief in the White House before he lived in it than afterwards. When doing a skit on the Spanish-American War Charlie, posing as a Spaniard, fell over a chair. Quentin descended on him with a saber and accidentally nicked his cheek. Charlie bled and Quentin, alarmed, hastily replaced the saber, which was a sacred relic that he was not supposed to touch. Other members of the gang smeared some of Charlie's blood over the brass feet of a chair to cover up for Quentin. When an usher marched the victim to Mrs. Roosevelt's room for first aid, the youngest Taft insisted that he had fallen over the chair. Charlie was only the best-publicized humorist among the Tafts. As his mother said: "We are a family that laughs. Both Mr. Taft and the children manage to get some fun out of almost everything." Mrs. Taft's own sense of humor was limited, but she enjoyed her family's merriment.

Charlie was by no means the average ten-year-old. He was an experienced boy who had traveled twice around the world and had seen strange sights in many lands. His thinking in the years to come would always have an international slant, as truly as Bob's would be based at home. He read with uncommon zeal, but his days were filled with a joyous round of parties and pleasure, even before he moved into the White House. Like all the other Tafts he flung himself deeply into the excitement of his father's campaign. Robert, who kept shrinking into the background at Yale when the subject was mentioned, played golf and tennis and made the second class crew in his sophomore year. Just before leaving to attend the convention in Chicago—his first experience of a national event that would both stir and agonize him in the future—he attended a dance at the Rosemary School in Greenwich and went to a house party in Washington, Connecticut, with four girls he had not known before. When it was over he wrote to his mother: "It was a great success, and we all fell in love but not seriously . . . we did quite a lot of driving and dancing, but there is no tennis or golf or anything else very much. Fussing is very well for two days, however," he finished.

The excitement in Chicago was intense. Robert slept at the Coliseum in a folding bed in his uncle Charlie's room, so that he had to retire late and get up early. He had never seen so many members of the family together at one time. Jane and Albert Ingalls had come in from Cleveland. Hulbert was there, a full-fledged newspaperman. All of Uncle Harry's family arrived except Walbridge, and all of Uncle Charles's but Howard. Robert had his first lesson in discretion with the press. "The reporters were thick," he noted, "but I managed to avoid most of them." However, newspapers were now a family heritage and the Tafts could never be dead to the necessities of journalism.

As the convention opened on June 16 the Ohio delegation marched in with Will Taft's face on a huge silk banner. Cheers broke loose, but any mention of Roosevelt still brought the loudest applause. On the second day a speech by Henry Cabot Lodge invoked a demonstration for the outgoing President that lasted for forty-nine minutes. Delegates jumped to their feet, yelling, waving their hats, clapping madly. Handkerchiefs, fans, and parasols fluttered in the galleries. On the day that his father was nominated, Bob could scarcely contain himself when the hall became a bedlam of shouts and cheers, placards bobbed up and down, and Taft was declared the winner on the first ballot.

The candidate received the returns quietly in his office in Washington, with Helen and Charlie at their mother's side. "Oh, my dear, my dear," Taft protested when his wife showed great distress over the prolonged applause for Roosevelt. When the nomination was made and it was Will's turn she listened attentively and counted the minutes it lasted. With characteristic frankness she said: "I . . . want it to last more than forty-nine minutes. I want to get even for the scare that Roosevelt cheer of forty-nine minutes gave me yesterday." It fell twenty minutes short of the Roosevelt ovation but it was enthusiastic, too. Charlie ran back and forth with bulletins as they came hot over the telegraph line. Newspapermen waited in the outside office of the War Department and the dispatches were read to them as fast as they arrived. Miss Boardman wrote enthusiastically to Mrs. Taft from Chicago: "It's all Will everywhere—buttons, flags, pictures. Nothing else to be seen or heard as far as the Presidency goes . . . it was a wonderful sight—and quite thrilling . . . tell Will the Philippine party were well to the fore."

Robert telegraphed to his father: "Congratulations on great victory from the whole family. Bob." Harry telegraphed to Delia: "Glorious victory. Will nominated first ballot. Over seven hundred votes." It was a family dream come true. Nellie kept a series of photographs taken of her husband's varying expressions as he followed the returns. He took it all quietly. But one member of the Philippine party who watched the outcome with mixed feelings was Alice Longworth, who was there with Nicholas. They stayed with Ruth and Medill McCormick and attended with her uncle and aunt, Mr. and Mrs. Douglas Robinson, and their daughter Corinne.

"I did not feel noble," Alice later wrote. "Not one little bit. All the same it was an interesting game—the game of putting Taft over. . . . I really do not believe I was boisterous. I was merely enormously keen and interested and occupied in having a very good time." But in her auto-biography, *Crowded Hours,* Alice confessed to the inner fire that burned her throughout:

> No one will ever know how much I wished, in the black depths of my heart, that "something would happen" and that Father would be re-nominated. It was against human nature, against mine anyway, not to feel that the prospect of all those great times coming to an end was something to be regretted, though most secretly.

Alice was scarcely aware of the presence of young Bob Taft, whom later she would come to admire and to back for the Presidency. On the surface Mr. and Mrs. Nicholas Longworth carried the Taft banner, and the President promptly announced that nowhere in the country could a man be found better fitted to be Chief Executive. In a burst of exuberance which he would soon regret he predicted that Taft would be as emphatic-ally a President of the plain people as Lincoln—"yet not Lincoln himself would be freer from the least taint of demagogy, the least tendency to arouse or appeal to any class hatred of any kind."

Annie wished that his mother might have lived to have seen Will so honored. Harry and Horace were quietly jubilant as they hurried back from Chicago to celebrate Horace's twenty-fifth anniversary at Yale. Again they were in the midst of a Taft accolade, since Will was the first Yale graduate to be a presidential candidate. Horace was interviewed and promptly apologized to Will for a gaucherie: "The New York *Herald* says I spoke feelingly of you as a father, brother & husband! D-n!"

But the next four months loomed like a nightmare ahead of William Howard Taft. Immediately after the convention he and Nellie went to Hot Springs for a rest. Taft's waistline, always so flexible, went down rap-idly after some horseback riding in the mountains and a week of steady tramping over the golf links. Nellie took baths for a mild case of rheu-matism. Charlie was learning to play golf. He fished, played tennis and, according to his father, "conducted an independent campaign on his own hook for enjoyment while Nellie looked on him fondly as the perfect boy, hard though it was to get him to brush his teeth, wear clean shirts, or otherwise observe the conventions."

Taft was fifty-one and he had been in public office almost continuously for nearly three decades. When accused of being an echo of the dynamic man in the White House he wrote that Roosevelt's views were his own long before he knew Teddy, so that he was not showing slavish imitation in arguing that the laws must apply to rich and poor alike, and that corporations must be brought into line under the statutes. He mustered all his forces for his acceptance speech and, as usual, he sought the advice of his brothers. Horace urged him to stand stiff as a ramrod on injunctions. He approved what he had to say on labor and the courts, but he thought him too florid in his allusions to Roosevelt and Nellie agreed. Harry pronounced the speech admirable. The President read it at Oyster Bay on a hot day in July and he too suggested less laudation of himself. Taft adopted some of his suggestions, but ignored others.

The family gathered again for the notification ceremonies which were held late in July, 1908, at the Pike Street house in Cincinnati. The historic porch was decorated with garlands, banners, flags. The thunder of guns and bursting of bombs ushered in the day and the flag was run up in the old Taft garden. Yale and Woodward students wore their class colors. Fred Grant was there with survivors of the Civil War, and a fife and drum corps of gray-haired veterans. The large hats and flimsy muslins of the Edwardian era gave the lawn a garden party air and Aunt Delia, who was never left out of anything by her nephew, primly took note of the scene. The city was crowded with celebrants. Japanese lanterns with Taft banners were strung along the hillsides, and sirens and whistles kept up a din. At night there were fireworks in Eden Park, for Ohio was en fête. Once again it was giving the nation a President.

With his speech effectively delivered Taft faced the strain and fatigue of campaigning. He was a most reluctant participant. As the mellifluous tones of William Jennings Bryan, Democratic candidate for the Presidency, cast their spell across the country, he hankered only for a restrained and dignified approach. This was what Horace had advised and his own instincts approved. But Theodore Roosevelt would not let it go at that. "Poor old boy! Of course you are not enjoying the campaign," he wrote to him from Oyster Bay on July 15, 1908. "I wish you had some of my bad temper. It is at times a real aid to enjoyment." He urged him to take the stump, to stay in hotels rather than in private homes so that more people could see him, to speak only once or twice in each state he visited, to choose his ground and fight aggressively, to put personality into the campaign. But when the time came for a smash it "should be conducted without ruth." Harry urged him to give a week to New York State and to speak in New York City's Lower East Side among the poorer classes, who were "both intelligent and not easy to fool." Will feared over-confidence in the East and watched Vermont with some anxiety.

In his campaign speeches Taft upheld the legal right of labor men to organize, to strike, and to enforce their demands in a peaceful way. He described the boycott in labor disputes as illegal and the closed shop as a weapon against the right of every man to work for whom he pleased.

Bryan, making the most of Taft's judgments during the Pullman strike, frequently called him the father of the injunction in industrial cases. Taft denied this, saying that the principles he laid down were not antagonistic to labor, and that they had even been used by labor to defend its rights in a subsequent controversy. He gave his audiences a precise statement on his stand as he went from one campaign meeting to another:

> I believe that there ought to be no favored class in litigation at all, that a man who has property and a man who has labor to sell shall stand on an equality in court, and that every man shall be entitled to be protected by all the writs and remedies that the law affords, by an impartial judiciary. . . .

Taft maintained that capitalists should be forced to obey the law like everyone else, but that the capitalist system was the best so far devised and should be preserved. He agreed with Bryan on one point only —that the high tariff rates were a weak link in the Republican policies. The jurist's views, as always, were dictated entirely by his respect for the law, and when speaking of labor he never failed to remind his audiences that in the War Department he had had 30,000 laborers working for him in Panama without complaint, and thousands more in other parts of the country.

The Democratic papers assailed him as he moved from point to point but, ever the citizen of the world, Taft could rise above the stifling waves of abuse and comment entertainingly to his wife on the landscape through which he passed, the colors, the crops, the sunsets, the manners and ideals of the people. Whether talking at Cooper Union Institute in New York or in his home territory Taft brought the same earnestness to his long speeches. Archie Butt thought that he pitched his campaign on a high plane, not making one demagogic appeal. Roosevelt tossed him a flowery bouquet in August: "You blessed old trump, I have always said you would be the greatest President, bar only Washington and Lincoln, and I feel mightily inclined to strike out the exceptions! My affection and respect for you are increased by your attitude about contributions. But really I think you are altogether oversensitive. . . ."

This comment was evoked by Taft's scrupulous attitude to party contributions. He shrank from those coming from large corporations. Roosevelt's campaign against Standard Oil was a fresh issue and he did not wish Taft or his campaign manager to accept a dollar from that source or from anyone connected with the company. But at the same time he felt his candidate was going too far in rejecting large contributions. By September Roosevelt felt that things were moving too slowly and he kept urging Taft on:

Hit them hard, old man! I feel that your nature shines out so trans-
parently when you do smile—you big, generous, high-minded fellow. . . . The trouble is that you would always rather fight for a principle or for a friend than for yourself. Now hit at them; challenge
Bryan on his record. . . . Do not answer Bryan; attack him! Don't
let *him* make issues and never define your religious belief.

By this time personal issues had cropped up and Roosevelt warned him
against publicity on his golf playing, and backed him up sternly on the
religious issue. Critical letters about Taft's golf were pouring in from
the West. The President took this seriously enough to write: "I don't
suppose you will have the chance to play until after election and whether
you have the chance or not, I hope you won't. . . . It is just like my
tennis. I never let any friends advertise my tennis, and never let a photo
of me in tennis costume appear."

But Taft not only enjoyed his golf; he considered it a health measure.
He was even more concerned over the censure of his Unitarianism, and
was particularly shocked when the pastor of the Second Presbyterian
Church in Cincinnati, attended by Charles and Annie, urged his con-
gregation to vote for Bryan. Actually, the Great Commoner's evangelicism highlighted this issue. He and others were highly critical of a candidate who did not accept the divinity of Christ. Taft had recently
joined the Unitarian church in Washington, where Dr. Ulysses G. B.
Pierce presided, and in October President Roosevelt made a point of
attending services with him. He reminded one of his enraged correspondents that in his Cabinet he had a Catholic, a Protestant Christian, and a
Jew, each man chosen for his special qualifications.

Prohibition also became a vexatious issue in the campaign, and
hatchet-slinging Carry Nation called on Taft in September, 1908, to
demand that he state his views on alcohol. When he did not answer her
questions she walked out and announced that he was a foe of temperance as well as an infidel. Taft, who was opposed to any law "that is not
enforced" was a completely temperate man all his life. "I am not a tee-
totaler, but I rarely drink anything," he explained. "It does not agree
with me and I know that I am better off without it. I am strongly in favor
of local option, because I believe in giving to the members of a locality,
either township or county, the opportunity to say whether liquor shall
be sold within the jurisdiction."

While Taft put up his somewhat halfhearted campaign, suffering
intensely from the brickbats hurled at him, and tired of ridiculous cartoons and jingles that had little relation either to his dignity or his intelligence, his family awaited the outcome with considerable assurance.
Charles was constantly at work behind the scenes, contributing time and

money to his brother's campaign. With Annie he visited Horace at his new summer home at Wainscott, Long Island, and with her quick eye for effect she pronounced it Turneresque and comfortable but flat compared with Murray Bay. Annie was cheered when John Drew came over from East Hampton to view the tableaux staged at the Taft School.

Horace was eager to speak on Will's behalf but both brothers were opposed to this. "I never felt so overpowered with discretion as I do in the present campaign," wrote the forthright Horace to Will. "Nothing would please me better than to tear loose and say things on all sorts of questions, but with you as the candidate I am a perfect model of conventional decorum." He assured Will that he was holding a place in his school for Charlie, who had been flirting with fame by having a letter published that he had written about his trip around the world.

In September the weary candidate took a brief rest with Nellie at Middle Bass Island in Ohio. He fished, in the presidential tradition, but failed to catch any bass. From there he wrote to Miss Boardman that if he were not elected he would not be in Washington that winter but would be living in a three-room flat in Cincinnati "rooting around for a living and trying to keep the bread in the mouths of my family." In the meantime Roosevelt confessed to Lodge that he was not tempted to snatch at the fringes of departing glory; indeed he was lucky enough to have strong tastes in more than one direction. "When I stop being President I will stop completely," he wrote. But Mrs. Taft felt that there was constant interference from the White House. When her husband was away and she was summoned suddenly for a conference she wrote: "I can't imagine what Teddy wants, but probably only to complain about something."

It was all bewildering to Taft, who rejected the public clamor that he wear a Rough Rider hat and frankly admitted that he could not be more aggressive than his nature allowed. The aura of Roosevelt's dynamism threatened to swamp him and the impression spread that the White House was doing all the work in the campaign. But if Taft did not have jubilant crowds as he moved from place to place he made a good impression and added to his own popularity by his temperate views on many issues and his self-evident honesty.

The Taft family gathered in strength in the Pike Street house on election day. The weather was clear and cold, ideal for getting out the Republican country vote. Will did not arrive from his last speechmaking stop until eight in the morning and except for going out to vote at four in the afternoon he passed the day in the house. Toward evening the returns were heard at the stately old mansion that had sheltered so many celebrities. Gus Karger read the bulletins to Mr. and Mrs. Taft and other members of the family. Alice Longworth had come in to hear them, too. By midnight the result was clearly indicated. Soon a band played outside and the Citizens Taft Club arrived to cheer the winner. A tired man went out on the porch and acknowledged their greeting. He had been talking for the preceding forty days and was exhausted. He promised that his administration would be a "worthy successor to that of Theodore Roosevelt."

A Taft would now be President. Nellie was quietly jubilant. Annie was madly happy. "Discipline gone to smash," Horace wired from Watertown as the boys ran wild, had a bonfire, rollicked around until early morning. Harry joined the family chorus by wire and Sheriff Maltais of Murray Bay telegraphed: "Murray Bay rejoicing at your victory." Alice later recalled: "I was delighted to see 'dear Mr. Secty.' win by such a huge figure." Taft gave all the credit to her father and his brother Charles. "My selection and election are chiefly your work," he wrote to Roosevelt on November 7, 1908. "You and my brother Charley made that possible which in all probability would not have occurred otherwise. I don't wish to be falsely modest about this."

Charles believed that he had everything to do with Will's election. So did Theodore Roosevelt, who was convinced that he alone had made it possible. Eventually the point became contentious and lay like a shadow between Roosevelt and Taft. But for the moment all was rejoicing at Pike Street. From there Mr. and Mrs. Taft went to Hot Springs, staying at a bungalow on a hill above the Bon Air Hotel. The limelight beat on them with all the intensity of their new role in the national life. Theodore Roosevelt now chose to address him as Mr. Taft instead of Will. But the President-elect was not elated. "I pinch myself every little while to make myself realize that it is all true," he said to a friend. "I feel just a bit like a fish out of water. However, as my wife is the politician and she will be able to meet all these issues, perhaps we can keep a stiff upper lip and overcome the obstacles that just at present seem formidable."

Helen entered Bryn Mawr that autumn and Charlie went off to the Taft School. It proved to be a fascinating world for him—a world of law and order. What he lacked in basic knowledge he more than made up for in worldly sophistication. All had waited with baited breath to see how Charlie would react to this environment. His Aunt Winifred hung up gay posters in his room and prodded him about brushing his teeth. He was more of a handful than Bob but a most beguiling one. Horace at this time bought three farms for $22,000 and invested another $8,000 in equipment. He had 300 chickens, 22 cows, several horses, and the dairy products and vegetables from his own land fed the school. But later he found this an impractical venture and sold his farms.

Immediately after the election Charlie wrote cheerfully to his father

that his marks were fairly good. History was his weak point, Latin his
strong one at the moment. He liked gymnasium and chinning himself,
and he had survived some rattling good snow fights. He was having a
great time and wished to stay at the Taft School for good, he announced.
There were ninety-one boarding students and ten day boys. "That's going some, from 13, in 18 years." Charlie commented and added: "Could
you please tell me where you are now and where you will be at Christmas. I'd like to keep better track of my father."

The President-elect, coping with more than 700 congratulatory messages, took careful note of Charlie's epistles and wrote to him with a humorous note of disapproval, reminding him what was expected of him
as a Taft:

> I am glad to note that you are enjoying your school days with Uncle
> Horace, but I fear that athletics and games and play are receiving a
> little more of your attention than history and some other of your
> studies, by the marks which you sent me. You know we have a pretty
> high standard in the family, with Robert and Helen before you, and
> we shall not be satisfied unless you keep up your end of the family. I
> hope that you will find it possible to study hard and play hard . . .
> all play and no work makes Jack a dull boy.

Charlie took heed. Between his father's promptings and Uncle Horace's firm challenge that he must come up to Bob's record, he was soon
making an average of 93. He was also manager of the Blues, an office that
Horace jestingly wrote was quite as important as the more exalted one
his father had. Aunt Winifred mounted guard on his comings and goings
and was scandalized when he went to Waterbury to meet his mother
without wearing a cap. Horace's wife was not thought to have a good understanding of small boys although she was in contact with them every
day.

Bob was starting on his junior year at Yale and he asked his father if he
would speak at the annual initiation banquet of his chapter of Psi U in
New Haven. The Yale Taft Club, which had worked enthusiastically for
his election, wished to present him with scrolls bearing their names. Bob,
quartered at Durfee Hall, had organized a debating club and was still
trying hard to polish his own style. "I really feel that I am improving a
great deal in speaking on my feet," wrote the future senator who would
never be at a loss for an argument.

The young Tafts were reunited with their parents in Augusta that
Christmas, to the satisfaction of their father, who thought that the no-
madic life he had been living had not been good for family discipline. "I
have to look over my children and see that they acquire a little more respect for their father now that he has fooled the country into making

him its chief magistrate," he wrote to Miss Boardman. He thought that Helen looked frail, and that her studies at Bryn Mawr might be too much for her. As usual, she was not enthusiastic about her marks. "If you pass here you are doing well," she explained, in humorous apology.

Bob went on from Augusta to Cincinnati to finish the Christmas holidays at the home of his Aunt Jennie—Mrs. Charles Anderson, who lived on the Grandin Road. She gave him a holiday whirl of parties with her own daughters, Jane, Katharine, and Harriet, and wrote to his father that he looked the "cutest thing, to borrow the girls' expression, in his swallow tail coat." She did her best for him as far as girls were concerned "but the time was very short and Bob does not put on as much speed in those matters as his father perhaps did at his age."

A family cloud hung over Pike Street that Christmas. Charles had tried for the Senate and had then withdrawn on the last day of the year. Joseph Benson Foraker, Theodore E. Burton, and he had all been in the running but Roosevelt, who was friendly enough to Charles Taft, thought that the most important thing of all was to beat Foraker. In addition to his other sins his name would now figure in the Standard Oil investigation. Will's hands were tied in the matter. When Charles withdrew he said that the party was more important to him than personal ambition. Foraker then dropped out and Burton, backed by Cox, was elected.

Annie was deeply hurt, not so much because her husband was out of the race as because of the bitter attacks of his newspaper competitors. She was convinced that Will had not wished him to run, and that the whole situation was embarrassing to the presidential nominee. Angry and saddened, Annie wrote to Will when her husband's withdrawal was ascribed, not to a sacrificial act on his part, but to a telegram from Will. Frantically she urged him to make a public statement giving Charles credit for his act and added:

> It drives me wild to see Charley worried. You know I care nothing for the position. . . . He could have had the whole thing any time if he had stooped to the usual political methods. He does not know I am writing this but I simply can't help it. It seems too hard that such a thrust should appear to come from you. . . . This may be a hysterical letter, but you know I have a great sorrow outside of politics—enough to upset one's life. On top of this to have Charley who is the most loyal honorable man alive abused in this time seems too much to bear. . . .

Charles and Annie were deeply worried, too, about their son Howard, who seemed to be heading toward a breakdown. As soon as Annie's letter reached Will he wrote to Charles from Augusta that he thought him wise to have pulled out. He did not doubt that he could have bought the votes but he was glad he had declined to do so. "I am delighted that

Foraker is out of the fight and out of politics," he wrote. "You stand better today in Ohio than you ever did before and I hope you will not lose the benefit of this experience." Charles replied mildly and without resentment: "Sometimes I think that the fellow with some money can not succeed in this kind of contest, because if he did, the members voting for him would be charged with bribery."

If Foraker had beaten Charles, at the same time Charles had beaten Foraker. They had canceled each other out. The presidential nominee wrote in a conciliatory tone to Burton that he was ready to start with a fresh slate. But clouds were already beginning to gather between Roosevelt and Taft, as the nominee went over the Cabinet lists and made his own decisions. Root's departure from the Cabinet made it difficult for him to find the right secretary of state. "The people I would select don't wish the places and those who would like the places don't commend themselves to me," he wrote to Delia on December 7, 1908.

But the affectionate note still prevailed between Taft and Roosevelt. On New Year's Day the outgoing President telegraphed to Taft at Augusta: "We believe that the coming years will be very happy for you and we know that through you they will be years of benefit to our people." Another message whipped off on impulse was typical of Teddy: "Ha ha! *You* are making up your Cabinet. *I* in a light hearted way have spent the morning testing the rifles for my African trip. Life has compensations!" Before Taft's election Roosevelt had written to William Allen White that his main reason for going to Africa for a year was so that he would be where no one could accuse him of running the job, or do Taft the injustice of accusing him of permitting Roosevelt to dominate him.

Nevertheless, Teddy was astonished to find how far Will Taft had traveled away from his wishes about the Cabinet. The President-elect mulled over his selections on the trip he made to Panama with Mrs. Taft in February, 1909. He wrote to Roosevelt from Culebra that he "felt very much torn up in his feelings" over leaving out men for whom he had high respect and a strong feeling of comradeship. But his object was to get appointees who would push through another stage of the reforms that the former President had initiated. Taft conceded that he would be attacked for having so many corporation lawyers in the Cabinet, but he did not feel he could get the best without selecting men with this type of experience. Six years later Roosevelt would accuse him baldly of breaking faith on the appointments and Taft would deny the charge.

Thus, before the Tafts entered the White House the shadow of one of the most famous feuds in presidential history hung over it. Major Butt spotted it early. Only slowly did he surrender to Taft's charm and Mrs. Taft's good sense. His adoration of both Roosevelts blinded him at first to the virtues of their successors. Archie decided that Taft's smile was

like a "huge pan of sweet milk poured over one," whereas Roosevelt elec-
trified those around him. It soon was clear that Mrs. Taft was an intellectual type with considerable executive ability. Butt expected startling
changes and they soon came to pass. He was told at once that automobiles would take the place of horses. Mrs. Taft was surprised to find that
the President paid for every dinner out of his own income. The Roosevelts had used Rauscher, the caterer, who charged $7.50 a serving, with-
out champagne. The new First Lady announced that all dinners would
be prepared in the White House kitchens. She ordered a big shakeup in
the staff and substituted liveried Negro attendants for the frock-coated
white ushers at the White House entrance.

Rather than wound Mrs. Roosevelt's feelings Major Butt maneuvered
things so that two of the ushers were kept as head men in charge of the
Negro footmen and the others were transferred to the Executive Office.
But Archie saw at once that Mrs. Taft was independent and did not welcome help or advice. He felt that she had been tactless in pushing
these matters through before inauguration and having them in operation
the moment she stepped into the White House. There certainly was no
hesitancy in the way she had taken hold.

When the President invited them to spend the night of March 3 in the
Executive Mansion Taft replied:

> People have attempted to represent that you and I were in some way
> at odds during this last three months, whereas you and I know that
> there has not been the slightest difference between us, and I welcome
> the opportunity to stay the last night of your administration under
> the White House roof to make as emphatic as possible the refutation
> of any such suggestion.

The Tafts passed the entire week before inauguration at the Boardman house on Dupont Circle. A reception given there in their honor on
March 2 brought out the cream of Washington society. A storm was raging as they arrived at the White House on March 3 to dine with the
Roosevelts and to spend the night in their new home. Their fellow guests
at dinner were Mr. and Mrs. Root, Admiral and Mrs. W. S. Cowles, Mr.
and Mrs. Nicholas Longworth, Henry Cabot Lodge, Miss Mabel Boardman, and Major Butt. It proved to be a melancholy function and Nellie
later remarked that it seemed like a funeral. Mrs. Roosevelt was visibly
depressed. There were tears in her eyes at one point in the evening.
Roosevelt and Taft told stories and cracked jokes but the atmosphere was
somber. Mrs. Roosevelt retired early, after expressing the hope that Mrs.
Taft's first night in the White House would be soothed by deep and
pleasant slumber.

Nellie, who had stayed in the White House when she was seventeen, slept that night in the Blue Suite, where Lincoln signed the Emancipation Proclamation. "It seemed strange to spend my first night in the White House surrounded by such ghosts," she later wrote in her autobiography. She was nervous about the following day and she studied the inauguration program before falling asleep. But the storm grew wilder and soon both she and her husband were roused by the flapping of shutters and the crackle of twigs and tree branches breaking under their burden of snow and ice.

When Roosevelt greeted Taft in the morning with a jest that it was nature's echo of a senator's denunciation of him, the towering Ohioan replied: "You're wrong. It is my storm. I always said it would be a cold day when I got to be President of the United States."

CHAPTER 16

THE WHITE HOUSE

Few inauguration days have been more blustery than President Taft's in 1909. The fierce storm that swooped down on the city during the night coated the streets with soft snow that quickly turned to slush. Plans were changed so that he took the oath and delivered his inaugural address in the Senate Chamber. The public plodded determinedly toward the Capitol through the side streets buried in snow. Wind tossed their umbrellas. Decorations were frozen stiff. Looped garlands of laurel joining gilded baskets of flowers were etched in ice. Eight pylons fifty feet high served as entrance and exit gates to the Capitol.

An army of street cleaners had gone to work in the early morning and by one o'clock Pennsylvania Avenue was officially cleared of snow. Dry sand was sprinkled along the parade route. As the bands began to play the sun broke faintly through the icicled trees and touched the flags over the President's head in the reviewing stand. The roaring wind died down. The tempo quickened as the soldiers appeared and horses came prancing into view.

The Taft and Herron families were gathered in strength. Robert, Helen, and Charlie, well bundled up against the cold, rode to the Capitol behind the leading figures in the day's events. Robert and Helen were excited. Charlie, for once, was glum. He felt he was going to be bored and he had brought *Treasure Island* to read, but he never opened it. All three were fully absorbed and Robert most of all. Years later he could relate step by step every detail of the ceremony. "Perhaps, unconsciously, it was there that he acquired his first ambition to become President," Helen wrote forty-three years later. "I wouldn't know, because we Tafts rarely discuss such things with one another. We don't ask one another's opinions as to our courses of conduct nor go along merely for the sake of family unity—as has been demonstrated by the divergency of opinion between us."

Aunt Delia was perhaps the most interested and attentive spectator present at her nephew's inauguration. Bright-eyed under a new hat, she took in every move, and was singled out for press attention. "Our new President is more *your* boy than anyone's," Mrs. Perry had written to her and Delia agreed. She had always had a special fondness for Will and now he had reached the summit. He looked immense, unsmiling and quite serious on this significant day in his life His inauguration address ranged over a wide field. He advocated revision of the tariff. He promised to continue the Rooseveltian antitrust reforms. He hoped for an "increase in the tolerance of political views of all kinds and their advocacy throughout the South." He urged an international policy to promote peace while the nation stayed armed, and he firmly outlined his own philosophy:

> In the international controversies that are likely to arise in the Orient growing out of the question of the Open Door and other issues the United States can maintain her interests intact, and can secure respect for her just demands. She will not be able to do so, however, if it is understood that she never intends to back up her assertion of right and her defense of her interest by anything but mere verbal protest and diplomatic note.

The moment he finished Roosevelt sprang up, gave his hand a mighty grasp and said: "God bless you, old man. It is a great state document." Taft greeted the crowd outside from the platform where he would have taken the inaugural oath had the weather been fine. Mrs. Taft looked on with satisfaction as the vow was taken and Will delivered his speech. She then proceeded to break precedent by riding back from the Capitol in the carriage with her husband, a decision she had made when she heard that Roosevelt would go straight to the station. She was well aware that this had never before been done by a First Lady and in her Recollections she commented: "For me that drive was the proudest and happiest event of Inauguration Day." She confessed to elation at doing what no woman had done before. Her responsibilities had not yet begun to weigh on her and she was enjoying the thought that her husband was now President of the United States. The crowd stared with interest at Mrs. Taft, gowned in a purple satin suit. Her large violet hat with gold lace had a white aigret that had suffered, to her family's amusement, from being singed by a gas jet a few days earlier.

But the powerful personality of Roosevelt still sparked the scene, and as he drove to the station to join Mrs. Roosevelt and the children, who had gone ahead, he was followed by cheering crowds. A band played "Auld Lang Syne" and Teddy shouted: "Good-bye and good luck to you." He left the Capitol for the station immediately after the ceremonies instead of returning to the White House. Four months earlier he had written to Whitelaw Reid that he would do this, since the traditional ride back of the outgoing and incoming Presidents had always struck him as being a "peculiarly senseless performance."

Meanwhile, at the White House, the Tafts gave a luncheon much delayed by the stragglers who were held up by the weather. Alice Longworth raged. She had been invited to this function but when she told Mrs. Taft at the Boardman home that she might not get there because she would be seeing her father off on the train, Nellie offered to send her a ticket to ensure her entrance in any event. Alice was outraged. In her own words:

> Instead of taking it as obvious routine, I flew shouting to friends and relatives with the news that I was going to be allowed to have a ticket to permit me to enter the White House—I—a very large capital I— who had wandered in and out for eight happy winters! Indeed, I gave myself over to a pretty fair imitation of mischief-making.

Alice was scornful, too, of the staff changes that Mrs. Taft had decreed, thinking them more pretentious than the Roosevelt ways and too hurriedly imposed. From then on she took occasion to mimic Mrs. Taft, conveying the impression that she was stiff and unyielding. "It was a really good piece of mimicry," she wrote with relish. Alice would sit on the front seat of the surrey with her family, pretending to look like Mrs. Taft. Then she would wickedly say: "This, my darlings, is what is coming after you."

The inauguration parade went off at a cheerful pace. The day had turned cold and bright and the streets were slippery. Charlie squeezed into the same seat as a friend to watch 30,000 marchers and sixty bands go past on Pennsylvania Avenue. It was a checkerboard effect, from the pink-coated fox hunters of Virginia and the Osage Indians to the governors of twenty states; from regimental gold braid to the Prince Alberts, top hats, and umbrellas of the Citizens Taft Club of Cincinnati, a bi-partisan body. Ohio was well represented in the day's proceedings and the veterans of the Civil War, the Spanish War, and the Philippine insurrection were in the line of march.

It was nightfall before the parade ended but Mrs. Taft left early for a tea she was giving to the members of the Yale class of '78. When the last of their guests had gone the Tafts stood alone in the State Dining Room and tried to realize that the White House was now their home. The President was the first to break the spell. Dead tired he suddenly exclaimed: "Let's go upstairs, my dears, and sit down."

The Tafts watched the evening's fireworks from the South Portico, a fantastic display over the snow-bound city, with trees and foliage laced in ice. They were late getting to the Inaugural Ball in the Pension Building, which was hung with spring greens and jewel-like clusters of electric lights. The Tafts marched around the tinted waters of the fountain in their grand promenade and later held a reception upstairs. The heavy white satin for Mrs. Taft's gown had been sent to Tokyo to be embroidered with a goldenrod pattern, delicately outlined with silver thread. This was the gown that formed the nucleus of the collection of inauguration costumes later assembled at the Smithsonian Institution. There were anxious moments while she waited for its arrival, but it came in from New York just in time for the ball. Her hairdresser had trouble with her hair, too, until finally she succeeded in mooring the diamond spray and aigret to her pompadour. But Mrs. Taft had a poised air as she proceeded on the President's arm into the full glare of observation that would now become part of her daily life. From the balcony she looked down on a brilliant spectacle of assorted uniforms, fashionable gowns, and jewels. Her own pearl dog collar seemed subdued in the dazzle of diamonds.

Delia sat erect in a box and took in the scene with visible enjoyment. The newly installed President bent over her with courtesy and a characteristic twinkle. All day long she had been the first to find her appointed place, and she did full justice to the late supper of game, salads, and ices. She was carefully turned out in black velvet, smothered in her best old lace. Her white hair had been dressed by a professional, a rare experience in her life. Helen was simply gowned in white mousseline with a touch of blue satin. She carried a bouquet of pink sweet peas and impressed observers as being a more demure White House daughter than Alice Roosevelt.

Charles and Annie had taken a house in Washington for the time being, but Annie was wary about being interviewed for her impressions. All she would say was: "I have the utmost confidence in the new President. Will Taft will act for the best interest of all classes." Horace and Winifred returned from the "rush of high life to being country jays" after the inaugural ceremonies. No one had more quiet satisfaction in his brother's success than Horace, who wrote to him from Watertown: "I came away with a glow of satisfaction at your being where you are and what it meant for the country." But he foresaw trouble with Congress and particularly with Speaker Joseph Cannon.

It was apparent at once to observers that Mrs. Taft was an initiate in statecraft and that she shared in official discussions. Her husband could rely on her remarkable memory for names and statistics. Henry Cabot Lodge was disturbed over the influence he thought she was going to have in the administration. He was convinced that the Taft family had been urging Will "to be his own King and to shake himself clear of the Roosevelt influence." Major Butt accompanied her to the opening of Congress and she was too absorbed to take time out for lunch. She decided on the spot that Joe Cannon, the rough-hewn Speaker whose blend of the sacred and profane in language was proverbial, whose tobacco-chewing and homespun philosophy covered a world of cynical realism, should be dismissed. Taft was more or less committed to the downfall of Cannon as the Insurgents launched their attack on the autocrat of the House. Root advised against war with the formidable Uncle Joe. In the end the President did not back the revolt, and he and Cannon came to terms and even had cordial relations. But Nellie did not change her mind and she kept a weather eye on the Speaker.

Butt had already discerned one of the fundamentals of her character. He found her uncompromising where principle was involved. She never deceived herself and therefore no one else. "I cannot but admire Mrs. Taft's honesty and directness," he wrote. After a month's scrutiny of the President he decided that Taft was "persistent in his antipathies . . . he is easily influenced to do what he wants to do, but he is stubborn as an ox when he gets set in the other direction."

The public as yet could see nothing but bland good nature in their new President. He was the personification of the genial man, with his spreading smile, his redundant chins, his winged collar and bowler hat. Taft had smooth, delicate skin and a fair mustache that turned tawny gray as he aged. His brows jutted over singularly clear blue eyes that held serenity as well as knowledge. His famous chuckle, rising in waves from the pit of his stomach, was a lifelong characteristic.

The White House dinner table quickly became a gathering place for legislators of differing views who were drawn within the nimbus of his hospitality. He chose to ignore personal squabbles and differences, and he staggered Washington at first with some of his combinations in a city where feuds flourished. He worked over the invitation lists himself and took some pride in them. "The White House is a big political asset when used wisely," he commented, as he made a point of inviting a Texas senator who a few weeks earlier had declared him less fitted to be President than any man who had ever held the office. None could assail his success as a host and raconteur. Mrs. Taft was more disposed to hold a grudge and let it show. She remembered those who had ignored her when she was the Solicitor General's wife.

Between them the Tafts broke down some of the formality of White House procedure. Guests were arranged informally around the Blue Room, and the President and Mrs. Taft went from one to another, greeting them as they might in a private home. Mrs. Taft and her partner went in to dinner at the end of the line—another innovation. At their first formal dinner she stirred up a flurry of talk by hurrying in ahead of the President. She was almost half way around the guests before he had finished shaking hands with the first couple. Mrs. Taft later confessed to Major Butt that she was extremely nervous. The President, too, conceded that it was the first time in his life he had felt stampeded and that it had seemed worse than taking the oath of office. But neither of the Tafts needed social coaching and the President delighted in inviting guests who had never before been in the White House.

The Tafts were the first to employ personal aides and the President often teased his wife about her liking for fuss and feathers. In the general upheaval Irwin (Ike) Hoover was retained as an usher and none would write more scathingly of the Taft administration than he in after years. He pictured Mrs. Taft as continually projecting herself into official discussions and joining her husband when she saw him deep in conversation with important politicians and, in particular, with Speaker Cannon. One of her first acts was to replace the White House steward with an English housekeeper, Mrs. Elizabeth Jaffray, who would flourish for years until Calvin Coolidge, thinking her extravagant, got rid of her. Mrs. Taft saw no reason to order new china, since she admired Mrs. Roosevelt's choice. For small luncheons and dinners she used the historic plates of earlier years. The china supply was important during this administration, for, like Herbert Hoover, Taft was one of the Presidents who invited people on impulse and in numbers. His wife at all times had to be prepared for the unexpected. He was apt to arrive late and he often had guests for breakfast, which in his case usually consisted during the presidential years of two oranges, a twelve-ounce steak, toast, jelly, and coffee. When his weight exceeded a certain point the steak was reduced to eight ounces.

Although wines were served by the Tafts in a discriminating way the President was at all times abstemious, observing the courtesies only. Their preferred punch was one quart-bottle of champagne to two bottles of charged water, with lemon, sugar, and ice. The head cook was Swedish and the White House fare during the Taft administration was discrim-

Sylvia Howard Taft (Mrs. Peter Rawson
Taft, I), in the 1850's. (*William Howard Taft
papers, Library of Congress*)

Peter Rawson Taft, I, 1859.
(*William Howard Taft Memorial Association*)

Alphonso Taft, 1876.
(*William Howard Taft Memorial Association*)

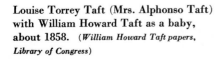

Louise Torrey Taft (Mrs. Alphonso Taft)
with William Howard Taft as a baby,
about 1858. (*William Howard Taft papers,
Library of Congress*)

William Howard Taft,
by Joaquín Sorolla y Bastida, 1909.
(*Taft Museum*)

Nellie Herron Taft (Mrs. William
Howard Taft) as First Lady, by B.
Kronstrand, 1910.   (*William Howard
Taft Memorial Association*)

Chief Justice and Mrs. William Howard
Taft as they were when presented to
King George V and Queen Mary, 1922.
(*William Howard Taft Memorial Association*)

William Howard Taft as Professor of Law at Yale, about 1913.
(*Library of Congress*)

William Howard Taft with
his aunt, Delia Chapin Torrey,
1910.   (*Library of Congress*)

Secretary of War William Howard Taft playing golf, 1908.　　*(Library of Congress)*

President William Howard Taft **on horseback, 1909.**　　*(Library of Congress)*

Charles Phelps Taft,
by Raimundo de Madrazo,
1902. (*Taft Museum*)

Annie Sinton Taft (Mrs. Charles Phelps
Taft), by Raimundo de Madrazo,
1902. (*Taft Museum*)

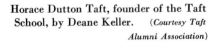

Horace Dutton Taft, founder of the Taft
School, by Deane Keller. (*Courtesy Taft
Alumni Association*)

Charles Phelps Taft, II, about
1907. (*William Howard Taft
Memorial Association*)

Helen Taft (later Mrs. Frederick
J. Manning), 1910.
(*Library of Congress*)

Robert A. Taft, *left*: aged five.
above: as a schoolboy.
(*Courtesy Mrs. Darrah Dunham Wunder*)

Senator Robert A. Taft, by
Karsh, 1946.

Martha Bowers Taft (Mrs.
Robert A. Taft), by Harry Carlson.
(*Courtesy Mrs. Darrah Dunham Wunder*)

Senator and Mrs. Robert A. Taft, by Harry Carlson.
(Courtesy Mrs. Darrah Dunham Wunder)

Senator Robert A. Taft fishing at St. Petersburg, Florida, during his campaign for the Republican nomination for President, 1940. *(William Howard Taft Memorial Association)*

Charles Phelps Taft, II, with President Franklin D. Roosevelt, when Taft was Chairman of the National Citizens' Committee for the Mobilization of Human Needs, 1938.   (*UPI*)

Bryn Mawr Commencement, 1939. Mrs. Helen Taft Manning, Dean of the college, Charles Phelps Taft, II, a speaker, and his daughter Eleanor K. Taft, a 1939 graduate. (*UPI*)

Charles Phelps Taft, II, and Eleanor Chase Taft (Mrs. Charles Phelps Taft), standing before the Sorolla portrait of William Howard Taft at the Taft Museum in Cincinnati. This picture was taken at their thirty-fifth wedding anniversary celebration. *(UPI)*

Charles Phelps Taft, II, second from left, with President Dwight D. Eisenhower and Vice-President Richard M. Nixon, during the campaign of 1952. Taft was Republican candidate for governor of Ohio. *(UPI)*

FOR ME & YOU IN '52
It's IKE & CHARLIE

Charles Phelps Taft, II, dedicating the marker designating the Taft Homesite in Mendon, Massachusetts, 1960
(Courtesy Mrs. Pearl Rawson)

Congressman Robert Taft, Jr.,
with Governor Nelson A.
Rockefeller, speakers at a
Women's National Republican
Club luncheon, 1963.
(*UPI*)

Seth Chase Taft in the early
1960's.

Chief Justice William Howard
Taft with his granddaughter,
Helen Manning.
(*Library of Congress*)

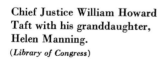

"Venetian Carnival" held in the Philippines in 1903. Standing, left to right: Major Noble an aide; Helen Taft; the children's German governess; and Fred Carpenter, Taft's secretary. Seated: Mrs. William Howard Taft; Charles Phelps Taft, II; and William Howard Taft. (*William Howard Taft Memorial Association*)

William Howard Taft's twenty-fifth wedding anniversary, the White House, June 19, 1911. Standing, left to right: Robert A. Taft, Maria Herron, Horace Dutton Taft, Helen Taft, Henry W. Taft, and Charles Phelps Taft, II. Seated, left to right: Mrs. Charles Anderson, Mrs. William Howard Taft, William Howard Taft, Delia Chapin Torrey, and Mrs. Henry W. Taft. (*William Howard Taft Memorial Association*)

Two generations of Tafts voting in the Ohio primaries of 1943. Standing, left to right: Mrs. Hulbert Taft, Senator Robert A. Taft, Lloyd Bowers Taft, Mrs. Lloyd Bowers Taft, Mrs. Robert Taft, Jr., and Robert Taft, Jr. (*UPI*)

All Want the Big Apple.

Speculation about William Howard Taft's presidential aims in newspaper cartoons published in the summer of 1906. The St. Louis *Star-Chronicle*, July 18, 1906, and the Rochester *Herald*, July 12, 1906.
(*William Howard Taft papers, Library of Congress*)

An Ohio cartoonist's impression of William Howard Taft's hesitation between a Supreme Court appointment and a presidential nomination. The *Youngstown Telegram*, July 16, 1906. (*William Howard Taft papers, Library of Congress*)

ANXIETY OVER TAFT'S CHOICE OF LIMBS

artoonist's reaction to President Taft's administra-
e policy. (*Cartoon by McCutcheon, courtesy Don Maxwell*
the Chicago Tribune)

Alice Roosevelt and Secretary of
War William Howard Taft
aboard the S.S. *Manchuria*, 1905.
*(Picture Collection, New York
Public Library)*

Secretary of War Taft campaigning for congressional candidates,
1906.   *(Picture Collection, New York
Public Library)*

Sky Farm, Indian Hill, in 1940.
Home of Senator Robert A. Taft
and, today, of Congressman
Robert Taft, Jr.   (*Courtesy*
Mrs. Darrah Dunham Wunder)

Charles Phelps Taft house on
Pike Street, Cincinnati. Now the
Taft Museum.   (*Taft Museum*)

Taft family home on Mount Auburn, Cincinnati—the birthplace of President William
Howard Taft—about 1868. Left to right: Henry W. Taft, William Howard Taft, Horace
Dutton Taft, Fanny Taft, Mrs. Alphonso Taft, Delia Chapin Torrey.   (*William Howard Taft*
Memorial Association)

William Howard Taft house at Murray Bay, Province of Quebec. Destroyed by fire in 1952. *(Courtesy Mrs. Darrah Dunham Wunder)*

The last White House cow, "Pauline Wayne." *(Courtesy Mrs. Ona Griffin Jeffries and the District of Columbia Public Library)*

President and Mrs. William Howard Taft in the first White House automobile. *(Picture Collection, New Yor Public Library)*

Architect Cass Gilbert's sketch for the Supreme Court Building, a favorite project of Chief Justice William Howard Taft. *(William Howard Taft papers, Library of Congress)*

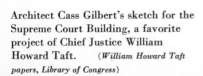

inating, if not inspired. The President insisted on good cigars. They were ordered from Cuba, 5,000 at a time—the Administration and the Cabinet brands—specially prepared for the White House. Taft, struggling always with a diet of one kind or another, was to become one of the world's most practiced banqueters. The dinner hour was changed from eight to half past seven because of Mrs. Taft's devotion to the theater. The musicales she gave were sophisticated, since no First Lady before her knew music as Nellie Herron did.

The White House seemed quiet and orderly after the din of the Roosevelt era. The Tafts lived as much downstairs as they did in their own quarters. Mrs. Taft's idea was to give the entire Executive Mansion a homelike air. Often they sat in the Red Room until bedtime. Fires were lighted and flowers were lavishly arranged in all the public rooms. The library held their treasures from the Orient—teakwood, tapestries, Japanese screens, and objects of art. The west end of the corridor upstairs was used as a family sitting room. After one night in the great bed in the Lincoln room Mrs. Taft had it removed and two smaller mahogany beds without canopies were installed. She bought a few colonial pieces and substituted heavy chintz for the brocade hangings and upholstery in this room. Helen had a suite across the hall which had been done in chintz for Ethel Roosevelt after Alice's marriage. This was left unchanged. The boys shared a gloomy room with dark red walls, and windows under the portico roof.

The President's study was lively with memorabilia—cartoons, news pictures, family snapshots, a pictorial record of his own career, and many pictures of his children. Mrs. Taft, who supervised the flower arrangements every day, sent him carnations for his desk. One of her favorite table decorations was a silver centerpiece rimmed with the engraved notes of a musical theme, a gift from the Cincinnati Orchestra Association. With this, Nellie often combined hothouse grapes and orchids. She had a vault installed for the White House silver which had always been kept in chests, and now for the first time it was cleaned by electricity. Major Butt soon came to the conclusion that Mrs. Taft had to fight continually against a fixed habit of economy that seemed to be part of her nature. Her husband was much more expansive when it came to entertaining. Major Butt thought he had never seen a man who more thoroughly enjoyed the role of host. But the first time Archie dined at the White House after his idols had left he "missed the marvelous wit and personality of Roosevelt and the sweet charm of his wife." However, he conceded that some of Mrs. Taft's changes were improvements. He noticed that Taft continued to speak of Roosevelt as the President. His wife corrected him sharply:

"You mean the ex-President, Will."

"I suppose I do, dear; but he will always be the President to me, and I can never think of him as anything else."

Instinctively Butt drew comparisons between the Roosevelts and the Tafts in all their ways, but by degrees he came to have hearty respect for them, if not as much love as he had for their predecessors. It did not take him long to see that Mrs. Taft was quite without vanity, and her coldness as she conferred with him each morning, sitting bolt upright in one chair while he faced her in another, was clearly due to embarrassment. But a bubbling fountain of news had dried up with the departure of the Roosevelts from the White House. In spite of his newspaper experience William Howard Taft had no conception of the press as an adjunct to his office. Mrs. Taft, like Mrs. Roosevelt, never gave interviews but occasionally handed out a statement on some formal function. Her purely social dinners were thought by the discriminating to have considerable charm and her guests noticed that her years in the Philippines had influenced her methods of entertaining. As soon as the weather became warm rugs were spread on the South Portico and the Tafts spent the evenings outdoors. The end terraces were transformed with flowers, shrubs, and tables. The President liked to settle there after dinner, and years later his wife wrote reminiscently of their evenings on the White House terrace with the faint smell of magnolia in the air, the tall column of the Washington Monument in the distance, the strings of lights close to the river, and the fountain playing in the foreground. But insects and damp defeated this outdoor living in the end.

No First Lady took more pleasure than Mrs. Taft in the abundance of flowers she could command from the greenhouses and nurseries. She liked softly arranged masses in assorted colors against the stiffer background of palms and ferns. Her favorites were the White House orchids and Killarney roses which she often used for her formal dinners. The music was apt to be by Verdi, Strauss, Gounod, Bizet, or Mascagni. The family had a victrola in the Blue Room and they liked to run off Caruso or Melba records, old English melodies, ragtime, or whatever appealed to old and young. On one occasion, when talking to Joe Cannon, the President could not resist getting up to waltz around the room when Archie put on the "Merry Widow Waltz," with Madame Sembrich singing it. Cannon followed suit with a ragtime shuffle, a scene that might have astonished the gentlemen of the Capitol. Archie was as surprised by the President's agility on the dance floor as he was by his seasoned way with a horse. "He dances well and is as nimble on his feet as a cat," he noted, adding to the testimony of others who had observed Will Taft on the dance floor. "I have found out three things he does well. He dances well, he curses well, and he laughs well."

Archie anticipated a decline in style when he went riding with President Taft after his exhilarating gallops with Theodore Roosevelt. But again he was surprised to find that the new President was an excellent horseman, out for exercise, and schooled in the best riding traditions. Now and then he became sensitive, thinking that spectators were amused by his bulk on a horse, but Archie assured him that they were merely responding to the atmosphere of good nature and geniality that he created wherever he went. In spite of his size and seeming clumsiness he walked lightly with a sure gait. His laughter matched his mighty frame but he was essentially thoughtful and judicial. He disliked public clamor, controversy, and criticism, and was well endowed with the social graces. His gallantry and good manners endeared him to women of all ages and he was particularly at ease with judges, lawyers, and witty women. People with rigid views and intolerant attitudes had small appeal for him. Taft could flare into sudden anger but the storm soon passed and he never sulked, nor was he vindictive in spirit. An angry exchange was apt to wind up with a hearty laugh and a pointed anecdote. Although conciliatory by nature and at heart a diplomat, some of these qualities were obscured during his years in the White House, when he seemed at times to move in a fog, and to show impatience and rage.

Above all Major Butt was impressed with his powers of endurance. He could go through the most grueling round without showing any sign of wear and tear. Yet once again his Brobdingnagian proportions, his gourmet tastes, his disposition to fall asleep in public, and his procrastination in preparing his speeches and making decisions tended to foster the impression that William Howard Taft was a lazy man. His son Robert always resented this aspersion on his father, since he had never known anyone who worked harder, but he conceded that the weight he put on while he was President slowed him up in some respects. Although he might knock off for a game of golf or a round of bridge he always made up for this with long stretches of highly concentrated work. Because of his long judicial experience he digested reports with ease and could clarify the knottiest points. Robert observed that he made up his mind slowly and liked to consult a great many persons before arriving at a conclusion.

Taft's personal correspondence in itself is testimony to his extraordinary industry. He believed in the family life in its richest sense and demonstrated this in his own history. He cherished his wife as long as he lived and never hesitated to tell her how much he loved her, to pay her compliments, to send her flowers on all their anniversaries, and to admire her looks and clothes. Even when his responsibilities seemed overwhelming he remained the thoughtful suitor he had been in the days of his courtship. Knowing how hard it was for Mrs. Taft to follow the brilliant

Roosevelt administration he said to Archie soon after he was inaugurated: "I am very proud of the way Nellie has taken hold of things in the White House." On another occasion he remarked that he loved to see her well dressed, but he had to urge her to spend money on her clothes. She had always bought in frugal fashion but now needed elaborate gowns. Still slim and small-waisted, it was her custom to go around Washington in trim suits, with the heavy hats fashionable at the time.

The public quickly realized that the White House again contained an interesting and affectionate family, although the children were away at school and college and appeared only during the holidays or on special occasions. Charlie's skylarking was periodic after his father became President. However, he showed great familiarity with the workings of the White House from the first day, and ran the elevator for his parents on their return from the Capitol. He could cope with the switchboard, too, when the operator went to lunch, and he enjoyed riding in the White House automobiles after the slow carriage pace. Charlie made friends with everyone and never had any reluctance about identifying himself as the President's son. Bob, on the other hand, shrank from attracting attention to himself. Archie Butt thought that Charlie understood the uses of publicity better than his father did. One day when he arrived unexpectedly from Watertown his mother asked him how he had managed to make the journey across New York from Grand Central to the Pennsylvania Station.

"Oh, I took care of that, Mamma," he cheerfully told her. "I know a Secret Service man who is now in New York. I sent him a telegram and asked him to meet me at Grand Central."

Mrs. Taft was keenly aware of the background the White House gave her growing children and she intended to make the most of it. Dinners and dances were arranged for Helen and Bob when they came home for the holidays, and she encouraged house parties for their particular friends. They all loved dancing and their passion for charades led to an awkward moment when a group of important visitors from abroad were being convoyed through the White House. The young were illustrating the word "dynasty" as "die nasty" and they were expiring dramatically outside the room where the Emancipation Proclamation was signed. Robert, an expert on Shakespeare, was Hamlet drinking poison and crying "I die, Horatio." Helen was committing hara-kiri and one of their friends was hanging when the visiting group arrived and viewed this tableau with some concern. Their father laughed heartily but advised them to post a guard when engaged in skulduggery of this sort.

The guessing game of the day was "Clumps" and another favorite was "Sardines," a hide and seek diversion which later came to be known as "Murder." In charades it was a family joke that Bob had always liked to play the bloodhound in *Uncle Tom's Cabin*. Both he and Helen were outgrowing these amusements when their father became President but the whole family were always ready for charades and guessing games. Their mother believed in a full social schedule for them and something was mapped out every night when they were at home. At the cotillions they liked to dance the Boston, which was in high favor at the time.

On Sunday mornings the young Tafts and their friends took trolley rides to Rock Creek Park and walked to Old Pierce's Mill for breakfast. At other times they drove to Lord Baltimore's Dower House in Maryland and had dinner in front of the enormous fireplace. They used the State Dining Room and their mother always arranged for someone to be on duty late at night to give them snacks after parties. Their life in the White House between 1909 and 1913 was quite informal. Their friends came and went without being checked by guards at the gate and one of Bob's classmates wrote letters all one night for the thrill of sending them out on White House stationery. The three Taft children were diverse in temperament but united on important issues. They had been taught by their father to consider all sides of a question and then to make up their own minds about it. Helen in later years said that they disagreed frequently among themselves and as a whole were a quick-tempered family. Bob was apt to get impatient with those who did not think as fast as he did. He would flare out at Helen when she made a stupid move at chess.

They had been in the White House little more than a month when Mrs. Taft gave the first of her musicales in the Blue Room, which she thought was not well adapted acoustically to this purpose. Rain drowned out her first garden party but the second was held in brilliant May sunshine, with Mrs. Taft moving among her guests in a pink silk gown draped with silver gauze, and a picture hat to match. She was soon responsible for two innovations that were to give lasting pleasure to Washingtonians. On April 17, 1909, Potomac Drive, which had been known as the Speedway, was formally opened for afternoon concerts, with President Taft giving this experiment his blessing. Remembering the Luneta in Manila Mrs. Taft had decided that concerts from five to seven two afternoons a week would popularize the driveway. A band stood at one end of the ellipse, and soon crowds gathered to hear Sousa marches under balmy conditions.

More lasting in its effect was her introduction of the cherry trees that bring thousands into the capital each spring. Mrs. Taft had become familiar with the cherry blossom festival in Japan and it occurred to her that a grove of cherry trees would beautify Washington. At first, blooming cherry tees were introduced from the nurseries of America. More than a hundred were planted along the Potomac Drive. Then Yukio Ozaki, mayor of Tokyo, who knew the Tafts, offered 3,000 trees from his municipality. But they arrived in an infected condition and had to be destroyed. Ozaki could not refrain from cracking an apt jest when he heard of this. "Oh, I believe your first President set the example of destroying cherry trees, didn't he?" The Mayor made another shipment of 3,000 saplings; these thrived and the tidal basin became famous for its pink and white mist of bloom in spring. Cherry trees soon flourished also in the Capitol grounds and in the suburbs of the city.

William Howard Taft was always proud of his wife's cherry trees. As long as he lived he sent her reports on them each spring if she were away. He had Oliver Wendell Holmes priming him on the subject when he was ill. The Japanese Government continued to send representatives in native costume to the festival, except during the war years. Young Robert Taft, in his freshman year in Congress, was present for the ceremonies of 1963, honoring his grandmother, who had always found such delight in the trees of the capital. President Taft rounded up their history for her, from the elm planted by John Quincy Adams in the south grounds to the two magnolias imported from France and planted in the 1850's. In the Taft era Washington had close to 150 varieties of trees and shrubs, with the silver maple, American ash, pin oak, and Norway maple predominating. Others that flourished in the capital were the elm, beech, linden, plane, mimosa, and tulip trees.

Soon after he became President, Taft sat for Joaquín Sorolla y Basida, the Spanish artist commissioned by Charles and Annie to paint the portrait that hangs today in the Taft Museum in Cincinnati. It is a joyous portrayal full of life and light that delighted Taft and made him feel younger. In the picture he holds a petition to delay the execution of a murderer in Panama to whom he had refused a pardon. The portrait hung for a time in the White House. Crowds flocked to see it when it was shown in Cincinnati in the summer of 1909, but first there was a private viewing in the Pike Street house, and Charles reported to the President:

> Annie thinks that "all conquering smile" ought to go down to posterity. She . . . suggests that some of your lady friends are glad to see that dimple immortalized. . . . The Sewing Circle met at the house yesterday and I think the portrait was the *pièce de résistance*.

Two months after President Taft's inauguration his wife had a stroke. She had given the last of six dinners, as well as two big garden parties and many smaller affairs. She had entertained every senator and all the more important members of the House. On the day of her collapse she had stayed with Charlie through an operation for the removal of his adenoids and this experience had upset her. The presidential party was sailing down the Potomac on the *Sylph* to attend a function at Mount

Vernon when she became ill. George W. Wickersham, Attorney General in the Taft cabinet, thought that she had fainted as he talked to her. He summoned Major Butt, who brought rye whiskey and ice to revive her. The yacht turned around and Mrs. Taft was only half conscious when she was taken upstairs at the White House. The President was stunned. "I have never seen greater suffering or pain on a man's face," Archie observed.

Mrs. Taft slept for sixteen hours and the doctors predicted her recovery. A formal dinner was scheduled for that night. The President appeared alone and showed the utmost self-control all evening. His guests were informed that Mrs. Taft was exhausted after her experience at the hospital with Charlie. In his letter to his children, explaining what had happened, Taft wrote that the doctor had assured him it was a "mere attack of nervous hysteria rather than a bursting of a blood-vessel in the brain, which is true paralysis." He reminded them that she had been subject to attacks of nervous exhaustion.

For weeks the secret was guarded, but the fact was that she had had a severe stroke, involving her face and speech. Although she recovered completely and was able later to share in public events and travel at will, a slight impediment in speech remained for the rest of her life. For a time she shrank from observation but she used great willpower to conquer her disability. Her husband became almost psychic in knowing what she wished to say, and he spent hours teaching her to enunciate again.

The papers soon learned that Mrs. Taft was ill but not how ill she was. Next day, in spite of his great anxiety, the President rose to the occasion and left for the celebration of the Mecklenburg Declaration in Charlotte, North Carolina. The entire family reacted with a disciplined sense of duty, and a few days later Helen joined her father at Gettysburg and unveiled a memorial shaft on the battleground. Messages on his wife's condition followed the President from point to point. Within a week after her collapse Nellie was able to stand at the window and watch Taft start for his daily ride. Archie was distressed when he first saw her. "She tried to smile, but it was only a ghost of the old smile," he wrote. On his return the President would not dismount until she had come to the window and waved. It seemed to Archie that he thought all the time of his ailing wife and watched for every chance to do little things for her. He detected a "world of misery" in Taft's looks and manner, and although he pretended optimism Archie saw new depths in the President.

But he never let his concern show when he was with Nellie. He laughed and tried to amuse her but when he came out of her room he was apt to sit for a long time, staring into space. In the months that followed all of her sisters took turns in being with her but soon she was

directing social activities from the second floor, almost as if she had
been well. The White House had now become a prison for Mrs. Taft.
In after years she never dwelled on the misery of this period; in fact, few
realized how handicapped she was, and her husband and children encouraged her in every way they could.

Bob wrote sympathetically to his mother from Durfee Hall, enlivening
his letters with college news. He had been to Cambridge with the freshman debaters from Yale and had seen them lose to Harvard. He feared
that his own coaching might have contributed to this disaster. After attending the Taft School reunion he reported that Charlie was exceedingly popular, a piece of news that he knew would cheer his mother. Until commencement he kept her primed on his examinations, sports, and
social engagements. Finally he reported that he had spoken for his
cousin Walbridge's rooms at the Harvard Law School a year from the
following September.

The Taft children were consistently optimistic about their mother's
condition; but Major Butt was less hopeful. It took time for her interest
in music, the theater, and card games to revive, but eventually she lost
herself for hours in these diversions. Her letters to her husband were
never quite so fluent again, for it tired her to write in detail. In response
to the great flood of warm and diverting correspondence that she received from Will as he traveled around, attended memorable functions,
and played a part in world affairs, were her cryptic little notes, telling of
the play she had seen, the concert she had heard, her luck at cards, the
book she had read. For a time her handwriting wavered but in later
years it was clear and legible again. Her husband worried constantly
over the danger of subsequent strokes and he watched every fleeting
change in her appearance or mood when he was with her. It was almost
an obsession with him for a time and he threw up a guard around her
lest she exert herself beyond her strength. None knew better than he
that his wife was a strenuous and ambitious woman, bitterly disappointed that the White House years, to which she had looked forward for so long, should be dimmed by a disabling illness. Her collapse
clouded his own days in office and may have contributed to his unhappy state in the role of President.

CHAPTER 17

A TARIFF STORM

PRESIDENT TAFT sweltered in Washington through most of the summer of 1909. The Progressives from the West were attacking him hard, suspicious that he was departing from the Roosevelt policies. They interpreted his association with Joe Cannon and Nelson Aldrich as indications that he was consorting with the ultra-conservatives. Debates raged on the Payne-Aldrich tariff bill and the President's letters to his wife mirrored the parade of party leaders to the White House and the political breakfasts, luncheons, and dinners involving discussion of this hot issue. His policy of downward tariff revision was scarcely upheld by the bill.

Early in August the bill was signed with a pen made of gold and pearwood from the Philippines. The margin was close and a Harmony dinner was held at the White House for members of the two committees that had framed it. "The close . . . was all very peaceful and sweet . . . and I think everybody left with a good taste in his mouth, except possibly Cannon," the President wrote to Horace. The table was decorated with crepe myrtle from the White House gardens. Carpets had been laid on the East Terrace and the legislators lounged outdoors, their work done. Taft was the genial host, smiling on those who had fought him. He knew that Cannon's downfall was imminent. In the long run Champ Clark succeeded him.

Between worry, dieting, and exercise, the President was down to 310 pounds when he left for Beverly, Massachusetts, where the family had taken a summer home. He had become less sluggish and Archie flattered himself that he had had something to do with this by riding with him, playing golf, and keeping him from dozing off. Butt disliked golf but he enjoyed the blue sky, the green grass, the entertaining flow of anecdotes from the President. Charles E. Barker had also had much to do with the enlivening process. Since the winter of 1905 this physical instructor had intermittently directed a stiff program of exercise for Taft. This was intensified at the White House. Every day except Sundays Barker passed an hour with him. First came thirty minutes of calisthenics, then a ten-minute rest period, then twenty minutes of boxing, wrestling, or tossing the medicine ball. Much as the President hated exercise he started this martyrdom at seven every morning. Usually he chatted with Barker while he rested. On his bedroom wall hung a verse by Henry Van Dyke that reflected his own stolid perseverance:

> Let me but live my life from year to year,
> With forward face and unreluctant soul;
> . . . My heart will keep the courage of the quest
> And hope the road's last turn will be the best.

Major Butt had discovered by this time that the President had a genuine passion for motoring. When tired or troubled he found it relaxing. Often he went driving before going to bed, knowing that the effect would be soporific. The day's worries tended to dissolve as the night air rushed against his face. The Taft cars were White Steamers and the whole family used them with enthusiasm. The President was granted an appropriation of $12,000 for four automobiles. In 1909 his salary was raised from $50,000 to $75,000, with an allowance of $25,000 for traveling expenses. Horace, too, was a motoring fan; he invested in a cheap car and was having a good time learning to drive, although his boys observed with amusement that he took up most of the road. He thought he was racing when he made twenty-five miles an hour but this was nothing compared with the speed favored by the President. "Coming back we made the machine sing; one and one-half hours to reach the White House from Baltimore," Archie reported. "The woodwork of the car caught fire from the heat generated by the speed. . . ." On another occasion four presidential automobiles started for Manassas but Taft's was the only one to reach Virginia.

The President was lonely in the White House with his family away for the summer, but he made the best of it, golfing at Chevy Chase and en-

tertaining or going out in the evening. He was the first Chief Executive
to visit extensively in Washington and the family link with the Larz
Andersons was so close that he was apt to wander into the kitchen
after the theater and watch the rarebit being prepared. He saw a good
deal of the Longworths, and Alice amused him when she arrived late at
one of his parties on a hot July night. Making her usual dramatic
entry, her apologies were so absurd that everyone laughed. The President took her hands in his and said: "Alice, if you will only stop trying
to be respectful to me, I believe you would become so."

"And then I would bore you to death as the other women do," said
Alice, with a sweep of the arm.

Archie Butt noted that while the President did not always approve of
Alice, he could never resist her wit and repartee. She was chagrined at
this time over his failure to reappoint Henry White Ambassador to
France. White was a particular favorite of her father's and before the
inauguration he had asked her to find out from Taft if the story that
he was repaying an old grudge happened to be true. He quickly told her:
"You must believe that I am big enough to forget that sort of thing."
But she was doubly surprised when White's resignation was promptly accepted. It struck her as adding to a "mounting list of black marks or be-
trayals, as they begin to seem." Taft took the attitude that his handling
of White was just a routine shift of diplomats. However, Charles
Phelps Taft disliked White and did not bother to call on him at the Embassy, and the President considered him a snob.

The Wright brothers, testing their airplane at Fort Myer, drew crowds
from Washington to watch their epochal efforts. Mrs. Longworth took
parties out nearly every day, running her own canteen and serving tea
and gin fizzes from her car. Aviation was beginning to be discussed in a
serious way and the President gave the Wrights a gold medal at a White
House ceremony attended by 1,000 guests. In making the presentation he said:

> You made this discovery by a course that we of America like to feel
> is distinctly American—by keeping your noses right at the job until
> you had accomplished what you had determined to do. . . . Many
> great discoveries have come by accident—but you gentlemen have
> illustrated the other and on the whole much more commendable
> method. You planned what you wished to find and then you worked it
> out until you found it.

On July 27, 1909, the President watched Orville fly for seventy-three
minutes against a gathering sunset. He had broken Wilbur's record,
made at Le Mans in France, and had brought aeronautics close to the
White House and to the American people.

Willie Schevill painted the President that summer and Taft found his work stern but in sound contrast to the laughing Sorolla. "Certainly the expression of the face is not all smiles," he noted. Taft was a much-photographed President and he always sought Nellie's opinion before accepting and using a picture of himself. This was one of many small matters in which he relied on her judgment. All summer long she read his letters eagerly as she sat on the veranda of their house at Beverly, Massachusetts, looking across Salem Harbor to Marblehead. The lawns sloped down to the seawall. The North Shore residents were near at hand with all their social claims on the First Lady, but she settled at once into a quiet routine of drives and reading. Mabel Boardman had helped the Tafts to find this summer home. As President, Taft was not anxious to leave the country, which meant that they could not go to Murray Bay.

Bob, Helen, and Charlie missed the freedom and rusticity of the Canadian resort as they were swept into a multitude of social engagements at Beverly. Major Butt suggested an extra chauffeur to cope with their comings and goings, but while relishing the good things of life the Tafts were always averse to display. There was a basic austerity in their approach to things, and a touch of New England thrift. Mrs. Taft, constitutionally averse to the prodigal spirit that infected her husband at times, objected to the extra chauffeur, but Will observed in his hearty way:

Let them have a good time while they can. In four years we may all have to become pedestrians again and I want them each to look back upon this portion of their life with the keenest relish. They are not children to be spoiled by a little luxury now.

Major Butt agreed wholeheartedly with this and wrote that he had never seen such a natural and wholesome family, with no sign of conceit in any of them. It would always be like this, even after they amassed some wealth. They were instinctively unostentatious, in keeping with their inherited principles and way of life. Although invitations poured in on them at Beverly, the elder Tafts responded only to friends they knew intimately, for the President's chief concern was to have Nellie build up her strength. They all watched the races at Marblehead from the *Sylph*. Helen hunted and played bridge and tennis while Bob golfed, bowled, and played tennis. Charlie belonged to an outing club and had his own dory. He was learning to sail and moved in a happy glow, having won his uncle's approval and also the first prize for the lower school at Taft. His weakest marks were in Bible study, which his father decided must be an inherited trait. He got 96 in English and algebra and 95 in Latin. His uncle Horace observed that he charged about like a buffalo on his skates, but he had adapted himself well to school life and his parents read the headmaster's analysis of Charlie with deep satisfaction:

> To my great delight he . . . fell into the life here in the most natural and simple way. He has a delight in every kind of fun that is simple and healthy and that is worth a fortune. . . . At the same time he is steady and attends to business. Whether he has as strong a mind as Bob is doubtful, though he is a year younger for his class than Bob was and it is hard to compare the two. He will find it easier, however, to take part in everything that comes up than Bob did. He is more facile in most ways.

The President was exhausted when he joined his family at Beverly. From the start he gave at least half of each day to his wife and would never let anything interfere with this arrangement. He talked to her by the hour, took her driving, helped her to forget her own enforced silence. "She is quite disposed to sit as a Pope and direct me as of yore, which is an indication of the restoration of normal conditions, which you will fully realize," he wrote to Horace on August 11, 1909. He golfed at the Myopia Club with William J. Boardman and John Hays Hammond. When he made 98 Nellie, never demonstrative in public, surprised onlookers by kissing him impulsively. But the needling over his golf continued during his years in the White House, and the public would never accept the theory that it was more than a game to him. Exercise was a medical necessity and the walking involved was doubly beneficial. By this time golf had become a popular pastime and nearly every small town had a Golf Club. On the President's speaking tours his hosts always knew that this would be positive bait for him. He played with considerable concentration, using long, heavy clubs. His driver and brassie were forty-seven inches long and weighed fourteen ounces.

Helen and Bob now made appearances in public with their father. They accompanied him to the Tercentenary Celebration in Vermont, a state for which he had strong ancestral feeling. He spoke in Burlington and reviewed the national and state troops, then attended an Indian pageant on the waterfront and was banqueted at the University of Vermont. Ambassador Jules Jusserand and Charles Evans Hughes, whose speech that day seemed brilliant to the President, were among the guests. Taft wrote proudly to his wife after watching their childrens' unassuming participation in the ceremonies: "I don't think we have any reason to be ashamed of Bob and Helen. They seem to be able to stake their places modestly and to entertain themselves. . . . I was very proud of my boy and girl and I know they made a good impression."

Delia joined the party at Beverly late in August and took special delight in driving around to see old friends, while the President entertained them en route with snatches of local history. They dined at the home of Henry C. Frick at Pride's Crossing and viewed his paintings and organ. But the President's visits then and later to the homes of Frick, J. P. Morgan, Murray Crane, and Nelson Aldrich gave his enemies a chance to ballyhoo his association with conservatives and they made the most of it. The Boardmans summered within close range at Manchester-by-the-Sea and the Charles Tafts stayed with them for a week on their way to Murray Bay that year. Annie wrote from Canada to the President: "By the way, if the Czar of all the Russias can go to Cowes why cannot you come to Murray Bay?"

Taft read with interest that Murray Bay was putting on airs. A race track with a grandstand had been built in the forest back of Cap l'Aigle and a clubhouse now had a little theater, with a French troupe giving plays three times a week. Charles had had the woods cleared behind their cottage and he called that area "The Philosopher's Grove." Maria was in Cincinnati nursing her dying father, and Annie missed her when they served afternoon tea on the rocks, or had moonlight picnics at Smugglers Beach, for Maria always gave spice to the proceedings. The President longed for Murray Bay when Charles wrote of the "balmy breezes and the mountain and river views with their changing colors" as he went around the golf course. But when it rained—as it often did—Annie still had tarpaulins spread over the roof of their house, with tubs and bowls arranged to catch the overflow. The primitive touch was still a matter of charm.

Major Butt had never known three brothers to be as devoted as the Tafts. Charles struck him as being quite insistent on the role he had played in getting Will to the White House. "I will agree not to minimize the part you played in making me President if you will agree not to minimize the part Roosevelt played," Taft commented when all three were discussing the matter. But Helen held to her own convictions on the subject. More than once she pointed to the fact that her father was well on his way to the White House when he went to the Philippines, and she knew that her mother had played a large role in the matter, too.

In September the President left for a 12,759-mile tour in his private car, the *Mayflower*. During his term of office he was to travel 114,558 miles in all and a special mattress was kept in readiness for him at Union Station at all times. At the moment his chief aim was to speak to the voters of the West who had been deeply antagonized by the Payne-Aldrich bill. The farmers had been looking for lower rates and the manufacturing elements in the East for full protection. Neither was satisfied with the bill, which left the tariff schedules nearly as high as before and in some important instances higher. The wool tariff was one of the most upsetting to the farmers, and the Progressives in the Republican party were in open revolt, insisting that Taft was abandoning the Rooseveltian policies. An increase in the duty on newsprint brought the wrath of the publishers to bear on Taft, and the newspapers were relentless in their attacks on his tariff stand. When the cost of living went up at this point the public blamed the rise in various commodities on the new tariff act.

The President did not help matters when he made a speech in Winona, Minnesota, characterizing the Payne-Aldrich as the "best tariff bill that the Republican Party has ever passed, and therefore the best tariff bill that has been passed at all." The headlines blazoned the primary quotation. Taft's qualifications were lost sight of in the ensuing din. The farmer, the laborer, the white collar worker, all took umbrage, and the forward steps taken in the bill were ignored. Both the Democrats and the Insurgents pounced on the carelessly spoken words and the Winona speech became a major point of attack on Taft. The offense was compounded when he artlessly admitted that he had dashed off his speech "between stations" as he traveled. He dictated it and "glanced through it only enough to straighten out the grammar."

Even his loyal brothers could find no excuse for him this time and Horace wrote to him on October 8, 1909: "The speeches have been fine, though as for the one in Winona about the tariff—I did not write to you about it, because my secretary is a lady and no language that suited the speech could be dictated. I will swear at you about it when I see you."

Taft was bewildered by all the uproar and he telegraphed to Nellie three days after he had delivered the speech: "I said what I thought and there is that satisfaction." However, his seeming appraisal of the tariff act as the best in history stuck in the public mind, like his observation when asked what the outcome of the labor situation would be: "God knows. Even a rat will fight when driven into a corner."

Day after day as he traveled the President wrote to his wife—on jolting trains, in hotel rooms and automobiles, whenever he had a moment—giving her an intimate and detailed view of each step along the way. It was becoming a familiar Taft refrain—banquets and speeches, school children lined up in flag formation, bands playing, gatherings of Yale alumni. The round was so exhausting that Major Butt finally insisted on all banquets being limited to an hour, on curbing the speeches preceding the President's, on cutting dessert from the menus. Taft did not encourage familiarity on these tours but he did not care for toadyism, either. Some of his friends found it just as well not to call him Will now that he was President. Although he deplored the pompous touch he had a keen sense of dignity and tradition, and he did not lend himself to every cam-paign trick. At Glenwood Springs, Colorado, he declined to don a bath-ing suit and take a dip before the entire population.

In Cincinnati on his cross-country tour he found Charles and Annie rejoicing in the possession of another Rembrandt. It was so costly that Charles had said he would not buy it, but when Frick threatened to get it unless Charles did, Annie felt that this was a challenge to a Sinton. It was exhibited later that year in New York when Scott & Fowles gave an exhibition of Taft paintings, including two by Frans Hals. "I think they made quite a sensation in the New York art world," Charles reported to Will. "Our Rembrandt was also a ten-strike." His first Rembrandt, "Portrait of an Elderly Woman," was bought in 1908 and his second, "Portrait of a Young Man," in 1909.

Early in September the President had a tremendous ovation in Chi-cago and he reacted as he always did to the mid-Western metropolis. "One can't touch the hem of Chicago without feeling an electric thrill," he wrote to Nellie. The crowds in San Francisco were more restrained but they tore loose in Los Angeles where he spoke in the Shriners Audi-torium from a dais facing an enormous map of the United States, with flashing lights marking his route across the continent. Fanny and Bill took him home for the night to their rambling ranch building, which the President thought was picturesque with its lacework of ivy and cling-ing vines. He wrote triumphantly to Nellie from Portland, Oregon, on October 3, 1909: "I have had a great reception in the Northwest; indeed from the time I left home it has been continual acclaim. . . . Good-night, my darling. I think of you always and every hour. It is still a long time before I shall see you but I love you, my dear, oh so much. Lovingly yours, Will."

But the most important event of his tour was his exchange of visits at El Paso and Juarez with President Porfirio Díaz, whose power was on the wane after a long dictatorship. Taft wrote to Nellie that the United States had two billions of American capital in Mexico that would be en-dangered if Díaz were to die or his government go to pieces.

The encounter went off with a flourish and had certain *opéra bouffe* aspects. The utmost ceremonial was observed and the two Presidents entered the banquet hall at Juarez arm in arm for a magnificent function at which they drank toasts from golden goblets. President Taft asked President Díaz if he thought that either of their wives knew to what ex-tent they had affected national affairs. The Mexican president humor-ously acknowledged that although his wife had not been responsible for his election as president she had probably assisted him in holding office, Taft responded that while his wife seemed to figure little in his official career, no one was as conscious as he of the effect that she had had. He reminded President Díaz that she had kept him from going on the bench and had thereby paved the way to the White House.

Taft was closely guarded on this occasion and when he heard afterwards that special precautions had been taken he roared with laughter. "Why should you have worried?" he inquired. "If anyone wanted to get me, he couldn't very well have missed such an easy target." After leaving the White House he wrote that he was never conscious of any personal anxiety while in large crowds. Security regulations had so improved that he believed no assassin could again walk up to a President with a revolver under his handkerchief, as in the case of McKinley. But he felt that a constant guard was a great burden to the President and, in his own words:

> It is a little difficult to get away from the feeling that one is under surveillance himself rather than being protected from somebody else. If a person is determined to kill a President, and is willing to give up his life for it, no such protection will save him. . . . The worst danger is from those who have lost part or all of their reason and whom the presence of a President in the community excites.

After his meeting with Díaz President Taft passed three days at La Quinta, Charles's ranch in southwest Texas. In 1885 David Sinton had bought 197,000 acres in the counties of San Patricio and Aransas. He purchased the stock for seventy-five cents a share and it paid enormous dividends over the years. Now the towns of Taft, Gregory, and Portland stood on the land and Sinton rose close to its borders. It was a patriarchal property that had always been of great interest to Charles. From time to time the Taft boys, Elihu Root's son, and other family friends had spent months in this toughening atmosphere. Charles and Annie had sent their own Howard there from time to time and Hulbert was thinking of settling on the ranch when he decided instead to work for the *Times-Star*.

La Quinta was scientifically run and contributed to the development of the Southwest. A large area had been sold to tenant farmers and five large farms of 1,000 acres each were operated directly by the company. This opportunity drew experienced cotton farmers from North Texas. Twenty different industries were developed on the property. There were stores, cotton gins, a cottonseed oil mill, a packing house, lumber, feed and implement yards, and two hotels. The Taft Oil and Gin Company, the Taft Packing House, and Taft's Crystal Shortening all became familiar trade names in the area. There were 30,000 head of cattle on the ranch and the famous Santa Gertrudis strain were bred there.

The major crop was cotton when the President visited La Quinta. Charles, Annie, and their daughter Louise met him at Gregory and they drove over a shell road to the ranch. There had been a flood and the golf course was in a sodden condition but Charles hoped that Will would enjoy the shooting. He did—as a spectator only. Annie deplored the fact that neither Will nor Charles was sportsman enough to carry a gun and shoot birds. But the party as a whole brought down sixty-eight mallards, teals, and redheads. Next day the President drove to the town of Taft and spoke to the ranch employees. He watched a roundup of 3,000 head of cattle at Rincon Ranch, adjoining Charles's place.

From La Quinta he went to the famous King Ranch near Corpus Christi and was the guest of Mrs. Henrietta King, owner of La Gertruda, the largest stretch of fenced property in the world. Mrs. King had 1,100,000 acres and the railroad crossing her land traveled for ninety miles. The President was surprised to find her a soft-spoken woman of seventy-six, still attending to the business of the ranch. She had been pictured as the swashbuckling cattle queen of Texas, moving around in khaki and sombrero. But he learned that day that no authentic pictures had ever been taken of her and that the legends built up around her were fictitious. He sat across the luncheon table from her, with a forty pound turkey between them, and wrote later to Nellie of Mrs. King's surprising grace and charm.

At St. Louis he was cheered by a batch of letters from home, telling him of his wife's improvement. From there he sailed down the Mississippi on the flagship *Oleander*, with a flotilla of thirteen vessels following. Congressmen, state governors, and politicians were on board and the public soon heard that Taft was fraternizing with Joe Cannon. At the same time he wrote to Nellie that Cannon would undoubtedly be the incubus of the 1910 Congress. With his usual leavening touch he wrote more romantically of "sitting for two hours watching the full moon rise over the Kentucky hills and flood the Mississippi with its moonlight."

The Southerners turned out to welcome their President. His gourmet tastes were whetted as he dined at Antoine's and the Pickwick Club in New Orleans. He attended the French opera *Les Huguenots* and every box was filled with the beauties of Louisiana. He was at the Unitarian church early next morning and then made a tour of the Vieux Carré. In Savannah twenty white pigeons floated like doves of peace in the banquet hall after dinner. The souvenirs were exotic. "I have never seen so much loot in my life," said the much-traveled President as the jewel boxes that held the ices, the silver coasters that contained the almonds, the china ashtrays with the President's initials in gold, the silver filigreed cut glass vases that held the punch, the chafing dishes with alcohol lamps that contained the stewed terrapin, all went home with the guests.

When the President reached Augusta, Georgia, he was again at home, since this was a familiar resting place and his golfing retreat. The people staged a big parade, thousands carrying Japanese lanterns on golf sticks in the line of march. The tour wound up in Richmond. The President had made 259 speeches in all and he now jested that he could recognize a caterer's dinner at a glance from the way the caviar sat on the toast. He had put on considerable weight from all the banqueting, and in climbing hills he now described his own state as "puffy." Archie Butt looked after him with all the care of a wet nurse, to see that he was properly attired and performed his duty as he ought, he wrote cheerfully to Nellie.

As his letters from point after point poured in Mrs. Taft drew comfort from the knowledge that so many people were getting to know her husband in person. She always felt that when he could apply the personal touch his cause was won, but she was already well aware of the political grumblings that flared into view in the press. Perhaps she was less convinced than Will that the warmth of his welcome everywhere was conclusive evidence of his standing with the people as a whole. He wrote to her from Texas on October 24, 1909:

> I cannot be mistaken in finding that the people are very friendly to me. Whatever their judgment as to particular things I have done, I certainly up to this time have their good will. . . . The one note that I could hear everywhere was that of contentment and satisfaction with conditions, and such a note is inconsistent with the defeat of the party in power. . . . Our friends, the insurgents . . . have become desperate . . . and their cry is heard above the quiet chant of contentment that exists everywhere in this country where I have been.

Behind the tour lay the ground swell of rising discontent, but Taft the man made a popular impression. The residents of cities, towns, and hamlets had a chance to judge him for themselves. The local newspapers presented him in a thousand different guises and his trip had all the glow of steady acclaim, of cheers and surging thousands. By the time it had ended Major Butt had come to the conclusion that Taft liked travel as the dipsomaniac loved drink. "I come back bedraggled and worn out, and he returns refreshed and invigorated," he wrote to his sister-in-law, Clara Butt. Archie had also accustomed himself to the hearty way in which the President entered into the gamboling of the Yale alumni who turned up at many points. "I have heard so much of the Spirit of Yale that I am really beginning to see what it means," he commented.

After studying Taft closely throughout the tour Archie decided that while he might be complacent his interest in all manner of people was sincere. He thrived on routine and could not be hurried or shaken from a given course. Although his nerves were steady the drumfire of press criticism got under his skin, and he asked Mrs. Taft and Carpenter to stop sending him antagonistic editorials. These merely angered him.

But in general Butt was impressed with his equable temper and good disposition. He considered him the cleanest-minded man he had ever known, although conceding a lively interest in harmless gossip. He was abundantly versed in the ancestry, marriage links, professional accomplishments, and idiosyncrasies of the better-known figures across the country. With his encompassing knowledge of people and their antecedents, and the fact that his career touched so many aspects of the national life, his impressions were rich with contemporary appraisal and comment. His letters to his wife and to Mabel Boardman were laced with material of this kind.

Taft listened attentively, if not always responsively, to the family chorus of suggestion and advice. Harry in New York, Charles in Cincinnati, Horace in Watertown, kept up a steady barrage. Horace alone gave him an acid bath of frank comment from time to time, perhaps because he was skeptical of all politicians and was a reformer at heart. Will, being innocent of guile, seemed to him to be hopelessly miscast among the intriguers. He listened to them all with true affection but their voices were dimmed during the clamorous days of the Presidency, while he moved uncertainly in an atmosphere of doubt and antagonism. There were times when the brothers felt that they could not reach him through the thicket of discord.

Taft was back from his travels in time for the family Christmas of 1909. With McKinley's assassination a fresh memory, he was closely guarded. Bob, who had not seen him for several months, telegraphed that he would be at the station to meet him. Six feet tall and moving now with more self-confidence Bob had just entered the Harvard Law School and was rooming in Craigie Hall. When he reached the gate leading to the train the stationmaster waved him off and shouted: "You'll have to get back, young fellow. This space is reserved for officials who are meeting the President." Bob stepped back without a word of protest. But in the midst of all the hand-shaking the President looked around and asked: "Where's Bob?" At this point his son worked his way into view and passed the surprised stationmaster. His father was as much amused by Bob's avoidance of the limelight as he was by Charlie's affinity for it. And he chuckled over Delia's welcoming note: "Welcome home! A thousand times welcome! You have escaped the perils of the railroads—the perils of indignation, the perils of assassination. Bless God from whom all blessings flow."

But death cast a shadow over the White House just before Christmas. In October Winifred had been taken to Johns Hopkins Hospital, where Dr. Harvey Cushing operated on her for a brain tumor. She died in December and the news reached the President as he was giving a Cabinet dinner. He had entered the Blue Room alone, for Mrs. Taft was not feeling well enough to appear that night. An announcement was made to the guests and he left at once for Watertown to attend his sister-in-law's funeral. She was cremated at Linden, Connecticut. "It is the kind of blow that divides a man's life in two," Horace wrote to Will as he pulled himself together three days before Christmas and went to work on his mail.

Washington had a white Christmas and the President went out in the snow to do some of his own shopping. He selected books at Brentano's and silver at Galt's. Books and umbrellas were always his standbys but this year there were silver knives to be bought for the secret service men and other gifts for the staff, including a traveling bag for Archie. The President was much too impressive in his proportions to move about unnoticed, and he was greeted on all sides like some great Santa Claus. Nellie's ill-health at this time dimmed his joy to some extent. She was steeling herself for the season ahead and the strain was great. Will and she passed the last evening of 1909 alone. Sitting together in the library on the second floor of the White House they saw the old year out and the new year in. Life had changed considerably for both of them in the course of a single year. Things had not turned out the way that Nellie Herron had planned them, yet the family flame burned unwaveringly. While addressing the students of the State Institute and College at Columbus, Mississippi, early in November, the President had said:

> I shall be glad that I shall not have any property to leave to my boys, of whom I have two, but only a good character and a pride in themselves and a good education; but for my daughter I am going to scrape together as much as I can give her and as good an education as I can so that she shall take in the lesson which I first sought to announce as the text of my discourse, that she marry only when she chooses to marry, and not because of circumstances.

The new year began with a successful reception, the first State function that Mrs. Taft had been able to attend since the start of her illness. Wearing a white crepe gown embroidered with gold, and carrying pink roses, she presided with poise and courage. It was not easy for her to stand at the head of her receiving line of Cabinet ladies and greet her guests. The diamond pin that they had given her hung as a pendant from her pearl dog collar. More than 5,000 streamed past but Mrs. Taft retired to her private quarters at the end of an hour. On this occasion the Tafts had limited the blue tickets of admission to avoid giving special privileges to some, a system that had caused dissatisfaction and jealousy in the past.

New orders had just gone into effect for the purpose of giving the White House a more homelike air. All the candles in the East Room, the Green Room, and the Red Room were lighted regularly. Masses of flowers and ferns were arranged wherever they might warm up the scene. Rugs were not taken up and guard ropes were abandoned. The furniture was left in place, except when certain pieces had to be pushed back to give more room. Soon after the Tafts took occupancy a huge and famous bathtub was installed to encompass the portly frame of the President.

Taft had a good deal to say in the plans for entertainment. Few Presidents have concerned themselves as much with the minutiae of party-giving as William Howard Taft. His wife's illness and his own flair as a host combined to enlarge his role in this respect. He was apt to argue with Nellie over the numbers invited and the fare provided. As an experienced trencherman he liked to see his guests well fed and he insisted on supper being served after receptions—not just for the favored few invited to the upper corridor of the White House but to everyone who came. Buffet suppers were frequently served to as many as 2,000 guests.

Special tickets were denied to the press. They were treated like the other guests and they resented their isolation after the intimacies of the Roosevelt era. News was rarely handed out to them direct. "I see very few newspapermen," the President observed. But if the press were out in the cold the diplomats and judiciary were never more at home. The Diplomatic Reception given early in January, 1910, was rated one of the best in White House history up to that time. Mr. and Mrs. Charles Phelps Taft of Cincinnati helped to receive and Annie's brilliant dark eyes glowed with excitement as she stood close to Nellie, who looked well that night in pink satin. The Judiciary Reception was equally successful. The President had taken a firm stand on precedence in giving the Chief Justice rather than the Speaker the place of honor. This had been a long-drawn-out battle and had provided a good deal of social chit-chat until Alice Longworth created a fresh diversion by smoking in the East Room. It was no dark secret that she was fond of cigarettes, but this time she was breaking ice on dangerous ground. Baroness Rosen, wife of the Russian ambassador, lit a cigarette quite casually and President Taft, who did not smoke himself, hastened to provide a flame for Alice's cigarette. Soon nearly every European woman in the room was smoking. Finally Alice moved into the Green Room and Archie Butt deduced—perhaps erroneously—that she had fled from the icy stares of the American wives. By this time the Major was persuaded that Alice was making a great mistake in not trying to placate Mrs. Taft. The only person she could not charm out of disapproval after one of her escapades was the President's wife and she underestimated Mrs. Taft's influence—or did not care. It was Nellie who kept Nicholas Longworth from being ap-

pointed minister to China, a post he coveted, because she thought that
Alice might stir up storms in the Celestial Kingdom.

By the end of February, 1910, the newspapers were commenting on
the President's weary look. He had lost much of his buoyancy and the
cares of office were beginning to show. From the start of his administration he had been involved in controversy and his worry over his wife's
condition was unabated. "He bears up beautifully under it, but as the
weeks go by and there does not seem to be any permanent improvement,
his hope sinks pretty low at times," Archie wrote at Easter. Mrs. Taft
went to the National Theater if she could do anything at all, and she
appeared in the gallery to hear the President read his message to Congress. Her interest in his career never flagged, although her spirits did.
When state dinners were given she was served at the same time in the
breakfast room adjoining the State Dining Room. There she had the
benefit of the music and the hum of the dinner table, but she never had
anyone dine with her on these occasions. Butt was struck by the scene
when he walked into the Blue Room on an April evening in 1910 and
found the President sound asleep on a long sofa with his wife, looking
wan and miserable, sitting beside him.

Aunt Delia was the President's guest at the White House early in
1910, and he went out of his way to honor his aged aunt. Her personality and character were often reflected in his speeches, particularly
when he addressed groups of college women. She was still vigorous, alert,
and did not wear glasses except for reading. Her writing was firm and
legible and she read insatiably. During the presidential years she was interviewed and quoted on all manner of subjects from her apple pies,
publicly lauded by Will, to the tariff and woman suffrage. Delia's opinions were delivered modestly but with conviction. No one appreciated
her qualities more than her boy Will and his pride in her was visible as he
escorted her across the East Room, took her to the Lincoln Day dinner
in New York that year, or introduced her to the celebrities who circled
around him.

Delia had no hesitancy about speaking up for Millbury and on her
return home she urged Will to back the local movement to get the Post
Office moved into better quarters. "The only thing lacking is consent
from Washington . . . it would be an immense convenience to our end
of the street, and nobody would be discommoded," she wrote with the
firm assurance that she had the President of the United States on her
side. However, he was dismayed when the New York *World* ran a
lively interview with Delia in which she discussed her visit to Washington
and some of Will's views on national questions. "I am sure that if all the
women in America showed that they wanted the suffrage Will would try
to get it for them," Delia announced, among other things. "Too bad

Will Taft can't have all he wants to eat," she added. She had found him the same old Will, bigger and busier but just as simple and as unaffected as of old. However, he had been cut off from her pies.

By the spring of 1910 the nation was aware that Mrs. Taft was having choice musicales at the White House. Fritz Kreisler charmed one audience and the quartet of the Boston Symphony Orchestra provided another musical evening of distinction. Young John McCormack paid the first of many visits and Mrs. Taft and the President went to Baltimore to hear Caruso sing. They enjoyed Maude Adams in *What Every Woman Knows* and De Koven's new opera, *The Wedding Trip*. The chorus marched to the footlights and saluted the President with flashing swords at the De Koven performance.

The Tafts did everything they could to encourage the arts during the President's term of office. A succession of gifted artists, musicians, and writers dined or performed at the White House, and Mrs. Taft gave them all Tiffany gold medals as souvenirs. She made a point of staging Shakespearean productions and Charles Coburn was chosen to present *A Midsummer Night's Dream* on the White House lawn. Taft's own tastes and sophistication led him instinctively to cultivate men of letters during his term of office and he was in his element at a dinner given in 1912 at Sherry's in New York for William Dean Howells, celebrating this writer's seventy-fifth birthday. Taft recalled his own graduation day at Yale when Howells, receiving an honorary degree, noticed how nervous he was and spoke to him reassuringly. He acknowledged his personal debt for the pleasure Howells had given him in the "pictures of American life and society and character he has painted." Gathered around Taft and Howells on this occasion were Ellen Glasgow, William Allen White, Mary Austin, Augustus Thomas, Alice Hegan Rice, and other stage and literary figures. Both Tafts were always at home with men and women of letters.

While her husband waged his political battles Mrs. Taft coped as well as she could with the social round, giving her musicales and garden parties, and entertaining for the young. One of her garden parties featured an Indian fete with Sioux dancers performing. Straw hats and informal clothes were decreed for the garden parties and none of his guests looked as jovial and expansive as William Howard Taft in a boater. Just before the first garden party in May, 1910, word came from Whitelaw Reid that King Edward VII was dying, followed by news of his death. The President immediately asked Theodore Roosevelt, who was still abroad, to represent the United States at his funeral. Cornelius Vanderbilt asked to be appointed special ambassador at the coronation of George V but his wish was not granted. Helen Taft was keen to go abroad to view this spectacle but her parents would not hear of it.

Theodore Roosevelt was now about to reappear on the American scene. Dismayed by the constant criticism of his actions in Congress and the press, President Taft had written to him in May, 1910, with a touch of humility and apology: "I do not know that I have had harder luck than other Presidents but I do know that thus far I have succeeded far less than have others. I have been conscientiously trying to carry out your policies but my method of doing so has not worked smoothly." Taft mentioned the added burden of his wife's illness and the "asphasia that for a long time was nearly complete." She was not an easy patient, he wrote, and any attempt to control her only increased the nervous strain. Then, setting forth his wife's condition with precision, Taft wrote: "Gradually she has gained in strength and she has taken part in receptions where she could speak a formula of greeting, but dinners and social reunions where she has had to talk she has avoided."

Roosevelt, who had already been well primed from many sources on Taft's ineptitudes as well as on his wife's condition, responded from London on June 8, 1910: "Indeed you have had a hard time, as you say, and of course the sickness of the one whom you love most has added immeasurably to your burden. We have followed with the greatest concern the news of her trouble, and feel very genuine pleasure at learning how much better she is."

The former President had a chance to see for himself how Mrs. Taft was when he visited the summer White House at Beverly on his return from the King's funeral. The returning hero, back from his safari, back from the pomp of the historic pageant in London, was rapturously greeted by the worshipers who had missed his exuberant ways. Taft had sent him an invitation to the ship. Again Archie Butt had been the bearer. Rumors of a break between the two men were in the air but their meeting was harmonious. Roosevelt arrived at the house in Beverly with Henry Cabot Lodge and at once took Taft's two hands in his dynamic grip.

"Ah, Theodore, it is good to see you," the President exclaimed.

"How are you, Mr. President. This is simply bully," Roosevelt replied.

"But why 'Mr. President?' " Will asked.

"Because it used to be 'Mr. President' and 'Will,' now it must be 'Mr. President' and 'Theodore.' "

Roosevelt stayed for two hours. Both men avoided politics and a floodgate opened when Taft suggested that Teddy discuss his experiences in London. In her Recollections Mrs. Taft read sympathetic comradeship into their meeting. But although the former President told Taft's friends that he intended to work for his renomination, it soon was apparent that a Roosevelt boom was in the making. Teddy's tour through the West was one continuous ovation, and Taft followed the flow of his speeches with bewilderment. He was upset by his attack on the Supreme Court, although Taft's own opinion of it at the time was far from high. The President expressed his astonishment over Roosevelt's attitude in a letter addressed to his brother Charles from Beverly on September 10, 1910:

> He allows himself to fall into a style that makes one think he considers himself still the President of the United States. In most of these speeches he has utterly ignored me. . . . His attitude toward me is one that I find it difficult to understand and explain. . . . But I have made up my mind . . . that the only course for me to pursue is to sit tight and let him talk. He is at the head of the Insurgents, and for the time being the Insurgents are at the top of the wave. . . .

In this same letter Taft alluded to many of the points at issue between Roosevelt and himself. He wrote that he did not know that Teddy was set on having Harry White reappointed; that apparently he was indignant over editorials in the Cincinnati *Times-Star*; that he regarded the letter sent to him at the boat as he left for Africa an "occasion for feeling bitterly toward me, because I dared to include you in the same class with him as assisting me in my canvass for the Presidency." In the final analysis President Taft concluded that his old friend was seeking justification for criticizing him. Before long it was quite clear to Will that Roosevelt intended to be a candidate in 1912. He confided to Horace that he had no desire himself for a second term but, if need be, he would run and "be beaten like a gentleman" rather than fail his supporters and let the battle go by default. As Taft had anticipated, he was accused of having a Cabinet overloaded with corporation lawyers. He was said to act always on the side of privilege and he was condemned for killing the Conservation Commission, a pet project of Theodore Roosevelt's.

The background of this decision involved the feuding all through 1909 and 1910 between Gifford Pinchot, chief of the Federal Forest Service, and Richard A. Ballinger, Secretary of the Interior. The dispute arose over a difference of opinion on national conservation policy and it ended with Ballinger resigning under fire and Pinchot being dismissed. Few incidents during his administration caused the President more suffering.

Roosevelt had given national conservation fresh impetus during his administration. He was annoyed when James Garfield, his own favorite, was dropped and Ballinger was appointed to succeed him. Taft, too, was keenly interested in conservation and, like Roosevelt, he liked the idealistic Pinchot, who took up a cause with uncommon ardor. Pinchot was a man of wealth who had studied forestry in Europe and had brought fresh ideas to bear on the subject. He belonged to Roosevelt's Tennis Cabinet and they had much in common.

The Alaska coal lands and vast tracts in the Pacific states were the points at issue. Pinchot charged that Ballinger favored the coal and mining companies, and the timber interests that he believed were exploiting the public lands of the West. He insisted that President Taft and his secretary of the interior were returning into private hands property that Roosevelt had withdrawn for conservation purposes. Taft, on the other hand, believed that Garfield had acted illegally in blocking them off.

Pinchot attacked furiously and the newspapers and magazines blew up the feud to major proportions. The master forester called it the most "critical and far-reaching problem this nation has faced since the Civil War" and went over Ballinger's head in an appeal to Congress. Taft looked on in bewilderment and wrote to Horace on December 27, 1909: "Gifford Pinchot is out again defying the lightning and the storm and championing the cause of the oppressed and downtrodden and harassing the wealthy and the greedy and the dishonest."

The President defended Ballinger, believing him to be the victim of an attack incited by a fanatic and magnified by the press. He wrote that life "is not worth living and office is not worth having if, for the purpose of acquiring the popular support, we have to do a cruel injustice or acquiesce in it." But Taft moved slowly in this, as in many other presidential crises, giving Pinchot his head while the public storm blew around them. He did not wish an open break with the powerful conservationist but Root at last told him: "There is only one thing for you to do now and that you must do at once." So he wrote calmly and judicially to Pinchot, dismissing him and informing him that he had destroyed his usefulness as a subordinate of the Government.

George W. Wickersham helped Taft draw up a defense of Ballinger. The President's stand was upheld in a congressional investigation but the Insurgents called it a whitewash for Ballinger and continued to belabor Taft as the agent of big business and a traitor to the cause of conservation. The President knew that Roosevelt, soon to return from Africa, would deplore the dismissal of his favorite. But Pinchot did not wait for Teddy to reach the United States. He went to Europe and primed the former President on the case from beginning to end. This feud widened the breach that had already developed between Taft and Roosevelt and remained a bitter issue down the years. Taft always considered the Ballinger-Pinchot controversy one of the most misunderstood of his problems, although evidence assembled years later tended to prove that he was right on the basic issue.

During the summer of 1910 the President found some relief from these troublesome matters in cruising up the New England coast with a party of friends. Horace, Maria, Mabel Boardman, Delia, Major Butt, and Mrs. Louis More, Nellie's sister who was most often with her at this time, were on board. Although never able wholly to forget his political worries the President found the nights restful, steaming along the rocky coast, or lying at anchor in harbors. Delia and Horace entertained them all with quotations ranging from Homer to Mr. Dooley. At Newport the President found a colony of friends who had winter homes in Washington. There were impromptu talks on the village green and larger meetings at which he met the politicians of Maine. At times the *Mayflower* moved through dense fog, but moonlight shone on the cruising party in Casco Bay and Delia went happily ashore the next day to explore the home of Longfellow. They drove to Campobello by buckboard but the President did not make the trip, since again it would involve leaving American soil. Although legally free to do so he left native territory only for official business.

Altogether it was a happy year for Delia, particularly when Will spoke at the unveiling of the monument erected in honor of the Pilgrims at Provincetown, with eight battleships rocking in the harbor. Nellie joined the President at the wharf, and hymns dedicated to the Pilgrim Fathers were sung by the Harvard Quartet. The Tafts later drove to Mendon where the President found the grave of Joseph Taft, from whom he was descended. He was able to trace the direct line through Peter Taft, Aaron Taft, Peter Rawson Taft, and his father, Alphonso Taft. Many times on this expedition the President's car was stopped while he greeted the descendants of some common ancestor. But he had to deny Delia's plea that he attend the Worcester Fair that autumn, since this would mean opening the door to many similar requests.

Charles paid a solo visit to Washington during the summer and held court under Ike Hoover's watchful eye. The President, amused by his son's independence, wrote to Nellie: "It is very full of humor to think of Charley sitting at the head of the table in the White House and formally presiding over it as though he were President of the United States. But nothing fazes him."

There were times when Charlie did not like all the restrictions that being the President's son involved. "Doggone the White House anyway," he exclaimed on one occasion. "It's no place for kids!"

He had come home from his first year at the Taft School in knickerbockers, so when autumn came his mother took him to be fitted for his first long trousers. When this item of family news got loose in the capital, a reporter called Charlie to ask him about it. Helen listened with interest to the one-sided conversation that followed:

"Who said so?"

"Certainly not."

"Well, somebody has been giving you misinformation."

"An absolute denial."

"Well, if you want to quote me exactly you may say that I said the rumor is false."

Helen wondered what momentous matter was under discussion and whether or not Charlie thought he was speaking for his father. She pressed the point and he finally admitted that he had been discussing his long trousers.

Because of her mother's health, Helen had decided to leave college for a year and act as hostess at the White House. She came out formally in December, 1910, at a tea attended by 1,203 guests, but she had already been hostess at a dinner given for Prince and Princess Fushimi of Japan. At her own tea the President helped her to receive. The White House debutante was quickly drawn into a round of dinners and dances. Although the newspapers tried to whip up a vogue for "Helen pink" as a fashionable color, it never had the impetus that the dashing Miss Roosevelt had given to "Alice blue.'" The snows were heavy but the younger set managed to get from one cotillion to another and to attend luncheons at the Chevy Chase Club. Helen showed quiet independence when taking her mother's place as hostess and she ruled out the royal curtsy when the Duke of Connaught and his daughter Princess Patricia visited the White House. She unveiled the Steuben statue in Lafayette Park and on the same evening the President and Mrs. Taft received the German Liederkranz Society of New York.

On Christmas Eve, 1910, the choir of St. Paul's sang carols at midnight under the North Portico. Next day the President did not deviate from his custom of going to the Unitarian church while his family went to St. John's Episcopal Church, but he compromised later by attending the Episcopal church with Charlie before his young son was confirmed by the Bishop of Connecticut. Although Charlie's marks in Bible study were low, he was already deeply interested in religious matters. He sang in the choir and helped lead a Y.M.C.A. boys club in Watertown.

Charlie and Annie, with their daughter Louise, arrived on New Year's Eve to attend the White House ball given for Helen. Masses of holly festooned the chandeliers and side brackets. Roses, orchids, and azaleas were used everywhere except in the East Room, which was without decoration. Window panes were removed and curtains were drawn to give more floor space for dancing. The Marine Band played on the East Terrace. Mrs. Taft and Helen received in the Blue Room and the President went from room to room, greeting the young people. Taft liked dancing for its own sake and he was one of the Presidents who most frequently whirled his guests around the ballroom floor. On this occasion he danced with Ethel Roosevelt, who had come to Washington for

Helen Taft's ball. At twelve the President rose and toasted the dawn-
ing year—1911.

Next day 5,625 guests streamed through the White House, with Mrs.
Taft shaking hands as often as she could. Major Butt had been told to
present each guest by name, an innovation on New Year's Day. Alice,
Kermit, and Ethel Roosevelt all passed down the line. Horace alone was
missing, since he was in a New York hospital recuperating from an
operation. After Winifred's death he had changed his mind about putting up a new school building on a nearby hilltop, and proposed instead
to add gradually to the Warren Hotel, using the old school until the new
buildings were ready. Horace was proud of the record Taft boys were
making at Yale. Bob had done brilliantly there, graduating in 1910, a
Phi Beta Kappa and first in his class. He won the Woolsey Scholarship
and the second Ten Eyck Prize. His roommates at Yale were Harry P.
Bingham and Adrian Van Sinderen, longtime friends. He rowed on the
sophomore crew and in his junior year was president of the University
Debating Association. But aside from Bob, Taft boys were first in the
senior and freshman classes at Yale and second in the sophomore class
that year, and Horace felt that he was making progress. Charlie showed
more flair for athletics than any other Taft who attended his school. His
average in his studies had slipped that year to 91 but his uncle told
the President not to worry, for the boy had ambition and the right
spirit. He lost marks through being careless, not from lack of ability.

It was an occasion for family rejoicing when Aunt Delia celebrated her
eighty-fifth birthday at the Waters home, with roses, candles, and a sip
of champagne. "My infirmities are few," she wrote to her White House
family. "My joints need lubricating, and my hair needs replenishing,
but as far as I know, my mind is not failing, for which I am truly thankful."

Charles and Annie had just given George Grey Barnard, then creating a stir with his bold sculpture, a contract to design a Lincoln memorial
for Lytle Park in Cincinnati. "He has done some wonderfully strong
things, and we are hoping that he will produce a great work of art,"
Charles wrote to the President. At the same time he suggested that
Barnard be considered for the proposed Lincoln Memorial in Washington. He knew how potent Will was in this matter, for in 1911 the President was drawn into the early plans for putting up the memorial, a profound and lasting interest of his.

The Lincoln Monument Association, created in 1867, had made no
progress in forty-four years and now Congress had appointed the Lincoln Memorial Commission, with President Taft as chairman. Its members were commissioned to choose a site and to get plans under way. A
year earlier, in 1910, the Commission of Fine Arts had been appointed

by Congress and Taft worked closely with its members—such distinguished architects and public figures as Cass Gilbert, Frederick Law Olmsted, Jr., Thomas Hastings, Charles Moore, Edwin H. Blashfield, Pierce Anderson, and Colonel William W. Harts. It was finally agreed that Henry Bacon should be the architect and Jules Guérin the mural decorator.

Cass Gilbert congratulated Taft on the decision to build the memorial on the Potomac Park site, where it stands today in classic majesty. This architect thought that it made the completion of the great plan for the development of Washington inevitable. C. S. Pietro, the sculptor who had done a bust of Taft that he had liked, was considered for the statue of Lincoln but Bacon insisted that Daniel Chester French was the ideal candidate. Taft and everyone involved were pleased with the result.

The memorial plans had a long and troubled history, with contractors, marble experts, and members of Congress battling it out, while Taft played the role of mediator. He told Elihu Root at one point that "sectionalism and political selfishness" were holding things up and even threatening its completion. The politicians of Georgia worked hard for the marble from their own quarries but Taft, acting on advice from experts, favored Colorado marble against the claims of Georgia. "The spirit of the design is that of a shrine, and that calls of course for the purest white marble we can get," he wrote to Woodrow Wilson on November 19, 1913. Robert Lincoln studied both types of marble and agreed with Taft that the Colorado variety was the better one. Henry Bacon was persuaded that even the Pentelic marble of Greece did not compare with it. In the end Colorado marble was used.

Taft followed developments on the Lincoln Memorial until it was dedicated in 1922 and he worked closely with the Commission of Fine Arts on other cultural interests in the capital. As he coped with one political crisis after another he often gave thought to Lincoln's course of action and he sometimes found comfort in his words, which were framed on Taft's desk:

> If I were to try to read, much less answer, all the attacks made on me, this shop might as well be closed for any other business. I do the very best I know how—the very best I can; and I mean to keep on doing so until the end. If the end brings me out all right, what is said against me won't amount to anything. If the end brings me out wrong, ten angels swearing I was right would make no difference.

Each day the President was reminded that his mother's words "uneasy lies the head that wears a crown" now applied to him. He was well aware that his administration was bogging down, although he was firmly convinced that conservative business people everywhere approved of his policies. Young Theodore Roosevelt wrote to his father that compromise and vacillation were Taft's undoing. He did not assert himself enough, said the son of the man who had played so dynamic a role as President. But the old warmth between the two families was not entirely extinct and Taft was always cheered by lively exchanges with Alice Longworth. When he sent her a gift for Chistmas, 1910, she wrote to him in the old affectionate vein: "I have just got back from Christmas at Sagamore and found your adorable present. It was *too* dear of you to think of me and a cigarette holder is just the very thing I need."

There were many days now when Taft's chuckle was not heard, when his great good nature was tried, and he needed the consolation of his family to balance the weight of his office. At times he reflected that the only mitigating circumstance of his wife's illness was the fact that she was now somewhat removed from the struggle and was spared knowledge of some of the torture he was undergoing.

CHAPTER 18

SILVER WEDDING

Present and Mrs. Taft celebrated their silver wedding anniversary on June 19, 1911, at a time when the man who had been the popular governor of the Philippines was fast becoming the unpopular and bewildered Man in the White House. Since he had never become hardened to public criticism he suffered considerably. There were flashes of temper, loud dictation, and some impatience with the details of office. "I am stronger than my party and I am not strong enough," he wrote to his wife that summer, as the 1912 election loomed up.

But as always where family matters were concerned, he was his most genial self on the day of his silver wedding. Mrs. Taft had had a relapse in May but had recovered in time for the festivities. She faced the evening with stamina and pride. By this time no sign of her stroke remained except for the obstruction in her speech. Major Butt considered the silver wedding ceremony the most brilliant function in White House history but Archie was apt to feel the glow of the moment. It was certainly unique in the display of gifts and the variety of its 3,400 guests. The White House was outlined by thousands of multicolored lights. Every tree and shrub on the grounds twinkled with tiny bulbs. Searchlights illumined the American flag waving above the White House and picked up the kaleidoscopic effect of the fountain. Paper lanterns hung from the trees and lit up the walks. The White House windows were golden blocks of light.

An arch embowered in smilax and palms was inscribed with the Taft wedding dates: 1886-1911. It was a balmy June night and the stars seemed pale and far away in the glitter of the grounds. The air was fragrant with honeysuckle at the spot where Mrs. Taft stood on the South Portico, leaning on the President's arm. The guests who streamed past had come from all parts of the country. The ambassadors were present in court dress, the Army and Navy in summer uniforms with the maximum of gold braid, the prelates in severe black, the women in an infinite variety of gowns and jewels. Mrs. Taft proudly wore the diamond tiara that Will had given her for their anniversary. Her gown was of white satin, with silver brocaded flowers and point lace and she carried pink roses. The Washington Saengerbund Society sang an epithalamium from behind a screen of foliage, followed by "My Old Kentucky Home" and "The Last Rose of Summer."

The President personally rounded up each member of the family for the occasion. Bob, who was about to go abroad, was involved in examinations but his father wrote to him firmly: "It would gratify your mother very much if you could be with us. We don't like to have a wedding without the presence of our three children." He adopted a humorous vein with Charlie:"Your mother . . . is anxious to have you here to show what we can do in the way of raising boys when we try." He wrote to his Murray Bay friend, Mrs. Thérèse D. McCagg, then in Paris: "I am trying to gather in the fruits of the original wedding to be examined at the silver wedding." But Delia was a problem. Her dressmaker had just died and she felt she did not have a suitable gown for so grand an occasion. She thought there would be no room for her in the White House; moreover, she was sure that her lameness would be conspicuous. She now used braces and springs and was having an elevator installed in the Millbury house.

But Will pooh-poohed every argument she brought up. "Am determined you shall be here," he wrote. "Any dress you have would be most becoming. Nellie and I would be greatly disappointed if you didn't come. . . . . We have plenty of room for you even if I have to sleep out myself." He asked Bob to stop at Millbury and accompany his aunt to Washington. In the end Delia was the liveliest member of the party. "I am filled with wonder, love and praise that I am allowed to live to see this anniversary and to see Helen and Robert grown to manhood and womanhood, and both so highly esteemed—and little Charlie, a wonder to all who know him," she exclaimed.

Having taken the plunge Delia was in her element. She strolled about on Robert's arm, a tiny black-clad figure with a white lace scarf thrown over her shoulders. Helen, Robert, Charlie, and several aides tried to keep her from wearing herself out. Elihu Root and Ambassador Jusserand devoted special attention to the New England spinster who had loomed so large in the Taft family history. Colonel Ulysses S. Grant, Jr., Mrs. Nicholas Longworth, Webb Hayes, Mrs. Mary Arthur McElroy, and a great-grandson of President Andrew Jackson were among the relatives of former Presidents who were present. Howard Hollister, Nellie's early suitor from Cincinnati, watched them attentively and wrote later to Will that he would never forget the scene as they walked down the steps from the portico. They had shared many memories together.

At 11 o'clock the State Dining Room was thrown open and a buffet supper was served. Small tables were arranged on the West Terrace for those who wished to have supper outdoors. Champagne and great bowls of Rhine wine punch were served. The anniversary cake had twenty-five crystal hearts embedded in scrolls. Cherubs rose from a frosted sea, and roses and turtledoves girdled the cake. Twenty-five silk Stars and Stripes and the President's flag finished off this confectionery marvel. By midnight Mrs. Taft, exhausted, went upstairs, where she sat for another hour in a dimly lighted room watching the scene from a window. Her father was on the brink of death that day in Cincinnati but at the last moment word had arrived that he was slightly improved. Her sisters, Maria and Jennie, were with her.

The dancers waltzed to the "Blue Danube," the "Dollar Princess," and "The Serenade." They two-stepped to the "Grizzly Bear" and "Red Wing." Mendelssohn's "Wedding March" drifted from the South Porch, reminding the dancers why they were there. No one wanted the music to stop and President Taft let it continue until two in the morning when "Home, Sweet Home" broke up the gathering. After that he sat alone on the South Portico for a time, deep in thought. He decided to open the grounds to the public the following night, with the same musical program. But however romantic this event, it was soon followed by a ground swell of criticism, reflected in the diary entry of Mrs. James L. Slayden, wife of the Democratic congressman from Texas, who wrote: "The wedding was a prodigous affair, the company promiscuous to a degree . . . it was crude like a fair or a circus. . . . The Tafts have such excellent taste usually, and I am sorry to hear them criticized so sharply for accepting carloads of presents." Mrs. Slayden was an admirer of the President, considering him the "most perfect everyday gentleman" of all the Chief Executives she had known, and that number eventually included McKinley, Roosevelt, and Wilson. She admired Taft's reverence for law, and his chuckle reminded her of the cluck of a whippoorwill who had been up to mischief.

Actually the outpouring of silver had become an embarrassment, as a constant stream of vans rolled up to the White House with gifts from far and near. The idea had snowballed beyond control, just as congratulatory messages had reached the Tafts from all parts of the world. They came from rulers like the Czar and from farmers at the crossroads. Among the wedding gifts was a silver box containing fragments of the small house where graduates of the first Yale class were taught. The Senate gave the Tafts a silver tea service. Mabel Boardman, who did not attend, sent silver compote dishes. Mrs. H. W. Forbush offered a slipper belonging to the President's great-grandmother and the Commercial Club of Cincinnati came to Washington in a body to give him a loving cup.

Annie and Charlie missed this event, since they were in London attending the Coronation of George V. At the last moment the King made special arrangements for their daughter, too, to have a seat in Westminster Abbey. President Taft consulted Lord Bryce about this recognition of his niece at a time when they were in close communication over the more important matters of reciprocity and arbitration. Taft was in the midst of a crisis over the Canadian Reciprocity bill, due largely to one of his own malapropisms and a lack of political prescience. It was an issue that would always be associated with the name of Taft, who, in actual fact, was deeply devoted to Canada and its people. His object was to get reciprocal tariff reduction on natural products, a matter of special interest in the farming belts of both countries. Canada was an excellent customer and in his message to Congress in 1911 the President said:

> The Dominion has greatly prospered. It has an active, aggressive and intelligent people. They are coming to the parting of the ways. They must soon decide whether they are to regard themselves as isolated permanently from our markets by a perpetual wall or whether we are to be commercial friends.

At the same time Taft wrote to Roosevelt that the "amount of Canadian products we would take would produce a current of business between western Canada and the United States that would make Canada only an adjunct of the United States." The phrase "adjunct of the United States" did not get into circulation but the "parting of the ways" was picked up out of context and created a furor. Champ Clark added fuel to the blaze in February, when he spoke in the House in favor of annexation and observed that he hoped "to see the day when the American flag will float over every square foot of the British North American possessions clear to the North Pole."

Thoroughly alarmed by this time President Taft said that the talk of annexation was "bosh." He described Canada as a great, strong youth, anxious to test his muscles, and added: "The United States has all it can attend to with the territory it is now governing, and to make the possibility of the annexation of Canada by the United States a basis for objection to any steps toward their great economic and commercial union should be treated as one of the jokes of the platform."

The measure was passed at a special session called by the President and the bill was signed in July, 1911, after bitter opposition from the lumber and newsprint interests. Canada, too, had favored reciprocity until Taft and Champ Clark made their statements, but now the Dominion was up in arms. Sir Wilfrid Laurier, the white-plumed veteran of many battles who had headed the Liberal party for twenty years, supported reciprocity, saying that it would benefit Canada more than it would the United States, but the cry of annexation would not be stilled. The Premier went to the people on the issue and lost. It was a tactical defeat for President Taft on an important measure that had almost been effected.

He was in Kalamazoo, Michigan, when the news reached him that Canada had rejected reciprocity. Characteristically he commented: "I presume we can get along doing business at the same old stand. . . . I thought, and still think, that it would have been a beneficial measure for both countries, but now it is an exploded issue." The British papers were caustic over Taft's plunge into the firmly knit relationship of Canada with the Empire. The London *Observer* picked up the phrase "parting of the ways" and Champ Clark's flag-waving statement with shattering effect.

President Taft was sorrowful over contributing to a major blunder in diplomacy. He was profoundly disappointed, since he regarded reciprocity as one of the best moves of his administration. But there was little time to brood over this one issue, as problems beset him on all sides. He sent troops to the border because of unrest in Mexico but refused to be stampeded into war by taking sides with either faction. All through his administration he had to cope with problems in Latin America and on one occasion, discussing the various leaders, he remarked that he yearned to knock their heads together to make them maintain peace among themselves.

When disorder broke out again in Santo Domingo toward the end of his administration he had to send special commissioners and 750 marines to maintain control. The warfare continued long after he had left the White House. In general Taft favored Dollar Diplomacy for Latin America, as for China, and efforts were made during his administration to persuade bankers to grant loans when the government of Nicaragua was floundering. But the Senate would not back him in applying to Nicaragua the same plan for financial rehabilitation that he had used in Santo Domingo. His policy here missed fire entirely, but he pointed to the stability achieved in Guatemala, Honduras, San Salvador, and Costa Rica.

Taft's greatest disappointment in foreign policy was his failure to bring to fruition his arbitration plans. His belief in arbitration rather than force was a fundamental in all his thinking, and he worked with Lord Bryce on arbitration treaties with Britain and France that came to nothing. The Senate refused to ratify them except with such restrictive amendments that Taft thought it futile to negotiate further. "The narrow view that the Senate took was inconsistent with any arbitration at all," he noted. "It destroys all hope of an international court for the settlement of international disputes."

It was inconceivable to the judicial-minded Taft that men of goodwill should object to questions of honor being submitted to a tribunal composed of their fellows who understood the implications of national honor. But he was neither the first nor the last President to find his hands tied in the foreign field by the United States Senate. Throughout his life Taft envisioned international law as the ultimate answer to discord between nations, and both he and Woodrow Wilson endorsed the American Society for the Judicial Settlement of International Disputes when it was organized by Theodore Marburg of Baltimore long before the League of Nations or World Court came under discussion.

President Taft liked to have what he called his Cabinet House Party when Congress sat in summer. This was the case during the summer of 1911 when meetings were called at the White House and the members sometimes stayed overnight as in a dormitory. Taft was not a man who liked to be alone and he moved aides and secretaries into White House quarters. Meanwhile he wrote to Mrs. Taft, telling her how much he missed her presence, her flower arrangements, her sympathetic understanding. He commented on the portrait Anders L. Zorn was doing of him. Alice Longworth decided that it made him look pudgy. "But I am," he assured her. "Not as pudgy as that, Mr. President, and I would not have it," she protested. Mabel Boardman, who also disapproved of the Sorolla, did not like it and Archie Butt thought that it made him look florid and gave him reddish hair, but the President accepted it with equanimity.

Mrs. Taft knew that her husband would never be at a loss in playing host by himself and she read with interest of his dinner for sixty, followed by a reception in honor of Admiral Togo, the Japanese naval hero who had destroyed the Russian Fleet. Will reported that he had two bands, a cavalry troop, and "all the fuss and feathers we could gather together." Although it drizzled they used the terrace after dinner and the congressmen turned out in force for their Japanese guest. Not many of the Insurgents attended but the bipartisan nature of Taft's foreign policy was reflected in the large turnout from both parties. More than most Presidents he had selected appointees for key posts from either camp.

Taft believed that although La Follette dominated the Progressives they did not like him. The Republican factions, quarreling all through 1909 and 1910, had now lost control of Congress. The Insurgents by this time were officially known as the Progressives and they were better organized. They did everything they could to prevent Taft's renomination and to bring Roosevelt back into the picture. With many elements working against him the President's chances of re-election had become so dubious that his closest friends worried about him. Whitelaw Reid wrote to Miss Boardman from Wrest Park, Bedfordshire, with veiled advice against the President tangling with Roosevelt, who had taken a strong counterstand on the Arbitration Treaty. As ambassador, Reid sent the President detailed accounts of brilliant social functions in London involving Americans, and when King George V remembered President Taft's birthday in September, Will noted that "We Kings have to be neighborly." He was fifty-four years old and he thanked Mabel for the bag she had given him to hold his ties, which he changed often "under the inspiration and direction of that *arbiter elegantium*, Major Arthur Brooks," his faithful Negro attendant.

The President increasingly needed powerful friends. Stung by the criticism that was flowing in on him from all quarters he wrote to Miss Boardman on November 21, 1911: "If the people do not want me I am entirely willing to retire." But on Christmas Eve he sent her a long, handwritten letter, saying that he had more confidence at that moment in his re-election than for some time past. He listed all the forces he believed to be against him—a formidable array of Progressives, of newspaper publishers, of potent women like Anne Morgan, of men like Roosevelt, Louis D. Brandeis, Albert J. Beveridge, and Albert B. Cummins. He knew the radical vote would go against him, but he did not consider it as formidable as a year earlier. He thought that his speaking tour in thirty states had been helpful and he hoped the public felt that he had given them a good administration. Taft was convinced that prosperity was on the way, that prices in many communities had come down, and that the business interests approved of his Tariff Board.

While his father coped with these problems Robert went abroad in the summer of 1911 with three of his college friends—Frank Nelson, Kim Townsend, and Jack Ewen. The President gave them letters to the ambassadors of twenty-two countries. "I keep the Baedecker and direct our movements generally, but we all four seldom agree on going anywhere and one person almost always goes in a grouchy sort of way to please the rest," Bob wrote to Helen from Amsterdam. Frank compared everything he saw in Europe with its parallel at home and announced his findings in ringing tones. Kim was amusing and good-natured but chose to affect the air of a Philistine. Jack wanted to see everything but spent so much time bathing, shaving, dressing, and sleeping that he usually missed the boat. Bob followed them only to a slight extent when they decided to paint a town red. He had never been counted a prig in college, and he did not parade his erudition, but it was always assumed at Yale that he was headed for success. He was now getting top grades at the Harvard Law School and would wind up as editor of the *Harvard Law Review* and president of the Law Review Board. Dean Ezra R. Thayer wrote to his father on August 24, 1911, while Bob was abroad:

> I cannot help expressing my pleasure at the news . . . that your son leads his class at the Law School. No success was ever better deserved. The faithfulness and severity of his work all through the year were remarkable and were only equalled by his modesty. . . . I was much impressed, even early in the winter, by his grasp of a law point, and the maturity and soundness of his thinking. He is a demonstration that a legal mind is heritable.

Donald J. Gallagher, a classmate at the Law School, wrote to his mother that young Taft did not care what people thought, but did exactly as he pleased. He seemed to have lofty ideals and the courage of his convictions. His clothes were sober and seemed out of date to some of the smart young Law School men. But Gallagher considered him the brightest member of the class and a well-built youth, although not at all good-looking—an appraisal that would not have been surprising to Bob. Feelers were already being sent out from the office of Charles S. Whitman, district attorney of New York, to draw the President's son within this orbit. But Bob had other ideas and they were firmly centered on Cincinnati.

The winter of 1911–12 was one of constant worry for the President, but everything else was forgotten when the *Titanic* sank in April, 1912. This event had special impact at the White House. Major Butt, who had gone abroad for a rest, went down with the ship. At first the President hoped that Archie might turn up among the saved, as dispatches poured in with details of the disaster. Among the many well-known figures who lost their lives was Major Butt's friend, the noted artist and writer Francis Davis Millet. The President and Mrs. Taft attended the memorial services in St. Paul's Church and St. John's. Later a memorial fountain for Butt and Millet was placed south of the White House grounds.

Archie was deeply missed by the Tafts, who had relied on him in many ways. The President had found him an accomplished and loyal aide and friend. He was quite unaware of the quiet chronicle of his White House days that Butt had embedded in his letters to his mother and sister-in-law,

and that one day would be made public. The President wrote affectionately of him to Miss Boardman:

> I cannot refrain from saying that I miss him every minute, and that
> every house, and every tree, and every person suggests him. Every
> walk I take somehow is lacking in his presence, and every door that
> opens seems to be his coming. He was a dear, sweet fellow, and if he
> had the choice of going, he could hardly have asked one that leaves
> a sweeter memory or a more lasting one.

Within a week after the Butt ceremonies the President was again a
mourner, this time at the funeral of his old friend, Frederick D. Grant,
in the Post Chapel on Governors Island. More personal still was the
death of John Herron, Nellie's father, a few days before the sinking of
the *Titanic*. Mrs. Taft was distraught over these combined events. Her
father had been ill for a long time and his death was expected, but the
sinking of the *Titanic* shocked the world. Butt had become so ill and
worn under the strain of watching the split developing between Roosevelt and Taft that the President had ordered him to take the trip which
led to his fateful voyage. Archie did not live to see the climactic events
that soon followed, although he was well aware of what was coming.

Taft was hurt to the core at this time by Roosevelt, and he wrote to
Miss Boardman that he must speak out in his own defense, however sor-
rowfully. He viewed it now as a tight fight and assured her that "we'll
buckle on our armor and fight for our institutions." An action brought in
the spring of 1912 to dissolve the International Harvester Company had
become a hot campaign issue since George W. Perkins, a director of the
company, was one of Roosevelt's backers. Once he had decided to attack
Teddy openly Taft was doubly miserable. Two months before the national convention he answered Roosevelt's charges in a speech he made in
Boston. At the same time he fired some broadsides of his own. From this
point on the warfare was pointed and deadly, with the country rocked by
the enmity of the two former friends. The bitterness of the fight was intense. The President, who scorned invective and mud-slinging, was up
against a past master in the biting phrase. Taft was neither eloquent nor
dramatic in his delivery; his legal training and his natural conservatism
tended to desiccate his oratory. Instinctively he rested his case on facts
rather than emotions.

As Senator La Follette's health failed Roosevelt took over the reins.
Although most of his old backers stood by Taft, in states where a direct
primary was held the vote showed Roosevelt to be more popular. President Taft had failed to popularize himself during his years in office; in
fact, his earlier image had been tarnished with the wear and tear of office.
The press had never warmed to him. Editorial comment on this battle of

the warriors was crushing and the cartoonists used it to the limit. Taft was drowned in dissension and waves of criticism beat on him from all sides. His family as a whole were deeply stirred by this historic battle. The Taft children had played for years with the Roosevelt children and they were all accustomed to the thought of their parents being close friends. Helen, who talked politics with her father more freely than any member of his family, wrote twenty-two years after his death that she believed his years in the White House to have been the only unhappy ones of his life.

She was close to her father as the breach developed between him and Roosevelt, and she knew how much he suffered over the change in their relations. The chill began with Taft's choice of Cabinet officers and deepened over the Pinchot-Ballinger controversy, the tariff, reciprocity, arbitration, and most of the moves initiated by the President. In spite of his protestations that he had gone to Africa immediately after Taft's inauguration so that no one could ever say he was still running the country, Roosevelt showed all the signs of chagrin and disaffection. He had picked Taft from among a group of able men, believing that he would be well attuned to the necessities of office. But the change in pace from his own dynamic style—the direct approach to every problem and the decisive move, right or wrong—had been disillusioning to Roosevelt. Reports kept reaching him of Taft's vacillation. Above all he had never expected his able secretary of war and governor of the Philippines to be ineffectual in office.

It was equally true that Roosevelt had not been long away from the White House before the old itch for office returned. His ambition and his energy were undimmed and he had been in the limelight for so many years that it irked him to play second fiddle. The situation, which had been more or less static while he was abroad, became highly charged on his return. He was quickly drawn back into politics while Taft, baffled and unhappy, followed this turn of events with dismay.

All through this painful period in her nephew's life Aunt Delia encouraged him to keep up his spirits. Her comments on Theodore Roosevelt were recurrent and tart. Finally he conceded to his faithful aunt the pain the situation gave him when he wrote:

> I can stand defeat as well as anybody. I have had a long and, I hope, an honorable career, and one in which good fortune has been with me at many crises. If now, fortune is to desert me for a time or permanently, it is my business to stand it, and I hope I will have the courage to do so. I have a sense of wrong in the attitude of Theodore Roosevelt toward me which I doubt if I can ever get over. But I have an abiding confidence, my dear Aunt Delia, in the eventual justice of the American people, and I am quite sure that in the end the hypocrisy, the insin-

cerity, the selfishness, the monumental egotism . . . that possesses
Theodore Roosevelt will make themselves known to the American people in such a way that his place in history will be accurately defined.

Delia cheerfully replied: "All the men I meet say 'I am for Taft, first,
last and all the time.'" She applauded him when he signed the bill for
the creation of the Children's Bureau, a major step in public health work.
An accomplished lobbyist where Will was concerned, she had been asked
to use her influence in this cause and she did, to good effect. Will took
pleasure in assuring her in April, 1912, that the measure was a *fait accompli*. She also gave him a pat on the back for appointing Julia Clifford
Lathrop, a friend of Jane Addams, to head the newly created bureau.
New Englanders were well aware that the sure way to reach the President
was to enlist the services of Aunt Delia. Horace reported to his brother
that she felt "a good deal of responsibility for the national government."

Mrs. Taft was so sensitive that she could not look at the papers when
Roosevelt carried Pennsylvania in the April primary of 1912. The President wrote to Horace, to Maria, to Charles, Harry, Fanny and Delia, assuring them of his own philosophical attitude as the picture darkened.
He pointed out that he represented a cause that would make it cowardly
for him to withdraw. "I am the only hope against radicalism and demagogy," he wrote, and in a brief summing up to Horace on May 12, 1912,
he was again the philosopher:

> Still, my dear old boy, I have had so much good fortune. I have had so
> much opportunity . . . to help along the cause of good government.
> Why should I mourn, or become a misanthrope or a pessimist because
> I may go down in a preliminary skirmish? . . . I shall be only fifty-five
> when I lay down my office and shall have some opportunity to strike a
> blow for decent government and the better things and I mean to do
> it. . . .

As the crucial convention opened in Chicago the President wrote to
Delia: "Of course, I would like to be nominated, but it is of much more
importance to the country that Roosevelt is beaten than that I be renominated." Meanwhile, Alice Longworth was so "full of bottled-up
savagery that I very nearly became ill," she later wrote. Her Longworth
relatives-in-law were as heatedly for Taft as she was for her father. Nicholas was in a quandary because of his devotion to Taft and his loyalty to
Roosevelt. Alice was convinced that no one suffered more than her husband in 1912.

It was a highly charged convention, lasting five days. Roosevelt arrived
in Chicago with a large black felt hat, his bulldog grin, and the utmost
confidence that he would be the winner. "I'm feeling like a Bull Moose!"
he exclaimed on his arrival and thereby gave his party its name. Crowds

gathered around him. Bands played "There'll be a Hot Time in the Old Town Tonight." The mob shouted "Soak 'em, Teddy." Twenty thousand people flocked to the auditorium to hear him speak on the eve of the convention.

Warren G. Harding nominated Taft, with William Jennings Bryan looking on as he covered the event for a news syndicate. Elihu Root presided and his keynote speech, quietly delivered, was directed more against Theodore Roosevelt than the Democratic candidate still to be chosen. Root made such resolute rulings that the anti-Taft delegates charged sardonically that they were steamrollered. In any event, Taft was the victor.

He stayed in the White House and when it was all over he wrote to Mabel Boardman with a touch of triumph: "Whatever happens in November, we have achieved the most important end and that is that Roosevelt can not be President, or the absorber of the Republican Party." He conceded that with a divided party his own chances were small but a "good deal of water flows under the bridge in four months," he ended hopefully.

The irrepressible Teddy promptly stunned the country by organizing the Bull Moose party. The National Progressives held a second convention and nominated him for President and Senator Hiram W. Johnson for Vice President. It was only a matter of weeks until the thunder of the Bull Moose campaign was heard throughout the land. The platform encompassed direct primaries, the initiative and referendum, suffrage for women, and various reforms in the social order. On a two months' speaking tour Roosevelt put more energy into fighting the standpatters in his own party than in challenging the Democrats.

But Woodrow Wilson was now in the field, nominee of the Democratic party and a more formidable opponent than he had seemed at first. In addition to his eloquence and personal gifts he had the great advantage of facing a divided party. Taft wrote to his wife with some bitterness on July 21, 1912: "If I can not win I hope Wilson will, and Roosevelt feels that if he can not win, he hopes Wilson will." At the moment Taft thought that the Republican party needed the discipline of defeat. Although he realized that the Bull Moose party would certainly affect the vote, he also felt sure that a party created around a "mere personality whose platform and candidate and purpose are all nothing but Theodore Roosevelt" could never become a permanent force in politics.

As the campaign progressed he found it difficult to believe that Roosevelt was the man they had all known as President. He expressed his bewilderment in a letter to Nellie over the "fakir, the juggler, the greengoods man, the gold brick man that he has come to be. . . . I have not any feeling of enmity against Roosevelt or any feeling of hatred. I look upon him as an historical character of a most peculiar type. . . ."

Taft was not a man given to hates or animosities. This would have been contrary to his genial habit of thought. He found that the appointment of Charles D. Hilles as chairman of the Republican National Committee met with favor on all sides. But Hilles was concerned when Wilson and Roosevelt each rated a column a day of political news in the papers, whereas the only comment on Taft concerned his golf. The President wrote impatiently to Nellie on July 22:

> I seem to have heard that before. It always makes me impatient, as if I were running a P. T. Barnum show, with two or three shows across the street, and as if I ought to have as much advertising as the rest. . . . Sometimes I think I might as well give up so far as being a candidate is concerned. There are so many people in the country who don't like me. Without knowing much about me, they don't like me— apparently on the Dr. Fell principle.

The sanctity that surrounded the Presidency did not seem to save him from the candor of friends or foes, he wrote. But since it was not the height of his ambition to be popular he had become philosophical about the dislike people felt for him; there were other and better things than being popular. He recalled the great popularity of Theodore Roosevelt "for reasons that I should not like to have attributed to me." Although it was still July and the election was four months off he wrote his own valedictory to his devoted wife: "I have held the office of President once, and that is more than most men have, so I am content to retire from it with a consciousness that I have done the best I could, and have accomplished a good deal in one way or another. . . . It is a very humdrum, uninteresting administration, and it does not attract the attention or enthusiasm of anybody, but after I am out I think that you and I can look back to some pleasure in having done something for the benefit of the public weal."

As always, Taft included his wife in his sense of accomplishment, inactive though she had been of necessity. She was all too well aware of the pain that her husband was suffering, in spite of his protestations of calm. In the past he had known more of popularity than of hate and he instinctively avoided the discordant and unpleasant. Nellie was nervous and anxious all through the summer of 1912. The White House had not brought much joy into her own life, and she could not bear to see Will being assailed by the man she had always distrusted.

She sat with Mrs. Leonard Wood at the notification ceremony in the White House. Elihu Root announced the nomination in one of his brief, forceful speeches. Four hundred guests were present in the East Room, a larger crowd than Nellie approved. She had bargained for seventy-five but Will had insisted on more and went over the menu personally with Mrs. Jaffray, ordering lobster Newburg, capon, and ham. Nellie's strength and interest were failing her at this time. She had always felt that Will had depths of energy and intelligence beyond his own awareness and she had encouraged him to follow the ambitious course. But neither her ambition nor her zeal burned so brightly as she watched him battle with Theodore Roosevelt. He admitted frankly that his heart was not in the campaign and this was plain for all to see. Years later William A. White, editor of the *Emporia Gazette*, recalled a luncheon at the White House during which the President said to him in some bewilderment: "White, I can't be a Roosevelt. I can't do things the way he does them. It just isn't me. I am not built that way!"

He was working desperately hard at this time and was usually dictating letters by seven in the morning. But he never failed to write almost daily to Nellie, and in longhand, because "in order to get the nicest shades of meaning, your intellect has to flow out through the ends of your fingers." He also knew that she disliked getting dictated letters from him. Mabel Boardman heard from him constantly, too, as he reported each step in the campaign. She was openly championing his cause but when asked to head a woman's committee working for him she declined because of her Red Cross connections, She praised his speeches, and particularly his acceptance, which was balm to the President. He considered Wilson's speech a "pink tea message," a milk and water oration, purring and lady-like. He thought that Roosevelt in his acceptance had outdistanced all the radicals, making a bold bid for "every crank and every dishonest man against the things that are."

On his final campaign tour he covered 18,000 miles, living for forty-one days on a special train and visiting between four and five hundred cities. Horace cheered from the sidelines. "Hit 'em again," he wrote. "I was delighted with your Ohio speeches and in my walk yesterday I got to speechmaking myself." Horace's old friend, Maria, had just taken off for a tour of the world with two Cincinnati friends, Ruth Harrison and Fanny Ramsey. Will gave her letters to rulers and dignitaries of every country she visited. It was a magnificent tour and Maria made the most of it, after her years at home, attending first her ailing mother and then her dying father.

In this same year—1912—Harry's wife Julia became a Catholic convert. She had been desperately unhappy about her daughter Louise, who had married against her parents' wishes and was now Mrs. George Snowden, living in British Columbia and the mother of a small son. It was some time before she and her mother became friends again and

Harry was greatly upset over this family split. Again he was working hard in New York for his brother's interests and his own legal business had reached formidable proportions. He had gone into partnership with George W. Wickersham.

Helen and Robert went west on a camping trip that summer with a dozen young people, going through Glacier Park by pack train, with the Great Northern supplying tents, horses, and guides. Bob was head man of the expedition and, as always, was a reliable guide. For the first time Helen was alive to the strong interest that Bob was showing in Martha Bowers, one of their young friends, whose father, Lloyd Bowers, had recently died. He was a noted lawyer and a close friend of President Taft's. At this time Bob and Helen were developing a strong friendship with Tom and Martha Bowers.

The President, too, was in the Far West, campaigning, and he found some hours of peace driving around the base of Mount Rainier. He wrote to Nellie urging her to tell the children to enjoy all the privileges they could on their trip because they might not long continue to be the son and daughter of a President. He was disappointed when Nellie's sister, Mrs. Charles Anderson, refused his offer to have her daughter Harriet married in the White House. She said that Helen should be the first to have that honor. Will jovially replied that he was not anxious to have Helen a bride at all and in any event there was plenty of room in the old mansion for two weddings.

Pauline Wayne, the last of the White House cows, had been sent out to pasture shortly before the young people left for their trip west. She had been giving the Tafts trouble for some time, since she had Bang's Disease. In 1911 the President had agreed to send Pauline for exhibition at the International Dairy Show in Milwaukee but he had to cancel the arrangement when it was learned that she was due to calve. Mrs. Taft had her sent to the Soldier's Home but she was not welcomed there, since her disease made her dangerous to other animals.

Pauline was well known to passersby who often paused to peer at her nibbling grass on the grounds. Mrs. Taft had insisted on a cow, for she had become used to one in the Philippines. Pauline was the gift of Senator Isaac Stephenson, and when she arrived in Washington by box car from Marinette, Wisconsin, in November, 1910, she was an object of great interest. She was a Holstein-Friesian, weighing 1,500 pounds and she was four years old at the time. Her final departure from the White House grounds marked the end of an old tradition.

The President was at dinner on an October night in 1912 when news reached him that an attempt had been made on Theodore Roosevelt's life while he was on his way to a rally in Milwaukee. John Shrank, a lunatic, shot at him, but he was saved from a second bullet when his stenographer took a flying leap from the sidewalk and diverted the assassin's aim. There was confusion in the early reports but it was soon established that Roosevelt's condition was not critical. He went on to the meeting and delivered his address. Taft, like others, was shaken by the news. Two days later he wrote to Miss Boardman: "The outrageous attempt on Mr. Roosevelt's life was a great shock, and I hope his recovery may be speedy. . . . The attempt of his supporters to charge my supporters with responsibility for the assault on the ground that the attacks upon him by the press were instigated by partisans of mine is ridiculous and, I think, will react."

But the election excitement was magnified by the assault on Roosevelt. The death of Vice-President James S. Sherman a few days before election was another stroke of ill-luck. Wilson had made a good campaign, putting much stress on tariff reduction. His speeches were effective. From the start they seemed to have the ring of history. "I do not want to promise heaven unless I can bring it to you," he told the voters. He viewed the Progressive platform as a "collection of impossible pledges." But President Taft refused to see Wilson as a serious threat until the returns were in.

It was a dark night for the Tafts. Nellie learned all too quickly that her husband had suffered the worst defeat in presidential history. Only Utah and Vermont, a family stronghold, had supported him, and Wilson had come into power against the divided Republicans. Taft and his family took his defeat philosophically, although slightly shaken by the magnitude of the Wilson victory. Delia, who had been speechless with indignation when Roosevelt men had dared to canvass Millbury, picked up her pen at once and wrote to Will on November 8: "I am writing to congratulate you, and you need not expect anything else from me. How preposterous to expect you to win, with a split party. I am entirely resigned to the result. . . . We shall always love you, for the perils you have saved us from."

Bob had a decision of his own to make within the next few days. Justice Oliver Wendell Homes had asked him to be his secretary. Tempting as this association seemed, he was anxious to get started without delay in Cincinnati. The President had no doubt about this at all and wrote to Professor John Chipman Gray, of Harvard, expressing appreciation of the compliment Justice Holmes had paid his son but pointing out that Bob was twenty-three, that he had spent four years on his academic studies and three more on law, and that he now needed the actual drudgery of practice.

With his cause lost Taft was considering returning to Cincinnati himself to practice law or to preside as a judge, but he hesitated, since six of the nine justices of the Supreme Court and forty-five per cent of the federal judiciary were his own appointees. With his scrupulous conscience he felt that this debarred him from practicing as an advocate. He also considered taking a trip around the world, like General Grant. But when invited to become Kent Professor of Law at Yale he quickly decided that this would be a congenial occupation for him and a dignified way of leaving the Presidency. He recalled that Grover Cleveland had gone from the White House to Princeton. Sick to death of conflict, he welcomed the thought of the quiet academic life that would remove him from the maelstrom of politics more effectively than the practice of law. The salary was $5,000 a year, a sum he could augment with lectures and magazine articles. And Charlie, soon to enter Yale, would be able to live at home, a strong point with both parents. But before making his final decision the President paid Aunt Delia the compliment of asking her for her advice. She assured him that she was all for it: "It will be a very dignified and honorable step from the Presidency and it will add lustre to the reputation of the college. . . . I am so delighted at the thought of keeping you and Nellie in New England . . . and so sure that Ohio is not worthy of you, that I rather chuckle at the idea." Delia reminded him that even though he was leaving the White House he and his family had made countless friends while there. Moreover, he would now be able to summer at Murray Bay.

The President and Mrs. Taft went to Panama before the end of the year. This was Taft's fifth trip and he knew more about the canal than anyone not actually engaged in its construction. By this time the Gatun Lock was more than half filled. Most of the excavation had been done in the Culebra Cut. The Tafts were the guests of Colonel George W. Goethals and they traveled by special train to each side of the locks so that Taft could view the construction from all angles. The president of Panama gave a ball in their honor, with a thousand guests.

They were back in Washington in time for the final parties of the administration. Helen had a dance for 250 young people on New Year's Eve. The reception next day was the largest the Tafts had had, with 6,054 guests moving along the line. In the afternoon the President went driving with his brother Harry, and they talked of the new life that would soon begin. In the evening young Charlie, growing up fast, gave a dance for his contemporaries. They had all had honest enjoyment in their White House days. Helen had had a full year of it and her personality, as in the case of her brothers, was well defined in the public consciousness. They had survived their father's years in office without spectacular newspaper attention. Helen's discreet course was always commented on with approval although toward the end she made headlines when she spoke in favor of the shirtwaist-makers when they were airing their grievances. She had a mind of her own and took an independent course, but Helen was quiet and thoughtful in public and only her intimates knew of the merry wit that always lay close to the surface. Bob was considered shy and he did not look the bright young man he was. Charlie had the visible sheen of brilliance from the start. All three were well mannered and unpretentious in their ways. They were indifferent to what they wore, to what they ate, to conditions around them. All were inclined to scoff at pomp and Helen had a deadly eye for humbug of any kind. They had been taught to respect scholarship and the truth.

Aunt Delia was in at the finish, arriving in February with a trained nurse for her last fling in the White House. She was badly crippled but bright and full of sprightly comment. Mrs. Taft made the most of the dying hours of her husband's administration. There were many big parties and the largest congressional reception they had had. Before gathering together his congenial companions of the judiciary for their final reception the President wrote to Joseph H. Choate: "I am proud of the Supreme Court as I have left it and I am anxious to bring to meet them on this valedictory occasion all the leaders of the bar who sympathize with my effort to strengthen the Court and to make it as permanent as the bodily health of the members can make it."

In the end 1,368 guests passed down the receiving line and the President started the dancing by swinging his niece Louise into the first waltz. Mrs. Grover Cleveland and her daughter Esther were present and caused a stir among the guests in the Blue Room. Mrs. Taft gave a dinner for her predecessor, with Mrs. Benjamin Harrison present, and all the Cabinet members of the Cleveland administration who were still alive. But a new First Lady was now on the horizon. Mrs. Woodrow Wilson wrote to the President, thanking him for the help he had given her in White House matters: "I am naturally the most unambitious of women and life in the White House has no attractions for me. Quite the contrary. But Mrs. Jaffray and the wonderful Brooks will rob the immediate future of much of its terror."

Remembering the fiasco of their night at the White House before his own inauguration Taft decided not to repeat this mistake with the Wilsons. Instead, Miss Boardman gave a dinner for the Tafts with the Chief-Justice and his associates, the French, German, and Russian ambassadors, and other intimate friends present to bid them farewell.

Next day the sun shone for Woodrow Wilson. The weather was balmy and quite unlike the blustery effect of the Taft inauguration. The temperature was fifty-one degrees and a great crowd had assembled at the Capitol. Taft and Wilson seemed extraordinarily unlike as they stood together—the outgoing President genial, massive, relaxed; his successor long-jawed, stiff in bearing, a tight smile finally breaking through. Unlike Theodore Roosevelt, Taft rode back to the White House with Woodrow

Wilson and shared in a hasty luncheon before the parade, but he was already the forgotten man. Mrs. Taft and Helen lunched with Mrs. Laughlin at her home on N Street and joined him later at the station. Helen walked away from the Executive Mansion as if she had just been in to pay a call. A group of their close friends, including Mabel Boardman, saw them off to Augusta. Mrs. Andrew Carnegie gave Nellie a necklace as a farewell gift.

Taft's chief regret as he left the White House was the Senate's failure to ratify the arbitration treaties, which he thought would have been a genuine step toward world peace. He made up his mind to speak in favor of international arbitration whenever the occasion arose. If the impression prevailed as William Howard Taft left office that his administration had been a blank, the cooler appraisal of later years gave him credit for much needed judicial reform; for the establishment of a court of customs appeals and a court of commerce; for the creation of a postal savings system and the parcel post; for tightening up the Panama Canal operations; for pinning down campaign contributions and expenditures in elections; for keeping peace with Mexico; for setting up a territorial government in Alaska; for opening Chinese ports to American products and establishing free trade between the Philippines and the United States; for pure food and irrigation measures; for the regulation of corporations; and for pushing arbitration principles, however unsuccessfully.

The outgoing President's tax on the income of all corporations was his own idea and was a shock to his more affluent friends. He made considerable headway with antitrust suits during his administration. With able and aggressive George W. Wickersham at his elbow as attorney general, operating under the Sherman Act, the work that Roosevelt had initiated was carried to a successful conclusion. Taft had the satisfaction of seeing the sugar, oil, and tobacco trusts finally dissolved, and a variety of other trusts, ranging from window glass to beef, lumber, and steel, come under attack. In Henry F. Pringle's opinion his work in this field was more effective, if less dramatized, then Roosevelt's. But Robert M. La Follette, William E. Borah, and George W. Morris, brilliant insurgents in his own party, kept pounding away at him. They spoke eloquently for the radical Republican element in the Middle West and La Follette maintained, with a certain lack of realism, that neither Taft nor Roosevelt ever took issue with the forces of reaction.

Taft was never known as a corporation lawyer nor would he accept the large retainers that might have come his way after he left the White House. But the impression prevailed as he stepped out of office in 1913 that he had accomplished little as President. His brother Horace, who understood him as no one else but Nellie did, considered the key to his unpopularity the fact that he was a poor politician; that he loathed the

methods involved and was clumsy in practicing them; that he underestimated the power of publicity and forbade any grandstand play in attacking the trusts; that his speeches were too long and dull; that he talked
indiscreetly about prominent politicians; and that his reliance on his
great capacity for work sometimes led him to put things off until the time
had passed for effective action. He scorned personal controversy until
forced into it by Roosevelt's attacks.

Charles Willis Thompson, a political observer of the period, thought
that he had a keen and powerful mind and displayed it in all matters
wherein he felt at home. But in politics he seemed to grope his way,
foggy and bewildered. Thompson noted that he was without egotism
and, in judging political events, was never misled by vanity or self-appre-
ciation. He considered his good nature "humorous sanity," the philosophical rather than the fatly stupid kind.

Oswald Garrison Villard, something of an insurgent himself, liked
Taft, while deploring his lack of political imagination. He thought his
administration a failure because Taft was never by nature intended for
the office of President, although he found him a "charming gentleman,
one of the finest who ever entered the White House." Villard viewed
him as kindly, well-meaning, absolutely honest, and true to his conservative training, but inclined to move too slowly and to be dead to the signs
of a rising crisis. He cited the fact that Taft opposed the initiative, the referendum, the recall, and the direct primary; but Robert Taft, looking
back on this period three decades later, wrote that his father believed
"law enforcement, law and order to be the first essentials of civilization,"
and that when he saw violence on the part of an employer he was just as
much against it as when the worker was involved.

William Allen White, the "Sage of Emporia," was equally devoted to
Roosevelt and Taft, and sometimes found himself in a quandary as their
feud raged openly. He described Taft as a "hewer of wood, a man to
whom work was his whisky, his cards, his revelry by night." But he
thought that he was born politically out of his time and as a President
was both a throwback to the 1880's in his conservative thinking, and a
forecast of the 1920's and 1930's in the liberal views he held on international affairs. White recognized the fact that never had the White House
been the scene of such "pulling and hauling, intriguing, contention, bick-
ering and strife" as it was in the years from 1909 to 1913. In the midst of a
tidal wave of liberalism Taft seemed to White to be battling "futilely,
desperately, stupidly, an unhappy, ill-fated figure who . . . figuratively,
used to come out upon the front stoop of the White House and quarrel
petulantly with the American people everyday."

The Kansas editor saw Taft as a simple-hearted man, who conceived
a statesman's job as an opportunity to do his work honestly, intelligently,

and courageously, yet was totally insensible to public opinion and the currents of public thought. White thought he was sunny and genial because he had never had to battle his way or fight for anything. His course through life had been direct and untroubled and the "easy gurgle of his laugh and the sweet insouciance of his answers" the natural traits of a gentleman who maintained a "vastly larger area of his consciousness in private life than in public." White agreed with Senator Jonathan P. Dolliver's observation that Taft was a "large, amiable island surrounded entirely by persons who knew exactly what they wanted." He deplored the President's tendency to trust to sudden inspiration in his speeches. Too often his delays in preparation were apparent and he delivered his speeches in a soft, high voice that did not travel far. But White liked Taft and enjoyed his company. On one occasion he summed him up as a "candid, big-hearted, bluff, affectionate man of the people who hooked up his wife's dress in the back and ignored diplomatic conventions when he stood in the presence of kings"—an astonishing appraisal of the suave Mr. Taft.

Like William Allen White, Will Rogers was conscious of Taft's deep humanity and wrote of him: "It's great to be great but it's greater to be human. He was our great human fellow because there was more of him to be human. We are parting with three hundred pounds of solid charity to everybody, and love and affection for all his fellow men."

A multitude of Americans questioned President Taft's capacity as he left the White House, but he was about to embark on a fresh career where his reputation would grow and his natural qualities find full expression.

CHAPTER 19

TAFT THE PROFESSOR

THE TRANSITION from President to professor was not a difficult one for William Howard Taft to make. The academic world was not alien to his instincts or training and he was as much at home with scholars as he was with lawyers. The students poured into College Street when he and Mrs. Taft arrived in New Haven on an April day in 1913. They marched in procession to Memorial Hall, where the new professor made a speech. He looked at the young faces around him and remembered that he, his father, his brothers, his son, had been closely identified with this campus. "As I hear your cheers and songs I feel young again, as if I had shed some of my years," he said. "I come here wanting to help what little I can the young men who are going out into the nation."

Mrs. Taft, all in black, clasping the huge bunch of violets the students had given her, knew that young Charlie would soon be among them. He was to live at home in the Victorian house with circular porch and pointed gables that they had taken on Prospect Street. In her practical way Mrs. Taft settled quickly into the simpler routine of private life. She did her own unpacking and soon was engaged in "fitting a beer diet to a champagne appetite." Guests were surprised to find the door being answered by the former First Lady. The change seemed to do her good. Sir William Osler, an old family friend then lecturing at Yale, was pleased with the progress she had made and the distinctness and freedom with which she now spoke. She played golf two or three times a week, went to the theater and concerts, entertained quite formally and made new friends. "Your mother . . . has a great deal of ingenuity and taste and energy about making a house homelike," his father wrote to Bob as Nellie once again established a Taft family base. But in May she had a hemorrhage in one of her eyes. Her husband, always fearful of her health, thought at once of another stroke but little damage was done on this occasion.

The former President worked twelve hours a day to keep up the academic pitch. He was relieved to pick up a newspaper at last and not find his name in the headlines. It was his intention to refrain from criticizing the Wilson administration and he reserved most of his comments on the new President for his letters to his family and to Miss Boardman. He decided that his successor had made a good start but he was surprised that Elihu Root should have been so laudatory of him at the Gridiron dinner.

The students found it a novelty to have the former President flapping in and out of classrooms in his robes. They were cut to measure and he liked this attire, since it tended to conceal his bulk. Taft was not considered a lively lecturer but his students regarded him with great respect and cheered him at every opportunity. He was apt to be late for classes and he lectured from notes and headings, never reading a formal speech. Taft was modest about his own qualifications and often told his fellow professors that he knew little of international law except what he had picked up from practical experience. His students were impressed to see him doing his own research, borrowing books from the college library, and keeping law books in his offices at the Hotel Taft. Constitutional law seemed to him to be a difficult subject to teach, because of the amount of reading involved. But it was a subject in which he had intense interest and he was in his element preparing his nine lectures on government.

Taft attended faculty meetings and voiced his opinion when asked, but in general he stayed in the background, so as never to dominate the gatherings of scholars. His college courses were elective but in the Law School his course was required for third-year students. Occasionally he brightened his lectures with thumbnail sketches of the personalities involved, describing the judge who had written a decision, or injecting an anecdote from his own abundant experience. He took his papers with him on his lecture trips and graded them wherever he chanced to be, working on them in hotels, in private homes, in automobiles, in public halls. Passersby in Grand Central Station sometimes caught glimpses of the former President doubled up on a bench hard at work correcting students' papers. "The crowd is considerable, but one is lost in it, and

there is solitude that is like what Robinson Crusoe enjoyed," he wrote to
Miss Boardman. At the end of the year he gave each student a diminu-
tive edition of the Constitution with his autographed card.

Taft was interested in the personal problems of the students and was
always willing to attend a Junior Prom, a student banquet, a smoker, or
a ball game. Undergraduate marriages on the campus were coming into
fashion and he regarded them with fatherly sympathy. He belonged to
the Friday Night Club which he thought gave him a "local atmosphere
in New Haven," attended as it was by the local scholars and professional
men. William Lyon Phelps, one of his colleagues at Yale, was his favorite partner at golf. When students demonstrated in front of his house in
April, 1914, to protest the refusal of Huerta, Mexico's provisional president, to salute the American flag, he was in sympathy with them. Huerta
had been denied recognition by the United States and had used this
gesture of defiance.

Taft's size presented some problems at Yale. Nellie saw to it that the
chairs at Murray Bay and in his New Haven house were ample. But as he
lectured around the country he frequently had to dodge a flimsy seat in
someone's drawing room. He became wary of period pieces and of folding seats. Dean Frederick S. Jones, of Yale, arranged for special chairs
for his use in classrooms and one was installed in the Yale University
Faculty Club, with a seat twenty-five inches wide. At a Lawrenceville
commencement he stuck fast to a leather seat on a blazing hot day. Elihu
Root liked to tease him about the cunning little Dutch bed eighteen
inches wide that Mrs. Root could offer him when he visited them at
their three-hundred-acre estate at Clinton, New York. His Ford sedan
was built with a side door, but none of the cartoons or jibes about his size
really troubled him. He had the wit to make fun of himself and he often
told stories at his own expense. The element of ridicule fell flat when he
outmatched the jokers themselves. When ushered to an extra-narrow
theater seat one night he turned to his schoolmaster brother with the
remark: "Horace, if this theater burns, it has got to burn around me."

The Professor applied himself consistently to a reducing regime after
leaving the White House. He went regularly to a health farm in West
Haven and took breathing exercises, vibrator, medicine ball, and massage. He rode and played golf regularly and reduced from 340 to 270
pounds in eight months. His weight when he left Yale in 1878 was 225
pounds and he was 270 pounds when he became a circuit judge in 1892.
When he moved to Yale he dieted under the direction of Dr. George
Blumer, dean of the Yale School of Medicine. At Murray Bay, Dr. James
Thacher, another Yale man, looked after his health. By 1922 he had reduced to 259 pounds and no longer looked out of proportion for his
height.

In spite of academic seclusion he could not escape the limelight altogether and news of his drastic swings in weight soon penetrated all parts
of the country. He was deluged with letters asking him for advice. His
correspondents all received the same answer. He told them that he
shunned potatoes, pork, salmon, or other oily fish, as well as pastry, sugar
in any quantity, and oil in salad dressings. He confined himself to lean
roast beef and mutton, salads, and vegetables lacking starch or sugar.
Taft often made the proviso before attending a dinner that he would
eat in advance so as not to violate his rules. When he felt faint on the
golf course in the summer of 1913 his physician slowed him up on his
dieting but gave him permission to eat fruit for thirty days. This meant
much to him since all his life Taft had helped himself to generous quanti-
ties of fruit. Soon after he went to Yale a sympathizer sent him a poem
about Aunt Delia's mouth-watering cooking:

To Our Well Beloved Ex-President

They say "Aunt Delia" has the trick
Of making pies both fine and quick
And yet the world has got to laugh
When she sends pies to Nephew Taft.
And even I am in a gale
To think what's going soon to Yale
Of Lemon-Apple-Pumpkin grand
Enough to stock a pastry stand.
"Aunt Delia"—don't you spoil the boy
Or let him die of cupboard joy
For *seniors* need him more and more
To lecture them on ancient lore.

Irrespective of Aunt Delia's pies, by the end of 1913 Taft had reduced
to the point where he was able to dispense with his valet and could dress
himself. His wife's maid pressed his clothes and kept his wardrobe in
condition. He was no Beau Brummell; in fact, he was apt to be untidy
about his tailoring, but Mrs. Taft kept a vigilant eye on these matters.
Will recognized this negligence in himself and when Mabel Boardman
gave him a leather golf bag for his birthday in September, 1913, along
with a copy of *The Professor at the Breakfast-Table,* he wrote to her: "In
spite of my natural tendency to be a slouch and to look seedy, you have
done much in your day and generation by your presents to give the impression that I really have some style about me." From time to time she
gave him luggage, a greatcoat, a golfing vest, a leather satchel to hold his
papers, a bellows to stoke his library fire, a great many luxury items in
leather, and a long succession of carefully chosen books. Mabel was
equally thoughtful in her gifts to Mrs. Taft and Helen.

The Tafts, who were no strangers to economy, now had to adjust themselves to their new way of living. The former President took three rooms in the Hotel Taft where he and W. W. Mischler, Carpenter's successor, worked until all hours of the night. He kept an office boy to run errands, but he could move about without attention now and this meant a great deal to the former President. However, there were moments when he still seemed to be in office. The entire audience rose and sang "America" when he entered the Music Hall in Cincinnati two months after leaving the White House. The twentieth May Biennial Festival was in progress and Annie was in her element as a chorus of 5,000, accompanied by Theodore Thomas's orchestra from Chicago, gave Mendelssohn's *Elijah*, with Madame Gadski as soloist. Later Annie and Charles took Will to a roof garden over the Orpheum Theater on Walnut Hills and he was struck all over again by the beauty of his native city.

He went to Boston for the Unitarian Festival and then attended a dinner in Cambridge for Bob's class. His oldest son had repeated his Yale record at the Harvard Law School and was first in his class. In introducing the former President, Dean Thayer said that among his claims to greatness none equaled that of being the father of Robert, whom he considered the most remarkable young man he had known at the Law School. Characteristically, Bob had not told his family of his standing; they learned first from the newspapers that another Taft academic record had been scored. The doors of several old law firms in New York were open to him but he was determined to settle in Cincinnati and arrangements were made for him to join the firm of Maxwell and Ramsey where he would be among friends, for Lawrence Maxwell was an old friend of Taft's. But first Bob had to pass his law examinations in Ohio.

The entire family returned joyfully to Murray Bay in the summer of 1913. They had been going there off and on for twenty-one years and had missed it during the presidential term. They had had more family reunions there than at any other place since leaving Mount Auburn. It was home to all of them, but they had lived in luxury for so long now that Mrs. McCagg felt they would find their cottage "too lowly a home" after the White House. Taft chuckled over this, since he knew of no place that he liked better than Murray Bay. He wrote cheerfully to Miss Boardman, urging her to visit them in their "wooden tent" with its one bathroom. "The fare is plain, but the air is good, the water is pure and cold, and the welcome will be warm," he wrote. Will added that it was full of sweet memories for his family "for here we have gathered all of our friends in the past."

Mrs. McCagg shared a house and garden with her sister, Mrs. Agnes B. Exston, whose son Frederick was Bob's old friend. By this time young Exston was with Doubleday, Page & Company. All of the old crowd were back—from Cincinnati, from Chicago, New York, Montreal, and Ottawa. Many new cottages had gone up since their last visit six years earlier and prices had risen, too. Parties were more formal than when there were only four or five families at Pointe au Pic and the Tafts and Mrs. Exston played penny-ante poker nearly every day.

Her parents regretted the absence of young men at this time for Helen, but she brought her own friends with her. She was busy in the summer of 1913, for she was writing an article about life in the White House and Mrs. Taft had been asked to write a book. Martin Egan and his wife Eleanor had persuaded them to take on these tasks and Taft was interested in having Helen cultivate her literary style. He hoped at this point that she might become a writer. Charlie now knew all the girls who visited Murray Bay and had become the favorite dance partner of the colony. The young people attended dances at the Manoir Richelieu and the Golf Club, and the atmosphere was joyous and free—a relief to Taft after the tensions of the White House. Mischler, who had remained with him as his secretary, now looked after the young Tafts' train reservations, sent them their allowances, got them their tickets for football games and the theater, and supplied them with ammunition for their debates.

But the former President was never free from work and responsibility, and even at Murray Bay he was busy on a speech he was to deliver before the Bar Association in Montreal, where he shared honors with Lord Haldane. McGill University gave him an honorary degree on this occasion. His engagements ranged from attending the opening of the Boston City Club, which he approved because it took in everyone irrespective of race and religion, to going to Rutland for the 125th anniversary of the first Congregational Church of Vermont. In December he went to Cincinnati to help celebrate the fortieth anniversary of the wedding of Charles and Annie. He had not expected his sister-in-law to observe the occasion, since she was sensitive about her age. Charles was seventy and looked his age but Will thought that Annie seemed young in looks and spirit. She was deeply absorbed in orchestra affairs and was sinking large sums of money into the Symphony Association. Bob was living with them while he studied for his bar examinations and they found him a considerate and adaptable guest. Annie was attempting to swing him into her own social pattern and he tried hard to improve his knowledge of music so as to please her. Bob attended the symphony concerts and confided to his father that he would do his best to learn to enjoy them, even to the point of studying a book called How to Listen to Music. Annie was full of bright and diverting ideas of her own on the subject, and she expressed them with considerable wit.

Her grooming of Bob included a dancing class, although he was never to match his father in the ballroom. He was only eight when he left Cincinnati, and most of his friendships had been formed elsewhere. Now he was being introduced all over again from one of the most hospitable homes in the city. He remembered some of the girls from his earlier days and he decided to lunch regularly at the University Club so as to get to know more of the men. His father was not anxious for him to get too deeply involved in business until he had taken his bar examinations. He had given him $500 to tide him over the winter. To outsiders Bob seemed a quiet, shy, hard-working youth, not out to beat the world. When autumn came he listened to the returns on the football games over a private wire. Neither Bob nor Charlie liked to miss a big football game, particularly when Yale and Harvard were playing. His uncle Charles gave a supper for Bob after the first symphony concert of the season; he was a new Taft on the scene, a President's son, and life looked rosy for him.

The family interest in symphony affairs was now extended to California where Fanny Edwards was helping to reorganize the Los Angeles Symphony Orchestra. Many good musicians had settled there from different parts of the world and Fanny's early interest in music was fully revived. After twenty years of silence she took singing lessons again. Bill and she now had two ranches in San Diego County, one for dairy products and one for fruit, Bill missed his quail-shooting in Mexico since they could no longer go to the hunting ranch because of Wilson's stand on Huerta and the trouble south of the border. Fanny wrote to Will on this subject:

> Wilson seems to think he will lead Mexico out of darkness! How glad I am you are out of it all! The history of your life since leaving the White House breathes contentment and happiness after you rested your tired nerves. I cannot picture you as nervous like us other mortals.

Now that the Tafts were settled in New Haven Will and Horace were closer friends than ever. They visited back and forth and exchanged telephone calls. Will enjoyed his brother's letters, which had a sparkle that reminded him of John Hay's. The Taft School had been incorporated in 1912, with Horace taking five-sixths of the stock, and Harley F. Roberts, head of the Latin Department, one-sixth. They had issued bonds and raised $300,000, with Charles and Annie helping them substantially. Early in 1914 Horace moved into the main building which had been designed by Cram, Goodhue and Ferguson. It reminded Will of a Tudor college at Oxford, yet with all the modern improvements. The boys now had a ball field and additional tennis courts.

Horace was choosing his students with great care and had a number who could not pay the full fees. They were the sons of friends and he considered them of worthy caliber—boys whose influence on the other students would be good. The former President often expressed his satisfaction that Bob and Charlie had had the advantage of being under Horace's care and had benefited by the thoroughness of the training of mind and character that he had given them. He expressed his view on this to Mabel Boardman:

> Even if he is my brother, I consider him a very remarkable man. He has so much humor and so much sanity, together with such high ideals and such practical methods of attaining them, I would like to be a boy again and go through such a training as Horace gives, just for the benefit and pleasure it would be. But alas, how much we know when it is too late to use the knowledge.

Horace's nervousness and gastric distress continued as he worried constantly about finances. He continued to criticize his brother's speeches, to comment to him on political affairs, to jest about his conservative views. Always an original and spirited thinker, he sometimes read Will's articles in advance and they had lively exchanges. He usually suggested cuts and once briskly urged Will to put all he had to say in a nutshell instead of letting his judicial habit of mind show up in long quotations. Will picked up academic stories from Horace that he used to good effect in his speeches. When he talked about the home backing the school he usually referred to his father Alphonso and the inflexible way in which he had stood by the school authorities. Horace's own credo was simple:

> In scholarship I am a perfect Democrat in wishing that every boy should have a chance to show what is in him, but a perfect Aristocrat in feeling that a boy who shows that he has the right stuff should have every opportunity for development and that all of our strength should not be expended on the "duffer."

When Will wrote "The College Slouch" for the *Ladies Home Journal* of May, 1914, Horace gave him pointers on the subject. He attributed the decline in youthful standards to lack of discipline in the family and to a transition period in society when the fundamentals of government, religious education, and economics were being questioned. Horace was worrying about the popularity of the tango and the turkey trot with the young and he had joined a movement of the private schools to organize a Parents League "to limit the extraordinary dissipation of boys and girls of school age."

The former President's magazine articles in the *Saturday Evening Post* and elsewhere were causing talk. Calvin Coolidge was so impressed with them that he wrote from Boston telling him he might be performing a public service in this way "greater and more important than what you could have done had you still been President." Taft's correspondence when he settled into the role of professor shows how keenly he followed the moves of his successor. Men of affairs continued to write to him from different parts of the world. Gus Karger, whom he expected ultimately to be his biographer, primed him constantly on what was going on at the seat of government. He sent him clippings, formal releases, cartoons that mirrored the political situation. Gus relayed to Taft Wilson's answers to questions at the press conferences, initiated some in needling fashion himself, visited the diplomats, observed the attitude of senators and the Cabinet to the President, and kept a close watch on Bryan. The old Taft crowd invited Gus to dinner and in general he was an astute observer in the capital, working for the Cincinnati *Times-Star* and keeping his finger on the pulse of government.

The former President was adept at picking up the strings, wherever they lay, and giving them judicial appraisal. Sophisticates like Ambassador Jusserand enjoyed corresponding with him. "Madame de Sévigné was supposed to be a good letter writer, but you beat her by many lengths—a rare acomplishment," this worldly Frenchman wrote. Miss Boardman's letters were laced with a combination of social and political comment, and both Mr. and Mrs. Taft encouraged her to continue writing the newsy letters they both enjoyed. She sent them detailed accounts of the Washington dinner parties, with sketches of seating arrangements, menus, and odds and ends that she thought might interest them. Ever alert to the swing of feeling regarding President Wilson she gave Taft a living picture of what went on among his friends and his foes. Mabel spotted new alignments and simmering feuds, and she made a point of relaying every compliment she heard relating to Taft or his family. Her reservations about the new President did not mitigate her resentment of Roosevelt. "I would like to have Wilson make good enough to offset any danger of Roosevelt in 1916," she wrote.

Miss Boardman reported on another Roosevelt in December, 1913. "I rather like young Franklin Roosevelt who took me out—and who does not seem overawed by his uncle, T.R. Young Mr. Roosevelt has the characteristic emphasis of words of his own family. Have you ever noticed the way they have of emphasizing every fourth or fifth word as they talk?" Meeting him at another dinner party she observed: "As he is a good Democrat without Bull Moose proclivities in spite of close family connections, I like him."

Mabel, at the very fountainhead of social Washington, dining with diplomats and ambassadors, with generals and senators, reported that many of the "old satellites had become Democrats now socially." Nothing escaped her, from the length of time President Wilson gave to his conferees, to the details of the wedding of his daughter Eleanor and William Gibbs McAdoo, in November, 1913. Mabel reported that Ambassador Jusserand had resurrected the Tennis Cabinet, that the Hammonds had sold the Pullman house to the Russian Government for an Embassy, that Lady Spring Rice still insisted on tramping up the hill to the British Embassy wearing her tailor-made suits and flat-heeled shoes, that the tango was being danced all over Washington. Meanwhile Mabel kept up with Professor Taft's schedule, followed his speeches as he traveled, commented on them, and advised him from time to time.

By the close of 1913 she was in a happier frame of mind about the Red Cross. She had resigned at the end of 1912, and as the President went out of office he was writing to her urgently from Augusta to hold on: "Write me that you have buckled on your armor anew for another struggle. Don't let the foolish notion that you are regarded as a woman with a fad affect you. The Red Cross is no fad. It is a great well-organized machine, the work of your hands. It has given you a world reputation." In this same letter Taft denied her charge that he had not stood behind her in a tussle over authority and added:

> There is no one in Washington whose friendship I value as I do yours. If you have gained a different impression, you are wrong. One of the great pieces of good fortune in my Washington experience has been that you and I have felt drawn towards each other and that Nellie has seen it on my part and has recognized its value to me and has welcomed your friendship for her.

Miss Boardman found herself in something of the same position as Clara Barton whom she had succeeded. Both women, strong individualists, found it difficult to work in tandem. Under Miss Boardman's direction the Red Cross had expanded enormously and she was now trying to raise funds for a National Red Cross building to honor the women of the Civil War. Toward the end of 1913 the Federal Government appropriated $400,000 for the memorial, predicated on public contributions of not less than $300,000. The square on which the building would rise was chosen. Miss Boardman staged a successful campaign for funds, with William Howard Taft helping her in some instances—notably in the case of Mrs. Russell Sage. It was hard work for Mabel. She had many affluent friends but she wrote to Taft: "If there is any star in a future crown—I'll deserve it not for work but for begging—against all my inclinations." She wrote to her old friend about each move she made—from the generosity of Jacob Schiff to the manner in which Mrs. E. H. Harriman gave her instant support. Before Christmas, 1913, President Wilson announced the success of the drive and Taft wrote triumphantly to Mabel. "The building is yours. The endorsement fund is at hand. You did it. . . . Really I bow before you as a greater one than he who conquereth a city." Mrs. Harriman gave her an etching of Zorn's portrait of Taft for Christmas and Jacob Schiff sent her an etching of himself.

By the end of the year Taft had modified his earlier estimate of Wood-row Wilson. If his admiration for him as a man had not increased, his respect for him as a politician had grown and he thought that the new President excelled even Theodore Roosevelt in his skill with the press. At different times, in letters to his intimates, Taft characterized Wilson as stubborn, thick-skinned, hypocritical, Jesuitical, a purist, an academi-cian, and the "most unblushing and most ruthless opportunist he had ever met," but he supported him strongly when the country went to war. He considered Henry Cabot Lodge a persistent officer-seeker and he was scathing about Bryan as secretary of state, although conceding that he had kindliness, mixed with a "supreme confidence in his own judgment upon matters upon which he had little knowledge." In commenting freely on the new administration he did not wish Miss Boardman to think, however, that he was the "old minister in the pulpit listening to the new sermon."

The Taft family gathered happily at New Haven for Christmas, 1913. Bob was in good spirits, having passed his Ohio bar examinations with the highest mark. The governor had wired his congratulations. He now knew many of the lawyers in his native city and was beginning to feel at home again. In a quiet way Bob was beginning to see the future opening up for him, but he had no delusions about the drudgery that lay ahead of him. His father had felt discouraged at the beginning of his legal career in Cincinnati but Bob could tackle the dullest job without re-sistance.

Both he and Helen took pride in their high-spirited younger brother who astonished them all that Christmas by arriving home a strapping giant, weighing 189 pounds. He was handsome, eloquent as always, and bent on projects peculiarly his own. Charlie was becoming a young man of affairs. During the holidays he attended a dinner in New York held by the editors of preparatory school newspapers. *The Papyrus* of the Taft School was his particular responsibility. He worked hard both at his studies and at sports and was popular with his classmates. It was clear to his family that Charlie, who had seemed so intractable, was fast be-coming a solid citizen.

He was more glib in debate than Bob and, like him, he seized every opportunity to practice the art and debated enthusiastically on whether or not the United States should have permanent possession of the Philip-pines. Of more interest to him at the moment, however, was the fact that the Taft baseball team had won seven games straight. But in March Charlie came to grief in a solid geometry exam. However, his uncle watched him leave next day, smiling and happy, ready for a good vaca-tion. "I have no doubt that he will get one," Horace wrote. "He belongs to the kind who never need a vacation and never fail to get one."

When his children's marks did not come up to scratch the Professor, like the President, always asked why and tried to find the answer. He knew it was not lack of ability. If Charlie's marks showed a decline the answer must inevitably lie with the playing fields, his father deduced. Helen was doing well at Bryn Mawr. "It is a great pleasure to have Miss Taft here this year," Miss Thomas wrote. "I am told that she is taking a prominent and influential part among the students and that in self-government and undergraduate meetings she shows something of her father's legal abilities."

Helen was now thinking seriously of working at Yale for her Ph.D., which delighted her father. She had matured into a steady, intellectual type but the same old bantering went on with her brothers. They had countless jests together and a common understanding, based on happy days at Murray Bay, on camping trips and family gatherings, on travel in distant lands and White House incidents. They all understood one another's jokes and conducted a sparkling correspondence from school and college. If Bob did not jest, except infrequently and in a wry way, he responded well to Helen's jokes. She wrote of all the reading and cramming she had to do for her exams but acknowledged that she had managed to work in some "grand coasting too." She described for Charlie's benefit a two mile slide, with buttons flying off and stockings splitting, all followed by a mad dash through the streets of Bryn Mawr and Haverford. "And wasn't the blizzard peachy?" she wrote on another occasion. "We weren't really blown away but the drifts on the campus were four or five feet high and it was hard to get around."

Her parents joined her at Bryn Mawr for the May Day festivities of 1914. Helen was Richard Coeur de Lion in *Robin Hood*. "I was tremendously admired and was indeed a lovely sight in old armour and purple velvet, and purple and gold legs," she wrote to Charlie. "I rode a magnificent horse and wore a crown and sword. My appearance was grander than my acting, I fear. . . ." But her parents watched her with pride and Taft wrote afterwards to Miss Boardman that he hoped she would do graduate work at Yale and prepare for a literary career or teaching. "A professorship, now that women are coming more to the front, is not beyond her reasonable ambition," he wrote. He added jestingly that in Nellie's eyes the family affection ran first to Caro the dog, then to Charlie, Helen, Bob, and finally to the "old man." He admitted that he seemed always to be moving at a mad speed while his wife kept track of the needs and whims of her family. He wrote:

> She is a philosophical woman and seems to be able to enjoy her own society without complaint. I feel often as if my life was too hard on her because I am away quite half the time, but she seems to be interested in the work I am doing and to regard it as part of my life's business.

She rejoices in the money that it brings me, though of course I do a great deal of work for which I get no recompense. She studies with Mischler over the various contracts and they confer as to the terms.

Taft's lecture fees ranged from $150 to $1,000, with $500 the average sum. His magazine articles usually brought in about $1,500 each, and Martin Egan sometimes helped him prepare them. He did not charge for speeches made at bar association meetings or before philanthropic and charitable organizations. Taft moved rapidly from point to point, from the meetings of the National Geographic Society to the gatherings of the bar associations, where he was always most at home. During his years at Yale he traveled thousands of miles, addressing a multitude of people of diverse interests, and in time he became known as the peripatetic professor. With Mischler he prepared a list of thirty subjects on which to lecture, from the "Duties of Citizenship" to "Judicial Recall." He might lecture in Iowa on a Saturday evening and be back at Yale ready for classes on Monday morning. Before the war he spoke chiefly on labor, woman suffrage, peace and the Mexican situation. At times he spoke of his life in the White House and gave his views on the Presidency. Addressing the students at the University of Virginia in January, 1915, he advocated a seven-year term for all Presidents, closer relations between the President and Congress, and better use of the art of persuasion from the White House before a bill reached the veto stage. He recalled his own feeling about the White House. "It is dignified, it is beautiful, it is comfortable," he said. "In all the world I venture to say, there is no more appropriate official residence for a chief executive, nor one better adapted to the simple, democratic tastes of the American people."

Taft warned his youthful audiences against a flippant lack of respect for the office of the President. For the time being, he reminded them, the President was the personal embodiment and representative of the dignity and majesty of the American people. Summing up he observed:

> The responsibility of the office is so heavy, the earnest desire that every man who fills the place has to deserve the approval of his countrymen by doing the thing that is best for the country is so strong, and the fear of just popular criticism is so controlling that it is difficult for one who has been through four years of it to remember many personal favors that he was able to confer.

The former President spoke often and fluently on the subject of peace. From 1915 to 1921 he was the chief promoter and president of the League to Enforce Peace, which was the actual forerunner of the League of Nations. Its object was to settle international disputes without arms and to use the united forces of the League to penalize nations that violated this rule. He was an active member of the World Court League and delivered many lectures for the New York Peace Society, advocating a World Court. This was a period when large sums of money were being raised to foster peace. Andrew Carnegie was building the court of arbitration at The Hague and was pushing his Endowment for International Peace in Washington. These were matters of great interest to Taft, although he did not always agree with Carnegie's methods.

When the war broke out in Europe Roosevelt preached preparedness in the most vivid terms but Taft continued to work for peace until the United States declared war. Then the tenor of his speeches changed. At the national convention of the League held in Philadelphia in May, 1918, he said: "Let us have Peace, but let us have War that we may have Peace. To sound the trumpet of stern, implacable war to the end, this convention was called." Roosevelt actively opposed the work of the League. Woodrow Wilson was chilly to it at first, but he endorsed the movement in 1916 and thereafter encompassed some of its ideals in his own peace plans.

The former President represented Yale at World Court Congresses in 1915 and 1916 and at other gatherings where his name spelled gold for the college. But he would not preach a sermon in Yale Chapel or anywhere else. "I don't feel that I am worthy to take the place," he commented. Always consistent in his faith he was elected honorary president of the American Unitarian Association in 1914 and president of the Unitarian General Conference in 1919. Taft was so liberal in his views that he was welcomed as a speaker by all religious organizations, Protestant, Roman Catholic, and Jewish. He frequently spoke to clubs associated with churches and at all times he strongly supported the Y.M.C.A. and work involving the welfare of the young. He was a favorite mark for dedication ceremonies but he particularly enjoyed the series of lectures he gave at various universities, and whenever he visited a college town he was immediately persuaded to talk in assembly rooms, at luncheons and banquets. Horace liked him "to go blazing away at education."

Taft never refused a chance to speak at the women's colleges, where he was a popular figure. He spoke at Smith College on Washington's birthday in 1914 and found the faculty clothed for the first time in academic garb. On this occasion he handed out what he called "good conservative doctrine." Wellesley was a revelation to him and he announced that he had rarely had a more inspiring audience. At Mount Holyoke he made a hit when he read some of his mother's old letters about the experiences she and Delia had had there in the distant past. His own gargantuan chuckle added to the gaiety of the hour as the students went into gales of merriment and even Miss Woolley looked amused. His visits to Bryn Mawr were always occasions of special interest and he was on extra-good terms with the greatly respected Miss Thomas. Taft had been

warned against speaking on woman suffrage at Swarthmore because he
was known to be opposed to it. Since the Friends favored it strongly he
decided not to ruffle their sensibilities; so he changed his topic and struck
the appropriate note on his visit to this Quaker college. He walked warily
in the suffrage field since Mrs. Taft, Mrs. Root, and Miss Boardman were
all strongly anti-suffrage, and he was so beleaguered that he had to use his
best brand of diplomacy on the subject.

Taft's life had never been more arduous than in the years immediately
following his term as President. He detailed the discomforts as well as
the joys of it to Nellie. Because of his size it was never easy for him to
cope with traveling conditions. He was troubled by gout and his weight
made him clumsy. For the sake of economy he now slept in sections
rather than in train drawing rooms, and dressing was a problem. "But
steps down from the luxury of Presidential life are essential to the development of character, and I am not kicking," he jested. However, if
traveling conditions were difficult, his receptions in private homes were
magnificent, from Rideau Hall, the Duke of Connaught's official residence in Ottawa, to the homes of the Crockers and the Hearsts in San
Francisco, or the Carnegies and Warburgs in New York. Mrs. Felix M.
Warburg was the daughter of Jacob Schiff, a good friend of his. "Warburg seems to be a man of very great poise, and they have a charming
family of boys and girls," he wrote to Miss Boardman. "There is among
the Jews as strong family affection as in any race that I know, and it is
very pleasant to see it in such attractive form as in the Schiff and Warburg families."

As time went on Taft found that almost the only way he could hold a
conference was in a taxicab or private car, going from one station to another. Horace regarded the vast amount of work he did during his years
at New Haven as clinching evidence of his abundant energy and ceaseless drive. The Tafts lived in four different houses in New Haven—at
"Hillcrest" on Prospect Street, at 70 Grove Street, at 113 Whitney Avenue, and at 60 York Square. The former President laid the cornerstone
of the post office in New Haven in 1914 and backed the work of the local
City Plan Commission. Since there was no Unitarian church in New
Haven he attended services in Yale Chapel from time to time, sitting in a
front pew and singing the hymns with the students. On the whole he
thrived on the new life, and his wife had fewer anxieties than when he
was President. Both were away from the constant scrutiny and criticism
that had worn them down. Taft crossed the campus with a feeling of
kinship and content, and at the end of his first year in private life he
wrote to Horace that he had had more real enjoyment than in many
years, although he had worked harder than at any time within his memory.

"The true attitude of a philosopher is that of enjoying what he has, without being blind to the probability of storms and the certainty of sorrows," he wrote to Miss Boardman. The waters of life seemed so untroubled after the stress of the Presidency that he scarcely hoped for continued peace. But all who knew William Howard Taft intimately recognized the fact that he was a man of sunny, optimistic spirit.

CHAPTER 20

BOB AND MARTHA

Robert was heading into the romance of his life during the winter of 1913–14. The girl who filled his thoughts was Martha Wheaton Bowers and he hurried away from the family Christmas party of 1913 to visit Mrs. Lloyd Bowers in Washington. Although his family had noticed his intense interest in Martha he had kept them all guessing during the White House years. He was deeply reserved in such matters but Bob was a man of purpose, and with his legal training finished he could afford to think seriously of marriage.

There was nothing impetuous about Bob's wooing of Martha. It was dogged persistence. He went after her with quiet intensity but his manner was so diffident that at times she thought he did not even care for her. When she went to Europe to study at the Sorbonne he turned up in Paris with George Harrison and followed her to Lucerne. Their camping trip in the West had also brought them together, but it was a serious riding accident that later precipitated matters. Martha was riding a spirited horse owned by Helen Taft when it bolted from the bridle path in Rock Creek Park and ran head-on into a streetcar. The horse's neck was broken and Martha was pitched over the car. As she recovered from her injuries Bob decided that the time had come to propose. He took her to dine at the Old Dower House on a March night in 1914 and asked her to marry him. Martha did not hesitate for a moment in saying yes.

She was fragile in appearance with expressive brown eyes in an oval face. Her smile was always radiant, and the young set in which she moved, and also their elders, recognized her as a girl of charm, wit, and balance. Their engagement was formally announced in April after various family preliminaries and Helen wrote gaily to Charlie: "They are delightful together—not sentimental but just beaming." She warned him to keep quiet about it until the engagement was announced. Charlie promptly went bounding in to tell his uncle Horace. Bob took care to write at once to Aunt Delia, who had a primary interest in all the family romances. "I am quite sure you will like her because there is no one who does not, but I do not intend to tell you how very much I love her, or the very good reasons for it. I think that Papa and Mama and Helen would have selected her for me themselves if I had allowed them, which I did not."

This was precisely true. The Tafts as a family could not have been more approving. Martha came up to their standards in all respects. The President, knowing her ancestry well, was heartily in favor of the match. He had loved and admired Lloyd Bowers, who had been solicitor general in his Cabinet, and he had always hoped that he and Bowers would sit together on the Supreme Court. Felix Frankfurter considered Bowers the most brilliant American lawyer of his generation, and Martha had heard good legal talk all her life. Mrs. Taft had been hoping for some time that Bob would propose to her and she had thought him unenterprising in holding off for so long. "Nellie and I are very happy over it," Will wrote to Horace. "We are very proud of Martha. If there is anything in eugenics, it is a wise match. She has a wonderfully bright mind like that of her father. He was one of the ablest men I ever knew."

Martha was born in Winona, Minnesota, on December 17, 1889. Her mother was Louise Wilson, daughter of an Irish immigrant who became chief justice of the Minnesota Supreme Court and later went to Congress. He was a man of boundless wit and mental vigor and Martha inherited some of his characteristics. Her ancestors were all sturdy patriots. She came of the combined stock of Jonathan Edwards, the theologian, and Timothy Dwight, president of Yale and a leader of the Connecticut Federalists. Her mother died when she was a small girl. By that time the family had moved to Chicago, where Bowers was counsel for the Chicago and Northwestern Railway. He later remarried and moved to Washington. Martha attended Rosemary Hall in Greenwich, Connecticut, and studied at the Sorbonne, since she planned to teach French. When she was seventeen Mr. and Mrs. George Wickersham took her on a trip around the world, along with Frances Noyes, daughter of Frank B. Noyes, owner of the Washington *Star*.

Helen considered Martha the most intellectual and keen girl in their set. In later years she expressed the opinion that Bob's wife actually had more interest in politics than her own mother had. Mrs. William Howard Taft would show impatience over a broken engagement, a dinner delayed because of her husband's political necessity, but Martha always considered herself a part of the political organization. She was prepared for any contingency. Helen believed that Martha—"the gayest, wittiest, most charming and sensible of women"—would be the perfect wife for Bob. His sister knew that behind his shy exterior was a bold and determined spirit, competitive, intense, devoted. She saw that Bob had a strong degree of primary color in him long before the voters realized it. He had always tried to make himself as nearly invisible as possible and the friends he brought home were not the big men at college but the quiet types. Although he dreaded cashing in on his father's fame he had a strong inner drive of his own.

While Bob's romance was brewing the family all laughed over a newspaper report that one of the Taft boys had become engaged to Miss Duke of North Carolina. Bob assured Charlie that he had never met the girl. Charlie was equally unaware of her existence. He read Bob's letter on this matter with the greatest interest:

> But you might like to know yourself that I *am* engaged to Martha Bowers. If you think of it you might write to her, and I am quite sure she would be very pleased, because I remember she once suggested that if you were a little older she might have chosen you instead of me.

At first Bob thought that he should wait until he was making enough to support a wife, but at the moment this seemed a distant prospect. Clients were not yet flocking to his office. Up to January 1, 1914, he had made six dollars at bridge and forty cents for notarizing a document. But he was learning how a law office functioned and he considered this valuable experience. Martha had a substantial estate left by her father, with an income that would help them to get started in a modest way. His parents knew that Bob would never let this circumstance prevent him from working his own way to success. More concerned about his father's opinion than any other, Bob gave his own view of this in a letter written just before the engagement was announced:

> As long as Martha has the money, it seems that we might as well be married next Fall and use it. We shall not be extravagant, and shall live very simply; and I don't believe that it will cause me to work any less hard. In fact, I shall not be entirely comfortable living on it. . . . You have given me the best opportunities, and the best ideals. I don't be-

lieve that in not waiting I am injuring either, and I will do my best to make as much of a success as I know you would like.

Martha wrote to the elder Tafts that her own mother had encouraged Bob shamelessly. In response to their good wishes she wrote: "I think I do know how splendid Bob is, and I shall always want to help him to do his very best at everything." During the Easter holidays she invited a group of her young friends to tea. She led Robert into the room and everyone knew at once what was in the wind. In May she was in Cincinnati at the time of the festival and Annie gave a big tea for her, with William Howard Taft present. Old friends swarmed around them. Bob was anxious to show Martha the place where she would live. They all attended the festival and heard Bach's *Mass in B Minor*, going later with the former President to hear him speak at Union Bethel, a settlement established by David Sinton.

Before leaving for Murray Bay that summer Taft gave the commencement address at Horace's school in June. Then he hurried back to New Haven to work on his Harvard Phi Beta Kappa address. President Lowell showed him the freshman dormitories in Cambridge, which he thought too luxurious. He decided that the Widener Library, then being completed, was the most usable university library in the country, with Yale second best. But he preferred the architecture of Yale, with its quadrangles, rather than what he called the higgledy-piggledy arrangement at Harvard. He returned to New Haven for commencement there and watched Yale beat Harvard in the ball game. Charles was present from Cincinnati and as enthusiastic as a freshman, but Annie did not relish the thought that it was his fiftieth anniversary. Old age and death were subjects never discussed at Pike Street. Taft always felt that the speeches he made at Yale were poor because he had talked there so much and had exhausted every subject. In 1913 he had turned his face against becoming dean of the Yale Law School. After leaving the White House he was also offered the presidency of Johns Hopkins University, of the College of the City of New York, of Lafayette College, of the University of Texas, and of Dartmouth. In 1914 he became honorary president of Hampton Institute and wrote of this connection: "The truth is I am very enthusiastic about the prospect that has come to the Negro and the South through the Negro . . . the South is awakening to community improvement. The Negroes are amenable, tractable and ambitious, have a land hunger, and regard education almost as a fetish. . . ."

The Tafts had a full family gathering at Murray Bay in 1914. The arrival of *Le Petit Juge*, no longer the President, was the signal for many friendly gestures among the local residents. Charles and Annie were at Mountain Ash Cottage with their daughter Louise. It stood close to the road but evergreens had been planted to screen them from view. Their living room was large enough for a ball and they had fine views from their upper and lower porches. Will's particular delight was to see so much of Horace at leisure, for usually his schoolmaster brother was hard to pin down in summer. He was apt to be found bicycling in Bermuda, mountain-climbing with Roberts, or taking long strides along the rocky coast of Maine. Now the brothers had days together on the golf course, long evenings on the porch, picnics, card games, the good conversation on which they flourished; and Will wrote appreciatively to Delia:

> As time goes on Horace grows more and more precious to me. His sunny disposition, his keen sense of humor, his catholic spirit and his high ideals are all a source of joy that I can not overstate. His school is becoming in excellence of moral and intellectual training the first preparatory school in the country.

Bob and Martha visited them briefly and all the young people went on fishing trips to Lac Gravelle. Mrs. Taft provided meals of fresh salmon, chicken, strawberries, and vegetables straight from the garden. The brothers went into conclave about Fanny, whose husband had developed acute neuritis in the arm and could no longer perform surgery, with the result that he was deeply depressed and in financial difficulties. Bill had a lemon ranch and part interest in a building in Los Angeles, and his income when he was able to practice averaged from $15,000 to $25,000 a year. With their customary family loyalty the brothers all rallied around Fanny and volunteered to send her money until her husband recovered. It was some time before he was able to resume his surgical work.

Taft's longing for the Supreme Court revived when his friend Justice Horace H. Lurton died that summer but he had little hope when he wrote to Miss Boardman: "Wilson would no more think of offering me the appointment than he would of flying." He thought that the appearance of the President at the meeting of the American Bar Association in Washington that summer had given distinction and a national character to the gathering, but he deplored his implied criticism of the courts in his speech. Taft was much impressed with Wilson's oratory, commenting on his antithetical and epigrammatical style, but although he thought it had beauty he was equally convinced that it lacked the practical touch required by a President.

Mrs. Wilson's death at this time awakened Taft's sensitive realization of the President's position. Recalling his own wife's collapse so soon after he took office he wrote that in a less acute way he understood the searing union of responsibility in office and private sorrow and anxiety. The White House would seem solitary without her, for it had a "splendid isolation that makes sorrow keener."

The Tafts were still at Murray Bay when the first World War broke out. It changed the course of the former President's life, as it did of countless others. He watched the electrifying way in which Canada rose to arms. Without hesitation he went to work at once, changing the tenor of his speeches. He wrote to Aunt Delia and others that the President's policy of neutrality should be supported and he predicted a long war. Colonel Roosevelt had now surrendered the front page to the Kaiser. Long before the United States went to war Taft toured the country, speaking in support of Wilson's policies, a respected voice in the midst of clamor.

Americans caught in Europe when the war began were arriving home, among them Edith Morgan, a niece of Herbert Parsons, who joined the Tafts at Murray Bay with breathtaking tales of the panic in France, and their own Maria, back from her tour of the world. Mrs. Bowers had just got out of Paris with Martha's trousseau. Since Delia was too frail to get to Washington for Bob's wedding the Tafts all gathered at Millbury for her birthday. She made a perfect New England picture, sitting on a straight chair under the trees, close to the flowers she carefully tended. With her high collar, her keen eyes, her crossed hands, Miss Torrey summed up a way of life. Horace, who lived nearest to her, was a frequent visitor. They talked of the war now and of the contrast with the old days in Vienna. Delia liked to hear about Horace's boys, some of whom came from famous American families. She had made a point of remembering Will's children at all the milestones of their academic life, and they never failed to treat her with respect. Now that they were mature they went out of their way to visit Millbury, where their grandmother had grown up, where their father had passed his boyhood summers, and not far from the spot where the first Taft had landed in America. It was a continuity of tradition that appealed to Aunt Delia, and in a way she held it intact in her own person. Now the first of Will's children was ready to found a family of his own.

Martha and Bob were married in St. John's Church in Washington on October 17, 1914. Helen was maid of honor and the bridesmaids— Marjorie Edgar, Louise Hellen, Frances Noyes, and Julia Thompson —wore autumn colors. Charlie, in his first cutaway, towered above the other ushers—Harry Bingham, Carroll Glover, John Herron, Stanhope Bayne Jones, Carl Leyman, Walter Logan, Stephen Philbin, and Adrian Van Sinderen. Mrs. Taft, looking on approvingly, wore sapphire-blue velvet. The judiciary, honoring the Taft and Bowers names, were present in impressive numbers. Martha's troop of ten Girl Scouts watched the ceremony from the church balcony. Will sent Delia a detailed account of the proceedings with an illuminating comment on his son's bearing:

> Bob looked trim and when he was asked the question, answered 'I will' as if somebody said to him 'You won't,' his answer was so positive and sharp. Martha was beautifully dressed and looked very sweet as a bride.

They went to The Manor at Asheville for their wedding trip and returned in time for Tom Bowers's wedding to Louise Hellen two weeks later. A few days after the wedding the entire family rejoiced when a telegram arrived from Horace announcing that Charlie had taken the Latin prize in his Yale entrance examination, first among 415 contestants. But the war that had just begun would shape the future of both young men. A new era had dawned and the headlines on Bob's wedding day proclaimed it.

Bob, settled with Martha in a plain brick house at 1812 Dexter Avenue and practicing law in an office in Union Central Building, sent Charlie letters filled with advice. He urged him to take every English course offered at Yale, and to let modern languages alone. He was now reading much that he should have read years earlier, Bob added. He also advised his brother not to become involved in meaningless activity. In retrospect he thought that he had wasted a good deal of time in college on things that were good in themselves but in which his participation meant nothing. Interesting courses mattered most, in Bob's opinion. He gave Charlie advice on football, too, and invited him to Cincinnati to show him what a young lawyer's life was like out there. Their wedding gifts had almost furnished their house and they particularly prized the mahogany bookcases that Annie and Charles had given them. But their books still overflowed the house since both were insatiable readers.

Charlie was on the freshman debating team at Yale and was president of the debating club. Soon he was captain of the basketball team but his father questioned the effect of this on his scholarship. He wished him to beat a brilliant student from Sherman Thacher's school and to lead the class, as Bob had done. He thought he should be president of the *Drama* and editor of the *News*. But Charlie insisted that football put him in the best condition for his work and Dean Jones reported that his academic results were admirable, too. Horace noted that Charlie seemed to have been inoculated by the virus of reform. He wished to widen the scope of the fraternities and called together twenty-five leading members of his class to help him revive Beta Theta Pi. Charlie, his uncle observed, "liked to play every instrument in the band." Among his classmates were John Farrar and F. Trubee Davison, who would become lifelong friends of young Taft.

Mrs. Taft's book, *Recollections of Full Years,* came out at the end of 1914 and was well received. She had been filled with doubts about its publication, lest it should be too revealing. It was anything but that, and Helen and her father, who had watched over its preparation, reassured her. Horace liked the part about the Philippines best and the White House section least. With its publication Aunt Delia remarked: "We are getting more and more illustrious every day." Mrs. Taft invested her profits on the book in five-per cent mortgages and set them aside as a nest egg for Helen, who used this money eventually to build a good tennis court at Murray Bay. Even in the midst of winter snows Taft was already yearning for Sassifern Cottage, which was then being remodeled. "No millionaire ever had more interest in the construction of his palace on Fifth Avenue than I have in that villa of mine under lease," he wrote to Charles.

It had been a year of ceaseless work for Taft, and as he traveled about on his lectures he now wore a gout shoe. He had become a fund-raiser as well as a public speaker. Anson Phelps Stokes had persuaded him to campaign for Yale Medical School, celebrating its hundredth anniversary in 1914. Both Dr. Harvey Cushing and Dr. Abraham Flexner were pushing for it, and Taft was soon engaged in trying to interest Carnegie and the Rockefeller interests in the needs of his alma mater. As his voice was heard across the country William Howard Taft was assuming a restored public image. He gained ground steadily and the New York *Evening Sun* summed up the feeling that he had grown in public estimation since leaving the White House: "He has been as slow to political criticism as to wrath, and the Democratic Party, as well as the country, owes much to his patriotic self-control and moderation." When he visited New York Harry and Julia usually gave imposing dinner parties for him, with leading figures in the Republican party present.

The realists of the Republican party, like Hilles, conceded that the European war had checked the tide that had set in for them, but Karger kept subtly whipping up the thought of the former President returning to office. Taft felt far removed from it all and refused to accept the suggestion of Hilles, Martin Egan, and Max Pam that he run for Congress, so as to be in the field for an ultimate presidential nomination. He was completely skeptical of the idea that he could ever be renominated but, as usual, he consulted his family before saying no. It was not pride that motivated him, he said, for he would willingly take any position in which he thought he could be useful because of his experience. But he felt he had been in the public eye long enough and he did not wish to expose his wife again to the excitement and mudslinging of a campaign. Miss Boardman, too, was against it. She wrote to him on Christmas Day, 1914: "Much as we want you back in Washington, I, for one, don't want you to undergo a second White House experience. Had you been re-elected I don't think you could have lived through another four years. The strain is terrific, and you did not know how to spare yourself as a more selfish man would have done."

Early in 1915 Taft felt that Root was in the lead for the Republican nomination but when he visited him in Albany his old friend scoffed at the idea. He felt unequal to undertaking the task and Taft observed that he did not look well. Shortly before his death Will wrote to Helen that Root filled the measure of statesmanship more fully than anyone with whom he had come in contact. He considered him an intellectual leader but lacking the courage and the instaneous grasp of a situation that Roosevelt possessed. Summing up his personal feeling for Root, Taft wrote:

> As I look back in my life, I think I have met few men for whom I have a higher respect than I have for him. He certainly is one of the strongest men intellectually whom I ever met, and he has a judicial cast of mind and a power of analysis that are much like Lincoln's. He has a fine wit, and while he has the reputation of being cold, I don't know anyone who responds more truly and certainly to an appeal to his affections and old associations than he does.

Taft had his first encounter with Roosevelt since his defeat when both men met in April, 1915, at the funeral of Thomas R. Lounsbury, a noted Yale professor. The two former Presidents were honorary pall-bearers and they met in the chapel vestibule. Taft was paired with Professor Henry A. Beers and Roosevelt with Brander Matthews. There were various accounts afterwards of what transpired between them. Some observers thought they greeted each other simultaneously. William Lyon Phelps insisted that Roosevelt gave no sign of recognition until Taft approached him, held out his hand, and said: "How are you, Theodore?" Governor Wilbur L. Cross, of Connecticut, recalled that Taft extended his hand with a genial "Hello, Teddy" and invited him to come to their New Haven home. Roosevelt said that he had to leave immediately after the funeral and "Taft was deeply hurt, as one could see, but his face quickly regained composure," Cross commented. Taft's own view of the encounter, as conveyed to Miss Boardman, was that it had been a stiff meeting, a kind of armed neutrality, but it relieved him from all uncertainty as to how they were to conduct themselves at future meetings.

Nelson Aldrich died close to the time of the Lounsbury funeral and Taft and John D. Rockefeller both were pallbearers at the service in Grace Church, Providence. "With the exception of Root, he is the great-

est statesman that I have met," the former President wrote to Miss
Boardman. "He was better able to control men, and he had greater courage, though of course he was not as great a jurist, and he had not the
power of the literary style or of learning that Root had." The Rhode
Islander had never tried to use his power in any way for his personal advantage, Taft assured Mabel, who was well aware that there had been
much public criticism of his association with the influential senator from
New England.

Taft was following Roosevelt's moves with interest in 1915, struck by
the influence he continued to wield. Karger wrote to him that fear of
the Bull Moose was responsible more than any other thing for the sharp
tone of the German notes. The sinking of the *Lusitania* in May had
changed the picture. This even threw the country into deep gloom
and Taft immediately wrote sympathetically to the President. He
urged him not to be stampeded into measures that might mean war, and
he suggested withdrawal of the United States ambassador and recall of
his German vis-à-vis. Taft doubted that Germany would make this a
casus belli, but he felt that if Congress were summoned, it would be
difficult to avoid a war. "Time is a great solvent of many of these troubles," wrote Taft, always the arbitrator at heart. He finished with a tribute to Wilson:

> I am glad to have the opportunity of expressing to you my confidence
> that you will take the wise and patriotic course and that you will avoid
> war, if it is possible. If you see no other course open than now to sum-
> mon Congress and declare war, of course the whole people will be with
> you without regard to party. With earnest prayer that you may good
> deliverance make, believe me, my dear Mr. President . . .

President Wilson responded with equal warmth: "I think the whole
country admires, as I do, the generous spirit in which you have sunk all
considerations of party and have come to my support at this critical junc-
ture in our history. You may be sure that the suggestions you make
have great weight with me and that they will constitute part of my most
serious thought in this time of perplexity. . . ."

Bryan's resignation in June took them all by surprise. "Bryan is a pacifist internationally, but I'll be hanged if he is a pacifist politically,"
Karger wrote to Taft, who was already out in the field backing Wilson.
He spoke at a League of Peace meeting in Philadelphia and took in the
Yale, Wellesley, Lawrenceville, Swarthmore, and Bryn Mawr commence-
ments. It was Helen's graduation year and she wrote to him: "It is
only your paternal duty to come and see conferred upon me the degree
of B.A. and all the rights thereunto appertaining in the Commonwealth

of Pennsylvania . . . tell Ma that, of course, she has to come along."
Since her illness Mrs. Taft was reluctant to leave her home except for
special occasions.

Helen had added to the family honors by taking the George W.
Childs Essay Prize. Miss Thomas assured her father that her English
teachers considered her the best writer in the senior class and able all
around. Were it not that they had a genius in the senior class that
year Helen would have received the European fellowship, Miss Thomas
added. The hapless victor was skillfully catechized by the former President after he had made the commencement address. He sent Aunt Delia
copies of his campus speeches and thanked her for the hundred dollars
she sent to Helen on her graduation. He told her to prepare herself to be
a great-great-aunt, for Bob and Martha were expecting a baby in August.
"But I guess you can stand it and carry it with as much dignity as I can
being a grandfather," he added. Helen passed on the news to Charlie,
with the usual warning not to tell anyone: "You are going to be an
uncle in August. I am all of a twitter over our new dignity."

Bob's first son, William Howard Taft, III, was born at Bar Harbor on
August 7, 1915. He weighed only five pounds but his father wrote that he
was "lusty and sonorous." Although Harry had a son named after the
President his parents always called him Howard. The Robert Tafts called
their son Billy from the start. At this time they moved to Indian Hill,
twelve miles from Cincinnati. After much hunting around they had
bought a farm on a tongue of land running into a bend of the Little
Miami River. It had sixty-five acres of arable land with an unpretentious old clapboard house that lacked running water and electricity but
had a commanding view of the surrounding country. They paid $15,000
for the property and were grateful for the owner's coal-oil lamps and his
well. In time Sky Farm, enlarged and developed, became the family
stronghold of the Robert Tafts. When the surrounding region came to
be known as "suburban château country" Martha remarked that moving
to Indian Hill was the only thing they ever did that turned out to be
fashionable. But when Père Taft went out to have tea with them
early in 1915 he wondered how they were going to manage with such in-
conveniences. A trolley line ran into town but he foresaw what their
winters would be like. However, he reported cheerfully to Horace:

> Bob and Martha seem to be like two cooing doves in a nest. They are
> sympathetic in their tastes, they are quiet in their manner, philosoph-
> ical in their temperament, considerate in their treatment of everybody
> and effective for work in their methods.

Bob golfed every Sunday with Hulbert Taft, Phil Wyman, and Harrison Smith. He frequently consulted his father about his law cases.

Business was piling up and Bob was beginning to have almost more than he could handle. He was deeply involved in his uncle Charles's business affairs. Annie was having trouble with the orchestra, since so many of the musicians came from enemy countries and were the victims of wartime hysteria. The concertmaster and the first violinist had been interned as Germans. Ernst Kunwald, the conductor, had been caught in Germany. With eighty men signed up for the season, she was concerned over the leadership of the orchestra. Since its cost was $150,000 a year, the revenue coming in from concerts was important. She and Charles were giving $60,000 a year at this time to keep things going, and she considered making an offer to Victor Herbert. The fact that he was Irish appealed to her but she feared he would be too light for their symphony. He drank champagne with the men and was popular with them. Henry Hadley, an American conductor and composer, also was considered.

Cincinnati had such a large German population that feeling about the war ran high and there were many arguments long before the United States took up arms. Feeling was constantly being whipped up as the war news came in from Europe. The Red Cross was already involved and Miss Boardman wrote to Taft: "I'm not pro-Allies nor pro-German but pro-Humanity, and so I will remain no matter what the criticism."

The elder Tafts went west in the summer of 1914 for the Panama-Pacific International Exhibition in San Francisco. Helen, Maria, and Louise accompanied them, but Charlie stayed behind with Mrs. McCagg and worked as volunteer secretary-treasurer of the Golf Club at Murray Bay. Nellie, who enjoyed sightseeing and touring more than her husband did, wrote regularly to her young son of their adventures as they visited Banff and traveled through the Rockies. They took a different route from Taft, who spoke at the American Bar Association meeting in Salt Lake City in August while they proceeded west by Canadian Pacific. He addressed bankers' clubs, the chamber of commerce, the Unitarian Conference, and a Red Cross convention. Some of his statements stirred up a storm with Hiram Johnson in California. The former President challenged the strong drive of the Progressives on the coast, meanwhile writing to Horace that he had been away from controversy for so long he did not relish being an object of attack again, but he was determined to state the truth as he saw it.

When the Tafts reached Los Angeles Fanny and Bill drove them through the hills and showed them the big estates and general development of the region. But the former President was not impressed. He felt that the people were living solely for luxury and pleasure and were overconfident in their power to overcome difficulties. It all seemed to him to be a "cult of the uplift and a parlor socialism that had made them anomalous in politics." Bill had regained his practice but Fanny looked thin and worn; they had suffered from hard times and bad investments. Harry, Julia, and their son Walbridge had traveled west for the exposition, too, and to see their daughter, Louise Snowden, who was now living in Seattle and had become wholly reconciled with her mother. Mabel Boardman traveled out for the Red Cross convention at the fair but she was in mourning for her father and avoided the social functions.

Taft observed his fifty-eighth birthday while in California, spending the day at Mrs. Phoebe Apperson Hearst's hacienda, but the major event of their tour was Taft Day, celebrated at the exposition with a luncheon and large reception for the former President and his family. Mrs. Taft sent Charlie by letter a full account of these events and told him that she had seen the great new picture—*The Birth of a Nation*— that everyone was discussing. The cinema was taking shape in California. Helen, who intended to enroll at Yale that autumn for her master's degree, hurried East with her father, leaving the others to travel home at leisure through the Panama Canal. But Nellie, Maria, and Louise were slowed up by slides in the Panama Canal and they finally had to cross the isthmus in the old-fashioned way.

On his return Taft found himself in the middle of a storm of protest from suffragists for his article on the subject in the *Saturday Evening Post*. He carried ballast diplomatically in both saddles until 1919 when he came out in the open in favor of suffrage. Among his best women friends were pros and cons, and each assailed him with humor or temper from time to time for his utterances on the subject. As the son of Louise Torrey and the nephew of Delia he was not exactly a captive of the anti-suffrage forces. "William, ah William!" Miss Boardman wrote to him playfully when he seemed to take a step with the pros. On the other hand, Mrs. Katrina Ely Tiffany, an old family friend with Murray Bay associations, was deeply reproachful when she learned that he was going to lecture at the Cosmopolitan Club in New York under the auspices of an association opposed to suffrage. "You, the most logical and honest-minded of men!" she protested, signing herself "Your dumbfounded admirer, Katrina Ely Tiffany."

Mrs. Root warned him that the mere sight of the committee of suffragettes who were going to present him with a petition would make him run or look the other way. He wrote back blandly that while he thought better of her sex's capacity for government than she did, he would wait until the "best women and all the women" had agreed that they ought to have the ballot. The issue became acute when Woodrow Wilson decided to haul down the flag of resistance, a piece of news that seemed to interlock with the startling announcement that he was about to marry Mrs. Edith Bolling Galt. Washington was immediately ablaze with gossip about the White House romance. Another four years would pass, however, and pickets would storm the White House and be hauled off to jail, before either man capitulated completely to the suffrage forces. Taft was finally won over by the evidence he gathered on his travels that women above all stood for peace and had the best right in the world to an equal voice in efforts to prevent war. His daughter Helen had never had any doubt on the subject, and Miss Thomas and she had worked hard for suffrage.

Miss Boardman took no public stand because of her position with the Red Cross, but she did not hesitate to express her views to Will. Toward the end of 1915 she was involved in major operations of a new kind. In organizing relief for European countries she had discovered how difficult it was to keep things on a neutral basis. A Red Cross relief ship had been chartered and sent abroad, but there had been delay, troubles with the crew, complications over neutrality, and now the feeling prevailed that a strong public figure was needed to head the organization. Miss Boardman sought a man with an international reputation. General George W. Goethals had declined the post. Elihu Root was not interested. She was now trying to get the former President to serve but he told her that his personality would give the post a political flavor that would be disastrous. However, at the end of 1915 President Wilson appointed him a member of the Central Committee of the Red Cross. This came as a great relief to Mabel, who was in the center of conflicting forces. But she soon found that he was paternally engaged in making her slacken her hold on the organization, since the Red Cross was now primarily associated with the Army and he felt it was entirely appropriate that high army officers should do the work. "Abate some of your highest ideals for the practical, my dear Mabel," he advised her.

While the former President backed Wilson in his war policies, if not in other respects, he was impatient with Root and some of his other friends for their intense desire to get into the war. He deplored the "Anglophile tendency of club circles in New York" to denounce Wilson for his failure to protest the invasion of Belgium. He assured Mabel that he would have made the same decision in the President's place. But the American people were getting restive as the slaughter continued in Europe. In April, 1916, he expressed himself clearly to Nellie: "We must stand by Wilson. Germany is wrong. Roosevelt's attack on Wilson is as mean as he could make it and as injurious. For a man who is exalting patriotism and Americanism, he is as lacking in them when personal hatred and egoism intervene as any one I know."

The Republicans were at odds among themselves over a presidential candidate. Roosevelt hovered constantly in the picture and still commanded a great following. He was vociferous in his support of the war, and was always the picturesque warrior who made newspaper copy. When Taft visited Cincinnati in June, 1916, he found both Bob and Hulbert Taft bitter over the Roosevelt boom. But when Roosevelt and the Progressive party came out for Hughes he felt sure that a Democratic landslide was in sight. Riding on a train a few hours before the returns were in, and trying to keep his mind on international law rather than on politics, he wrote: "It will be hard for me to bear another administration of Wilson. . . . He is perfectly ruthless and unscrupulous but many people regard him as a saint. He will ruin the Supreme Court."

News of Wilson's triumph reached him in Iowa. He wrote at once to Nellie: "You and I have had defeat before and we can stand it after we grow used to it. We must buckle down. With Democrats so strongly entrenched, our usefulness will be much narrowed so far as public matters are concerned but we must now go to work and earn some more money and make ourselves better fitted for the professorial life." It was Taft's ambition to leave $250,000 to his family, between his insurance policies and his private fortune, and in the end he exceeded this sum.

In writing to Mabel Boardman he attributed the Republican defeat to the "emotional nature of women just endowed with the right to vote, and the besotted comfort and lethargy of farmers in the West. . . ." His own support of Wilson's policies had not moved him any nearer to the Supreme Court. When a vacancy occurred in 1916 there was speculation again that he might be appointed, but Wilson's choice was Louis D. Brandeis. Taft was one of the group of lawyers who protested this appointment. Later he was to become the friend and admirer of this jurist but he felt no enthusiasm for him in the beginning. Only to his wife did Will reveal his deep-seated disappointment. Outwardly he jested with light good humor. When Henry Ford invited him to go to Europe on the Peace Ship he considered it a "fool performance" and would have nothing to do with it.

When next Taft visited Pike Street he found Charles spreading out in new directions. He had invested in the McAlpin Hotel in New York and the Hotel Taft in New Haven. Both were doing well. The McAlpin was making $300,000 a month and a million-dollar addition was planned. Charles had given Will sixty shares of the common stock so that he could become a director in the New Haven Hotel Company. He had also sold the Cubs for half a million dollars. The gas company in which he and Annie were interested was booming. He had organized the Dixie Terminal Company as a focus in the heart of Cincinnati for all the lines of the Newport and Covington Street Railway system. An office building and modern arcade were planned and he had bought additional property on Fourth, Walnut, and Third streets.

Early in 1917 he and Annie were agitated over the statue of Lincoln

that they had commissioned Barnard to do. They intended sending replicas to London and Paris but Robert Lincoln protested against giving
such a grotesque image of President Lincoln to the peoples of other nations. He thought the statue uncouth and that it did his father a great
injustice. He asked Taft to intercede with Charles but Will was hesitant, knowing how angry Annie would be. "Barnard will blow up
about it and R.L. will continue his rage," Taft wrote to Miss Boardman.
"Lincoln said he could not prevent the Cincinnati statue but he was
anxious to stop the London and Paris ones." Replicas were finally sent
to Louisville, Kentucky, and to Manchester, England, but a lively controversy preceded the gift, and George Bernard Shaw upheld Barnard's
conception of the Emancipator. He said that a sloppily-dressed Lincoln
would be appropriate near Parliament, which housed the worst-dressed
men in the country. Some time earlier Taft, one of the most photographed of Presidents, had a bust of himself done by C. S. Pietro for
John Wesley Hill, the active agent of the Peace Forum, who wanted it
for the Hague Tribunal.

CHAPTER 21

CHARLIE AND ELEANOR

LIKE ROBERT, Charles Phelps Taft II found the romance of his lifetime in his college years. In 1917 he joined the Army and he also fell in love with Eleanor K. Chase, a fluffy-haired, blue-eyed girl who had attended St. Margaret's School in Waterbury and Bennett College. Her father, Irving H. Chase, was president of the Ingersoll Waterbury Company. Like the Tafts, the Chases of Waterbury were a spreading clan, with a family fortune founded in brass and copper. Their watches and clocks were internationally known.

Charlie met Eleanor at a dance and he never had any doubt that she was the girl he wished to marry. His father observed his devotion to her in April and by June Charlie was writing exuberantly to his friends about his engagement. Taft had just sent flowers to Mrs. Taft, with an accompanying card reading: "1886–1917. With love and gratitude for thirty-one years of unalloyed happiness." The marriage of Charlie and Eleanor would continue in the same tradition.

By this time the youngest Taft had developed into a formidable young man, endowed with good looks, presence, drive, and capacity. He was six feet one and a half inches tall and weighed 190 pounds. Articulate and optimistic as ever, he was always noticed wherever he appeared and he was still an individualist to the core. While other members of his class were going to officers' training camps or were learning to fly Navy airplanes with the First Yale Unit, Charlie enlisted in May, 1917, as a buck private in the Third Field Artillery. He was in his junior year and was slightly below the officers' age level. His parents were proud of this move and were not disposed to push his cause at headquarters. "I am content to have my boy serve in the war as a Sergeant—I am not ambitious for his military promotion but only for his usefulness," his father wrote to Newton D. Baker, Secretary of War.

The Tafts now shared the anxiety of countless other parents across the land. His father wrote moralistic letters to Charlie, then at Fort Myer, Virginia:

> It is a great comfort to me that you are a member of the church, that you don't smoke, and that you don't drink, and that you have those high ideals that enable you to elevate the people about you rather than to yield to their levelling or lowering tendency.

Helen, who had just been appointed dean of Bryn Mawr, wrote her usual gay and jesting letters to "Dear Charley-Boy," dwelling particularly on life at Murray Bay. She had gone on a camping trip to Grand Lac de Ha-Ha and they had forded a deep stream where the beavers had dammed the river and the bridge was down. They went without food from 8 A.M. to 8 P.M., walking fifteen miles in the pouring rain, singing hymns for all they were worth. There was also the tragedy of Caro to report. Charlie had no sooner donned uniform than the beloved family dog, known variously as Caro, Caruso, or Karuse, died of rabies. His family conspired to break the news to him as gently as possible. Mrs. Taft had adored the caramel-colored Caro, and Helen and Charlie had made him their special pet. Taft frankly detested the dog but he joined in the general chorus of mourning, knowing how much Caro had meant to his family. "My heart goes out to you, dear, in your personal loss," he wrote to Nellie from Atlantic City, as if one of their friends had just died. He knew that Caro had kept her company during many lonely hours while he was "grasshopping about the country." And to Charlie he wrote: "I am very, very sorry because your mother and Helen loved him so and he was so much company for your mother. . . . Our love and thoughts are all and always with you, my dear boy."

Amazed at her father's attitude Helen wrote to Charlie: "Pa actually called up yesterday morning after Caro had been carried off and said: " 'Well, we must have another dog.' . . . I think he is quite ready to write to Queen Marguerite for a cousin to Caruso. Goodby, my darling, I love you much better than Caro, appearance to the contrary notwithstanding. Do write to us often. I hope that you are getting enough to eat." She told him that Caro had missed him after he left but had attached himself to Aunt Delia. The family pet had survived many adventures at Murray Bay, landing in bogs and bramble bushes as he chased the young Tafts across the golf course.

The new dean of Bryn Mawr made a cake for her soldier brother but put salt in it instead of sugar on the first try. She bought him a tie but her mother reminded her that Charlie liked to pick his own. But if Helen was not yet an expert cook her other gifts were many. She had taken her M.A. degree at Yale and her father, sending her $2,000 in Liberty Bonds, had written to her with deep satisfaction:

> Your taking your M.A. degree and your election as Dean of Bryn Mawr constitute one of the great joys of my life and gives me the greatest pride. They open for you a career of great usefulness and great distinction. It is quite probable you will marry, though you may not. But now whatever course you may take, you will take it because you prefer it after due consideration and judgment uninfluenced by a duress which in so many cases has brought unhappiness.

Taft explained to Helen that he hoped to leave an estate large enough to yield her an income. He was always watchful of his children's financial interests, and particularly of Helen's. At all times he gave generously to philanthropic causes. A $5,000 fee he received for arbitrating the claim of the New Haven Railroad against the Adams Express Company, for damages in the destruction by fire of Hartford Station, went to his Yale class fund at this time. His idea was to give back to his college a large part of his salary, because the financial strain of the war years was serious at Yale.

Taft never ceased to be thankful for the quiet success of his children. "When I think how up to this time, your mother and I have been blessed in the remarkable children we have had, it makes me very grateful to God," he wrote to Helen. "Bob and you and Charlie should and do make your mother and me profoundly happy." While Charlie was wooing Eleanor, his uncle Charles's daughter Louise was married at the family home on Pike Street to William H. Semple, assistant Latin professor at the University of Cincinnati. Charles, seventy-three years old, was shaky on her wedding day, for he was just recovering from injuries he had received in a fall at a friend's house.

Annie and he had invited 500 guests, and the house with its choice paintings made an impressive setting for the wedding. Jane Ingalls, in pink, was maid of honor, and little Ann Ingalls and Catherine Moore carried flower baskets. The wedding party seemed to William Howard Taft to be academic in spirit because of the number of young professors present. Will gave Nellie a full description of all that transpired, from

Annie's costume to the cases of champagne that emptied rapidly. He thought Louise, usually so shy, seemed happy and self-possessed—even radiant.

Maria was a focus of attention, as always. Since her father's death she had been living with the Mores, but after Louise's wedding Taft invited her to stay with them in New Haven. But Maria, who now had independent means, was going abroad to do war work. However, she joined them briefly that summer at Murray Bay. Pointe au Pic no longer seemed the same to the elder Tafts. For fifteen years they had been planning a house large enough to hold all their children and their children's friends. Now that they had it, not one of the younger group was there with them to enjoy it, and his father wrote dolefully to Charlie: "You and Helen and Bob, the bright particular souls with whom I filled it, are not here. Your mother and I alone occupy the ten bedrooms, the four bathrooms, the study, your mother's sitting room and the big downstairs room."

Taft's study was upstairs, with French windows opening out toward the St. Lawrence and the hills beyond, always a satisfying view to the former President. Mrs. Taft had a room with French doors looking into the hall. The living room, dining room, and hall had been greatly enlarged and they had three big open fireplaces downstairs. Nellie used her Philippine shields, helmets, baskets, and swords for decoration, together with Moro mats. Filipino hats were used for wall decorations and Navaho blankets for rugs. Japanese pictures of the Russo-Japanese War papered the dining room, toning down the rawness of the white pine. The national flag, the President's naval flag, and two Ohio flags hung in the hall.

The woods around their house had been cleared and the ravine had been opened into a glade with a heavy fringe of trees. The stone wall in front of the house enclosed the flower beds, which had been enlarged. Maria and Helen had labored over the lupines and columbines. The new pine ceiling and walls gave the house its own fragrance. An entire new suite was ready for Bob and Martha. The servants had their own porch and Maggie, their treasured cook, presided over the kitchen. Helen had designed the kitchen and its closets, with an eye to good storage space.

Murray Bay was a never-ending source of delight to William Howard Taft. He longed for it when he was President; he dreamed about it when he sat on the Supreme Court bench. As each new child was born in the family his first thought was to get the baby to Pointe au Pic as soon as possible. He was a strongly sentimental man where his family was concerned and the house at Murray Bay did much to strengthen the Taft pattern of life. His associations there were deep-rooted and he could dwell at length on the rustic days before plumbing and artificial light;

the nights of cards and good talk; the sunny and misty days on the golf links; the play of light on river and sky; the picnics on the beach at St. Irenee, the fishing trips to Lac Gravelle; the endless outdoor delights of the St. Lawrence resort.

Not all members of the family shared the patriarch's enthusiasm. Julia and Harry chose to sample more worldly resorts. Horace liked variety and while Winifred was alive she pulled him away from Murray Bay, although he always returned with zest. Martha's hay fever improved at Bar Harbor and she also liked to go abroad. Eleanor had her own family to visit at Miramer, Narragansett Pier. But for the most part they gathered habitually at Murray Bay, with Helen and Charlie the most devoted. Pointe au Pic was a Taft colony, so recognized by Canadians, and as the years went on a succession of handsome children filed into the little church, picnicked, and ran about with the sense of freedom their parents had enjoyed in the same setting.

Long before the United States entered the war the Tafts were deeply conscious of the heavy cloud that rested over Canada. Her men were dying in France and Belgium. Canadians were critical of American nonintervention and Taft could feel the sadness and sternness that prevailed. But now the picture had changed. The United States, too, was at war and both of the Taft sons were serving their country in separate ways. After being rejected twice for active service because of poor eyesight Bob went to work for Herbert Hoover, who was running the Food Administration. He and Martha moved to Washington, where he worked night and day. At first he was engaged chiefly in drafting regulations in different fields, but soon he had additional responsibilities.

The former President had intensified his efforts as a speaker, throwing his support behind Wilson as the quick thrust of wartime emergencies developed. He made close to fifty speeches on the war in August, 1917, convinced that people across the country needed to be awakened to the need for full participation. He wrote to Charlie: "I do what little I can to explain what the war means to us and to the world, why we are in it and why we must win." He hammered away at Mayor William H. Thompson of Chicago as a "blathering numbskull and demagogue." This was a strenuous trip for Taft and he became very ill in Kansas City. He was stricken on the train and was taken to the Mayo clinic, where he was kept for eight days. Although he arrived home in a state of collapse he recovered rapidly in Murray Bay and was glad to find Martha there with her two small sons. Before leaving Cincinnati she and Bob had had a second son, born in February, 1917. This was Robert Taft, who would follow his father to the Capitol in 1963. "Bobbie is a great chubby infant," Taft remarked after looking him over at Murray Bay. Bill had grown tall and was the most active youngster he had ever seen.

After their stay in Murray Bay the family gathered in strength at Waterbury on October 6, 1917, for the wedding of Charlie and Eleanor at the Chase mansion. Uniforms, flags, and autumn flowers were in evidence and Lieutenant Walter Wolf was Charlie's best man. Bob was a solemn-faced usher on this occasion. Mr. and Mrs. William Howard Taft looked on benignly as their youngest son married the girl whose beneficence would be strongly felt in Cincinnati in the years to come. Helen had come from Bryn Mawr, Harry and Julia from New York, Annie, Charlie, and the Semples from Cincinnati, to see the young sergeant-major take his vows. Helen scarcely knew how she would scrape up the money for a wedding gift but she looked on them with love. They set up simple housekeeping at St. Asaph's close to Fort Myer until orders came for Charlie's battalion to sail for Europe. In December his parents were suddenly alerted that Eleanor was to meet him at the Biltmore Hotel, for his unit had moved to Hoboken to embark for Europe. Taft had asked to go abroad but Woodrow Wilson had vetoed this suggestion. Bitterly disappointed he wrote to Charlie on December 19, 1917, as his son prepared to sail:

> He has made a great mistake, I think, in not wishing to strengthen the bond between us and England but it is his responsibility and I bow. And now Charlie dear, my heart goes out to you. You are a constant source of pride and joy to me. Not, my dear boy, in your mental power and application, not in your fine face and form, not in your physical strength and capacity but in your fine character, in your purity of soul, in your high ideals, in your spurning of the low and unmoral. . . . It is hard, my darling boy, to let you go. You are the apple of our eye. But we would not have it different. If sacrifice is to be made who are we that we should escape it. . . . You are a knight *sans peur* and *sans reproche*. God bless and keep you.

This was the last letter that Taft sent to Charlie before he sailed. The young sergeant was not permitted to go home for Christmas but he stayed in New York and he and Eleanor dined with F. Trubee Davison. After that the darkness of censorship prevailed. Maria stayed with Mrs. Taft until it was time for her, too, to sail. She was going abroad to do canteen work for the Y.M.C.A. but in the meantime she had what Will liked to call a spree, going to the opera with Nellie, and seeing George Arliss and John Drew on Broadway.

With the beginning of the new year Taft was more deeply involved than ever in patriotic work. He had agreed to tour the cantonments for the Y.M.C.A., explaining to the soldiers why they were in the war. He rode around the camps, visiting the generals, speaking to the men. The war fever was at its height and he moved in a haze of flags, patriotic songs, and cheers. Drums rolled around the peace-loving William Howard Taft. He saw familiar faces wherever he went and at Camp Gordon he had a vociferous welcome. The San Antonio *Express* told the story with its headline: "Private Charlie Taft's pa is given rousing greeting by Gorden men." The Tafts at home enjoyed this characteristic trail left by Charlie.

Taft's throat, always delicate, was continually strained by exertion and his voice at times was thin and high. Between his Y.M.C.A. work, the Red Cross, his Liberty Loan speeches, and his addresses on the League to Enforce Peace, he moved at express speed, a condition not discernible to the crowds that viewed the hearty-looking Mr. Taft. He was particularly popular at the loan rallies. Enormous sums were rolling in and wartime relics eventually went up for sale—the first American flag carried over German soil, the cane Marshal Joffre carried at the battle of the Marne. After attending a Victory Loan meeting in the Metropolitan Opera House at which $125,000,000 worth of bonds was sold, he wrote to Nellie: "They throw everything on me. I kick, but yield. . . . I hate money begging. They ought to arrange that without me but they say they can't. . . ."

Helen, too, had thrown herself enthusiastically into war work. The Bryn Mawr girls were running a wartime farm. She drove the college truck to their farm at West Chester where the girls worked for seven and a half hours a day, and swam in the lake belonging to the man whose fields they were cultivating. The combination of a former President's daughter at the wheel, and Bryn Mawr girls working as farmerettes, entailed considerable publicity. "You will probably see a terrible picture of me pushing a cultivator with an affected leer on my face," Helen wrote to Charley-Boy. "The reporters are after me hot and heavy." It was an old story to Miss Taft but one that she never enjoyed. She was emerging in the role of a public speaker, too, somewhat to her own chagrin and to her mother's consternation. Again she wrote to Charlie:

"I have been leading a pretty reckless life since I wrote you & have developed into a very prominent public speaker. It doesn't matter what the subject—Liberty Loan—women in agriculture—women's education—or just patriotism in general. I turn on my flow of eloquence and every audience is spellbound. . . . At Richmond I spoke at all the prominent seminaries for young ladies and urged their inmates as a part of their patriotic duty to come to college.

Helen's sense of humor was constant. She was a popular dean as well as a good one and she sometimes backed the girls in their moments of rebellion. One crisis arose when Miss Thomas decided that more students should be dropped, to make way for brighter newcomers. There was instant panic among the girls. "The whole college rose in wrath and in-

sisted that we shouldn't do such things without warning," Helen reported to Charlie. "Explanations & soothing syrup were unavailing and
we had to pretty well eat our words. So now there is peace once more
but we still don't know what to do with our freshman class."

Miss Thomas and Miss Taft were good friends, and however much
Helen might jest with Charlie over her own muddle-headedness in
straightening out the courses of a hundred-odd freshmen, she was a remarkably able dean. Although she made a good deal of fun of herself
for the benefit of the family no one else presumed to do so. She was
surprised to find herself on the same platform as her father at a meeting
of the Congress of the Security League in Chicago. Helen, Miss Thomas,
and the former President were all speakers on this occasion and Taft reported to Nellie that he thought Helen's "sense of humor and her common sense gave her poise." He decided that she was becoming a good
speaker. Again she toured New England with Miss Thomas, an architect, and six undergraduates, studying existing college buildings. They
visited Smith, Mount Holyoke, Wellesley, and Radcliffe.

But Helen was being led ever more deeply into the suffrage agitation
and her mother was ready to cast her off for a speech she made at a
woman's luncheon in Washington along with Mrs. Carrie Chapman
Catt and Dr. Anna Howard Shaw. Her father approved of Dr. Shaw,
liking her quiet irony and her hatred of sham. She worked with him on
the League to Enforce Peace and he thought she had a "sweet reason-
ableness that endeared her to all who had the privilege of knowing her."
By this time he had been all but won over to a cause that was already
close to victory, but Nellie feared that her daughter might run into
trouble in so controversial a matter.

Whenever Helen had a chance she visited Bob's family. In the summer
of 1917 she found them growing potatoes, corn, and beans on Indian
Hill. She reported to Charlie that their house was large and airy, far from
stylish, but with the most beautiful vista one could imagine. Helen observed that Bobby was a handsome child "who eats and sleeps and cries
the whole time." On a later visit to the young Tafts in Washington she
described him as being "more beautiful than the day" with his brown
curls and dark eyes. However, he showed signs of temper "which I think
he must have inherited from his uncle Charles," she wrote gaily. By this
time Bob was so busy in the Hoover administration that the family
heard nothing at all from him.

In France Charlie learned with surprise that his father and Theodore
Roosevelt were moving closer together. The country's need, and the
death of young Quentin, had brought the two warriors into sympathy
again. Quentin's death in July, 1918, had startled them all. Taft telegraphed at once to the Colonel from the Ritz-Carlton Hotel in Mont-

real: "His was a noble life gloriously ended. Our sympathy for you is deeper when we remember that Quentin and Charlie were boys together and babes in the same year." Taft promptly wrote to Charlie that Roosevelt faced Quentin's death with the spirit of a soldier and a fighter. The shock was doubled when Kermit was wounded, but the fact that he was decorated for bravery was consoling to his father.

Earlier in the year, when Roosevelt was desperately ill with an abscess in the inner ear, Taft had sent him a telegram of sympathy. It was a tentative gesture well received, and the events that followed warmed up the atmosphere between them. Elihu Root and Harry Taft were trying to persuade Roosevelt to run for governor of New York State against Whitman. Teddy decided to show his old enemy an important speech he intended to make in Maine. It reached Taft first through Root and he returned it without reading it. But Alice Longworth then brought it to him. This time he read it, made some suggestions, and to his surprise Roosevelt accepted them. Charlie received a letter from his father written on March 16, 1918, directly after this incident:

> Roosevelt did me a great injury and great injustice, but he did himself more. He would certainly have been President during the war had he held his hand against me. . . . Of course he is now a candidate for the Presidency and if the war lasts to the Presidential election he is likely to be the Republican nominee. He will make a good President for war because things will move under him. . . . I cherish no resentment against Roosevelt because such attitude of mind is not congenial to me. It only worries the resenter and works little harm to the resentee. If opportunity came to get even, I would feel myself above it. . . . I am glad to be on good terms with a man for many of whose traits and abilities I have great admiration, to whom I am indebted for many generous acts, and many great opportunities.

Thus the wheel had turned. Taft was sorry for Roosevelt, whose health was failing. He had lost the sight of one eye and his hearing was impaired. Moreover, he suffered from the tropical fever he had picked up in Brazil. But his spirit and energy were unflagging and his hatred of Wilson was so acute, said Taft, that "when my indignation breaks over bounds, I cool it off in the thought that Theodore is swearing harder than I would like to." Wilson had kept Roosevelt from taking a regiment to France, as he had prevented Taft from going to Britain in a good-will capacity.

The country learned quickly that the two antagonists had buried the hatchet and were solidly aligned against Woodrow Wilson. Some approved, others were critical; but the two men had resumed correspondence and Taft insisted that life was too short "to maintain these quarrels no matter what the justice of them." A crowd cheered them when they met accidentally in the dining room of the Blackstone Hotel in Chicago. Taft noticed Roosevelt alone at a table as he walked in and he went over to him at once. Roosevelt jumped to his feet and clasped Taft's hand. The party leaders were urging a united front against a formidable foe and the dove of peace was again hovering over the Grand Old Party.

Roosevelt wrote to Henry L. Stimson on June 5, 1918, that Taft and he were now in "absolute accord about present needs and about our failures and shortcomings and the cause of them during the past year." By July both men were on intimate terms again, although Taft was not convinced that Roosevelt had changed his opinions, nor that he had changed his. But he believed that if Teddy had been the war President things would have been a year ahead of where they stood. Taft thought that his old antagonist now longed for his earlier associations, having measured the emptiness of newer friends on whom he had relied.

Bob, doing the major part of the legal work for the Hoover administration, was getting restive in 1918. Hoover, receiving an honorary degree at Yale that year, told Taft when he met him on the campus that his son was still searching for some way to get into the Army. The Food Administrator said he could not afford to let Bob go. "It is rather hard on Bob," Taft wrote to Charlie on Independence Day, "but I think it takes as much moral courage for him to continue his work there, without compensation, and without being in uniform, as it would to get into uniform and never be where he could smell gunpowder."

But both Mr. and Mrs. Taft agreed that Bob always made up his mind for himself and whatever he decided would seem right to them. He had made an impression on his colleagues from the start. His father heard echoes of his work in Washington and wrote proudly to Charlie that Bob had got up at a food conservation meeting and had made a statement "so clear and so convincing that even those who had taken a different view yielded to his."

Other members of the Taft family besides Bob, Charlie, and Helen were involved in war work. David S. Ingalls, the oldest son of Jane and Albert Ingalls of Cleveland, was already a great flying ace. Harry's sons, Walbridge and Howard, were in the Army. Tom Bowers was with the Marines. Fanny in California received a gold medal from the French Government for her services on behalf of the French Red Cross, and she and Dr. Edwards were impatient because the surgeon's health kept them from going abroad.

When the big American push began in March, 1918, Mr. and Mrs. William Howard Taft read the papers anxiously every morning, trying to figure out where Charlie might be. Actually, they knew more than he did of the action going on, since he was now caught in the mass flow of troops. Letters moved slowly and his parents suffered torments over long silences. His father wrote to him on March 24: "My dear boy, our prayers go with you. Whatever happens we know that you will do your duty and face death with a pure heart and a clear conscience and a spirit that either in you or in others will win the war for the right. . . . You of the younger generation render service at the front of a dangerous character, and some of us in the rear try to help with wind."

After being under fire east of Verdun Charlie was ordered to the Saumur Artillery School for three months. He was again the student and his father was pleased to hear that he was making progress in French as well as in the science of field artillery. Taft wished to know if he was taking trigonometry, surveying, and mathematics. "Push it, my dear boy, push it," he wrote. "It will earn you promotion . . . keep your books on hand, study them and accept every chance to talk." Again the professor spoke. Charlie's letters were vivid and interesting. They were copied and passed around in the family but most of them were now addressed to his young bride. When his commission finally loomed in view Helen wrote: "I couldn't really think what Generals Pershing and Foch were about when you were put off from week to week. Don't they know what they're losing in the way of an officer?"

Charlie was graduated from the Saumur Artillery School on August 1 and in October he became a first lieutenant, but he was still dreaming of the day when he would coach the basketball team at Yale. His father reminded him in one of his letters that his ambition in this direction showed he did not quite realize his college days were over. He would be a householder on his return and would have to dig his nose into law. On the anniversary of the declaration of war Taft wrote: "How much has happened in your life, enlisted, married, promoted to a top sergeant and subjected to the dangers of hostile fire all in a year."

Because of his high standing at Yale a decision was made to give young Charles Taft his degree on the strength of his marks. This would clear the way for him to enter the Law School as soon as he got back instead of finishing his college term. President Arthur T. Hadley wrote to General Pershing that his record at Yale was magnificent. Dean Jones added testimony that Charles had been the most conspicuous man at Yale during his three years there—a remarkable scholar, highly respected, and winning the Gordon Brown Prize by unanimous vote.

While Charlie was still at Saumur Maria landed in the headlines in the summer of 1918. She was one of thirty Y.M.C.A. workers driven away from their posts by the German advance near Soissons. They burned their stores and buildings before the enemy arrived, and Maria and Jane Bowles, both of Cincinnati, were reported to have distin-

guished themselves under fire. Will wrote at once to Nellie: "It is evident that Maria was right in the midst of it, was under fire and did her
part. What a stormy petrel she is. But I would know that when the test
of bravery and duty came she would meet it. . . ."

Katherine Wulsin, also of Cincinnati, cabled that Maria was safe and
Maria herself soon wrote to Charlie, making light of the heroics of the
situation. With the forthright Herron touch she announced that they
had got away before the bombing began but things were exciting
enough as it was. The *foyer* directors came in the morning and left
chocolate and other fare for the American troops crowding in. Maria
and Jane fed them until the last possible moment. A major from
Belleau had his office in Maria's *foyer*, and she could follow on his maps
the rapid strides that the Germans were making towards them. At 4:30
P.M. an automobile arrived with orders for Maria and her helpers to
leave at once.

"I shall never forget that ride," she wrote, describing the road crowded
with refugees, dragging their pitiful belongings in anything from a
child's wagon to a haycart. Some had nothing but bundles. The women
and children were crying, the men were scolding, and the cattle
were mooing. Coming in the other direction were French reinforce-
ments with long strings of cannon. At Meaux everyone was preparing to
flee and the hotels were closed. For a week Maria messed in her room
with an alcohol lamp—cooking eggs and bouillon tablets. She went
around doing odd jobs so as not to be sent back to Paris and for four
nights she worked in the receiving ward of the hospital, seeing grim
sights. When the military authorities arrived they did not want volunteers, so Maria went to Paris for a few days, then returned to Meaux,
where she ran a canteen near the station until the Frenchwomen to
whom it had been promised came on the scene.

Not to be frustrated by red tape Maria set up a little canteen of her
own. From 7:30 A.M. until 9 P.M. she was rushed to death, pouring out
coffee and chocolate in an endless stream, her dark eyes blazing with
excitement, her white hair curling around her trim cap. Maria never
forgot those war days, and many whom she had helped remembered
her. "When I look back on all I have in my life it seems too much for
one person," she wrote to Charlie. And again, after Château-Thierry:
"Hurrah for our side! Isn't it all too extraordinary, what has happened
to the Boche? I am so thankful to think that you will go home intact &
Bob will never come at all."

Mabel Boardman, too, went abroad in the spring of 1918 with
seventy-two Red Cross workers and forty-five from the Y.M.C.A. There
had been a serious rift between her and Taft since a crisis in 1917 over
Red Cross matters had almost ended their friendship. Although they

soon patched things up there was a coolness until Mabel sailed for France, when Will wrote to her in a conciliatory tone: "You and I have had differences upon some things, Mabel, and in the words which have been used were some suggestions that I hope are now all forgotten in a friendship which I value as one among the most precious that I have. God bless you and bring you safely back to your mother, friends and family."

She landed on an April day on a French dock alive with khaki-clad men. As she traveled up to Paris past blooming fruit trees, and viewed the winding roads, the red-roofed houses, the villas and châteaux, war seemed to her an anachronism. She inspected the Red Cross headquarters in Paris and visited General Pershing with an introduction from Taft. In Rome she found the Palazzo Quirinale functioning as the Italian Red Cross Hospital. Most of the patients were mutilated men, a strange and pathetic sight against a background of Gobelins. In London she was again with Red Cross friends and was entertained by Mrs. Whitelaw Reid. A letter from Taft in May informed her that $150,000,-000 had been raised for the Red Cross, an unprecedented sum in its history. This included large donations but also countless small ones. "Of course this feature of enlarging the constituency of givers is one much to be desired," he commented. Henry P. Davison was by this time chairman of the Red Cross Council and had directed its great drive.

Taft was summoned suddenly to Washington to work with Frank P. Walsh on the creation of a National War Labor Board. Expecting to have trouble with Walsh, he found that they got on remarkably well. Both were anxious to create an effective war organization at a time when strikes were becoming an embarrassment to the administration. When Taft was appointed to serve as co-chairman of the board some of his friends considered the position undignified for a former President, but Taft replied that it was not a question of dignity but of useful service. Josephus Daniels, Secretary of the Navy, jested that he would wind up in overalls in order to be helpful.

While Mrs. Taft relaxed at Murray Bay in 1918 her husband sweltered in Washington, trying to find relief from the heat in long automobile drives before going to bed. Among his many hosts was Bernard Baruch, whom he described to Nellie as the most powerful man in the capital except for the President and McAdoo. When in New York he visited Julia and Harry at the Garden City Hotel on Long Island and observed that it was made to order for Julia, who loved the excitement of seeing people and the "parade up and down the Peacock Alley."

Martha and her children were at Spring Lake, New Jersey, during the hot months, and Eleanor was in Murray Bay, awaiting the birth of her first child. Helen busied herself in the garden and she wrote to Charlie that she had bought a Corona and was learning to type, an art that would come in handy in completing her thesis. Aunt Delia had given them all a scare early in the year by coming down with pneumonia. They were sure she could not survive and Will wrote to his wife: "Her strength has been great and her New England fiber is tough. But she has lived to a green and sweet old age. It is a great pleasure to me that she lived to see me President and to visit us in the White House. She enjoyed every minute of it."

But Delia rallied and stayed with them a little longer. She was alive to rejoice in the birth of Charlie's first child in September, 1918. Another large Taft family—five girls and two boys—was on its way when little Eleanor (later known as Nonie) was born at Rose Hill, the Chase home at Waterbury. The young mother helped prepare supper the night before; she wakened at three in the morning with labor pains and the baby was born at 4:20 A.M. Taft promptly wrote to his wife: "Our granddaughter appeared the day after my birthday. Charlie is now a second lieutenant, a graduate of Yale and a father all before he is twenty-one. Certainly he is making progress." On the following day he wrote to Charlie from the McAlpin Hotel in New York: "There is nothing that helps as much to keep a boy in proper form as an older sister. Then the girl does wind the tendrils about your paternal heart. . . . We live our lives over in our children. I felicitate you on escaping the sorrows of childlessness. See Uncle Horace and think what a father he would have been and how he must miss them as he grows older."

Will and Horace walked seven miles to Waterbury to see the new baby and then his father wrote to Charlie: "Now I don't claim to be able to distinguish much between small pieces of protoplasm such as babies generally are, but I am bound to say, Charlie, that this little Eleanor seemed to me to be as well developed, as well trained, and as healthy a looking baby as I have seen."

That autumn influenza swept over America like the Black Plague. There were more than a thousand new cases and a hundred deaths a day in Washington. Soldiers were used to dig graves and the suffering in army camps was severe. Masked women worked everywhere and the Red Cross used its great network of facilities to cope with this national emergency. Professional nurses were not to be had. Horace had eighty cases at the Taft School. Bob, Martha, and Mrs. Bowers were all in bed with it at the same time and their grandparents meanwhile took care of Billie and Bobbie. Helen came down with it, too. While it still raged the Armistice was signed and bedlam broke loose across the nation.

The life of young Robert Taft broadened out when Herbert Hoover asked him to sail for Europe immediately to act as counsel and administrative assistant for the American Relief Administration. This was the

young lawyer's introduction to international politics and the experience
had a lifelong effect on him. His sturdy Americanism, deeply rooted in
his heritage, was challenged as he watched the European statesmen in
conclave. His own straightforward outlook was alien to the atmosphere
of intrigue in which he found himself. Bob became a close observer
and a disillusioned skeptic. For the rest of his life he was destined to
give careful thought to foreign entanglements of any kind, but for the
time being he was an invaluable aid to Herbert Hoover.

It was part of his mission to help shape policies for the spread of relief
from Finland to Albania, with thirty-two nations getting help. The
operations were of gigantic proportions, and his well-established knowledge of finance widened from the problems of Ohio to those of a
hungry world. It was a steep step in his own development.

Hoover was alternate chairman of the Supreme Economic Council
and a member of the advisory committee of the United States delegation to the Peace Conference, so that Robert was drawn into the larger
picture during a crucial period in world affairs. He shared in all of
Hoover's interests and attended some of the meetings of the Peace
Conference. This was an eye-opening experience for him and he wrote
to his father of an atmosphere "so secretive that you cannot overcome
the impulse to talk in whispers." Hoover had offices at the Crillon with
the Peace Commission, although he had taken a private house for his
staff.

Inevitably Bob was an interested observer of President Wilson on his
visit to Paris and he sent his father detailed impressions of what he saw
and heard. He felt that the whole structure of international policies had
reappeared suddenly in much the old form. "I almost wish considering
our representation that we had let them settle their own troubles when
we had licked the Kaiser," he wrote. He thought that Wilson's status
at the Peace Conference was greatly affected by the criticism at home
of his mission in Europe, and no one he met had anything good to say
of the League of Nations. Bob felt that Wilson's Fourteen Points were
so indefinite that "he can take whatever he can get and say that it was
the particular thing he intended."

Young Taft's cool gray eyes were in no way dazzled by the mirrors and
prisms of Versailles. He saw the rocks ahead and wrote to his father
on January 5, 1919:

> Bolshevism is certainly growing and has more force in it than any other
> movement outside the Allied Countries. Food is the principle thing
> that can stop it and so we are trying to hurry things up. . . . Mr.
> Hoover has suggested to the President that he come out openly against
> the Bolshevists, and say that the Bolshevists get no food, because they
> are incapable of distributing it fairly and make any distribution impos-

sible. . . . So far he has not done so, and he has a little of that Progressive bug. . . ."

Bob expressed the fear that Wilson would take "too Bolshevistic an attitude" and would also be unduly easy with the Germans. He believed personally that the food blockade of Germany should be stopped, since nothing but Bolshevism could result from starving a nation. But Bob preached moderation in giving and cited Belgium as a good example of a country receiving so much help that nothing was being done by the people themselves to revive their industries. Bob commented scathingly to his father on the huge indemnities demanded by various countries—the Saar Valley by France, the Adriatic coast by Italy. Knowing how close the cause of peace was to his father's heart he discussed at length the proposed League of Nations, in which they both believed. He considered Clemenceau the most determined opponent of the plan and he was not wholly convinced of Wilson's sincerity. "At least I believe he would accept almost anything if it was called a League of Nations, whether it had any force or not," Bob wrote. "I am not convinced that an international police force or executive would work, but a League without an agreement to use force, military and economic, against anyone who makes an aggressive war, would be worse than useless."

The elder Taft, reading Bob's analysis of the situation attentively, was soon convinced that Clemenceau, Lloyd George, and Wilson were not sincere about the treaty, which he had viewed in the beginning as a glimpse of the promised land. He was profoundly interested in the League of Nations and was one of the best friends it had in the United States. Much of the work of the League to Enforce Peace had dovetailed into the League of Nations, and Wilson had incorporated three and rejected many more amendments suggested by Taft for the second draft of the covenant. These were the proposals that a nation might withdraw on two years' notice, that domestic questions were outside this scope of the League, and that plans for the limitation of armaments should be revised periodically.

"Wilson seeks to make this peace his and his alone," her father wrote to Helen. "He regards himself as an arbiter and schoolmaster for the world." He had disapproved the President's sending Colonel Edward M. House abroad to help frame the covenant of the League of Nations, but Bob reported back to his father that House was the "most sensible and reasonable man on the Commission though certainly not of extraordinary ability."

Taft toured the country speaking on behalf of the League and Wilson thanked him from Paris for his nonpartisan support. The former Presi-

dent disapproved of the Republicans who allowed their animosity to
Wilson to blind them to the potentialities of the League. But he was
disillusioned when the President on his return made his own cross-country
tour. When he collapsed Taft commented: "He has so insisted on hog-
ging all the authority—trusting no one—that he has broken himself
down." By this time Taft had turned against Wilson and had begun to
look to Warren G. Harding as the potential prince of peace. Both he and
Bob were profoundly disappointed when the United States failed to ratify
the treaty or join the League of Nations.

Harding was being pushed for the Presidency and at the moment
Taft thought that it was anybody's race, although he leaned to the
Ohioan because of his stand on the League of Nations—a confidence
that was to be shattered by Harding's inaugural address. Taft assured
Nellie that he would never permit his friends to get him into a scramble
for the nomination. He was again a popular figure with the public. His
years of teaching, writing, and lecturing; his sportsmanship on public
issues; his humane approach to international affairs, had not only gone
far to restoring the earlier image of William Howard Taft but had created
a new one. Millions had heard him speak and he had epitomized the
patriotic American, in spite of his profound aversion to war and his work
for peace.

One great fighter had passed from the scene in 1919. Taft was on his
way to New York from Washington when word reached him at Newark
that Theodore Roosevelt was dead. He at once wrote a warm editorial
about his old friend for the syndicated column he was then doing for the
Philadelphia *Ledger*. At the funeral he was led to a pew directly behind
the family, but Archie approached him and said: "You're a dear personal friend and you must come up further." He then placed him behind the Vice-President and in front of the Senate committee which
was headed by Senator Lodge. Taft accompanied them to the grave. A
significant chapter in his personal and public life ended with the death
of Roosevelt. He often spoke of him in his addresses after that and always in an admiring way. It was his belief that without the cohesive
power of its dynamic leader the Progressives would thin out into personal factions.

Aunt Delia died within a month of Roosevelt, and Charlie, who had
returned to the United States in January, 1919, hurried to Millbury for
the Unitarian rites held in the Torrey parlor. She left her grandfather
clock to Will, who was on a lecture tour too far away to get home for
the funeral of his beloved aunt. By Christmas of that year the elder
Tafts were back in New Haven. The work of the War Labor Board
was finished and Taft had thrown his weight into such problems as
the eight-hour day, the minimum wage, the right to organize—all mat-

ters that would preoccupy his son Robert in the future. The former President felt that the board had been influential in its wartime operations, and that the measures put through might have some lasting effect on labor conditions. Helen joined them all at Christmas and Taft followed his usual custom of reading Dickens's *Christmas Carol* aloud. "Although I sniffled, I managed to get through it this time," he wrote to Miss Boardman, who had given him a golfing vest for his present that year. His blood pressure was up and he had to cut out meat, reduce the number of eggs he ate, and resume the Spartan regime required from time to time when his weight soared.

Hulbert Taft went abroad for interviews that winter and Will gave him letters to Lord Bryce, Lord Reading, and Jules Jusserand. His fellow Cincinnatian, Howard Hollister, died at this time, making a break in a lifetime association. Both Mr. and Mrs. Taft had been devoted to Hollister for many years, although he had followed a different course from theirs in his thinking. Perhaps remembering how Howard and he had courted Nellie at the same time Will wrote to her a little wistfully from Toronto in February, 1920, reminding her that she had not acknowledged his valentine. "Is it possible, my dearest, that you are losing sentiment and don't like these little reminders?" he addressed her reproachfully.

Martha had left the children with Mrs. Taft while she joined Bob in Paris. She accompanied him to various countries and saw at firsthand the harvest of war. In Poland thousands of bare-footed children greeted young Taft with songs and flag-waving. Paderewski, as premier, gave him a Polish decoration. King Albert decorated him for his relief work on behalf of Belgium. He was the first American to receive the White Rose, Finland's highest award. Hoover's work had made a tremendous impression on Europe as a whole and Bob, as his active assistant, was recognized for his share in the great relief program. This was one of his earliest steps to fame and the beginning of a warm friendship with Herbert Hoover.

Bob had returned from Europe to a country that had undergone the convulsion of war and would not be the same again. People were shaken by the knowledge that the Monroe Doctrine no longer blanketed their shores. There were strikes, frenzied gaiety, the devastation of the influenza epidemic. Woman suffrage had come to pass and prohibition was introducing a gaudy era of crime and corruption. There were new political groupings and Bob worked actively for the nomination of Herbert Hoover as President. In April, 1920, he informed his father that he believed his conversation and correspondence had influenced the Food Administrator to run against Johnson in a Republican primary in California.

"It would be funny if Bob's chimerical dreams of Hoover's nomination were to come true but I can't think it," Taft wrote to his wife in June. He had declined to report the presidential convention in Chicago for his syndicate since he was now on the sidelines, he explained, but firm in his belief that "we must end Democratic and Wilsonian rule."

When Taft learned that Franklin D. Roosevelt had been nominated by the Democrats for the Vice-Presidency along with James M. Cox, he took mild note of this choice in another letter to Nellie. "He is a good fellow and will make a good running mate for Cox. He is a pretty good speaker and an attractive looking man. He will not add any particular strength anywhere but he will give the ticket a good social flavor."

A star of magnitude had sailed into view but Taft, like his compatriots, saw nothing exceptional yet in the man who would soon change the course of history for the American public.

A WEDDING AT MURRAY BAY

Early in 1920 it became known that Helen Taft was engaged to marry Frederick Johnson Manning, who was then a professor at Yale. He was from Braintree, Massachusetts, and had served with the Field Artillery. The dean of Bryn Mawr, busy raising funds for her college, tried to keep the romance a secret at first. Her father had to fend off reporters as he traveled about making speeches. Although he gave her his blessing at once he had some reservations about his clever daughter's plunge into matrimony. He urged her to wait a year until she had her Ph.D., since he doubted that she would ever write her thesis if she married first. But he conceded that she must carve out her own future, and be responsible for the consequences. He misread that future when he wrote to her on January 13, 1920:

> I have been very proud of the success you have thus far attained and perhaps my feeling in the matter has been colored by my ambition for a career for you so auspiciously begun. Your marriage will probably end that career, if your married life is as happy as I hope it may be. You have a right to welcome married life. It is probably wiser for you to insist on it. Certainly you are and ought to be the arbiter of your own future in this regard. I hope you are . . . not unconsciously stimulated

in your enthusiasm for this marriage by the thought that you are approaching thirty and yearn for the happiness of family life. You are a woman of poise and level headed and I can not think this.

Taft added that he did not mean to suggest that the academic life was not a happy and useful one, or that the prospect of having to live with economy should turn her from her purpose. He did not wish her to think him cold or unsympathetic, and he would be glad to be proved wrong in thinking that she should continue with her work. At this point he stated a family truth: "You and I are a good deal alike, more so I think than the boys and I; and when we differ, we differ." Bob was extremely like his mother, both in looks and nature. Charlie combined many of his grandfather Alphonso's views with his father's warmth and geniality.

Helen had no doubt whatever about the course she was following and she wrote blithely to Miss Boardman: "I am going to marry a most unusual young man on July 15th (probably) in Murray Bay. Unusually poor and unusually young, but also unusually clever and nice. And most unusually fond of me." The Tafts all liked jingles with the Gilbert and Sullivan touch and this announcement was in character. Meanwhile, Helen toured successfully for funds and besought her father's help in approaching such men as Elihu Root. When the two-million-dollar objective was passed Taft wrote to her from Twin Falls, Idaho, that this fittingly ended her service to her college. But Helen was by no means finished with it and she would always be as warmly associated with Bryn Mawr as her father and brothers were with Yale.

Shortly before their daughter's wedding Will, perhaps stirred to sentiment by the coming event, wrote to Nellie as he journeyed to Canada past a string of lakes strewn with pond lilies:

> I never see a Jacqueminot rose that I don't think of my efforts to send you the finest when love's dream was young. I always thought them more beautiful than American Beauties but they are rare now. . . .
> We are running through lakes of pond lilies. Do you remember the pink pond lilies I got up at five in the morning to go out and get for you? . . . I hope you permit yourself to be reminiscent and romantic at times, darling.

Helen was married on July 15, 1920, in the Union Church at Murray Bay, where the Episcopalians and Presbyterians had finally joined forces to worship at alternate services. A gray stone building, opened in 1910, had taken the place of the old wooden church that had served Pointe au Pic since 1861. A memorial service for President McKinley was held in it in 1909. Helen, Maria, Lucy Herron, and Laura Harlan all sang in the choir and Taft attended regularly, taking up the collection and serving as a trustee. He liked to stand outside under a tree greeting the

churchgoers and swapping stories with the rector and his fellow parish
ioners.

No setting could have been more suitable for Helen's wedding than
Murray Bay and her father was well aware of this as he observed her
happy look, the familiar summer friends, the deep flow of the river
the outlines of Cap l'Aigle in the distance. The sun shone for her that
day. She wore white taffeta draped with Brussels lace and carried
sweet peas and white roses. Edith Morgan was her maid of honor and
Billie and Bobbie Taft were her trainbearers.

"I hope you and Fred are still friends and that life has the color of
the summer skies under which you were married," her father wrote to
Helen five weeks after this event. In the years that followed it was to his
daughter that he wrote most exhaustively of his political and judicial interests. Helen had definite theories on public affairs and a liberal point
of view. Their correspondence in the next decade would illumine the
inner life of William Howard Taft. He was sixty-three in the year of
Helen's marriage and Charles and Annie gave him a birthday party at
Murray Bay. Their daughter, Louise Semple, who had recently had a
baby, was with them at Mountain Ash Cottage and Annie found fresh
joy in her grandchild.

In August Charlie and Eleanor had a second daughter, Sylvia, and
William Howard Taft noted that his son carried pictures of Nonie and
the baby in every pocket. The younger Tafts lived in the family home
at New Haven, first on Grove Street, then in the stately house they
took on Whitney Avenue. Charlie, who had led his class in his freshman
year at Yale and been second in his sophomore and junior years, was
now coming to grips with drudgery at the Yale Law School. He was still
a notable figure on the campus and it was remembered that he had won
the Gordon Brown Prize when he was eighteen, an award for the
student who summed up the best in manhood, scholarship, and capacity
for leadership. Now, while studying law, Charlie also coached the
freshman football line at Yale, an old ambition that had stayed with
him throughout his service in France. Bob sent him books from Indian
Hill that would help him prepare for the Ohio law examinations, and he
promised him a job whenever he was ready to move west.

With the national election looming up Taft urged Nellie and Helen
to register and vote. "You must not allow the ignorant women to exercise
their right and neglect to do your duty yourself," he wrote, with a
change of front. Helen needed no prompting and her mother moved
with the tide. With Warren G. Harding the victor, the task of choosing
Cabinet officers began and Taft breakfasted with the Hardings just before Christmas, 1920. He had commended Senator Harding to Miss
Boardman as a suitable subject for hospitality when the Ohioan first

moved to Washington. "He is a handsome man, a gentleman, and a man of courage and of much ability," he wrote. "He is a journalist and a very good speaker. Added to that he has the trait . . . of loyalty. I have summered and wintered with him and I know."

Taft was now to get a closer view of him. Mrs. Harding had already been to the White House and had let Mrs. Jaffray know that she intended to be mistress there. Taft praised both Mrs. Jaffray and Arthur Brooks to the incoming First Lady. They discussed social customs at the White House and Harding indicated that he was disposed "to chuck ceremony." Mrs. Harding took a different view and Taft supported her in this and insisted that it was essential. She asked him about precedence and they discussed the never-ending fuss between the ambassadors and members of the Supreme Court, and the Cabinet members and senators.

When Harding was out of the room Taft told his wife that all his friends except his family should call him Mr. President rather than Warren. He was surprised to find that Mrs. Harding knew so little about the White House and had never been entertained there. She asked his advice on garden parties and suggested informal teas and a continuation of the coterie of Senate wives. Both commented on the meager amount of entertaining that the Wilsons had done because of the President's ill-health. Taft advised Mrs. Harding to ride with her husband after the inauguration, if Wilson did not do so. "She is a nice woman, who will, I think, be all right," he wrote to Nellie after this interview. "She is a little disposed to be anxious not to be backward but she will readily adapt herself."

The talk with Harding that followed was full of surprises for Taft. When he proposed Elihu Root for the State Department Harding seemed to consider him an elder statesman of a different generation. He had made up his mind to have Charles G. Dawes as Vice-President and he was considering the Department of the Interior or the Department of Commerce for Herbert Hoover. Taft proposed Max Pam, his Cincinnati friend for solicitor general if Harry Daugherty were to be attorney general. He recommended Pam as an able lawyer, a prominent Jew, and a confidential adviser of the inner propaganda circle of the Catholic church. As an alternative he suggested Pam as minister to Czecho-Slovakia. Harding did not respond on Pam but he said he would like to recognize the Jews and he spoke of Edward Lasker, of Chicago, for the Department of Commerce. Taft said that he thought Hughes would like to be chief justice but Harding did not agree. He believed that Hughes did not wish to return to the bench. Harding said he would appoint George Sutherland as an associate justice, and at that moment he asked Taft if he would accept an appointment to the Supreme Court.

Directly faced with the issue at last, Taft quickly told him that it had always been his ambition, that he had refused it before but that now, having been President, and having appointed three of the incumbent justices and protested the elevation of Brandeis, he could not accept anything less than the Chief Justiceship. Harding said nothing more and Taft was again left in doubt about his future. He was afraid to tell Nellie, lest her hopes should be dashed again, but he told Horace and then awaited developments.

He and Nellie had gone to Bermuda for a rest when word reached him from Gus Karger that he had made a "deep and lasting and agreeable impression" on the Hardings and that the appointment would go through. Nellie flourished in Bermuda but Taft gained weight from all the entertaining by the Colonial and British authorities, and he disliked the hilly golf course with crabgrass on the greens. From Bermuda he went to Montreal to sit at an arbitration hearing involving an attempt by the Canadian Government to take over the Grand Trunk Railway System. The next few months were crucial and anxious ones for Taft as his last chance to become chief justice seemed to hang in the balance. He heard nothing from Washington. In the meantime he lived at the Ritz-Carlton and was lavishly entertained, Montreal was lively now that the wartime pressure had eased. He dined with Sir Montague Allen, Sir Vincent Meredith, Lady Shaughnessy, Sir Walter and Lady Cassels, Sir Frederick Williams Taylor, Gordon MacDougall, and Sir George and Lady Drummond. Taft enjoyed the lively Lady Drummond, who had run a hospital in England during the war. He exchanged quips with the humorist Stephen Leacock and was on close terms with Sir Arthur Currie, the war hero who had become president of McGill University. Taft went to McGill to do his own research for his speeches and he described himself to Nellie as flapping along in the snow, with his heavy coat getting shabbier by the day. The lining was worn through. "I hope I'll not be taken for a tramp in Washington," he jested.

Nicholas Murray Butler thought that he should be appointed ambassador to Great Britain, but Taft said that he could not afford a post of that sort, since it required a private fortune. When inauguration day arrived Taft was snug in the Ritz-Carlton. He recalled for Nellie the "dreadful dinner the Roosevelts gave us with Lodge and Root trying to make things bright and Mrs. Roosevelt teary and distraught." Writing of the blizzard that had awakened them he reminded her that together they had lived through a good many interesting and uncomfortable times. It pleased him that Mrs. Harding had taken his advice about riding with the President. But his overwhelming impression of the day's events was that Woodrow Wilson's condition was revealed to the American people in full for the first time, when the shattered man rode to the Capitol with Warren Harding but was too ill to get out of the car. "It is clear he was very much disabled and that Marshall ought to have taken his place for a while," Will wrote to Nellie. "They have been lying to the American people about him. Had Marshall been in when the Treaty was passed with reservations Marshall would have accepted them and conditions would have been years in advance of what they now are."

Taft further observed that after inauguration Harding went to Grasslands to spend Sunday with some companions instead of going to church. "The old man will have to wake up and select a Washington church and go there or his fellow Baptists will begin to inquire," he wrote to his wife three days after Harding's inauguration. The President's speech was a bitter disappointment to him, specifically for what he said about the League of Nations. Nellie, who had worked so hard to keep her husband from the Supreme Court in years gone by, now feared that in his "blue condition of mind over Harding's inaugural" Will might decline the post if it were offered to him.

"I don't think there is any danger on this head," he assured her on March 15, 1921. "I don't object to you hoping and continuing to hope, darling, if you don't allow yourself to be made unhappy by having to live on in New Haven. I love you, my dearest, and I want you to be happy, to be happy myself." Both were preparing for another disappointment and by April Nellie had given up all hope. Taft had written to Miss Boardman that the Chief Justiceship was a shining prize that might well go to a younger man. He knew he was not popular with the Progressives in the Senate. His own deep feeling in the matter shows in a letter he wrote to J. M. Dickinson six weeks after Harding's inauguration:

> I don't hesitate to say to you that I would rather have been Chief Justice than President and that now it would give me the greatest joy to end my career by useful service in that exalted office. . . . Considering everything I have had to be grateful for to God and to the American people, it is absurd for me to be thinking of something else, and I must suppress my ambitious thoughts, which force themselves on me uninvited. . . . I shall be not only foolish but blind if I do not settle down to my work at Yale as a graceful ending of my activities. I have enough to live on. I have children and wife who give me joy and a consciousness of having tried to be useful. What more can I ask?

The Tafts were now comfortably settled in a neo-classical house on old York Square in New Haven, having moved once again. Charlie's children had plenty of room for play in their large garden. Although close to busy Elm and Broad streets Taft found it as quiet for work as an isolated square or church close in the heart of London. Helen and Fred, who were now expecting a baby, had an apartment nearby and came in every day for lunch. While Taft waited patiently for developments in Washington, Horace was at Ormond in Florida and had called again on John D. Rockefeller. They were good friends by this time but he thought the oil king had failed since he had last seen him. "Shall I bring you a million?" he wrote to Will, but the bounty of another millionaire was about to come Taft's way. He had been advised at this time to accept the Carnegie annuity that he had refused while the steel magnate was alive. Some years earlier Carnegie had asked his corporation to make arrangements to pay former Presidents and their widows $25,000 a year. This move was so widely criticized that he drew back, but in making his will he named William Howard Taft an annuitant. Wickersham, Root, and Hilles all urged Taft to accept the annuity, now that Carnegie was dead.

In May Taft was still on tenterhooks about the Supreme Court appointment when the death of Chief Justice Edward D. White focused attention again on the matter. Taft had appointed him and he said on more than one occasion that no act of his administration had given him greater satisfaction. Late in June Karger telephoned to Montreal that his own appointment was going through. "I'll wait until the golf ball is in the hole," Taft wrote to Nellie on June 29. But this time the appointment was assured. He was dining with Sir Walter Cassels when news reached him that the Chief Justiceship was his. Sir Walter ordered a bottle of Pol Roget and Taft drank a glass with him to celebrate, the first he had had since Helen's wedding. He wrote at once to Nellie:

> Well, that has happened which I have always doubted coming true. I am now Chief Justice of the United States lacking only the qualifying oath. . . . The immediate confirmation of the Senate was unexpected and was engineered I doubt not by [Frank B.] Brandegee who wired me. I am curious to see who the four were who voted against me but I can guess.

Taft learned later that Borah, for one, had attacked his legal qualifications. By chance the new Chief Justice had just rejected an offer from the New York Telephone Company to serve as chairman of the board at $50,000 a year, working only three days a week. To add to the family joy Charlie was graduated *magna cum laude* from the Yale Law School in June, a few days before his father's appointment went through. Taft hurried from Montreal to Washington, where he paid his respects to President Harding and Calvin Coolidge, the Vice-President. His old friend, Harry Daugherty, now attorney general, welcomed him, and Max

Pam and Gus Karger shepherded him around Washington but were not with him when his car skidded in a rainstorm and his knees were badly bruised.

That night he dined at the White House in the room where he and Nellie had always had their breakfast. The President read the bonus message to him for comment and criticism, and he and Daugherty persuaded Harding to make some changes in it. Taft now worked with speed and direction. He felt that at last he was removed from the world of controversy that had seared his spirit and could go his way in peace, without a constant barrage of criticism. Mrs. Anna Roosevelt Cowles, sister of Theodore Roosevelt, was among the first to send him a congratulatory message. Uncle Joe Cannon, with whom he had waged many battles, called to see him, and Senator Frank B. Kellogg warned him against the disposition of the House and Senate to increase the number of federal judges without regard to the need for them. His salary would be $15,000 a year, he informed his wife, but he had no qualms about giving up the honorariums for the speeches, articles, legal opinions, and arbitrations that had been swelling the family income considerably. He discontinued his syndicated newspaper feature at once. One of his first moves was to visit his friend George Wickersham at his Long Island estate to consult him on the reorganization of the United States courts. They walked together in the Japanese garden and he found Wickersham "so bright, sympathetic, and responsive that he makes a fine host."

Pleased that his older brother had reached the goal he sought, Harry was restive that year about getting into public life. He had always longed for office but his family expenses were such that he did not feel he could afford it. Like Will, he strongly supported the League of Nations. In 1919 he visited Russia and was a vigorous critic of communism, often writing on this and other subjects for The New York Times. In 1919 and 1920 he headed the New York State Bar Association and in his constant drive for civic improvement he directed the coalition campaign committee in the mayoralty election of 1921, but the effort to oust the controversial John F. Hylan and install Henry Curran failed.

With Harry working to clean up politics in New York, Charles and Annie were dispensing large sums for the improvement of Cincinnati. The Chief Justice thought they were spending freely at this time, even for them. They had just given the University of Cincinnati $100,000 to start its drive for funds. "Charles evidently believes in giving in his life time," Will commented in his next letter to Nellie. They had recently sold their Texas ranch for a million dollars.

The meeting of the American Bar Association was held in Cincinnati that year and many of the visiting jurists were entertained at the Pike

Street house. Sir John Simon, over from England, was particularly impressed with the family paintings. He had the interest of an expert, since he had recently proved a picture sold to Lord Huntington as a genuine Romney to be a fraud. With William Howard Taft present they all discussed the great collection of pictures that Frick had given to New York, and his Fifth Avenue house that would be turned into a museum. Will speculated on what Charles and Annie might do with their collection. In course of time they did much the same as Frick.

Bob was helpful to the visiting jurists and his father wrote to Nellie that he was a "sweet fellow, so kind and attentive in an unobtrusive way." As always when he was in Cincinnati Taft went out to Indian Hill to see his grandchildren. He was impressed on this occasion with the changes that his son had wrought in his acres, for he was now going in seriously for farming and had a hired man. He had added a porch to the house on the side with the best view, and had sleeping porches upstairs. He had built a farm cottage and had cows, three calves, a good stock of pigs and chickens. All of the Robert Tafts seemed to be thriving, and Martha had finally lost the pale and fragile look that had always been commented on by those who knew her, and particularly by her father-in-law, who favored a hearty look in his young friends. Martha's dinner of lamb and farm vegetables, with home-made ice cream, made Taft forget entirely about his own diet.

He observed that Bob's car needed washing and painting but the young lawyer who had recently strolled in the halls of Versailles was now deep in a flourishing law practice in Cincinnati and enjoyed being a farmer on the side. He and Martha had picked out a site for Charlie on an adjoining hill but Charlie had already settled for a house at the junction of Lawrence and Ludlow streets, opposite the park and close to a schoolhouse. Their grandfather observed that Bobbie and Billie were dressed in the suits they had worn at Helen's wedding. Billie had grown very tall and seemed to Taft "to be as sweet-natured as ever." He had just started going to school and he reminded the Chief Justice of Bob, because he always wanted tasks to do and was a grubber for work.

Taft toured the old Mount Auburn region with Harry, who was attending the meeting of the Bar Association. The corporation lawyer from New York had not been back to his native city in fifteen years and the two aging men paid a nostalgic visit to the home of Mrs. Herman Groesbeck and had a long talk with her mother, Mrs. Elizabeth Perry, who had been so close to their family in the early days. The region was almost unrecognizable to Harry and they thought that the old house on Mount Auburn looked seedy. They walked through Oak Street into Walnut Hills, then to Park Avenue and down through Eden Park, without seeing a single person they knew. Taft wrote to Nellie of climbing the hill he had used so much when he was going to school and when he was courting her. Now he was wearing a gout shoe and it was no longer a pleasure to engage in his marathon walking.

Taft was conscious, too, of the changes in Charles and Annie. He noticed how deaf his sister-in-law had become. Annie O'Gara, small, spare, and thoroughly Irish, had joined the household as her personal maid. She was to stay with Mrs. Taft for the rest of her life and to look after countless details for her employer. Will and Nellie thought that Annie in many respects was like a child, careless of the ways of the world. She wrote checks generously but seldom handled money. It was her habit to tuck bills in her pocket and then forget all about them. Once she had liked to be photographed; now she avoided the camera. Always good-looking, there was a certain wistfulness about the aging Annie. She was unfailingly kind to her employees and would rather take taxis than dismiss an alcoholic chauffeur, because she regarded him as an old retainer. She had had her own way for so long that some of the younger generation thought her imperious. Martha and she could work up an argument but she was devoted to all of the Robert Tafts.

The Chief Justice found her effervescent over a concert at which D'Indy, the French composer, led the orchestra, with Eugène Ysaye, the Belgian violinist then at the height of his fame, looking on. Both men had played at her house the night before, not for money but for love of Mrs. Taft. Ninety guests had been present, and a quartet from the orchestra had rounded out the program.

Before assuming his place on the Supreme Court bench the Chief Justice joined Mrs. Taft briefly in Murray Bay and the family gave him a big birthday party. His wife was adept at running a function of this sort and she rounded up thirty lobsters, four turkeys, and ten chickens to feed eighty guests arranged at small separate tables in Sassifern Cottage. Her husband thought that she carried things off with as much style as if it were a White House party.

But there were other family joys in store for the Chief Justice soon after he mounted the bench. The Court was in session when a telegram reached him early in October, 1921, saying that Helen had given birth to a daughter. He showed it joyfully to his fellow justices and received their congratulations. The infant bore the same name as her mother and her grandmother. Fred, with paternal enthusiasm, wrote to Taft that the baby had a dimple in her chin and resembled her grandfather. The Chief Justice promptly sent off a note to Helen: "I hope Fred proves to be a good entertainer of the baby. I never was with our babies, but perhaps he will be. P.S. You should train Fred by making him walk at night with the baby. I did that with you. Hence my career."

The Chief Justice had at last found total happiness in his work. His court duties were strenuous but he assured Helen that he could not wish for anything better. He rose at a quarter past five, worked until eight, breakfasted for half an hour, worked again until a quarter past ten, then walked the three miles from his home at 2215 Wyoming Avenue to the Capitol. There he bathed and changed, had a rub-down, and went to work. The Court members all lunched together, taking half an hour. They adjourned for the day at half past four. Tom, the Taft chauffeur, met the Chief Justice with the Dodge and drove him home. Taft worked both before and after dinner unless they had evening engagements. He was finding already that the Court members were congenial. "Brandeis and I are on excellent terms," he wrote to Helen. There had not been any clashes of opinion up to that time, although he knew these must come.

The house they had taken on Wyoming Avenue needed painting, new electrical fixtures, and plumbing, but on the whole it was in good order and the Chief Justice found it comfortable. It was the first of their many houses that they actually owned, except for Sassifern Cottage at Murray Bay. They had too much furniture for their quarters and there was ample room for guests. Outdoors the shrubs, trees, and vines needed pruning. The Chief Justice hung a large portrait of Horace where he could see his "fine old kindly face smiling down on me a benediction" when he wakened in the morning.

The Tafts dined out twice a week at first. The dinners, many of which were given in their honor, mounted in number but they ended early and did not tire the Chief Justice as much as countless functions he had attended across the nation. He found them relaxing after hours of hard, concentrated court work. On December 4, 1921, he gave his views on this in a letter to Helen:

> To go out and sit between agreeable women, to eat a good dinner without eating too much and avoiding dangerous viands, is not a physical strain but in some sense is a rest. Since the first of October I have walked a full hour a day—indeed usually something more than that, and generally part of it uphill. That I consider one of the best aids to health I can pursue.

Miss Boardman, back in power at the Red Cross, frequently entertained for the Tafts. She had been elected secretary at the annual meeting held in Washington in 1919. Its war record had added enormously to the power and prestige of the Red Cross and the organization had grown to mammoth proportions. Soon after her appointment Mabel was mourning the death of her brother-in-law, Murray Crane, who had been a power in the Republican councils for many years, the friend both of Taft and of Calvin Coolidge.

In 1922 the Chief Justice was invited to England to be honored by the British Bar, but before sailing he had the satisfaction of presenting the Lincoln Memorial to President Harding at ceremonies held in January. It was an occasion of great moment to him, since he had an intimate sense of association with this noble monument. He made many visits to it in the years that followed, often showing it off to friends by moonlight. Taft took genuine pride in the finished work, for he had watched it from the blueprint stage. But he did not approve of the electrical illumination that he felt gave it the rawness of a plaster mold and robbed it of "all mystery, all delicacy and all refinement." Charles Moore agreed with him and wrote to the Chief Justice: "This nation has got a very great thing in the Lincoln Memorial, and I hope the achievement may be regarded with dignity and not as a plaything." Taft was equally critical of the illumination of the Capitol and the Washington Monument, except for special occasions.

Before sailing for England the Tafts visited Lucy Herron in Providence. After the death of her first husband she had married the popular Senator Henry F. Lippitt, of Rhode Island. They now had a large farm and an abundance of beautiful children. There were Lippitt's children, and Lucy's children, and the children of Lippitt and Lucy. He was a widower when he married Nellie's sister, Mrs. Laughlin, and they now divided their time between Washington, Providence, and Newport. The Senator gave a dinner in Taft's honor, attended by the leading judges and lawyers of Rhode Island.

The Chief Justice's last public act before sailing was to speak at a dinner for Miss Thomas at Bryn Mawr on her retirement. He felt that he had made a poor speech on this occasion and he was haunted by the recollection of a slip in a Latin quotation. It was neither the time nor the place for a lapse of this kind, but he was consoled by the good speech that his only daughter delivered that night.

As he sailed on the *Regina* in April, 1922, Samuel Gompers and Robert La Follette, Jr. were denouncing his decisions in a case involving the right to sue unincorporated labor unions. The Court was deeply involved in measures designed to divest the Government of some of the emergency powers it had assumed during the war years. Railroads, taxation, monopolies, labor, and prohibition were all matters of discussion. But the Chief Justice placidly confided to his family that in John Marshall's time threats against the Supreme Court had been equally violent.

CHAPTER 23

A MASTER BENCHER

THE VISIT of Chief Justice Taft to Britain in 1922 was one of the high points of his career. He had hoped to visit the English courts again, ever since he had sat in the cooped-up galleries on his wedding trip in 1886, listening to judges whose decisions he knew as well as many members of the British Bar. He returned now as former President of the United States, as chief justice of the Supreme Court, as a widely known and admired public figure. From first to last he was in his element and on his return he dictated a full account to Bob from breezy Murray Bay of all that had happened on his trip.

George Harvey, the new United States Ambassador to Britain, was host to the Tafts. Although the Chief Justice had been lukewarm about his appointment he came to like Harvey and was gratified to find that he got on particularly well with Lord Curzon, Secretary of State for Foreign Affairs. The burning issue of the hour in Britain was the Sinn Fein revolt in Ireland, and Mrs. Taft was lunching with Mrs. Harvey at the American Embassy when Sir Henry Wilson, the Irish member of Parliament deeply involved in the controversy, was shot in the street two squares from where they were. They heard the shot and an aide rushed out and saw the assassins running away. They were waving pistols and shouting at a policeman whom they managed to hit. After their capture the aide went to the law courts, where Chief Justice Taft was lunching, and informed him that Sir Henry was dead. Nothing else was talked of for days.

Taft's first view of Winston Churchill was a memorable one. He had gone from a luncheon at Lady Astor's to the House of Commons. Churchill spoke that day on the Irish question and on the assassination of Sir Henry. He read his speech, but in such a way that he seemed not to be using his manuscript. The Chief Justice considered it the great speech of the day; in fact, it impressed him as much as anything he heard while in Britain. He thought that Churchill had complete command of himself and of the House of Commons. He and Lloyd George both glanced up at Taft in the gallery when George N. Barnes, the Labor member whom he had met at Lady Astor's, said that Woodrow Wilson was chiefly responsible for the false "application of the doctrine of self-determination."

Taft found Bonar Law, who was succeeding Lloyd George as prime minister, persuasive but not assertive. He seemed to the Chief Justice to speak with the exactness and force of a Scot. Lady Astor, at the moment in sympathy with the Government, buttonholed her fellow countryman in the lobby, introduced him to some of the members, and took him to tea with the press correspondents. Then she guided him to Lloyd George's quarters and soon Churchill strolled in, but it was the outgoing premier who fascinated Taft at close quarters. He found Lloyd George "quick in motion, a little knock-kneed, direct, graceful and anxious to be agreeable but not to a tiresome degree." His words flowed so easily and effectively that the Chief Justice asked him if his training in Welsh singing had given him this sense of rhythm and he said he thought that it had. They discussed Woodrow Wilson, and Lloyd George revealed that he had never received an answer to his letter which had urged more war activity on the part of the United States.

The Chief Justice was astonished at the candor with which King George V discussed public affairs with him on two occasions during his visit to London. They talked freely when he was privately received at Buckingham Palace and again at a dinner the Harveys gave, with King George and Queen Mary as guests. The King told him that he considered Theodore Roosevelt and Cecil Rhodes the two most remarkable men he had ever met. Taft got the impression that Woodrow Wilson was not popular at the palace and the King commented astringently on his statement about "being too proud to fight." He said that if America had been in the conflict earlier many lives might have been saved but he was "full of appreciation of what we did when we got in." The King then discussed the labor question and the debt which loomed significantly at

the time between Britain and the United States. Taft came to the conclusion that the British monarch seemed to be hinting strongly at can-
cellation. Taft told the King that anything of the sort would be unpopular in America. The labor unions were next discussed and then the
conversation turned to the assassination of Sir Henry Wilson. The Chief
Justice congratulated the King on the speech he had made at Belfast and
on the courage it had taken to go there for the purpose. It was clear to
Taft that George V was greatly stirred up over this incident and favored
quick execution for the captured assassins. But he shortly reminded the
Chief Justice that he was a constitutional king and so could not say
anything that his ministers did not allow him to say, regardless of what
he thought.

Both Lloyd George and Lord Birkenhead (F. E. Smith) were troubled
over the King's heated comments to Taft, and it was suggested to the
Chief Justice that he had talked too freely on this subject. Taft agreed
that the King's remarks might have been unguarded, but he described
him in his letter to Bob as a "man of direct method, candid in his statement, very free in his expression of opinion and . . . loyal to the cause
which he espouses."

The Tafts considered it a feather in Harvey's cap that the King and
Queen should have dined with them, since they rarely went to the Embassies. The dinner was a great success and the Chief Justice beamed
across the table at such fellow Americans as Mrs. Whitelaw Reid, James
Beck, Paul Cravath, James W. Gerard, and Frank Munsey. In addition
to his compatriots, Lloyd George, Lord Balfour, and Lord Birkenhead,
then Lord Chancellor, were all present and the Chief Justice had a
lively time sitting between Queen Mary and Lady Astor. Up to this time
he had felt rather prejudiced against Lady Astor because of what he had
read of her in the papers, but he now decided that she was charming,
direct, and sympathetic, in spite of her whimsical antics. He was much
amused when she remarked that Alice Roosevelt abused her privileges
by mixing insolence with her natural brightness but he noticed that Lady
Astor had thought nothing of delaying the procession into the dining
room while she chatted with the King. She was determined to show that
she was not overcome by his presence.

At the table Lady Astor was irrepressible, and even embarrassing to
the Chief Justice at times, as when she punched him in the leg because
she thought he was not getting along comfortably with the Queen.
But she was quite mistaken about this. Actually the Chief Justice, a
master diplomat on the social front and always particularly tactful and
gallant with women, got on famously with Queen Mary. He did not
find her at all stiff and they moved easily from subject to subject. They
discussed Woodrow Wilson and John W. Davis, who was highly regarded

in London. The Queen told him she wanted to read *The Life and Letters of Walter H. Page* and Taft sent her this book when he returned to the United States. They had a lively interchange on prohibition and she told him that liquor had been banned from the royal table during the war until the King's physician had ordered some stimulant for his health. At this point Queen Mary suggested that he discuss this subject further with his other partner, Lady Astor, whose strong views on prohibition were well known.

"Isn't it awful?" the Virginian had asked him in a loud whisper, but the Chief Justice had not found it awful at all. He could see that things were much less animated where Mrs. Taft sat between the King and Lord Balfour. Nellie, who found the evening absorbing, if somewhat heavy going, considered the Queen exquisitely dressed, in spite of all the prevailing comments on Queen Mary hats. When she and the Chief Justice were presented at court Mrs. Post Wheeler, who had gone halfway round the world with Taft and Alice Roosevelt, helped Nellie with her court presentation gown and gave her the necessary train from her own wardrobe. Mrs. Harvey added the three feathers. Harvey had arranged that the Chief Justice should wear his judicial robes over evening dress. A private audience was held before the ceremony and then the Tafts were taken to the Throne Room. Since Taft was troubled by a rheumatic knee he was relieved to be able to sit through the long ceremony of 200 presentations. During the supper that followed he fell in with old friends, such as the Duchess of Devonshire, who had entertained him in Canada, and Lord and Lady Beatty, whom he had known in Washington. On their return to the Embassy he told Nellie that he must send Bob and Martha the picture of her wearing her three feathers, to add to their growing gallery of family portraits.

In the midst of all the social fuss the Chief Justice was well aware that the British statesmen were making subtle approaches on reparations in the hope that their views might filter through him to President Harding and Charles Evans Hughes, the Secretary of State. It was not the social display, however, but the honors paid him by his colleagues and the functions in the law courts that mattered to William Howard Taft. His initiation into the Middle Temple as a Master Bencher was one of the great moments of his life. In the hall where "Shakespeare acted before Queen Elizabeth, in that Hall that has come down for centuries, with its beautiful paneling and its great pictures" the traditional forms were preserved. The Benchers all drank from a loving cup. A formal Latin grace was said by the Master of the Temple. They cheered Taft and he returned and bowed several times. They then went into the dessert room, where the treasurer made a speech of welcome and Taft one of acceptance, and of tribute to the Inns of Court and the English bar. The Chief

Justice noted that the Benchers were seated according to seniority, not rank, and the names of the men who had been members of that Inn seemed to him to have been the greatest in British jurisprudence.

Mrs. Taft went with Mrs. Harvey to see Mrs. Patrick Campbell in *The Second Mrs. Tanqueray* on this momentous evening in her husband's life, but she and a few other women were permitted to sit in the gallery on the night of the Bench and Bar dinner given in the Middle Temple in honor of the Chief Justice. The acoustics were poor and Taft felt that he had made a deplorable speech, leaving out essential bits, but he confessed to being more moved and overcome than at any time in his experience. He was also received at Gray's Inn, which honored Francis Bacon as its patron saint, and he passed an interesting evening there, listening to discussion of famous trials and their judges. Justice Charles J. Darling, who had donned the black cap many times for some of the most spectacular murderers in nineteenth-century history, was enthralling to Taft, but he was disillusioned in listening to the talk of Lord Birkenhead's relations with Horatio Bottomley, the editor of *John Bull*, who was then facing five years' imprisonment for misappropriation of funds.

Taft took special note of Lord Birkenhead throughout his stay in London. As Lord Chancellor he was his own vis-à-vis in the British system of government, and he was much in evidence at all the functions given for the Chief Justice. Taft was fascinated by his virtuosity but thought him hard and critical. The tall, muscular Birkenhead, lean and driving, seemed to him as "ambitious as the devil" and overly eager to be prime minister. He preferred Sir John Simon, whom he had met earlier in Cincinnati, and who appealed to him as being mild, careful, and judicial. Birkenhead, too, recalled dining with Mr. and Mrs. Charles Phelps Taft on Pike Street and finding himself ill-prepared for the art treasures he found in their house. "I do not think that I have ever seen in one private home a collection of masterpieces with which I was so much delighted," he told the Chief Justice, who was finding that wherever he went in England he heard unexpected echoes of Charles and Annie. Birkenhead took him to the House of Lords where a debate was in progress over Lady Rhondda's right to vote on political questions in that body.

The British jurists were struck by Taft's close knowledge of their cases. He was able to follow their allusions with ease for he had studied the English Reports since first borrowing them from his father's library at the age of twelve. He continued this study throughout his career so that he knew a great deal about the personalities of the English bench. Lord Mersey told him that he was better informed than many men then at the bar in England.

Charles Evans Hughes had urged the Chief Justice to sound out the

Englishmen who were active in the League of Nations on the question of divorcing the World Court from the League. Taft made a special point of discussing the political situation, the peace negotiations, and world affairs with Lloyd George and with Lord Cecil, who had helped to draft the League of Nations covenant. Driving to the Law Courts with Lord Cecil—"long-legged and bent over"—Taft introduced Hughes's suggestion of a change in the constitution or the statutes of the World Court, so that the United States might be induced to join it. Lord Cecil blandly said that he would be glad to cooperate. But Taft was staggered when he listened to Lloyd George say that President Wilson had made a mistake in not sending a representative to the Peace Conference instead of coming himself. "We had to treat him on our level, and when we got him over here then he was at our mercy," Lloyd George told the Chief Justice. "We could teach him a few things."

Although this had been common talk among politicians in the United States the Chief Justice was surprised to hear the facts so baldly stated by British diplomats. They also discussed the difficulty of getting Woodrow Wilson "to reply or explain when confronted with an inconsistency." Taft was closely questioned about the former President's physical state. He told the British statesmen that he did not believe Wilson was dying and that he still seemed to be exercising influence in his party. In this he was as genuinely baffled as other American political leaders who groped blindly in their estimate of the true state of affairs.

Both Tafts attended the banquet given annually by the Lord Mayor to the Judge and the Bar. They were summoned to the royal box at a charity ball held at Albert Hall under the auspices of Princess Mary. The Chief Justice felt that he had "put his foot in it" when he asked the Queen where Princess Mary was. Actually she had gone to the races at Newmarket with Lord Lascelles, and there was adverse comment on her absence. The golden-haired Prince of Wales, just back from a world tour, recalled that William Howard Taft had presided at a dinner given for him in New York.

"I am glad to see you and I hope you have done well since," the Prince remarked. "By the way, haven't they made you something since? Haven't you been made a Secretary, or put in the Cabinet, or something?"

Taft enjoyed this. It enabled him to tell the Prince that he had been made chief justice—a fact that had been considerably emphasized during his visit to London, since every move he made was reported, from buying pinks from a pretty actress on Queen Alexandra Day to his initiation as a Master Bencher. "It came home to me with considerable force that one may exaggerate the importance of his own status and situation," he wrote jestingly to Bob.

All branches of the Taft family read this long and informative letter with appreciation. The Chief Justice shared with them his impressions of the various celebrities he had met, from Lord Asquith, whom he found to be a man "of exact knowledge, of compact statement and scholarly tastes" to Sir Thomas Willys Chitty, Chief Master of the King's Bench, whom he considered "reserved, modest and a trifle cold." When he watched Justice Darling and Sir Thomas in operation in the courts he thought Darling severe, but his admiration for Sir John Simon increased as he listened to a "masterly cross-examination in a suit brought to break the Earl of Shrewsbury's will." Taft met Lady Asquith at a luncheon given at their home, with their children and Lady Beerbohm Tree present. He thought his hostess intense and a good deal of an actress, with little restraint on her tongue or her disclosures, but she was warm and agreeable with the Tafts. They agreed that Lady Astor's celebrated imitation of Margot Asquith, which they had seen, was true to life.

The Chief Justice thought the two women much alike, saying bold things verging on impudence and abusing the immunity often extended to bright and audacious women. But when he visited Cliveden and saw Lady Astor in her own background he found her pert, forcible, and fascinating. Taft thought her a good mother, running her household with verve and understanding. When he was leaving England she sent him grapes and peaches from the Cliveden gardens.

The Chief Justice and Mrs. Taft visited some of the stateliest homes of England during this visit. Taft thought 10 Downing Street neither a dignified nor an adequate dwelling for the Prime Minister but he was impressed with the country houses. Sir John received him warmly at Fritwell Manor, his Elizabethan house, and together they paraded in the gardens and talked of art, politics, and the law. Lord Balfour entertained them in his Regency house in Carlton Gardens at a time when he was acting in place of Lord Curzon as temporary minister of foreign affairs. Taft learned that he was more popular than Curzon, because he was less of a driving force. The Chief Justice found Lord Balfour responsive but slow and hesitant in choosing his words when they discussed the League of Nations. He was profoundly interested in Lord Curzon and decided that he was a zealot in his work and greatly enamored of the pomp of his position. "Curzon's passion is to hold office," he wrote to Bob.

Both he and Mrs. Taft studied Lady Curzon with interest. She was born Mary Leiter of Chicago, an heiress long famous for her beauty and for the love her husband bore her. The Chief Justice decided that although she must have been good-looking in the past she now seemed artificial. He considered Princess Patricia stolid and her father, the Duke of Connaught, whom he had known in Canada, a "nice old boy." He told Rudyard Kipling how much his books had meant to him as he lay ill in Manila. Taft met another literary figure when John Masefield joined him in the procession of those receiving honorary degrees at Oxford. Taft walked with Lord Birkenhead at the head of the procession, wearing the brilliant scarlet gown faced with purple and the beefeater hat of Henry VIII's time. The Harveys later gave him the gowns he wore at Oxford and Cambridge as mementos of his trip. One was for Bob, one for Charlie. Lord Birkenhead took him to Wadham and Merton, Wadham being his own college and Merton Sir John Simon's. They visited the Bodleian Library and the Warden of All Souls showed them the original announcement of Sir William Blackstone's lectures, subsequently embodied in his books. At Oxford Taft met the Bishop of Salisbury, who told him that he, too, had been a guest of Mr. and Mrs. Charles Phelps Taft in Cincinnati during an Episcopal convention held there. On their way to Warwick Castle the Tafts called on Mrs. Antonio de Navarro, the American actress Mary Anderson, then living in the town of Broadway.

Gordon Selfridge, the American-born merchant who had made a fortune in Britain, gave an elaborate party for the Chief Justice and Mrs. Taft, and before they left for Scotland the Harveys gave a final reception for them. The Chief Justice took time to attend a meeting of the Unitarians in Essex Hall. In Aberdeen, where he received a degree, he had a rowdy time. He was met at the train by Sir George Adam Smith, the Scottish biblical scholar, and was quickly exposed to the strongest student ragging of his career. This custom still prevailed in all its glory in Scotland, Professor Taft observed. The students cheered the ulster-coated figure vociferously and when he sat down they shouted: "Take two seats, Bill." The Chief Justice, used to the ways of students, accepted this good-naturedly but it was not the end. They closed the gate which was his exit, jumped on his automobile, chased him on foot to his hotel, where they yelled for a speech. He finally talked to them from a window but showed resistance when they tried to seize him. His bulk made this a difficult matter.

Mrs. Taft stood all the excitement well, although the trip had been tiring for her. She had enjoyed the shops and theaters as well as the magnificent functions they had attended. While in London the Chief Justice heard that he had been elected to the Yale Corporation. "I suppose I shall be considered a reactionary but perhaps it will not hurt to have one who is more conservative on the board," he wrote.

On their arrival home Mrs. Taft went straight to Murray Bay but her husband crossed the country to attend the meeting of the American Bar Association in San Francisco. John W. Davis, whom he greatly admired, was elected president after a close fight, although Will had hoped that his brother Harry would win this honor. Fresh from his triumphs in London the Chief Justice was the star of the occasion. He thought that the

American Bar Association was growing in strength and usefulness and he told Nellie that he intended to help it as much as he could. Taft strongly believed in tightening the links between the judiciary of both countries and he invited Sir Thomas Chitty, who attended the meeting in the West, to visit him at Murray Bay.

Crossing the country Taft read *The Little Minister, Stella Maris*, and Ralph Connor's *To Him that Hath*. He could move easily from international law to the lightest fiction, and he often picked up mystery books as relief from his political cares. He had done so much technical reading in his time that this was recreation for him. His wife shared this taste although she, too, was exceptionally well read.

After all the excitement in the early part of the summer, Murray Bay exerted its usual charm the moment he breathed the air of the St. Lawrence. Charlie was as popular as ever and Bob was enjoying a real vacation, but Helen was missing. She and Fred had gone to London to do research in the Public Record Office for their theses. Helen's topic was the colonial policy of Great Britain in the eighteenth century. Her father showered her with introductions to prominent Britons and he particularly urged her to call on Lady Simon, whose two daughters were at Girton. The Mannings settled first on Dorset Square, then at 4 Greville Place, and Helen sent her family amusing letters describing her experiences, from the flighty ways of the "chars" to the freezing winds of Oxford. In the House of Commons she heard the speech introducing the bill "to retaliate against Papa's decision as to liquor on foreign ships."

Characteristically Helen did not make any use of the Taft name when she was presented at court in the spring of 1923. Her father was slightly surprised when Mrs. Frederick J. Manning, of Bryn Mawr, was not identified as the daughter of a former President. "I am glad that you went through the procedure of presentation at Court," he wrote to Helen. "It is a good deal of a bore, but it is something to have seen it and to understand what it is." On another occasion he jested on this same subject: "We have a picture of you and the Queen of Belgium which we are having framed, because when we of our family are associated with royalty, we wish to put it in permanent form."

Because Mrs. Harding was ill the White House schedule was cut to nothing in the winter of 1922–23, although the Chief Justice attended a luncheon given there for Clemenceau in December. He did not feel that the Frenchman's visit had much significance, although everyone was interested in seeing the Tiger and hearing him talk. In commenting to Helen on this visit Taft wrote that he had never seen any reason to regret his efforts to get the United States into the League of Nations, nor had he forgiven Woodrow Wilson "for not taking us there when he had the opportunity." He felt that all the negotiations had been badly bungled and that Wilson's ego had alienated sympathy for his cause. He blamed Wilson and Henry Cabot Lodge equally for the defeat of the treaty that created the League of Nations.

The Chief Justice observed on his return from England that the bloom of office was wearing off for Harding, although he felt that the President's "equanimity, his sweet nature and his wish to do right" kept him in a good frame of mind. The undercurrents of the Harding administration were muted and Harry Daughtery was a potent figure at the White House. Taft felt that Mrs. Harding had made herself ill from overwork and her "high ambition to fill her place worthily." He considered her conscientious in trying to fulfill her social duties, to cope with her correspondence, and to accompany the President on his trips.

The Chief Justice's own health had not been good since his trip abroad, and at Murray Bay he had been forced to play golf on the lower links, which was the children's course. He was dieting furiously and was losing two pounds a week in his never-ending battle to keep down his weight. By Christmas, 1922, he was down to 255½ pounds and he and Mrs. Taft went out very little. She was in mourning for her brother, Will Herron, who had died of a heart attack while working in the Justice Department. Thereafter she had stopped holding her Monday receptions for the time being.

As the Supreme Court convened on a June day in 1923 Justice Holmes told Taft that they had finished the most pleasant Court year in his experience. He attributed this to the Chief Justice, who had brought kindness and geniality to bear in dealing with his colleagues and had brightened their work with flashes of wit. He had also pushed the speeding-up process that was one of his great contributions to jurisprudence.

Immediately afterwards he went to Cincinnati with Mrs. Taft for the unveiling of a monument to Salmon P. Chase. In his usual happy vein when discussing law he recalled the criticism of the Supreme Court in Chase's time and drew a parallel with contemporary attacks. Afterwards Bob took his parents to the graves of Alphonso and Louise in Spring Grove Cemetery, where Taft studied the monument that his mother had put up in Alphonso's memory and gave thought to the vigorous and affectionate father who had done so much for them all.

From there they drove to Indian Hill and had their first glimpse of Alphonso's newest descendant—Lloyd Bowers Taft, a blue-eyed boy who seemed to his grandparents to be quiet and well behaved. Next they visited Charlie and Eleanor and found that their new son, Seth Chase Taft, was the image of his father. Nonie and Sylvia had grown into blond elfin beauties and their grandparents observed them with satisfaction. Taft noticed that Eleanor, their mother, was quiet in all her kindnesses. She seemed content but did not surround herself with friends in the typical Taft fashion.

Both of the Taft sons were doing well. The tax bill on which Bob had worked long and hard had finally been passed by the Ohio legislature and his father considered it a measure "in which he has made himself the master of the science of taxation in Ohio." He had just gone into a law partnership with John Stettinius and John Hollister. His father observed that Indian Hill was fast becoming fashionable and the Country Club had bought a stretch of land for golf links within two miles of Sky Farm. Hulbert Taft had taken ninety acres close to Bob's farm.

The Chief Justice learned on this trip that his brother Charles was faced with an operation for cataract and his sight was failing badly. His chief editorial writer, Russell Wilson, had just become engaged to Elizabeth Smith, an old family friend of the Tafts who had been at Bryn Mawr with Helen and was the daughter of a Cincinnati judge. "I cannot think of anything that really has pleased me more in recent history," Bob Taft wrote to her with his usual brevity. He and Martha had been friendly with both of them for years, and Wilson was an important link with the newspaper world.

No sooner had the Chief Justice settled at Murray Bay in the summer of 1923 than the news of Harding's death in San Francisco and Coolidge's succession to office brought him hurrying back to Washington. He found the new President looking remarkably cool and self-possessed. The Chief Justice stood with him at the station as Harding's body was brought in from the coast. He rode back with Charles Evans Hughes and they discussed Harding and Coolidge and the extraordinary chain of events that had made the silent lawyer from Vermont President of the United States. Hughes recalled that Coolidge had attended every Cabinet meeting and thus knew much of the detail of the executive branch. He described Mrs. Harding as an able woman and Harding as a man who had never spared himself in the hours he put in on work, exercise, or social enjoyment.

The Chief Justice described the funeral in detail in his letters to Mrs. Taft—the ceremonies in the rotunda of the Capital, the train trip to Ohio, and the cortege moving through the streets of Marion to the house where Dr. George T. Harding lived. The room where the service was held was small and close. Harry Daugherty, feeling faint, collapsed in a chair. Taft thought that Mrs. Harding, stoical throughout, bore up strongly and directed everything. Henry Ford and Charles A. Edison both were present and George Harvey whispered a greeting to Taft in passing.

On their train journey the Chief Justice was invited to the presidential car to pay his respects to the new President and Mrs. Coolidge. "As I had no office to seek I kissed her hand to show my foreign training and she did not seem to dislike it," Will wrote to Nellie. "I told her that I thought there would be no suspicion of an infusion of a spirit of royalty into the function because of that. She is very nice." The President's act in having his father swear him in by lamplight in the parlor of their home in Plymouth, Vermont, was already the talk of Washington. It would soon become a national legend, although it had to be done all over again in the capital to make it official.

Late in September Taft had a talk with the President about the judiciary and came to the conclusion that Coolidge would ignore political considerations in the appointment of judges. Always prepared to see the best in everyone the Chief Justice reported to Nellie that the dour Vermonter's "cordial smiles were frequent." He thought that Coolidge talked freely to him and was anxious to do the right thing. Reassured by his attitude Taft wrote to his wife:

> He asked me what I thought he ought to do now. I told him that I thought the country was delighted to have a rest before Congress came together and that with approaching and present prosperity the people wanted to be let alone, confident that with him in the White House, nothing would be done for effect and quiet would be maintained if there was no real reason for affirmative action.

From the beginning Taft and Coolidge got on well and treated each other with mutual respect. The Chief Justice thought that the President's message to Congress that year was especially good—"great in its comprehensiveness and style, great in the soundness of its economic statesmanship, and great in the courage that it took to say what he had said." Taft was never to agree with the critics who called Coolidge's utterances trite but in course of time he jested occasionally about his lack of geniality.

By the end of 1923 the Mannings were back from England and had settled in a new apartment in New Haven. The Chief Justice feared that it might take Helen some time to settle down to her thesis, now that she had finished her research. "But the sooner the better, my dear girl," he reminded her. Helen did not need this warning for she was already hard at work, preparing for her examinations in French, German, and Latin for her Ph.D. degree. In Washington the elder Tafts had settled down to a second year of Supreme Court activity. They continued in their hospitable ways and visitors from out of town were always sure of a welcome at their house. Nellie had a regular program in which they shared. She gave them luncheons and card parties, took them to Mount Vernon, showed them the Lincoln Memorial, Arlington, the Capitol, and the Supreme Court. When the Gridiron Club invited the sons of

Presidents to be their guests Bob and Charlie both came on from Cin-cinnati. Ten in all attended this dinner.

"Your mother is an exceptional woman," the Chief Justice wrote to Helen as he pictured Nellie taking in concerts and plays, having gowns fitted, looking after her household with energy and good management, and keeping track of her children and her grandchildren. In the spring of 1924 she decided to go abroad and join Maria in Spain. By April she was strolling under the horse chestnuts in Paris, and Oliver Wendell Holmes was giving the Chief Justice reports on her cherry blossoms in Washington. He arrived in court one morning with a glowing account of their beauty. Taft finally drove out to see them himself and found the crowd so dense that it was impossible to get near them. "That was a great thought of yours," he wrote to Nellie next day. Their magnolia tree was doing well, too, and the birds were making themselves melodious around the house.

All of the older members of the Court were ailing that spring. The Chief Justice usually took Holmes and Brandeis home in his car from their Saturday conference, since Mrs. Holmes used the family coupe on that day of the week. Taft thought Holmes marvelously robust for a man of his years. He was careful of his health, and his wife would not let anyone near him unless a card was sent to her. McReynolds had what he called gout and Taft called old-fashioned lumbago. The Chief Justice thought that he took more vacations than anyone else on the Court and was most censorious of its functionings, its decisions, and Taft's manner of conducting it. He had predicted that the Chief Justice would not last a year. "McReynolds may be right," he conceded ruefully to Helen. "One can not tell what a year will bring, but I'll do my best."

The fact was that Taft, having at last reached the place he had long desired, was now having serious trouble with his heart. He had had two severe attacks. The first was on the day of Woodrow Wilson's funeral. He was to have been a pallbearer but was unable to attend at all. At the end of April he had a second attack and was warned against excessive exercise. He was treated with quinine and digitalis and had to spend some time in bed, but his chief thought was for Nellie's safety and comfort as she traveled in Europe. He urged her to be careful of the traffic in Paris and not to economize on taxi fares. As his condition improved he decided to give his usual Easter dinner and Mrs. Coolidge charmed him by sending him a pot of lilies for this function. He thought her modest and retiring—a "thoroughly nice woman" who would make a most worthy First Lady when she felt entirely at home in her new surroundings, he reported to Mrs. Taft. Coolidge, he observed, was making headway by keeping his mouth shut and talking only when he had something to say.

Lucy Lippitt, his sister-in-law from Rhode Island, helped Taft draw up a menu for his Easter dinner. He stopped in at Small's himself and ordered Easter flowers. Ambassador Jusserand was in top form and they all drank Mrs. Taft's health in "sparkling cider." By this time it was known on the social circuit that the Chief Justice must be protected in his diet. Mrs. Coolidge, who arranged for roast beef to be slipped before the President, no matter what the menu, was equally punctilious about providing whole wheat toast and nothing else for Taft at some of the White House functions. Among his new friends in the capital were Mr. and Mrs. Eugene Meyer. He considered Meyer a clever man and his wife a great beauty.

Charles and Annie visited him late in May. They drove around Washington and studied the house where they had lived when Charles was a congressman in 1895. Will took them to the Supreme Court where they "saw the show but could not hear the judges deliver opinions." He drove them to Rock Creek Park, to Chevy Chase, and to see the unfinished cathedral. Then he took them inside the Lincoln Memorial, his special pride, and on to the White House for luncheon. Their deafness and the President's reserve made this a stiff occasion, but after it was over Mrs. Coolidge took them upstairs and broke the ice. Will described it all to Nellie, who was then in Biarritz, but who always had great interest in anything that had to do with unpredictable Annie.

> Of course they suffer much in not understanding what people talk about, because they are both quite deaf. Annie felt that the President was most uncommunicative, and sympathized with his wife because he was so silent. But the Coolidges were very nice and we went upstairs after luncheon, and Annie had quite a talk with Mrs. Coolidge, while we went into the other room to have the President smoke. I think it was a pleasant reminiscence of old White House days for them to go there and see the old Mansion just as it is.

Taft took interested note of all that the President said and did. By this time it was clear that Herbert Hoover's friends were working in his behalf for 1928, but Charles D. Hilles thought that the Vermonter topped him in finesse and cunning. He found Coolidge direct and more practical than the traveled and worldly Mr. Hoover. Taft did not share the President's enthusiasm for the *Mayflower* and thought yachting the least pleasurable of recreations, particularly in the rain. He was always reluctant to go on one of these trips, and was quite amused over the "deuce of a time" the President had persuading the public that he went to church before setting off for his Sunday jaunt. Her father wrote to Helen about this: "The older one grows the more convinced one becomes that real comforts are those which one moderately enjoys, and that extreme luxuries to which one is not accustomed tire one and are demoralizing."

The President was maintaining a stony front as the oil investigation opened up floodgates of censure, and the corruption of the Harding administration was spread on the record. Harry Daugherty was at the storm center, but was ultimately acquitted on the charge of conspiring to defraud the Government. At first Taft thought the Attorney General was being "greatly and most unjustly traduced" but should resign to spare Coolidge further embarrassment. As the story unfolded he was shocked but reluctant to believe the worst of his old friend—the man who had been largely responsible for his appointment to the Supreme Court. As chief justice he held his peace through the Teapot Dome investigation, except for an occasional note of regret or dismay that crept into his family letters. When Daugherty was in the deepest trouble he wrote to Horace: "I am still of the opinion that Daugherty is honest personally." Taft felt that in the various ill-judged moves he made as the investigation proceeded he was covering up for Harding. The Attorney General, in his opinion, was "one of the finest fellows I know . . . loyal, hard-working, disinterested, honest and courageous," but he also considered him a man of boundless ambition who was never fitted for the post he held in the Cabinet.

Taft had hoped to join Nellie and Maria in Europe but his second heart attack made this impossible. He had devotedly followed their journey, from their audience with the king and queen of Spain to relaxing hours spent at Biarritz. Early in June he dashed off the good news that Eleanor had had another baby. This one was named Lucia, after her aunt, Lucia Chase, the famous ballet dancer. The Chief Justice was disappointed that he was not on the bench when the telegram announcing the new arrival came in. "I would like to have the Court realize that telegrams mean babies to me," this most human of judges wrote to his wife. "Four children for a man of twenty-seven is doing pretty well." But everyone was aware of Taft's strong devotion to his family; it was a matter of comment on the Supreme Court bench. Because of his illness he missed the meeting of the Bar Association in London but to his greater consternation he was unable to get to Yale to see Helen receive her Ph.D. degree. This worried him, particularly since Fred was unable to be present, but he assured Nellie that their daughter was independent enough not to mind their absence.

The Chief Justice was at Murray Bay when news of young Calvin Coolidge's death from blood poisoning reached him. He sent off a telegram at once to the boy's parents. "It would seem as if the White House always carries domestic burdens for the occupants," he wrote to Nellie. Coolidge suffered in silence and a shadow fell over his gracious wife. Neither one had any zest for the election campaign that followed. Taft was relieved when John W. Davis was nominated by the Democrats. Although anxious for Coolidge to win, it meant that, should the Democrats be returned to power, a "sound and conservative man" would be President—one who in the Chief Justice's opinion would not impair the weight of the Court or appoint any but seasoned lawyers. The choice surprised him since Davis had been counsel for J. P. Morgan & Company and Standard Oil. Taft did not think that Charles G. Dawes, the Republican vice-presidential nominee, would be as strong as Hoover might have been, and he feared the outspoken Ohioan might get the ticket into trouble with his blunt speech. But he would add a picturesque touch to the fight and Taft liked his independence.

The Chief Justice knew that he must now go slow, even at Murray Bay. He had never passed so inactive a summer there and he had to be pulled up the hills in a *planche*. It pained him that he could no longer swing around the golf course, but had to sit on the porch of the clubhouse and watch the others go off. His diet had never been so restricted. Eleanor and Charles, with their four children and two nurses, joined him, and Horace marched across the golf course "like Father Anchises walking taller than all," his brother observed. In October he had further heart warnings, which gave him great concern, for he believed that he must resign the moment he felt unable to carry on his full share of work. But he soon picked up strength again. Miss Boardman was ailing at this time, too, and his Christmas gift to her in 1924 was a cane for the hills of Murray Bay.

Early the next year Helen bore a second daughter whom she named Caroline. Her father was in church when Mischler brought him a note saying that the baby was born. "The little girl was a little in a hurry to get here just as her mother was a good many years ago when she beat me to Cincinnati and East Walnut Hills," he wrote to Helen from the Supreme Court. He noted that she weighed three quarters of a pound more than Alice Longworth's Paulina, born on Valentine's Day that year. Fred had just been appointed assistant professor of history at Swarthmore and the Mannings were able to remain in their comfortable home at Bryn Mawr. On top of this came the news that Helen was to be dean of Bryn Mawr. Things were turning out well for her. She was happily married, had two little girls, and she would now be able to resume her career. Her parents were pleased.

Taft continued to miss Nellie desperately when she was away and while she was abroad in 1924 he wrote to Charlie:

It is hard to realize that she is gone for four months. It will come on me with more and more force as I live all alone in this house. We have had our sitting rooms next to one another, and I don't remember that we have ever been absent from one another for four months since we were married. It is easy to agree to such an arrangement, but it is hard to bear it.

They had had few disagreements in their years together, except over prohibition and Theodore Roosevelt. As Taft's health failed he was more than ever grateful for the happy years they had spent together. Mrs. Taft, Mrs. Newlands, and Miss Boardman sat together to watch him swear in Calvin Coolidge on March 4, 1925. "I observe he is to have his own family Bible," the Chief Justice wrote to Helen. "Ordinarily, Presidents have been sworn in on the Bible of the Supreme Court, but I presume it is the same Bible and it will not vary the character of the obligation." They joined the Coolidges later to watch the parade and the Chief Justice chatted with Colonel John Coolidge, the hardy Vermonter who had sworn in his son the first time. He admired the President's inauguration address and wrote to Charlie that Coolidge had acquired great aptness of expression. Taft thought that his speeches were as good to read as to hear.

The Chief Justice had been working at top speed. The Court had delivered more than forty opinions in one day immediately before the Coolidge inauguration. There were 558 cases in arrears and Taft was determined to move this backlog. He was exultant when his pet bill passed in February, simplifying the appellate procedure of the Supreme Court and the Court of Appeals. This gave them selective power in hearing cases and went far to ease the crowded dockets of the state and federal courts. Van Devanter, McReynolds, and he had carried it through. Senator Thomas J. Walsh of Montana fought it, but when he surrendered victory followed. This was a real step in the history of the Supreme Court. When Justice Harlan F. Stone became one of the associates early in 1925 Taft reported that he was the right age, a hard worker, and a learned lawyer, as well as being a straightforward, judicially-tempered man. At this time the Chief Justice wrote to Charlie: "I have to be careful, and when I wake up in the morning and get dressed and come to breakfast, I thank the Lord for another day." He had just told Holmes that that great jurist would probably live to bury all his colleagues. When Nellie made the unusual gesture of accompanying him to the Unitarian church on a blustery spring morning he was touchingly grateful. "I am glad to rescue her as a brand from the burning," he wrote in the bantering tone he often adopted with his children about their mother. "She is a bit like a cat and she loves the pew in St. John's Church where she sat when she was First Lady of the Land."

When Bob and Martha had a fourth son in April, 1925, they named him Horace and the Chief Justice wrote to Miss Boardman: "Dear old

Horace ought to have some worthy member of the new generation to bear his name—I think it would warm the cockles of his heart." Bob repeated history that April by making a speech opposing a bill involving Bible reading in the public schools passed by the Ohio Senate. "I wonder if he read his grandfather's opinion . . . back in 1872," the Chief Justice commented to Charlie. His young son and Eleanor went abroad that summer. Their trip was a gift from the elder Chase, or "Popsy" as he was known in family circles. Fred Manning, a brilliant scholar who took his Ph.D. with ease at Yale that spring, set off for Spain on a walking tour. Helen, as usual, was heading for Murray Bay, and her father was building a cottage for the Mannings close to his own. British Columbia fir was being used throughout, and he intended to furnish it, too.

Maria, still abroad, was supplying the family with table talk as usual. When Nellie returned home she went on to Italy, where she struck up a friendship with Mrs. Frances Noel Hall, who had gone abroad to get away from the whispered charges that she had murdered her husband, the Reverend Dr. Edward Hall, and his choir singer, Mrs. Eleanor Mills. For months the newspapers had been headlining the details of the double murder committed under a crabapple tree in a small New Jersey town—one of the classic crimes in American jurisprudence. Mrs. Hall was tried and acquitted with her brothers in the following year, 1926, but in the meantime Maria was enthusiastically championing her cause. She believed that the clergyman's wife was much maligned. "It is the fate of Maria to always be in it," the Chief Justice wrote to his daughter. "I wonder that she wasn't in the neighborhood of New Brunswick at the time."

But another headliner was developing in the Taft family. In September, 1925, Charlie stepped suddenly into the limelight in Cincinnati when he made what he considered his first political speech at a meeting in Chester Park. A small crowd of loyal voters had turned out to hear him plead the cause of the Charter candidates for the new city council. Alphonso's liberal strain was beginning to show in Charlie. Horace's early observation at the Taft School that he was a reformer at heart was coming true. His father viewed this tendency in Charlie with some concern. Was he devoting all the time that he should to his law practice? Actually, Charlie was fast becoming attuned to the needs of the world. In 1924 he had started his long fight for civic reform and righteousness in Cincinnati when he was elected president of the Cincinnatus Association, a group of young business and professional men who organized a City Charter Committee, pledged to give the city a new kind of government.

This was where the two young Tafts, Bob and Charlie—both brilliant, both dedicated to the public good—chose separate paths. Charles became a leader of the insurgents. Bob stayed with the party machine, hoping to reform matters from within. In a sense it was a perpetuation of the fight waged long before by Alphonso, and more briefly by William Howard Taft. By this time Rudolph K. Hynicka, a former Cincinnatian who bossed the Republican organization from New York, operated like Cox, controlling city jobs and spreading patronage. Civic institutions were badly run; taxes were exorbitant; the city was in poor repair; and the streets were peppered with holes. Democrats merged with independent Republicans to form the City Charter Comittee. The idealistic amateurs were pitched against hardheaded politicians, who oozed unction and experience.

Charlie proved to be a lively campaigner. He rang doorbells, hit hard, and helped to put across the new charter that cut the council from thirty-two members to nine, installed a city manager, established civil service, and gave the minority a vote in government. The reformers managed to elect six out of nine council members and in the next decade they made Cincinnati one of the better governed cities of the nation. Charlie continued to exercise these principles down the years, going to any remote part of the city at any hour of the day or night to push a good civic cause.

The Chief Justice took careful note of the veering paths of his sons. The course of things was clear when the Cincinnatus Club took political action against two prominent local officials. "The elder of your sons favored deliberation and the younger radical action," he wrote to Nellie on July 4, 1924. On another occasion he observed: "In our family we have one vote for the practical good and another vote for the ideally good, which is usually cast into the wind, accomplishing nothing." His father thought that Charlie should resign from the Cincinnatus Club, since his membership would bring him into conflict with Bob. "You are not called upon to make the sacrifice involved in family feelings," the patriarch pointed out to his younger son.

But family loyalty held intact down the years, whatever the political divergence. The Taft brothers could not be neutral on any issue. They bore Cincinnati's most distinguished Republican name. They had a strong heritage—political, social, humanitarian. Charlie supported the Republican ticket in state and national elections. He applied another rule to Cincinnati's involved affairs. Bob took the bad with the good and was rewarded in the long run with organization support. The brothers voted for each other when they ran for office and Charlie campaigned vigorously for Bob when he ran for the Senate and the Presidency. They visited each others' homes and congregated at Murray Bay. They joined forces in family gatherings and forged strong links in the Taft line of succession.

But before his death the Chief Justice warned Charlie against spreading his interests too thin as he threw himself into all manner of extra-curricular work. He was called on to make many speeches and his work for the Y.M.C.A. took time. When it became obvious that Charlie could never turn down a chance to help, his father treated him to all the time-honored homilies of the dogged spirit needed for success, and of sticking on the job instead of answering calls to make speeches in California. "When you have done that, all that you desire will come to you in the way of usefulness to the community and the gratifications of a legitimate ambition," he wrote to Charlie at the close of 1925.

The disparate natures of the Taft sons had been evident quite early in their lives. Bob was like his mother, intense, practical, ambitious, not given to flattery or the meaningless word. Charlie was like his father—free in manner, warm, responsive, ambitious too, but without Bob's hard drive. Even their faces bespoke their natures. There was nothing about Bob to suggest his traveled youth, as there was about Charlie. Bob's life was firmly based from the day he entered school, and he lived with clear-headed purpose when he returned to Cincinnati. The wives both men married accentuated their differences. Martha Bowers was as politically inclined as her husband. She was a born campaigner, quick, practical, witty, and extroverted. Eleanor was a quiet idealist, deeply religious and interested in social service. Gentle in manner, she was strong and steady in her convictions and sympathies, with an inflexible will. Both Tafts had found the perfect wives for their particular natures and their marriages were singularly happy. All four were given to community service, but Bob concentrated his forces on political issues while Charlie diffused his.

Hulbert Taft, always a conservative, opposed the Charter group, and with his journalistic power he could fight it on many issues; but the Taft blood made itself felt here, too. He could not turn his face against Charlie and on many occasions gave him qualified support when he ran for office. No Taft would work to keep another from moving ahead, and all of Charlie's interests were geared to what he thought to be the good of mankind. Hulbert recognized this fact and the Taft name was always prime news in the Cincinnati papers.

As things grew wild in the flaming 1920's the Chief Justice, a toler-ant man, surveyed the social scene with some concern. He deplored the exploitation of football and general athletics in the colleges, and was critical of the use of campus papers to attack the faculty and established institutions. Taft considered this the spirit of demagoguery. But the decade of jazz, big football games, prizefights, gangster murders, and pro-hibition was at its peak. Boys in raccoon coats, with Stutz roadsters and pocket flasks, invaded the football stadiums in autumn. Jazz whined out of countless night clubs as the Charleston was danced with frenzy and speakeasies flourished. The churches were at odds on doctrinal issues of Fundamentalism versus Modernism. Fortunes were made overnight and Coolidge and prosperity were synonymous. The theater, with such playwrights as Eugene O'Neill, blossomed with rich and lasting fruit. The book world was lit with fresh and brilliant talent as Sinclair Lewis shook up his generation. An era of spending, speed, and license had followed the first World War, but it was also an era of creative advances in the arts. This was as true of Ohio as of New York or San Francisco, but all branches of the Taft family continued to live in the austere tradition of public service.

In November, 1925, Helen landed in the headlines by permitting the Bryn Mawr girls to smoke under fixed rules. It was years since Alice Longworth had stirred up Washington on this issue, and it was fully forty years since Mrs. Taft had done some experimental smoking in Cincinnati and at Narragansett Pier. The Chief Justice was accustomed to seeing some of his most respected women friends puffing at cigarettes, but he still did not like it. However, he conceded in a letter to his daughter that girls could no longer be treated like hothouse flowers; they must judge for themselves the danger or folly of their diversions, and restrictions would not help.

The Mannings had settled at 215 Roberts Road, Bryn Mawr, in a large house with four bathrooms and five fireplaces, plenty of room for guests, a Negro butler named Jerome with a wife who cooked biscuits in the best Virginia manner, a secondhand Franklin sedan, and what Fred described as an avalanche of bills. Small Helen was attending a kindergarten and her mother was getting along well in her familiar environment. They dined out at least twice a week and they scraped up tickets for an occasional Stokowski concert. They had many friends and Fred, teaching history at Swarthmore, was finding it a big change from his work at Yale.

They all joined the elder Tafts in Washington for Christmas, 1925, and the failing Chief Justice sat happily by the Christmas tree with small Helen on his knee. He was always at home with children and in spite of his size he did not overawe them. Charlie and Eleanor spent this Christmas with their children at the Chase home in Waterbury. With one handsome child following another through Bob, Helen, and Charlie, the Taft grandparents now looked forward to such events with special joy.

Soon after this the Chief Justice was asked to write his memoirs but he declined. Early in 1926 he had a relapse and he did not feel equal to the effort; moreover, he felt that his position on the bench set a book of this kind beyond the pale of consideration. Once he had counted on Gus Karger being his biographer but Gus was dead. In the end Henry F. Pringle performed this task, and his book *The Life and Times of William Howard Taft* was published in 1939.

CHAPTER 24

GENTLEMEN OF
THE COURT

ASIDE FROM HIS FAILING HEALTH, Chief Justice Taft was finding great contentment on the Supreme Court bench. Under his directing hand the justices had become a more genial and good-tempered group in spite of the increased pace of their work. By this time he understood the gifts, idiosyncracies, and humanity of his colleagues, and he had learned to apportion cases to those he thought could handle them best. Both Holmes and McReynolds kept their opinions short and Taft thought that Holmes gave special piquancy and character to his by sententious phrases. He acknowledged to his children that his own opinions ran too long, even though he tried to restrain this tendency. But he believed that the bar did not always appreciate the brief opinion, preferring the old-time method of quoting lavishly from early authorities. This suggested that more homework had been done on their cases.

Henry L. Stoddard, who had studied a number of Presidents, considered Taft as surefooted on the Supreme Court as he had been blundering in the political field. William Allen White took a fresh look at him and described him in this role as "one of the high gods of the world, a smiling Buddha, placid, wise, gentle, sweet and noble as a man may be in this poor, worm-eaten earth." His own values were most akin to those of Justices Willis Van Devanter, Pierce Butler, George Sutherland, and James C. McReynolds. But he often struck out with complete independence, as when he wrote a much discussed dissent in favor of upholding a minimum-wage statute. In general he viewed the use of federal power over commerce in a broad way.

The aging gentlemen on the bench were somewhat competitive about their staying power. Taft's worldly sense and academic interests made him responsive to the ways of Oliver Wendell Holmes, who was determined to outmatch Chief Justice Roger B. Taney in the length of his service. His predecessor had lived to be eighty-seven and had presided to the end. As each year passed Holmes embarked on every new case with gusto and gloried in his youthful vigor. The Chief Justice marveled at his colleague's mental acumen and his power for rapid work. "I am very fond of him and he certainly adds to the interest of the Court," he wrote to Helen. "I often don't agree with him but he has been so long on the Court, and I have had sufficient judicial experience to realize that differences of that kind make no difference in our kindly and fraternal relations." The two jolly gentlemen of the court compared notes on their reading and Justice Holmes would recommend *Leave it to Psmith* and *The Greek Commonwealth* in the same breath. Both enjoyed Wodehouse.

Taft thought that Holmes's age made him more subordinate and yielding to Brandeis, his constant companion, than he would have been in his prime. Their dissents ran a parallel course, and the Chief Justice disliked dissents. In working with him Taft had come to like and admire Brandeis, although he usually differed from him in the field of social economics. He had once called this powerful and original thinker a "muckraker and emotionalist" but now he found him his ally in such vital matters as speeding up the work of the courts. Brandeis was a hard worker who wished the Court to be consistent and strong, and Taft thought that he "pulled his weight in the boat." Brandeis, who had said of Taft that he was a "first-rate second-rate thinker," in the end acknowledged that he could reason with the Chief Justice because he had an open mind. He conceded that Taft was able at reconciling the more obstinate elements in the Court. "The judges go home less tired emotionally and less weary physically than in White's day," Brandeis conceded. "When we differ we agree to differ without any ill-feeling. It's all very friendly."

The two jurists, who had contacts outside the court, were close neighbors and Taft was always touched by Brandeis's devotion to his invalid wife. He never failed to send them yellow roses on anniversaries. All the members of the Supreme Court were pleased when the Chief Justice's salary was raised from $15,000 to $20,500 and theirs from $14,500 to $20,000 in 1926.

Taft wrote freely but with discretion to his daughter Helen about his judicial work. Fred was thinking of taking up law and he was encouraging him in this purpose. On October 24, 1926, Taft informed Helen that next day he would deliver one of the most important opinions he had ever written. It concerned the power of the President to remove executive officers without the consent of the Senate. For years he had been pointing out in his lectures that Congress had exceeded its legislative discretion in the Tenure of Office Act and that it dated back to partisan anger against Andrew Johnson when he removed Edwin Stanton from the War Department. Taft's opinion in this instance was unmercifully long—fifty-five pages. McReynolds, who dissented, had prepared forty-nine pages and Brandeis, also dissenting, thirty-two. Holmes managed to dissent in five lines. The vote was six to three.

Taft's evaluation of his other colleagues varied. He thought that Justice Sutherland worked fast and well. Justice Van Devanter, often his mainstay, wrote fine opinions but was slow and turned out too few. Justice Joseph McKenna was pugnacious and was apt to make up his mind on what Taft called the impressionist principle. To the Chief Justice he was a "Cubist on the bench," a man given to foggy language. He found Justice McReynolds able, grouchy, and full of prejudice.

After his relapse at the beginning of 1926 the Chief Justice acknowledged that he no longer worked as fast on his own opinions as he had done in the past. He was suffering from kidney stones as well as from heart trouble and his powers were waning. Some months later he wrote to his daughter that he could no longer assemble his thoughts as readily as he should. In this letter, dated February 20, 1927, he summed up his own way of working:

> The framing of an opinion is always for me the most important part of the work. The array of your facts and the sequence of your statement of principles and the strategy of the opinion, if I may call it such, devoted to stating the facts with fairness but with force, usually consume the greatest time with me, and it seems to me that it takes longer now than it used to, but I don't wish to express the view that I am discouraged. I suppose others have the same difficulty.

Taft's one final ambition was to have a building put up that would be worthy of the Supreme Court. This entailed a long fight, with Holmes, McReynolds, Brandeis, and Sutherland opposing the plan. "I beat them five to four," he finally wrote to Helen. "My predecessors had always been against it but I think the present opponents are beginning to see how shortsighted their policy has been." Congress appropriated $1,500,-000 to buy the lot he had chosen and Cass Gilbert drew up plans for the building. "What I am praying for is that I can live and be on the court until we can move in," Taft wrote to his daughter on February 27, 1927. But this was not to be, although he functioned faithfully on the bench as long as he could. In the long run Senator Reed Smoot of Utah led the congressional fight for the ornate building to which the Supreme Court moved from a room in the Capitol. But the marble pile remains the most visible memorial to William Howard Taft in the capital.

The heat was extreme in the summer of 1927 and Taft could not sleep, but Justice Holmes would arrive in court like a fresh breeze in the morning and announce jubilantly that he had slept until 8 o'clock under a blanket. "He ought to live in the tropics," the Chief Justice commented. He was half-amused and half-annoyed by the old man's buoyancy; it happened to be his own fate always to feel heat intensely. Mrs. Taft was having their house done over with an eye to her husband's comfort, and an elevator now took him upstairs to his bedroom. She had brought up old treasures from the cellar that Louise had bought in Vienna, including one of the brass chandeliers with glass crystals that matched the one given to Annie. Nellie had it fitted with electric lights and the Chief Justice thought it magnificent. He teased his wife gently on her endless supply of silver for wedding presents, dating back to the flood of gifts that had reached them on their anniversary. They had few dinner parties now because of the jurist's health. Although Mrs. Taft still went to the theater when she could, for the most part she spent her evenings with Will in his new study. There they read for an hour or two before going to bed and they talked often of the old Cincinnati days. The death of her early friend, Alice Keyes Hollister, saddened Nellie in the spring of 1927.

Bob's family visited them on their way to Europe that summer. The small boys were taken to the Supreme Court where young Billie donned his grandfather's robes and sat on the bench when the Court was not in session. They visited the zoo, the parks, and the Lincoln Memorial, the Capitol and the White House. Their grandfather wished to fix this visit in their minds but they were in no danger of forgetting it, because they sailed on the day that Charles A. Lindbergh made his sensational trans-Atlantic flight. Bobbie, the future congressman, and his brother Billie were indignant because they had to carry their small brothers' kiddie cars from point to point, but Lloyd and Horace got plenty of mileage out of the little cars, whizzing around the decks of an ocean liner.

After a month of sightseeing in Paris they went to St. Jean-de-Luz, the Basque resort greatly favored by Martha. This proved to be the first of many trips made by the Robert Taft family. They went abroad again

in 1929, touring Italy, Austria, Germany, and Great Britain. In 1937
Mrs. Taft went to Scandinavia and in 1939 to Brittany. In 1949 she flew
over the Atlantic for the first time, to visit her son Bill in his Georgian
house outside Dublin. The Senator was too busy to accompany his family
on their later trips but he took two of his sons to the Chicago Exposition
in 1934.

Eleanor stayed with Charles in Cincinnati through the summer of
1927. She did not mind the heat and the children had their own swimming pool. The Charter Committee had asked Charlie to run for the
office of prosecuting attorney for the county and he had won. He was
now dealing with criminals, a new phase in Taft legal history. But he got
more than he bargained for in prosecuting George Remus, a powerful
bootlegger who had killed his wife, Imogene, in October, 1927. Remus
pleaded insanity and there was melodrama in the courtroom. Charlie
was faced with experienced lawyers and as one Cincinnati colleague observed: "To be a good prosecutor you've got to believe in punishment.
You've got to be a killer. Charlie isn't a killer."

Just before Christmas the Chief Justice, greatly interested in his son's
plunge into criminal law, wrote to Russell Wilson that Charlie apparently was born for publicity. "He is up against it now," he added. The
jurors found Remus insane. They had a champagne celebration over the
verdict in the courthouse corridors and the defendant was freed after six
months in an asylum. Taft feared for Charlie's life when word seeped
through from the underworld that Remus would kill him and the man
charged with being the dead woman's lover. He warned his son to take
precautions and he was outraged by the court procedure in this case.
Charlie was defeated for re-election as prosecuting attorney and in the
spring of 1928 he became attorney for the Amalgamated Clothing Workers of America. In May he and Eleanor had another daughter, Cynthia,
bringing the number of Taft grandchildren to eleven.

That same month Horace was in Washington, staying with Will, and
he visited the White House. His brother commented ironically after he
had paid his call: "I have no doubt you had a most informative conversation with President Coolidge. He is always full of information and
most anxious to impart it." Horace's worries about his school finances
had been somewhat allayed by this time. The Taft School had been
turned over to fifteen trustees, to be run as a non-profit institution. A two-
million-dollar endowment had been raised, to which Edward S. Harkness
contributed $500,000 and Mr. and Mrs. Charles Phelps Taft—who had
helped Horace from the start—another $300,000. Mrs. William Rocke-
feller had given the school an athletic field shortly after the Armistice
was signed.

The Coolidge days in the White House were coming to an end. Herbert Hoover had been nominated and Bob was deeply involved in his campaign. Martha organized the Hoover Woman's Committee in Cincinnati and worked hard for the man she had come to know well and to admire. The Chief Justice wrote to Horace that he thought Hoover would get the support of the women of the country, and this would represent a formidable vote. But one feminine member of the Taft family who worked industriously for his opponent, Alfred E. Smith, was Julia. Fred Manning also cast his vote that year for the Democratic candidate. Taft observed with surprise that his brother Harry was not particularly enthusiastic about Hoover as a candidate. The Chief Justice wrote to Helen that the New York capitalists and Wall Street men seemed not to favor him, but he did not consider this a good reason for failing to back Hoover. Taft was one of those who had expected the Republican convention to turn to Coolidge in spite of his famous "I do not choose to run" declaration. But when Hoover was named Taft predicted that he would make an excellent President. He considered the candidate a man of force and courage, with great powers of organization. Hoover also interested him as a widely traveled and scholarly man, and he appreciated the small human touches, like the occasion when the future angler of the White House sent him trout he had caught in a Pennsylvania stream on a spring day in 1928. Always interested in the nation's First Ladies, Taft found Mrs. Hoover a woman of charm.

Mrs. Boardman died that spring and the Chief Justice was an honorary pallbearer at her funeral. He wrote to Mabel that he had known her mother when he visited Cleveland half a century earlier and had always found her "encouraging, sympathetic, helpful, overflowing with hospitality." The house where the Chief Justice had spent so many pleasant evenings had been left to Mabel by her father. Her sisters, Mrs. Murray Crane and Mrs. Florence Keep, had independent means. In Cincinnati Charles, now eighty-four years old, fell desperately ill and the Chief Justice had to hurry west. Louise Semple was abroad but Jane Ingalls was hastily summoned from Cleveland. Annie, still sorrowing over her little grandson, Charles Semple, who had died of asthma in Florida three months earlier, was inconsolable when Charles collapsed. Will, believing that he was dying, wrote to Helen about him with the utmost affection:

> He has lived to a great age and has done great good in his life, and he will leave a remarkable record. What he has done for me I can hardly overstate, and his loyalty to the entire family has been intense. It was almost the strongest feeling he had. I don't know what poor Annie will do, and there have been so many who have felt the touch of his generous feeling that grief will come to a host.

But Charles had a brief resurgence of strength at Murray Bay that summer and Will and he rested on the porch and talked of days gone by. Both men knew that their days were running short. Will had attended the Yale commencement, his fiftieth and last. He had never ceased to back his college, to help raise funds for it, to give it his undivided loyalty, and he had attended all but three of his class reunions.

There were new bells at the Murray Bay church that year and the *habitants* noticed that *Le Petit Juge* and his brother Charles moved slowly to answer them. The children went about in a Dodge station wagon and the walls of Sassifern Cottage were constantly being adorned with new pictures of them at various stages in their development. Helen had added a study to her house and her father was having his own cottage re-roofed. On his return to Cincinnati Charles resumed his visits to the *Times-Star* offices and took long drives in the country. "I think it is wonderful how that Murray Bay trip revived him," Will noted, but the fine air could no longer do much for either of them. Bob was asked by his father at this time if he wished to go on the bench but the successful young lawyer had other ideas. He had enjoyed his legislative experience in Columbus and it was clear to the Chief Justice that he was thinking in terms of Congress or the Senate.

The downpour at the Hoover inauguration reminded Taft of the wild day twenty years earlier on which he had been sworn in. He thought well of Hoover's Cabinet appointments and all the Tafts were interested in the choice of David Sinton Ingalls as assistant secretary of the Navy for aeronautics. F. Trubee Davison had suggested him for this post, since Ingalls had distinguished himself as a flier in World War I. He had trained in England and flown with a scout squadron of the Royal Naval Air Service while the American naval air services were being organized in France. Ingalls shot down a number of enemy planes and was the first aviator to receive the Flying Cross. After the war he resumed his studies at Yale and then attended Harvard Law School. In 1922 he married Louise Hale Harkness, of the Standard Oil family, and in the following year became a partner in a well-known Cleveland law firm. Ingalls, who was born in 1899, was descended from Edmund Ingalls, a Lincolnshire man who moved to Salem in 1628. When Albert Ingalls married Jane, the daughter of Mr. and Mrs. Charles Phelps Taft, another early American strain was introduced into the Taft family.

Ingalls became an important figure in the swift development of aeronautics during President Hoover's administration. From the beginning of his term the new President was heading into a storm. As early as March, 1929, Taft felt the shadow of the approaching depression. He wrote to Helen, then acting president of Bryn Mawr, about investments he had made for her: "I have no doubt we must expect a depression

and a change from the present very prosperous condition in these stocks."
He wished to know how his daughter's finances stood. Her mother's
Kennicott copper stock and his own Otis Elevator stock were doing
well. Mrs. Taft was sixty-eight that summer and he took affectionate delight in her good health and the active life she led. He wrote about her
to Helen on June 2, 1929:

> She is youthful and she is very active, and her figure is such as to make
> some of the younger dames a little impatient about it. She goes without
> hesitation everywhere, accepts all the invitations that she wishes to ac-
> cept, goes out at night when there is anything that is attractive to her,
> and apparently is encouraged to face any exigency, with Tom on the
> box ready to serve her purpose. She is as impatient with Tom and with
> Annie as usual, but takes it out in scolding me, which is an entirely
> safe way of doing things.

When Mrs. Taft gave a reception for the Colonial Dames they came in
great numbers and "I had to get back into my White House manner,"
the former President jested. Although now exhausted most of the time,
and greatly troubled by his gout, his good nature still prevailed. Every
Saturday he drove to a circulating library to pick up detective stories
that Nellie and he might both enjoy. In June he went to Cincinnati but
he would never take an airplane "lest he capsize it." He visited his two
sons in the offices of Taft, Stettinius & Hollister and found them with a
corps of assistants. Charlie had just returned from California where he
had attended a Y.M.C.A. convention, and his father could see that he
was getting a considerable reputation in the social service field. The boys'
law business was in good order and their father reported to Helen:
"What with your uncle Charley's business and the Emery business and
Mary Hanna's business and the new railroad depot terminal, they need
all the force they can get." Among their clients in the 1930's were the
P. Lorillard Company, the R. J. Reynolds Tobacco Company, the Cincinnati *Times-Star* Company, and the Dixie Terminal Company. Bob
was handling Annie's finances with dexterity and had saved her $100,000
in taxes in the spring of 1929. The Emery estate was a business in itself.
Mrs. Thomas Emery, who had survived her husband by twenty-one
years, died in 1927 at the age of eighty-three. Her benefactions were legendary. She gave a $3,500,000 collection of paintings to the Art Museum
and built Mariemont, a model suburb for people of modest means. She
had long lived on Indian Hill and was closely associated with the Robert
Tafts.

The Chief Justice was relieved that Charlie had moved into this
abundant field. He had not considered the prosecutor's role the ideal
one for his brilliant younger son. He toured the city with Charlie, who

wished to draw his attention to civic improvements in Cincinnati. Taft was struck by the cleanliness of the streets, the freshly painted houses, the good pavements, the improved lighting. It looked almost like another city and young Charlie was proud of the changes that had been wrought. But the terminal was not yet completed and Mill Creek was just as dirty as ever, the Chief Justice observed.

As always, he stayed in the Pike Street house, which now had an elevator that made things easier for him. He was saddened to see how depressed Annie was over the trips she made to Rhode Island with Annie O'Gara to visit her son Howard in his sanitarium. Taft had his last round of visits with all his relatives in Cincinnati. He called on Maria, then living in the Phelps apartments, surrounded by the treasures she had picked up on her travels. He visited Louise and Will Semple in the pleasant little house they had, with a barn adjoining. He went out to Indian Hill and lunched with Bob, Charlie, and Hulbert. Each trip west, he now felt, might be his last.

Six months later, in January, 1930, he had to return once more, this time for the funeral of Charles who had died on the first day of the year. He had been unconscious for three days, suffering from pneumonia. Annie clung to him to the end, determined not to let him die, but Charles, worn-out and emaciated, slipped away with his immediate family gathered around his bed. At the end he was recognized as an internationally known publisher and philanthropist, a quiet man who had helped to spread the fame of Cincinnati. For half a century artists, writers, musicians, world statesmen, jurists and diplomats, royalty and struggling poets, had dined at his board. William Howard Taft had made his acceptance speech from his porch, and other high points of his career were associated with the Pike Street house. King Albert of Belgium, Cardinal Mercier, and Eugène Ysaye had been recent guests. They joined the ranks of prominent figures who had visited the house before the Tafts owned it—from Robert Owen and Mrs. Frances Trollope to President William Henry Harrison.

The Chief Justice was shaken by Charles's death. He remembered that "nothing ever diminished the ardour and enthusiasm of his loyalty to the family and every member of it." On his return from Cincinnati he became so ill himself that he was taken to Garfield Hospital for treatment and from there went to Asheville with Mrs. Taft for a rest. Late in January President Hoover was notified that unless he soon showed improvement the Chief Justice would resign from the Court. Robert delivered his father's resignation on February 3, 1930, and Charles Evans Hughes was appointed to succeed him. It was thought at first that Taft might linger for months but he became steadily weaker. The President and his fellow Justices called to see him, and saw that his splendid mind was failing. Horace had thought him as alert as usual on the day after Charles's funeral, but he declined rapidly after that and Nellie was informed by his physicians that the end was close at hand. "It is like some sturdy oak tottering," Mischler wrote in agony of spirit when Taft could no longer focus his attention on a given point. But he seemed to listen when a last message was read to him from his colleagues of the Supreme Court. It was composed by Justice Holmes, who wrote of his voluminous capacity for getting work done, his humor that smoothed the tough places, his golden heart that brought him love from every side, and the tasks that he had made happy and light. The Chief Justice feebly signed the reply that was drafted for him. "Only the advice of my doctors and my own conviction that I would be unable to continue adequately the great work of the court, forced me to leave you," it ran. The worker, the humanitarian, the understanding judge, had come to the end of the road. He died in a coma on the afternoon of March 8, 1930. Taft was seventy-two and the day of his death was also the eighty-ninth birthday of Oliver Wendell Holmes, who lived to be ninety-four and retired from the bench only three years before his end.

President Hoover was out driving when the Chief Justice died. He hurried at once to the house on Wyoming Avenue and later issued a proclamation:

> Mr. Taft's service to our country has been of rare distinction and was marked by a purity of patriotism, a lofty disinterestedness, and a devotion to the best interests of the nation that deserve and will ever command the grateful memory of his countrymen. . . . His private life was characterized by a simplicity of virtue that won for him a place in the affection of his fellow countrymen rarely equaled by any man. In public and in private life he set a shining example, and his death will be mourned throughout the land.

Troops followed the caisson that bore the coffin from the Taft house to the Capitol where the former President lay in state for several hours. A simple service was held at All Souls Church, where he had always worshiped. Two of his favorite hymns "Lead Kindly Light" and "Abide with Me," were sung, and Dr. Pierce read Wordsworth's "Happy Warrior" and Tennyson's "Ode on the Death of the Duke of Wellington." He was buried in Arlington National Cemetery, near the summit of the long sloping hillside and close to the grave of Robert Todd Lincoln. He was the only President to be buried at Arlington until the death of John F. Kennedy in 1963.

The long companionship of the years had ended for Nellie. Messages rained in on the Taft family from around the world. The President and Fellows of Yale University adopted a resolution: "Greatly loving he was greatly loved. . . . We shall remember him always. We shall love him always. We shall always be the better for what he was." His friends in the Philippines remembered Governor Taft, naming a town for him on the east coast of Samar. The Taft Memorial Bridge connecting Malacanan with Taft Avenue was a tribute to him. And in Murray Bay where Taft the man, rather than Taft the public figure, was much beloved, a memorial service was conducted in the stone church by the Reverend Dr. F. J. Moore, who recalled him as a familiar figure on the village street, a genial companion on the links, a witty member at a party, a gracious host in his own home.

Le petit Juge was lost to Murray Bay, as to the larger world. His opinions would continue to be quoted in the courts when his political speeches were long forgotten. He had lived to see the crash of 1929 and the end of the golden days in which he had flourished. The second generation of notable Tafts was passing. The third was in the ascendant as Bob and Charlie each moved forward in his own particular way. But a year later Annie, who had never recovered from the loss of Charles, died suddenly and was buried at Spring Grove on a February day in 1931. The Art Museum and Eden Park were closed for her funeral and the Symphony Orchestra, which she had nursed with ceaseless devotion, added Richard Strauss's *Death and Transfiguration* to the regular program in honor of their patron saint. The men of the *Times-Star* composing room drew up a resolution that they would ever be mindful of the "high plane on which she strove to place our community in music, education and the fine arts."

She had been a familiar figure at the office on election nights, when big news was breaking, or when she was especially interested in some cause. In recent years she had been a little lost in the world of the deaf, but for four decades she had contributed much to the gaiety and advancement of her native city. Annie had always resisted shifting her focus to Washington or New York. She was a flower of native growth, potent, wilful, original. With her pink cheeks and white hair, a velvet ribbon with a cameo around her throat, and her emeralds sparkling against her warm-toned velvet gowns, she was remembered by many as they had seen her moving about at her musicales and parties. It had been her habit to toss out Celtic quips under the shadow of her Rembrandts, her eyes keen, her fan waving as she talked. Her witty, free spirit was legendary in Cincinnati—like her cuisine, her champagne, her art collection. In her last years she drove around, ramrod-straight in her car, with a high-boned collar and large hat, appraising the look of the Queen City as its hills sparkled with life, tall new buildings went up, and business flowed swiftly in its downtown streets. She knew its history as few did, and much that had happened behind the scenes. The Taft impress was visible on all sides. The list of their benefactions told its own story when Mr. and Mrs. Charles Phelps Taft died, although they had been dispensing large sums of money for a lifetime.

They gave $1,000,000 to the Cincinnati Symphony Orchestra and Annie left $2,000,000 to the University of Cincinnati in memory of her husband. Characteristically she wrote that she wished to endow the study of the humanities, particularly literature and language, philosophy and history. Without wishing to lessen or regard lightly the material and physical betterment of mankind to which large funds were being devoted, she felt that there was a lack of emphasis on the value of thought, conduct, and character, and so she wished her own bequest to be used toward this end.

"What finer memorial could anyone have than that?" the Cleveland News commented. It was in keeping with the history of the Tafts.

Charles had given the Alphonso Taft Hall to the university in memory of his father. Here William Howard Taft studied and taught law, and he was present for the opening of the memorial building in 1925. The interests of the Charles Phelps Tafts had a catholic range. From time to time Charles made substantial gifts to Yale, Princeton, Harvard, Johns Hopkins University, and the Hebrew Union College of Cincinnati. The Charles Phelps Taft Hall at Yale was named in his honor as well as a building at the Taft School. He served for seventeen years on the Union Board of High Schools of Cincinnati and from 1900 to 1902 was a member of the board of directors of the Associated Press. Charles held stock in many Cincinnati public service corporations, utilities, and transportation companies.

Mrs. Taft established the Anna Louise Home for girls with small earnings and she endowed Sinton Park. The May Festival and summer operas owed their existence largely to the two Tafts. With Mrs. Emery they saved the Zoological Garden from extinction. The Taft Auditorium, used as a theater, was named for Charles Phelps Taft, who helped to finance it. Bob acted as legal adviser for his uncle and aunt in pushing through a large-scale plan designed to promote all the arts in Cincinnati. In 1927 they had given their house, the land on which it stood, the art it contained, and $1,000,000 if another $2,500,000 could be raised. Thus the Cincinnati Institute of Fine Arts was formed and was dedicated in 1932, when both Mr. and Mrs. Taft were dead.

The Taft Museum was opened as part of the institute and soon the public was flocking through the rooms in which Charles and Annie had given so many notable entertainments. Duncan Phyfe pieces were introduced to preserve the spirit of the past, and reproductions of the original carpets were used. The rooms were not roped off, museum-fashion, but visitors wandered at will through one of the most distinguished small museums of the twentieth century, with Miss Katherine Hanna as its director. Raimundo de Madrazo's paintings of Mr. and Mrs. Charles Phelps Taft and Joaquín Sorolla's of William Howard Taft hung with Gainsborough's "Maria Walpole." Van Dyck's "Paolina Adorono," Reynolds's "Mrs. Weyland and her son John," Turner's "Old London Bridge," and other works of art. Hiram Powers's bust of David Sinton was another family touch in this unique museum. The collection of Chinese vases and porcelains of the K'ang Hsi and Ch'ien Lung periods and an important assemblage of Renaissance enamel plaques and dishes, jewelry and watches, represented years of discriminating buying by Mr. and Mrs. Taft.

In the restoration of the mansion all the original woodwork remained intact, except the mantels and chair rails. Old frescoes on the walls were uncovered and it was found that some of the ceilings retained the original plaster ornamentation of classical moldings, acanthus leaves, and eagles. The garden, laced with paths and picturesque with shrubs as in the days of Longworth, was dedicated in 1949 as a memorial to the men and women who served in World War II.

For many years before the deaths of Charles and Annie, Hulbert Taft was a potent force at the *Times-Star*, yielding great influence in the Middle West through the family newspaper. He had joined the staff at the turn of the century as a young reporter fresh from Yale and had worked his way up to being editor and chairman of the board of directors. He was in executive control although his aunt and uncle continued to go to the office, advise on editorial policy, and play a large role in running the family paper. Hulbert became both editor and publisher after Charles's death.

A lean, quiet, unassuming man, Hulbert Taft was described by John Gunther in *Inside U.S.A.* as the most conservative man he had encountered in forty-eight states. His conservatism was interpreted by some as solid dependability and he was unquestionably a master of his own craft. Hulbert was a man of many interests, a student of world history, who had traveled widely and covered every type of story from local politics in Cincinnati to interviews and political developments abroad. In 1929 he talked to Mussolini in Rome and noted that "liberty in the American sense does not exist here." Later in Mexico City he interviewed Trotsky, the Russian revolutionist exiled by Stalin. In 1954 Roy Howard wrote to Hulbert Taft that no single competitor had more unfailingly demonstrated E. W. Scripps's belief that journalism was a gentleman's game. He added: "I would like to say that never in my newspaper experience have I encountered a competitor who, over the years, gave me a more complete feeling of confidence in his word, who demonstrated greater sportsmanship in his competitive activities, or for whose integrity I developed greater respect than that which runs to you."

Hulbert Taft was deeply loyal to his employees. No one was laid off during the depression and he fought the decision to sell the papers to the Scripps-Howard chain in 1958. He had remained chairman of the board of directors up to that time and he died in the following year. In 1954 a bronze plaque was unveiled in the lobby of the *Times-Star* building to mark his fifty-fifth anniversary. Like his uncle Charles he supported civic, business, and cultural projects. He worked for smoke abatement and the purification of the Ohio River, for retail trade expansion, industrial growth, and the building of new schools. He was a familiar first-nighter at the opera, and he gave support to the May Festival, the Symphony Orchestra, the Taft Museum, and the Institute of Fine Arts.

He was a prominent figure in the world of sport, going in for horses and dogs and appearing often at the race tracks. As president of the Cincinnati Riding Club, and chairman of the Cincinnati Charity Horse Show, he was closely identified with sports events in his native city. His hobby was photography and he took striking shots as he traveled. After his first wife, Nellie Leamon, died of cancer in 1927, Hulbert married Virginia Kittredge. She died in 1942 and four years later he married the beautiful Eleanor L. Gholson, a well-known Cincinnatian. Hulbert had four children by his first wife.

The Robert Tafts and the Hulbert Tafts were neighbors and close friends on Indian Hill. Although the region was rustic when they settled there large estates were soon carved out of twenty square miles of land, looped together with forty-two miles of smooth roads. Where the Miamis, Shawnees, and Delawares had established villages J. J. Emery, Julius Fleischmann, Stanley M. Rowe, Hulbert Taft, and others built up a unique community. Soon there were only hares in the thickets where wolves, panthers, bears, and even buffalo had once roamed. Robert and Hulbert Taft had much to do with the modernization of Indian Hill. Bob agitated for electricity in 1919. The Camargo Country Club, where they all golfed, was organized in 1925 and the village itself was incorporated in the late 1930's. A fire department, a country day school, tennis courts, bridle paths, and baseball diamonds followed. At the same time every effort was made to keep Indian Hill a region of gardens and woods, fields and pastures. In 1942 the population was nearly 2,000. By 1962 there were 4,800 residents, occupying 1,240 houses. The community had grown two and a half times in twenty years, and the Taft name was closely linked with its development and fame.

CHAPTER 25

MR. REPUBLICAN

W ITHIN A DECADE of his father's death Robert Alphonso Taft had moved with momentum into the national picture. He emerged at a significant moment in American history. The social order was being turned upside down in the great upheaval of the New Deal. Strong, resistant, a conservative and fighter, he stood firm on major issues and breasted the abuse that followed. As a freshman senator in 1939 he lashed out, made headlines, and became a thorn in the flesh of Franklin D. Roosevelt. Taft's leadership was so decisive, his attacks so sharply pinpointed, that he quickly became the unchallenged leader of the opposition. Within a year he was viewed as a presidential possibility. After titanic battles and three tries for the White House he had won the respect of friend and foe and eventually was enshrined on the national scene as Mr. Republican. To his grandchildren he was a quiet and kindly gentleman whom they knew as GOP.

In 1938 he was little known outside Ohio except for the name Taft, which carried weight. When he ran for the Senate against Robert J. Bulkley, who was backed by Roosevelt, he defeated him by a large majority. Martha joined forces with him and they were soon known as the whirlwind team of Bob and Martha. She had campaigned with him for Alfred M. Landon. Why not for her own Bob? she asked. Singly and together they covered 50,000 miles and made roughly a thousand speeches in eighty-seven counties. Martha had been studying public affairs for years. Politics and law were in her blood. She gave the campaign the verve and wit that her husband lacked as he battled in the primaries and then on the national ticket. A series of radio debates with a smooth New Dealer was the clinching touch. Here Taft's skill with facts, his sharp thrusts, his political sophistication, all told.

The Senator's rise was laborious and hard fought. He had worked extraordinarily hard all his life, from ringing doorbells in Cincinnati in the early days to the most grueling cross-country campaigning and high-powered mental effort on involved financial issues. He had slaved on tax revision for six years in Ohio. Those who watched his useful service during three terms in the House of Representatives and a later term in the Ohio State Senate foresaw that he was headed for Washington. The political inheritance had flowed direct from Alphonso Taft to William Howard Taft and then to young Robert, but he had more concentrated drive and ambition than any other Taft.

His father's career had been shaped by the accidents of fate. William Howard Taft was the first to acknowledge that one opportunity after another had come to him without any effort on his part. His genial spirit had helped to pave the way to fame. But observers felt that Bob had shaped his own destiny, chosen high goals, and worked relentlessly to achieve them. He was always more the politician than his father, more forceful, more decisive, more effective in action; yet to many he seemed a man of severe limitations, an unbending zealot when he championed a cause. Only his intimates knew how intensely he suffered when he met with defeat. Even as a boy he had wept when worsted in a game or when his father was outplayed on the golf course. Bob longed for the Presidency as ardently as his father had hankered for a place on the Supreme Court bench, but he kept an iron grip on himself through three defeats.

When Herbert Hoover was President he might have had one of several appointments on the national scene but he stuck close to Ohio until he felt he was thoroughly prepared for national politics. "One with a family name has a lot to live up to," he observed when he finally moved to Washington, a newcomer whose high voltage was apparent to none in the beginning. When he walked into the Capitol to take his seat a touch of provincialism seemed to envelop him. Actually he was widely traveled; he had conferred with world leaders, and he was as familiar with the White House and the ways of government as a man could be. But Helen Manning, who understood him better than most, pointed out that he was forty-nine and in the Senate before he had full confidence in himself or made friends with ease. The rawboned effect was the essence of the man. It was part of his strength and his sincerity.

Bob was indifferent to what he wore or how he looked. His tall figure was beginning to show the aldermanic tendency that his experienced father had detected. His light brown hair, thinning at this time, was brushed to cover his scalp and sometimes had a straggly look. His large gray eyes, behind rimless glasses, could be icy, aloof, or full of thoughtful interest. Sometimes his brooding stare was disconcerting to his opponents, but his friends could find warmth and humor in it. The dry wit that underlay Taft's austere manner delighted his intimates but flashed out only rarely in public. However, both friends and foes found his wide and bashful grin disarming. He had a way of sprawling in his chair, with his glasses dangling from one ear, while he bluntly voiced his views. He never hesitated to grapple boldly with a difficult issue and the force behind his diffident manner was soon recognized by his fellow senators. In course of time everyone knew what he stood for, and that he would fight for his convictions.

A major disaster in speechmaking came early in his Washington career when he appeared without preparation before the Gridiron Club, one of the most critical audiences in the world. He had not gauged the importance of the occasion and his dull and inept talk left the baffled correspondents dubious about the qualities of the new senator from Ohio. Thomas E. Dewey, on the other hand, fashioned his arguments precisely to the shrewd audience he faced. But Bob did not repeat this mistake. In his conscientious way he practiced his speeches after that, drilling himself in inflection and emphasis, and working hard to overcome the fact that he was no charmer. His voice on the air was harsh but he did well on television, a medium that seemed to reflect his sincerity. After he had pitched his tones as instructed and worn the colors suggested he would ask one question: "Did they get what I was talking about?" He was always a provocative subject for comment by the press and in general the reporters liked him. Radical writers who sniped at him ceaselessly in the early years gave him grudging admiration at the end. Martha, with her wit and charm, inevitably made news. Helen recognized the effect that she had on Bob's political fortunes but, unlike their mother in the case of William Howard Taft, she did not make any of the family decisions when it came to politics. As Helen put it:

> Before Bob decides any question he consults all the available authorities and his wife is only one of them. Any person who ever overheard political arguments between Bob and Martha—arguments which she often lost—would never charge that Bob Taft hasn't a mind of his own. However, Bob is not so adamant that he isn't quick to admit that

he was wrong when conditions change or when further search proves
that his judgment of the facts was incorrect. He has proved that in his
political career.

In this statement his sister pointed straight at one of the fundamentals
of Robert Taft's character and history—his willingness to concede a
point when he was proved wrong, or had responded to persuasion. He
may have lacked magnetism but he was never at a loss for the essential
fact, and she understood why his fellow senators soon turned to him instinctively in matters involving labor, industry, housing, and education.
He could disentangle the complexities of federal finance and taxes, foreign trade and tariff issues, faster than anyone on the floor. Helen attributed this to his early love of mathematics. She had often listened to him
at Murray Bay, hoping to catch the drift of his monumental revision of
the Ohio tax system. In general she believed that his sincerity and honesty were misunderstood in the political world. Actually she differed from
him herself on many issues for Helen was always liberal in her outlook.
But time and again she saw his factual, persistent drive take effect, and
whether or not she agreed with him she always loved Bob and believed
in him. When asked by friends why she did not tell him when she
thought he was in the wrong, Helen would mildly reply: "He wouldn't
pay any attention to me."

By her own admission she was one of the most surprised persons in
the country when it became clear that Bob wished to be President. His
Ohio friends had helped to talk him into it. So had Alice Longworth.
His mother was invited to attend the Republican convention of 1940
and Helen went with her. Having lived through the presidential years
with her husband, Mrs. Taft had never expressed the wish that one of
her sons should run for this office. But when she learned that Bob
yearned for the White House she was solidly behind him. Some of her
old ambition revived and she wrote him earnest letters. In spite of the
usual family loyalty none of them really expected Bob to get the nomination on this occasion. Nevertheless, the stampede for Wendell L. Willkie
came as a great blow to the Tafts. On his way out of the hall Robert
said: "Never again!" When he ran the second time Helen again learned
of his intention from the newspapers, not from him. He did not discuss
this particular aspiration with her, knowing how she felt about the Presidency and believing that she could not be an unprejudiced witness.
Helen later said that had he asked her she would have advised him to do
as he thought best, since the Tafts all cherished independent opinions.

No one doubted that Bob would feel at home in the White House.
No other American family had more familiarity with the Executive
Mansion. Alphonso had first gone there in the time of Polk, and was

again a welcome guest at the family dinner table when Ulysses S. Grant was President. Mrs. William Howard Taft's family frequently visited the White House in the days of Benjamin Harrison and Rutherford Hayes. Bob, Helen and Charlie had come to know it well in the time of Theodore Roosevelt and had then lived in it as White House children. But Alice Longworth's ardent support of Bob in the early 1940's caused much comment. "A daughter of a Roosevelt has a different attitude toward the Presidency from that of a daughter of a Taft," wrote Helen, with a long backward view of her father's sufferings during his term of office. Alice went all-out for Bob in an article she wrote for the *Saturday Evening Post* of May 4, 1940, on "Why I am for Bob Taft."

> I am for Bob Taft because I do not yearn any longer for the man who is always on his toes, waving his hat, raising his voice, raring to go here, there, anywhere. I want one whose feet will be firmly on the ground and whose mind will be upon finding solutions for the national problems rather than in becoming the shining hero of the undiscriminating masses. Miss Columbia has had a long and giddy spell of being the girl friend of the whirling dervish. It's time she stopped revolving, chose another partner.

Alice went on to say that Bob Taft would lead Americans back to their old ways of self-reliance. She considered him singularly lacking in the wiles that came naturally to most politicians and she applauded the team of Taft and Taft, scoffing at the critics who believed voters would be antagonized by the spectacle of a candidate's wife backing him up on the platform. Alice thought that both had political sportsmanship. She cited the "wholesome, sane, serene character" of their family life, their unpretentious home, their way of staying out of the limelight that reminded her of their father. In the final analysis she said that if Taft were elected he would follow Franklin D. Roosevelt "like a glass of milk after a slug of benzedrine."

If he never became one of the great orators of the Senate, Taft was generally rated one of the most informed, persistent, and persuasive. History of a new order was being made as he hammered away at public spending. The era of internationalism had dawned in America and it was soon apparent that President Roosevelt and Senator Taft were poles apart in their philosophy and candid in their antagonism. On the domestic front the letter agencies were wearing thin and Taft quickly established himself as a voice calling for economy against an avalanche of public spending. "The New Deal has discovered the secret of perpetual emotion," he commented. Bob was a strong dissenter, a home-grown politician who had seen enough at Versailles to make him skeptical and wary of foreign entanglements. To some he seemed cold-blooded and a figure of granite as his mathematical mind focused on fiscal problems and he argued ceaselessly for a balanced budget.

Often misled on international issues, he ruefully admitted his errors and reversed himself when proved wrong. He was drastically mistaken in his predictions before Pearl Harbor and storms of criticism and the frost of disfavor enveloped Bob and Martha in the early 1940's when they were thought to be isolationist in their sympathies. Although three of the Taft sons were in service and a fourth was in military intelligence, the Senator voted against lend-lease, the transfer of destroyers to Britain, the arming of American merchant ships, and the draft—although he conceded the need for selective service and even for universal military training in time of war. He backed appropriations to build up the Army and Navy and stood behind most of the wartime measures.

Taft supported the United Nations Charter and indeed, as far back as 1943, had urged the formation of a worldwide organization of sovereign nations. But he brought his critical touch to bear on the charter, too, arguing that it was not based primarily on a system of law and the administration of justice, a foundation as essential to Robert as it had been to his father. Speaking before the Senate in behalf of ratification on July 28, 1945, he said:

> My father was one of the original supporters of the League to Enforce Peace, and of the League of Nations. While I was not then in politics myself, I always strongly supported his position. I always maintained that an international organization was the best method of reducing the danger of war.

However, the public as a whole found it difficult to view Robert Taft as an internationalist. In spite of the fact that his father had been so articulate on the subject, with a strong slant toward peace, arbitration, and international alliance, Robert could be stubbornly insular, an attitude that his supporters defined as strong Americanism. The Marshall Plan was one of the measures on which he reversed himself, opposing it at first, then voting for it, but believing that its bounty should taper off.

It was after the war, when Truman took office, that the real tussle began. Then Taft became an irritant as well as a force in public life. In course of time he was called an obstructionist, a moss-backed reactionary, a boring grind, the best nineteenth-century mind in the twentieth century, and the man who reached more wrong decisions more ably than any other figure in public life. The chorus in his favor was equally insistent. He was ever the advocate, where his father had been the judge. Taft was also one of the great dissenters, a tendency that William How-ard Taft had always deplored in his Supreme Court colleagues.

In spite of Bob's intense convictions he could compromise on legislation when the necessity arose, and he had some of his father's power of mediation when a basis could be found for common agreement. Facts alone swayed him, and he would listen to reason if not to the sentimental aspects of any given situation. He summed up his own history when he said: "A man who is always in favor of change is a radical. A man who always prefers existing institutions is a conservative, but either of them may be liberal or the reverse." By his own definition Taft considered himself a liberal in action but a conservative in general outlook and in particular problems, where he favored individual justice.

The Senator came to the fore commandingly when he established a new party line after the war. The public was tired of controls, and in 1946, with Republican majorities in both houses, he was chairman of the Republican Steering Committee. He served on many committees during his years in the Senate and in particular was the fiscal and labor expert, while Senator Arthur H. Vandenberg dominated the foreign field. Taft's command of facts was stupefying and the effort he expended on studying domestic bills amazed even the most hard-headed occupants of the Press Gallery. He had the largest staff of researchers on Capitol Hill and took the floor armed to the hilt on any given bill, his sharp mind quickly sorting out the wheat from the chaff. He usually wrote the amendments that his party desired; and when no bill met their requirements he drafted one himself.

One of his favorite coups was the Wagner-Ellender-Taft bill which provided $88,000,000 in federal funds for 500,000 units of low-rent public housing, a measure that proved helpful to many Negroes. When he first read the Wagner-Ellender bill he called it socialism. But after absorbing the studies that had been made by the New Dealers he approved its principles and gave his own particular twist to the bill, making it a workable measure that became law. In this and other instances he showed his ability to come up with a substitute bill of his own when he did not like a New Deal measure but approved the underlying principles. Characteristically, he told his Republican colleagues at a policy meeting that it was senseless to sneer at welfare. He consistently supported bills for civil rights, the anti-poll tax and anti-lynching measures, and in 1948 he introduced a bill to establish a Fair Employment Practice Commission to offset discrimination in employment. He voted for a bill requiring the Ku Klux Klan and other secret organizations to file their membership lists.

The issue that projected Senator Taft most dramatically into public view was the Taft-Hartley Act, passed in 1947 over President Truman's veto. This stirred up a storm of protest and set the labor forces on his trail. He insisted that it was designed to restore justice and equality in labor relations and to eliminate special privileges, but this was not how the union leaders viewed it. As he campaigned Taft took pains to explain the new labor law, which he always felt was not properly understood by the public. He argued that it strengthened collective bargaining and that it made no attempt to curb strikes or any other union activity. Union shops could be established only if a majority of the employees desired them, and union dues were not to be used for political purposes. The bill provided for an impartial mediation board with a national labor manager and a panel of twelve men.

The closed shop was ruled out and jurisdictional strikes and secondary boycotts were declared illegal. Unions as well as employers were held accountable for unfair labor practices and the unions could be sued for breach of contract. The eighty-day injunction was provided for in national health and safety strikes, and unions were required to make public their financial affairs.

But the field was wide open for attack on Taft. John L. Lewis said that he was born with "velvet pants," a statement that outraged Mrs. Manning, who remembered how hard up they had always been as children. He was called "Mr. Moneybags," the grandson of a rich man, although Alphonso was almost penniless when he died. With perhaps more truth he was said to have had a rich father. Plain, hard-working Bob Taft suddenly assumed the image of a gilded aristocrat and the labor forces poured money into Ohio to defeat him.

Another controversy had blown up over a speech he delivered on the Nuremberg trials at Kenyon College in October, 1946. He questioned the legal validity of trying the war criminals under *ex post facto* law. It was not his intention to defend the Nazi leaders but he argued that the trial of the vanquished by the victors could not be impartial. "About this whole judgment there is the spirit of vengeance, and vengeance is seldom justice," he said. Although there were other jurists who agreed with him on strictly constitutional grounds, Bob Taft stood in the limelight as the author of a statement that could scarcely have been more unpopular.

The Senator opposed subsidies for farmers but maintained that they should receive technical assistance through their local soil conservation districts. He believed in a "reasonable, flexible price support program for farm products," and favored cooperatives. Measures to fortify the soil and increase the productivity of the land were supported by the Senator, but he sternly opposed giving Russia and other lend-lease countries scarce farm equipment that he felt was needed on American farms.

To large segments of the country he seemed a double-dyed conservative as he opposed reciprocal trade treaties, the relaxation of trade restriction, and the Senate ratification of the North Atlantic Treaty Alliance; yet right-wingers were baffled at times by Bob Taft's dramatic switches.

Senator Joseph McCarthy was riding high as the 1950's dawned and, although on amicable terms with him, Taft took pains to observe on April 19, 1950: "I notice that some commentators credit me with being back of the McCarthy charges and advising McCarthy. As a matter of fact, I never heard of the charges until he made them. He has never consulted me about his course and I have given him no advice."

Bob did not live for the public hearings of 1954 but when McCarthy fought the appointment of Charles E. Bohlen to the Foreign Service Taft stood firmly behind President Eisenhower and voted for his appointment. He viewed McCarthy judicially, as he did all else, although he praised him for his anti-Communist work. He did not endorse him because by his own admission he never interfered in state primaries. But Taft never ceased to attack the Communist influence wherever it developed. At Versailles he had been one of the first to spot the rising danger of Bolshevism. In a pamphlet he issued in 1949 the Senator said: "Communism is the greatest threat to freedom the world has ever known. . . . We can win the war against Russia only by defeating the Communist philosophy in the minds of the people of the world." He blamed the Korean crisis on the weak policy of the State Department toward China, Formosa, and Korea. In his book *A Foreign Policy for Americans* Senator Taft explained his attitude on foreign affairs:

> I do not believe it is a selfish goal for us to insist that the overriding purpose of all American foreign policy should be the maintenance of the liberty and the peace of the people of the United States, so that they may achieve that intellectual and material improvement which is their genius and in which they can set an example for all people.

Senator Taft favored using Chinese Nationalist troops to win the war in Korea. No member of the Senate was more interested than Bob when General Douglas MacArthur came home, dismissed, and made his famous address to the joint House of Congress. There must have been faint echoes in his memory of his father and General Arthur MacArthur in the Philippines.

Altogether Senator Taft was a dynamic figure during six years of the Roosevelt administration and eight years under Truman. None could ignore him, whether he was pushing through a measure he favored or blocking one he disapproved. The older generation of Tafts were all gone by the time he reached the peak of his career, but he and Charlie were carrying on the family tradition and their wives were deeply involved. Martha's training had led her logically into the field of national politics. In the year that Bob was elected to the Ohio House of Representatives she helped start the League of Women Voters in Cincinnati and became its first president. She resigned from this organization in 1941 in a disagreement over foreign policy. She was national treasurer at the time and her close friend, Mrs. Darrah Dunham Wunder, was executive secretary. Martha was an America Firster, but she always maintained that she was a pacifist, not an isolationist. Pearl Harbor silenced the group that had been working to keep the United States out of war and in the years that followed she helped through Quaker societies to relieve wartime distress in Europe and concerned herself with the plight of the victims of the Nazis and Fascists.

Martha was the first woman in Cincinnati to serve on the board of directors of the Community Chest and she was associated in one way or another with virtually every social agency functioning in Cincinnati. She was a trustee of the Children's Hospital, and was active in Girl Scout work, both in Cincinnati and Washington. She headed the first Cincinnati relief drive during the depression. In later years she was one of the founders of the American-Israel Society, a non-sectarian group created to promote cultural interchange between the United States and Israel. After the first World War both Bob and Martha advocated American membership in the League of Nations.

She was already known as a community worker when she worked for Alfred M. Landon in 1936, but she came into national prominence when she campaigned for Bob. After he won his Senate seat in 1938 an Ohio newspaper headline ran: "Bob and Martha Win." By the time her husband made his bid for the Presidency in 1940 Martha was already an accomplished campaigner who could make a rousing speech and cope with hecklers better than Bob could. Her political understanding and wholesome sincerity endeared her to the professionals as well as to the thousands of average Americans she addressed during the whirlwind Taft tours. It was easy for her to establish rapport with all manner of women —the sophisticated and the simple, the hostile and the friendly. Martha made her audiences laugh where Bob made his think. She simplified the facts that he presented and gave them color; indeed, she was as nimble-witted and as ready with a wisecrack as Lady Astor.

Martha ripped into the New Deal and its begetters. She deplored wage rises and price controls, attacked the Marshall Plan, urged tax reductions, and pleaded for economy in government. Her talks were practical but she laced them discreetly with anecdote and metaphor. When they appeared together she tried to keep the spotlight on Bob, although the audience was apt to turn to her sunny self. With full understanding of the ways of publicity she neither sought it nor shunned it. When separated Bob and Martha discussed strategy over the telephone. It was her custom to follow the papers and keep a clip file for her husband.

When asked at Philadelphia for three good reasons why her husband should be nominated she did not hesitate a moment before replying:

"Brains, character, and experience." She scorned the mock apology of the demagogue. During Bob's campaign against Bulkley she faced a hostile gathering of coal miners who had been listening to a "humble origin" tirade. She quickly took a counterstand and in her deep melodic voice remarked:

> My husband is not a simple man. He did not start from humble beginnings. My husband is a very brilliant man. He had a fine education at Yale. He has been trained well for his job. . . . Isn't that what you prefer when you pick leaders to work for you?

The miners reacted with enthusiasm to this novel approach. On another occasion Martha's car skidded and turned over three times as she tried to avoid a dog in her path. She was bruised and battered, but she got to the meeting and had the wit to say: "Well, anyway, that probably got us the S.P.C.A. vote." She drove over the roughest roads and could change a tire in a pinch. Neither she nor Bob minded the fatigue, the hard work, the endless hours. In Cleveland they attended thirty meetings between them in one night and were still talking at 2:30 A.M. Martha would return to Washington from these fatiguing trips fresh as a daisy and would weave her spell all over again at a Republican women's luncheon, with a glittering array of national figures grouped around the tables.

In their early days of campaigning both wrote their own speeches and they traveled without the usual entourage of secretaries, publicity men, and managers. Martha would sit up in a train until three in the morning typing a fresh speech to deliver next day. Minnesota, her home state was a favorite visiting ground for Lloyd Bowers's energetic daughter. When they hit the trail in 1948, the last time that Martha was able to campaign, Bob was dogged by abuse along the way. The labor forces fought him at every turn. In Seattle his audience stamped out of the hall as he spoke and pitched vegetables at his car. By mischance his guard slammed shut the door on his hand. He was badly hurt and his palm had to be stitched but he spoke to a large crowd that night.

Robert Taft took defeat with good grace but suffered deeply, although by heritage and training he understood the political game and accepted its cruelties. Speaking at the Burning Tree Club in 1948 at a party given in his honor after he had lost his second bid for the Presidency, the Senator spoke from the heart: "It isn't the honor or the glory of the office; the yacht and the White House and all the protocol. I believe deeply in my principles, and I want to put them into effect. The office of President has the power and the prestige to put these principles into effect. That's why I keep running for the job." In the following year a hundred Washington newsmen in a *Look* magazine poll chose Taft as the senator who had contributed most to the nation's welfare.

His later campaigns were expertly managed by his cousin, David Ingalls, and a group of interested Ohioans. Behind the barnstorming was a powerful alignment of wealth and prestige. While serving with Hoover young Ingalls had added to his earlier honors by becoming well known as the flying Cabinet officer, staging national air shows and traveling about with motion picture films to illustrate his speeches popularizing his branch of the Government. He pushed technical development of the Navy and speeded up appropriations for this purpose. During World War II he served in the Pacific area from 1942 to 1945 and was awarded the Legion of Merit for his contribution to the development of the Naval Air Transport Service. After the war he became vice-president of Pan American World Airways, resigning in 1949 to take part in Robert's political campaign. He took over the management of the *Times-Star* in 1954, with Lloyd Taft serving as assistant publisher. At this time he bought a home on Indian Hill where he lived until the paper was sold to the Scripps-Howard chain.

But before the handsome and able David Ingalls stepped into the campaign picture, Martha was Robert Taft's most effective aid, representing considerable momentum in herself. She was five feet five and Alice Roosevelt described her neatly as being "alert, crisp, collected with that home-brushed look no beauty parlor ever gives." Her large brown eyes were alive with thought or laughter. The fragility of her earlier years had changed to robustness and she now had to watch her weight. In a burst of virtue she would order a salad, then impetuously finish up with a rich dessert. She could dress smartly when the need arose but clothes were not a preoccupation with Martha. The younger generation deplored the scarcity of mirrors in her home and she scarcely knew what she wore; nor did she ever own any jewels.

On one of her trips the impression spread that Mrs. Taft was "dressing down" to her audience. The fact was that she was wearing her usual clothes. But some of her smart colleagues in the League of Women Voters persuaded her to go to a famous couturier and buy something special for a convention at which she was to preside. Martha did not really believe that a dress made that much difference, but she donned the black print creation and was amused when a Minnesota woman showed up wearing exactly the same model—but in size 54.

"You see what you girls are doing to me," Martha jested.

After that she went happily on her way where clothes were concerned, continuing to buy at random. She made special efforts when her son Robert married Blanca Duncan Noel in St. James's Episcopal Church,

New York, in 1939; when Bill married Barbara Bradfield in Grand Rapids in 1942; and when Lloyd married Virginia Stone in St. Joseph, Michigan, in 1947. Mrs. William Howard Taft was able to be present at young Robert's wedding and she looked as smart and trim as in her earlier years. Martha wore a short print dress of white and maroon at the garden party given in June, 1939, for the king and queen of Great Britain. On this occasion Bob mentioned the fact to the King that his father had met George V in 1922.

At one rally where the two Tafts were speaking from the same platform Bob had to dash off to catch a train. His wife stepped up promptly and caused shouts of laughter when she introduced herself by saying: "I am the most miserable woman in the world. My husband has just told a story on which my whole speech was based and I have just discovered a run in one of my stockings."

Martha indulged in all sorts of quips and tossed off such puns as "To Err is Truman" and "Delirium Trumans." Among the sallies whipped off by vivacious Mrs. Taft from the platform were these:

"The Torch of Liberty is like your husband or a furnace—if you don't do something about it, it will go out."

"A $2 bill is not unlucky any more. You can buy a dollar's worth of goods with it."

"We've got a highboy government in Washington. One bureau on top of another. And there are termites in the drawers."

"Bob is not severe. He's just departmentalized."

"Fellow traveler will have a new meaning—a fellow traveling away from Washington."

"The difference between his [Bob's] 'eat less' and the President's 'conserve more' is the difference between plain language and double talk."

"Truman should have the balcony made portable so that he could take it back to Missouri with him."

Snipe as she did at President Truman, Mrs. Taft was on good terms with his wife and took Spanish lessons with the First Lady. She gave one of the family high chairs to Mrs. Henry Wallace for a grandchild, and she could always swap jokes with her husband's critics, rubbing in salt at the same time. Occasionally Bob made wryly witty remarks without the ghost of a smile. When an interviewer cited the critic who had likened him to Marie Antoinette in her callousness to the starving French mobs, Bob gravely asked: "Is that because of my glamour?"

The Senator went around Sky Farm singing the Lord Chancellor's words from Iolanthe: "And in my Court I sit all day, Giving agreeable girls away," on August 1, 1942, when Mrs. Wunder's daughter Lucy was married to Dudley Allen Levick, Jr., of Philadelphia. The wedding was to have been held at the Church of Our Savior on Mount Auburn, but when Mrs. Wunder's mother died suddenly the plans were switched and the ceremony was held at Sky Farm. The Senator, who was to have given the bride away in church, performed the same function in his home. He also fastened the groom's tie and helped the Wunder family through an emergency. George William Wunder, Darrah's nephew whom she had brought up as a son, was a Captain of Engineers in the Pacific, and so could not be present.

Bob liked to sing hymns, usually off key, and *habitant* songs. He tossed off Gilbert and Sullivan verses in a loud, grating voice and was also given to reciting the Bab Ballads and other nonsense verses when in the mood. The personal life of the Robert Tafts, both in Cincinnati and Washington, had much of the quality that had characterized Bob's own early days. There was the same affection, the same family loyalty, the zest for family gatherings and summer days at Murray Bay, for golf and games and puzzles and quizzes, for hard work and scholarship. Bob was as gentle and quiet at home as he was austere and harsh in the Senate. He could work with great concentration, with television, conversation, or any sort of noise going on around him. He jested that he did his best thinking at symphony concerts, which he frequently attended in the old Taft tradition. Martha, too, had the family feeling for music although her major interest was art, and she treasured her father's distinquished collection of Japanese prints, which she had inherited. Bob liked a game of bridge but Martha rarely played. She liked small dinner parties, and the theater, although no member of the family could match Mrs. William Howard Taft in this respect. Like Bob, Martha read insatiably and she was always ready to take off on a trip with the children and their nurse, an Englishwoman named Mary Ball who had been with them for years and who stayed on after the children grew up. Martha had brought her own bright and highly cultivated strain into the Taft family line. By 1952 she and Bob had four children, all boys, and nine grandchildren.

Since the Robert Tafts lived and breathed politics on Indian Hill their growing children heard endless discussion of public affairs, so much so that while still in college young Robert had his heart set on a political career. After the first World War they had remodeled their house, adding rooms, installing modern plumbing, and giving it the four white pillars suggestive of the colonial tradition. They made a point of preserving its simplicity as great estates were developed around them on Indian Hill. Their books, pictures, and period furniture reflected the life of the Tafts, from the dining room table at which so many vital political discussions had taken place to the side porch with its view of the hills and valleys around Cincinnati.

Although Bob chose to think of himself as a dirt farmer there was little time in his later years for work of this sort, even though some thought that he took more pride in his asparagus and strawberry beds than he did in his speeches. When they remodeled the house Martha had flower gardens planted along the slope on one side, and they went in for market gardening. They practiced it scientifically, experimenting with soils, fertilizers, and insecticides. They consulted books and pamphlets, since Martha insisted on things being done in the right, rather than the amateur, way. Bob was so determined to produce a fine variety of strawberry that he bought balloon tires for his truck rather than a new car for Martha, who was then driving the children to school in a rattling Model T. But visitors to Cincinnati liked to savor the large and juicy strawberries provocatively listed on the hotel menus as "Taft Strawberries." However, Bob did not make a fortune on this venture, or break even with it.

Martha enjoyed gardening and was an active member of the Indian Hill Garden Club. One day she was hurrying down to the terrace below the porch to cut tulips when she fell with a pair of scissors in her hand. They pointed straight at her eyes. Bob rushed down the steps, picked her up in his arms, and carried her into the house, muttering, "My darling, my darling." It was a serious moment but Martha's sight was not affected. Bob's excitement was most unusual for one so undemonstrative. Only those who knew him intimately ever saw the more tender side of the Senator. He coveted privacy but could no longer find it once he became prominent in Washington.

"I'll wear my tweed suit," he told Martha as he set off for his first day in the Senate.

"Well, you'll look sharp in that," said Martha briskly. "Oh, Senator, you will wear something else." And he did, but the baggy look never left him. He usually bought two suits a year and wore "all purpose pants" for golf, with his sleeves rolled up. He considered Martha's taste in ties splashy but in general he scarcely noticed what he wore. He would leave umbrellas or galoshes wherever he chanced to be but he never forgot the big cowhide briefcase that his wife had given him, or the papers he needed at any given time. Senator Taft might fumble, drop things, forget names, scorn hand-shaking and back-patting, get angry or irritable, but he was reassuring to voters drowned in the flattery of the slick politician. He knew that he must pose for pictures but it went against the grain to be photographed holding a dead turkey, catching a fish while wearing a business suit and hat, mowing a lawn, or otherwise acting up for the camera. He had to be sincere in all that he did. Bob was not censorious or narrow-minded among worldly men and was amiable enough in the locker room, but he had grown up with politics and he knew that posed shots were part of the game, however little they had to do with good government.

Martha, however, could enter into the spirit of things with warmth and sincerity, and laugh as she faced the camera whereas Bob was inclined to look grim. Actually, he was no amateur when it came to fishing. Both he and Martha were enthusiastic about trout fishing and the French-Canadian guide noted that Madame Taft cast with a *pique féroce*. For years Bob had been taking his sons on canoeing trips at Murray Bay. He had a cabin where they roughed it eighty miles from Pointe au Pic. They had to ride for six miles, then go by wagon over a rough road, and finally walk and canoe the rest of the way to this retreat that came to be known as "The Eternity Fish and Game Club."

The tenor of their lives changed considerably when they moved to Washington, although they always liked to go back to Indian Hill and this remained the family stronghold. Bob was more or less indigenous to Ohio but Martha had lived a good deal in the capital and knew her way around. They had several houses before settling in the one they finally owned in Georgetown, a twelve-room Victorian dwelling with high ceilings, tall azaleas outside the door, and no pretension. They had previously rented a furnished Legation house and then an imposing mansion with marble statuary and ornate furnishings that Bob found oppressive. In fact, Martha came downstairs one morning and found that he had placed a cake of soap in the hand of a marble goddess on the stairway.

Mrs. Robert Taft soon became noted in the capital for the dignity of her dinner parties, the good conversation, the clever minds that threw off sparks. Bob scarcely knew what he ate. He was by no means a gourmet but, like his father, he ate a good deal of meat and avoided potatoes. He liked to have lobster once a week and his only food aversion was parsnips. At dinner parties Martha usually served simple American fare, not forgetting the ice cream with crushed fruit that Bob preferred. For special occasions a caterer was called in. Bob mixed the cocktails himself and liked a bourbon before dinner.

Martha never pretended to care for cooking even though Alice Longworth said of her that "Martha Taft's home is the kind that has a cookie jar in the pantry instead of a bar." But she briskly wheeled a wire basket through the supermarket and hunted for bargains. She usually had some merry tale to tell over the dinner table but Bob, with his aloof eyes and his hidden drive, would discuss the issues of the day and keep up a steady drumfire of hardheaded conversation on the political point that interested him at the moment. He could never drop his guard for the relaxed hour, except in the company of his family and most intimate friends. He played golf in the middle eighties but he did not share his father's intense passion for the game and his friends recognized the fact that he was a dogged rather than a spectacular player. Bob was prone to make medium-length drives and cautious approach shots. He was always observed with interest at Burning Tree, at Camargo or on the golf course at Murray Bay.

Bob was without fads or hobbies of any sort but he liked the company of amusing and even slightly wacky people at times. He was thrifty, like his mother, and was disposed to refuse the Cadillac with driver assigned to majority leaders until he was persuaded that he must not make things hard for his colleagues. Actually, he preferred to drive his own car, and would sometimes arrive at the most formal parties in his well-worn Buick, which he parked among the chauffeur-driven limousines. As he left a dinner party one night the doorman shouted: "Senator Taft's car."

"Well, it's a good car, but it won't come when it's called," he quietly observed, as he moved off to the parking lot.

When he abandoned his Buick he bought a Plymouth and drove it for years. Early in 1951 he surprised his family by investing in a robin's-egg-blue Oldsmobile. He liked this car but felt that it might be considered showy. "Do you think it too flashy for me?" he asked Mrs. Wunder. She assured him that he need not worry on that score.

The Senator did not like to have others do anything for him that he could do for himself, and he sometimes confounded MacAllister Gray, his butler-chauffeur, by insisting on carrying his own bags up three flights of stairs. He drove fast and absentmindedly, and was apt to take his meals in the same fashion. Mac would observe him at breakfast, busily taking notes and not knowing what he was eating. He was so short-sighted that he often passed people without recognition. When asked on "Meet the Press" what her husband's most irritating habit was, Martha quickly replied: "Forgetting to do the things I tell him to do on the way to the office." He thought nothing of tucking his napkin across his white waistcoat as he dined at Mrs. Longworth's, and he had no small talk, but if not a social lion, he was a terror in the Senate. With each defeat he threw himself more intensely into his senatorial work until his power seemed matchless to some of the correspondents watching from the sidelines.

William S. White, one of his admirers, noted that he seemed "to bestride" the Senate after 1944, the year in which he stepped aside to let Senator John W. Bricker, of Ohio, seek the nomination. After that his voice rang out with authority on many issues. Although shy he could also be haughty, as his opponents knew to the full. He was a ruthless prober in committees, an impatient listener, a heckler, and a master of the subjects under discussion, in spite of his blind spot on foreign affairs.

He demanded precision and invariably challenged inaccuracies. Senator Taft was expert at helping to draft the Republican party platforms and his son Robert was repeating history when he gave the Taft touch to the platform of 1960. White was not one of those who thought that Senator Taft acknowledged error readily but he wrote that he had a "luminous candor of purpose that was extraordinarily refreshing in a chamber not altogether devoted to candor." Lyndon Johnson was one of the few men in the Senate who could heckle Taft and not be subjected to his icy glare. There was good feeling between these two senators, far apart though they were in temperament and outlook. Both were accomplished politicians, pragmatic and dogged in their aims. They knew how to influence men and beat down opposition.

CHAPTER 26

FOR GOD, FOR COUNTRY, AND FOR YALE

IN THE 1940's Charles Phelps Taft, II, known to everyone as Charlie Taft, became a crusader at large, a man of many causes, a nationally known figure devoted to war work and the good of mankind. "For God, for Country, and for Yale" was a phrase that seemed to have been made for him, his sister thought. Charlie appeared in many guises, always smiling, handsome, courteous, in a hurry, intent on moving mountains. He headed committees and ran campaigns. He organized community work and drew on a vast list of friends to support his causes. A telephone call from Charlie Taft across the country would galvanize local forces into action. He could never ignore an appeal for help and the field of public service remains his natural setting today.

For three decades the youngest son of William Howard Taft has been involved in public affairs: fighting civic corruption, intolerance, and hate; backing slum clearance; testifying before the Senate on trade policies; presiding at religious conferences; working as labor mediator; or raising funds for Yale. His idealism persisted through the war years and the ambiguous peace that followed. "Democracy," said young Charles on one occasion, "can only exist while we look at each man, woman and child as a person, a child of God who in some degree can make his contribution to the common good."

In the war years Charlie was brought face to face with Bob on the national level, as well as in Cincinnati. The crosscurrents of the 1940's highlighted the separate paths down which they traveled. Each fulfilled his destiny in his own particular way and along the lines their earlier history had indicated. The public took note that Bob was a conservative to the right of his father and Charlie a liberal to the left of his father. Although worlds apart in their outlook each respected the independence and achievements of the other. Charlie recognized the fact that Bob would never listen to his advice but still regarded him as the little brother. Bob felt that Charlie was too prone to take on the color of his surroundings. Charlie campaigned ardently for his brother and tried to swing some of the liberal vote for him when he ran for the Presidency. Similarly, Bob never stood in Charlie's way; their disassociation of ideas was conducted on a courteous level.

Charlie had friends everywhere and wanted nothing more than to be known as a good citizen, a title he earned in a variety of ways. He might easily have been an affluent lawyer, but his practice was always secondary to his humanitarian interests. When he was not fighting the political machine in Cincinnati he was giving unlimited time and effort to difficult and sometimes thankless causes. In the 1960's he was still the reformer, the last of the Charterites and the longest-lived champion of integrity at City Hall. On the national level he was backing the late President Kennedy's trade expansion bill. As co-founder and general counsel of the Committee for a National Trade Policy, this was an old interest of his since he had worked on the Reciprocal Trade Agreement Act of 1934. While serving in the State Department during World War II he presented to Congress President Roosevelt's proposal to extend and expand the reciprocal trade agreements. Bob and he disagreed sharply on foreign trade policy. The Senator stayed away from the hearings at which Charlie testified, but his son, Robert Taft, Jr., wrote a liberal trade-policy plank for the 1960 Republican platform. Charlie was also named to serve on President Kennedy's American Food for Peace Council.

As a tax and trial lawyer, a labor consultant, a housing expert, a tariff authority, his career has touched the national interest at many points. In his pyrotechnic course he has stirred up trouble and has had to face formidable opposition at times. Charlie has stepped out in so many different directions as to leave even some of his admirers baffled. He was for aid to Britain before Pearl Harbor. He supported lend-lease, selective service, Bretton Woods, the British loan, and the reciprocal trade agreements, all of which were opposed by Bob. Although sometimes voting for Democrats in Cincinnati he has remained staunchly Republican on the national front. When Landon was nominated he joined his staff of campaign advisers and drafted much of the platform. He stumped vigorously for Willkie and his "One World."

Although always predicting a Republican victory when Franklin D. Roosevelt ran, he was quickly drawn into the network of war effort. The New Dealers eyed liberal-minded Charlie Taft as a likely captive when he accepted one tough wartime job after another. But he remained stubbornly Republican, a Taft of Ohio. However, he was just as much at home in Washington as in Cincinnati, where he might be seen hurrying along the streets munching an apple as he went lunchless from one meeting to another. In Washington it was natural for him to dine at the White House or with the Washington Old Guard who had known his parents well. Some of them remembered Charley-Boy from his short-pants' days.

He was busy with the Greenhills Home Owners Corporation, a housing development for workers in Cincinnati, when he was drawn into the complex picture of the capital in time of war. As attorney for the Cincinnati Board of the Amalgamated Clothing Workers of America from 1928 to 1940 he had mediated steel strikes and had become deeply involved in the politics of the labor forces. He had launched a private attack on the housing shortage and building trades unemployment and had been active in helping people on relief.

His work in Washington began in February, 1941, and by the time he returned to live in Cincinnati at the end of 1945, he had been a director of the Division of Health and Welfare for the Federal Security Agency, a member of the President's War Relief Control Board, and director of Wartime Economic Affairs for the State Department. When selective service came into effect he was asked by Henry L. Stimson to take charge of the program the Government was launching to provide health, recreation, and welfare facilities in the boom towns swollen by army camps and defense installations. Charlie soon was directing the care of children whose mothers were doing war work, and was promoting entertainment and welfare causes. In his various jobs he had to smooth out the bickerings among economic control agencies, persuade religious groups and foundations to consolidate their foreign relief activities, and fight his own way through a forest of red tape. But Charlie, like his father, had the conciliatory touch, the diplomatic approach that overcame obstacles, and his own fame spread as he impressed his image on innumerable national agencies.

While busy with war work he was elected once again to the city council of Cincinnati in 1941. He flew once a week to Ohio to attend the council meetings and collected only half of his government salary, merely to cover his travel expenses. But various factions objected and proved by court decision that he could not work for the United States Government and for the city of Cincinnati at the same time, so he resigned from the council. For once Charlie had tackled more than he could handle. On his return in 1945 he was defeated for the council, but was back in office in 1948.

At the end of the war he was a director of seven corporations, a trustee of the Twentieth Century Fund and the Carnegie Institution, chairman of the board of trustees of the Taft School, labor relations consultant to Monsanto Chemical Company, and a member of many other agencies, both local and national. For a time he was a director of Farrar, Straus & Young, the publishers, working with his old Yale classmate, John Farrar. At all times Charlie was the sparkplug of the Cincinnati Community Chest and a national leader in Y.M.C.A. work. He headed two fund-raising campaigns for the Episcopal Church and another to raise a million dollars for the Yale Law School Library.

Young Taft became president of the Federal Council of Churches in 1947, the first layman to hold this office. In his first speech he plunged boldly into the need for the churches to concern themselves with race relations and industrial problems, and to encourage laymen of sound character and religious conviction to work for what they thought to be right. In his own local councils on Sunday afternoons he brought union leaders and industrialists together to present their points of view. He created a sensation with the stand he took in 1948 at the World Council of Churches, meeting in Amsterdam. For the first time the Protestant churches of Europe and America were brought together by the council, with forty-four countries represented in the picturesque processional at Amsterdam.

The tall, handsome Ohioan made his presence felt in this gathering. He helped to shape a report on "The Church and the Disorder in Society" that shocked many of the churchmen by its radical terms. It was modified before being accepted by the World Council. Charlie was all for Christian principles being brought to bear concretely on international politics. As its first lay president he injected new life into the Federal Council of Churches. He and Eleanor were unfailing churchgoers. At Murray Bay, in Cincinnati, wherever he chances to be, he is always the devout Episcopalian, and for years has been senior warden at Christ Episcopal Church in Cincinnati.

During the war and in the years that followed the Charles Tafts exemplified their humane spirit in the long succession of displaced persons they housed. All the international sympathies Charlie had were shared by his small dynamic wife and they made a strong team in the field of succour. The world was Eleanor's parish. Refugees swarmed over the large stucco house that they had built on three acres of land in East Walnut Hills. Their home was so arranged that their own five daughters and two sons could come and go their separate ways but maintain friendly contact with the family protégés. Before resettlement sixty-five refugees found shelter with them at one time or another, including a Latvian family with nine children who stayed for five years before settling in Kentucky.

Eleanor had almost as many projects under way as Charlie, and all on the humanitarian level. Her interests lay in church work, international relief, and municipal affairs. She was in charge of the refugee service and overseas clothing needs for the Episcopal Diocese of Southern Ohio and for the Cincinnati Council of Churches. She was chairman of the UNICEF committee for Cincinnati, and a trustee of the United States Board of the Japanese International Christian Union in Tokyo, and of Anatolia College in Salonika. Another of Eleanor's strong interests was the Experiment in International Living at Putney, Vermont.

There was always excitement around the Taft household. Taft was usually campaigning for one cause or another and his wife was invariably engaged in good works. From 1955 to 1957 he was mayor of Cincinnati and he brought a distinctive and experienced touch to this role. Three years earlier he had one of the great disappointments of his life when he lost the governorship of the state to Frank L. Lausche, who won his fourth term that year on the Democratic ticket. Charlie was nominated but he had only lukewarm organizational support. He campaigned hard for Bob, who was re-elected as senator on a landslide at the same time that Charlie went down to defeat.

Eleanor and the children had campaigned for him, too. In typical Taft fashion they were independent in their outlook and one of the girls wore a Roosevelt button in the 1940's. Nonie, Sylvia, Seth, Cynthia, Peter, Rosalyn, and Lucia were brought up in the old family tradition of Murray Bay, with big family gatherings, a healthy outdoor life, a concern for other people. Mrs. Charles Taft was slim, intense, a graceful dancer. Her dark hair framed a vivacious face with blue-gray eyes. She cared as little about clothes as Martha Taft and had been known to show up at the opera with a brocaded Chinese cloak over a T-shirt. She was interested in the Noyes Rhythmic Camp at Cobalt, Connecticut, and was expert at eurythmics. The visits of her sister, Lucia Chase, were always of great interest to the entire family. When she came with the Mordkin Ballet in 1938 Charlie and Eleanor rounded up all their friends for the occasion. Both Tafts attended concerts and the cinema but did not play bridge. They liked to entertain at big Sunday dinners, and neither of them smoked or drank. Eleanor, as well as her husband, made speeches and she was a persistent advocate when she took up a cause. Her strong will was belied by her fragile air. Although her New England background gave her strength of purpose she was gentle and mild in her social relations.

As the years went on Charles Taft was decked with laurels of one kind or another, receiving honorary degrees from seven universities, including Yale. The National Conference of Christians and Jews conferred on him its eighth annual citation in the Cincinnati area for "outstanding achievements in public service, religion, professional activites and human relations." He has been variously associated over the years with the law firms of Taft & Taft; Taft, Stettinius & Hollister; Headley, Taft & Headley; Headley, Sibbald & Taft; and Taft and Lavercombe.

Mr. and Mrs. Taft had profound family sorrows, too. Rosalyn died of polio in 1941 and Cynthia was paralyzed from the waist down at the same time. With enormous courage she faced the future as if nothing ailed her. She was graduated from Vassar in 1949, took her M.Sc. at the London School of Economics in 1951, and her Ph.D. in economics at Yale in 1959. She married Donald R. Morris, a foreign service officer, and while they were stationed in Beirut, Lebanon, she bore a son named David Taft Morris. In 1963 she was using her training in economics as a policy consultant in the State Department.

In 1955 Lucia Taft, aged thirty-one, a graduate of Vassar and a teacher, died by her own hand at their house on Garden Place. Both beautiful and clever, the fourth daughter of the Charles Tafts had been in the East, teaching at the School for Nursery Years and living at International House in New York. She worked at a summer camp near Stockbridge but returned home in autumn, discouraged and depressed. On her first day back she helped distribute packages for city council campaign workers and showed her usual interest in her father's campaign for office. She talked of going West to work but two days later she was dead.

Her parents learned of this tragedy when they telephoned the house after being in the inaugural procession for President Walter Langsam at the University of Cincinnati. They wanted her to join them at the football game that afternoon but instead they were informed that Lucia had brought an end to her own unhappiness. After that they wrote to all their friends on October 31, 1955, that a "very high courage, misguided though it was, had taken her home and at last she possessed the quietness and trust and stability that she had struggled to achieve but never quite could reach."

Lucia's oldest sister, Eleanor K. Chase (Nonie) married Dr. Donald T. Hall and settled in Seattle with their four children. Sylvia Howard married Dr. William Lotspeich and lives in Rochester. They have a daughter and two sons. The two Taft boys, Seth Chase Taft and Peter Rawson Taft, adhered to the family tradition and both went into law. Like his grandfather Alphonso, Seth studied the field before settling in Cleveland. Many doors were open to him but he followed an independent course. He decided that there were too many Tafts in Cincinnati and after considering Boston, Providence, Philadelphia, Pittsburgh, Chicago, and the West Coast, Cleveland seemed just right to Seth. He wanted to settle in a place that would grow, yet not be too overwhelmingly large, and he had a general belief that the Middle West was the "swing area" of the country. As a management center for many businesses he felt there was plenty of room for expansion.

Seth is a product of the Taft School and of Yale, where he was a Phi Beta Kappa, president of the Political Union, and an enthusiastic member of the debating and current affairs teams; he also did work for the Yale *Daily News*. From his undergraduate life he promptly stepped into an ensign's uniform and was assigned to the U.S.S. *Doran*, a destroyer convoying troops to Europe. Seth was a junior grade lieutenant when the war ended, and he was soon repeating his father's history, for on his return he went straight to the Yale Law School, where his interests again were channeled toward public service and politics. He was graduated in 1948, near the head of a class of one hundred, and he was only twenty-six when he settled down to the practice of law with Jones, Day, Cockley & Reavis. As a partner in this firm he is principal attorney for the Cleveland Development Foundation, which works with the city on an urban renewal program, and for the University Circle Development Foundation.

Seth quickly made a place for himself in the political, civic, and legal life of the city, serving as president of the Citizens League and then as a member of the Cuyahoga County Charter Commission. He ran ahead of all other Republicans in his first race for office. Public housing became one of his special interests and he has taken a firm stand against race bias. One of his ideals is the preservation of human values in a metropolitan community and he believes strongly in home rule for counties. "Local municipalities are the foundation for good government," Seth maintains. He helped to create the Cleveland Metropolitan Services Commission that made a massive study of the governmental problems of Greater Cleveland between 1955 and 1959 and recommended various improvements.

Seth enjoys being a lawyer, and in the practice of corporate law sees opportunities for public service in the large-scale foreign operations of today. Like his father he is interested in the extension of foreign trade and reciprocal benefits. Although his law practice flourished from the start Seth could not stay on the sidelines. His well-developed civic consciousness, a Taft inheritance, drove him into one activity after another. As co-chairman of the Cleveland Welfare Federation's legislative committee he pushed health and welfare measures. He worked for the Phillis Wheatley Association, designed to benefit Negroes, and was chairman of its Friendship Hunt in 1948. He is a trustee of the Urban League of Cleveland, the Cleveland Guidance Center for Disturbed Children, and the Cleveland Council on World Affairs. In 1956 Seth Taft, personable, ambitious, and able, was chosen Young Man of the Year by the Junior Chamber of Commerce. He campaigned hard in 1960 for the Nixon-Lodge ticket and he ran unsuccessfully himself for the Ohio Senate in 1962. It is his policy to work from within the Republican party and he serves both on a precinct committee and on the executive committee of the party.

Like the other Taft sons Seth married immediately after graduation. Frances Prindle grew up near the Yale campus and he first met her in Poughkeepsie when he was visiting one of his sisters at Vassar. When Frances was graduated from Vassar in 1942 she promptly enrolled in the Waves and both had the rank of ensign when they were married. While Seth was at sea his wife was teaching naval communications. She took her master's degree at Yale and taught for a time in New Haven schools. Today Mrs. Taft teaches the history of art at the Cleveland Institute of Art and is vice-president of Karamu House, Cleveland's nationally known theater and settlement. She is a crack tennis player and has frequently won honors in tournaments. The Tafts have four children— Frederick (Ricky), a freshman at Yale in 1963; Tucker, born in 1953, Cynthia in 1950, and Thomas in 1948. They live in a small community of about a dozen families on Pepper Ridge Road. Together the residents have built contemporary houses and share a village common, with a skating pond, swimming pool, baseball diamond, tennis court, and other recreational facilities for the children. The Tafts did much of the interior work on their house themselves. "I like to build things," Seth cheerfully volunteers.

The youngest of Charles Taft's children is also one of the most brilliant of all the Tafts—an outstanding scholar, an athlete, a traveled young man. Peter Rawson Taft, who was law clerk to Chief Justice Earl Warren during 1962–63, joined the firm of Edward Bennett Williams after passing his bar examinations in the summer of 1963. This was a fresh twist for a Taft, since Peter will be involved in criminal law, whereas most of his lawyer relatives have been experts in corporation law. But he welcomes the drama of the courtroom.

Peter attended the Lotspeich School in Cincinnati and then the Walnut Hills School. He was at the Taft School from 1950 to 1953, graduating *cum laude* with a letter in track. He attended Radley College in

Berkshire, England, on a scholarship and then entered Yale, where he won the Gordon Brown Prize that had also gone to his father. He was graduated *magna cum laude*, his field being physics and philosophy. True to family tradition he went on to the Yale Law School and while there was managing editor of the *Yale Law Journal*. After graduation in 1961 he worked in the Deep South for Justice Richard T. Rives, of the fifth circuit court. During this period he studied the civil rights question, an old family interest.

Peter Taft is a handsome youth, lean, vigorous, and ambitious. He was captain of the swimming team at Yale and is a mountain climber who has tackled Zermatt, the Cascades, the Sawtooth Mountains in Idaho, and the Olympic Mountains in Washington. From the age of seven he has hiked and camped and is one of the fishing enthusiasts of Murray Bay. Before settling down in his law firm he hiked a hundred miles in the Rockies with Ricky, Seth Taft's son. In 1958 he sailed to Australia on a tramp steamer and is proud of the fact that the trip cost him only seventy dollars. Photography is a major hobby of his and in odd moments he plays the flamenco guitar, an instrument that he picked up in Geneva on one of his summer tours. When in the mood he does water colors, for his gifts take a wide range.

Peter is quick-witted, original, and his thoughts are already veering toward a political future. He bears the name of the great-great-grand-father who moved from Vermont to Cincinnati in the 1840's and helped the Tafts take root there. Peter is the first of the Tafts to choose the capital as a starting point.

During the 1940's, as new young Tafts appeared on the scene the older generation was dying off. Mrs. William Howard Taft had lived on in Washington through the early years of Bob's tempestuous rise in the Senate, and Charlie's appearance on the national scene. With all the old interest alight she followed each move made by her sons with the closest attention. Bob and Martha visited her regularly when they lived in Washington and their oldest son, William Howard Taft, III, often stayed with her or dined at the house on Wyoming Avenue when he was an instructor at the University of Maryland. The elder Mrs. Taft went on in the old tradition, going to the theater and concerts, visiting friends, attending family gatherings, and taking a keen interest in political affairs.

She watched the rise of the New Deal with mental reservations but was an honored guest early in 1941 at a luncheon given by Mrs. Franklin D. Roosevelt for Supreme Court wives. They all gathered in the Blue Room, which Mrs. Taft surveyed with many memories of the past. Although not given to reminiscence, in her aging years World War II stirred up echoes of the Philippines, but she did not live to learn of

General Douglas MacArthur's landing at Luzon to free the Filipinos from the Japanese. From time to time she visited the Mannings in Pennsylvania and it was still her custom to go to Murray Bay. Year after year she franked her mail from Canada and nothing would convince her that "Helen H. Taft" written across an envelope was not as good as a stamp. This caused confusion at the local post office until the postmaster finally agreed to let the letters go through. At the end of the season Bob paid up for all his mother's letters. The frank had no validity in Canada in any event, but this solution left everyone satisfied. Bob was watchful of his mother's comfort in Washington, too, and when she was snowed in he attended to her furnace himself before going to the Senate.

Mrs. Taft was ill for a year before she died on May 22, 1943. She would have been eighty-two that June. Charlie, who was then assistant director of the Office of Defense, Health and Welfare, was with her at the end. Bob was at Grove City College in Pennsylvania, attending a commencement. Helen at this time was head of the History Department at Bryn Mawr. Mrs. Taft's two sisters, Maria and Lucy Lippitt, survived her, as well as twelve grandchildren and two great-grandchildren.

Six First Ladies had impressed themselves on the public consciousness since she had ridden so proudly to the White House at her husband's side. But all who knew inside Washington history were well aware of the potent role she had played. At the end, as in the beginning, she was a woman of great independence. She had never been able to hide her antipathies and Theodore Roosevelt had headed her list of dislikes. Actually she was shy, but she rarely gave any indication of lacking social poise. On political questions she was essentially conservative and she watched her husband's antitrust operations with some misgivings. Mrs. Taft considered it imprudent to rock the boat and she was slow to respond to the evolving social pattern. Although a rebel in her adolescent days, eager to carve a career for herself, in her mature life Mrs. Taft was never in any doubt that woman's place was in the home and she fought suffrage until it became the law of the land. On humanitarian questions her outlook was broad and sympathetic.

She had deep understanding of her husband's noble qualities and also of his weaknesses and indecision. Of all his varied achievements she regarded the work he did in the Philippines as his most enduring monument. Her own collapse so soon after Taft became President was the great tragedy of her life, for no First Lady ever harbored more ambition for this role, or worked more persistently to achieve it. Although she lacked the magnetic and popular touch that came easily to her husband Mrs. Taft was always a respected figure in public life. She was resourceful and self-contained, and her common sense and good management were proverbial among her family and friends. No one who knew them ever questioned the devotion of the Tafts. In small things, as on large issues, they were altogether harmonious. Taft valued his wife's advice and never underestimated the role she played in his life.

Her sister-in-law, Mrs. Henry W. Taft, died at her home in New York in the winter of 1942. She was two years older than Nellie and had celebrated her golden wedding anniversary with Harry at White Sulphur Springs in 1933. A requiem mass was celebrated at St. Patrick's Cathedral for Julia, who had worked for many Catholic charities and was honorary president of the New York Foundling Hospital.

Their beloved Horace died on January 28, 1943. After forty-six years as head of the Taft School he had retired in 1936 and had continued to cast his benign shadow over the school as headmaster emeritus. For a short time after retiring he stayed at El Cajon, close to San Diego, with his sister Fanny, but he was glad to get back to the house that had been prepared for him at Watertown. He kept up affectionate relations with the faculty, and gave civil government classes to the seniors and weekly talks at Vespers.

Horace was a fighter to the end. In 1937 he criticized President Roosevelt for failing to take action against the United Automobile workers who staged the first sit-down strike against General Motors. When the President was accused of "packing" the Supreme Court Horace Taft took up the issue with considerable fire and made speeches criticizing Franklin D. Roosevelt. He watched a new generation of boys grow up, some of them the sons and grandsons of earlier pupils, and in the early 1940's he passed tranquil days writing *Memories and Opinions*, his own reminiscences. Paul Cruikshank was Horace's successor and in 1963 John C. Esty, Jr., became the third headmaster of the Taft School.

Harry Taft survived Horace by two years and died in 1945, some time after having a severe fall. His civic interests were all in the Taft pattern. He was a strong supporter of the League of Nations, a foe of communism, a founder of Town Hall, a trustee of the New York Public Library, a backer of the Salvation Army. He drafted the chapter of the New York City Charter dealing with the public school system and was chairman of the high school committee of the Board of Education.

His had been a strong voice in legal circles in New York for three decades and he had been active in state politics. He became an authority on the relation of the press to the courts and he turned out a succession of books, ranging from *An Essay on Conversation* in 1927 to *Legal Miscellanies: Six Decades of Change and Progress* in 1941. Harry was a man of wide culture, traveled, knowledgeable, prone to set forth his views in the newspapers, earnest always in pursuing what he considered to be the common good. In spite of his childhood on

Mount Auburn most of his life had been lived away from Ohio. He rarely went back, although his association with Charles and Annie was strong and constant. He liked to play host in New York to all the traveling Tafts, as they moved back and forth, and many family gatherings were held at his house. Julia and Harry left two sons, Walbridge S. Taft and William Howard Taft, II, seven grandchildren, and three great-grandchildren. Their only daughter, Louise, died in 1926 and her husband, George Snowden, was later killed in an automobile accident. They left two sons and one daughter.

CHAPTER 27

THE TEAM BREAKS UP

MARTHA was not with Bob when he made his last bid for the Presidency in 1952. She had suffered a stroke and so had to watch her husband from the sidelines. Her collapse was a stunning blow for Robert Taft and it took some time to accustom himself to the sight of capable Martha in a wheelchair. Her intelligence was as keen as ever but there was no more of her spirited conversation, her quick response to life, her zest as a campaigner. Bob wheeled her around when he was in Washington and lifted her in and out of cars. As her condition slowly improved she dined out, visited friends, and went to the Senate. Although she had difficulty talking she would listen attentively and respond when she had the strength.

As Bob campaigned Martha followed every move he made. She clipped newspaper items about him and monitored both his television and radio programs. He usually called her at nine in the evening, to hear about her day, to tell her what he was doing, to get her comments on his speeches. Since only her left side was affected by paralysis she was able to carry on a letter-writing campaign for him. This was the year that the members of Bob's family really believed that he would win. They had not always thought so before. The pace of his campaign was terrific. No county or township was too remote, no meeting too unimportant, no factory group too small to be addressed. Bob traveled 46,000 miles by plane, bus, train, and automobile. He made 524 speeches, crossed the country three times, and campaigned in forty-one states. A Taft organization functioned in every state, with Ingalls and his colleagues controlling the master keyboard, and Jack Martin working close to Taft.

It was like old-time campaigning, the sort of thing that his father had disliked but that Bob threw himself into with quiet determination. There were airplanes, television, and radio now to speed up the message. Taft had his own bi-partisan following of voters who stood ruggedly with him for the established order. The country had come to know him well, not only as a strong senator but as a living presence. He showed unlimited endurance throughout this campaign. There was no repetition of the scene at the Youngstown Steel Mills during his run for re-election to the Senate in 1950. On that occasion he had been warned that neither the mayor nor the police could guarantee him protection from the angry mob at the mill gates. Bob drove right into their midst, stepped out of his car, and held out his hand to the nearest group of men. His bashful grin was disarming and the workers responded. Soon they were all shaking hands and as he drove off they cheered. Robert Taft had been re-elected to the Senate that year by a majority of 430,000 votes. Now he sought the larger prize.

Shortly after Martha's collapse he asked Mrs. Wunder, one of her oldest and best friends, to live in their home, act as hostess, and help her in every way she could. This was to give her companionship, in addition to the trained nurses who attended her around the clock. When at home Bob would rehearse his speeches before Martha and Mrs. Wunder. He reported cheerfully to Mrs. Manning at the close of 1951 that he thought Martha was improving and he felt greatly encouraged about her. Helen had just finished an article for the *American Magazine* on Robert and his family life. He told her that he liked it, although he did not usually enjoy reading anything about himself, good or bad.

Just before Christmas, 1951, Robert had a tonsilectomy, and when friends gathered at his house for a party they found him wearing a cardboard placard that Darrah Wunder had devised. She had printed the message in large letters with India ink:

> HAD MY TONSILS OUT FRIDAY
> BY DR. HARRY HAGGART
> EATING SOMEWHAT DIFFICULT
> CONVERSATION LIGHT
> MERRY CHRISTMAS!

This hung around Bob's neck with a red ribbon and he wore it to a dinner given for him on Indian Hill by Mr. and Mrs. Stanley Rowe. Martha had just begun going to parties and concerts again and Washingtonians were becoming used to the sight of Senator Taft pushing her around in her wheelchair. Only once did she break down and he looked at her sadly as tears streamed down her cheeks in the Senate restaurant. It was never Martha's habit to weep.

"What's the matter?" he asked.

She made no reply.

Mrs. Wunder accompanied her to Chicago for the convention of 1952. Both women helped Bob at a reception he gave in their hotel. Martha did not go to the convention hall but she was all ready to join him at a moment's notice if he were nominated. They were all prepared for victory. The indications were that he would win. However, it was Dwight D. Eisenhower's day and the echoes of this frenzied occasion and the charges and countercharges of stolen votes reverberated for months to come. Bob took it stoically. He was soon on the telephone talking to Martha. Each tried to say precisely the right thing to the other, but this time it was not easy. It was the final collapse of a lifelong dream for Bob and Martha knew it.

General Eisenhower telephoned to Senator Taft at once and asked if he might call on him in his hotel across the street. He thought that the defeated man had had every right to think of himself as the logical candidate of the Republican party. Senator Henry Cabot Lodge had played a large part in the sudden turn of events. The General noted sad faces above Taft buttons and ribbons, even as the crowd cheered him enthusiastically. As the victor and the vanquished shook hands Senator Taft asked if he might have his sons present and the General immediately agreed to this. Lights flashed on the faces of the two men as pictures were taken. Taft smiled gamely and said to the nominee: "You will win." Commenting on this historic moment Arthur Krock wrote:

His disappointment must have been shattering, yet he bore it with dignity and graciousness. As he stood with General Eisenhower before the flashing lights of television, many thought this his finest hour; that even had he become President, he could have left no finer memory to the people.

Before hurrying off to Murray Bay Senator Taft sent his political staff a letter of 2,200 words, going over the ground and making it clear that he had no fault to find with anyone who had worked for him. In September General Eisenhower invited him to have breakfast with him at Columbia University, an occasion on which each man set forth his views. Taft argued against reprisals in the new Republican administration, asked that there be no repudiation of the Taft-Hartley Act, and suggested steady resistance to socialization. This meeting assumed dramatic overtones in the press at the time but in his book *Mandate for Change*, published in 1963, General Eisenhower scoffed at the suggestion of "surrender on Morningside Heights" and wrote:

> The fact was that Senator Taft and I had agreed emphatically on the need for fiscal sanity in the government, as on most other issues, long before the breakfast talk. In the succeeding weeks he evidenced his enthusiasm for our common cause by a rugged round of campaigning which included more than thirty speeches in nineteen states.

Senator Taft campaigned hard for Eisenhower and he stood by with a smile on his face as the popular general was sworn into office. He had watched his father take the oath forty-three years earlier and, according to Helen, had never forgotten a detail of that occasion. "I'm a three-time loser now," he said to a friend at this time. "I ought to be getting good at it."

His arduous political career was nearly over but in the short time he had left he was again the rock-like figure in the Senate, the majority leader often fighting his own party as well as the opposition. Three wars had not basically changed the nature of his thinking. He had fought his way through the New Deal, the Fair Deal, and now he weighed every measure as it came up and fought stubbornly for the things in which he believed. Little more than two weeks after his inauguration the President made a diary entry: "Senator Taft has been the model of cheerful and effective cooperation." Some time later he commented: "Senator Taft and I are becoming right good friends. The relations between the Executive Branch and Republican leaders in Congress are getting better and better." But close in-fighting on federal spending irked Eisenhower. Tempers boiled over the budget and the President observed that Taft was "very much a man" as he staged one of his last fights, with no one present knowing that he was already dying of cancer. He wrote of their relationship:

> During the weeks we worked together a sound friendship developed between Senator Taft and me. It was not a Damon-Pythias affair, nor was there any unfailing compatibility of political viewpoint. On the one or two occasions when he voiced his differences impatiently and in vehement fashion . . . his behavior seemed at the time inexplicable; his illness then was unsuspected. . . . In some ways I found him unexpectedly "liberal," specifically in his attitudes on old-age pensions, school aid, and public housing. . . .

Taft and Dean Acheson were both members of the Yale Corporation and had met in harmony on social occasions in spite of the deep party differences between them. But the Senator and John Foster Dulles, Acheson's successor in the State Department, were close personal friends. The Tafts gave a dinner party almost every week after the election and Vice-President Richard Nixon, Mrs. Nixon, and Mr. and Mrs. Dulles often dined with them. Early in June, 1953, the Tafts gave a tea in their garden for Mrs. Eisenhower and the President arrived unexpectedly— a special compliment to Senator and Mrs. Taft, since he did not often leave the White House for social engagements.

Taft's favorite room was on the third floor of their house. He liked the high ceilings and wide fireplaces of his Georgetown dwelling and after his wife became ill he had a small elevator installed for her comfort. Mrs. Manning always stayed with them when she visited Washington; she was devoted to Martha, as she was to Bob. In 1952 they all grieved when the main Taft house at Murray Bay burned down. The shabby, hospitable old place went up like tinder when a spark landed on the roof from brush being burned along the railroad track. Treasures from all parts of the world, collected over a period of sixty years, were lost. Fine Japanese prints that hung on the dining room walls, Oriental rugs, china, silver, and linen were burned and only the most ephemeral of their books were saved. The grandchildren regretted the destruction of the large playroom at the back of the house and the enclosed yard in which they had all played. Barbara Taft, Bill's wife, called it "The Goat Pen."

Charlie later put up a modern house, designed by the Ohio architect Robert Little, on the site of the old Taft home. It is large enough to accommodate fourteen guests and from its wide windows a magnificent view of the St. Lawrence unfolds. The house has every modern device, in contrast to the early days of rusticity at Murray Bay, and on its walls hang the pictures of the large and handsome clan founded by Louise and Alphonso Taft. Mrs. Semple used Mountain Ash Cottage, the house that had belonged to Charles and Annie, until her death; then Lloyd Bowers Taft inherited it. Mr. and Mrs. Manning continued to use the house that the President had built for them, so that the Taft colony at Murray Bay stayed comparatively intact.

The Robert Tafts returned to Indian Hill at every opportunity and the last glimpse Mrs. Russell Wilson had of the Senator was just before Christmas, 1952, when he stopped to leave a book with her. He was on his way to buy ice cream for the family dinner. In recent years the breach between the Tafts and the Wilsons, based on their differing political views, had been healed, and Mrs. Wilson was one of the old friends whom Bob asked to visit Martha regularly while he was away campaigning. Both families had been close associates all through the 1920's. At that time they had helped to found the Hyde Park Culture Club, a name they gave it in jest, for its real purpose was "to have fun and good times without drinking or gossiping." They delivered weighty papers and others that were merely amusing. Bob, with his thorough mind, would review a book as if he were tearing a fiscal bill to tatters. The Wilsons attended the club meetings separately before their marriage and together afterwards. It was all reminiscent of Nellie Herron's salon in the 1880's, where William Howard Taft first wooed his future wife.

This club was a source of enjoyment for about ten years, until politics tore it apart when Bob became the national symbol of conservatism and Russell Wilson, mayor of Cincinnati for several terms and a Charter reformer from scratch, held to a more liberal line. Wilson died in 1946 and in the early 1950's his widow and Martha recalled the old joyous days of the club as Martha sat in her wheelchair and waited for the next telephone call from Bob.

Toward the end of April, 1953, President Eisenhower invited Taft to Augusta, Georgia, for a golf holiday. He also wished to consult him about political affairs, for he leaned heavily on his counsel in some matters. As they went round the course on a raw, damp day Bob was conscious suddenly of stiffness in his hip. He told the President that it had been troubling him vaguely for some time. They were at the seventh hole but he insisted on finishing the round, which he lost. President Eisenhower urged him to go at once to the Walter Reed Hospital for tests, which he did, meanwhile continuing his work at the Capitol. Actually Bob had not felt well since he had a severe bout of influenza while campaigning for General Eisenhower. He went on making speeches and, although seemingly recovered, he coughed nearly every morning in the early winter.

The Tafts were not at all health-conscious until Martha had her stroke and Bob became ill. They were a healthy family and paid little attention to the medicine cabinet. But now Bob continued to run a fever. He was anemic, and arthritis or a tumor was suspected. Although he kept all his appointments he had trouble getting up to his bedroom, but he refused to move to one on the ground floor. All his detective stories were up there, he jested; so was his favorite campaign button, pinned to a curtain. It read: "Don't be Daft. Vote for Taft."

In the middle of May Bob joined Martha at Hot Springs. When he tried to carry her up the steps of the train as they were returning home, he collapsed into his seat after getting her safely in her place. He had been concealing from his wife the fact that anything was wrong but now he admitted that he was having a little trouble with his hip. Immediately afterwards he went to Cincinnati to address the National Conference of Christians and Jews. He took his medical records with him and he was not allowed to leave Holmes Memorial Hospital in his native city to deliver his speech. He asked if he might give it over the telephone, but this did not work and young Robert jumped to his feet and read a copy of his father's speech to the gathering in the Netherlands Plaza Hotel.

By this time metastasis had set in and it was apparent that Senator Taft had widespread cancer. Knowing that he was not a man who could be fooled by evasion, three doctors interrupted him while he was doing a crossword puzzle and told him the truth about his condition. He took the news calmly and did not ask how long he might live but he cross-examined them and learned that they had not found the focus of the malignancy. A postmortem showed that it began with a tiny growth in one of the branches of the air tube leading to his right lung.

The Senator left the hospital on crutches and went straight to Indian Hill, where he passed a cheerful evening with his grandchildren. Next day he flew back to Washington with his son Robert. It was apparent as he sank wearily into a chair in his Georgetown house that he was a sick man. He had lost a great deal of weight and looked frail. After dinner he said to Martha and Mrs. Wunder in a quiet, conversational tone: "I think I should tell you girls that the doctors think this is a malignancy but great progress has been made in this field in the last few years, so there is nothing to worry about."

Martha refused to accept the grim knowledge that had been conveyed to her or, if she did, she managed to conceal the fact from everyone.

"Oh, they said that about Father and it wasn't true," she commented.

The Senator never mentioned the matter in front of her again, and outwardly she gave no sign of apprehension although those who knew her best believed that she played a game in the weeks that followed, knowing that distress on her part would add to Bob's anxiety. Mrs. Wunder kept up a cheerful front, in spite of the certain knowledge that the Senator was slipping away, a fact that became more apparent every day. He was staving off the exploratory operation that had been recommended, for he was determined to finish his legislative work. "In all of life defeat is necessary—sometimes," he had said to Martha after the 1952 convention. "No man should go into politics if he's afraid to be defeated. Once he gets that fear he'll lose his courage."

He needed all his courage now as he began to appear around Washington in great anguish and on crutches. He used them publicly first at a dinner given by John Foster Dulles. Next he showed up with them in the Senate and jested lightly about his hip muscle. In the Senate office that he soon would leave for the last time he had a picture of Martha and his four sons. A small bronze statue of his father, with back-swept coat and right hand on his hip pocket, stood on the mantelpiece and a large photograph of President Taft leaned against the fire-place.

Early in June President Eisenhower learned that Senator Taft might be "seriously incapacitated." The Senator entered New York Hospital under an assumed name and underwent further tests. On June 10 he was back in Washington, ready to give up the majority leadership to Senator William Knowland. The President was shocked when this piece of news reached him in Minnesota. He telegraphed to Bob: "Take every step to restore your health. The country needs you." On June 12 the Senator visited Herbert Hoover's apartment in New York on his crutches and said he was going to have a checkup later that day. He had lost weight and looked pale and ill. For two hours they talked about the political situation at home and abroad, and Taft gave no indication that he would soon be bowing out. On his return to New York Hospital he used his own name. Hoover visited him and although Bob did not say what ailed him, his old friend was no longer in any doubt about it. Bob read, worked over his puzzles, looked out the window at the East River, and watched the ships go by. He said he felt too well to be in a hospital. He jested with his doctors, saying that inoculations were making a pincushion of him and he told one nurse: "Don't pretty me up. I'm not a television star." Among his visitors was Thomas Dewey, who had helped to defeat him.

Late in June the Senator insisted on returning to Washington. President Eisenhower first saw him on crutches when he attended a conference at the White House. He returned for a breakfast and a luncheon with other legislative leaders and took part in the discussion with his usual brusque acumen. Greatly alarmed over Bob's persistence in attending to his duties Herbert Hoover followed him to Washington to urge him to return and have the exploratory operation that surgeons from Memorial Hospital had advised. He was amazed to find Bob still conferring with party leaders, attending committee meetings, and taking an active and intelligent part in the proceedings. The Senator told him he must finish up some legislative work, and when the distressed Mr. Hoover protested Bob's answer was simple and to the point: "My friend, you know what is the matter with me. I know what is the matter with me. I'm going to die with my boots on!"

At the moment Bob looked much better. President Eisenhower, having an informal conversation with him at the end of June, thought that his color was good and that he was almost jovial. Bob told him that although he had lost twenty-five pounds since first becoming ill, he had gained back four and he even talked of recovery at this point. But the President was soon informed by physicians that the temporary improvement was due to treatment he was getting which would have no effect in the long run. He had again put off having surgery done because he felt so much better, but it was self-evident now to observers that he was in trouble.

Senator Taft returned to New York Hospital on July 4 and was operated on four days later. Cancer was widespread but Bob picked up briefly after the operation. He was deluged with flowers, fruit, and messages. Meanwhile he read the papers with care and commented: "I've got to snap out of this in a hurry now. Eisenhower needs me." When the President talked to him on the telephone on July 21 the Senator said that he would leave the hospital in a week and return to Washington. But grim realization touched him when he found that he could not finish a puzzle he had started. The words escaped him, an incredible circumstance for Bob Taft, who had prided himself all his life on his skill with puzzles.

Mrs. Wunder told Martha gently that Bob was worse and that they must go to New York to see him. The news was received with total quiet and acceptance. "They're made of stern stuff, these Tafts," said Mrs. Wunder, sure now that Martha had accepted the truth all along. As her constant companion, Darrah understood her moods better than anyone else at this time. Together they flew in a chartered plane to New York with Mrs. Manning, Lloyd Taft, Jack Martin, and Dr. Bretney Miller, a close family friend. Horace had arrived from Los Alamos. Bill had flown in from Ireland. Young Robert was with his father. Up to this point the Senator had been telephoning regularly to Martha from the hospital and had discussed his illness matter-of-factly with other members of the family.

Martha, Lloyd, and Dr. Miller went straight to the hospital on their arrival. Bob made a mighty effort for his last meeting with his wife. His bed was cranked up before she was wheeled into the room. He asked for an extra pillow so that he could sit up. He chatted with Martha and told her how well she was looking; then he discussed plans for the remodeling that autumn of Sky Farm. When fifteen minutes had passed he kissed her and watched her being wheeled out of the room. She last saw him waving at her with the old wide grin. He waited until she had disappeared from view before sinking back on the pillows. On her return to the Carlyle Hotel, where they were all staying, Martha remarked that Bob had looked well.

Mrs. Manning and Mrs. Wunder went to the hospital next morning and saw the Senator separately. Bob was having a blood transfusion when Darrah appeared but he smiled broadly when he saw her, although his voice was strangely weak for Senator Taft. He said at once that he thought Martha looked well and he questioned her on what was going on at the Georgetown house. Mrs. Wunder told him of the friends who called, and the way in which they spent their time. His concern was all for his wife and he told Darrah how much he appreciated what she was doing for Martha. He clasped her hand in farewell and she staggered speechless from the room. "I knew he was near the end," she later recalled. Helen then went in to spend some time with the brother to whom she had always been so deeply devoted. Some hours later he sank into a coma.

Martha and Darrah Wunder were back in Washington when the news of the Senator's death was flashed across the country. He died on the morning of July 31, 1953, at the age of sixty-three and at the height of his career. He had lived only three months from the day on which he became noticeably ill. His physicians had all been impressed with his quiet courage and one of them had said: "He gave us all a lesson in how to die."

Mrs. Wunder waited for the arrival of Dr. Miller before breaking the news to his wife that Bob was dead. Martha lay quietly on a couch in their upstairs sitting room and wept silently as she listened, but said nothing. No one knew what her thoughts were in the weeks that followed but months later she said to Darrah one day: "I wish I had been with him to hold his hand."

The deep impression Robert Taft had made on his times, the manner of his dying, brought a universal reaction from friends and foes. There were plenty of both. Word reached Senator Knowland and Senator Lyndon B. Johnson on slips of paper from a ticker machine in the Senate lounge. Johnson silenced Clinton P. Anderson, who was rising to speak. Then Senator John W. Bricker, of Ohio, deeply moved, announced Robert Taft's death. It was a dramatic moment in the history of the Senate. Everett Dirkson, the senator who had nominated him in Chicago, spoke of his friend. Then Senator Johnson, to whom he had said when he last left the Senate, "I'll be back in January," added his tribute: "I think Bob Taft was one of the truly great men who have walked our way. He was characterized by a rock-like integrity, unconquerable common sense at all times, and an unswerving devotion to the principles in which he believed." Joseph McCarthy, Harry F. Byrd, and John Sparkman eulogized their colleague, who had staged so many tough battles in the Senate.

Herbert Hoover, whose political life had been closely linked with Bob Taft's, said of him on the day he died: "He was more nearly the irreplaceable man in American public life than we have seen in three generations." General MacArthur wrote to Mrs. Taft: "I felt he was the indestructible bulwark upon which we could base the welfare and future of our beloved country."

The dead senator received all the honors usually reserved for Presidents. Thousands filed past his coffin in the Rotunda of the Capitol where he had long been so dominant a figure. President Eisenhower led the mourners at the memorial service and Senator Bricker delivered the eulogy. Martha held her head high but wept quietly as she was wheeled in to sit by her four sons. Most members of the Taft family were buried in Spring Grove Cemetery but she had decided that Bob should rest in the little cemetery on Indian Hill. On a warm and windy day in August she attended a simple family service in the small Episcopal church that Bob had helped to build. A public memorial service was held in Christ Church, which he had attended before his own suburban parish was formed.

Portraits of the five men considered the greatest senators were unveiled in the Capitol in March, 1958. Each was an irreconcilable in his own particular way and one had battled William Howard Taft. They were Henry Clay, Daniel Webster, John C. Calhoun, Robert M. La Follette, and Robert A. Taft. In the following year the Robert A. Taft Memorial on Capitol Hill was dedicated, a bell tower with twenty-seven bells chiming the hours, and at its base a bronze statue of Robert Taft, reminding passersby of the fighting senator. The memorial was created from a dollar-fund and was the gift of the people to Congress. President Eisenhower made the presentation and said of Robert Taft that to the people of the United States he was a "liberal in his championship of individual right and opportunity, but he was also the very symbol of informed and responsible conservatism in everything affecting the nation's economy. . . . Whenever I needed him most, he was there, with all his vast knowledge of government—all his wisdom and experience."

Vice-President Nixon accepted the gift on behalf of the Senate and Speaker Sam Rayburn for the House. Herbert Hoover, who knew him best, spoke with deep feeling:

> When these great bells ring out, it will be a summons to integrity and courage. . . . His interest in the rights and dignity of men was paramount; his efforts for the workers and their families were endless; his concern with housing and health, untiring. . . . He became in the Senate a bulwark against those forces of reaction that would tear the United States into sects and cults of warring theorists. He brought to the social problems of his country a trained and political mind.

Robert Taft's own words were engraved on the marble shaft: "Liberty has been the key to our progress in the past, and is the key to our progress in the future. If we can preserve liberty in all its essentials, there is no limit to the future of the American people."

In his *Profiles in Courage* John F. Kennedy, who would hold the office that had eluded Robert A. Taft and die from an assassin's bullets in 1963, selected him as one of his subjects. He wrote that Taft gave new dimensions to the conservative philosophy, frequently flinging to the winds the restraints his own analysis advised, refusing to bow to any group, refusing to keep silent on any issue. Kennedy pointed out that the Senator had antagonized the friends of the Taft-Hartley Act and had endangered his own leadership in the Republican party by his support of education, housing, health, and other welfare measures. He cited his stand on the Nuremberg trials, the personal tragedy of his three bids for the Presidency, and his fearless attitude in face of almost universal criticism.

Martha sold the Georgetown house in 1953 and went back to Cincinnati. But in the following year she returned to Washington and took an apartment at 2500 Massachusetts Avenue. From her sunroom she could see the Japanese Embassy and the new Moslem minaret. She continued to go out when she could, driven by MacAllister Gray, the family chauffeur. Martha had the satisfaction of seeing her four sons fulfilling themselves in the family tradition of politics, law, education, and government. All four had served their country during World War II. Horace, her youngest son, pursued the scholar's course without interruption except for his war service. He saw action at Okinawa and went into Japan with the Eighth Army. Home again, he took his degree at Yale under the G.I. Bill of Rights; then added a postgraduate course in physics and did further work in Zurich, Switzerland. Horace moved quite logically from youthful star-gazing through a telescope given him by his father to becoming a research assistant at the University of Chicago Institution for Nuclear Studies. Then Yale claimed another Taft when he was appointed associate professor of physics. Of all the sons he most closely resembles his father in appearance.

Lloyd Bowers Taft became in turn a newspaperman, radio and television executive, and investment banker. After attending Yale and the University of Michigan he worked as a reporter for the *Times-Star* and was its assistant publisher from 1954 to 1959. He was associated in his radio-television work for the Taft Broadcasting Company with Hulbert Taft's two sons, David G. Taft and Hulbert Taft, Jr. David, who was wounded in action during World War II, died of a heart attack in Maine in 1962 at the age of forty-six, leaving a widow and six children. He had survived his father only by three years, for the elder Hulbert Taft died on Indian Hill on January 19, 1959, at the age of eighty-one. He had been the newspaperman par excellence of the Taft family, the reporter as well as the owner. Services were held for him at the Indian Hill Church that Bob and he had helped to establish and he was buried in Spring Grove Cemetery. He left thirteen grandchildren and his wife

Eleanor, whose history of the region, *Hither and Yon on Indian Hill,* was published in 1962.

Lloyd, who has four children, lived in the suburb of Mariemont at the foot of Indian Hill, until moving to New York. His wartime service was in the Navy and he is the champion golfer of the family. His oldest brother, William Howard Taft, III, became a permanent member of the Foreign Service in 1962, working in the office of International Scientific Affairs. His career has involved both education and diplomacy. Closely resembling his father in features and manner, he is tall, angular, accomplished, and quietly witty. Bill, as he is known to his intimates, was graduated from the Taft School in 1933 and from Yale in 1937. He took his Ph.D. at Princeton in 1942 and was a freshman instructor at the University of Maryland in 1940, moving from there to Haverford College where he taught English and also met Barbara Bradfield, the Grand Rapids girl he married in 1942. Advanced academic degrees abound among the women in the Taft family and, like her husband, she holds the degree of Ph.D. Bill and Barbara have four children, who have had an interesting upbringing, since their father's career has taken them from Ireland to Mozambique.

During World War II Bill left Haverford and worked for Army Intelligence in Washington for three years. After the war he taught English at Yale from 1945 to 1948 and while there studied the Irish language from the linguistic historian's point of view. From 1948 to 1951 he was in Dublin working for the Marshall Plan mission and in his free moments he studied Irish. Today he delights his friends with his wit and scholarship in this field.

When his work under the Marshall Plan ended Bill returned to the United States, did some writing, and considered going into politics. He campaigned for his father in the South Dakota primary of 1952 but a round of hand-shaking and extemporaneous speaking persuaded him that he was not cut out to be a politician. In 1953 he was back in Ireland, this time as United States ambassador. In the next four years his growing children enjoyed life in Dublin, and Ambassador Taft had the satisfaction of putting into practice some of the projects he had worked for under the Marshall Plan. On his return he joined the Policy Planning staff of the State Department and was at once involved in the rapidly developing problems of Africa. He visited the fomenting continent in 1958 and in January, 1960, was assigned to Mozambique as consul general, staying at Laurenço Marques for the next two years. On his return he was a reserve officer in the Foreign Service until 1962, when he became the first ambassador to join the Foreign Service on a permanent basis.

Mrs. Robert Taft did not live to see her son, Robert Taft, Jr., follow his father to the Capitol as congressman-at-large from Ohio in 1963. She died of a heart attack on October 2, 1958, and was buried with Bob in the cemetery on Indian Hill. When Darrah Wunder suggested that Robert, running for the Ohio legislature, should instead be running for the United States Senate, Martha promptly said: "I think he must make his own decisions." She and Bob may have shaped their sons' lives through their early training but they never dictated to them.

Young Robert, the inheritor of the Taft political tradition, was born on February 26, 1917, the year his parents moved to Indian Hill. He attended the Cincinnati Country Day School and was a healthy youngster, strong and bright, but not the superlative scholar that his father had been. He attended the Taft School and today he is chairman of the board of trustees. At Yale he was a football enthusiast but never got beyond the junior varsity team. Robert was inclined to be a quiet and serious student. With him on the campus were two of the men whose paths would cross his later on the national scene—McGeorge Bundy and William W. Scranton. Robert was graduated from Yale in 1939 and took his law degree at Harvard in 1942. The war experiences that followed matured and developed him. As naval officer on an attack transport he had the searing experience of the landings at Guadalcanal, Sicily, Salerno, Normandy, and Okinawa. He returned with widened vistas and when he entered Congress in 1963 he was a seasoned lawyer and an experienced legislator as well as a war veteran.

It was inevitable that young Robert Taft should get prime attention when he walked into the Capitol a decade after his father's death. He brought the Taft name, the Taft image, and some of the Taft philosophy back to the Capitol. His fine presence and his potentialities in the political field were recognized at once as he settled easily into his place as a congressman-at-large. At the close of 1963 he announced that he would run for the Senate, and he emerged from the April primary in Ohio with a majority of 445,000 votes. From the start he freely acknowledged that the family name was an asset but that this could work in reverse and make failure more obvious if he did not move ahead. He was soon at work on the labor, education, and banking committees, and was deeply involved in congressional machinery. Robert played a modest role on the floor but took care to be on hand for the significant vote. Always the staunch Republican, he declared himself complimented when the Americans for Democratic Action gave him a voting score of zero. Instead of rushing in with a flourish at the beginning he quietly took stock and recalled for one of his earliest audiences the story of Abraham Lincoln greeting a new congressman with the line: "Come in here and tell me what you know. It won't take long."

Robert proved himself to be a practical politician but not a headline seeker. Observers quickly decided that he had some of his father's political acumen with a good deal of his mother's charm. He avoided rhetorical crescendo and was direct and factual, if perhaps less abrasive than his father; but, like him, he was invariably well primed on his subject. Unlike the senior senator, he made his points smoothly and without emphasis, so that they neither stung nor burned. He showed the same general interests as his father and at the end of 1963 introduced a bill to provide for the medical and hospital care of the aged through voluntary health insurance. He proposed this bill as a substitute for the King-Anderson bill backed by the Johnson administration.

Young Robert made it clear from the start that he was not trying to pattern himself after his father, although his admiration for the late senator is profound. He accepted the fact that the world had changed in the last ten years and that the politician has to think in terms of the particular era in which he lives. His own experiences have made him somewhat more of an internationalist although he always maintains that his father was never isolationist in spirit. He likes to recall that both Senator Taft and William Howard Taft supported international law and the League of Nations.

The true test of liberalism, in Robert's opinion, rests in maintaining the freedom of the individual to think, act, and express himself and to manage his own life instead of straitjacketing him with laws and regulations. In his many speeches since winning his congressional seat he has pounded away at the need to curb federal spending and federal controls, except for defense and space development. He does not believe in tax cuts without balancing reduction in federal spending. He is a liberal on civil rights, and takes a tough stand on such matters as loan funds going to any institution that discriminates against Negroes. "Final equality must come from the hearts of people as much as the laws of the land," he says on this issue. He voted enthusiastically for the Civil Rights Bill, approving every phase of it. He proposed putting the Antipoverty program under the Department of Labor, an amendment defeated by the Democrats.

The Congressman has special interest in housing, as his father had. The elder Taft supported federal aid to education and young Robert is not against it, but he believes that it should be carried out in a controlled fashion. He is the avowed foe of communism and came out for a blockade of Cuba more than a month before this measure was taken. But he is not an enthusiast about banning subversive speakers from university campuses. He believes that the "continued success of our private enterprise system is the one dominating weapon which we have in the entire conflict with international communism." During the primary fight Robert was accused by his opponent, Ohio Secretary of State Ted W. Brown, of holding views more akin to those of his uncle Charlie than of his father, the Senator. He said that the Congressman was abandoning the traditional principles of Ohio Republicanism for the more liberal views of Eastern Republicans. In general Robert Taft has emerged, both in the State House and on Capitol Hill, as a moderate-liberal on human rights, a conservative on fiscal measures.

Congressman Taft is profoundly interested in broadening the base of foreign trade, but through Congress and without granting excessive power to the President. In labor he insists on keeping collective bargaining strong and he is opposed to compulsory arbitration in labor disputes, favoring a cooling-off period for fact-finding, with provisions guaranteed to prevent either side from obtaining an advantage during this period of abeyance. Robert is convinced that no one labor union should be allowed to become too powerful and he has given careful thought to legislation that would meet such emergencies as the newspaper strikes of 1962–63.

Like his cousin Seth, Robert Taft enjoys the practice of law. He quickly announced when he reached Washington that every politician should have some solid interest to fall back on in case of defeat, since this would tend to make him more independent if pressures were applied. In his own case he knows that an excellent law practice awaits him in Cincinnati should he find himself out of office; he has built up a solid reputation as a corporation lawyer with the firm of Taft, Stettinius and Hollister.

While still in college he was thinking in terms of a political career and he campaigned for his father on various occasions. He could find no residue of bitterness in the Senator's attitude and to his son the elder Taft seemed a warm-hearted man behind the cool front that the public knew, a politician who tried to be realistic rather than emotional. After his death strong pressure was applied to young Robert to run for the Senate, but he made the same decision that his father had done years earlier—to get his training in his own state before aiming for the national scene. He ran for the state legislature in 1954 and won with ease, after campaigning in much the same style as Senator Taft—barnstorming the counties of Ohio, wading ankle-deep in mud at country fairs, and shaking hands with more genuine enthusiasm than the elder Taft was ever able to muster.

When he reached the State House in Columbus it was clear that another Taft was on his way. For the next three terms he found deep satisfaction in a combination of his legislative work and his private practice. While majority floor leader he did not often share in debate but showed a special gift for working with committees on controversial legislation. When he made his bid for Congress he campaigned hard, as before, but breezed his way into office. It was a foregone conclusion that he would win and he did not regard it as any sacrifice to give up his corporate earnings for his salary of $22,500, which he considers a "fair wage."

In Washington he was quickly drawn into the social life of the capital, where his father, his grandfather, and his great-grandfather had made their mark before him. It soon was apparent that he was not as far to the right as his father. He chose to call himself a liberal-conservative, a characterization that had also been applied to the Senator. But young Robert qualifies this with the warning that the word "liberal" has been so misconstrued and confused in its application that it has no meaning any longer. He defines the conservative as one who knows and appreciates the importance of stability.

His own approach is more relaxed than his father's. He is genial but shrewd, and absorbs what is said with legal understanding. He can drink beer with the rank and file, enjoys speaking and campaigning, and feels at ease in the company of politicians. He has less trouble than his father in flashing a wide grin at the electorate. Behind his candid manner lies a thoughtful nature, with a touch of the combative spirit. Young Robert Taft is six feet one, weighs 200 pounds, and moves with the controlled gait of the athlete. He is dark-haired and has a stubborn, pointed chin, along with his mother's dark and intelligent eyes. Physically he closely resembles Martha Taft. Robert has more authentic reserve than his free and easy campaigning suggests and his wide grin fades quickly when a nerve is touched. His laughter is high-pitched and relaxed but in essence he is a grave young man. His hobbies are golf and trout fishing. His wife, Blanca Noel, daughter of Louis W. Noel, a New York banker, dislikes public attention and is not the campaigner that Martha Taft was. They have four children—Robert A. Taft, II, who was at Yale when his father took his seat in Congress, and on graduation joined the Peace Corps and went to Tanganyika; Sarah Butler Taft, who married Winfield Payne Jones, II, in the summer of 1963 while she was still a student at Radcliffe; Deborah, who attends Concord Academy; and Jonathan, who was enrolled in the Beauvoir School in Washington when his family moved to the capital and took a house in the Cleveland Park section.

Until his father's death Robert lived in a white clapboard house close to his parents on Indian Hill and raised Angus cattle. Later he moved into the big house, which remains the Robert Taft home. He has returned frequently to his native state to speak and to keep warm currents flowing between Cincinnati and Washington. True to family tradition, he has always been active in the social welfare field, working for the Children's Home and for the Community Chest, with which his mother was always identified.

Robert does not like the sound of the word dynasty, yet when the William Howard Taft Memorial Association was organized in 1962 for the restoration of the old family house on Mount Auburn, the thought was inescapable that the Tafts were dynastic in their spread. The plan was to restore the house as it was in 1857, the year of President Taft's birth. Descendants of Alphonso and Louise rounded up old furniture, silver, objects of art, letters, and family memorabilia of one kind and another, under the guidance of Mrs. Willa Beall, executive director of the association. Japanese cherry trees were planted close to the square old mansion which was no longer in Taft hands but was divided into separate apartments by E. R. Bellinger, who owns it and has lived in it since 1940.

Charlie Taft, the family historian, has worked to link up the history of his ancestors. He hurried back from Scotland in 1960 for the memorial dedication service at the home site of the first Robert Taft at Mendon. On that occasion he was the speaker and, looking back nearly 400 years, he said: "They started right here, somewhere on this land. Here they began to scratch and dig and prosper. . . ." Today no one knows how many Tafts there are across the country but large numbers assemble periodically at Uxbridge. The first of these gatherings was in 1874 when Alphonso Taft, who had compiled a history of the family, was the guest of honor and more than 500 Tafts heard him speak. Some came from as far west as Nebraska. Another big reunion was held in 1894. Many Tafts still live in the Mendon-Uxbridge region, although they are not closely related to the Tafts of Ohio. Charlie treasures a family tree that he hopes to hang one day in the restored birthplace on Mount Auburn. The first Robert's name is at its base, with branches for his five sons. The last entry was Charles Phelps Taft, I, who was born in 1843. In 1964 there were 167 living descendants of Louise and Alphonso Taft.

Always responsive to family reunions, Charlie was present at the Chase home in Connecticut for Christmas, 1962. On this occasion 65 of the 254 living Chase descendants sat around the family board, but the Chase who mattered most to Charlie was no longer there, for his wife Eleanor died of cancer at their Avondale home on August 28, 1961. She was sixty-seven years old and she left five children and four sisters —Mrs. Edward Carmody, Mrs. John Griffith-Davies, Mrs. William H. Feeter, and Mrs. Thomas Ewing, known professionally as Lucia Chase, of the American Ballet Theater.

The William Howard Taft family strain by this time had narrowed down to Charlie Taft and Mrs. Manning, whose interest in the academic world had remained unchanged down the years. She retired from Bryn Mawr in 1957, after serving as dean, acting president, professor of history, and chairman of the History Department. She was executive direc-

tor of the alumnae drive for funds and has always been as closely associated with the college as her father and brothers with Yale. During the
winter of 1962-63 she was a visiting lecturer at the University of Texas,
after spending the previous summer doing research in the Public Record
Office in England. In her busy life Mrs. Manning has found time to have
two books published—*British Government After the American Revolution 1782–1820* and *The Revolt of French Canada 1800–1835*. Her
family, too, are deep in the academic tradition. Her oldest daughter,
Helen, married Holland Hunter and they have three daughters and a
son—Ann, Barbara, Christine, and Timothy. Her youngest daughter,
Caroline, married Frederic Cunningham and their children are Sarah,
Mary, and Constance. All four parents teach at Bryn Mawr or Swarthmore, and the Manning tradition remains strong in Pennsylvania, as
the Taft heritage does in Ohio, California, Rhode Island, Massachusetts,
Maine, Connecticut, New York, and Washington.

Mrs. Manning likes now to holiday on an island in the Caribbean
as well as at Murray Bay. Both she and Charlie were at the St. Lawrence
resort in the summer of 1963. They had a long way to look back and
were thinking now in terms of their children and their grandchildren.
The place was full of memories for the two remaining children of William Howard Taft. The echoes of history were always close to them as a
family. After his wife's death Charlie continued to foster the spirit of
tolerance that Eleanor and he had always upheld. He backed the can-
dlelight memorial ceremony for John F. Kennedy, acting as co-chairman
of America's Conscience Fund, established to help repair damaged
churches in the South, and to combat hate.

From first to last the Tafts have dedicated themselves to public service
of one kind or another, leaving their impress on government, the judiciary, education, the arts, and the philanthropy of the nation, as well as
of their native state. Their talents have been well divided among the
men and women of each generation. They have always been willing to
stand up for their beliefs, however unpopular, and to weather criticism
without giving ground. But for the most part the sun has shone on the
Tafts as a family. The recurrence of special gifts and qualities, of lofty
aims and integrity, has been marked in their history. They have touched
the national life at many sensitive points—often with distinction, always
with high intent.

SOURCES

Chapter 1: *From Vermont to Cincinnati*

Mabel T. R. Washburn, *Ancestry of William Howard Taft*; John G. Metcalf, *Annals of the Town of Mendon from 1659–1880*; C. F. Jewett, *History of Worcester County*, 2 vols.; *Taft Family Gathering at Uxbridge, Mass.*, 1874; Alphonso Taft's address at Uxbridge, August 12, 1874; *A Meeting of the Descendants of Ebenezer and Mary (Howard) Taft at the Chestnut Hill Meeting-House in Blackstone, Mass.*, August 11, 1891; Russell W. Taft, *Taft Family News*, Vol. I, May 1910; Anson Titus, "The Taft Kin," Boston *Evening Transcript*, March 4, 1909; Newburyport *Daily News*, July 18, 1908; Taft family papers, Lib. Cong.: Fanny Phelps Diaries, 1842 and 1848; Peter Rawson Taft's Diary; Peter Rawson Taft to Sylvia Howard Taft, October 17, 1833, November 1, 1833; Sylvia Howard Taft to Peter Rawson Taft, October 12, 1833; Alphonso Taft to Sylvia Taft, March 9, 1834, February 14, 1836, January 1, 1837, November 15, 1838; Sylvia Taft to Alphonso Taft, September 16, 1835, June 3, 1837, August 17, 1837, September 5, 1837, March 9, 1844, June 17, 1850; Peter Rawson Taft to Alphonso Taft, August 10, 1836, January 1, 1837, March 17, 1839, April 1, 1839, October 5, 1843; Alphonso Taft to Peter Rawson Taft, September 7, 1835, October 27, 1838, March 30, 1839, June 13, 1848; Alphonso Taft to Fanny Phelps, September 18 and 27, 1838, October 5, 9 and 21, 1838, November 12, 1838, January 7 and 15, 1839, March 17 and 30, 1839, April 3, 1840, May 17, 1840, August 11, 1840, September 21, 1839, December 28, 1839; Alphonso Taft to Fanny Phelps Taft, June 11, 1848, July 2 and 9, 1848; Fanny Phelps Taft to Alphonso Taft, June 4, 1848, July 2, 1848, August 21, 1848, September 11, 1848, April

5, 1849, January 7, 1851; Charles Phelps to Fanny Phelps, July 18, 1842; Mrs. Charles Phelps to Fanny Phelps, September 26, 1841, September 29, 1842; James Phelps to Fanny Phelps, July 10, 1845; Elisa Phelps to Fanny Phelps, April 16, 1837; Alphonso Taft to Sylvia and Peter Rawson Taft, September 28, 1832, March 30, 1834, November 8, 1835, October 22, 1836, May 28, 1837, November 13, 1838, April 1, 1839, July 28, 1840, September 12, 1840; Aaron F. Perry to Alphonso Taft, August 12, 1848, April 29, 1849, March 5, 1851, February 17, 1852, December 21, 1852; *Memoir to Fanny Phelps Taft by Her Husband*, 1852; Alphonso Taft to Daniel Webster, January 29, 1844, February 26, 1847; Alphonso Taft to Charles Phelps Taft, Dec. 1, 1884; Alphonso Taft to William Howard Taft, October 26, 1884; Charles Phelps Taft to W. H. T., July 20, 1900; Martha Willard, mss., 1935, Swarthmore College, "Notes for a Biographer, based on the Taft private papers 1810–1891," Lib. Cong.: Lewis Alexander Leonard, *Life of Alphonso Taft*; Francis McHale, *President and Chief Justice*; Alvin F. Harlow, *The Serene Cincinnatians*; Charles Frederic Goss, *Cincinnati: The Queen City 1788–1912*; Charles Cist, *Sketches and Statistics of Cincinnati in 1851.*

Chapter 2: *The Torrey Sisters*

Frederic C. Torrey, *The Torrey Families and Their Children in America*, 2 vols.; *Centennial History of the Town of Millbury, Mass.*; C. F. Jewett, *History of Worcester County*; George Walter Chamberlain, *Genealogy of Weymouth Families*; Taft family papers, Lib. Cong.: Susan H. Waters to Serafina G. Waters, September 25, 1822, February 4, 1824; Mrs. Susan Waters Torrey to Delia Chapin Torrey, September 13, 1837, February 12, 1845, March 3, 1845, January 15, 1846, October 7, 1846; Mrs. Susan Waters Torrey to Louise Torrey, August 4, 1847, October 5, 1857, December 24, 1854; Louise Torrey to Mrs. Susan Waters Torrey, September 3, 1841, July 13, 1843, October 13, 1843, January 1, 6 and 14, 1846, May 30, 1846, March 15, 1847, March 26, 1847, February 10, 1853, January 12, 1854, January 5, 1855; Louise to Delia Torrey, March 31, 1841, February 19, 1846, March 30, 1848, August 17, 1848, February 8, 1849, January 5, 1850, April 26, 1850, May 22, 1850, March 12, 1851, January 4 and 30, 1854, February 7, 1854, June 5, 1854, February 22, 1857; Delia to Louise Torrey, January 1 and 18, 1854, February 10, 1854, June 2, 1854, August 24, 1857, October 11, 1857, November 22, 1857; Delia to Mrs. Susan W. Torrey, January 31, 1844, January 21, 1845, January 7, 1846, September 3, 1847, December 26, 1854; Delia Torrey's Graduation Book, November, 1837, Uxbridge Female Seminary; Delia to Mr. and Mrs. Samuel Torrey, November 25, 1843; Delia to Alphonso Taft, March 2, 1857, January 1, 1858; Delia to Samuel Torrey, October 2, 1854; Delia to W. H. T., October 30, 1914; Delia to W. Moody, March 17, 1858; Louise Torrey to Samuel Torrey, November 12, 1847, January 22, 1853, February 1, 1857; Alphonso Taft to Samuel D. Torrey, Dec. 30, 1853; Alphonso Taft to Louise Torrey Taft, June 2, 1854, July 8 and 31,

1854; Alphonso Taft to Delia Torrey, August 3 and 6, 1854, November 19, 1854; Samuel Torrey to Louise Taft, February 8, 1858; Anna Torrey to Louise Taft, July 6, 1857; Alphonso to Mrs. Samuel Torrey, April 15, 1854, November 26, 1854; Increase V. Tarbox to Mrs. Alphonso Taft, April 15, 1854; November 26, 1854; Martha Willard mss.; Clara (Longworth) de Chambrun, *Cincinnati: Story of the Queen City*; Charles Cist, *Sketches and Statistics of Cincinnati in 1859*; *The Cincinnati Miscellany or Antiquities of the West*, 2 vols.; Harriet Martineau, *Retrospect of Western Travel*; Charles T. Greve, *Centennial History of Cincinnati*; Alvin F. Harlow, *The Serene Cincinnatians*; Charles Frederic Goss, *Cincinnati, the Queen City 1788–1912*; Dr. Paul Herget to author.

Chapter 3: *Birth of a President*

Peter Rawson Taft's Diary 1850–1866; Alphonso Taft to Increase N. Tarbox, September 21, 1857; Delia Torrey to Mrs. Alphonso Taft, August 24, 1857, November 22, 1857, January 2, 1858, February 3, 1858, March 3, 1858, April 4, 1858, January 15, 1859, March 1, 1859, December 8, 1859; Mrs. Alphonso Taft to Delia Torrey, February 22, 1857, June 20, 1857, November 8, 1857, February 12, 1858, April 4, 1858, May 3, 1858, September 26, 1858, December 13, 1858, January 26, 1859, April 10, 1859, May 15, 1859, June 10, 1859, March 4, 1860, December 30, 1860, January 2, 1861; Alphonso Taft to Delia Torrey, February 1, 1857, February 20, 1857, March 8, 1857, July 5, 1857, October 16, 1857, December 13, 1857, October 8, 1858; Delia to Alphonso Taft, March 2, 1857, September 20, 1857; Delia to Anna Torrey, May 10, 1858; Delia to W. Moody, March 17, 1858; W. Moody to Delia, August 15, 1858; Louise Taft to Mrs. Samuel Torrey, May 10, 1857, February 28, 1858, March 22, 1858, April 10, 1858, November 14, 1858, February 6, 1860, March 6, 1859, June 19, 1859; Mrs. Alphonso Taft to Samuel Torrey, February 1, 1857; Louise (Mrs. Alphonso Taft) to Alphonso Taft, July 15 and 18, 1858, August 23, 1858, August 1 and 25, 1859; Alphonso Taft to Louise, *Inter Nos*. undated, 1854, June 9, 1857, July 21, 1859, August 28, 1860; Alphonso Taft to Mrs. Torrey, February 19, 1860; Alphonso Taft to Samuel Torrey, February 7, 1855, September 15, 1858, January 10, 1859; Mrs. Torrey to Mrs. Alphonso Taft, February 19, 1855, October 5, 1857, December 15, 1859, October 22, 1860; Mrs. Torrey to Samuel Torrey, September 30, 1859; Samuel Torrey to Mrs. Alphonso Taft, September 27, 1857, October 5, 1857, January 11, 1858; Charles Phelps Taft to Alphonso Taft, September 4, 1859, November 2 and 6, 1859; Charles Taft to Mrs. Alphonso Taft, September 28, 1859, October 9, 1859; Mrs. Alphonso Taft to Peter Rawson Taft II (Rossy), August 3, 1858; Mrs. Alphonso Taft to Susie Torrey, November 3, 1857, January 2, 1858; Mrs. Alphonso Taft to Anna Torrey, July 15, 1857; David G. Ray to Alphonso Taft, April 5, 1858; Alphonso Taft to Aaron F. Perry, January 3, 1861, W. H. T. papers, Lib. Cong.; Lewis Alexander Leonard, *Life of Alphonso Taft*; Horace Dutton Taft, *Memories and Opin-*

ions; Edward H. Cotton, *William Howard Taft, a Character Study;* Martha Willard mss.

Chapter 4: *The Civil War*

Mrs. Alphonso Taft to Mrs. Samuel Torrey, September 22, 1861, April 21, 1861, July 1, 1861, January 4, 1863, June 24, 1863, August 15, 1864, November 16 and 21, 1864, December 15, 1864; Mrs. Alphonso Taft to Samuel Torrey, June 11, 1861, March 28, 1862, March 13, 1865; Mrs. Samuel Torrey to Mrs. Alphonso Taft, October 22, 1861; Mrs. Samuel Torrey to Delia Torrey, June 23, 1861, November 1, 1863, June 9, 1864; Mrs. Alphonso Taft to Charles Phelps Taft, September 22, 1861; Mrs. Alphonso Taft to Delia, August 25, 1861, September 25, 1861, December 9, 1861, March 9 and 30, 1862, December 5, 1862, February 1 and 15, 1863, April 21, 1863, November 29, 1863, December 13, 1863, March 2 and 13, 1864, August 4, 1864, September 4, 1864, October 26, 1864, October 5, 1865; Mrs. Alphonso Taft to Anna Torrey, February 23, 1863, May 14 and 30, 1864, June 6 and 28, 1864, July 10, 1864, August 27, 1864, October 17 and 24, 1864; Mrs. Alphonso Taft to Susie Torrey, January 13, 1863, March 1 and 29, 1863, July 9 and 19, 1863; Alphonso Taft to Delia, August 18, 1861, June 15, 1862, October 5, 1862, June 7, 1863, January 23, 1864, November 24, 1865, March 21, 1873; Alphonso Taft to Mrs. Torrey, March 18, 1865; Alphonso Taft to Samuel Torrey, November 17, 1861, January 10 and 29, 1864, March 13, 1865; Alphonso Taft to W. H. T. (Willie), January 23, 1864; Alphonso Taft to Rossy, September 26, 1863; Alphonso Taft to Anna Torrey, September 3, 1864; Alphonso Taft to Salmon Portland Chase, December 7, 1864 (Chase papers); Delia Torrey to Anna Torrey, November 22, 1864; Delia to Louise, November 3, 1861, February 16, 1862; Delia to Samuel Torrey, April 25, 1864; May 1, 1864; Delia to the Rev. Samuel Dutton, February 2, 1864, October 4, 1864, December 2, 1864, January 21, 1865, March 21, 1865, May 28, 1865, September 2 and 29, 1865; Delia to Susie Torrey, March 5, 1864; Delia to Alphonso Taft, January 5, 1862, May 5, 1862, June 9, 1862, January 17, 1863; Delia to Anna, November 22, 1864; Increase Tarbox to Delia, December 30, 1862; Anna Torrey to Mrs. Samuel Torrey, November 7, 1864; Anna Torrey to Charles and Rossy Taft, February 21, 1864; Anna Torrey to Mrs. Alphonso Taft, September 23, 1861, November 24, 1861, February 15, 1862, March 30, 1863; W. H. T. papers, Lib. Cong.; *Henry Howe Historical Collections of Ohio,* Vol. 1; Alvin F. Harlow, *The Serene Cincinnatians;* R. Ernest Dupuy and Trevor N. Dupuy, *The Compact History of the Civil War;* Bruce Catton, *The Coming Fury* and *The Terrible Swift Sword.*

Chapter 5: *Peace At Last*

Correspondence between Charles Phelps and Peter Rawson Taft and their parents, Louise and Alphonso Taft, from Europe, 1867–1869, Taft family papers, Lib. Cong.; Mrs. Alphonso Taft to Anna Torrey, March 7, 1865, April 18, 1865, August 7, 1866; Delia Taft to Samuel Dutton, January 2, 1865, March 2 and 21, 1865, April 11 and 21, 1865, May 7, 17 and 28, 1865, June 14, 1865, July 2, 1865, September 2 and 5, 1865, November 24, 1865; Mrs. Alphonso Taft to Delia, October 5, 1865, January 28, 1866, February 26, 1866, April 24, 1866, May 16, 1866; Delia to Alphonso Taft, November 5, 1865; Mrs. Alphonso Taft to Samuel Dutton, June 3, 1865, October 5, 1865; Mrs. Alphonso Taft to Mrs. Samuel Torrey, January 2, 1865, May 23, 1865, July 2 and 3, 1865, August 12, 1865, December 10 and 24, 1865; Mrs. Alphonso Taft to Samuel Torrey, June 6, 1866, April 2, 1869; Anna Torrey to Delia Torrey, April 15 and 30, 1867, June 2 and 30, 1867; Anna Torrey to Samuel Torrey, May 15, 1867; Alphonso Taft to Anna Torrey, July 25, 1869, September 15, 1869; Alphonso Taft to Samuel Torrey, April 22, 1865, July 17, 1865, October 16, 1872; Mrs. Alphonso Taft to Susie Torrey, June 26, 1866; Willie to Alphonso Taft, July 16, 1869; Willie to Mrs. Alphonso Taft, August 2, 1868; Alphonso Taft's Passport, May 19, 1869; Alphonso Taft to Delia, November 5, 1865, October 14, 1869, December 24, 1869; Mrs. Alphonso Taft to Anna Torrey, February 17, 1866, March 28, 1866, June 17, 1866, August 7, 1866, November 18, 1866, July 14 and 26, 1869; Mrs. Alphonso Taft to "My Dear Boys," September 12, 1869; Peter Rawson Taft (Rossy) to Alphonso Taft, May 21, 1865, July 2, 1865, November 12, 1865, May 16, 1868, July 18, 1868, November 8, 1868, December 27, 1868, February 3, 1869, April 14, 1869, December 5, 1869, May 22 and 31, 1870; Rossy to Willie Taft, December 12, 1869; Charles Phelps Taft to Alphonso Taft, February 22, 1867, March 31, 1867, July 27, 1867, December 18, 1867, August 30, 1868; Alphonso Taft to Willie, August 1, 1869, September 4, 1869; Alphonso Taft to Henry Waters Taft (Harry), August 8, 1869, September 10, 1869; Alphonso Taft to Willie and Harry, July 15, 1869; Martha Willard mss.; Charles Frederic Goss, *Cincinnati; the Queen City 1788–1912*; Charles T. Greve, *Centennial History of Cincinnati*; Alvin F. Harlow, *The Serene Cincinnatians*; Alphonso Taft to Salmon Portland Chase, December 7, 1864, Chase papers, Lib. Cong.

Chapter 6: A *Sinton Marries a Taft*

Cincinnati *Enquirer*, December 5, 1873; Taft family papers, Lib. Cong.: David Sinton's invitations to wedding of Annie Sinton and Charles Phelps Taft; Mrs. Alphonso Taft to Delia Torrey, January 26, 1873, April 23, 1873, January 2, 1874, March 8 and 23, 1874, April 1 and 10, 1874, August 16, 1874, September 13, 1874, October 22, 1874, September 19, 1875, July 9, 1877, January 22, 1878, September 7, 25 and 28, 1878, July 31, 1879, August 26, 1879, June 6 and 23, 1880, January 26, 1882; Mrs. Alphonso Taft to Anna Torrey, February 26, 1874, May 31, 1876; Alphonso Taft's nomination address at Columbus, Ohio, for Rutherford B. Hayes as governor, June 2, 1875; White House invitation to dine with President and Mrs. Grant, March 27, 1876; Alphonso Taft's wedding anniversary, Cincinnati *Gazette*, Dec. 27,

1878; Alphonso Taft to Colonel Asa Waters, January 11, 1877, July 27, 1877, Asa Waters' papers, American Antiquarian Society, Worcester, Mass.; Adelia Waters Tarbox to Asa H. Waters, June 14, 1865, Waters papers; Taft family papers, Lib. Cong.: Alphonso Taft to Delia, April 30, 1875, July 23, 1877, August 1 and 21, 1877, September 29, 1877, December 11, 1877, October 21, 1877, August 8 and 29, 1879, September 10, 1879, June 13, 1880, October 17, 1880; W. H. T. to Alphonso Taft, September 13, 1874, March 19, 1876, June 18, 1876, March 11, 1878, April 14, 1878, June 4, 1882; W. H. T. to Mrs. Alphonso Taft, October 1, 1874, November 1, 8 and 15, 1874; August 23, 1882; Alphonso Taft to W. H. T., July 2, 3 and 7, 1879, September 10, 1880, May 30, 1882; Mrs. Alphonso Taft to W. H. T., September 22 and 29, 1875, January 30, 1878; W. H. T. to Delia, April 25 and 30, 1875, May 30, 1875, September 14, 1878; W. H. T. to Fanny Taft, May 21, 1882; Charles Phelps Taft to Alphonso Taft, March 14, 19 and 30, 1876, May 23, 1876, May 30, 1876, June 30, 1876, August 25, 1876, September 2, 6 and 11, 1876, November 15, 1876, February 22, 1877; Peter Rawson Taft to Alphonso Taft, May 28, 1876, April 2, 7, 11, 19 and 26, 1878; Dr. W. S. Chipley to Mrs. Peter Rawson Taft, March 27, 1878; Edwards Pierrepont to Alphonso Taft, June 29, 1875; Fanny Taft to Mrs. Alphonso Taft, April 24 and 30, 1876, May 16, 1876, August 7, 1880; Mrs. Alphonso Taft to Fanny Taft, July 6, 1878; Delia to Samuel Torrey, May 18, 1876; Harry Taft to Delia, March 29, 1880, July 22, 1880; Mrs. Alphonso Taft to Alphonso Taft, June 27, 1877; Mrs. Charles Phelps Taft (Annie) to Alphonso Taft, March 19, 1876; Horace Taft to Alphonso Taft, March 17, 1875; Horace Taft to W. H. T., May 3, 1882, June 4, 1882; Harry Taft to W. H. T., May 30, 1882; Alphonso Taft to Samuel Torrey, November 4, 1875, March 12, 1876; Mrs. Henry Waters Taft (Julia) to Alphonso Taft, May 27, 1882; Rutherford B. Hayes to Alphonso Taft, May 22, 1876; William Dore to Alphonso Taft, October 30, 1884; Harry Taft to Alphonso Taft, October 22, 1876, November 5, 1876; Justice M. R. Waite to Alphonso Taft, Dec. 13, 1874, Waite papers, Lib. Cong.; Alphonso Taft to Justice M. R. Waite, December 7, 1874; William Allen White to W. H. T., March 31, 1908, William Allen White papers, Lib. Cong.; Eugene P. Lyle, Jr., "Taft: A Career of Big Tasks. The Beginning of Public Service," World's Work, July, 1907; Arthur Wilson Davis, History of Mount Auburn, Historical and Philosophical Society of Ohio; Robert Lee Dunn, William Howard Taft, American; Julia B. Foraker, I Would Live It Again; Joseph B. Foraker, Notes of a Busy Life; Horace Dutton Taft, Memories and Opinions; Francis McHale, President and Chief Justice; Lewis Alexander Leonard, Life of Alphonso Taft; Harriet Martineau, Retrospect of Western Travel, Taft Museum Catalogue; Alice Roosevelt Longworth, Crowded Hours.

Chapter 7: *Vienna Days*

From Taft family papers, Lib. Cong. and William Howard Taft Memorial Association, Cincinnati: Diary of Delia C. Torrey, 1884; Diary of Fanny Taft;

Fanny Taft to Horace Taft, September 17, 21 and 30, 1882; October 30, 1882; President Arthur to Mrs. Alphonso Taft, March 8, 1883; Julia W. Smith to Fanny Taft and Mrs. Alphonso Taft, March 10, 1883, May 26, 1882; Delia to Susie Torrey, September 16, 1883, November 2, 1883, January 8, 1884; Delia to W. H. T., June 18, 1882; Alphonso Taft to Delia, May 12, 1882, January 19, 1883; Charles Phelps Taft to Alphonso Taft, August 26, 1882, March 4, 1883, January 2, 1884, January 6, 1885; W. H. T. to Alphonso Taft, June 4 and 25, 1882; July 9 and 24, 1882; August 13 and 20, 1882; September 2, 1882; January 22, 1883, April 22, 1883, May 31, 1883, March 8, 1883, July 20, 1883, April 30, 1883, November 11, 1883, December 9, 1883, January 13, 1884, February 10, 1884, March 13, 24 and 31, 1884; May 13, 1884, June 16, 1884, July 15, 1884, September 13, 1884, October 22, 1884, February 8, 1885, April 9, 1885; Alphonso Taft to Horace Taft, October 7, 1884, January 17, 1885, February 15, 1885; Alphonso Taft to Charles Phelps Taft, July 15, 1882, January 10, 1883, June 12, 1883, January 6, 1884; Horace Taft to Alphonso Taft, July 27, 1882, September 24, 1882, October 26, 1884, January 4, 1885, June 13, 1885; Horace to Mrs. Alphonso Taft, September 5, 1882, September 8, 1884, October 22, 1884, January 4, 1885, February 8, 1885; W. H. T. to Mrs. Alphonso Taft, July 16, 1882, August 8, 23 and 28, 1882, January 2 and 6, 1883, February 21, 1883, April 15, 1883, May 14, 1883, September 20 and 24, 1883, October 6 and 12, 1883, October 28, 1883, November 4, 1883, January 20, 1884, May 5, 1884, August 28, 1884, October 26, 1884, March 1, 20 and 21, 1885, April 27, 1885; Horace to W. H. T., May 3 and 28, 1882, June 4, 1882, July 6 and 7, 1882, September 25, 1882; Mrs. Alphonso Taft to W. H. T., September 6 and 27, 1882, July 18, 1883, January 6 and 27, 1884, March 23 and 31, 1884, April 4, 1884, June 6, 1884, November 8 and 21, 1884, May 18, 1885; Alphonso Taft to W. H. T., June 19, 1882, July 8, 11 and 21, 1882, September 3 and 30, 1882, January 20, 1883, February 1, 1883, March 12 and 13, 1883, April 8, 15 and 24, 1883, November 4, 1883, January 12, 1884, March 2 and 3, 1884, April 29, 1884, June 10, 1884, June 24, 1885; Alphonso to Charles Phelps Taft, June 27 and 29, 1882, July 15, 1882, September 11, 1882, January 10, 1883, March 1, 19 and 26, 1883, June 12 and 17, 1883, August 12, 1883, January 6, 1884, December 1, 1884; January 24, 1888; Mrs. Alphonso Taft to Mrs. Charles Phelps Taft, June 29, 1882; Harry Taft to Alphonso Taft, August 15, 1882, January 31, 1883, March 9, 1883, December 8 and 29, 1883, May 10, 1884, May 2, 1885; Harry Taft to Mrs. Alphonso Taft, August 21, 1882, September 8, 13 and 27, 1882, January 23, 1883; Harry Taft to Delia Torrey, January 5, 1882, May 30, 1882, March 16, 1883; Mrs. Alphonso Taft to Harry Taft, June 5, 1882; Mrs. Alphonso Taft to Susie Torrey, July 19, 1882; Mrs. Alphonso Taft to Delia, January 26, 1882, June 29, 1882, August 1, 1883, March 19, 1884, October 23, 1884, January 7, 1885; Mrs. Alphonso Taft to Horace Taft, August 29, 1882, September 26, 1882; Fanny Taft to Mrs. Alphonso Taft, August 24, 1882, August 21, 1884; W. H. T. to Fanny Taft, May 21, 1882, February 28, 1883, August 20, 1884; Fanny Taft to W. H. T., June 11, 1884, August 2, 15 and 28, 1884, September 10, 1884; Horace Taft to Fanny Taft, September 28, 1884; Horace Taft to W. H. T.,

September 25, 1882; Mrs. Alphonso Taft to Delia Torrey, March 19, 1884, October 23, 1884; Mrs. Henry W. Taft (Julia) to Alphonso Taft, May 27, 1882, March 14, 1883; Mrs. Henry W. Taft to Mrs. Alphonso Taft, March 10, 1883, May 12, 1883, July 8, 1883, May 15, 1884, January 26, 1885; Delia to Mrs. Alphonso Taft, August 3, 1884, March 2, 1885; Delia to Susie Torrey, September 16, 1883, November 2, 1883, January 8, 1884, March 2, 1884; Alphonso Taft to Peter Taft, June 15, 1883, July 20, 1883; Peter Taft to Alphonso Taft, February 8, 1885, May 24, 1885; Mrs. Elizabeth W. Perry to Mrs. Alphonso Taft, January 10, 1883; Fanny Taft to Delia, August 20, 1884; Benjamin Butterworth to Alphonso Taft, January 5, 1885; Edward Orton to Mrs. Alphonso Taft, May 23, 1885; Mrs. Charles Phelps Taft to Alphonso Taft, May 6, 1883; Alphonso Taft to Mrs. Alphonso Taft, August 28, 1884, September 13, 1884; *New York Tribune*, August 30, 1885; *New York Times*, March 20 to April 4, 1884; Mrs. Alphonso Taft, "Impressions of Foreign Housekeeping," mss. Taft family papers, Lib. Cong.; Horace Taft, *Memories and Opinions*; Lewis Alexander Leonard, *Life of Alphonso Taft*; Martha Willard mss.; Eugene P. Lyle, Jr., "Taft: A Career of Big Tasks. The Beginning of Public Service," *World's Work*, July, 1907.

Chapter 8: *Will Taft and Nellie Herron*

Nellie Herron's Diaries, 1879–1884; valentines and poems; W. H. T. to Nellie Herron, July 1, 2, 4, 5, 6, 9, 10, 12, 15, 16, 17, 19 and 22, 1885, August 16, 19, 20, 23, 24, 25, 26, 27, 28, 29 and 31, 1885, September 1, 2, 3, 4 and 5, 1885, October 5, 1885, January 25 and 29, 1886, February 22, 1886, March 1, 2, 4, 6, 7, 8, 9 and 10, 1886, W. H. T. to Nellie Herron, April 21, 1885, June 17, 1885, July 10, 12 and 13, 1885, August 21, 25, 29 and 31, 1885, January 29, 1886, February 22, 1886, March 1, 2, 4, 5, 7, 9, 10 and 11, 1886, April 10 and 14, 1886; W. H. T. to Mrs. Alphonso Taft, August 28, 1882, January 2, 1883, February 12, 1883, March 2, 1883, May 14, 1883, December 15 and 25, 1883, March 17, 1884, April 13, 1884, January 27, 1884, March 1 and 8, 1885, May 5 and 24, 1885; W. H. T. to Alphonso Taft, July 24, 1882, December 30, 1883, February 10, 1884, June 16 and 22, 1884, October 22, 1884, January 6, 1885, March 21, 1885, July 12, 1885; Alphonso Taft to W. H. T., September 2, 1882, March 2, 1885, June 22, 24 and 25, 1885, September 23, 1885; Alphonso Taft to Mrs. Alphonso Taft, August 28, 1884, September 11, 1884; Alphonso Taft to Fanny Taft, April 23, 1886; Alphonso Taft to Nellie Herron, July 29, 1885; Alphonso Taft to Horace Taft, February 15, 1885, June 1, 1886; Alphonso Taft to Delia Torrey, October 12, 1885; W. H. T. to Delia Torrey, February 23, 1886; W. H. T. to Mrs. Alphonso Taft, May 13, 1884, October 26, 1884, August 22, 1885; W. H. T. to Fanny, January 6, 1882; Fanny Taft to W. H. T., June 11, 1884, August 2, 1884; Mrs. Alphonso Taft to Delia Torrey, January 7, 1885, March 19, 1884; Harry Taft to Delia Torrey, March 29, 1880; Harry Taft to Alphonso Taft, August 2, 1885; Mrs. Alphonso Taft to W. H. T., June 6, 1884; Horace Taft to Mrs. Alphonso Taft, October 22, 1884; Horace

Taft to W. H. T., September 2, 1885, April 10, 1886; Peter Taft to Alphonso Taft, February 8, 1885; Mrs. Charles Phelps Taft to Mrs. Alphonso Taft, June 29, 1885; Charles Phelps Taft to Alphonso Taft, January 6, 1885; Delia Torrey to Mrs. Alphonso Taft, March 2, 1885, May 26, 1885, July 26, 1885, August 21, 1885; Mrs. Henry W. Taft to Mrs. Alphonso Taft, January 26, 1885; Nellie Herron to Alice Keys, July 5, 1880, Taft family papers, Lib. Cong. and William Howard Taft Memorial Association, Cincinnati; Lewis Alexander Leonard, *Life of Alphonso Taft*; Alphonso Taft interviewed in *New York Tribune*, August 30, 1885; Horace Dutton Taft: *Memories and Opinions*.

Chapter 9: **A** *Day in June*

Taft family papers, Lib. Cong.: Mrs. W. H. T.'s Wedding Diary Journal, 1886, and Diary, 1888; Theater and concert programs, menus and memorabilia of wedding trip; Horace Taft to W. H. T., June 24, 1886; Mrs. W. H. T. to John Herron, July 4, 1886; Mrs. W. H. T. to Mrs. Herron, July 20, 1886; W. H. T. to Mrs. Herron, June 20, 1886; Mrs. W. H. T. to Maria Herron, June 26, 1886; Horace Taft to Mrs. W. H. T., February 4, 1887, March 30, 1890, July 10, 1890; W. H. T. to Mrs. W. H. T., August 15, 23 and 27, 1890, May 17 and 18, 1891; W. H. T. to Alphonso Taft, July 24, 1888, April 10, 1889, February 26, 1889, July 5, 9, 15, 1889, August 10 and 18, 1889, September 15, 1889, January 6 and 23, 1891, February 9 and 14, 1891, March 7 and 18, 1891; Mrs. Alphonso Taft to W. H. T., July 11 and 22, 1886, May 15, 1890, March 15, 1891, June 11, 1891; Alphonso Taft to W. H. T., February 7, 1890, May 21, 25 and 28, 1890, June 6, 1890, July 10, 1890, March 15 and 18, 1891; Alphonso Taft to Delia Torrey, January 30, 1887, September 12, 1888; Horace Taft to Mrs. W. H. T., March 30, 1890, June 2, 1890; Horace Taft to Fanny Taft, April 1, 1888, October 13, 1888, March 9, 1889; Horace Taft to W. H. T., June 24, 1886, August 4, 1886, August 6, 1891; W. H. T. to Horace, June 17, 1889; Horace Taft to Mrs. Alphonso Taft, February 27, 1891; Mrs. W. H. T. to Delia Torrey, October 11, 1888, October 2, 1889; Delia Torrey to Mrs. Alphonso Taft, June 18, 1889; Alphonso Taft to Fanny Taft, April 23, 1886; W. H. T. to Mrs. Alphonso Taft, November 2, 1889; Alphonso Taft to Charles Phelps Taft, December 2, 1889; Charles Phelps Taft to W. H. T., April 29, 1890, May 21, 1890, October 20, 1890, April 4, 1891; Mrs. W. H. T. to W. H. T., June 9, 10 and 11, 1890; August 14, 15, 21, 22, 27 and 29, 1890; August 3 and 24, 1890; September 2 and 17, 1890; July 18 and 23, 1891; September 1 and 4, 1891; Harry Taft to Alphonso Taft, June 3, 1889; Bishop Boyd Vincent funeral address, June 5, 1889, Taft family papers, William Howard Taft Memorial Association, Cincinnati; Mrs. William Howard Taft: *Recollections of Full Years*; Martha Willard mss.; Allan Nevins, *Henry White: Thirty Years of American Diplomacy*; Horace Dutton Taft: *Memories and Opinions*; Helen Taft Manning, "My Brother Bob Taft," *American Magazine*, January,

1952; Clara (Longworth) de Chambrun: *Cincinnati: Story of the Queen City*; Alvin F. Harlow, *The Serene Cincinnatians*.

Chapter 10: Le Petit Juge

Taft family papers, Lib. Cong.: W. H. T. to Mrs. W. H. T., June 1, 1891, June 20, 1892, October 31, 1892, November 18, 1892, February 6, 1894, September 27, 1894, November 27, 1894, June 25 and 28, 1895, July 2, 11 and 13, 1895, March 18, 22 and 25, 1896, July 6, 11 and 14, 1896, September 20, 1896, June 19, 20 and 29, 1897, July 2, 3, 4 and 5, 1897, July 2, 5, 8 and 10, 1898, September 13, 17 and 25, 1899, December 9, 14 and 16, 1899; Mrs. W. H. T. to W. H. T., May 19, 1891, June 12, 1891, July 13, 18, 20, 23, 24, 25, 26, 27 and 28, 1891, August 17, 18, 23, 27 and 29, 1891, September 1, 13 and 16, 1891, March 8 and 10, 1892, May 4, 1892, November 19, 1892, December 8, 1892, May 15, 1893, June 2, 7, 10 and 17, 1893, November 13 and 16, 1893, July 13, 1894, November 23, 1894, March 28, 1895, July 5, 1895, November 23, 1896, July 6 and 10, 1898, December 6, 8 and 15, 1899; W. H. T. to Mrs. Alphonso Taft, November 27, 1891, January 5, 1893, March 19, 1893, June 29, 1894, September 9, 1897; Mrs. Alphonso Taft to W. H. T., February 10, 1892, March 19, 1893, May 10 and 20, 1894, September 15, 1894, October 25, 1894, October 22, 1895, March 14, 1896, October 29, 1896, November 10, 1896, March 14, 1897, April 28, 1897, January 1, 1898, July 9, 1898, September 22, 1898, October 11, 1898, November 14, 1898, January 8, 1899, February 6 and 19, 1899, August 23, 1899, September 12, 1899; Mrs. Alphonso Taft to Mrs. W. H. T., March 8, 1892, April 28, 1892, January 10, 1903; Helen Taft to W. H. T., September 25, 1898; W. H. T. to Harry Taft, January 23, 1899; Harry Taft to W. H. T., Feb. 10, 1894, November 13, 1894, January 4 and 23, 1899; Horace Taft to W. H. T., January 12, 1892, February 8, 1894, October 10, 1894, November 10, 1896, June 18, 1897; Charles Phelps Taft to W. H. T., January 6, 1896; Fanny Taft to Mrs. W. H. T., June 13, 1896; Mrs. Alphonso Taft to Charles Phelps Taft, June 6, 1894; Mrs. Alphonso Taft to Delia Torrey, July 29, 1898; Mrs. Alphonso Taft to Horace Taft, August 22, 1898; W. H. T. to Lucien Wulsin, April 12, 1895, Historical and Philosophical Society of Ohio; Mrs. W. H. T. to Lucien Wulsin, June 24, 1895, Historical and Philosophical Society of Ohio; "The Cincinnati Plan," *Musical Courier*, November 14, 1894; Maria Longworth Storer, *In Memoriam Bellamy Storer*; Edward H. Cotton, *William Howard Taft, a Character Study*; Rev. F. J. Moore to author; Al Laney, *Preparatory Schools*; Henry F. Pringle, *The Life and Times of William Howard Taft*; William H. Taft: *Political Issues and Outlooks*.

Chapter 11: Governor of the Philippines

Taft papers, Lib. Cong.: W. H. T. to Charles Phelps Taft, diary letter, May 27, 1900, April 15 and 23, 1900, June 2, 12 and 23, 1900, July 7, 1900,

August 11, 23 and 31, 1900, September 1, 6 and 21, 1900, October 15 and 30, 1900, November 6, 15 and 30, 1900, December 6, 1900, January 9, 1901, March 17, 1901, May 26, 1901, September 16 and 30, 1901; Charles Phelps Taft to W. H. T., January 4, 1900, April 4 and 7, 1900, May 8, 1900, June 3, 23 and 27, 1900, July 3, 5 and 16, 1900, August 1, 1900, September 1, 1900, October 8, 1900, November 7, 22 and 24, 1900, December 20, 1900, January 23, 1901, February 5, 1901, May 2 and 11, 1901, June 10, 1901, July 30, 1901, September 16, 1901, October 4, 1901; Horace Taft to W. H. T., January 31, 1900, June 7, 1901, July 4 and 11, 1901, October 4, 1901, May 12, 1902; Harry Taft to W. H. T., January 30, 1900, March 28, 1900, July 6, 1900, September 7, 1900, June 7, 1901, July 30, 1901, November 8, 1901; Mrs. Alphonso Taft to W. H. T., February 8, 1900, April 9, 1900, June 8, 24 and 25, 1900, July 9 and 27, 1900, August 10, 1900, October 26, 1900, November 12 and 22, 1900, December 9 and 29, 1900, January 12, 1901, February 26, 1901, April 14, 1901, May 24 and 29, 1902; William Howard Taft to Theodore Roosevelt, February 15, 1900, Theodore Roosevelt papers, Lib. Cong.; W. H. T. to Mrs. W. H. T., February 17, 1900, May 8, 20 and 30, 1900, June 6, 8, 10, 12, 13, 14, 18, 26, 27 and 28, 1900, July 8, 1900, August 12, 1900, January 30, 1902, February 8, 17 and 24, 1902, May 25, 1902; Mrs. W. H. T. to W. H. T., May 25, 1900, June 14 and 27, 1900, July 5 and 10, 1900, February 1 and 8, 1902; Mrs. Horace Taft to Mrs. Alphonso Taft, June 23, 1900; Mrs. W. H. T. to Mrs. Alphonso Taft, June 25, 1900; Mrs. W. H. T. to Mrs. Herron, July 19, 1901; Horace Taft to W. H. T., July 4, 1901; W. H. T. to Mrs. Alphonso Taft, June 14, 1900, September 9, 1900, December 26, 1900, April 12, 1901, July 19, 1901; W. H. T. to Harry Taft, April 25, 1901; W. H. T. to Mrs. Herron, January 19, 1901; W. H. T. to Horace Taft, April 12 and 25, 1901, January 30, 1902; W. H. T. to Nancy G. Roelker, April 16, 1900; W. H. T. to Elihu Root, June 11, 14 and 15, 1900, July 14, 1900, August 18 and 23, 1900, September 13, 1900, January 9, 1901, February 10, 15 and 24, 1901, March 17, 1901, July 8, 1901, September 11, 26 and 30, 1901, Taft-Root correspondence, Lib. Cong.; Elihu Root to Taft, January 21, 1901, February 26, 1901, Taft-Root correspondence, Taft-Root Letter books, 1900 and 1901, Lib. Cong.; James Creelman, "The Mystery of Mr. Taft," Pearson's Magazine, May, 1907; Manila Times, May 2, 1900; Helen Taft Manning, "My Brother Bob Taft," American Magazine, January, 1952; Eugene P. Lyle, Jr., "Taft: A Career of Big Tasks; His Work in the Philippines," World's Work, October, 1907; Edward H. Cotton, William Howard Taft, a Character Study; Phyllis Robbins, Robert A. Taft: Boy and Man; Caroline Thomas Harnsberger, A Man of Courage: Robert A. Taft; Oscar King Davis, William Howard Taft: The Man of the Hour; Mrs. William Howard Taft's Vigan Diary, June, 1891; Mrs. William Howard Taft, Recollections of Full Years; Alice Roosevelt Longworth, Crowded Hours; Henry F. Pringle, The Life and Times of William Howard Taft, Vol. I; Dean C. Worcester, The Philippines, Past and Present; W. Cameron Forbes, The Philippine Islands, Vol. I; Nicholas Roosevelt, The Philippines, a Treasure and a Problem.

Chapter 12: *Taft at the Vatican*

Taft family papers, Lib. Cong.: W. H. T. to Mrs. W. H. T., February 11, 12, 13, 17, 19, 20 and 24, 1902, March 1, 1902, May 6, 1902, June 11 and 12, 1902, July 18, 1902, August 5, 1902; Mrs. W. H. T. to W. H. T., October 20 and 28, 1901, (telegrams), October 25 and 26, 1901, February 1, 4 and 6, 1902, July 6, 1902, August 26, 1902; W. H. T. to Mrs. Alphonso Taft, October 21, 1901, March 4 and 25, 1902, May 6, 1902, March 7, 1903; Hulbert Taft to W. H. T., July 17, 1903; W. H. T. to Hulbert Taft, September 7, 1909; W. H. T. to Horace Taft, August 19, 1903, October 26, 1903; Horace Taft to W. H. T., January 28, 1902, April 3, 1903, May 13, 1903, July 24, 1903, October 24, 1903; W. H. T. to Mrs. Herron, January 19, 1901, November 18, 1901, April 3, 1903; W. H. T. to John Herron, March 24, 1903, June 10, 1903, September 23, 1903; John Herron to W. H. T., May 3, 1903; W. H. T. to Harry Taft, October 21, 1901, March 30, 1903, April 16, 1903; Harry Taft to W. H. T., November 8, 1901, January 10, 1903, March 2, 1903, June 16, 1903, September 26, 1903; Mrs. Alphonso Taft to W. H. T., September 15, 1901, November 3, 1901, January 19, 1902, May 4, 1902, January 25, 1903, March 11, 1903, May 16, 1903, August 9, 1903, October 17, 1903; W. H. T. to Mrs. Henry W. Taft, October 26, 1903; Charles Phelps Taft to Mrs. Alphonso Taft, December 6, 1901; Fanny Edwards to W. H. T., January 23, 1902; W. H. T. to Fanny Edwards, February 14, 1902; Edward Orton to W. H. T., January 27, 1902; Delia Torrey to W. H. T., August 31, 1902; W. H. T. to Delia Torrey, July 14 and 27, 1902; Fanny Edwards to Delia Torrey, May 18, 1903; Charles Phelps Taft to W. H. T., July 3, 1900, October 4, 1901, August 31, 1902, November 6 and 24, 1902, December 26, 1902, February 11, 1903; April 18, 1903, May 6, 8 and 25, 1903, June 3, 1903, July 12 and 31, 1903, September 2, 1903, October 19, 1903; W. H. T. to Charles Phelps Taft, July 7, 1900, October 15, 1901, November 9, 1901, December 9, 1901, June 7 and 10, 1902, July 5, 1902, January 26, 1903, February 4, 1903, March 27, 1903, April 18, 1903, June 15, 1903, August 20, 1903, October 21, 1904; Helen Taft to W. H. T., July 28, 1902, August 19, 1902; W. H. T. to Helen Taft, September 24, 1902; W. H. T. to Charlie Taft, November 11, 1902; Charlie Taft to "Dear Mama," 1902; Charlie Taft to W. H. T., October 4, 1901; W. H. T. to Robert A. Taft, October 27, 1903; Robert to Mrs. W. H. T., November 15 and 22, 1903, April 10, 1904; Theodore Roosevelt to W. H. T., February 14, 1903, June 9, 1903, Taft papers, Lib. Cong.; W. H. T. to Theodore Roosevelt, April 27, 1903, Roosevelt papers, Lib. Cong.; W. H. T. to Elihu Root, November 17, 1901, Root papers, Lib. Cong.; Mrs. William Howard Taft, *Recollections of Full Years*; Henry F. Pringle, *The Life and Times of William Howard Taft*, Vol. I; Horace Dutton Taft, *Memories and Opinions*; Roger Butterfield, "Possible Presidents. Robert A. Taft," *Ladies Home Journal*, February, 1948.

Chapter 13: *The War Office*

Taft family papers, Lib. Cong.: Robert A. Taft to Mrs. W. H. T., November 15 and 22, 1903; February 12, 14, 21 and 28, 1904; March 13, 1904, April 10, 1904, May 1, 1904, March 5, 1905, April 23, 1905, May 7, 1905, June 4, 10 and 21, 1905; W. H. T. to Robert A. Taft, October 27, 1903, February 6, 1904; Robert A. Taft to W. H. T., March 17, 1904; Mrs. Alphonso Taft to W. H. T., May 16, 1903, February 8 and 27, 1904, May 10, 1904, September 5 and 21, 1904, June 2 and 25, 1905, July 2, 1905; W. H. T. to Mrs. Alphonso Taft, February 4 and 14, 1904, June 14, 1904, July 16, 1904, September 11, 1904; Mrs. W. H. T. to W. H. T., October 4, 1904; W. H. T. to Mrs. W. H. T., February 1, 2, 4, 15 and 27, 1904, March 4, 10, 11, 13, 14, 15, 18, 22, 25 and 31, 1904; April 5, 12 and 16, 1904, May 11, 1904, August 3, 12 and 27, 1904; Horace Taft to W. H. T., June 21, 1903, March 4, 7 and 29, 1904, April 27, 1904, August 1, 1904; Charles Phelps Taft to W. H. T., February 9 and 13, 1904, March 15 and 19, 1904, May 10 and 28, 1904, October 20, 1904, November 9, 1904, December 8, 1904, May 4, 1905; W. H. T. to Charles Phelps Taft, February 1 and 27, 1904, June 20 and 23, 1904, August 20, 1904, October 21, 1904, November 11 and 17, 1904, December 30, 1904, April 8, 1905; W. H. T. to Howard Hollister, February 8, 1904, August 23, 1904, September 16, 1904, November 10, 1904; W. H. T. to Harry Taft, November 3, 1903; Harry Taft to W. H. T., July 19, 1904; W. H. T. to Charles W. Eliot, May 26, 1904; W. H. T. to Beekman Winthrop, February 6, 1904; W. H. T. to Mrs. Therese McCagg, February 4, 1904; W. H. T. to Luke E. Wright, November 12, 1904; W. H. T. to Elihu Root, February 7, 1904, Taft-Root correspondence, Lib. Cong.; Taft to John Hays Hammond, November 13, 1904, Taft papers, Lib. Cong.; Theodore Roosevelt to W. H. T., July 11, 1904, September 19, 1904, October 11, 1904; Taft papers, Lib. Cong.; Theodore Roosevelt to W. H. T., April 8, 1905; Henry F. Pringle, *The Life and Times of William Howard Taft*; W. H. T. to Miss Eva Keys, February 8, 1904, Taft papers, Lib. Cong.; W. H. T. to Mrs. John A. Logan, March 9, 1904; W. H. T. to Mrs. Susan W. Longworth, February 9, 1904; Dr. William Edwards to W. H. T., May 23, 1905; Charlie Taft to W. H. T., May 14, 1904; Helen Taft to W. H. T., May 10, 1904; Mrs. William Howard Taft, *Recollections of Full Years*; Edward H. Cotton, *William Howard Taft, A Character Study*.

Chapter 14: *Alice Roosevelt and Mr. Taft*

Taft family papers, Lib. Cong.: Charlie Taft to Mrs. W. H. T., December 3 and 5, 1905; Charlie Taft to W. H. T., December 4, 1905; Mrs. W. H. T. to W. H. T., July 8 and 13, 1905, August 2, 13, 14, 20, 24 and 31, 1905, September 4, 20, 26, 27, 28 and 29, 1906, October 27, 1906, March 29, 1907, August 11, 13 and 15, 1907; Helen to W. H. T., August 1, 1905; Helen to

Mr. and Mrs. W. H. T. Taft, November 18, 1906; Robert A. Taft to W. H. T., October 5, 1905, November 12, 1905, December 16, 1905; W. H. T. to Robert Taft, October 4, 1906; Robert A. Taft to Mrs. W. H. T., July 9 and 13, 1905, November 3, 1905, December 16, 1905, February 19, 1907; Maria Herron to W. H. T., September 28, 1905; Mrs. Alphonso Taft to W. H. T., May 1, 1905, September 22, 1905, February 21, 1906, November 9, 1906, April 29, 1907, June 21, 1907, October 4, 1907; Mrs. Horace Taft to W. H. T., May 24, 1906; Charles, Annie, Will, Nellie, Harry, Julia, and grandchildren to Mrs. Alphonso Taft, September 11, 1906; Mrs. Alphonso Taft to Delia Torrey, June 11, 1907; Lily W. Grosvenor, to W. H. T., July 26, 1907; Mrs. Therese McCagg to W. H. T., October 10, 1907; Charles Phelps Taft to W. H. T., July 24, 1905, November 13, 1905, December 3 and 25, 1905, October 18, 1906, December 11 and 17, 1906, April 16, 1907; W. H. T. to Charles Phelps Taft, July 24, 1905, December 3 and 25, 1905, January 1, 1907, August 18 and 21, 1907, September 11, 1907; Harry Taft to W. H. T., December 30, 1906; Harry to Mrs. Alphonso Taft, July 30, 1907, August 16, 1907; W. H. T. to Mrs. Alphonso Taft, August 16 and 18, 1907, September 11, 1907; W. H. T. to Miss Boardman, September 16, 1905, December 25, 1905, April 11, 1906, June 29, 1906, November 10, 1906, July 15, 1907, August 17, 1907, September 11 and 27, 1907; Mabel Boardman to Mrs. W. H. T., November 4, 1907; Mabel Boardman to Mrs. William Boardman, August 8, 1905, Boardman papers, Lib. Cong.; W. H. T. to Theodore Roosevelt, March 15, 1906, Roosevelt papers, Lib. Cong.; Theodore Roosevelt to W. H. T., July 29, 1905, March 15, 1906, July 26, 1907, August 6 and 21, 1907, Taft papers, Lib. Cong.; Joseph F. Green to W. H. T., June 12, 1907; Fanny Edwards to W. H. T., September 10, 1907 (telegram); W. H. T. to Horace Taft, December 3, 1905, January 9, 22 and 29, 1906, July 30, 1906, August 27, 1906, July 2, 1907, September 1 and 10, 1907; Horace Taft to W. H. T., March 7, 1905, October 5, 1905, November 16, 1905, December 2, 1905, January 13 and 25, 1906, March 1, 1906, October 4, 1906, July 29, 1907, August 9, 1907; Hermann Hagedorn, *The Boys Life of Theodore Roosevelt* and *The Roosevelt Family of Sagamore Hill*; Alice Roosevelt Longworth, *Crowded Hours*; H. H. Kohlsaat, *From McKinley to Harding*; Irwin (Ike) Hoover, *Forty-two Years in the White House*; Henry F. Pringle, *Theodore Roosevelt* and *The Life and Times of William Howard Taft*, 2 vols.; Bess Furman, *White House Profile*; Mrs. William Howard Taft's Diary, September, 1907; Helen Taft Manning, "My Brother Bob Taft," *American Magazine*, January, 1952; George von L. Meyer Diaries, 1907–1909; Eugene P. Lyle, Jr., "As Secretary of War," *World's Work*, November, 1907; Raymond Patterson, *Taft's Training for the Presidency*; Mrs. William Howard Taft, *Recollections of Full Years*; William Howard Taft, *Presidential Addresses and State Papers*; William H. Taft, *Political Issues and Outlooks*.

Chapter 15: *Around the World*

Taft family papers, Lib. Cong.: Mrs. William Howard Taft's Diary, September 1907–December, 1907; Helen Taft to Mrs. W. H. T., November 14, 1907; Robert Taft to W. H. T., January 20, 1908, June 18, 1908, October 16, 1908; Robert Taft to Mrs. W. H. T., May 12 and 24, 1908, June 3, 1908; Robert H. Murray, *Around the World with Taft*; Mrs. Charles Phelps Taft to W. H. T., December 20, 1907; Harry Taft to W. H. T., December 9, 1907, September 11 and 24, 1908, November 3, 1908; Mrs. Anna M. Smith to Delia Torrey, December 10, 1907; Mrs. Elizabeth Perry to Delia Torrey, November 24, 1907; W. H. T. to Charles Phelps Taft, October 10, 1907, November 13, 1907, February 20, 1908, September 9, 1908; W. H. T. to Mabel Boardman, July 14, 1908, September 1, 1908, December 24, 1908, January 5, 1909; Mabel Boardman to Mrs. W. H. T., November 4, 1907, June 17, 1908, Taft papers, Lib. Cong.; W. H. T. to Mrs. W. H. T., May 7, 1908; Mrs. W. H. T. to W. H. T., February 15, 1908; W. H. T. to Mrs. Charles Anderson, January 10, 1909; Delia Torrey to W. H. T., December 21, 1907, May 15, 1908, September 7, 1908; W. H. T. to Delia Torrey, December 26, 1907, December 7, 1908; Harry Taft to Delia Torrey, June 19, 1908; Charles Phelps Taft to Delia Torrey, November 21, 1907; Mrs. Lucy Laughlin to Mrs. W. H. T., February 9, 1908; W. H. T. to Horace Taft, September 12, 1908; Horace Taft to W. H. T., December 21, 1907, May 20, 1908, July 11, 1908, September 5, 1908, November 3, 1908, December 2, 1908, January 26, 1909, March 12, 1909, May 25, 1909; Mrs. W. H. T. to Helen Taft, November 7, 1908, January 6, 1909; Dr. Ella B. Everitt to Mrs. W. H. T., January 14, 1909; Charlie to W. H. T., November 18, 1908; Charlie to Mrs. W. H. T., May 8, 1908; W. H. T. to Charlie, November 30, 1908; W. H. T. to Theodore Roosevelt, July 12, 1908, November 7, 1908, January 4, 1909, Fred Carpenter correspondence, Taft papers, Lib. Cong.; Theodore Roosevelt to W. H. T., July 15 and 21, 1908, August 7 and 29, 1908, September 1, 5, 11 and 24, 1908, January 1, 1909, Taft papers, Lib. Cong.; Theodore Roosevelt to J. C. Martin, November 6, 1908, Elting E. Morison, *The Letters of Theodore Roosevelt*, Vol. IV; Theodore Roosevelt to Kermit Roosevelt, October 20, 1908, Roosevelt papers, Lib. Cong.; W. H. T. to John Wesley Hill, August 12, 1908, Taft papers, Lib. Cong.; W. H. T. to Theodore E. Burton, January 5, 1909, Taft papers, Lib. Cong.; W. H. T. to Nicholas Longworth, September 21, 1908, Taft papers, Lib. Cong.; W. H. T. to William Allen White, March 31, 1908, White papers; Sydney Brooks, "Presidential Possibilities," *Fortnightly Review*, May, 1908; Walter Wellman, *The Review of Reviews*, June, 1908; George von L. Meyer Diary; Archie Butt, *Taft and Roosevelt: the Intimate Letters of Archie Butt*, 2 vols.; Helen Taft Manning, "My Brother Bob Taft," *American Magazine*, January, 1952; Alice Longworth, *Crowded Hours*; William Henry Harbaugh, *Power and Responsibility*; Cincinnati *Times-Star*, July 27, 1908; William Howard Taft, *Political Issues and Outlooks*.

Chapter 16: *The White House*

Official Diary of the President, compiled by Major Archibald Butt and
Major Thomas L. Rhoads; *White House Social Functions*; William Woodward, *A Memorial of the First Inauguration of William Howard Taft*; *New
York Times*, *New York Herald Tribune*, Washington *Post*, March 4 and 5,
1909; Archie Butt, *Taft and Roosevelt: the Intimate Letters of Archie Butt*;
Mrs. William Howard Taft, *Recollections of Full Years*; Helen Taft Man-
ning, "My Brother Bob Taft," *American Magazine*, January, 1952; Katherine
Graves Busbey, "Mrs. Taft's Home-Making," *Good Housekeeping*, Septem-
ber, 1911; George von L. Meyer Diary; Theodore Roosevelt to Whitelaw
Reid, November 26, 1908, Elting E. Morison, *The Letters of Theodore
Roosevelt*, Vol. VI; Delia Torrey to W. H. T., April 16, 1910, June 19, 1910;
W. H. T. to Delia Torrey, August 20, 1909; Horace Taft to W. H. T., March
4 and 27, 1910, April 22, 1910, August 19, 1910; Harry Taft to W. H. T.,
January 19, 1909; Charles Phelps Taft to W. H. T., May 13, 1909; Mrs.
Elizabeth Perry to Delia Torrey, January 15, 1909; Mrs. Elizabeth Perry to
W. H. T., July 28, 1909; Robert Taft to Mrs. W. H. T., May 19, 1909, and
undated letters May and June, 1909; W. H. T. to Robert Taft, May 18,
1909; Robert Taft to Henry F. Pringle, May 30, 1938, Pringle papers, Lib.
Cong.; "Charlie Taft's Big Chance," *Fortune*, August, 1947; James Creel-
man, "The Mystery of Mr. Taft," *Pearson's Magazine*, May, 1907; Bess Fur-
man, *White House Profile*; Ona Griffin Jeffries, *In and Out of the White
House*; Amy Jensen, *The White House and Its Thirty-two Families*; Nanette
Kutner, "My Life in the White House," *American Weekly*, March 23, 1952;
Eleanor Roosevelt, "Cherry Blossom Time," *Reader's Digest*, April, 1938;
Irwin (Ike) Hoover, *Forty-two Years in the White House*; Henry F. Pringle,
The Life and Times of William Howard Taft; Charles Hopkins Clark, *The
Independent*, April 9, 1909; Edward H. Cotton, *William Howard Taft, a
Character Study*, William Howard Taft, *Presidential Addresses and State
Papers*.

Chapter 17: *A Tariff Storm*

Official Diary of the President, compiled by Major Archibald Butt and
Major Thomas L. Rhoads; *White House Social Functions*; *Presidential Addresses and State Papers of William Howard Taft from March 4, 1909, to
March 4, 1910*; Taft papers, Lib. Cong.; Delia Torrey to W. H. T., September 10, 1909, November 13, 1909; W. H. T. to Delia Torrey, August 20,
1909, November 13 and 24, 1909, April 2, 1910, October 8, 1910; Mrs.
W. H. T. to W. H. T., July 17, 1909, August 4, 1909, November 5, 1909;
W. H. T. to Mrs. W. H. T., July 15, 18 and 25, 1909, July 6, 7, 9, 11, 13
and 29, 1909, August 10 and 23, 1909, September 19, 1909, October 3, 15,
24 and 28, 1909, November 2 and 7, 1909, March 19 and 28, 1910, June 3,

1910, September 23, 24 and 28, 1910; "Sister Anne" (Mrs. Charles Phelps Taft) to W. H. T., August 5, 1909; Walter J. Travis, "Golfing with President Taft," *The Century Magazine*, September, 1910; Delia Torrey, "Too Bad Will Taft Can't Have All He Wants to Eat," New York *World*, February 21, 1910; Theodore Roosevelt to W. H. T., June 8, 1910, September 16, 1910, November 28, 1910, Taft papers, Lib. Cong.; Archie Butt to Theodore Roosevelt, August 17, 1909; to Mrs. Theodore Roosevelt, June 22, 1909, Roosevelt papers, Lib. Cong.; Whitelaw Reid to Mabel Boardman, August 23, 1909, Boardman papers, Lib. Cong.; Charles Phelps Taft to W. H. T., April 18, 1903, July 10, 1909, September 6, 1909, November 15, 1909, June 24, 1910, July 2, 1910, December 16, 1910; Taft family papers, Lib. Cong.; W. H. T. to Charles Phelps Taft, September 10, 1910; Alice Roosevelt Longworth to W. H. T., Dec. 22, 1910; Horace Taft to W. H. T., June 4 and 19, 1909, August 6, 1909, October 8, 1909, December 12 and 22, 1909, March 4 and 27, 1910, April 22, 1910, August 19, 1910, November 3 and 23, 1910; W. H. T. to Horace Taft, June 27, 1909; W. H. T. to Mabel Boardman, June 14, 1909, Boardman papers, Lib. Cong.; W. H. T. to Gifford Pinchot, September 13, 1909, Gifford Pinchot papers, Lib. Cong.; address to the students of the State Institute and College at Columbus, November 2, 1909; tariff speech at Winona, September 17, 1909; Mary Kohler mss., April 13, 1939, Swarthmore, "Background and First Stages of the Passage of the Payne-Aldrich Bill, 1897–June 8, 1909"; John H. Powell thesis, 1934, Swarthmore, "President Taft and the Payne-Aldrich Tariff; Helen Taft Manning, "My Brother Bob Taft," *American Magazine*, January, 1952; Alice Roosevelt Longworth, *Crowded Hours*; Mrs. William Howard Taft, *Recollections of Full Years*; Archie Butt, *Taft and Roosevelt: the Intimate Letters of Archie Butt*; Horace Dutton Taft, *Memories and Opinions*; Charles E. Barker, *With President Taft in the White House*; Irwin (Ike) Hoover, *Forty-two Years in the White House*; Phyllis Robbins, *Robert A. Taft, Boy and Man*; Caroline Thomas Harnsberger, *A Man of Courage; Robert A. Taft*; Henry L. Stoddard, *As I Knew Them*; Henry F. Pringle; *The Life and Times of William Howard Taft*, 2 vols.; William Henry Harbaugh, *Power and Responsibility*; "Delia Torrey," *Harper's Bazaar*, October, 1910; William Howard Taft: *Presidential Addresses and State Papers*.

Chapter 18: *Silver Wedding*

Official Diary of the President; White House Social Functions; Washington *Post*, Washington *Herald*, New York *Times*, New York *Tribune*, June 20, 1911; King George V to W. H. T., December 15, 1912; W. H. T. to King George V, December 15, 1912, Taft papers, Lib. Cong.; W. H. T. to Mrs. W. H. T., July 11, 12, 15, 18, 22, 24, 26 and 28, 1911, May 17, 1911, August 8, 1911, September 15 and 18, 1911, July 14, 15, 16, 22, 24, 27 and 1912, August 9 and 26, 1912, November 1, 1912, February 26, 1913, Taft family papers, Lib. Cong.; Mrs. W. H. T. to W. H. T., July 22, 1912; Mrs. W. H. T. to Mrs. Andrew Carnegie, February 25, 1913, Taft papers, New

York Public Library; W. H. T. to Delia Torrey, June 15, 1911, November 29, 1911, March 5, 1912, April 12, 1912, May 12, 1912, August 1, 1912, November 1 and 8, 1912, December 12, 1912, September 3, 1912, Taft family papers, Lib. Cong.; W. H. T. to Robert Taft, June 15, 1911, August 27, 1911, November 19, 1912; Delia Torrey to W. H. T., June 13, 1911, July 19, 1911, March 2, 1912, May 9, 1912, November 21, 1912, December 16, 1912, January 18, 1913, February 27, 1913; Horace Taft to W. H. T., February 2, 1912, May 15 and 29, 1912; W. H. T. to Fanny Edwards, August 2, 1912; W. H. T. to Horace Taft, June 19, 1912, April 14, 1914, September 16, 1912; Howard Hollister to W. H. T., June 26, 1911; Maria Herron to W. H. T., July 21 and 23, 1912, August 13 and 17, 1912; W. H. T. to Mrs. Jennie H. Anderson, March 28, 1912; W. H. T. to Mabel Boardman, May 25, 1911, June 21, 1911, September 8 and 15, 1911, December 24, 1911, April 22, 23 and 30, 1912, June 23, 1912, August 7 and 17, 1912, October 24, 1912, November 10, 1912, February 26, 1913, February 10, 1914, Boardman papers, Lib. Cong.; Delia Torrey to Mabel Boardman, December 30, 1912; Robert Taft to W. H. T., November 13, 1912; Robert Taft to Helen, July 23, 1911; Helen Taft to Bob Taft, March 1, 1914; Mrs. W. H. T. to Charlie Taft, March 4, 1914, Charles Phelps Taft's papers, William Howard Taft Memorial Association, Cincinnati; W. H. T. to Charles Phelps Taft, May 29, 1911, Taft papers, Lib. Cong.; W. H. T. correspondence on Pauline Wayne, last White House cow, Washington *Evening Star*, November 3, 1910; Mrs. Whitelaw Reid to Mabel Boardman, undated, 1911, Boardman papers; W. H. T. to Professor John Chipman Gray, November 19, 1912; W. H. T. to Joseph H. Choate, January 14, 1913; W. H. T. to Elihu Root, November 20, 1912, Taft-Root correspondence, Lib. Cong.; Oscar Garrison Villard to Mabel Boardman, January 30, 1912, Boardman papers; William Allen White to Henry Pringle, September 7, 1939, Pringle paprs, Lib. Cong.; Ezra Ripley Thayer to W. H. T., August 24, 1911; Whitelaw Reid to Mabel Boardman, September 8, 1911, Boardman papers, Lib. Cong.; W. H. T. to Lord Bryce, August 26, 1911, Bryce papers, Lib. Cong.; Mrs. Cornelius Vanderbilt to W. H. T., May 9, 1911; *The Nation*, March 6, 1913; *Harper's Weekly*, June 24, 1911; W. H. T.'s address at dinner for William Dean Howells, March 2, 1912; Washington *Post*, January 3, 1911; Leonard Wood Diary, June 30, 1912–December 3, 1912, Wood papers, Lib. Cong.; Mrs. William Howard Taft, *Recollections of Full Years*; Horace Dutton Taft, *Memories and Opinions*; Helen Taft Manning, "My Brother Bob Taft," *American Magazine*, January, 1952; Archie Butt, *Taft and Roosevelt: the Intimate Letters of Archie Butt*; Charles Willis Thompson, *Presidents I've Known*; Oswald Garrison Villard, *Fighting Years*; Ellen Maury Slayden, *Washington Wife*; William Allen White, *Masks in a Pageant*; Frank K. Kelly, *The Fight for the White House*; Ona Griffin Jeffries, *In and Out of the White House*; Phyllis Robbins, *Robert A. Taft: Boy and Man*, Belle (Case) La Follette and Fola La Follette, *Robert M. La Follette*, 2 vols.; Robert Marion La Follette, *Autobiography: A Personal Narrative of Political Experiences*; William Howard Taft to Theodore Roosevelt, January 10, 1911; William Howard Taft: *Presidential Addresses and State Papers*.

Chapter 19: *Taft the Professor*

New York Times and *New York Tribune*, April 2, 1913; Frederick C. Hicks, *William Howard Taft, Yale Professor of Law & New Haven Citizen*; Elihu Root (Athos) to W. H. T. (Porthos), November 3, 1912, June 4, 1914, Taft-Root correspondence, Lib. Cong.; W. H. T. to Elihu Root, November 8, 1913; W. H. T. to George W. Wickersham, November 5, 1913, Taft papers, Lib. Cong.; Robert Taft to Mrs. W. H. T., October (undated), 1913; Robert Taft to W. H. T., November (undated), 1913, January 20, 1914; Robert Taft to Delia Torrey, January 1, 1914, W. H. T. papers, Lib. Cong.; W. H. T. to Robert Taft, November 20, 1913; Jules Jusserand to W. H. T., February 11, 1915; Horace Taft to W. H. T., November 6, 8 and 20, 1913, January 9, 1914, February 12, 1914, March 16, 1914; Horace Taft to Mrs. W. H. T., September 1, 1914; W. H. T. to Horace Taft, April 26, 1914, September 4, 1914; W. H. T. to Charles Phelps Taft, June 12, 1915; W. H. T. to Delia Torrey, August 29, 1914, September 25, 1914, December 18 and 28, 1914; Delia Torrey to W. H. T., December (undated), 1913, November 11, 1914; W. H. T. to Mrs. W. H. T., April 22, 1913, January 30, 1914, February 2, 1914; Fanny Edwards to W. H. T., October 27, 1913, September 24, 1914, October 1, 1914; Wendell W. Mischler to Charlie Taft, November 13, 1913, January 26, 1914; Charlie Taft to Wendell W. Mischler, January (undated), 1914, May 14, 1914, William Howard Taft Memorial Association, Cincinnati; Mrs. W. H. T. to Charlie Taft, April 6, 1913, May 10 and 11, 1914; Helen Taft to Charlie Taft, May (undated), 1914, William Howard Taft Memorial Association, Cincinnati; M. Carey Thomas to W. H. T., April 29, 1914, Taft papers, Lib. Cong.; Ezra R. Thayer to W. H. T., December 19, 1913; Mabel Boardman to W. H. T., October 26, 1913, November 29, 1913, December 14, 16 and 25, 1913, January 5, 17 and 20, 1914, May 24, 1914; W. H. T. general correspondence, Taft papers, Lib. Cong.; W. H. T. to Mabel Boardman, December 31, 1912, February 26, 1913, March 11 and 13, 1913, April 13 and 22, 1913, May 2, 4 and 27, 1913, June 29, 1913, July 3 and 19, 1913, August 3 and 20, 1913, September 2, 1913, October 30, 1913, November 25, 29 and 30, 1913, December 2, 9, 14 and 27, 1913, January 5, 17 and 20, 1914, March 28, 1914, April 4 and 5, 1914, May 19, 1914, June 27, 1914, July 27, 1914, August 10, 1914, September 6, 1914, December 22, 1914, April 19, 1915, Boardman papers, Lib. Cong.; Woodrow Wilson to W. H. T., August 26, 1914; William Howard Taft, "The College Slouch," *Ladies Home Journal*, May, 1914; Horace Dutton Taft, *Memories and Opinions*, Henry F. Pringle, *The Life and Times of William Howard Taft*; William Howard Taft, *The Presidency*.

Chapter 20: *Bob and Martha*

W. H. T. papers, Lib. Cong.; Robert Taft to W. H. T., April (undated), 1914, October 22, 1914, December 2, 1914, June 29 and 30, 1915; Robert Taft to Delia Torrey, April 5, 1914; Martha Wheaton Bowers to W. H. T., April 7, 1914; Horace Taft to W. H. T., April 15 and 22, 1914, October 2, 1914, January 22, 1915, November 27, 1915; W. H. T. to Horace Taft, April 1 and 11, 1914, Dec. 7 and 27, 1914, September 11, 1915, November 29, 1915; W. H. T. to Delia Torrey, September 25, 1914, October 19, 1914, November 28, 1914, June 12, 19 and 20, 1915, September 15 and 22, 1915, November 21, 1915; W. H. T. to Mrs. W. H. T., April 22, 1916, May 4, 1916, June 2, 1916, October 5 and 31, 1916, November 10 and 11, 1916, January 8, 1917, March 3, 1917, June 4, 1917; Delia Torrey to W. H. T., November 1, 1914, January 19, 1915, February 5, 1915, March 27, 1915, April 22, 1915, October 9, 1915; W. H. T. to Charles Phelps Taft, February 6, 1914, October 21, 1914, December 6 and 24, 1914, September 13, 1915, February 15, 1915; W. H. T. to Horace Taft, April 21, 1914, September 9, 1914, October 5, 1914, December 8 and 10, 1914, March 2, 1915, September 4 and 5, 1915, October 8, 1915, December 15, 1915; Mabel Boardman to W. H. T., August 23, 1913, September 2, 1913, February 2 and 24, 1914, March 11, 1914, April 1, 5, 12 and 19, 1914, May 14 and 24, 1914, June 27, 1914, July 15, 1914, August 5, 6, 10, 16, 23 and 29, 1914, November 9, 1914, December 19, 22 and 25, 1914, January 3, 20 and 25, 1915, February 3, 1915, March 1, 1915, April 9, 1915, May 6, 24, 30 and 31, 1915, June 25 and 27, 1915, July 3, 1915, August 2, 9 and 11, 1915, September 4 and 26, 1915, October 8 and 10, 1915, November 1, 4, 5, 8, 19, 20 and 21, 1915, January 11 and 18, 1916, February 20, 1916, March 16, 1916, April 4, 1916, May 31, 1916, November 14 and 27, 1916, March 27, 1917, Taft papers, Lib. Cong.; W. H. T. to Mrs. Charles Phelps Taft, September 9, 1914; Mrs. Charles Phelps Taft to W. H. T., December 28, 1914; Mrs. Charles Phelps Taft to Fanny Edwards, September 20, 1914; W. H. T. to Fanny Edwards, September 9, 1914; Charles Phelps Taft to W. H. T., July 9, 1914, October 25, 1915, W. H. T. papers, Lib. Cong.; Horace Taft to Charlie Taft, October 16, 1915; Robert Taft to Charlie Taft, March 1, 1914, undated but probably April or May, 1914; Helen Taft to Charlie Taft, 1915 (undated); Mrs. W. H. T. to Charlie Taft, October 9, 1914, Charles Phelps Taft correspondence, William Howard Taft Memorial Association, Cincinnati; Helen Taft to W. H. T., October (undated), 1914, March (undated), 1915; W. H. T. to Dr. William Edwards, October 7, 1915, W. H. T. papers, Lib. Cong.; Daniel Chester French to W. H. T., January 15, 1915; M. Carey Thomas to W. H. T., March 29, 1915, May 8, 1915; Charles D. Hilles to W. H. T., August 31, 1914; Gus J. Karger to W. H. T., March 8, 1914, October 23, 1914, December 23, 1914, June 10, 1915, October 11, 1915; W. H. T. to Max Pam and Martin Egan, August 10, 1914; Charles D. Norton to Helen Taft, October 28, 1915; Mrs. Katrina Ely Tiffany to

W. H. T., March (undated), 1914; W. H. T. to Mrs. Henry Wade Rogers, May 28, 1914; W. H. T. to Charles Moore, October 8, 1917; Woodrow Wilson to W. H. T., October 28, 1915, W. H. T. papers, Lib. Cong.; Dewey L. Fleming, "A Helpmate Indeed," *Current History*, April, 1940; Cass Gilbert to W. H. T., February 5, 1912; Robert Lincoln to W. H. T., January, 1914; W. H. T. to Robert Lincoln, January 13, 1914; George W. Wickersham to W. H. T., April 20, 1914, June 3, 1914, November 5, 1914; W. H. T. to P. C. Knox, April 21, 1914; Elihu Root to W. H. T., December 22, 1913, December 30, 1914; Theodore Roosevelt to Henry L. Stoddard, September 28, 1916, Elting E. Morison, *The Letters of Theodore Roosevelt*; New York *Evening Sun*, January 6, 1915; Joseph Alsop and Robert Kintner, *Life*, March 18, 1940; Helen Taft Manning, "My Brother Bob Taft," *American Magazine*, January, 1952; Phyllis Robbins, *Robert A. Taft: Boy and Man*; Caroline Thomas Harnsberger, *A Man of Courage, Robert A. Taft*; Frederick C. Hicks, *William Howard Taft, Yale Professor of Law & New Haven Citizen*; Henry F. Pringle, *The Life and Times of William Howard Taft*.

Chapter 21: *Charlie and Eleanor*

W. H. T. papers in Lib. Cong. and Charles Phelps Taft II's papers in William Howard Taft Memorial Association, Cincinnati: W. H. T. to Charlie Taft, May 23 and 30, 1917, July 19, 1917, August 23, 1917, September 5, 1917, December 19, 1917, February 25 and 27, 1918, March 11, 16, 19 and 24, 1918, April 6, 19 and 24, 1918, May 6, 7 and 30, 1918, June 9, 1918, July 4 and 24, 1918, August 19, 1918, September 17 and 20, 1918, November 6, 1918, December 22, 1918; Maria Herron to Charlie Taft, June 23, 1918, July 22, 1918, October 19, 1918; Helen Taft to Charlie Taft, May 30, 1918, June 30, 1918, May and October letters, 1917 and 1918 (undated); Fanny Edwards to Charlie, September 28, 1918; W. H. T. to Eleanor Taft, March 11, 1918; Robert Taft to Charlie Taft, 1918 (undated); Irving Chase to W. H. T., September 6, 1918; Robert Taft to W. H. T., December 4, 1918, January 5, 1919; W. H. T. to Mrs. W. H. T., May 23, 1917, June 4, 22 and 27, 1917, October 25, 1917, February 17, 1918, May 9, 1918, June 2, 5 and 26, 1918, July 22 and 24, 1918, September 16, 1918, January 20 and 21, 1919, March 6, 1919, May 9, 1919, June 13, 1919, July 31, 1919, November 20, 1919, December 3, 20, 23 and 29, 1919, February 6, 1920, April 3, 1920, June 8, 1920, July 7, 1920; W. H. T. to Helen Taft, July 3, 1917, November 6, 1919; Horace Taft to Charlie Taft, July 27, 1918; W. H. T. to Mabel Boardman, April 9, 1917, October 4 and 30, 1917, March 19, 1918, May 31, 1918, December 10 and 27, 1919, February 21, 1920; Mabel Boardman to Mrs. William Boardman, April 14 and 28, 1918, Boardman papers, Lib. Cong.; President Wilson to W. H. T., April 2, 1918; W. H. T. to Newton D. Baker, August 31, 1917; W. H. T. to Gilbert M. Hitchcock, July 21, 1919; Arthur T. Hadley to General John J. Pershing, March 20, 1918; W. H. T. to Theodore Roosevelt, July 17, 1918; San Antonio *Express*, February 5, 1918; Horace Dutton Taft: *Memories and*

Opinions; Frederick C. Hicks, *William Howard Taft, Yale Professor of Law
& New Haven Citizen;* Oswald Garrison Villard, *Fighting Years, New York
Times,* October 7, 1917.

Chapter 22: A *Wedding at Murray Bay*

New York Times, July 16, 1920; W. H. T. to Helen Taft Manning, January
13, 1920, June 3, 1920, August 1 and 29, 1920, September 15, 1920, April
4, 1921, May 16, 1921, June 8, 1921, September 16, 1921, October 13, 1921,
December 4, 1921, Helen Taft Manning papers, Lib. Cong.; W. H. T. to
Mrs. W. H. T., December 4, 1918, January 16, 1920, February 13 and 29,
1920, March 12, 1920, May 14, 1920, June 3, 1920, July 5, 1920, September
20, 1920, December 26, 1920, January 30, 1921, February 24 and 28, 1921,
March 5, 6 and 30, 1921, May 11, 1921, June 8, 21, 28, 29 and 30, 1921,
July 2, 10, 11 and 12, 1921, August 4, 1921, September 1, 2, 3 and 7, 1921,
December 29, 1921; Horace Taft to W. H. T., March 20, 1921; W. H. T. to
the Rev. F. J. Moore (undated); Rev. F. J. Moore to W. H. T., September
15, 1921, W. H. T. papers, Lib. Cong.; Robert Taft to Charlie Taft, August
10, 1920, May 22, 1920, William Howard Taft Memorial Association, Cin-
cinnati; W. H. T. to Mabel Boardman, May 4, 1920, November 3, 1920,
January 9, 1921, March 3 and 8, 1921, April 6 and 25, 1921, May 21, 1921,
Boardman papers, Lib. Cong.; Helen Taft to Mabel Boardman, May 4, 1920,
Boardman papers, Lib. Cong.; W. H. T. to J. M. Dickinson, March 7, 1921,
April 25, 1921; Gus Karger to W. H. T., January 14, 1921, W. H. T. papers,
Lib. Cong.

Chapter 23: A *Master Bencher*

William Howard Taft to Robert A. Taft, Narrative of trip to Britain in summer of 1922, July 29, 1922, W. H. T. papers, Lib. Cong.; Queen Mary to
W. H. T., November 13, 1922; W. H. T. to Helen Taft Manning, August
24, 1922, October 6, 1922, November 5 and 26, 1922, January 2, 21 and 28,
1923, March 25, 1923, April 1, 8 and 16, 1923, May 2, 6 and 27, 1923, June
3 and 11, 1923, September 30, 1923, October 14, 21 and 28, 1923, January
11, 1924, February 17 and 23, 1924, March 2 and 8, 1924, April 20, 1924,
May 2, 1924, October 12, 1924, November 30, 1924, January 18, 1925, February 8, 15 and 22, 1925, March 1, 1925, April 5, 12, 19 and 29, 1925, May
10 and 31, 1925, June 7, 1925, November 29, 1925, Dec. 20, 1925, January
17, 1926, Helen Taft Manning papers, Lib. Cong.; W. H. T. to Mrs.
W. H. T., May 21 and 22, 1922, August 10, 1922, April 13 and 14, 1923,
May 25, 26 and 27, 1923, August 7 and 11, 1923, March 20, 1924, April 2,
5, 7, 8, 11, 13, 20 and 26, 1924, May 4, 11, 15, 20, 27, 28, 29 and 31, 1924,
June 9, 10, 12 and 14, 1924, July 1, 4, 8 and 10, 1924, October 5, 1925;
Helen Taft to Mrs. W. H. T., May 17, 1923; Charlie to Mr. and Mrs. Wil-
liam Howard Taft, April 15 and 30, 1925, November 10 and 15, 1925,

W. H. T. papers, Lib. Cong.; Helen Taft to Charlie, February 26, 1925; W. H. T. to Charlie Taft, February 22, 1925, March 2, 8 and 9, 1925, April 19, 1925, May 3, 1925, June 7, 1925, November 1, 8, 15 and 22, 1925, William Howard Taft Memorial Association, Cincinnati; Charlie to W. H. T., January 14, 1925, September 12, 1925; Fred Manning to Charlie Taft, November 4, 1925; Eleanor Taft to Mrs. Irving Chase, February 22, 1925; W. H. T. to Eleanor Taft, December 25, 1925, William Howard Taft Memorial Association, Cincinnati; Charles D. Hilles to W. H. T., June 8, 1925; W. H. T. to Calvin Coolidge, December 22, 1923, Calvin Coolidge papers, Lib. Cong.; Robert Taft to Liz Smith, July 6, 1923, Mrs. Russell Wilson papers, Historical and Philosophical Society of Ohio; Mrs. Robert Taft to Liz Smith, July 19, 1923; W. H. T. to Mabel Boardman, July 4, 1922, September 4 and 12, 1922, July 12, 1924, September 14 and 17, 1924, December 6 and 24, 1924, April 5, 1925, September 14 and 17, 1925, December 25, 1926, Boardman papers, Lib. Cong.; Jerome Beatty, "The Other Taft," *American Magazine*, July, 1947; "Charlie Taft's Big Chance," *Fortune*, August, 1947.

Chapter 24: *Gentlemen of the Court*

W. H. T. papers, Lib. Cong.; W. H. T. to Helen Taft Manning, May 8, 1924, January 10 and 17, 1926, March 15, 1926, April 1, 18, 25 and 28, 1926, October 17, 24 and 31, 1926, November 3 and 14, 1926, December 12 and 19, 1926, January 2, 9 and 28, 1927, February 6, 13, 19, 20 and 26, 1927, March 6, 1927, April 10 and 24, 1927, May 6 and 22, 1927, June 5, 1927, August 31, 1927, October 23, 1927, November 14, 1927, December 4, 11 and 18, 1927, January 8 and 29, 1928, March 3, 10 and 25, 1928, April 1 and 8, 1928, May 12, 1928, October 14, 23 and 28, 1928, November 17 and 25, 1928, December 2 and 9, 1928, January 13, 1929, February 10, 1929, March 10, 1929, April 7 and 20, 1929, May 12, 19 and 25, 1929, June 2 and 7, 1929, September 3, 1929, December 1, 1929, Helen Taft Manning papers, Lib. Cong.; W. H. T. to Mabel Boardman, January 1 and 15, 1928, May 21, 1928, June 7, 1928, December 25, 1928, Boardman papers, Lib. Cong.; George W. Wickersham to W. H. T., May 24 and 28, 1928; Roy W. Howard to Hulbert Taft, April 26, 1954 (courtesy Mrs. Hulbert Taft); Charles Evans Hughes to Herbert Hoover, March 8, 1937, February 25, 1937, Henry F. Pringle papers, Lib. Cong.; Robert A. Taft to Henry F. Pringle, August 31, 1939, Pringle papers, Lib. Cong.; W. H. T. to Robert Taft, November 6, 1927 and March 25, 1928; W. H. T. to Horace Taft, January 28, 1929, March 20, 1928, May 20, 1928; Mrs. W. H. T. to Helen Taft, October 23, 1928; W. H. T. to Russell Wilson, December 19, 1927; Mrs. Russell Wilson to author; W. H. T. to the Rev. F. J. Moore, November 15, 1928; Rev. F. J. Moore to author; Herbert Hoover Proclamation on death of William Howard Taft, March 8, 1930; Washington *Post*, *New York Times*, *New York Herald Tribune*, March 9–13; Last message from Supreme Court colleagues; Henry F. Pringle, *The Life and Times of William Howard*

Taft; Helen Taft Manning to Charles Moore, October 18, 1930, Moore papers; W. H. T. to Mrs. W. H. T., May 26, 1923, September 26, 1927, October 3, 1927, September 25, 1928, W. H. T. papers, Lib. Cong.; W. H. T. to Charlie Taft, November 1, 1925, January 31, 1926, March 25, 1928, William Howard Taft Memorial Association, Cincinnati; Charles Moore to Patrick H. Hurley, March 14, 1931, National Archives; Mrs. Hulbert Taft to author; Mrs. Darrah Dunham Wunder to author; Mrs. Willa Beall to author; *Times-Star* and *Enquirer*, January 2, 1930; Rev. F. J. Moore's memorial address at Murray Bay, August 3, 1930 courtesy Dr. Moore; Alexander M. Bickel, *The Unpublished Opinions of Mr. Justice Brandeis*; Edward H. Cotton, *William Howard Taft, a Character Study*; William Allen White, *Masks in a Pageant*.

Chapter 25: *Mr. Republican*

Robert A. Taft to Helen Taft Manning, August 24, 1932, Manning papers, Lib. Cong.; Helen Taft Manning, "My Brother Bob Taft," *American Magazine*, January, 1952; Official campaign family records; Robert A. Taft to Hulbert Taft, January 10, 1942, W. H. T. papers; Mrs. William Howard Taft obituary, Washington *Post* and *New York Times*, May 23, 1943; Alice Roosevelt Longworth, "Why I am for Bob Taft," *Saturday Evening Post*, May 4, 1940; Joseph Alsop and Robert Kintner, "Taft & Taft," *Life*, March 18, 1840; Arthur M. Schlesinger, Jr., "His Eyes Have Seen the Glory," *Collier's*, February 22, 1947; Frank Gervasi, "Bob Taft and Martha," *Collier's*, April 3, 1948; Felix Morley, "The Case for Taft," *Life*, February 9, 1948; "Martha Taft Meets the Press," *Life*, March 15, 1948; Richard H. Rovere, "Taft: Is This The Best We've Got?" *Harper's Magazine*, April, 1948; William Mylander, "The Trouble with Taft," *Look*, October 15, 1946; Bess Furman, "Candidate's Wife," *New York Times Magazine*, November 2, 1947; Beverly Smith, "Bob and Martha Take the Stump," *American Magazine*, September, 1939; Kenneth Crawford, "Taft the Presidential Candidate," *The American Mercury*, June, 1948; Benjamin Stolberg, "Robert A. Taft, American Liberal," *The American Mercury*, October, 1950; Robert S. Allen, "Men Who Would be President. Taft for Safety," *The Nation*, May 25, 1940; Roger Butterfield, "Possible Presidents. Robert A. Taft," *Ladies Home Journal*, February, 1948; Walter Davenport, "Bashful Buckeye," *Collier's*, April 6, 1940; Samuel Lubell, "How Taft Did It," *Saturday Evening Post*, February 10, 1951; Dwight D. Eisenhower, *Mandate for Change*; Darrah Dunham Wunder, "My Most Unforgettable Character," *Reader's Digest*, June, 1962; Phyllis Robbins, *Robert A. Taft: Boy and Man*; Caroline Thomas Harnsberger, *A Man of Courage, Robert A. Taft*; Darrah Dunham Wunder to author; Mrs. Hulbert Taft to author; Mrs. Russell Wilson to author; Robert Taft, Jr., to author; William Howard Taft, III, to author; news magazines and newspapers on Robert A. Taft's political activities; Robert A. Taft, *A Foreign Policy for Americans*.

Chapter 26: *For God, for Country, and for Yale*

Family records at William Howard Taft Memorial Association, Cincinnati (courtesy Charles Phelps Taft, II, and Mrs. Willa Beall); Eleanor and Charlie Taft "To Their Friends," October 2, 1938, October 31, 1938, and September 15, 1941, Historical and Philosophical Society of Ohio; "Charlie Taft's Big Chance," *Fortune*, August, 1947; Charles P. Taft, "Why the Bells are Ringing Today," *New York Times Magazine*, August 22, 1948; Jerome Beatty, "The Other Taft," *American Magazine*, July, 1947; Charles P. Taft, *City Management: the Cincinnati Experiment, Democracy in Politics and Economics, Trade Barriers and the National Interest, Why I am for the Church, You and I—and Roosevelt*; Sanford Watzman, "The Taft Family Tree—It's a Forest," Cleveland *Plain Dealer*, November 17, 1963; Cincinnati *Post*, September 7, 1933; Frank C. Porter, "New Vistas Opened by Trade Bill," Washington *Post*, October 14, 1962; Charles Phelps Taft, II, to author; Seth Chase Taft to author; Peter Rawson Taft to author; Mrs. Donald R. Morris to author; Darrah Dunham Wunder to author; Charles T. Greve, *Centennial History of Cincinnati*; Alvin F. Harlow, *The Serene Cincinnatians*; "The Tafts of Cincinnati," *Life*, May 26, 1952; *Newsweek*, January 12, 1948 and August 22, 1955; *Time*, January 12, 1948; Cincinnati newspapers, 1954–56; L. B. S. open letter to Charlie Taft, Cleveland *Press*, January 22, 1958; Cleveland *Press* and Cleveland *Plain Dealer*, February–March, 1962; "Seth Taft Advises on Home-Rule fight," *New York Times*, November 19, 1963; Cleveland *Plain Dealer*, December 29, 1961; Washington *Post*, April 26, 1963; *New York Times*, October 12, 1958; *Christian Century*, July 2, 1958.

Chapter 27: *The Team Breaks Up*

Robert A. Taft to Helen Taft Manning, December 29, 1951, Manning papers, Lib. Cong.; Robert A. Taft, "The Dangerous Decline of Morality," *Reader's Digest*, November, 1950. Robert A. Taft dies, *New York Times*, *Herald Tribune*, Washington *Post*, Washington *Star*, Cincinnati *Enquirer*, August 1–5, 1953; William S. White, *The Taft Story*; Jhan and June Robbins, *Eight Weeks to Live*; Dwight D. Eisenhower, *Mandate for Change*; John F. Kennedy, *Profiles in Courage*; Phyllis Robbins, *Robert A. Taft: Boy and Man*; Mrs. Robert A. Taft dies, *New York Times*, *New York Herald Tribune*, October 3, 1958; Hulbert Taft dies, Cincinnati *Enquirer*, *New York Times*, January 20, 1959; William Collins, Cincinnati *Enquirer*, October 3, 1958; Morris Edwards, "A Contemporary View," paper read at Literary Club, Cincinnati, April 16, 1956; Commercial Club of Cincinnati booklet, January 6, 1954; "The Tafts of Cincinnati," *Life*, May 26, 1952; Mendon *Evening Gazette*, June 9, 1955; Cincinnati *Enquirer*, February 3, 1954 and December 5, 1962; Cincinnati *Post*, July 31, 1952; *Time*, June 2, 1952; "William

Howard Taft Memorial Association," Cincinnati *Pictorial Enquirer*, May 13, 1962; Eleanor Chase Taft dies, Cincinnati *Enquirer*, August 29, 1961; David G. Taft dies, *New York Times*, September 28, 1962; Richard Armstrong and Robert Massie, "A New Taft and a Young Kennedy go to Washington," *Saturday Evening Post*, January 19, 1963; Marquis Childs, "The Newest Taft on the Horizon," Washington *Post*, February 27, 1963; Robert Taft, Jr., to run for Senate, *New York Herald Tribune*, December 6, 1963; Text of speeches by Robert Taft, Jr. before the Women's National Republican Club, New York, January 26, 1963; Akron Chamber of Commerce, February 12, 1963; Lincoln-Jefferson dinner, Fairfax County Republican Committee, March 26, 1963; Baltimore County Republican Victory Dinner, Pikesville, Maryland, March 20, 1963; Robert Taft, Jr. to author; William Howard Taft, III, to author; Robert A. Taft, *A Foreign Policy for Americans*; Caroline Thomas Harnsberger, *A Man of Courage*; Dwight D. Eisenhower, *Mandate for Change*; Stewart Alsop, "Rough Ride for a Hero," *Saturday Evening Post*, March 14, 1964.

Manuscript collections explored, Library of Congress:

Nelson Aldrich
Newton D. Baker
Albert J. Beveridge
William Jennings Bryan
Mabel Boardman
William E. Borah
Lord Bryce
Andrew Carnegie
Henry C. Corbin
Walter Fisher
James R. Garfield
Gist-Blair
Lloyd C. Griscom
Benjamin Harrison
James Hay
John Hay
Rutherford B. Hayes
Gilbert M. Hitchcock
Charles Evans Hughes
Gertrude Lane
Horace H. Lurton
William McKinley

Daniel Manning
Helen Taft Manning
Theodore Marburg
Benjamin Marcus
Charles Moore
Harry S. New
Gifford Pinchot
Henry F. Pringle
Theodore Roosevelt
Elihu Root
Carl Schurz
Henry L. Stimson
Willard Straight
William Howard Taft family papers
    General Correspondence
    Presidential Series, 1 and 2
M. R. Waite
Daniel Webster
Henry White
William Allen White
Woodrow Wilson

New York Public Library: William Howard Taft papers, Andrew Carnegie papers, James S. Sherman papers.

Historical and Philosophical Society of Ohio: William Howard Taft papers, Mrs. Charles Phelps Taft papers, Charles Livingood papers.

William Howard Taft Memorial Association, Cincinnati: Taft family papers Courtesy Mrs. Willa Beall).

American Antiquarian Society, Worcester, Massachusetts: Asa Waters family papers.

BIBLIOGRAPHY

Baker, Ray Stannard. *Woodrow Wilson, Life and Letters.* Vols. 3 and 4. New York: Doubleday, Doran & Company, 1931; London: William Heinemann, Ltd., 1932.

Barker, Charles E. *With President Taft in the White House.* Chicago: A. Kroch & Son, 1947.

Bickel, Alexander M. (ed.). *The Unpublished Opinions of Mr. Justice Brandeis.* Cambridge: The Belknap Press, 1957.

Bickley, G. W. L. *A Critical Cyclopedia of Literature, Science & Art.* Vol. I. Cincinnati: Abbott & Bentley, 1853.

Bishop, Joseph Bucklin. *Theodore Roosevelt and his Time.* 2 vols. New York: Charles Scribner's Sons, 1920.

Bowen, Catherine Drinker. *Yankee from Olympus.* Boston: Little, Brown & Company, 1944.

Bowers, Claude G. *Beveridge and the Progressive Era.* Boston: Houghton Mifflin Company, 1932.

Brown, F. W. *Cincinnati and Vicinity.* Cincinnati: C. J. Krehbiel & Company, 1898.

Bruckberger, R. L. *Image of America.* tr. by C. G. Paulding and Virgilia Peterson. New York: The Viking Press, 1959; London: Macmillan & Co., Ltd., 1960.

Bryan, William J., and Bryan, Mary Baird. *The Memoirs of William Jennings Bryan.* Philadelphia: John C. Winston Company, 1925.

Bryce, James. *The American Commonwealth.* New York: The Macmillan Company, 1888.

Butt, Archie. *Taft and Roosevelt: the Intimate Letters of Archie Butt, Military Aide.* 2 vols. New York: Doubleday, Doran & Company, 1930.

Centennial History of the Town of Millbury, Mass. Published under the direction of a committee appointed by the Town of Millbury, 1915.

Chamberlain, George Walter. *Genealogy of Weymouth Families.* Weymouth: Weymouth Historical Society, 1923.

Chambrun, Clara (Longworth) de. *Cincinnati: Story of the Queen City.* New York: Charles Scribner's Sons, 1889.

———— *The Making of Nicholas Longworth.* New York: R. Long and R. R. Smith; London: Putnam & Co., Ltd., 1933.

Cincinnati, Past and Present. Cincinnati: Elm Street Printing Company, 1872.

Cist, Charles. *Sketches and Statistics of Cincinnati in 1851.* Cincinnati: W. H. Moore & Company, 1851.

———— *Sketches and Statistics of Cincinnati in 1859.* Cincinnati: W. H. Moore & Company, 1859.

———— *The Cincinnati Miscellany or Antiquities of the West.* Vol. I. Cincinnati: Caleb Clark, 1845.

———— *The Cincinnati Miscellany or Antiquities of the West.* Vol. II. Cincinnati: Robinson & Jones, 1846.

Cooke, George Willis. *Unitarianism in America.* Boston: American Unitarian Association, 1902.

Corwin, E. S. *The Twilight of the Supreme Court.* New Haven: Yale University Press; London: Oxford University Press, 1934.

Cotton, Edward H. *William Howard Taft, a Character Study.* Boston: The Beacon Press, 1932.

Cowles, Anna Roosevelt. *Letters from Theodore Roosevelt.* New York: Charles Scribner's Sons, 1924.

Davis, Oscar King. *William Howard Taft: The Man of the Hour.* Philadelphia: P. W. Ziegler Company, 1908.

Dawson, James W. *Picturesque Cincinnati.* Cincinnati: The John Shillito Company, 1883.

Dickens, Charles. *American Notes.* New York: Harper & Brothers, 1842.

Duffy, Herbert S. *William Howard Taft.* New York: Minton, Balch & Company, 1930.

Dunn, Robert Lee. *William Howard Taft, American.* Boston: The Chapple Publishing Company, 1908.

Eisenhower, Dwight D. *Mandate for Change.* New York: Doubleday & Company, Inc., 1963.

Foraker, Joseph B. *Notes of a Busy Life.* New York: Appleton, 1916.

Foraker, Julia B. *I Would Live It Again.* New York: Harper & Brothers, 1932.

Frankfurter, Felix, and Landis, James M. *The Business of the Supreme Court.* New York: The Macmillan Company, 1927.

Furman, Bess. *White House Profile.* Indianapolis: The Bobbs-Merrill Company, Inc., 1951.

Goldman, Eric. *Rendezvous with Destiny.* New York: Alfred A. Knopf, 1952.

Goss, Charles Frederic. *Cincinnati: The Queen City 1788–1912.* Chicago: S. J. Clarke Company, 1912.

Greve, Charles T. *Centennial History of Cincinnati.* Chicago: Biographical Publishing Company, 1904.

Hagedorn, Hermann. *The Boys Life of Theodore Roosevelt.* New York: Harper & Brothers, 1918.

―――― *The Roosevelt Family of Sagamore Hill.* New York: The Macmillan Company, 1954.

Hammond, John Hays. *The Autobiography of John Hays Hammond.* New York: Farrar & Rinehart, Inc., 1935.

Harbaugh, William Henry. *Power and Responsibility: The Life and Times of Theodore Roosevelt.* New York: Farrar, Straus & Cudahy, 1961.

Harlow, Alvin F. *The Serene Cincinnatians.* New York: E. P. Dutton & Co., Inc., 1950.

Harnsberger, Caroline Thomas. *A Man of Courage: Robert A. Taft.* Chicago: Wilcox and Follett Company, 1952.

Hicks, Frederick C. *William Howard Taft, Yale Professor of Law & New Haven Citizen.* New Haven: Yale University Press, 1945; London: Oxford University Press, 1946.

Hoover, Herbert. *Memoirs of Herbert Hoover,* Vol. II, New York: The Macmillan Company, 1952.

Hoover, Irwin (Ike). *Forty-two Years in the White House.* Boston: Houghton Mifflin Company, 1934; London: Williams & Norgate, Ltd., 1935.

Howe, Mark DeWolfe. (ed.). *Justice Oliver Wendell Holmes: The Proving Years, 1870–1882.* Cambridge: Harvard University Press, 1963.

Howells, William Dean. *Stories of Ohio.* New York: American Book Company, 1897.

Hughes, Charles Evans. *The Supreme Court of the United States.* New York: Columbia University Press; London: Oxford University Press, 1928.

Jeffries, Ona Griffin. *In and Out of the White House.* New York: Wilfred Funk, Inc., 1960

Jensen, Amy (La Follette). *The White House and its Thirty-two Families.* New York: McGraw-Hill Book Company, 1958.

Jessup, Philip C. *Elihu Root.* 2 vols. New York: Dodd, Mead & Company, 1938.

Jewett, C. F. *History of Worcester County, Massachusetts,* 2 vols. Boston: Jewett & Company, 1879.

Jones, Edward Alfred. *American Members of the Inns of Court*. London: The Saint Catherine Press, 1924.

Kelly, Frank K. *The Fight for the White House*. New York: Thomas Y. Crowell Company, 1934.

Kohler, Mary. *"Background and First Stages of the Passage of the Payne–Aldrich Bill, 1897 to June 8, 1909."* Lib. of Cong., Unpublished mss., Swarthmore, 1939.

Kohlsaat, H. H. *From McKinley to Harding*. New York: Charles Scribner's Sons, 1923.

La Follette, Belle (Case), and La Follette, Fola. *Robert M. La Follette*. 2 vols. New York: The Macmillan Company, 1953.

La Follette, Robert Marion. *Autobiography: A Personal Narrative of Political Experiences*. Madison: University of Winconsin Press, 1960.

Laney, Al. *Preparatory Schools*. New York: Doubleday & Company, Inc., 1961.

Leech, Margaret. *In the Days of McKinley*. New York: Harper & Brothers, 1959.

Leonard, John William. *The Centennial Review*. Cincinnati: J. M. Elstner, 1888.

Leonard, Lewis Alexander. *Life of Alphonso Taft*. New York: Hawke Publishing Company, 1920.

Leopold, Richard W. *Elihu Root and the Conservative Tradition*. Boston: Little, Brown & Co., 1954.

Link, A. S. *Wilson: The Road to the White House*. Princeton, New Jersey: Princeton University Press; London: Oxford University Press, 1947.

Lodge, Henry Cabot. *The Senate and the League of Nations*. New York: Charles Scribner's Sons, 1925.

Longworth, Alice Roosevelt. *Crowded Hours*. New York: Charles Scribner's Sons, 1933.

McAdoo, Eleanor Wilson, and Gaffey, M. J. *The Woodrow Wilsons*. New York: The Macmillan Company, 1937.

McHale, Francis. *President and Chief Justice*. Philadelphia: Dorrance & Company, Inc., 1931.

Makepeace, LeRoy McKim, *Sherman Thacher and His School*, New Haven: Yale University Press; London: Oxford University Press, 1941.

Manning, Helen Taft. *The Revolt of French Canada 1800–1835*. New York: St. Martin's Press, Inc., London: Macmillan & Co., Ltd., 1962.

——— *British Colonial Government After the American Revolution 1782–1820*. New Haven: Yale University Press, 1933; London: Oxford University Press, 1934.

Marburg, Theodore, (ed.). *Taft Papers on League of Nations*. New York: The Macmillan Company, 1920.

Martineau, Harriet. *Retrospect of Western Travel*. London: Saunders & Otley, 1838.

Maxwell, Sidney D. *The Suburbs of Cincinnati: Sketches, History and Descriptive*. Cincinnati: George E. Stevens & Company, 1870.

Metcalf, John G. *Annals of the Town of Mendon from 1659–1880*. Providence: Freeman & company, 1880.

Metzman, Gustav. *Cincinnati and Ohio, Their Early Railroads*. Address delivered at 1948 dinner of the Newcomen Society of England. Printed for American branch of the Newcomen Society by Princeton University Press, 1948.

Morison, Elting E. (ed.). *The Letters of Theodore Roosevelt*. 8 vols. Cambridge: Harvard University Press; London: Oxford University Press, 1951–1954.

Morison, S. E., and Commager, H. S. *The Growth of the American Republic*. 2 vols. New York: Oxford University Press; London: Oxford University Press, 1937.

Morris, Lloyd R. *Postscript to Yesterday*. New York: Random House, 1947.

Murray, Robert H. *Around the World with Taft*. Detroit: F. B. Dickerson Company, 1909.

Nevins, Allan. *Henry White: Thirty Years of American Diplomacy*. New York: Harper & Brothers, 1930.

Official Diary of the President, 1911, 1912 and 1913. Compiled by Major Archibald Butt, Major Thomas L. Rhoads, John E. Fenwick and Colonel Spencer Cosby. Unpublished diaries in Library of Congress.

Ohio Guide, The. Ohio Writers Project. New York: Oxford University Press, 1940.

Patterson, Raymond. *Taft's Training for the Presidency*. Boston: The Chappel Press, 1908.

Powell, John H. "President Taft and the Payne–Aldrich Tariff." Lib. of Cong., Unpublished thesis, Swarthmore, 1934.

Pringle, Henry F. *The Life and Times of William Howard Taft*. 2 vols. New York: Farrar & Rinehart, Inc., 1939.
——— *Theodore Roosevelt*. New York: Harcourt, Brace & Company, Inc., 1931.

Proceedings at the meeting of the Taft Family at Uxbridge, Massachusetts, August 12, 1874. Uxbridge: Spencer Bros., 1874.

Pusey, Merlo John. *Charles Evans Hughes*. 2 vols. New York: The Macmillan Company, 1951.

Ragan, Allen E. *Chief Justice Taft*. Columbus: Ohio State Archaeological and Historical Society, 1938.

Randall, E. O., and Ryan, D. J. *History of Ohio*. New York: Century History Company, 1912–16.

Rhodes, James Ford. *The McKinley & Roosevelt Administrations 1897–1909.* New York: The Macmillan Company, 1922.

Robbins, Jhan, and Robbins, June. *Eight Weeks to Live.* New York: Doubleday & Company, 1954.

Robbins, Phyllis. *Robert A. Taft: Boy and Man.* Cambridge: Dresser, Chapman & Grimes Inc., 1963.

Rogers, Will. *The Autobiography of Will Rogers.* Boston: Houghton Mifflin Company, 1949.

Roosevelt, Theodore. *An Autobiography.* New York: Charles Scribner's Sons, 1920.

Rose, George M. *Cincinnati: The Queen City of the West.* Cincinnati: C. J. Krehbiel & Company, 1895.

Slayden, Ellen Maury. *Washington Wife.* New York: Harper & Row, 1963.

Smith, Gene. *When the Cheering Stopped.* New York: William Morrow & Company, 1964.

Smith, T. V., and Taft, Robert A. *Foundations of Democracy: a Series of Debates.* New York: Alfred A. Knopf, Inc., 1939.

Stewart, Kate M. "The William Howard Taft Papers." *Quarterly Journal of the Library of Congress,* November, 1957.

Stoddard, Henry L. *As I Knew Them.* New York: Harper & Brothers, 1927.

Stokes, Anson Phelps. *Memorials of Eminent Yale Men.* 2 vols. New Haven: Yale University Press, 1914.

Storer, Maria Longworth. *In Memoriam Bellamy Storer.* Boston: The Merrymount Press, 1923.

Stowe, Lyman Beecher. *Saints, Sinners and Beechers.* Indianapolis: Bobbs–Merrill Company, 1934; London: Ivor Nicholson & Watson, Ltd., 1935.

Taft, Charles P. *City Management: the Cincinnati Experiment.* New York: Farrar & Rinehart, Inc., 1933.

———— *Democracy in Politics and Economics.* New York: Farrar, Straus & Young, Inc., 1950.

———— *Trade Barriers and the National Interest.* Dallas: Southern Methodist University Press, 1955.

———— *Why I am for the Church: Talks on Religion and Politics.* New York: Farrar, Straus & Co., Inc., 1947.

———— *You and I—and Roosevelt.* New York: Farrar & Rinehart, Inc., 1936.

Taft, Eleanor Gholson. *Hither and Yon on Indian Hill.* Cincinnati: The Indian Hill Garden Club, 1962.

Taft Family Gathering, Uxbridge, Mass., 1874. Privately printed by George M. Ellis, 1891.

Taft Family Gathering Proceedings at the Meeting of the Taft Family at Uxbridge, Mass. Uxbridge: Spencer Bros., 1874.

Taft Genealogy. Family tree showing the descendants of Robert Taft. Cincinnati: Ehrgott, Forbriger & Company, 1910.

Taft, Henry W. *A Century and a Half at the New York Bar.* Privately printed, 1938.
—— *An Essay on Conversation.* New York: The Macmillan Company, 1927.
—— *Kindred Arts: Conversation and Public Speaking.* New York: The Macmillan Company, 1929.
—— *Legal Miscellanies; Six Decades of Change and Progress.* New York: The Macmillan Company, 1941.
—— *Opinions, Literary and Otherwise.* New York and London: The Macmillan Company, 1934.
Taft, Horace Dutton. *Memories and Opinions.* New York: The Macmillan Company, 1942.
Taft, Robert A., and Smith, T. V. *Foundations of Democracy; a Series of Debates.* New York: Alfred A. Knopf, Inc., 1939.
Taft, Russell W. *Taft Family News.* Vol. I, No. I. Burlington, Vermont: May, 1910.
Taft, William Howard. *Ethics in Service.* New Haven: Yale University Press, 1915.
—— *Our Chief Magistrate and his Powers.* New York: Columbia University Press, 1938.
—— *Political Issues and Outlooks.* New York: Doubleday, Page and Company, 1909.
—— *Popular Government; its Essence, its Permanence and its Perils.* New Haven: Yale University Press, 1913.
—— *Presidential Addresses and State Papers.* New York: Doubleday, Page & Company, 1910.
—— *The Anti-Trust Act and the Supreme Court.* New York: Harper & Brothers, 1914.
—— *The Presidency.* New York: Charles Scribner's Sons, 1916.
—— *The United States and Peace.* New York: Charles Scribner's Sons, 1914.
—— *World Peace:* a written debate between William Howard Taft and William Jennings Bryan. New York: George H. Doran Company, 1917.
Taft, Mrs. William Howard. *Recollections of Full Years.* New York: Dodd, Mead & Company, Inc., 1914.
Thompson, Charles Willis. *Presidents I've Known and Two Near Presidents.* Indianapolis: Bobbs–Merrill Company, 1929.
Titus, Anson. *The Taft Kin.* Reprinted from Boston *Evening Transcript,* March 4, 1909.
Torrey, Frederic C. *The Torrey Families and their Children in America.* 2 vols. Lakehurst, New Jersey: 1929.
Villard, Oswald Garrison. *Fighting Years.* New York: Harcourt, Brace & Company, Inc., 1939.
Washburn, Mabel T. R. *Ancestry of William Howard Taft.* New York: Frank Allaben Genealogical Company, 1908.

Werner, Morris R. *Bryan*. New York: Harcourt, Brace & Company; London: Jonathan Cape, Ltd., 1929.

White, William Allen. *Masks in a Pageant*. New York: The Macmillan Company, 1930.

White, William S. *The Taft Story*. New York: Harper & Brothers, 1954.

Willard, Martha. "Notes for a Biographer, based on the Taft private papers 1810–1891." Lib. of Cong., Unpublished mss., Swarthmore College, 1935.

Woodward, William. A *Memorial of the First Inauguration of William Howard Taft*. Lib. of Cong., Privately printed in Worcester, Mass., 1909.

Worcester, Dean C. *The Philippines, Past and Present*. 2 vols. New York: The Macmillan Company, 1921.

INDEX